Greek Cypriots in the UK

A directory of who's who

compiled and produced by

Michael Yiakoumi

First published in Great Britain by
Pen Press Publishers Ltd
39-41, North Road
Islington
London N7 9DP

ISBN 1-905203-81-0

Printed and bound in the UK

A catalogue record of this book is available from
the British Library

Cover design by Matthew Ward Design
matthew.ward10@btinternet.com

Greek Cypriots in the UK, 111 St Thomas's Road, London N4 2QJ
Tel: 020 7503 3498
Email: cypriotwhoswho@aol.com

EDITED BY

KYRIAKOS L TSIOUPRAS
SPECIAL THANKS TO SOPHIA TOUMAZIS

ACKNOWLEDGEMENTS

Cyprus High Commission
Greek Orthodox Church Great Britain
London Greek Radio
Parikiaki Newspaper
Eleftheria Newspaper
Gabriel Gabralatsou
Vasilis Panayi
Koulla Anastasi
Dinos Nicolas
Vasilia Michael
Peter Pentayiotis
Panicos Michael
Matthew Ward

CONTENTS

Editor's Note

When my nephew, Michael Yiakoumi, mentioned to me for the first time the idea of producing a book about achievers within the Greek Cypriot community in Britain, I reacted negatively.

I do not like the idea of classifying people according to their success without reference to their background, notably if they had enjoyed a privileged position or were deprived of any advantage. If one judges achievement by result, one runs the risk of missing the main point which is related to the amount of effort made. One may try very hard, but for one reason or another which maybe beyond an individual's control, one may fail to reach a successful goal.

But after further consideration of the suggestion for a book of achievement, I agreed. Three main considerations influenced my decision:

1. The tremendous attachment Greek Cypriot parents feel towards their children. Any Greek Cypriot parent who settled here as an immigrant would tell you his decision to emigrate was taken for the sake of his children's future.

One can think of all the hard experiences of the Greek Cypriot immigrant and marvel at the way he had managed to survive and prosper. Not speaking the native language in a foreign land - in some cases being illiterate in his own language. These were not unusual phenomena among the very first wave of Greek Cypriot immigrants - in the late 20s, in the 30s, and, in a lesser degree, after the war; there was also the antiforeign feeling to overcome in a society that had kept its insular isolation for decades. The Greek Cypriot immigrant endured all these adversities mostly for the sake of the children. One can truly feel admiration and respect for this perseverance.

2. The considerable effort made by the second and third Greek Cypriot generations to overcome disadvantages at school and in life. Greek Cypriot children born in this country do indeed find themselves facing a number of disadvantages. They

are brought up in a family environment different from local customs and usages, the language which they hear constantly at home is so different from the one that they hear at school, not to mention the different traditions with which they have to get familiarised. When at the age of five at nursery or school, they find themselves in a different atmosphere alien to what they got used to at home, they do feel isolated and strangers especially when they are separated from other children in order to attend special classes in English.

Experiences like these are especially traumatic for children who arrive from Cyprus with no knowledge at all of the English language and with a different background of family and social life. Yet they manage to go through these difficulties effectively overcoming at the same time other problems and obstacles in order to compete on equal terms with their classmates to university studies and, indeed, in some cases with excellent results. The least we can do for these young people from the Greek Cypriot community is to applaud their achievement and recognise it as a proud record for themselves and the Greek Cypriot community and their country of origin - Cyprus.

3. The high rate of achievement in so many walks of life, as one will notice going through this book, is in itself, a living proof of the right balance they have struck between their national identity and their contribution as citizens of this country in its everyday life. The second and third generation Cypriot has one part of himself with his parental family and the other part with the wider world of this country. There is no magic formula by which one can find the right balance between the two worlds. The part with the parental family is stronger with regard to ethnic origins and roots. The other part, in the wider society of this country, is stronger with regard to present experiences and future orientation. The right balance is one which avoids any contradiction between the two concepts. For one to know his roots is like a tree able to resist strong winds. For one who does not know his roots, where he came from, is like a tree not able to stand in a storm. On the other hand, if one lives with the past, being satisfied with his roots without looking forward to the future is like a tree not bearing any fruit. As much as one needs to know one's past one must try and understand the future world and one's obligations to it. We like to think we are a community with the right approach within a multi-national an a multi-cultural society that British society is today. Yes to the creative integration. No to assimilation.

If one can find these concepts reflected in this book, the project will be worthy of the effort. It is for you, the reader, to judge.

Kyriacos L Tsioupras

The Idea and How it Materialised

I first had the idea of publishing this book while I was working for Parikiaki newspaper a few years ago. I approached the editor, my uncle, Kyriacos Tsioupras, and PR Consultant, Sophia Toumazis for their opinions. A number of discussions followed, and with their support, I started collecting material for the profiles. I never imagined at the time that this would become such a big project.

Writers, doctors, actors, politicians, social workers, and footballers - these are just a few of the dozens of professions occupied by Greek Cypriots.

The reader will find profiles of the Archbishop of Thyateira and Great Britain, the High Commissioner, Mr Petros Eftychiou and Mr Haris Sophoclides, the President of the National Federation of Cypriots in the United Kingdom.

Many people included in the book are virtually unknown among our community in the UK and Cyprus. But I believe they are people we should be proud of and that the least we can do is to acknowledge and recognise them.

While many of the entries are first and second generation, it is amazing just what incredible inroads were made by the original immigrants from Cyprus, most of whom came in the late 40s, 50s and early 60s. Many had not even finished primary school but 'education, education, education' was an adage of Greek Cypriot immigrants long before Tony Blair coined the phrase and you can see why.

Who would have guessed that the Prime Minister's special advisor on education and former policy unit head would originate from the scenic village of Yialoussa? But Andrew Adonis, now Lord Adonis, and junior minister for education has achieved this at the age of 42.

While high-profile people will strike a chord with most - pop star, George Michael, Easy-Jet entrepreneur, Stelios Hajioannou, and Brit artists Dinos and Jake Chapman - many others have contributed to life in the UK and beyond in ways almost unimaginable a generation ago and often against huge odds.

Professor Kypros Nicolaides, based at Kings College Hospital, London, has transformed the way obstetrics is practised and is the director of the biggest foetal research medical centre in the world.

Janet Paraskeva is the Chief Executive of the Law Society and Maggie Koumi was the first editor of Hello! magazine at a time when it changed the face of British glossy publishing.

There are many others: actor and singer, Eve Polycarpou and brother, Peter Polycarpou, footballer, Jason Koumas, TV psychologist, Linda Papadopoulos, and headmistress, Mary Karaolis.

The criteria related to people who have distinguished themselves in various walks of life - including medicine, academia, business, the arts, music, media, sports, journalism etc. - as well as those who have helped the community socially, professionally and culturally. Nominations were generally received via a third party through announcements in local and community press and radio.

The book took more than four years to produce and was a labour of love. I am particularly proud to be able to showcase some of Andy Nicola's amazing photographs in the picture section of this book and thank his family warmly for this privilege.

Many people supported me on this venture - especially Uncle Kyriacos Tsioupras and Sophia Toumazis - and I much appreciate their encouragement.

This book is a celebration of what our community has achieved - a kind of social snapshot of where it is today - and one which looks forward to tremendous potential for the future. I hope you will find this book a useful resource.

Michael Yiakoumi

With thanks to all the advertisers and sponsors

ARTEMIS ACHILLEOS
Community Work

DATE OF BIRTH: 28.06.53
PLACE OF BIRTH: Larnaca.
MARITAL STATUS: Married to Lilia (Paramaxis), a Fashion Designer, from London.
CHILDREN: Nicolas and Alexis.
SCHOOLS/COLLEGE: Copeland Senior High School
HOBBIES AND INTERESTS: Community work, film and TV.
PERSONAL PROFILE: Currently Chairman of the PTA at Chancellors School, Brookmans Park, Hertfordshire. Former Vice Chairman at Twelve Apostles Greek Orthodox Church, Hertfordshire. Past committees: Potters Bar Greek School, Wembley Round Table, Secretary of London branch of British Boot & Shoe Institute, youth organisations Ekon, Brent Cypriot Youth Club. Shoemaker based in Barnet under the name Baboucha. In 1986, was commissioned to make the bridesmaids' shoes for the royal wedding of Prince Andrew and Sarah Ferguson.

SOTOS ACHILLEOS
Inventor/Illustrator/Designer

DATE OF BIRTH: 02.09.55
PLACE OF BIRTH: London. Father, Andreas, from Vokolida; Mother, Eleni, from Eptakomi.
MARITAL STATUS: Married to Tanya from Auckland, New Zealand.
CHILDREN: Helen, Leonida, Alexander and Lilly Carole.
PROFESSIONAL QUALIFICATIONS: BA Honours in Commercial Design and Illustration.
HONOURS/AWARDS: National Association of Toy & Leisure Libraries Gold Medal for inventing reflection puzzles - Time Out's Good Toy Guide Puzzle of the Year 2001
HOBBIES AND INTERESTS: All arts but specifically painting and sculpture. Is now a professional inventor. The source of all his inventions is painting and drawing, so his work is really his hobby although he does have a particular interest in the steroscopic image and optical illusions.
PERSONAL PROFILE: Trained as a Commercial Artist/Designer and has, for most of his career, worked as a Freelance Illustrator/Designer. Over the years, his work has appeared in various publications, books, toys and games. His close association with the toy business prompted him to become an inventor within this industry. He is also a painter and some of his early canvasses are on permanent display at the Whitechapel Hospital.
Email: sotos@tesco.net

ANDREA ACHILLEOS
Magazine Designer

DATE OF BIRTH: 01.07.75
PLACE OF BIRTH: London. Father from Ayios Theodoros Karpasia.
MARITAL STATUS: Single
SCHOOLS/COLLEGES: Queen Elizabeth Girls' School, Barnet College, Central Graphics Academy.
ACADEMIC QUALIFICATIONS: A Levels in Art, Theatre Studies, Computing & Economics
HOBBIES AND INTERESTS: Travelling and socialising.
PERSONAL PROFILE: Senior Designer working for EMP Plc one of the biggest publishers of celebrity and sports magazines in England. Also project manager for the *At Home* magazines. Works with and helps many charities including Cancer Research, United Airlines Charity Ball for action for children in Battersea, and various others.

ANDREAS ADAM
Professor

DATE OF BIRTH: 04.05.51
PLACE OF BIRTH: Nicosia
MARITAL STATUS: Married to Jane, Consultant Radiologist at St.Georges, from London.
CHILDREN: Sophie and Clio.
SCHOOLS/COLLEGE: First Greek Gymnasium for Boys, Famagusta. Middlesex Hospital Medical School.
QUALIFICATIONS: MB, BS Honours FRCP, FRCR, FRCS
MEMBERSHIPS: Numerous medical societies.
HOBBIES & INTERESTS: Current affairs and music
PERSONAL PROFILE: Professor of Interventional Radiology University of London.

GINA ADAMOU
Councillor

DATE OF BIRTH: 06.02.45
PLACE OF BIRTH: Psymolophou.
MARITAL STATUS: Married
CHILDREN: Christina, Social Worker; Andreas Project Manager; Niki, Special Needs Teacher.
SCHOOLS/COLLEGE: Schooling in Cyprus, then North London College as a mature student for four years.
MEMBERSHIPS: Labour Party
HONOURS/AWARDS: Award in celebration of Lifetime Achievements from Greek Cypriot Women's Organisation of Haringey.
HOBBIES AND INTERESTS: Reading
PERSONAL PROFILE: Councillor since 1990 (Haringey Council), chairing Social Services 1993-7 and 1999-00 Ethnic Minorities Organisation, Women's Organisation and more voluntary sector organisations.

MOYSIS ADAMOU
President of Achna Association UK

DATE OF BIRTH: 06.08.40
PLACE OF BIRTH: Achna, Famagusta.
MARITAL STATUS: Married to Maria Nicola.
CHILDREN: Adam Graphic Designer; Helen, Travel Agent.
SCHOOLS/COLLEGE: Primary education.
HOBBIES AND INTERESTS: Gardening and politics.
PERSONAL PROFILE: Fish and chip shop owner. President of Achna Association in Britain.

LORD ADONIS IS THE FIRST GREEK CYPRIOT LORD AND FIRST GREEK CYPRIOT TO HOLD A MINISTERIAL POSITION IN THE UNITED KINGDOM

LORD ANDREW ADONIS
Former Head of Prime Minister's Policy Unit. Now Department for Education and Skills Parliamentary Secretary and Under Secretary of State for Schools.

DATE OF BIRTH: 22.02.63
PLACE OF BIRTH: UK. Father from Yialloussa.
MARITAL STATUS: Married to Kathryn Davis.
CHILDREN: Two
SCHOOLS/COLLEGE: Kingham Hill School, Keble College, Oxford; Christ Church, Oxford.
ACADEMIC QUALIFICATIONS: BA 1st Class Honours Modern History, D Phil.
PERSONAL PROFILE: Member of the HQ Secretariat British Gas Corporation 1984-85. Fellow in Politics, Oxford University, 1988-1991. Financial Times Public Policy correspondent 1993-1994, The Observer 1996-98. 1987-1988 member of Oxford City Council. A member of the Prime Minister's Policy Unit since 1998, former Head of the Policy Unit. Has written five books: *Parliament Today* (1990), *Making Aristocracy Work - the Peerage and the Political System in Brtiain 1884 to 1914* (1993), *A Conservative Revolution: the Thatcher-Reagan Decade in Perspective* (1994), *Failure in British Government; the politics of the Poll Tax* (1994), and *A Class Act - the Myth of Britain's Classless Society* (1997). Made a Lord and department for education and skills parliamentary secretary in 2005.

FRANCESCA ADONIS
Assistant Merchandiser

DATE OF BIRTH: 27.08.74
PLACE OF BIRTH: Dhekelia (The intention of the family was to go and live in Cyprus - as a result of the outbreak of the war in 1974 Francesca was born in the British bases).
MARITAL STATUS: Single
SCHOOLS/COLLEGE: Parliament Hill, Islington 6th Form Centre, London Guildhall University.
ACADEMIC QUALIFICATIONS: BA in Business Studies.
HOBBIES AND INTERESTS: Travel, reading and theatre.
PERSONAL PROFILE: Worked overseas for BHS as Assistant Merchandiser, now at Dorothy Perkins as Assistant Merchandiser in womenswear.

GEORGE ADONIS
Barrister

DATE OF BIRTH: 13.01.42
PLACE OF BIRTH: Vasilli.
MARITAL STATUS: Married to Irene from Scotland.
CHILDREN: Francesca, Assistant Merchandiser and Nicholas, at Middlesex Univesity studying for a degree in Film Studies and Arts.
SCHOOLS/COLLEGE: North West London Polytechnic, Lincolns Inn, called to the Bar in 1973.
PROFESSIONAL QUALIFICATIONS: Barrister at Law
HOBBIES AND INTERESTS: Theatre, tennis and football (Arsenal fan).
PERSONAL PROFILE: Barrister of Law Chambers at the Temple. Member of the Leonarisso Vassilli Association. On the Executive Committee of the National Federation of Cypriots. Executive member of the Estia. Member of the Anglo Cypriot Law Association.

ARIAN AGHABABAIE
Musician

DATE OF BIRTH: 06.04.87
PLACE OF BIRTH: London. Grandmother from Rizorkapaso. Grandfather from Koma Tou Yiallou.
SCHOOLS/COLLEGES: Queen Elizabeth Boys', Barnet.
MEMBERSHIPS: Royal Academy of Music.
HONOURS/AWARDS: Distinction for piano grades 1-7 by Associated Board of the Royal Schools of Music 1995-2000. Silver medal winner in the North London Music Festival, sight reading competition 1999. Winner of two bursaries for Outstanding Musical Achievement at Queen Elizabeth's School 2000 & 2002.
HOBBIES AND INTERESTS: A keen light aircraft pilot with interests in the RAF and NASA. Enjoys sports and martial arts. Future plans include publishing his orchestral, vocal and piano compositions.
PERSONAL PROFILE: Featured child pianist in the BBC Documentary 'Teaching Today' highlighting children of talent in 1997. Played the lead child role in Peter Sondheim's *Merrily We Roll Along* at the Royal Academy of Music. Principal boy in Mozart's *Magic Flute* with the English National Opera at the London Colliseum. Also with the ENO performed in *Carmen* and *Cunning Little Vixen*. Performances with Chicken Shed Theatre Company: Children's charity concert at the Royal Albert Hall with singer Gabrielle, and Queen Mother's 100th Birthday Celebrations televised by BBC.

KYRIAKOS AKATHIOTIS
Chairman of Birmingham Greek School

DATE OF BIRTH: 11.02.46
PLACE OF BIRTH: Lefkoniko
MARITAL STATUS: Married to Elenitsa Flasou from Solea, now deceased.
CHILDREN: Four sons and one daughter.
MEMBERSHIPS: Member of Action for Cyprus
HOBBIES AND INTERESTS: Football, Manchester Utd fan.
PERSONAL PROFILE: Chain of fish and chip shops and restaurants in the Midlands and a travel agency called Azure Travel.
Chairman of Birmingham Greek School.

STEPHEN ALAMBRITIS
Political Advisor

DATE OF BIRTH: 22.02.57
PLACE OF BIRTH: Aradippou
MARITAL STATUS: Married to Athanasia, from Nicosia, Senior Haematologist at Charing Cross Hospital.
CHILDREN: Maria and Andreas.
SCHOOLS/COLLEGE: Elliot School, London School of Economics
ACADEMIC QUALIFICATIONS: BA (Politics), MSc (Economics), MA (Business Law).
MEMBERSHIPS: National Union of Journalists, Amicus.
HOBBIES AND INTERESTS: Fulham FC, Class 1 Referee. Enjoys real ale and is a member of CAMRA.
PERSONAL PROFILE: Advisor Parliamentary Affairs to the UK-wide Federation of Small Businesses. On a number of Government Task Forces at the Cabinet Office and at DfES and DEFRA. Recently elected Labour Councillor for the London Borough of Merton. Came close to being selected by the Labour Party's National Executive Committee for a safe seat in the 1997 and 2001 General Elections. Now on the Party's official list of Parliamentary Candidates for the next General Election.
Address: 2 Catherine Place, Westminster, SW1E 6HF
Tel: 020 7592 8100 alambritis@fsbdial.co.uk

KATHY ALEXANDER
Solicitor/Lecturer/Writer

DATE OF BIRTH: 16.12.58
PLACE OF BIRTH: Myrtou village, Kyrenia.
MARITAL STATUS: Single
SCHOOLS/COLLEGES: University of London, Birbeck and Bedford Colleges. University of Ghent, Belgium, University College London, Queen Mary & Westfield College.
ACADEMIC QUALIFICATIONS BA Honours, 1st Class Classics, MA Ancient History, PhD (Distinction) in Sciences, Philosophy and Literature, Diploma in Law, Postgraduate Diploma in Law, Solicitors Professional Exam.
HOBBIES & INTERESTS: Writing, production of plays, active participation in TV chat shows, campaigning on behalf of the Cypriot community and for animal welfare.
PERSONAL PROFILE: Three-time parliamentary candidate for the Liberal Party, first ever Cypriot candidate. Leader of the newly formed Democrat Liberal Reformist Party of United Cyprus.

ALEX ALEXANDROU
Optician

DATE OF BIRTH: 23.12.69
PLACE OF BIRTH: Famagusta
MARITAL STATUS: Married to Hayley Vowles from Deal, Kent.
CHILDREN: Haris and Emily.
SCHOOLS/COLLEGE: Pancyprian Gymnasium in Nicosia; City-Islington College; City University London.
PROFESSIONAL QUALIFICATIONS: Qualified Dispensing Optician & Ophthalmic Optician.
HOBBIES AND INTERESTS: Running, diving and football.
PERSONAL PROFILE: Qualified Optician for the last five years. Shop owner of Optikal Opticians with Kiki Soteri. eyes@optikal.co.uk

JAMES ALEXANDROU
Actor

DATE OF BIRTH: 12.04.85
PLACE OF BIRTH: London. Grandparents from Akanthou.
MARITAL STATUS: Single
SCHOOLS/COLLEGE: Anna Scher Theatre School.
HOBBIES AND INTERESTS: Keen basketball player, swimming (has swam at County level), football, is an Arsenal fan.
PERSONAL PROFILE: James is an actor and appears regularly in the *East Enders* BBC TV Drama as Martin Fowler. He has also appeared on TV in *Friends Like These, Celebrity Special Live and Kicking,* and *Diggit.*

DEMITRIS (Douglas) ALEXIOU
Solicitor

DATE OF BIRTH: 24.04.42
PLACE OF BIRTH: London. Father, Augustis, from Paphos; Mother, Maria, from Akanthou.
MARITAL STATUS: Married to Shirley Wale.
CHILDREN: Mark and Katie.
SCHOOLS/COLLEGE: Eaton House Prep School, St. Paul Public School, Kings College, University of London.
ACADEMIC QUALIFICATIONS: LLB Honours
HOBBIES AND INTERESTS: Football, tennis, golf and collecting fountain pens.
PERSONAL PROFILE: Became a Solicitor in 1970. In 1971, went to Gordon Dadds as Assistant Solicitor and went on to become Senior Partner. Left July 2001 and formed Alexiou, Fisher Philipps. Member of the Greek Cypriot Brotherhood. Voted one of the top three family Law Solicitors in England. Acted for Duchess of York, Sarah Brightman and Mel B. Went on Spurs Board of Directors in 1980, Chairman 1982-84, currently club Vice President.

ENTRANTS IN GREEK CYPRIOTS IN THE UK HAVE BEEN NOMINATED FOR THEIR ACHIEVEMENTS AND CONTRIBUTIONS. YOU CAN NOMINATE SOMEONE OR YOURSELF WHO DESERVES TO BE IN THE BOOK. ENTRIES ARE FREE.
SEND IN YOUR NOMINATIONS, INCLUDING NAME, CONTACT ADDRESS, TELEPHONE NUMBER AND EMAIL TO
GREEK CYPRIOTS IN THE UK
111 ST THOMAS'S ROAD LONDON N4 2QJ   TELEPHONE 020 7503 3498
EMAIL cypriotwhoswho@aol.com

MARK ALEXIOU
Owner of Pangaea Nightclub

DATE OF BIRTH: 17.06.75
PLACE OF BIRTH: London. Father, Douglas Alexiou, from Akanthou; Mother, Shirley, from UK.
MARITAL STATUS: Single
SCHOOLS/COLLEGE: Stowe Public School.
HOBBIES AND INTERESTS: Films, snowboarding, DJ-ing, fast cars, football, Tottenham supporter.
PERSONAL PROFILE: Former Nightclub DJ in Metropolitan Turnmills, Icini, KBar. Owns Lunasa Bar in Kings Road Chelsea where clientele has included Kylie Minogue, Jodie Kidd, Mel B, Max Beesley, Gianfranco Zola and Jay Kay. Also owns Pangaea Nightclub in Piccadilly.

SAVVAS ALEXANDROU
Chairman of St Spyridon Church in Great Yarmouth

DATE OF BIRTH: 23.1.50
PLACE OF BIRTH: Pelendri, Limassol
MARITAL STATUS: Married to Despo from Limassol.
CHILDREN: Alex, Qualified Electronics Engineer and Soulla, Qualified Beauty Therapist.
HOBBIES AND INTERESTS: Football (Man Utd fan), and swimming.
PERSONAL PROFILE: Has small catering business in Great Yarmouth. Chairman of St Spyridon Church in Great Yarmouth.
Email: Alex1sav@aol.com

ADONIS ALVANIS
Musician

DATE OF BIRTH: 31.07.65
PLACE OF BIRTH: London. Father from Nicosia.
MARITAL STATUS: Single
SCHOOLS/COLLEGES: Westminster City School, Guildhall School of Music and Drama.
QUALIFICATIONS: AGSM, FLCM
MEMBERSHIPS: MU, PRS, PAMRA, SPNM
HONOURS/AWARDS: Lennox Berkeley Prize for Composition (1992).
PERSONAL PROFILE: Violinist and Composer. Performed in renowned concert halls throughout Europe. Recordings for BBC, LWT, Carlton, Virgin Records America, MCA, EMI, Sony Classical.

LOUIS DEMETRIUS ALVANIS
Musician

DATE OF BIRTH: 21.12.60
PLACE OF BIRTH: London. Father from Nicosia.
MARITAL STATUS: Married
CHILDREN: Triplets.
SCHOOLS/COLLEGES: Royal Academy of Music, London.
PROFESSIONAL QUALIFICATIONS: Dip Ram, ARCM
HONOURS/AWARDS: Hellenic Foundation Arts Award 1990, RAM scholarships and top prizes in piano and composition.
HOBBIES AND INTERESTS: Classic cars. Organising exhibitions of works by contemporary painters.
PERSONAL PROFILE: Concert pianist. First public performance aged nine at South Bank Centre, London. Royal Festival Hall, concerto debut in 1981 before a capacity audience. Has gained an international reputation as a musician of outstanding technical brilliance and sensitivity. Performs extensively in major concert halls in UK and throughout Europe, appearing with leading orchestras and conductors. Has broadcast widely on radio and television. Commercially available CD recordings feature works of Bach, Brahms, Chopin, Schumann, Scriabin.

CHRISTAKIS AMERICANOS
Chartered Certified Accountant

DATE OF BIRTH: 26.10.35
PLACE OF BIRTH: Yialousa
MARITAL STATUS: Married to Stella, from Leonarisso.
CHILDREN: Maria, Sylvia, John - all Accountants.
SCHOOLS/COLLEGE: Yialousa Gymnasium, Nicosia College.
HOBBIES AND INTERESTS: Music, swimming and reading.
PERSONAL PROFILE: Consultant partner in John Alexander Ltd Accountants in Southgate. Was Chairman and Treasurer of Yialousa Association in Uk. Treasurer of Twelve Apostles Church in Hertfordshire.

KOULLA ANASTASI
Programme Buyer for the History and Biography Channel and Contributor to 'Greek Cypriots in the UK'

DATE OF BIRTH: 29.11.76
PLACE OF BIRTH: London. Father from Kapedhes. Mother from Yialousa.
MARITAL STATUS: Married to Greg, an Accountant, born in London (Parents from Lymbia and Tymbou).
CHILDREN: Jack, born 2004.

SCHOOLS/COLLEGE: Southgate School, Churchill College, Cambridge.
ACADEMIC QUALIFICATIONS: MA History
HOBBIES AND INTERESTS: Reading and travelling.
PERSONAL PROFILE: Programme Buyer for the History channel and the Biography channel. Contributor to 'Greek Cypriots in the UK'.

MARIA ANASTASI (née DEMETRIOU)
Social Worker, Child Protection

DATE OF BIRTH: 29.09.61
PLACE OF BIRTH: London. Family from Voni, Nicosia.
MARITAL STATUS: Married to George, Youth Centre Manager (Parents from Achna).
CHILDREN: Pavlos and Neove.
SCHOOLS/COLLEGE: Tollington Park School, Middlesex University, South Bank University.
ACADEMIC QUALIFICATIONS: B.Ed (Honours)/ Diploma in Applied Social Studies (Postgraduate)
PROFESSIONAL QUALIFICATIONS: QSW Certificate for Qualified Social Workers.
MEMBERSHIPS: British Association of Social Workers.
HOBBIES AND INTERESTS: Reading, cooking, watching football and spending time with family.
PERSONAL PROFILE: Currently a Child Protection Advisor for LB Haringey. Previously employed by LB Barnet as a Child Protection Co-ordinator. Former Social Worker in Haringey (1988-1999), starting as a Section II funded worker specifically for the Cypriot community. Was a member of EKON for many years and taught in Greek community schools, teaching Greek to English-speaking adults.

NATASHA ANASTASIADES (Stage name Natasha Anastasi)
Actress/Singer (Deceased)

DATE OF BIRTH: 09.12.82
PLACE OF BIRTH: London. Father, Mario, from Nicosia; Mother, Klida, from Ayios Dometios.
MARITAL STATUS: Single
SCHOOLS/COLLEGE: Sylvia Young Theatre School.
HOBBIES AND INTERESTS: Swimming and dancing.
PERSONAL PROFILE: Does acting, dancing and singing; appeared on TV in *Grange Hill, East Enders, Queens Nose, Esther Rantzen Show*. Part in *Evita* the film. Also did Haliborange advert. Was in the girl group In 2 You. Performed on the *Pepsi Chart Show, Pop 2000*. Produced own singles including *Into You, Unbelievable* and *Call Me*.

PETER JAMES ANDREA (Known as Peter Andre)
Entertainer

DATE OF BIRTH: 27.02.73
PLACE OF BIRTH: London. Father from Kyrenia (Harja and Ayios Amvrosios); Mother from Angastina.
MARITAL STATUS: Married to glamour model Jordan.
SCHOOLS/COLLEGES: Sudbury Junior School; Wembley High, London; Benowa High School, Australia.
PROFESSIONAL QUALIFICATIONS: In entertainment.
HONOURS/AWARDS: From *Smash Hits* – Monaco World Music Awards.
HOBBIES AND INTERESTS: Martial arts, jet-skiing and eating.
PERSONAL PROFILE: Pop singer who has had several chart hits and a sell-out concert at Wembley Arena. Recently entered the Aussie Jungle as a contestant in *I'm a Celebrity, Get Me Out of Here!*, making £214, 932 for his chosen charity, the National Society for the Prevention of Cruelty to Children (NSPCC). Peter released the single *Mysterious Girl*, which went straight to number one for the third time round, thus ensuring him a place in *The Guinness Book of Records*. 300, 000 copies of the record were sold and even more money was made for the NSPCC. His single *Insania* went to number three in the charts.

SOPHOCLES C ANDREADIS
Teacher and Writer (Deceased)

DATE OF BIRTH: 20.04.21
PLACE OF BIRTH: Yialloussa.
MARITAL STATUS: Married to Jeannie from Manchester
CHILDREN: Three daughters.
SCHOOLS/COLLEGES: Yialloussa Elementary School; Famagusta Gymnasium; Manchester University.
ACADEMIC QUALIFICATIONS: LLB (Honours)
HOBBIES AND INTERESTS: Reading.
PERSONAL PROFILE: Taught Greek in Manchester schools and at Manchester University. Has written books such as a text book of *Modern Greek, My First Rains*, and a Personal History of the Greek Community in Manchester and its Church (1843-1990).

DIMITRI ANDREAS
Actor

DATE OF BIRTH: 06.01.42
PLACE OF BIRTH: Rizokarpasso, Cyprus.
MARITAL STATUS: Married
CHILDREN: Andreas, a student.
SCHOOLS/COLLEGES: Webber Douglas School of Music and Dramatic Art.
MEMBERSHIPS: Equity
PERSONAL PROFILE: Has appeared on TV in *The Jury*, *Sam's Game*, *The Bill*, *Sunburn*, *London's Burning*, *Casualty*, *Minder* films, *Family Money*, *Demob*, *Into the Blue*, *Top Secret*. Founder member of Theatro Technis.

LISA ANDREAS
Singer

DATE OF BIRTH: 22.12.87
PLACE OF BIRTH: Chatham, Kent. Father from Canterbury, Kent; Mother and maternal grandparents from Pano Lakatamia, Nicosia, Cyprus.
MARITAL STATUS: Single
SCHOOLS/COLLEGES: Chatham Grammar School for Girls.
MEMBERSHIPS: Member of Music Union.
HONOURS/AWARDS: School Form Captain, two years running.
HOBBIES AND INTERESTS: Singing, dancing, drama, ice-skating, netball, song-writing, poetry, music and playing keyboards.
PERSONAL PROFILE: In 2000, whilst still at primary school, one of Lisa's poems was published in a book (Celebration 2000 Northern Kent) representing young poets from around the UK. She started singing at eleven years old, and has won many talent competitions, including the Strand Festival. She has also raised money in her local area for Children in Need, and appeared in a concert featuring Atomic Kitten, Damage and other well-known acts, before an 8000-strong audience. Lisa has been on CYBC over the Christmas period, and appeared on television in the UK, as well as singing live on radio, in many road shows and in a showcase in central London. She has recorded some of her own songs, worked with songwriters and recording studios, and been interviewed by several newspapers and radio stations and also represented Cyprus in the 2004 Eurovision Song Contest.

Address: c/o Management, 62 Lake Rise, Romford, Essex RM1 4EE
Tel: 01708 760544
Email: foxrecords@talk21.com

DR ANDREAS DEMETRIOU ANDREOU
Scientist/College Principal

DATE OF BIRTH: 04.09.50
PLACE OF BIRTH: Amargeti, Paphos, Cyprus.
MARITAL STATUS: Married to Efrosini, from Famagusta.
CHILDREN: Demetrios and Neovi, both at university.
SCHOOLS/COLLEGES: Paphos Gymnasium; City of Westminster College; Kings College, London; Brunel University.
ACADEMIC QUALIFICATIONS: BSc in Biochemistry; PhD in Organic Chemistry.
HOBBIES AND INTERESTS: Sport, reading, chess and community affairs.
PERSONAL PROFILE: Vice Chair of Governors, St Cyprians Greek Orthodox Primary School; President of Church Council, St Constantine and St Helens Church in Croydon; Principal of Dean College, London N7.

ANDY ANDREOU
Financial Controller

DATE OF BIRTH: 19.11.68
PLACE OF BIRTH: London. Father from Patriki; Mother from Argaki, Morphou.
MARITAL STATUS: Married to Paula.
CHILDREN: Sofie-Eliza Price; Zoë Marie Andreou; Emilia Louise Andreou.
SCHOOLS/COLLEGES: Ashmole School, Southgate, London; Warwick University.
ACADEMIC QUALIFICATIONS: BSc Engineering and Business Studies.
PROFESSIONAL QUALIFICATIONS: Chartered Management Accountant (ACMA).
MEMBERSHIPS: C.I.M.A.
HOBBIES AND INTERESTS: Five-a-side football, reading and theatre.
PERSONAL PROFILE: Former Treasurer of Local Residents' Association. Current occupation: Financial Controller.

ANTONIOS MICHAEL ANDREOU
Hellenic Brotherhood, Manchester

DATE OF BIRTH: 02.04.47
PLACE OF BIRTH: Ormidia, Cyprus.
MARITAL STATUS: Married to Chrystalla Andreou, a Book-keeping Assistant, from Larnaca, Cyprus.
CHILDREN: Iacovos; Costas; Michael.
SCHOOLS/COLLEGES: Hull University, Manchester Poly-technic.
ACADEMIC QUALIFICATIONS: BSc in Mathematics.
PROFESSIONAL QUALIFICATIONS: PGCE
PERSONAL PROFILE: Taught for five years at secondary schools, then became a self-employed bookkeeper from September 1978. Got involved with the Hellenic Brotherhood, Manchester, and then served the Church as Secretary and Chairman of the Committee. After a short break, was appointed a Trustee of the Church.

PAULA ANDREOU
Primary School Teacher

DATE OF BIRTH: 20.11.68
PLACE OF BIRTH: London. Mother from Nicosia
MARITAL STATUS: Married to Andy Andreou.
CHILDREN: Zoë Marie and Emilia Louise.
SCHOOLS/COLLEGES: Winchmore Primary School; Southgate Secondary School; North London Poly.
ACADEMIC QUALIFICATIONS: B.Ed Honours (2:1)
MEMBERSHIPS: NUT
HOBBIES AND INTERESTS: Reading, gardening and dancing.
PERSONAL PROFILE: Primary school teacher at Garden Suburb Infant School.

PERICLES ANDREOU
Chairman of Kontea Association UK

DATE OF BIRTH: 25.11.42
PLACE OF BIRTH: Kontea, Cyprus
MARITAL STATUS: Married to Elizabeth, from Kontea.
CHILDREN: Soulla, Joanna, Andreas.
SCHOOLS/COLLEGES: English School, Nicosia; Commercial School, Famagusta; London College of Fashion.

HOBBIES AND INTERESTS: Sport, football (Manchester United fan) and politics/current affairs.
PERSONAL PROFILE: Started work as a pattern cutter, then, in 1977, opened his own dress manufacturing business. Chairman of Kontea Community Association, former member of Ashmole Greek School Parents' Association. Representative of the Greek Parents' Association; also Representative of Ekeka, and of the National Federation of Cypriots. Member of the Planning Council Panel for Youth Clubs.

PETROS STELIOU ANDREOU
Ophthalmic Surgeon

DATE OF BIRTH: 08.09.66
PLACE OF BIRTH: London. Parents from Koma Tou Yiallou and Aradippou.
MARITAL STATUS: Married to Anita (Father Maltese, Mother English).
CHILDREN: Joseph
SCHOOLS/COLLEGES: Chase School for Boys (11-18); Southampton University.
ACADEMIC QUALIFICATIONS: 3 A Levels (2 at grade A); 10 O Levels (6 at grade A).
PROFESSIONAL QUALIFICATIONS: MBBS; FRCOphth.
MEMBERSHIPS: Royal College of Ophthalmologists.
HONOURS/AWARDS: Fellowship of Royal College of Ophthalmologists.
PERSONAL PROFILE: Specialist Ophthalmic Surgeon and Certified Specialist in Ophthalmology.

SOULLA ANDREOU
Teacher

DATE OF BIRTH: 12.11.69
PLACE OF BIRTH: London. Parents from Kontea.
MARITAL STATUS: Married to Andrew Sophocli from London (Father from Pyrka, Mother from Rizokarpasso).
SCHOOLS/COLLEGES: Osidge Primary, Ashmole Secondary, Middlesex Polytechnic
ACADEMIC QUALIFICATIONS: BA (Honours) in English.
PROFESSIONAL QUALIFICATIONS: PGCE, Counselling Course in Youth Work.
HOBBIES AND INTERESTS: Singing and theatre.
PERSONAL PROFILE: Taught from 1992-1996 at the Cyprus American Academy in Limassol. 1996-present: English teacher and community officer at Southgate School. Helps the 'Make a Wish' Foundation, which grants the wishes of children with terminal illnesses. Used to run the Kontea Youth Association, and taught the choir of the Greek Parents' Association.

ANDREW ANDREWS
Clay Pigeon Shooting

DATE OF BIRTH: 03.10.80
PLACE OF BIRTH: London. Parents from Nicosia, Cyprus.
MARITAL STATUS: Single
MEMBERSHIPS: Clay Pigeon Shooting Society.
HONOURS/AWARDS: GB Junior Championships, World Silver Medallist and European Gold Medallist in Clay Pigeon Shooting.
HOBBIES AND INTERESTS: Shooting and fishing.
PERSONAL PROFILE: An engineer who has won many competitions and trophies in clay pigeon shooting.

NIKOLAS ANDRONICOU
Actor

DATE OF BIRTH: 22.01.54
PLACE OF BIRTH: Liverpool, England. Father, Christopher, from Lefkara. Mother, Panayiota, from Kato-Drys.
MARITAL STATUS: Married to Charlotte, a Company Director from Denmark.
CHILDREN: Katerina and Christofina.
SCHOOLS/COLLEGES: West Derby High School; Harold Ackerley Drama School.
ACADEMIC QUALIFICATIONS: O and A Levels.
PROFESSIONAL QUALIFICATIONS: From LAMDA (in Drama)
MEMBERSHIPS: Equity; OFS World Net.
HOBBIES AND INTERESTS: Singing and bridge.
PERSONAL PROFILE: TV actor. Principal Shakespearean actor at Curium Amphitheatre. Has raised money for charity (Committee for Chest Diseases) over the years.

PAUL ANTONIOU ANENOMYLOS
Poet and Writer

DATE OF BIRTH: 02.07.49
PLACE OF BIRTH: Ormidia, Larnaca, Cyprus.
SCHOOL/COLLEGE: Ormidia Elementary Pancyprian Gymnasium.
HONOURS/AWARDS: In 1997 he was awarded 1st prize at Theatre of Mankind in London. A year later he won 1st prize at the European Jean Monet competition in Italy. He also won this competition again in 2002, when he was awarded 1st prize in Belgium. In the latter part of 2002 he was awarded the Millennium award for Haringey and Enfield.
HOBBIES & INTERESTS: Writing and reading.

PERSONAL PROFILE: Poet and writer, has written three books, two in Greek and one in English. They include: *Love for Freedom*, *My Soul Eyes* and *Breaking the Chains*.

STEVEN ANDREW ANGELI
Estate Agent/Property Developer

DATE OF BIRTH: 11.11.69
PLACE OF BIRTH: London Father from Ayios Loucas, Varosi, Cyprus; Mother from Trikomo, Cyprus.
MARITAL STATUS: Married to Ria, General Manager of Angeli Property Services (parents both from Larnaca).
CHILDREN: Andrew.
SCHOOLS/COLLEGES: Ashmole School, London N14, up to sixth form (Head Boy); Southbank University.
ACADEMIC QUALIFICATIONS: Eight O Levels, three A Levels; BSc (Honours) in Architectural Technology (2:1)
PROFESSIONAL QUALIFICATIONS: NAEA Practising Estate Agency.
MEMBERSHIPS: National Association of Estate Agents (NAEA); Vice Chairman of Green Lanes Business Association; Founding Chairman of Bounces Road Business Association.
HONOURS/AWARDS: Recognition by Government-backed management training scheme for management success, which led to a full-page feature in the *Daily Mail*. Angeli Property Services is the only company in Enfield to sit on the Local Authority Housing Advice & Scrutiny Panel.
HOBBIES AND INTERESTS: Music (has played the bouzouki for over ten years); fitness; travel and reading.
PERSONAL PROFILE: Estate Agent. Does a lot of charity work, both through the Rotary Club and personally.

CHRISTOS EMILIOS ANGELIDES
Group Product Director, Next

DATE OF BIRTH: 27.03.63
PLACE OF BIRTH: UK. Father from Nicosia, Cyprus.
MARITAL STATUS: Married to Suzanne, a self-employed garment agent, from USA.
CHILDREN: Nicole-Taylor and Max-Emilios.
SCHOOLS/COLLEGES: Langley School; Solihull College; Leicester Polytechnic.
ACADEMIC QUALIFICATIONS: BA (Honours) in Business Studies (2:1).
PROFESSIONAL QUALIFICATIONS: MDIP, Marketing
HOBBIES AND INTERESTS: Gym and golf.
PERSONAL PROFILE: Joined Next Main Board as an Executive Director in 2000.
Email: Christos_angelides@next.co.uk

MARLAIN ANGELIDES
Singer/Actor/Dancer

DATE OF BIRTH: 6.9
PLACE OF BIRTH: Athens, Greece. Father from Athens; Mother half-English, half-Cypriot from Paphos, Cyprus.
MARITAL STATUS: Single
SCHOOLS/COLLEGES: Falcon School, Cyprus; Imperial College of Science, Technology and Medicine, London; Boston Conservatory, USA; Royal Academy of Music, London.
ACADEMIC QUALIFICATIONS: Bsc in Biochemistry with Management; PGDip Musical Theatre.
HOBBIES AND INTERESTS: Dance, water-skiing, basketball, swimming, running, weight-training, theatre, cinema and socialising.
PERSONAL PROFILE: Represented Cyprus in the Eurovision Song Contest in Jerusalem, 1999 (with *Thane Erotas*).

PROFESSOR FLOYA ANTHIAS
Professor of Sociology

DATE OF BIRTH: 31.05.45
PLACE OF BIRTH: Nicosia, Cyprus. Father, Tefcros Anthias, from Kontea; Mother, Anastasia, from Aradippou.
MARITAL STATUS: Married to Ronald Ayres, Professor of Economics.
CHILDREN: Alexander, IT Specialist & Musician; Natasha, Research Assistant.
ACADEMIC QUALIFICATIONS: BSc in Sociology; MSc, PhD.
PROFESSIONAL QUALIFICATIONS: PGCE, Sociology; ACCS
MEMBERSHIPS: British Sociological Association.
HOBBIES AND INTERESTS: Reading, theatre and cinema.
PERSONAL PROFILE: Professor of Sociology at Oxford Brookes University. Member of the inter-university Research Committee on Cyprus. Author of numerous books and articles.

ANDREAS ANTONA
Restaurateur/Chef

DATE OF BIRTH: 24.09.57
PLACE OF BIRTH: Cuckfield, Sussex. Parents from Achna.
MARITAL STATUS: Married to Alison from Kenilworth, Warwickshire.
CHILDREN: Four children.
SCHOOLS/COLLEGES: Ashton House Preparatory School; Ealing College School; Ealing Technical College.
HONOURS/AWARDS: Michelin Rosette 2000 Guide; 1999 Craft Guild of Chefs; Hotel and Restaurant Chef of the Year Award.
HOBBIES AND INTERESTS: Reading and golf.
PERSONAL PROFILE: Owner of Simpsons Restaurant in the Midlands, which has achieved the Michelin star. Committee member and former chairman of the Midlands Association of Chefs. Governor at Birmingham College of Food, Tourism and Creative Studies.

VASSILLIS ANTONAS
Psychotherapist

DATE OF BIRTH: 30.05.74
PLACE OF BIRTH: Nicosia
MARITAL STATUS: Single
SCHOOLS/COLLEGES: Tasis Hellenic High School, University of La Verne Athens, South Bank University, Middlesex University.
ACADEMIC QUALIFICATIONS: BSc Psychology Graduate Diploma Psychotherapy, MSc Psychotherapy.
MEMBERSHIPS: Hellenic Medical Society, Association of Humanistic Psychology Practitioners.
HONOURS/AWARDS: Certificate of Honour for serving the Hellenic Medical Corps as a psychologist
HOBBIES AND INTERESTS: Motor sports, diving, reading and martial arts.
PERSONAL PROFILE: Worked as psychotherapist for the NHS for three years. Currently in Private Practice in Islington, London.

ANTONIS ANTONIADES
Businessman

DATE OF BIRTH: 1957
PLACE OF BIRTH: Paphos.
MARITAL STATUS: Married
CHILDREN: Christopher and Ariana.
SCHOOLS/COLLEGE: Southgate College.
ACADEMIC QUALIFICATIONS: OND Business Studies.
MEMBERSHIPS: Member of the Institute of Commercial Management.
HOBBIES AND INTERESTS: Football and travel.
PERSONAL PROFILE: Shortly after studying in England he returned to Cyprus to join the National Guard and complete his Military Service. Returning to the UK at the age of 25 he joined a property company that was involved in the purchasing and development of property in the residential and commercial sectors. In 1989, he set up C&A Agencies with Petros Petrou which developed to the Capital Accomodation company a major property business within the UK.

ANTONIS ANTONIADES
Journalist

DATE OF BIRTH: 25.02.29
PLACE OF BIRTH: Anaphotia, Larnaca.
MARITAL STATUS: Separated.
CHILDREN: Melanie, Material Designer; Anthony, doing Business Studies.
SCHOOLS/COLLEGES: Pancyprian Lyceum, Larnaca; Regent Street Polytechnic, London.
PROFESSIONAL QUALIFICATIONS: In Journalism
MEMBERSHIPS: National Federation of Cypriots in the UK; AKEL, and the Democratic Left.
HOBBIES AND INTERESTS: Writing and reading.
PERSONAL PROFILE: General Manager of Vema (Newspaper); Chair and Secretary of the Cyprus Committee of the Democratic Left.

ATHOS ANTONIADES
Martial Arts Expert

PLACE OF BIRTH: Platres, Cyprus.
MARITAL STATUS: Married to Susan Antoniades, a Beauty Therapist.
CHILDREN: Helen and Marianne.
SCHOOLS/COLLEGES: Westminster University
ACADEMIC QUALIFICATIONS: BA (Hons), ACEA, FMAAT
PROFESSIONAL QUALIFICATIONS: 5th Dan American Kenpo.
MEMBERSHIPS: Founder Member of American Kenpo Taiji Association.
HONOURS/AWARDS: Inducted into 'Martial Arts Hall of Fame'.
HOBBIES AND INTERESTS: Martial Arts.
PERSONAL PROFILE: Revolutionised American Kenpo by incorporating internal aspects of the arts.

GEORGE ANTONIADES
Solicitor

DATE OF BIRTH: 17.07.47
PLACE OF BIRTH: Ktima, Paphos, Cyprus.
MARITAL STATUS: Divorced
CHILDREN: Yolanda has a degree in Psychology; Alexander, in final year of a Classics degree at Bristol University.
SCHOOLS/COLLEGES: William Ellis School, Highgate; Jesus College, Oxford.

ACADEMIC QUALIFICATIONS: BA (Oxon); MA (Oxon)
PROFESSIONAL QUALIFICATIONS: Solicitor of the Supreme Court. Passed Finals with distinction in Land Law and Accounts.
MEMBERSHIPS: Club Secretary, Woodford Archery Club.
HONOURS/AWARDS: Award for bravery from High Sheriff of Essex.
HOBBIES AND INTERESTS: Classical History, archery and gardening.
PERSONAL PROFILE: As a solicitor in private practice, has helped many Cypriots to get their rights.
Current Essex Archery Champion and double record-holder at 180 yards.

RENO ANTONIADES
Solicitor

DATE OF BIRTH: 27.07.66
PLACE OF BIRTH: London. Father, Mikis, from Davlos; Mother, Joy, from London.
MARITAL STATUS: Married to Julie Cunningham from London (Originally from Ireland).
SCHOOLS/COLLEGES: Alleyns School in Dulwich; Leicester University; London Law School.
ACADEMIC QUALIFICATIONS: LLB (Honours)
HOBBIES AND INTERESTS: Football (Tottenham supporter), cinema and travelling.
PERSONAL PROFILE: Worked for Herbert Smith Law Firm from 1989-1993, and for Olswang (1993-4); From 1994-present, he is working for Lee and Thompson, expert Film and Television Lawyers.

Address: Lee and Thompson, Green Garden House, 15-22 St Christophers Place, London W1V 1NL
Email: renoantoniades@leeandthompson.com

ANDREAS ANTONIOU
Restaurateur

DATE OF BIRTH: 11.06.43
PLACE OF BIRTH: Koma tou Yialou
MARITAL STATUS: Married
CHILDREN: Three
HONOURS/AWARDS: London Weekend Award, Evening Standard Award and London Tonight Award 2003 for his restaurant.
HOBBIES AND INTERESTS: Driving cars and Arsenal FC.
PERSONAL PROFILE: Owner of Vrisaki Restaurant, North London (founded in 1981). Chairman of the Koma tou Yialou Association, UK.

ANTONIOS VARNAVAS ANTONIOU
Obstetrician/Gynaecologist

DATE OF BIRTH: 28.10.67
PLACE OF BIRTH: London. Parents from Milia, Cyprus.
MARITAL STATUS: Engaged to Dr Evanthia Frangos, born in Greece.
SCHOOLS/COLLEGES: Kings College, London; Hunterian Institute; Royal College of Surgeons; Guys & St Thomas Medical School, London
QUALIFICATIONS: BSc Honours in Immunology, PhD, Faculty of Medicine; MBBS; MRCOG
MEMBERSHIPS: Royal College of Obstetrics & Gynaecology. British Society of Immunology. British Medical Association.
HONOURS/AWARDS: Cochrane Prize for medical students. Enid Linder Foundation Award. Foulkes Foundation Fellowship.
HOBBIES AND INTERESTS: Travelling, scuba diving, photography, listening to jazz and Greek music.
PERSONAL PROFILE: Obstetrician/gynaecologist with special interest in keyhole surgery. Previously Senior Registrar, University College Hospital. Was President of Democratic Movement of Cypriot Students in Britain and Co-editor of Students Voice. Consultant at Newham University Hospital, London.

ANTONIS STAVROS ANTONIOU
Head of Compliance, Laiki Bank

DATE OF BIRTH: 08.08.64
PLACE OF BIRTH: Hillingdon, Uxbridge. Father from Kato Varosi; Mother from Rizokarpasso.
MARITAL STATUS: Married to Maria Antoniou.
CHILDREN: Three, Katrina; Christina; Alex – all still at school.
SCHOOLS/COLLEGES: William Ellis and Queen Elizabeth Boys'; City of London Polytechnic.
ACADEMIC QUALIFICATIONS: HND Business & Finance (Distinction).
PROFESSIONAL QUALIFICATIONS: Associate of Chartered Institute of Bankers (ACIB).
MEMBERSHIPS: Member of Institute of Bankers.
HOBBIES AND INTERESTS: Spending time with his family, football, badminton, swimming, films, classical and Greek music.
PERSONAL PROFILE: From 2002, was Branch Manager of Laiki Bank at their main West End branch. Now Head of Compliance Dept. Loves getting involved in the Radiomarathon Appeal for children with special needs.

GREGORY ANTONIOU
Barrister/Councillor

PLACE OF BIRTH: London. Father from Famagusta. Mother from Ayios Theodoros, Karpassia.
MARITAL STATUS: Single
SCHOOLS/COLLEGES: Firs Farm and Winchmore Schools, Imperial College London, Hughes Hill Cambridge, University College London.
QUALIFICATIONS: BSc (Honours) ARCS, Dip. Comp. Sc, LLM. Called to the Bar March 2000 (Inner Temple).
MEMBERSHIPS: Inner Temple, Conservative Party, MENSA.
HOBBIES AND INTERESTS: Politics, history and music.
PERSONAL PROFILE: Barrister-at-Law, Councillor in the London Borough of Enfield (elected May 2002).

Address: Members' Room, Enfield Council, PO Box 50, Civic Centre, Silver St, Enfield EN1 3XA

KATRINA ANTONIOU
Dancer

DATE OF BIRTH: 12.07.85
PLACE OF BIRTH: London; grandmother from Rizokarpasso; grandfather from Famagusta.
MARITAL STATUS: Single
SCHOOLS/COLLEGES: Rush Croft School, Epping Forest College.
ACADEMIC QUALIFICATIONS: 10 GCSEs and 2 A Levels.
MEMBERSHIPS: British Theatre Dance Association
HONOURS/AWARDS: Has passed many dance examinations and entered various competitions. Qualified for the All-England Championship Finals, in which she achieved runner-up in the Tap Section in 1999 (aged 14), runner-up in the Song and Dance Section in 2003, and third place in the Tap Section (aged 18).
HOBBIES AND INTERESTS: Dancing
PERSONAL PROFILE: After A Levels, joined Kounnis & Partners Plc and is currently part of the payroll department. Now training to become a dance teacher.

MICHAEL ANTONIOU
Scientist/Senior Lecturer

DATE OF BIRTH: 20.02.55
PLACE OF BIRTH: Famagusta. Father from Komi Kebir.
MARITAL STATUS: Married to Janey Antoniou (neé White), formerly Research Scientist, now Mental Health Trainer, from London.
SCHOOLS/COLLEGES: Hampstead Comprehensive School; University of Oxford (Hertford College); University of Reading.
ACADEMIC QUALIFICATIONS: BA (Oxon), Biochemistry; PhD .
HOBBIES AND INTERESTS: Light aircraft flying, transcendental meditation, organic food and farming.
PERSONAL PROFILE: Senior Lecturer in Molecular Genetics, GKT School of Medicine, Guy's Hospital, London. Helps the UK Thalassaemia Society and the Muscular Dystrophy Campaign. Biotechnology Advisor to Greenpeace, Friends of the Earth, Soil Association. Professional research interests: human gene control mechanisms; safe and efficacious gene therapy for thalassaemia and muscular dystrophy.

MICHAEL ANTONIOU
Chartered Accountant

DATE OF BIRTH: 26.02.62
PLACE OF BIRTH: London. Parents from Milia, Cyprus.
MARITAL STATUS: Married to Lisa, from Achna, Cyprus.
CHILDREN: Andrianna and Kristina.
SCHOOLS/COLLEGES: Chace School for Boys, Enfield; London School of Accountancy; Westminster University.
QUALIFICATIONS: FCCA, Postgraduate Certificate in Management.
MEMBERSHIPS: Fellow of the Association of Chartered Certified Accountants.
HOBBIES AND INTERESTS: Chess, organic gardening, swimming and distance running.
PERSONAL PROFILE: Worked in public practice for (taxation, auditing, systems implementation and business development). Moved to industry, assisting in the expansion of an insurance mutual. Currently on contract with an international re-insurer (turnover $100 million), and in the process of setting up Business Support (UK) Ltd, a financial services company.

Email: ma@accamail.com

NICK ANTONIOU
Accountant

DATE OF BIRTH: 04.11.60
PLACE OF BIRTH: London. Parents from Rizokarpasso and Larnaca.
MARITAL STATUS: Married to Christalla from London, parents from Akaki and Aradippou.
CHILDREN: Phillipa & Miranda - still at school.
SCHOOLS/COLLEGES: Stationers, Barnet College, North London Polytechnic.
PROFESSIONAL QUALIFICATIONS: FCCA
HOBBIES AND INTERESTS: Football, music, gardening, travel, DIY and cars.
PERSONAL PROFILE: An Accountant Partner/Director in Smith & Williamson Chartered Accountants, ranked eleven in the UK League Tables of Accounting Firms. A regular contributor to articles on accounting, financial and taxation issues in the national press and has featured in the *Daily Telegraph, Evening Standard*. Writes regularly for the Building Magazine and Drapers Record. Active member of the governing body of the Hellenic School of High Barnet. Past Chairman and currently Vice Chairman, now also Treasurer, Independent Greek Schools of England.

TONY ANTONIOU
Chairman Omonia Youth FC, London

DATE OF BIRTH: 27.07.60
PLACE OF BIRTH: London. Father from Leonarisso; Mother, Tymbou.
MARITAL STATUS: Married to Maria, a Financial Adviser, (father from Xylotymbou).
CHILDREN: Christopher, at school.
SCHOOLS/COLLEGE: Clerkenwell & St William of York.
PROFESSIONAL QUALIFICATIONS: Advanced Financial Planning Certificate.
HOBBIES AND INTERESTS: Football and music.
PERSONAL PROFILE: Independent Financial Adviser at Thomas Anthony Mortgage & Financial Services. Former Secretary of New Salamis FC, currently Chairman of Omonia Youth FC. Qualified Football Association Coach.

NICK APOSTOLIDES
Senior Lecturer

DATE OF BIRTH: 10.04.50
PLACE OF BIRTH: London. Father from Limassol; Mother from Platres.
MARITAL STATUS: Married to Phoebe from Nicosia.
CHILDREN: Kiki, Victoria and Michael.
SCHOOLS/COLLEGES: George Monoux, Walthamstow; Lancaster University; City University.
ACADEMIC QUALIFICATIONS: BA Economics.
PROFESSIONAL QUALIFICATIONS: MBA Finance
HOBBIES AND INTERESTS: Football (Leyton Orient fan), sport, travel, cars and music.
PERSONAL PROFILE: Senior Lecturer at the University of the West of England (UWE). Research interest: annual general meetings.

EVANGELOS APOSTOLOU
Solicitor/Barrister

DATE OF BIRTH: 23.06.69
PLACE OF BIRTH: London. Father from Mandres; Mother from Moniatis.
MARITAL STATUS: Single
SCHOOLS/COLLEGES: Holloway School, University College London, Lincolns Inn.
PROFESSIONAL QUALIFICATIONS: Called to the Bar of England and Wales. Admitted as Advocate by the Cypriot Bar Association. Admitted as Solicitor of the Supreme Court.
PERSONAL PROFILE: Solicitor and Barrister. Has worked in Cyprus with Christos Pourgourides & Co. Now legal counsel for Europe, Middle East and Africa for Fujitsu Services.

SOFIA NEOPHITOU APOSTOLOU
Fashion Editor

DATE OF BIRTH: 21.12.65
PLACE OF BIRTH: London. Father from Morphou; Mother from Episkopion.
MARITAL STATUS: Married to Apostolos Demos Apostolou.
CHILDREN: Zacharia
SCHOOLS/COLLEGES: Southgate College; Middlesex University.
ACADEMIC QUALIFICATIONS: 9 O Levels, 3 A Levels, BA Honours, Interior Design.
HOBBIES AND INTERESTS: Cinema, galleries, travel, music and theatre.
PERSONAL PROFILE: Fashion Editor of Independent Saturday Magazine, 10 Magazine, Italian Vogue and Sunday Times.

ARIS SAVVA ARESTIS
Civil Engineer

DATE OF BIRTH: 01.02.43
PLACE OF BIRTH: Polemi, Paphos, Cyprus
MARITAL STATUS: Married to Helen Margery (née Fraser), a Medical Secretary, from Glasgow.
CHILDREN: Nikolas, Doctor in Edinburgh; Christina, Dancer with the Royal Ballet in London; Alexandros, Architectural student at King's College, Cambridge.
SCHOOLS/COLLEGES: Elementary School, Ktima, Paphos; Greek Gymnasium, Paphos; 5th Boys' Gymnasium, Athens, Greece; Glasgow University.
ACADEMIC QUALIFICATIONS: BSc in Civil Engineering.
PROFESSIONAL QUALIFICATIONS: Eur Ing; Bsc C'Eng; FICE; MCS.
MEMBERSHIPS: Fellow of the Institute of Civil Engineers.
HOBBIES AND INTERESTS: Hunting, fishing and walking.
PERSONAL PROFILE: Civil Engineer Divisional Director. Member of Governing Council of the Greek Orthodox Cathedral of St Luke's, Glasgow.

FANOULLA ARGYROU
Researcher/Journalist/Author

DATE OF BIRTH: 09.08.48
PLACE OF BIRTH: Nicosia, Cyprus.
MARITAL STATUS: Married to Demitrios Argyrou, Manager with Bank of Cyprus UK, from Yialloussa.
CHILDREN: Katina and Antonis.
SCHOOLS/COLLEGES: St Joseph's School, Nicosia.
HOBBIES AND INTERESTS: Reading, writing and gardening.
PERSONAL PROFILE: Has had articles published in Greek-Cypriot newspapers, including Simerini, Eleftherotypia and others in London. Also published in Parikiaki, Ta Nea and The Times of Barnet. Has been London Correspondent for Simerini and Radio Proto, and for Radio Elios in Larnaca. Is one of the founders of the Greek Women's Philanthropic Association of Finchley and Barnet. Books published include: *Cyprus Under the Hammer*; *This is How They Destroyed Cyprus*; *From Union to Occupation*; *Conspiracy*; *Genocide*; *Hypocrisy*; *Conspiracy or Blunder*.

GEORGINA ARGYROU
Radio presenter

DATE OF BIRTH: 21.07.72
PLACE OF BIRTH: London. Father from Mazotos; Mother from Akanthou.
MARITAL STATUS: Married to Michael Sergeant, a BBC reporter from London.
SCHOOLS/COLLEGES: Woodford County High School for Girls; University of London (School of Slavonic and East European Studies).
ACADEMIC QUALIFICATIONS: BA Honours, Russian and Soviet Studies.
PROFESSIONAL QUALIFICATIONS: Radio Broadcasting Foundation; CNN Internship
MEMBERSHIPS: Amnesty, NSPCC.
HOBBIES AND INTERESTS: Jazz, singing, theatre work and writing (currently working on a novel).
PERSONAL PROFILE: Georgina is a journalist employed as a presenter and newsreader for LBC 97.3 FM and Heart 106.2 FM, and is currently the voice of the Sky Patrol. Other radio work includes presenting on ITN News Direct and newsreading for LGR. TV employment includes editorial and production work (mainly foreign news at ITN, Channel Four News, the BBC and APTN). She was a reporter and assistant producer on BBC Newsround, and has also worked in the Press, including reporting for the *Cyprus Mail*.

GEORGE ARISTIDIS ARISTIDOU
Dental Surgeon/Lecturer

DATE OF BIRTH: 15.07.71
PLACE OF BIRTH: London. Parents from Akanthou.
MARITAL STATUS: Single
SCHOOLS/COLLEGES: St Dunstan's College, Catford; King's College School of Medicine and Dentistry, University of London; Eastman Dental Institute, University of London.
ACADEMIC QUALIFICATIONS: 9 O Levels and 3 A Levels.
PROFESSIONAL QUALIFICATIONS: BDS (Lon); MSc Prosth.
MEMBERSHIPS: British Society for the Study of Prosthetic Dentistry; British Dental Association; Angloakanthou Aid Society.
HOBBIES AND INTERESTS: Bouzouki-playing, football and basketball.
PERSONAL PROFILE: Dental surgeon, Lecturer in prosthetic dentistry.

CHRIS ARNAOUTI
Consultant Engineer/Lecturer

DATE OF BIRTH: 30.1.42
PLACE OF BIRTH: Ayios Georgios, Famagusta, Cyprus.
MARITAL STATUS: Married to Margaret Grace Redruth, a Charity Worker, from Cornwall.
CHILDREN: Maria and Nicos.
SCHOOLS/COLLEGES: English High School, Famagusta, Cyprus; University College, London; University of Aston, Birmingham.
ACADEMIC QUALIFICATIONS: BSc (Eng), University College, London (1967); PhD, University of Aston (1972).
MEMBERSHIPS: Corporate Member of the Institute of Civil Engineers, 1977; Senior Vice Chairman of the Chiltern Branch of the Institute of Civil Engineers; Reader at the University of Hertfordshire.
HOBBIES AND INTERESTS: Wild flowers, with particular emphasis on orchids; history of London, particularly the development of tunnelling and underground transport.
PERSONAL PROFILE: Academic posts include Senior Research Fellow for the University of Warwick (financed by the Transport, Road Research Laboratories), and Principal Lecturer and Reader at the University of Hertfordshire for over 20 years. Senior Chairman of the Institute of Civil Engineers for the Chiltern Branch, representing the counties of Hertfordshire, Bedfordshire and Buckinghamshire. Involved with the Greek School in Coventry.

DR DEMETRA ARSALIDOU
Lecturer

DATE OF BIRTH: 06.08.72
PLACE OF BIRTH: Nicosia
MARITAL STATUS: Single
SCHOOLS/COLLEGES: Lyceum Archbishop Makarios, Nicosia; University of Lancaster; University of Exeter.
ACADEMIC QUALIFICATIONS: LLB (Lancaster); LLM, PhD (Exeter).
PROFESSIONAL QUALIFICATIONS: Accreditation as an Associate Teacher in Higher Education (University of Exeter).
HOBBIES AND INTERESTS: Singing, gym and long walks.
PERSONAL PROFILE: Lecturer in Law at the University of Exeter. Has been contributing to the organisation 'Children in Need' for the past four years. Author of *The Impact of Modern Influences on the Traditional Duties of Care, Skill and Diligence of Company Directors* (published by Kluwer Law International).

PAUL ARTEMI
Inventor

DATE OF BIRTH: 27.08.69
PLACE OF BIRTH: London. Father from Limassol; Mother from Famagusta.
MARITAL STATUS: Engaged to Laura Voyle, a Fashion Designer from England.
SCHOOLS/COLLEGES: Aylward
HONOURS/AWARDS: Queen's Award for Enterprise 2000
HOBBIES AND INTERESTS: Greek history, football and wine.
PERSONAL PROFILE: Invented the Artemi Spacemaker Hook, which is now sold in over 15 countries.

MICHAEL ARTEMIS
Educational Psychologist

DATE OF BIRTH: 28.01.56
PLACE OF BIRTH: London. Father from Xylotympou; Mother from Mazoto.
MARITAL STATUS: Single
SCHOOLS/COLLEGES: Universities of East London, Greenwich and London; Thames Polytechnic.
ACADEMIC QUALIFICATIONS: MSc in Educational Psychology; MA in Psychology; BEd Honours.

PROFESSIONAL QUALIFICATIONS: CNAA.
MEMBERSHIPS: Association of Educational Psychologists; National Union of Teachers; Executive Member of the Hackney Community and Police Consultative Group.
HOBBIES AND INTERESTS: Sport, reading and travel.
PERSONAL PROFILE: Counsellor and group leader at a summer camp in Massachusetts, USA (1986-90). Youth and community trainer and development worker with the London Borough of Haringey (1987-91). Secondary school teacher (1991-96). Senior specialist educational psychologist and specialist consultant to behaviour support team with the LB of Hillingdon (1997-present). Management member of Greek-Cypriot special needs group (1995-6). Chairman of Hackney Crime Prevention Conference (1995). Chairman of Amhurst Park Action Group (1993-2001) Numerous sporting qualifications include: 1st Dan, karate-ashindo; basketball coach (EBBA); gymnast, 1st class (BAGA); 1st degree black belt in Brithai karate; and the National Martial Arts Award for services to martial arts.

GEORGE ASTANIOU
Project Manager

DATE OF BIRTH: 21.10.43
PLACE OF BIRTH: London. Parents from Kaimakli.
MARITAL STATUS: Married to Melia, a part-time hospital Admininstration Assistant, from Yialoussa.
CHILDREN: Athena, Pharmacist; Christine, Trainee solicitor; Helen, Student at Royal Holloway, University of London.
SCHOOLS/COLLEGES: St Marylebone Grammar School; the Open University.
ACADEMIC QUALIFICATIONS: Full Tech Certificate; BA
PROFESSIONAL QUALIFICATIONS: I. Eng; MIIE
MEMBERSHIPS: Member of the Institution of Incorporated Engineers.
HOBBIES AND INTERESTS: Reading, gardening and DIY.
PERSONAL PROFILE: Installed major traffic control systems all over the world. Currently active in Brazil, Republic of Ireland and UK. Committee member of an independent Greek School for approximately ten years, and Chairman for one year.

ARGYROULLA (Loulla) ASTIN
Restaurateur/TV Presenter

DATE OF BIRTH: 23.06.51
PLACE OF BIRTH: Avgorou, Cyprus.
MARITAL STATUS: Married to Stewart Astin, also a restaurateur, from Manchester.
CHILDREN: Solos, Restaurant Manager; Vasos, in TV Production; Stefanos, still at school.
SCHOOLS/COLLEGES: Avgorou School; Salford College
ACADEMIC QUALIFICATIONS: Fashion Design Diploma
MEMBERSHIPS: The Restaurant Association.
HONOURS/AWARDS: Granada TV Woman of the Year Award, 1995.
HOBBIES AND INTERESTS: Cookery and travel.
PERSONAL PROFILE: Opened the Kosmos Taverna in Manchester with her husband. The restaurant is listed in the Egon Ronay Guide, the AA Top 500 Restaurants, and was Perrier Restaurant of the Year in 1990. Success brought media attention, and Loulla started with a programme called Eggs and Baker, after which she appeared many times on This Morning, and was eventually given her own series, Simply Greek. She then created the TV series Restaurant Dishes and World on a Plate, as well as appearing on Light Lunch. Loulla can be seen once a week on Granada Regional (The Afternoon Show) on satellite television. She contributes regularly to *Nurse to Nurse* magazine as their cookery correspondent, is involved with the Vegetarian Society, and is appearing in their promotional video, which will be shown in schools to promote vegetarian food.

VASOS ASTIN
TV Producer

DATE OF BIRTH: 31.05.77
PLACE OF BIRTH: Manchester, UK. Mother from Avgorou, Cyprus.
MARITAL STATUS: Single
SCHOOLS/COLLEGES: North Cestrian Grammar School; North Area College of Technology.
ACADEMIC QUALIFICATIONS: HNC
MEMBERSHIPS: BECTU (Broadcasting, Entertainment, Cinematography and Theatre Union)
HOBBIES AND INTERESTS: Music and cars
PERSONAL PROFILE: Works in production for Granada Television.

PANAYIOTIS ATAOU
Hairdresser

DATE OF BIRTH: 1.10.49
PLACE OF BIRTH: Avgorou, Cyprus.
MARITAL STATUS: Married to Anna N. Sialou, a Dressmaker from Sotira, Cyprus.
CHILDREN: Maria, Travel Advisor; Martha, Nursery Nurse.
PROFESSIONAL QUALIFICATIONS: Diploma in Ladies & Gents Hairdressing.
MEMBERSHIPS: AKEL; Greek Cypriot Brotherhood, Cardiff; Multicultural Crossroads; Race Equality.
HOBBIES AND INTERESTS: Fishing and gardening.
PERSONAL PROFILE: Chairman of Greek School of Cardiff for two years. Member of Greek Cypriot Brotherhood of Cardiff for 20 years, Chairman for two years.

Tel: 01446 744072

KATE ATHANASI (née PANAYIOTOU)
Marketing Manager

DATE OF BIRTH: 13.07.66
PLACE OF BIRTH: London. Father from Mesayeitonia, Limassol; Mother from Vatili, outside Larnaca.
MARITAL STATUS: Divorced
CHILDREN: Sophia Nicole.
SCHOOLS/COLLEGES: South Haringey Junior School; Michenden Secondary; GC School of Careers, Nicosia; College of NE London; the London Institute.
ACADEMIC QUALIFICATIONS: 9 O Levels, 2 A Levels; HNC in Business (with distinction; won award for top student in the UK for that year).
PROFESSIONAL QUALIFICATIONS: CIM Post-Graduate Diploma in Marketing.
MEMBERSHIPS: Chartered Institute of Marketing
HONOURS/AWARDS: School scholarships; HNC Student of the Year.
HOBBIES AND INTERESTS: Reading and psychology.
PERSONAL PROFILE: Global Marketing Manager for Chivas Regal. Set up Seagram's Charity Committee, as part of a team. Launched Chivas 200, the world's largest online charity auction, benefiting over 100 charities worldwide.

GEORGE ATHANASIADES
Company Director and Property Consultant

DATE OF BIRTH: 07.08.48
PLACE OF BIRTH: Tricomo
MARITAL STATUS: Married to Andre, from Marathovouno.
CHILDREN: Julie and Peter.
SCHOOLS/COLLEGES: Greek Gymnasium, Famagusta; Institute of Foreign Languages; Ecole Superieure de Journalisme.
MEMBERSHIPS: British Institute of Journalists, NUT.
HOBBIES AND INTERESTS: Writing, theatre, politics and music.
PERSONAL PROFILE: Worked with Islington Council as Chief Executive, Neighbourhood Office. Former General Manager of Lazari Investments Ltd. Worked for several Greek Newspapers and for Cyprus Radio Broadcasting. Contributor to the *Vema* newspaper, and Editor-in-Chief of the newspaper Parikiakos Typos. General Secretary of Ekeka (Cyprus Refugees Association). Secretary of Desy (Democratic Rally). Speaks Greek, French, English, German and Italian. Currently Director of Mayfair London Properties Ltd, and Cyprus Mayfair Properties.

BISHOP ATHANASIOS OF TROPAEOU
(Secular name: **Constantinos Kyriacou Theocharous**)
Bishop

DATE OF BIRTH: 20.11.43
PLACE OF BIRTH: Marathovounos, Famagusta, Cyprus.
SCHOOLS/COLLEGES: Pancyprian Gymnasium; Theological School, University of Athens
ACADEMIC QUALIFICATIONS: Degree in Theology.
HOBBIES AND INTERESTS: Byzantine music.
PERSONAL PROFILE: Ordinations: as a Deacon on 6.8.69; as a priest on 10.8.69; consecrated as Bishop on 12.4.97 (all took place in London). Based at the Greek Orthodox Church, Wood Green, London.

ANDREAS ATHANASIOU
College Principal

DATE OF BIRTH: 09.11.47
PLACE OF BIRTH: Lapathos, Famagusta.
MARITAL STATUS: Married to Maria from Pedhoulas.
CHILDREN: Nicholas, Economist/Accountant; Nelina, Solicitor.
SCHOOLS/COLLEGES: Gymnasium B', Famagusta, Cyprus; Walbrook College, London; City of London Polytechnic, Newport University USA- Distant Learning.
ACADEMIC QUALIFICATIONS: BA in Business Administration.
PROFESSIONAL QUALIFICATIONS: In Financial Accountancy and Management.
MEMBERSHIPS: Fellow: Institute of Financial Accountants; Fellow: Institute of Cost & Executive Accountants; Member: Institute of Management; Member: Association of Business Executives.
HOBBIES AND INTERESTS: Golf, gardening and DIY.
PERSONAL PROFILE: Founder and Principal of City College, London, since 1979. Prior to this, worked for the Bank of Cyprus in London for two years, in the manufacturing industry for four years, for a firm of Chartered Accountants for two years and for another private college for three years.

Website: www.citycollege.ac.uk

MICHALIS ATTALIDES
Cyprus High Commissioner in London, 1998-2000

DATE OF BIRTH: 15.11.41
PLACE OF BIRTH: Cyprus.
MARITAL STATUS: Married to Alexandra Alexandrou.
SCHOOLS/COLLEGES: London School of Economics; Princeton University.
ACADEMIC QUALIFICATIONS: BSc Econ; PhD.
PERSONAL PROFILE: Lecturer in Sociology at Leicester University, 1966-8. Sociologist, Cyprus Town and Country Planning Project, 1968-70. Military service, 1973-4. Journalist, 1974-5. Ministry of Foreign Affairs and Ambassador to France and Morocco, 1989-97. Ambassador to Spain and Portugal, 1991-5. Delegate to EU, 1995-8. High Commissioner in London, 1998-2000. Currently Permanent Secretary, Ministry of Foreign Affairs, Cyprus.

ANDREA AUGOUSTIS
Chairman of St Cosmas and St Damian Greek Church, Gospel Oak

DATE OF BIRTH: 07.03.25
PLACE OF BIRTH: Akanthou
MARITAL STATUS: Married to Christalla Lefkara.
CHILDREN: Nicholas, Headteacher; Thalia, Housewife; five grandchildren.
SCHOOLS/COLLEGES: Akanthou Elementary School
HONOURS/AWARDS: Archon Ecumenico Patriarchiou from the Greek Orthodox Church
HOBBIES AND INTERESTS: Church and travelling.
PERSONAL PROFILE: Came to England and went into the catering and grocery business. Agent for Metaxas for thirteen years. Chairman of St Cosmas & St Damian Greek Church (Gospel Oak) for 30 years.

NICHOLAS AUGOUSTIS
Deputy Headmaster

DATE OF BIRTH: 1950
PLACE OF BIRTH: London. Father, Andreas, from Akanthou; Mother, Christalla, from Lefkara.
MARITAL STATUS: Married to Jane, from Birmingham.
CHILDREN: Eleanor, in Promotions; Melanie, BSc in Marketing, Manchester University; Marianna, at school.
SCHOOLS/COLLEGES: Holland Park School; Teacher Training College; Birmingham University.
ACADEMIC QUALIFICATIONS: BPhilosophy (Education).
HOBBIES AND INTERESTS: Soccer (Tottenham supporter), and travel.
PERSONAL PROFILE: Deputy Head at Sheldon Heath Comprehensive School, Birmingham.

TINA AUGUSTI
Marketing Manager

DATE OF BIRTH: 13.06.74
PLACE OF BIRTH: Famagusta, Cyprus.
MARITAL STATUS: Single
SCHOOLS/COLLEGES: Southgate School
ACADEMIC QUALIFICATIONS: In Business Studies.
HOBBIES AND INTERESTS: Photography.
PERSONAL PROFILE: Marketing of council services and major campaigns for Enfield Council.

LATE ENTRIES

CHRISTINA ANDREOU
Production Journalist

DATE OF BIRTH: 31.05.76
PLACE OF BIRTH: London. Parents from Kalogrea.
MARITAL STATUS: Married to self employed Stavros Kallis from Dhali, Cyprus.
CHILDREN: None
SCHOOLS/COLLEGE: Haberdashers' Aske's Hatcham College Girls' School, Middlesex University, Westminster University. **ACADEMIC QUALIFICATIONS:** 12 GCSEs, 3 A Levels
PROFESSIONAL QUALIFICATIONS: BA Honours Media, Cultural and Communication Studies, Post Graduate diploma in Journalism, awarded with Merit.
MEMBERSHIPS: National Union of Journalists.
PERSONAL PROFILE: Production Journalist for London Tonight at ITN (Independent Television News) on ITV 1. Writes the news and helps put together the bulletins and programmes, seen by around a million people each day

STELIOS ANDREW
Creative Coach at Rush Hairdressing Salon

DATE OF BIRTH: 31.10.64
PLACE OF BIRTH: Stockwell, South London. Parents from Davlo and Trikomo.
MARITAL STATUS: Married to Nicky, a Housewife, from Rizokarpaso.
CHILDREN: Eleni and Demi.
SCHOOL/COLLEGE: Norbury Manor, Selhurst, Robert Fielding Hairdressing College **ACADEMIC QUALIFICATIONS:** 3 O Levels.
PROFESSIONAL QUALIFICATIONS: Hairdressing Honours with Distinction.
HONOURS/AWARDS: Andrew was responsible for training the team at Rush Salons, who have won the following awards:
Guild Photo Stylist, 2001. British Southern Hairdresser of the Year, 2001. Master Hairdresser of the Year, 2001. British F.A.M.E Team Member, 2001 & 2002. Southern Hairdresser of the Year, 2002 & 2004. Guild Art Team of the Year 2002 & 2003. Fellowship for British Hairdressing Team of the Year 2003. British Newcomer of the Year, 2003. British Artistic Team of the Year, 2004.
The above are the biggest prizes you can win in the Hairdressing Industry.
HOBBIES AND INTERESTS: Football and art.
PERSONAL PROFILE: As Creative Coach of Rush Hairdressers, Andrew's job is to train hairdressers and them to the highest standards in the world.

DR JOHN BEHIRI
Senior Lecturer/Associate Director, International Office

DATE OF BIRTH: 14.09.56
PLACE OF BIRTH: London. Parents from Rizokarpasso.
MARITAL STATUS: Married to Martha, from London.
CHILDREN: Christopher and Panayiotis.
SCHOOLS/COLLEGE: Creighton, Queen Mary, University of London.
ACADEMIC QUALIFICATIONS: B.Eng in Material Science, PhD Fracture, Mechanics of Bone Post Doc.
MEMBERSHIPS: Institute of Materials, Institute of Bio Medical Engineers.
HOBBIES AND INTERESTS: Squash and tennis.
PERSONAL PROFILE: Senior Lecturer in Bio-Medical materials at Queen Mary's University of London, specialising in the area of synthetic replacement materials used in the body. Director of the International office as well. Nominated by the Cyprus Government to act on the creditation panel to assess higher education colleges in Cyprus.

Email: J.C.Behiri@qmul.ac.uk

ANGELOS BESHONGES
Chairman of Ayios Amvrosios Association

DATE OF BIRTH: 05.12.54
PLACE OF BIRTH: Ayios Amvrosios. Father, Kyniakos Beshonges, teacher at English School, Nicosia.
MARITAL STATUS: Married to Michelle Koulafas, from London, (parents from Ayios Amvrosios and Ireland).
CHILDREN: Michael and Chantel.
SCHOOLS/COLLEGE: The English School, Nicosia.
HONOURS/AWARDS: Duke of Edinburgh Gold award.
HOBBIES AND INTERESTS: Shooting and tennis.
PERSONAL PROFILE: Chairman of Ayios Amvrosios Association.

ANDONEA (TONIA) MICHAEL BUXTON
Journalist/Presenter

DATE OF BIRTH: 12.05.68
PLACE OF BIRTH: Camden, London. Father from Larnaca; Mother from Latsia.
MARITAL STATUS: Married to Paul Buxton, an Architect.
CHILDREN: Antigoni Scarlet Delilah and Sophia Daisy Grace.
SCHOOLS/COLLEGE: St Marthas Convent, Hadley Wood, University of North London (UNL).
ACADEMIC QUALIFICATIONS: BA (Honours) Classical History & Philosophy.
PROFESSIONAL QUALIFICATIONS: P.G.C.E (Post Graduate Certificate in Education) A.N.B (Assoc of Natural Bodybuilders).
MEMBERSHIPS: NSPCC, Amnesty, World Family (Child Sponsor).
HONOURS/AWARDS: A.N.B (Association of Natural Bodybuilders), South East Britain 1997.
HOBBIES AND INTERESTS: Exercise, skiing, tri athlete, alternative complementary therapics, acting, singing and dance.
PERSONAL PROFILE: Part-time teacher, Lea Valley Primary. Presenter Satellite Channel R.M.N (Revolutionary Motoring Network), Author of *Have A Baby And Look Better Than Ever*, Angel Publications. Multi-Media and Web Journalist on Holistic Therapies, Make-up/Beauty, Well Being, Exercise/Nutrition for Boots.com, health.com.

SOTERIOS PETROU CHAKLIDES
Accountant

DATE OF BIRTH: 31.08.51
PLACE OF BIRTH: Ayios Epiktitos, Kyrenia.
MARITAL STATUS: Married to Anastasia, an Accountant, from Gerani Famagusta.
CHILDREN: Petros, studying Computer Science at university.
SCHOOLS/COLLEGE: 1963-1969, Terra Santa Cyprus, 1971-1973, Waltham Forest and Wandsworth, 1975-1976, Emily Wolf College.
ACADEMIC QUALIFICATIONS: 8 GCE O Levels, 3 GCE A Levels.
PROFESSIONAL QUALIFICATIONS: Part 3 ACCA.
HOBBIES AND INTERESTS: Football, politics & helping the Cypriot community in London.
PERSONAL PROFILE: Accountant (Own Practice) Cypriot Football League, UK Treasurer.

JOHN CHAMBI
Project manager for Radio Marathon and Chairman of UK Greek Business Directory

DATE OF BIRTH: 11.10.1971
PLACE OF BIRTH: London. Parents from Spathariko and Famagusta.
SCHOOLS/COLLEGE: Chase School, Barnet College, University of North London, Middlesex University.
ACADEMIC QUALIFICATIONS: BTEC Nat Dip, BA Honours in Business Studies, MSc BIS.
HOBBIES AND INTERESTS: Sport, basketball, was going to play for EPA in Cyprus, music and travel.
PERSONAL PROFILE: Worked for Lombard Trinity Finance as Strategic Marketing Analyst. Then with Barnet Council as Performance Indicator Analyst. Now with Radio Marathon as Project Manager - a registered charity that was set up in response to special needs identified within the Cypriot community, an initiative first lauched in Cyprus, by Cyprus Popular Bank. Since March 2000, Chairman of Greek Contacts Ltd, publisher of the UK Greek Business Directory and owners of www.Greekcontacts.com.

Contact details: Greek Contacts Ltd, 36 High St, London N14 6EE
Tel: 020 8351 0821
Email:contactjohnChambi@hotmail.com

TRIAS CHANIDOU (TSIANIDOU)
Voluntary Worker

DATE OF BIRTH: 13.10.20
PLACE OF BIRTH: Kaimakli, Nicosia
MARITAL STATUS: Widow.
CHILDREN: Cassius Chanides, Microbiologist (Retired); Dr Alex Chanas, Central research manager; Mary Kalymnios, teacher.
PROFESSIONAL QUALIFICATIONS: Professional dressmaker.
HOBBIES AND INTERESTS: Reading both English & Greek, gardening, knitting and dressmaking.
PERSONAL PROFILE: Daughter of the violinist Alexis (deceased), sister to musicians, violinist & teachers George Averof & Theseus Volantis, both deceased. Has musical knowledge, plays violin. A dressmaker. Involved with charity work, member of various organisations and associations such as The Womens Health Group, Cypriot Elderly Club, one of the original founders of the Academy Social Club in London founded in early 70s. Gives a lot of voluntary time and involved with Greek Cypriot cultural and social events and Greek schools.

DINO CHAPMAN
Artist

DATE OF BIRTH: 1962
PLACE OF BIRTH: London. Mother is Cypriot from Larnaca area, Cyprus
SCHOOLS/COLLEGE: Ravensbourne College of Art, Royal College of Art.
ACADEMIC QUALIFICATIONS: BA Art, MA Art.
PERSONAL PROFILE: Artist. Work shown in White Cube Gallery in London, Tokyo, Paris, New York, Toronto, in public collections such as Saatchi collection London, British Museum London, has appeared on TV Channel 4 on TV Sculpture.

DINOS AND JAKE CHAPMAN WERE SHORTLISTED FOR THE TURNER PRIZE 2003 WIDELY CONSIDERED TO BE ONE OF THE MOST IMPORTANT AND PRESTIGIOUS AWARDS FOR THE VISUAL ARTS IN EUROPE

JAKE CHAPMAN
Artist

DATE OF BIRTH: 1966
PLACE OF BIRTH: Cheltenham. Mother from Larnaca area.
SCHOOLS/COLLEGE: North East London Polytechnic, Royal College of Art.
ACADEMIC QUALIFICATIONS: BA Honours.
PERSONAL PROFILE: Brother of Dino Chapman. Work shown at the White Cube Gallery in Hoxton London, in Paris, New York, Tokyo, Toronto, Work shown in public collections such as Saatchi, London, British Museum, London, appeared on TV Channel 4 on TV Sculpture.

ANDREAS KLEARCHOU CHARALAMBIDES
Accountant

DATE OF BIRTH: 11.08.53
PLACE OF BIRTH: Pentayia,
MARITAL STATUS: Married to Paula, from Cardiff.
CHILDREN: Nicholas and George.
SCHOOLS/COLLEGE: B Gymnasium Morphou, City and East London College, Hammersmith and West London College.
ACADEMIC QUALIFICATIONS: Higher National Diploma in Business Studies (HND with Distinction). Post HND Diploma in Business Studies.
PROFESSIONAL QUALIFICATIONS: Chartered Certified Accountany FCCA.
MEMBERSHIPS: The Association of Chartered Certified Accountants.
HOBBIES AND INTERESTS: Football, The Cyprus Problem, Education, Greek Language & Customs.
PERSONAL PROFILE: Practice Accountant, a partner in Andrew Steale & Co. Treasurer to: The Greek-Cypriot Association of Hammersmith and Fulham 1988-1995, St Nicholas Greek School 2000- present, Parents Association. On the committee of the Greek Church of St Nicholas.

ARIS L CHARALAMBIDES
Accountant

DATE OF BIRTH: 16.04.37
PLACE OF BIRTH: Nicosia
SCHOOLS/COLLEGE: Pancyprian Gymnasium, Nicosia, Balham & Tooting College of Commerce.
PROFESSIONAL QUALIFICATIONS: Accountant. FAIA, FPAA Registered Auditor.
HOBBIES AND INTERESTS: Travelling, theatre and football - Chelsea fan.
PERSONAL PROFILE: In 1961 started own accountancy practice A.L. Charles. Vice President of the Greek Cypriot Brotherhood.

CHARALAMBOS CHARALAMBIDES
Consultant Orthopaedic Surgeon

DATE OF BIRTH: 02.05.62
PLACE OF BIRTH: Nicosia, Cyprus.
MARITAL STATUS: Married to Dr Irene Hadjikoumi, a Consultant Paediatrician, from Nicosia.
CHILDREN: Maria, at school, Stavros, eighteen months.
SCHOOLS/COLLEGE: Graduated from Kykko's Lyceum, Nicosia and from Aristotle University Medical School, Thessaloniki, Greece.
ACADEMIC QUALIFICATIONS: MD.
PROFESSIONAL QUALIFICATIONS: FRCS, FRCS (Trauma and Orthopaedics).
MEMBERSHIPS: Fellow of the British Orthopaedic Association.
HOBBIES AND INTERESTS: Swimming, photography and clay shooting.
PERSONAL PROFILE: Consultant Orthopaedic surgeon. Honorary Senior Lecturer, University College London, Medical School. Whittington Hospital, London.

CHARALAMBOS THEODOROU CHARALAMBIDES
Barrister

DATE OF BIRTH: 10.10.29
PLACE OF BIRTH: Moutoullas.
MARITAL STATUS: Married to Panayiota.
CHILDREN: Georgia and Theodora.
SCHOOLS/COLLEGE: Commercial School of Pedulas, Regent St Polytechnic.
PROFESSIONAL QUALIFICATIONS: Called to the Bar in 1959.
HOBBIES AND INTEREST: Snooker, poetry, reading and walking.
PERSONAL PROFILE: Barrister, London. Former representative of the British Hellenic chamber of Commerce. Worked for the Royal Courts of Justice for nearly 20 years as a Supreme Court Associate. Since his retirement in 1984, works as an Educational Consultant representing several institutes. In 1984 established the Academy of Negotiating.

ELENITSA CHARALAMBOU
Charity Events Organiser

DATE OF BIRTH: 27.6.29
PLACE OF BIRTH: Komi Kebir
MARITAL STATUS: Widow of George Charalambou, from Eftakomi.
SCHOOLS/COLLEGE: Komi Kebir Elementary School
CHILDREN: Harry, Chartered Accountant; Christine, Co.-Director; Katia, Co.Director.
HOBBIES AND INTERESTS: Organising charity events, socialising and travelling.
PERSONAL PROFILE: Pattern cutter, running the sample departments of the House of Nicholas Bridal Co., of which she is one of the founders.

MARTINE CHARALAMBOU
Artist

DATE OF BIRTH: 09.07.77
PLACE OF BIRTH: London. Grandparents from Akanthou and Angastina.
MARITAL STATUS: Single
SCHOOLS/COLLEGE: Highlands Junior, Wanstead High School, Camberwell College of Art & Design, Central St Martins College of Art & Design.
PROFESSIONAL QUALIFICATIONS: BA Honours in Visual Arts.
HOBBIES AND INTERESTS: Singing, dancing, good music and swimming.
PERSONAL PROFILE: Artist and Photographer. Has had over 16 one-woman exhibitions.

NICHOLA CHARALAMBOU
Community Worker

DATE OF BIRTH: 12.07.72
PLACE OF BIRTH: London. Grandparents from Angastina and Akanthou.
MARITAL STATUS: Single
SCHOOLS/COLLEGE: Wanstead High School, De Montford University, Leicester.
ACADEMIC QUALIFICATIONS: BA Honours in Combined Arts & Humanities (Drama, English Literature and Art History).
HOBBIES AND INTERESTS: Theatre and writing. Has been a theatre assessor for the Arts Council in London for several years and has written reviews for various newspapers and magazines. Also attended a creative writing workshop in New Mexico and has written short stories. Enjoys travelling and socialising.

PERSONAL PROFILE: Currently the General Manager for a charity providing workshops in visual arts for learning disabled people in London. Formerly Advocate for the Homeless in East London; Community Worker at Fitzrovia Neighbourhood Centre; Tour Co-ordinator for a homeless theatre company and Co-ordinating Tutor for a young carer's club - teaching English to children who are carers for their parents or siblings.

Contact tel: 07941091313
Email: nichc18@hotmail.com

SOTIRAKIS CHARALAMBOU
Artist

DATE OF BIRTH: 07.03.47
PLACE OF BIRTH: London. Father from Akanthou; Mother from Angastina.
CHILDREN: Nichola, BA Honours, Theatre Critic, Writer & Community worker; Martine, BA Honours, Artist and Photographer.
SCHOOLS/COLLEGE: Saint Martins School of Art, University London of Institute of Education.
QUALIFICATIONS: BA Honours Fine Art painting; PG.CE; ATC.
HOBBIES AND INTERESTS: Music, science, poetry, film and literature.
PERSONAL PROFILE: Independant Visual Artist. Has exhibited in Germany, Holland, England and USA. Works as a part-time Lecturer. Work featured in newspapers and books.

ALEXANDRA CHARALAMBOUS
Actress

DATE OF BIRTH: 04.10.77
PLACE OF BIRTH: London. Parents from Vathilaka and Gastria.
SCHOOLS/COLLEGE: Winchmore Secondary School University of Surrey.
ACADEMIC QUALIFICATIONS: 7 GCSEs, 3 A Levels, BA Honours degree in Drama, Film & T.V. Studies.
QUALICATIONS: Vocational Acting Training, The Academy Drama School, 2001.
HOBBIES AND INTERESTS: Singing, aerobics, writing and cinema.
PERSONAL PROFILE: A trained Actor, has performed in panto over christmas, three short films & worked at Theatro Technis Theatre.

ANDREW LAMBROU CHARALAMBOUS
Barrister

DATE OF BIRTH: 12.03.67
PLACE OF BIRTH: Highgate, London. Parents from Episkopi, Paphos.
MARITAL STATUS: Married to Anastasia, a computer operator, from London. (parents from Larnaca and Famagusta).
SCHOOLS/COLLEGE: Southgate Technical College, Queen Mary College, University of London, Inns of Court School of Law.
ACADEMIC QUALIFICATIONS: LLB, PhD, Barrister- At - Law.
PROFESSIONAL QUALICATIONS: Barrister-At-Law
MEMBERSHIPS: Member of Institute of Directors, Fellow of the Royal Society of Arts, Honourable Society of Gray's Inn, Honourable Artillery Company- Light Cavalry Unit. Metropolitan Police Detachment.
HOBBIES AND INTERESTS: Martial Arts; chief instuctor for UK in Pencak Silat Cimande. Instructor in Thai Boxing, Shaolin, Brazillian Jiujitsu & Internal Arts. Master of Yoga & Meditation initated in Borneo and India. Advanced Master of Five Reiki Healing System.
PERSONAL PROFILE: Company Director for a successful private residential property developers in North London. Parlimentary candidate, Conservative Party, for Tottenham Constituency general election 1992.

PAMPOS CHARALAMBOUS
Managing Director Parikiaki Newspaper London

DATE OF BIRTH: 09.04.56
PLACE OF BIRTH: Morphou, Nicosia.
MARITAL STATUS: Married to Soulla, a Housewife, from Morphou.
CHILDREN: Elbida, George, and Christopher.
PROFESSIONAL QUALIFICA-TIONS: Secretary of Omonia FC (London) from 1989-2000.
PERSONAL PROFILE: Managing Director of Parikiaki Haravgi from Dec 2001.

ANDY CHARALAMBOUS
Stockbroker

DATE OF BIRTH: 05.10.71
PLACE OF BIRTH: London. Parents from Sia, Nicosia.
MARITAL STATUS: To Maria, a Housewife.
CHILDREN: Pantelis Andreas and Kyriacos Andreas.
SCHOOLS/COLLEGE: School of St Davids, St Katherines Secondary & Sixth Form.
ACADEMIC QUALICATIONS: 9 GCSEs, 3 A Levels.
PROFESSIONAL QUALIFICATIONS: SFA- (Securities & Futures Authority) General representative
MEMBERSHIPS: ISMA (Interrnational Securities Market Association) General representative.
HOBBIES AND INTERESTS: Football, squash and current affairs.
PERSONAL PROFILE: Stockbroker, Deputy Managing Director Lewis Charles Securities. Helped create Sharelinks UK subsidiary in UK.

Lewis Charles, 47 Chiswell Street London EC1 Y4UP

BAMBOS CHARALAMBOUS
Councillor

DATE OF BIRTH: 02.12.67
PLACE OF BIRTH: London. Parents from Kalo Chorio and Fasoulla.
MARITAL STATUS: Single
SCHOOLS/COLLEGE: Chace Boys' School; Tottenham College; University of North London; South Bank University; Liverpool University.
ACADEMIC QUALIFICATIONS: LLB Honours.
PROFESSIONAL QUALIFICATIONS: Qualified Solicitor.
MEMBERSHIPS: Labour Party, Law Society, Enfield Law Centre.
HOBBIES AND INTERESTS: Chelsea football club, reading, politics, current affairs, cinema, the arts and walking.
PERSONAL PROFILE: London Borough of Enfield Councillor, and Councillor for Palmers Green Ward. Chair of Special Projects Security Panel, Enfield Council. Chair of Enfield Law Centre. School Governor at Eversley, St Michael at Bowes. Cabinet member of the Council.

Email address: bambosc@yahoo.com
Address: The London Borough of Enfield Members' Room, PO Box 50, Civic Centre, Enfield, Middlesex EN1 3XA

BAMBOS CHARALAMBOUS
Rally Driver

DATE OF BIRTH: 16.11.60
PLACE OF BIRTH: Limassol. Father was Melis Charalambous, marathon champion of Greece from 1952 to 1956.
MARITAL STATUS: Married to Katerina.
CHILDREN: Three children.
SCHOOLS/COLLEGE: Limassol Gymnasium, William Penn School in Dulwich, Southwark College, Camberwell School of Art & Craft.
HOBBIES AND INTERESTS: Rallying and football (Tottenham supporter).
PERSONAL PROFILE: Owns a printing company called The Press - printing work for ICI, Fords, BMW, Jaguar. Bambos is a Rally Driver - started 1993 won motoring News Group N Championship in 1994. Won Twyford Wood Forest Stages in 1998 & 2000. Won Bournemouth Winter Rally in 1997 in group A.

CHRIS CHARALAMBOUS
Music

DATE OF BIRTH: 15.04.47
PLACE OF BIRTH: London. Parents from Achna and Eptakomi.
MARITAL STATUS: Married to Miro, from Famagusta.
CHILDREN: Melina, Paulina and Gabriella.
SCHOOLS/COLLEGE: London School Of Economics.
ACADEMIC QUALIFICATIONS: BA Honours in Economics.
PROFESSIONAL QUALIFICATIONS: Certified Accountant.
HOBBIES AND INTERESTS: Music and travelling.
PERSONAL PROFILE: Sony Music Vice President for European Strategic Marketing.

CONSTANTINOS CHARALAMBOUS
Barrister

DATE OF BIRTH: 01.01.55
PLACE OF BIRTH: London. Father from Kontea; Mother from Morphou.
MARITAL STATUS: Married to Androulla from London, (parents from Leukoniko).
CHILDREN: One daughter, one son.
SCHOOLS/COLLEGE: Alexandra Park School, City of London College, North East London Polytechnic.
ACADEMIC QUALIFICATIONS: BA Honours in Law.
HOBBIES AND INTERESTS: Reading and travelling.
PERSONAL PROFILE: Worked at the Financial Times for twelve years in Accounts, then did Law Degree part time whilst working. Then did four years Bar exams. Now a Criminal Defence Barrister.

DINO CHARALAMBOUS
T.V. Director

DATE OF BIRTH: 02.07.70
PLACE OF BIRTH: London. Father born in Ayios Domedios, Nicosia.
MARITAL STATUS: Single
SCHOOLS/COLLEGE: North Bridge House, London (Prep School), University College School.
ACADEMIC QUALIFICATIONS: 7 O Levels.
HOBBIES AND INTERESTS: Sports, Music, Travelling, Reading & Meze! Passionate Arsenal fan.
PERSONAL PROFILE: T.V. Director. Credits include, *The Big Breakfast* (Channel 4), *GMTV*, *Nickelodeon*, *Disney Channel*, *Richard & Judy* on Channel 4, and various travel programmes. Has his own production company, Angelic Pictures.

Email address: dinocharalambous@hotmail.com

HARITHEA CHARALAMBOUS
Company Director and Voluntary Worker

DATE OF BIRTH: 03.05.49
PLACE OF BIRTH: Limassol
MARITAL STATUS: Married to Miltiades Charalambous, Director of Property Company, from Avlona, Cyprus.
CHILDREN: Katina, Solicitor; Sophia, Musician/Personal Secretary Stylianos, Recruitment Consultant.
SCHOOLS/COLLEGE: School for Girls, High School both in Cyprus.
PROFESSIONAL QUALIFICATIONS: Diplomas in interior design, designing, cutting, making ladies', men's and children's clothes, bridesmaids and christening gowns.
HOBBIES AND INTERESTS: Dressmaking, flower arranging, all craft generally. Also Manchester United
PERSONAL PROFILE: Many years voluntary involvement serving as a member of the Independent Greek School Southgate and the Twelve Apostles Church in Brookman Park.

HARRY JOHN CHARALAMBOUS
Founder, Scottish Hellenic Association
(Deceased)

PLACE OF BIRTH: Kato Drys
MARITAL STATUS: Married to Galatia fom Larnaca.
CHILDREN: John, Chartered Accountant at Cooper and Lybrands, Cyprus.
SCHOOLS/COLLEGE: Pancyprian Gymnasium, American Academy.
MEMBERSHIPS: Founder of Scottish Hellenic Association; Amnesty Intenational; Church Committee over 50 years; two other local Associations.
HONOURS/AWARDS: Archon Deputators of Ecummenical Patrichate. Was Honorary member of the committee of St Lukes Cathedral. Educational advisor for Scotland and Life Honorary Chairman of the school committee. Also Honorary Life President of Cypriot Hellenic Association Of Scotland.
HOBBIES AND INTERESTS: Cyprus/Chinese Lace and Embroidery.
PERSONAL PROFILE: Founder of Scottish Hellenic Association. Was an Honorary member of the commitee of St Lukes Greek Church in Glasgow.

JOHN CHARALAMBOUS
University Professor

DATE OF BIRTH: 13.01.37
PLACE OF BIRTH: Nicosia
MARITAL STATUS: Married to Elma, an International Compliance Manager for Elizabeth Arden, from Canada.
CHILDREN: Alexia, Technical Development Manager at Katsouris Fresh Foods.
SCHOOLS/COLLEGE: Pancy-prian Gymnasium, University of London, University of Western Ontario.
ACADEMIC QUALIFICATIONS: BSc, PhD (Lond).
PROFESSIONAL QUALIFICATIONS: Chartered Chemist, Fellow of the Royal Society Chemists.
MEMBERSHIPS: Member of Society of Chemical Industries.
HONOURS/AWARDS: Professorship by the University of North London, Archon Megas Ieromnimon by the Ecumenical Patriarchate of Constantinople.
HOBBIES AND INTERESTS: Gardening and preservation/ restoration of old buildings.
PERSONAL PROFILE: Following a period in Cyprus as Head of the Central Chemistry Laboratory of the Cyprus Agricultural Research Institute, joined the University of North London where he has taught chemistry for several years and has been active in research and consultancy in this field. Has examined MSc and PhD degrees at the Universities of North London, London, Manchester, Greenwich, Kingston and the King Abdul Aziz University, Saudi Arabia. Co-author of over 100 papers, books and patents. Has acted as consultant to the Ministry of Defence, the Goverment of Cyprus, Unilever, Filtrona and Marks & Spencer. Has been Secretary/Vice President of the Greek Cypriot Brotherhood and Secretary of National Federation of Cypriots in Great Britain. Life Member of the Hellenic Centre. Established the Cyprus Community Centre at the University of North London in 1987 from which time has been its Director. Via this position has been involved in researching the community and in organising conferences, seminars and exhibitions in the UK, Greece and Cyprus concerned with the community. Has edited five books relevant to the Cypriot Community in the UK and Cyprus.

MARINOS CHARALAMBOUS
Marketing

DATE OF BIRTH: 08.02.73
PLACE OF BIRTH: London. Parents from Kalochorio and Fasoula.
MARITAL STATUS: Married to Nancy from Portugal.
CHILDREN: One son.
SCHOOLS/COLLEGE: St Michaels at Bowes, Chase Boys, Enfield College, University of North London.
HOBBIES AND INTERESTS: Football.
PERSONAL PROFILE: Was marketing assistant at Bank of Cyprus, then head of marketing at the Popular Bank. Former head of marketing in Channel Marketing at Siemens. Involved in the Radio Marathon, Prince of Wales Trust Business advisor. Now Director of a Marketing & Design Agency.

MILTIS CHARALAMBOUS
Former Chairman of Twelve Apostles
Greek Orthodox Church in Brookman's
Park

DATE OF BIRTH: 03.06.45
PLACE OF BIRTH: Avlona Nicosia District.
MARITAL STATUS: Married to Charoulla, from Limassol.
CHILDREN: Katina, a Solicitor; Sophia, Musician; Stylianos, Recruitment Consultant; two Grandchildren.
HOBBIES AND INTERESTS: Manchester United and Greek Music.
PERSONAL PROFILE: Founder member of Southgate Greek School, Chairman for three years then Honorary Chairman. Former Vice Chairman of Independant Greek Schools of London. Former Chairman of Twelve Apostles Greek Church Committee. Freeman of the City of London, Dress Manufacturer for thirty years, now runs his own Property Company.

PHILLIPOS CHARALAMBOUS
Businessman

DATE OF BIRTH: 08.01.37
PLACE OF BIRTH: St Demetrianos, Paphos.
MARITAL STATUS: Married to Katina, from Rizokarpasso.
CHILDREN: One son, one daughter.
SCHOOLS/COLLEGE: Technical School, Paphos.
HOBBIES AND INTERESTS: Travel and reading.
PERSONAL PROFILE: Runs Valentina Fashion Group, producing ladieswear for multiples. Owns hotel and property business in UK & Cyprus. Does a lot of charity work and fundraising.

ANDREW MICHAEL CHIALOUFAS
Community & Schools

DATE OF BIRTH: 26.07.30
PLACE OF BIRTH: Alithinou.
MARITAL STATUS: Married to Christalla, from Omodhos.
CHILDREN: Jenny, Stella and Michael.
SCHOOLS/COLLEGE: Samuel Commercial School, Cyprus.
MEMBERSHIPS: AKEL.
HONOURS/AWARDS: Brent Council Citzenship of the year 1995.
HOBBIES AND INTERESTS: Politics.
PERSONAL PROFILE: Educational chairman of Kingsbury High Greek school for over 20 years. General Manager of Parikiaki Newspaper from 1984 to 1995. Was a member of the main commitee of OESEKA. Now retired living in Cyprus.

ANDREAS STYLIANOU CHIMONAS
Community/Schools

DATE OF BIRTH: 04.04.44
PLACE OF BIRTH: Xylotympou, Dhekelia.
MARITAL STATUS: Married to Anna, from London.
CHILDREN: Stelios and Helen.
SCHOOLS/COLLEGE: Famagusta Gymnasium, Kilburn Polytechnic, North London University, London University.
MEMBERSHIPS: Institute of Electrical Engineers.
HOBBIES AND INTERESTS: Football - Man United; Cars and DIY.
PERSONAL PROFILE: Chairman of OESEKA, Secretary of EFEPE, Chairman of Greek Parents Association, Chairman of Hazelwood Greek School.

STELIOS CHIMONAS
Teacher

DATE OF BIRTH: 25.02.69
PLACE OF BIRTH: London. Father from Xylotympou, Dhekelia.
MARITAL STATUS: Married to Helen.
CHILDREN: One daughter.
SCHOOLS/COLLEGE: Winchmore, University of South Bank, Middlesex University.
ACADEMIC QUALIFICATIONS: HND in Civil Engineering, B ENG Honours in Civil Engineering.
PROFESSIONAL QUALIFICATIONS: P.G.C.S.E. in Design & Technology.
HOBBIES AND INTERESTS: Dancing and Liverpool Football Club.
PERSONAL PROFILE: Teacher at Hatch End High. School in Pinner. Taught dancing at Greek Schools Hazelwood and Queenswell. Member of the Datcha Dance group performed on the Michael Barrymore Show and Generation Game.

STELIOS CHIOTIS
Singer/Songwriter

DATE OF BIRTH: 1943
PLACE OF BIRTH: Famagusta, Cyprus.
MARITAL STATUS: Married to Carol.
CHILDREN: Two sons.
SCHOOLS/COLLEGE: Eric Gwilter Jazz School.
HOBBIES AND INTERESTS: Travel.
PERSONAL PROFILE: Singer/Songwriter. One of the first radio presenters on LGR radio.

VAS PETROS CHIOTIS
Construction/Football

DATE OF BIRTH: 21.09.71
PLACE OF BIRTH: Islington; Dad from Lefkosia, Mum from Lithrothonda.
MARITAL STATUS: Married to Stella, a Corporate Hospitality Manager, (mother from Edinburgh, father from Karpasia).
ACADEMIC QUALIFICATIONS: Qualified Personal Fitness Trainer, New Roads & Street Works (NRSWA) Assessor.
PROFESSIONAL QUALIFICATIONS: NVQ Level 3 Management, HND Civil Engineering, BSc Honours Project Manager.
HOBBIES AND INTERESTS: Football and music.
PERSONAL PROFILE: Project Manager in Construction. Director of Delta Developments. Secretary of Trent Park in the Mercury Waltham Football League.

ANGELIQUE CHRISAFIS
Journalist

DATE OF BIRTH: 30.10.75
PLACE OF BIRTH: London. Father from Eptakomi; Mother is English.
MARITAL STATUS: Single
SCHOOLS/COLLEGE: Pembroke College, Cambridge University.
ACADEMIC QUALIFICATIONS: BA Honours Modern Languages (Spanish & Portuguese) Cambridge.
PROFESSIONAL QUALIFICATIONS: Post Graduate Diploma in Journalism, University of Central Lancashire.
HONOURS/AWARDS: Riley Prize for undergraduate achievement, Cambridge; Cambridge University Modern Languages prize.
HOBBIES & INTERESTS: Writing, travel and film.
PERSONAL PROFILE: Was Northern Correspondent, then Arts Correspondent, general news reporter, now Northern Ireland Correspondent for *The Guardian*, which she joined in 1998. Prior to that, worked as a features writer on a portuguese National Newspaper in Lisbon, was a voluntary worker with street kids in Mexico and a runner in special effects department of the film industry.

PETROS CHRISOSTOMOU
Artist

DATE OF BIRTH: 22.02.81
PLACE OF BIRTH: London, Parents from Koni Kebir and Lythrodontas.
MARITAL STATUS: Single
SCHOOLS/COLLEGE: Holy Trinity, St Martins School of Art.
ACADEMIC QUALIFICATIONS: 10 GCSEs, 4 A Levels.
PROFESSIONAL QUALIFICATIONS: Currently in 2nd year of BA Honours degree at St Martins.
HONOURS/AWARDS: Queens Heritage Trust Fund.
HOBBIES AND INTERESTS: Art, literature, cinematics photography and sport.
PERSONAL PROFILE: Artist who has started exhibiting frequently. Most recent one is a corporate project involving the US Law Firm Paul Hastings. Has also been commissioned to paint portrait of Sir Patrick Moore for National Portrait Award 2003. Worked to raise money for charities such as War on Want.

PETER CHRISTIANSON
Founder of Greek City

DATE OF BIRTH: 26.12.41
PLACE OF BIRTH: Lythrodontas, Nicosia, Cyprus.
MARITAL STATUS: Separated.
CHILDREN: None
SCHOOLS/COLLEGE: English School, Nicosia.
PERSONAL PROFILE: Founder of Greek City Music Centre. One of the first to put Greek films onto Video and DVD. First to promote Greek music in UK having managed Greek bands from the 1970s. Known in the community as 'Mr Entertainment' after the successful concerts, including one with Parios with Haris Alexiou at the Royal Albert Hall in 1986.

ANDREW CHRISTIE
Surveyor

DATE OF BIRTH: 15.04.61
PLACE OF BIRTH: London. Parents from Kilani and Vassa.
MARITAL STATUS: Married to Victoria from Cheshire.
CHILDREN: Joseph
SCHOOLS/COLLEGE: Christchurch North Finchley, Kingsway College, Westminster University.
ACADEMIC QUALIFICATIONS: BSc in Quantity Surveying.
MEMBERSHIPS: Member of the Royal Institute of Chartered Surveyors and of the Association of Planning Supervisors.
HOBBIES AND INTERESTS: Football - Chelsea fan. Keeping fit, theatre, music and model cars.
PERSONAL PROFILE: Formerly a player for, and on the commitee of, Thiella Football Club. Partner in private surveyor's practice.

DR DAPHNE A. CHRISTIE
Scientific Editor

DATE OF BIRTH: 16.01.59
PLACE OF BIRTH: London. Parents from Katodrys and Paphos, daughter of Erasmia Stakis.
MARITAL STATUS: Married to Mr D Economides.
CHILDREN: Margarita and Alexandra, both at school.
SCHOOLS/COLLEGE: Heathfield School for Girls, Ascot, Eton College, Windsor, University College, London, Trinity College, Cambridge.
ACADEMIC QUALIFICATION: BSc, Mphil, PhD.
HOBBIES AND INTERESTS: Travel, music and tennis.
PERSONAL PROFILE: Scientific Editor for Wellcome Trust Centre for the History of Medicine at University College London. Co-organizes Witness Seminars, History of Twentieth Century Medicine group. Governor, St Christopher's School, Belsize Lane, NW3.

NICHOLAS CHRISTIE
Surveyor

DATE OF BIRTH: 21.08.57
PLACE OF BIRTH: London.
Parents from Kilani and Vassa.
MARITAL STATUS: Divorced
CHILDREN: Madison and Yasmin.
SCHOOLS/COLLEGE: Christchurch North Finchley, Kingsway College, Barnet College, Reading University.
ACADEMIC QUALIFICATIONS: Degree in Estate Management
MEMBERSHIPS: Member of The Royal Insitute of Chartered Surveyors and of the Association of Planning Supervisors. Fellow of the National Association of Estate Agents.
HOBBIES AND INTERESTS: Cycling, keep fit, skiing, and football, (Chelsea fan).
PERSONAL PROFILE: Chartered Surveyor with own practice.

Email: ncmail@amserve.com

MICHAEL D CHRISTODOULIDES
Teacher and Author

DATE OF BIRTH: 12.05.21
PLACE OF BIRTH: Ikos, Marathassa.
MARITAL STATUS: Married to Niki, a Housewife, from Kalopanayiotis.
CHILDREN: Nearchos, Quantity Surveyor; Lenia, Chemistry; Maria, Computer Science.
SCHOOLS/COLLEGE: Teacher Training College.
ACADEMIC QUALIFICATIONS: B.A., DIPL. Adolescent Development.
PROFESSIONAL QUALIFICATIONS: Teacher
HONOURS/AWARDS: Patriarchate Offico.
HOBBIES AND INTERESTS: Reading, writing and gardening.
PERSONAL PROFILE: Promoting community education, G.C.E Associate examiner 1971-1991, co-founder of community organisations: Muswell Hill, Barnet. Kalopanayiotis-Ikos Association, parents guidance centre. Author of books: *Comparative History, Australia Visit, First Reading, Parents & Young Generation of UK*. Regular article writing in community newspapers.
Address: 14 Wetherill Road, London N10 2LT

ANASTASIOS CHRISTODOULOU CBE
Founding Secretary of the Open University (Deceased)

DATE OF BIRTH: 01.05.32
PLACE OF BIRTH: Akanthou, Cyprus.
MARITAL STATUS: Married to Joan.
CHILDREN: Two sons and two daughters.
SCHOOLS/COLLEGE: Marylebone Grammar School, Queens College, Oxford University.
HONOURS/AWARDS: CBE in 1978 for contribution to the establishment of the Open University. Honorary Doctorate from the Open University and by eight other universities in the Commonwealth. Professor of the universities of Mauritius and Surrey.
PERSONAL PROFILE: First Secretary of the Open University from 1968-80. Previously Deputy Secretary of Leeds University. Joined colonial service and spent six years in what is now called Tanzania as a District Officer and Magistrate. Was Secretary General of the Association of Commonwealth Universities form 1980-1996.

ANDREAS G. CHRISTODOULOU
Optometrist

DATE OF BIRTH: 30.01.34
PLACE OF BIRTH: Makrassyka, Famagusta.
MARITAL STATUS: Married to Loulla, from Ayios Amvrosios Kyrenia.
CHILDREN: George, Certified Accountant with own office & Company in Highgate; Ambrose, Optician; Despina, Optometrist.
SCHOOLS/COLLEGE: Studied in Cardiff South Wales, City University London, Refraction Hospital.
ACADEMIC QUALIFICATIONS: F.B.O.A, F.B.C.O.
PROFESSIONAL QUALIFICATIONS: Ophthalmic Optician Optometrist.
HONOURS/AWARDS: Patriarchate Officialos from the Greek Orthodox Church
HOBBIES AND INTERESTS: Swimming, reading and socialising.
PERSONAL PROFILE: First Optometrist in the community, established 1966 small chain of optical practices. 1960-1964, General Secretary, 1970-1976 Greek Cypriot Brotherhood, 1976-2001, Chairman of the Cypriot Estia of London. Founder member & first secretary of the Cypriot Centre at Wood Green. Share holder & Director of LGR also spokesman on behalf of the Board of Directors, founder member of the Hellenic Centre and member of the executive board since 1992. Vice-chairman since 2000.

DR ARISTOPHANES CHRISTODOULOU
Radiologist

DATE OF BIRTH: 08.02.62
PLACE OF BIRTH: London. Parents from Limassol.
MARITAL STATUS: Divorced
CHILDREN: Andreas and Carolina, both students at Mill Hill School.
SCHOOLS/COLLEGE: Agios Georgios Gymnasium, Larnaca to 1976, Tottenham Technical College 1976-1979, Middlesex Hospital Medical School 1979-1984.
ACADEMIC QUALIFICATIONS: 5 A Levels.
PROFESSIONAL QUALIFICATIONS: MB.BS. FRCR (1)
MEMBERSHIPS: Royal College of Radiologists.
HOBBIES AND INTERESTS: Swimming and clay shooting.
PERSONAL PROFILE: Set up number of businesses, including Construction Company, Medical Service Provisions, Nursing Home and others. Helped to offer MRI scans to a large number of Greek Cypriots in the UK who suffered and had to wait for months, sometimes years, to have this expensive examination performed.

JOHN CHRISTODOULOU
Property Developer/ Investments

DATE OF BIRTH: 24.05.1965
PLACE OF BIRTH: Nicosia
MARITAL STATUS: Married
SCHOOLS/COLLEGE: Creighton School
HOBBIES AND INTERESTS: Fitness training and water sports.
PERSONAL PROFILE: Property Developer Investments Chairman of Yianis Holdings Property Investment Co. One of their investments is a freehold of Canary riverside in Canary Wharf, over 1.1 million square feet which includes a leisure and residential complex. John is a known philanthropist in the community. One of his ambitions is to enter into politics in Cyprus.

KYRIAKOS CHRISTODOULOU
Community work

DATE OF BIRTH: 15.08.57
PLACE OF BIRTH: Agios Amvrosios.
MARITAL STATUS: Married to Allison, from Watford.
CHILDREN: Two
SCHOOLS/COLLEGE: Agios Amvrosios Gymnasium, North London College, Tottenham Tech, North London Polytechnic.
ACADEMIC QUALIFICATIONS: BSc Statistics and Computing.
HOBBIES AND INTERESTS: Football (Arsenal Supporter).
PERSONAL PROFILE: IT Development Manager.

Was Secretary and played for Ethnikos FC in Cypriot League. Former Secretary of Agios Amvrosios Association, still a commitee member. Lobby for Cyprus Co-ordinator.

LEFTERIS CHRISTODOULOU
Honorary Commissioner for Cyprus in Birmingham

DATE OF BIRTH: 18.05.48
PLACE OF BIRTH: Lymbia
MARITAL STATUS: Married to Anastasia from Birmingham, (parents from Aradippou).
CHILDREN: One son, one daughter.
SCHOOLS/COLLEGE: University of East London.
ACADEMIC QUALIFICATIONS: BSc in applied Microbiology.
HOBBIES AND INTERESTS: Football, (Aston Villa Fan).
PERSONAL PROFILE: Owner of a catering business and Director of a company selling holiday homes in Cyprus. Chairman of West Midlands Cypriot Association for 9 years. Committee of St Andrews Church in Birmingham. Honorary Commissioner for Cyprus in Birmingham.

LEONDIOS CHRISTODOULOU
Former Chairman of Yialousa Association

DATE OF BIRTH: 23.08.36
PLACE OF BIRTH: Yialousa.
MARITAL STATUS: Married to Katerina.
CHILDREN: Four.
SCHOOLS/COLLEGE: Cyprus.
PROFESSIONAL QUALIFICATIONS: Master Baker.
MEMBERSHIPS: Shooting, Cookery and Food Associations.
HOBBIES AND INTERESTS: Shooting and snooker.
PERSONAL PROFILE: Owner of Leons Patisserie. Chairman of Twelve Apostles Greek Orthodox Church for six years. Chairman of Yialousa Association for two years.

LOULLA CHRISTODOULOU
Dispensing Optician

DATE OF BIRTH: 16.07.44
PLACE OF BIRTH: Ayios Amvrosios, Kyrenia.
MARITAL STATUS: Married to A.G. Christodoulou, from Makrasyka.
CHILDREN: Three
SCHOOLS/COLLEGE: City and East London College.
PROFESSIONAL QUALIFICATIONS: FADO (Honours) C.L specialising in contact lenses.

MEMBERSHIPS: Member of the Association of Dispensing of Opticians & Contact Lenses Practitioners
HOBBIES AND INTERESTS: Reading, walking and charity work.
PERSONAL PROFILE: Member and first Chairwoman of the Woman's Committee of the Cypriot Estia of London. Deputy Chairwoman/Treasurer of the Greek Cypriot Brotherhood Ladies Committee 1974-1982.

SAVVAS CHRISTODOULOU
Businessman

DATE OF BIRTH: 20.09.51
PLACE OF BIRTH: Strovolos, Nicosia, Cyprus.
MARITAL STATUS: Divorced
CHILDREN: Pavlos
SCHOOLS/COLLEGE: Stratford Grammar School, London School of Economics. Graduated 1974.
ACADEMIC QUALIFICATIONS: BSc (Economics) Honours
PROFESSIONAL QUALIFICATIONS: ACA. Admitted to the Institute of Chartered Accountants in England & Wales in 1978.
PERSONAL PROFILE: Founder and proprietor of the Erotica Festival, the world's largest public adult lifestyle event, held annually at London's Olympia.
For 18 years, operated the biggest residential care homes for the elderly in the London Borough of Havering. Over the last 20 years, has owned, managed and operated a series of nightclubs, and in addition has owned and managed small hotels in the UK and the Greek Dodecaneses islands.

ANDRIANA CHRISTOFI
Singer/Actress

PLACE OF BIRTH: London, daughter of Varnava Christofi the Cyprus International Goalkeeper and Rita both from Famagusta.
MARITAL STATUS: Single
SCHOOLS/COLLEGE: Edmonton Senior School, Brits Performing Arts technology School in Croydon.
HOBBIES AND INTERESTS: Gym
PERSONAL PROFILE: Singer/Songwriter. A professional singer, sessions, performance and studios, backing singer for BoyZone, Michael Bolton. Appeared in commercial for Holsten Pils appeared in Blue Peter and performed in Wembley Arena.

APOSTOLOS CHRISTOFI
Senior Building Services Consultant

DATE OF BIRTH: 19.11.48
PLACE OF BIRTH: Analyondas, Nicosia.
MARITAL STATUS: Married to Irene (née Klanga), a Qualified Childminder, also from Analyonda
CHILDREN: Maria, High School Teacher; Michael, IT Consultant; Andreas, at school.
SCHOOLS/COLLEGE: Analyonda Primary School, Wandsworth Secondary School, Lewisham Technical College, South Bank University.
ACADEMIC QUALIFICATIONS: City & Guilds in Electrical Installations, Higher National Certificate (HNC) in Electrical & Electronics, Engineering, BSc in Electrical and Electronic Engineering.
PROFESSIONAL QUALIFICATIONS: Registered Chartered Engineer.
MEMBERSHIPS: Member of the Institute of Electrical Engineers.
HOBBIES AND INTERESTS: Reading, swimming, charity work.
PERSONAL PROFILE: Came to England in 1962 and attended secondary school. At 16 joined an apprenticeship scheme with an Electrical Contractor and at 27 left and joined a firm of building services consultants, where given the opportunity to study for degree. Currently works for a firm of Building Services Consultants as an Associate Director. Has been actively involved with the St Demetrios Community in Edmonton for the last 16 years, serving for ten of them as President of the committee.

FLORA CHRISTOFI (née LOIZOU)
Teacher

DATE OF BIRTH: 11.01.74
PLACE OF BIRTH: London. Father from Komi Kebir; Mother from Kiti.
MARITAL STATUS: Married to Chris from London, (parents from Styllous).
CHILDREN: Maria and Louis.
SCHOOLS/COLLEGE: Bishops Hatfield Girls School, Woodhouse 6th form College, Kingston University, University of London.
ACADEMIC QUALIFICATIONS: BA French Studies.
PROFESSIONAL QUALIFICATIONS: P.G.C.E.
HOBBIES AND INTERESTS: Travel and theatre.
PERSONAL PROFILE: Teacher in French at Edmonton County School. Previously assistant head of the year.

LUCY LOUKIA CHRISTOFI
Actress

DATE OF BIRTH: 24.10.66
PLACE OF BIRTH: London. Father from Vasili; Mother from Eptakomi.
MARITAL STATUS: Single
SCHOOLS/COLLEGE: Rose Brunford School of Speech And Drama, Royal Academy of Dramatic Art, London.
ACADEMIC QUALIICATIONS: BA in Drama & Theatre Studies.
PROFESSIONAL QUALIFICATIONS: Professional Actress.
MEMBERSHIPS: Equity Actors Union.
HOBBIES AND INTERESTS: Theatre, film, photography, literature, ski-ing and history.
PERSONAL PROFILE: Professional Actress, has worked in radio, theatre, film and televison, both in UK and in Cyprus. Appearances include *The Bill*, *Road to Ithaca*, *Family Affairs* and concrete Canvas films. Voice-overs in *Captain Corelli's Mandolin*, House of Cards. Appeared in Theatre Macbeth, Ajax, Writing on the Wall at prominent London Theatres.

MARIA CHRISTOFI
Teacher

DATE OF BIRTH: 26.05.77
PLACE OF BIRTH: London. Parents from Analyonda, Nicosia.
MARITAL STATUS: Single
SCHOOLS/COLLEGE: Chase Lane Primary, Rushcroft Secondary, Monoux College, North London University, Goldsmith University.
ACADEMIC QUALIFICATIONS: BA Honours in History and Education, PGCE in History and Social Science, presently studying for MA in Education.
HOBBIES AND INTERESTS: Reading, swimming, aerobics, music, theatre and travel
PERSONAL PROFILE: Head of History at Aveling Park Secondary School.

MICHAEL CHRISTOFI
IT Consultant

DATE OF BIRTH: 22.04.79
PLACE OF BIRTH: London. Parents from Analyonda, Nicosia.
MARITAL STATUS: Single
SCHOOLS/COLLEGE: Chase Lane Primary, Rushcroft Secondary, Enfield College, London Guildhall University.
ACADEMIC QUALIFICATIONS: BSc Honours in Computer Science.
HOBBIES AND INTERESTS: Football, basketball, reading and swimming.
PERSONAL PROFILE: IT Professional for an international firm of consultants.

VARNAVAS CHRISTOFI
Footballer

DATE OF BIRTH: 23.04.43
PLACE OF BIRTH: Famagusta. Father from Achna; Mother from Famagusta.
MARITAL STATUS: Married to Rita, from Famagusta.
CHILDREN: Christakis, works for Quantas Airlines in IT; Andrianna is a singer.
SCHOOLS/COLLEGE: Emporiko Lykeion, Famagusta.
MEMBERSHIPS: Cypriot Golf Society, Player of the year 1999/2000.
HOBBIES AND INTERESTS: Golf
PERSONAL PROFILE: Goalkeeper for six years with Salamis in Cyprus. Two years in North American League with Vancouver Whitecaps, who were managed by Ferenc Puskas. Played for Olympiakos for one year. Represented the Cyprus National team 25 times. Also played in the Cypriot League in London for Athletic United, and managed the teams Anorthosis, Dynamo and New Salamis. Also managed the Cypriot League team which won the League Cup. Captain of Enfield Golf Club.

ANDREAS G CHRISTOFIDES
Structural Engineer

DATE OF BIRTH: 01.01.50
PLACE OF BIRTH: Ayios Nicolaos Lefkas.
MARITAL STATUS: Divorced.
CHILDREN: Phivos and Timeon.
SCHOOLS/COLLEGE: Queen Mary College, Univerity of London, City University.
ACAMDEMIC QUALIFICATIONS: B.Sc (Eng), MSc.
PROFESSIONAL QUALIFICATIONS: CEng, MICE.
MEMBERSHIPS: Member of Institute of Civil Engineers.
HOBBIES AND INTERESTS: Reading, Travel, Art Exhibitions.
PERSONAL PROFILE: Structural Engineer, doing project management. Involved in Greek Schools.

GEORGIOS C CHRISTOFIDES
Former Chairman of Bank Of Cyprus

DATE OF BIRTH: 04.12.15
PLACE OF BIRTH: Nicosia
MARITAL STATUS: Married to Mona, (née Papadopoulos), from London.
CHILDREN: Christakis and Stelios, business in Cyprus.
SCHOOLS/COLLEGE: Pancyprian Gymnasium and London School of Economics.
PROFESSIONAL QUALIFICATIONS: AIB.
MEMBERSHIPS: Institute of Directors and RIIA.
HONOURS/AWARDS: Awarded an Honorary Doctorate by the University of North London.
HOBBIES AND INTERESTS: Studies, participation in Conferences and Seminars.
PERSONAL PROFILE: Former Chairman Bank of Cyprus Group, later Chairman of Bank of Cyprus (London), currently Director. Served as Director-Chairman of Cyprus Employers Association.

GEORGE CHRISTOFIDES
Former President of the National Federation of Cypriots in the UK

DATE OF BIRTH: 09.09.31
PLACE OF BIRTH: Apesha, Limassol.
MARITAL STATUS: Married to Yiota from Kilani, Limassol
CHILDREN: Zeza and Anna Maria, both Barristers at Law.
SCHOOLS/COLLEGE: Limassol Gymnasium, Balham & Tooting College, Grays Inn.
PROFESSIONAL QUALIFICATIONS: Fellow International Accountant and Barrister at Laws.
PERSONAL PROFILE: Barrister at Law and Business Consultant, has a practice in Cyprus with representative office in London. President of the South London Cyprus Association, and a member of the board of directors of Theatro Technis. Former member of the Council of the Hellenic Centre and past President of the Rotary Club of Clapham. He served for over ten years in the Committee of the Greek Orthodox Cathedral of Camberwell. He was the Secretary of the Greek Cypriot Brotherhood for a number of years, and one of the founder members, and for 15 years the President, of the Democratic Party of Cypriots in the UK. Former President of the National Federation of Cypriots in the UK. Former Vice-Chairman of PSEKA and former President of the World Federation of Overseas Cypriots and is the Honorary President of POMAK.

DR GEORGE CHRISTOFINIS
Microbiologist

DATE OF BIRTH: 11.03.26
PLACE OF BIRTH: Limassol
MARITAL STATUS: Married to Annie from Denmark.
CHILDREN: Maria, Irini and Adonis.
SCHOOLS/COLLEGE: Limassol Gymnasium, Iowa State University and Oklahoma State University U.S.A; London University.
ACADEMIC QUALIFICATIONS: BSc Bacteriology Oklahoma University, PhD Virology, London University.
MEMBERSHIPS: Royal Society of Medicine, Society for General Microbiology.
HOBBIES AND INTERESTS: Theatre, music, politics, nature and gardening.
PERSONAL PROFILE: A Microbologist who has worked in several institutes and pharmaceutical companies, working on vaccine development and production, and on the classification of viruses. Has had work published in several scientific journals all over the world. Was President of the Union Of Cyprus in Britain. Also Vice President of the Federation of Cypriots in Great Britain.

Address: 9 Roundhill, London SE26 4RF

CHRISTOPHER CHRISTOFOROU
Estate Agent

DATE OF BIRTH: 28.05.50
PLACE OF BIRTH: London. Parents from Sylikou and Yerakies.
MARITAL STATUS: Married to Betty, from Lebanon.
CHILDREN: Nicholas and Alexis.
SCHOOLS/COLLEGE: Middlesex University.
ACADEMIC QUALIFICATIONS: HND, BA Honours in Business Studies.
HOBBIES AND INTERESTS: Walking, travelling and skiing.
PERSONAL PROFILE: Started Christo & Co in 1983, Estate Agents, Surveyors and Valuers for pension funds, banks and building societies. One of the top 100 Estate Agents in the UK. Company does property management, lease renewals and rent reviews.

ERRICOS ALEXANDROS CHRISTOFOROU
Veterinary Nurse

DATE OF BIRTH: 30.05.67
PLACE OF BIRTH: Manchester. Parents from Achna and Lympia.
MARITAL STATUS: Married to Jenny, a Vet, from Greece.
SCHOOLS/COLLEGE: Croydon.
HOBBIES AND INTERESTS: Football and music.
PERSONAL PROFILE: Trained as a Graphic Designer, now a Veterinary Nurse in Croydon. Teaches Greek Dancing in Croydon and also a member of LYRA Greek Dancers.

ANDREAS CHRISTOFOROU
Businessman

DATE OF BIRTH: 03.03.43
PLACE OF BIRTH: Milia
MARITAL STATUS: Married to Kika, also from Milia.
CHILDREN: Maria, owns Estate Agents The Property Company in North London; Lakis, a Property Developer; Pamela, at university.
SCHOOLS/COLLEGE: School in Milia.
HOBBIES AND INTERESTS: Shooting, snooker and backgammon.
PERSONAL PROFILE: Worked with Brother Michalakis who owned Milia & Co. Then started own business, Salamis & Co wine supplier. Agent for Hajipavlou Wines for 27 years. Agent for six years for Peoples Coffee Co, and ETKO for 25 years. In 1999 sold business now retired.

CHRISTIANA MARIA CHRISTOFOROU
Accountancy Award Winner

DATE OF BIRTH: 21.12.78
PLACE OF BIRTH: London. Father from Leonarisso; Mother from Larnaca.
MARITAL STATUS: Single
SCHOOLS/COLLEGE: Winchmore School, Southgate Sixth Form, Brunel University.
ACADEMIC QUALIFICATIONS: GCSEs 8As, 2Bs; A Levels ABC; BSc Mathematics & Statistics with management studies (1st class Honours).

PROFESSIONAL QUALIFICATIONS: ACA (ICAEN).
HONOURS/AWARDS: Railton Prize for Business management (ACA paper), achieving the highest mark.
HOBBIES AND INTERESTS: Socialising with friends and family, drama and dance, gym, member of the St John's Ambulance.
PERSONAL PROFILE: Trainee Chartered Accountant, Price Waterhouse, Coopers.

DESPINA CHRISTOFOROU
Optometrist

DATE OF BIRTH: 22.08.68
PLACE OF BIRTH: UK. Parents from Kyrenia and Famagusta.
MARITAL STATUS: Married to Demetris Christoforou, a Banker, from Limassol
CHILDREN: George and Stefanie.
SCHOOLS/COLLEGE: Brooklands School, Channing School, City University.
ACADEMIC QUALIFICATIONS: 9 O Levels, 3 A Levels, Optometry degree.
PROFESSIONAL QUALIFICATIONS: Optometrist
MEMBERSHIPS: British College of Optometrists (MBCO).
HONOURS/AWARDS: B.S.C. (Hons), MBCO
HOBBIES AND INTERESTS: Reading, swimming, travelling, cooking, cinema and music
PERSONAL PROFILE: Optometrist.

HAMBIA (HARALAMBIA) IRENE CHRISTOFOROU (née TOFI), MBE
Art Teacher

DATE OF BIRTH: 27.08.50
PLACE OF BIRTH: London. Parents and grandparents born in Cyprus, mother's family from Asha and father's family from Koma-tou-Yialou.
MARITAL STATUS: Married to Christopher Christoforou, a London born Greek Cypriot.
CHILDREN: Anthony, a History Honours graduate, University of Bristol; Chrisanthy, a second year Geography undergraduate (University of Oxford).
SCHOOLS/COLLEGE: Tufnell Park Primary School, Shelbourne Secondary School, Hornsey College of Art, North-east London Polytechnic, North London Polytechnic.
ACADEMIC QUALIFICATIONS: BA (Fine Art) Certificate in Education.
HONOURS/AWARDS: MBE (for services to art education).
HOBBIES AND INTERESTS: Reading, painting, drawing, theatre and spending time with my family.
PERSONAL PROFILE: Art Teacher, Assistant Headteacher and an accredited Art Inspector.

GEORGE CHRISTOPHER
Solicitor

DATE OF BIRTH: 17.12.46
PLACE OF BIRTH: Mazotos, Larnaca.
MARITAL STATUS: Married to Maria from Oroklini, Larnaca.
CHILDREN: Peter, Stephanie.
SCHOOLS/COLLEGE: Imus of Grant School of Law, Law Society.
PROFESSIONAL QUALIFICATIONS: Barrister/Solicitor.
PERSONAL PROFILE: Solicitor.

OLIVIA CHRISTOPHI
Local Newspaper

DATE OF BIRTH: 04.10.77
PLACE OF BIRTH: London. Father from Varosi; Mother from Ayios Sergios.
MARITAL STATUS: Single
SCHOOLS/COLLEGE: Salisbury School in Edmonton, Enfield College.
ACADEMIC QUALIFICATIONS: GCSEs, NVQ Administration level 1 & 2, Word Processing Certificate.
HOBBIES AND INTERESTS: Sports and dancing.
PERSONAL PROFILE: Advertising Manager for the Enfield Council Newspaper.

BISHOP CHRISTOPHOROS COMMODATOS
Bishop (Deceased)

DATE OF BIRTH: 21.12.36
PLACE OF BIRTH: Anaphotia, Larnaca.
MARITAL STATUS: Single
SCHOOLS/COLLEGE: Anaphotia Elementary School, Pancyprian Commercial Lyceum Larnaca, Greek College of Paphos, Athens University.
PERSONAL PROFILE 1955-1957 arrested and kept in Detention Camp for 2 years during EOKA struggle. 1962 ordained Deacon Priest archmiandrite. In 1963 came to England put in charge of New Community of Virgin Mary South London until now. Taught Greek at various South London English Schools. Has written books including *Church of Virgin Mary, South London; The Diary of a Detainee; Ascensions of the Heart; 208 Cypriot Proverbs.*

ANGELA CHRISTOU
Hairdresser

DATE OF BIRTH: 03.12.65
PLACE OF BIRTH: UK. Parents both from Akanthou.
MARITAL STATUS: Married to Constantinos, owns Contract Cleaning Company, from Paphos.
CHILDREN: Twins, Christopher and Rianna.
SCHOOLS/COLLEGE: Hornsey School for Girls, Alan International Hairdressing Academy.
PROFESSIONAL QUALIFICATIONS: World Federation of Supreme Hairdressers, Distinction.
MEMBERSHIPS: W.F.O.S.H.
HONOURS/AWARDS: Distinction in cutting, styling and technical work.
HOBBIES AND INTERESTS: Gardening, floristry, painting
PERSONAL PROFILE: Worked with Daniel Galvin, then the top salon in South Molton Street where she was Manageress for ten years. Did session work, i.e newspaper and magazine work and commercials, plus top stars such as Joanna Lumley, Shirley Bassey, Joanne Whalley Kilmer, Kevin Kline, DJs Steve Wright, Gary Davis, and top fashion designer Ronit Zilka.

ARTEMIS CHRISTOU
Schools

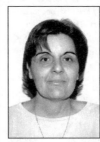

DATE OF BIRTH: 26.10.50
PLACE OF BIRTH: Aradhippou, Larnaca.
MARITAL STATUS: Married to Stelios Christou, a Businessman, from Nicosia, Cyprus.
CHILDREN: Christo, own Business; Toulla, Teacher.
SCHOOLS/COLLEGE: Convent For Girls, Larnaca.
ACADEMIC QUALIFICATIONS: School Leaving Certificate.
PROFESSIONAL QUALIFICATIONS: Cambridge RSA/ Celta, (Certificate in English Langauge Teaching Adults).
HOBBIES AND INTERESTS: Reading
PERSONAL PROFILE: Founding member and Secretary of Moss Hall Greek School. Founding member and Chair for 15 years of The Greek Women's Philanthropic Organisation Finchley & Barnet, Chair of The Ladies Committee of St Katherines Church in Barnet.

HARRY ISAIA CHRISTOU
President of Pendayia Association

DATE OF BIRTH: 08.06.56
PLACE OF BIRTH: Pentayia
MARITAL STATUS: Married to Christine, a Company Secretary, from the UK, (parents are from Agios Elias).
CHILDREN: Katrina, at University of Surrey, Roehampton; Mario, doing course in MCSE; Nicola, at Mill Hill County High School.
SCHOOLS/COLLEGE: Pallaris College Cyprus, Ackland Burghley, Waltham Forest College.
MEMBERSHIPS: Greek Cypriot Brotherhood, National Federation of Cypriots, Lobby for Cyprus.
HOBBIES AND INTERESTS: Football, Greek music, food and wine.
PERSONAL PROFILE: President of Pendayia Association. Served as Director of Enfield FC.

NICK (NEOCLIS) CHRISTOU
Headteacher

DATE OF BIRTH: 17.07.57
PLACE OF BIRTH: Episkopi, Paphos.
MARITAL STATUS: Married to Janet, a teacher of Computer Studies at East Barnet School, from London.
CHILDREN: Eleni and Katerina, both attend East Barnet School.
SCHOOLS/COLLEGE: Highgate Wood School, Haringey, University of Sussex; King's College, University of London.
ACADEMIC QUALIFICATIONS:
Bsc (Honours) in Biochemistry.
PROFESSIONAL QUALIFICATIONS: PGCE (Chemistry), National Professional Qualification for Headship (NPQH).
MEMBERSHIPS: Secondary Headteachers Association (SHA), National Association of Headteahers (NAHT)
HOBBIES AND INTERESTS: Football (Tottenham), Greek Music, sharing good food and wine with close friends and family, reading *The Guardian* and the *Cyprus Weekly*, keeping abreast of the latest scientific developments.
PERSONAL PROFILE: Headteacher of East Barnet School, one of the largest Secondary Schools in Barnet (1250 students). Has introduced the ' I want to learn' philosophy, which has brought much success to the school and generated a huge demand for places. Previously Deputy Headteacher of Hendon School and Head of Science at Highbury Grove. Also Chair of Barnet Secondary Headteachers' Forum.

PAUL CHRISTOU
Footballer

DATE OF BIRTH: 29.06.74
PLACE OF BIRTH: Limassol
MARITAL STATUS: Married to Panayiota, from Nicosia.
CHILDREN: Koulla
SCHOOLS/COLLEGE: St John Boston, Leeds Deaf School.
HONOURS/AWARDS:
FA Youth Cap.
HOBBIES AND INTERESTS: Football and snooker.
PERSONAL PROFILE: Paul is deaf he was on Y.T.S. at Leeds United football club and played for Leeds under 16s. He now plays and manages St Johns, a deaf club that plays in the Cypriot football league. Works tirelessly fundraising and organizing events for them. Paul is a Carpenter but now works as a Chef.

RICHARD CHRISTOU
Chief Executive of ICL

DATE OF BIRTH: 12.44
PLACE OF BIRTH: Cyprus.
MARITAL STATUS: Married
CHILDREN: Two sons.
SCHOOLS/COLLEGE: Eltham College, London, Trinity College, Cambridge.
ACADEMIC QUALIFICATIONS: Double first BA Honours in Law, later an MA.
HONOURS/AWARDS: He was Senior College Scholar and Prizeman. Won the Lizette Bentwich Prize for law.
PERSONAL PROFILE: Christou was general legal advisor latterly Director and General Manager of Lanitis Bros Ltd, Cyprus, 1970 to 1974. In 1975 was Company Secretary to STC Telecommunications Ltd. In 1990 moved to ICL as commercial and legal affairs Director. Now Chief Executive of ICL, which is one of Europes leading business services companies.

LEONTIOS CHRISTOUDIAS
Business Development Manager

DATE OF BIRTH: 17.04.48
PLACE OF BIRTH: Asha, Famagusta, Cyprus.
MARITAL STATUS: Married to Maria, a Housewife, from Famagusta.
CHILDREN: Christina, Teacher; Georgios, at Brighton University studying Business and Marketing.
SCHOOLS/COLLEGE: Pancyprian Gymnasium and Pancyprian Economic Lyceum in Nicosia.
MEMBERSHIPS: ASHA Association and Famagusta Association.
HOBBIES AND INTERESTS: Football and gardening.
PERSONAL PROFILE: Has worked for Laiki Bank for 26 years (from 1975). Branch Manager since 1984. Now Business Development Manager. Served in the Army in Cyprus from 1966-1968, with the rank of Second Lieutenant, and in 1974 from July to December. Moved to London in 1975.

ANDREAS CHRYSANTHOU
University Lecturer

DATE OF BIRTH: 12.01.60
PLACE OF BIRTH: Nicosia
MARITAL STATUS: Single
SCHOOLS/COLLEGE: Imperial College.
ACADEMIC QUALIFICATIONS: B.sc (Eng), PhD, ARSM, DIC
MEMBERSHIPS: Institute of Materials.
HOBBIES AND INTERESTS: Traditional Greek Dancing.
PERSONAL PROFILE: Senior Lecturer, Dept of Aerospace Civil and Mechanical Engineering, University of Hertfordshire. Vice President of The Anglo Hellenic Society of the Midlands 1993-1995.

EVA CHRYSANTHOU
Managing Director

DATE OF BIRTH: 23.07.59
PLACE OF BIRTH: London. Parents from Cyprus.
MARITAL STATUS: Single
SCHOOLS/COLLEGE: St Marthas Senior School, Southgate College.
HOBBIES AND INTERESTS: Travel and squash.
PERSONAL PROFILE: Managing Director, Belgrave Graphics Ltd. Committee member of Eleni Pericleous Trust Fund in aid of Leukaemia since its conception 18 years ago.

SAVVAS CHRYSANTHOU
Clothing Manufacturer

DATE OF BIRTH: 23.06.49
PLACE OF BIRTH: Akaki
MARITAL STATUS: Married to Flora, a Housewife from Larnaca.
CHILDREN: Maria, Myroulla, Niki, Chrysanthos, all in business.
SCHOOLS/COLLEGE: Pancyprian Gymnasium, Nicosia, evening classes at Fogel Academy for Design and Patterns.
HOBBIES AND INTERESTS: Reading and travelling.
PERSONAL PROFILE: Clothing Manufacturer. Involved with Independent Greek Schools of London, Manor Hill Greek School, UK Thalasssemia Society. Founder of Eleftheria Newspaper, London. Managing Director of Fosby Ladies' Clothing Manufacturers and Pomilo Ladieswear Retailers.

YIORGOS CHRYSANTHOU
University Lecturer

DATE OF BIRTH: 18.09.67
PLACE OF BIRTH: Nicosia
MARITAL STATUS: Married
SCHOOLS/COLLEGE: Queen Mary and Westfield College.
ACADEMIC QUALIFICATIONS: BSc 1st Class Honours, Computer Science and Statistics, University of London studentship, 1991-1994, overseas Reward Scheme PhD studentship, 1991-1994.
MEMBERSHIPS: IEEE Computer Society; ACM and ACm SIGGRAPH; European Association for Computer Graphics.
HOBBIES AND INTERESTS: Cycling, climbing, DIY and interior design.
PERSONAL PROFILE: Lecturer in Computer Science Department, University College London, 1998-present. Teaching undergraduate and postgraduate courses on Computer Graphics and Virtual Environments. Involved in numerous research projects. Has written books and published articles for numerous

ALICA SOPHIA CHRYSOSTOMOU
University Lecturer

DATE OF BIRTH: 05.05.66
PLACE OF BIRTH: London. Father from Avgorou.
MARITAL STATUS: Single
SCHOOLS/COLLEGE: Schoil Mhuire, Trim, Co Meath, Ireland; Athlone Regional Technical College, Co Westmeath, Ireland; University of North London, Holloway, London.
ACADEMIC QUALIFICATIONS: National Certificate in Polymer Engineering, Grad. PRI; MSc Polymer Engineering and Technology; PhD.
PROFESSIONAL QUALIFICATIONS: Teaching and Learning in Higher Education; PG Dip SEDA certificate from the Institute for Learning and Teaching.
MEMBERSHIPS: Institute of Materials, Minerals and Mining.
HONOURS/AWARDS: Governors Award - UNL for meritorious research project. James Walker Award - IoM for best technical publication. New Zealand Federation of University Women Visiting Scholar Award.
HOBBIES AND INTERESTS: Craftwork, genealogy, travelling and exploring new countries.
PERSONAL PROFILE: Lecturer at London Metropolitan University (previously known as the University of North London), where specialist field is in polymer engineering. Has lectured primarily in England but has also worked as a lecturer in New Zealand.

Contact: London Metropolitan Polymer Centre, London Metropolitan University, Holloway, London N7 8DB

ANDREAS CHRYSOSTOMOU
Businessman

DATE OF BIRTH: 24.03.47
PLACE OF BIRTH: Boghazi. Father from Patriki; Mother from Spathariko.
MARITAL STATUS: Married to Valentina, from Milia.
CHILDREN: Lucy, Lakis, Stephanie and Alexi.
SCHOOLS/COLLEGE: Laycock.
HOBBIES AND INTERESTS: Music.
PERSONAL PROFILE: Chairman United Buying Services. Director Nisa Today. Managing Director and Chairman of Venus & Co and Eurovenus, co-formed in 1972.

ANDREAS CHRYSOSTOMOU
Businessman

DATE OF BIRTH: 08.02.52
PLACE OF BIRTH: Sotira, Famagusta.
MARITAL STATUS: Married to Niki, from Famagusta.
CHILDREN: Dino, at Westminster University; Lakis and Elena at school.
SCHOOLS/COLLEGE: 2nd Gymnasium, Famagusta, Princeton College, Holborn, Middlesex Polytechnic, now Middlesex University.
ACADEMIC QUALIFICATIONS: HND in Hotel Management.
HOBBIES AND INTERESTS: Tennis, swimming and basketball.
PERSONAL PROFILE: First worked in Intercontinental Hotels as a trainee Manager, then Food & Beverage Manager. Now has own Estate Agency Network Agencies in Finsbury Park. Also Director of Mayfair London Properties Ltd with offices in Mayfair and Cyprus Mayfair Properties with offices in Cyprus. Vice chairman of Famagusta Association for five years. Involved with Bowes Greek School

ANGELA CHRYSOSTOMOU
Actress

DATE OF BIRTH: 17.08.81
PLACE OF BIRTH: London. Father was born in Egypt; Mother from Larnaca.
MARITAL STATUS: Single
SCHOOLS/COLLEGE: Redroofs Theatre School, St John The Baptist Greek School, St David and St Katherines Secondary School.
ACADEMIC QUALIFICATIONS: 1 A Level, (Greek and Greek Literature), 11 GCSEs
PROFESSIONAL QUALIFICATIONS: Diploma in Performing Arts.
MEMBERSHIPS: Equity, PAMRA and Spotlight
HONOURS/AWARDS: Diploma Pass with Honours
HOBBIES AND INTERESTS: Performing, theatre, literature and fitness.
PERSONAL PROFILE: Has done few shows for local charities. Formerly a civil servant. Currently has an agent and is promoting her Greek album named *Turning Point.*

EVDOKIA CHRYSOSTOMOU
Singer

DATE OF BIRTH: 03.04.80
PLACE OF BIRTH: London. Father from Morphou; Mother from P. Zodhia.
MARITAL STATUS: Single
SCHOOLS/COLLEGE: Cuffley Primary School, Chancellors School, Goffs School.
ACADEMIC QUALIFICATIONS: GCSEs, A Levels, studying for BMus Music degree.
PROFESSIONAL QUALIFICATIONS: Royal Academy of Music, Grade 8 Piano, singing, saxophone.
MEMBERSHIPS: NYFC Youth.
HONOURS/AWARDS: 1st prize in Cypriot singing/songwriting competition in 1998, won award for best performance. Honoured by EKON in 1999
HOBBIES AND INTERESTS: Singing, dancing, swimming
PERSONAL PROFILE: Studying at Goldsmith University in London. Gave two concerts at Millfield Theatre. Has released 3 CDs. Has appeared in theatre productions.

KYRIACOS CHRYSOSTOMOU
Accountant

DATE OF BIRTH: 01.07.48
PLACE OF BIRTH: Ayios Loucas, Famagusta.
MARITAL STATUS: Divorced
CHILDREN: Jason, at university; Christopher, at Secondary School.
SCHOOLS/COLLEGE: Ayios Loucas Primary School, Greek Gymnasium of Famagusta, City of London Polytechnic.
ACADEMIC QUALIFICATIONS: Gymnasium Apolitirion, GCE O Levels & A Levels.
PROFESSIONAL QUALIFICATIONS: F.C.A. (Fellow of Institute of Chartered Accountants).
HOBBIES AND INTERESTS: Sport, chess and reading. Played football for Anorthosis of Famagusta before coming to UK.
PERSONAL PROFILE: Finished Gymnasium at age of 18. Did National Service in Army for two years and at the age of 20 came to London to study Accountancy. Has been in practice since 1978.

MARCOS CHRYSOSTOMOU
Director of Citizens Advice Bureau at Haringey Council

DATE OF BIRTH: 09.12.46
PLACE OF BIRTH: Labithos, Father, the late Chrysostomos Costi, Co Founder of the Greek Schools in London.
MARITAL STATUS: Married to Julie whose father was the late Taki Patata from Komi Kebir.
SCHOOLS/COLLEGE: Thornhill Road Primary School, Barnsbury Boys School, N.W. London Polytechnic, London School of Economics.
ACADEMIC QUALIFICATIONS: BA Geography, Postgraduate MSC.
HOBBIES AND INTERESTS: Politics, social activities, arts, radio and travelling.
PERSONAL PROFILE: For four years was a teacher at Upton House Hackney. Then a Director of G & S Formwork. Then became manager of Islington Advice Bureau. Founder Barnet Youth Club in 1975, then formed Dynamo Football Club in 1977. Secretary of the Cypriot Football League. Now Chairman. Currently Director of Citizens Advice Bureau at Haringey Council.

MIKKOS CHRYSOSTOMOU
Football Journalist

DATE OF BIRTH: 12.12.46
PLACE OF BIRTH: Ayios Loukas, Famagusta.
MARITAL STATUS: Married to Catherine, a Director's PA, from Wood Green, London.
CHILDREN: Vassos, IT Manager; Alex, Graphic Designer & Studio Manager; Nicos, has Computing degree from Hatfield University.
SCHOOLS/COLLEGE: Ayios Loukas, Lykeion Famagusta, William Grimshaw, Tottenham Technical College.
ACADEMIC QUALIFICATIONS: O Level GCE 5, A Level Maths.
PROFESSIONAL QUALIFICATIONS: HND Structural Engineering.
HOBBIES AND INTERESTS: Football and all sports.
PERSONAL PROFILE: Founder of Anorthosis FC London 1975, Founder of Famagusta FC London 1988. Worked with the Cypriot League since the start 1975. Helped form youth league, generally involved in promoting football for the Cypriot community and encouraging youth to participate through Community press and KOPA for 26 years. Columnist with *Parikiaki* for several years, now with *Eleftheria Newspaper*.

TAKIS CHRYSOSTOMOU
Charity Worker

DATE OF BIRTH: 29.11.44
PLACE OF BIRTH: Rizokarpaso.
MARITAL STATUS: Married
CHILDREN: Three.
SCHOOLS/COLLEGE: Primary and Secondary at Rizokarpaso and Peter St College London.
PROFESSIONAL QUALIFICA-TIONS: Sales Rep, Silver Service Waiter and Hairdresser.
MEMBERSHIPS: Rizokarpaso Association and Kisos EDEK.
HONOURS/AWARDS: Gold medal from Rizokarpaso Association and several gold, silver and bronze from British Heart Foundation.
HOBBIES AND INTERESTS: Reading, history, biking, travelling and gardening.
PERSONAL PROFILE: Raises money for charity by cycling from London to Brighton every year.

SALOMI COLMAN
Charity Worker

DATE OF BIRTH: 15.06.59
PLACE OF BIRTH: Paphos
MARITAL STATUS: Married to Vernon, an Architect and Chairman of the IF Group, charity for disabled people, from England.
CHILDREN: Two stepsons, Oliver, at school and Christopher, at college.
SCHOOLS/COLLEGE: Vale Road School, North East London College, Enfield College & Middlesex University.
ACADEMIC QUALIFICATIONS: GCSEs in English & Sociology. Diplomas in Counselling & Access. BA Honours Sociology & Criminology.
HOBBIES AND INTERESTS: Travelling, theatre, reading, socialising, and writing short stories and poems.
PERSONAL PROFILE: Disabled - Tetraplegic due to catching/having Encephalitis. There is a 1 in 5,000 chance of surviving Encephalitis, this was helped by having a determination to deal with a disablity. Mrs Colman is a member of various organisations/charities that deal with disabilities. ie: Haringey Community Health Council, Primary Care Working Party, The Haringey Joint Services Planning Team for Physical Disabilities, The Wheelchair Users group, Haringey Council Direct Payments Pilot Scheme Advisory Group. A member of the IF Group management committee and on the Mulitiple Sclerosis (MS) management committee.

VAS CONSTANTI
Actor

DATE OF BIRTH: 23.04.67
PLACE OF BIRTH: London. Father, Kyriako from Gerani; Mother, Despo Neophytou, from Avgorou.
MARITAL STATUS: Single
SCHOOLS/COLLEGE: Winchmore, Guildford School of Acting.
PROFESSIONAL QUALIFICA-TIONS: Actor.
PERSONAL PROFILE: Organised Crusaids, charity midnight matinee for Rocky Horror Show, starred Robbie Williams, Shane Richie. Wrote Musical *Golden Fleece*. Appeared on TV in *The Bill*, in theatre in *Miss Saigon*, *Grease*. Film: *Road to Ithaca*

LENIA CONSTANTINE
Pshychiatrist

DATE OF BIRTH: 17.11.52
PLACE OF BIRTH: Polis Chrysochous, Paphos.
MARITAL STATUS: Married to George, a doctor, born in Alexandria.
CHILDREN: Andrew & Natalie, both at Edgbaston High School.
SCHOOLS/COLLEGE: Gymnasium Morphou, Cyrychov University, Prague, Charles University
PROFESSIONAL QUALIFICATIONS: MU DR, MRC Psych.
MEMBERSHIPS: Mental Health Foundation, Cancer Research, Ladies Committee Greek Church Birmingham.
HOBBIES AND INTERESTS: Swimming, music and philosophy.
PERSONAL PROFILE: Consultant Psychiatrist, working at Kidderminster General, Worcestershire Mental Health.

STEPHEN CONSTANTINE IS THE INDIAN NATIONAL FOOTBALL TEAM MANAGER

RICKY CONSTANTINE
Karate Champion

DATE OF BIRTH: 14.02.52
PLACE OF BIRTH: Psemadismeno, Nicosia.
CHILDREN: One daughter.
SCHOOLS/COLLEGE: Camden Town Primary, North Haringey Secondary.
HOBBIES AND INTERESTS: Martial Arts.
PERSONAL PROFILE: 7th Dan in Karate WADO-RYU, European Martial Arts Champion 1970-1973, British National Champion, 1967 to 1970, 1972 to 1973. South East area national coach. Teaches Martial Arts at David Lloyd Centre Finchley.

STEPHEN CONSTANTINE
Football Manager/National Team Coach

DATE OF BIRTH: 16.10.62
PLACE OF BIRTH: London. Father from Paphos.
MARITAL STATUS: Married to Lucy, a Housewife, English/Cypriot.
CHILDREN: Paula and Christiana.
SCHOOLS/COLLEGE: Southgate, the Grammar School, Limassol.
PROFESSIONAL QUALIFICATIONS: FA Advanced Licence, UEFA Licence FIFA Instructor.
MEMBERSHIPS: FA Coaches (FACA) FIFA.
HONOURS/AWARDS: Nepalese OBE received medal from King of Nepal.
HOBBIES AND INTERESTS: Military Modelling.
PERSONAL PROFILE: Football manager, Nepal National Team, APEP, and Achilleas in Cyprus. Assistant Manager at Apollon in Cyprus. Bournemouth FC Youth Team Manager. Played for AEL in Cyprus, Enfield Town in UK. Now India National Team Manager.

ANDREAS CONSTANTINIDES
Former Mayor of Enfield

DATE OF BIRTH: 25.02.43
PLACE OF BIRTH: Pera Pedhi
MARITAL STATUS: Married to Maroulla from Paleomylos.
CHILDREN: Theodhotos, Chartered Quantity Surveyor; Joanne, IT Support.
SCHOOLS/COLLEGE: Paedagogical Academy of Cyprus, Aston University, Birmingham.
ACADEMY QUALIFICATIONS: BSC Honours in Chemical Engineering.
HOBBIES AND INTERESTS: Gardening, football and backgammon.
PERSONAL PROFILE: Councillor for Enfield Council, was Mayor of Enfield. Director of Millfield Theatre and Governor of Oakthorpe School. Chair of St Barnabas Greek School. Andreas is currently a Teacher of mathematics at a secondary school.

ANTHONY GEORGE CONSTANTINIDES
University Lecturer

DATE OF BIRTH: 01.01.43
PLACE OF BIRTH: Acheritou
MARITAL STATUS: Married to Pamela Maureen Bowman, an Anthropologist, from England.
CHILDREN: George, completed his PhD.
SCHOOLS/COLLEGE: Pancyprian Gymnasium, Regent Street Polytechnic, Imperial College.
ACADEMIC QUALIICATIONS: B.Sc (Eng), phD, Honours. Dsc (NTVA).
PROFESSIONAL QUALIFICATIONS: Fellow IEE, Fellow IEEE, Fellow RSA.
HONOURS/AWARDS: Chevalier Palmes Acadeniques, Officier Palmes Acadeniques (France).
HOBBIES AND INTERESTS: Reading.
PERSONAL PROFILE: Professor of signal processing; author of more than 300 learned papers and six books. Honorary Professor of Archaeology, University College London.

DORA CONSTANTINIDES
Greek Traditional Dance Teacher

DATE OF BIRTH: 14.08.46
PLACE OF BIRTH: Nicosia
MARITAL STATUS: Married to Chris.
CHILDREN: Athina, Alexandros, Nicolas, Andreas, Dimitra and Dimitrios.
SCHOOLS/COLLEGE: Tollington Park School, Adolf Walters School for Hairdressing and Beauty.
HONOURS/AWARDS: Millennium Award Winner.
HOBBIES AND INTERESTS: Music and travelling
PERSONAL PROFILE: Teaches Greek Dancing at Bowes School, Oakthorpe, St Andrews Church, City & Islington College, Community Centre at Wood Green and at the Cultural & Health Centre for Greek Cypriot Women. Has appeared on TV in the Generation Game with one of her dance groups.

CHRIS CONSTANINIDES
Football

DATE OF BIRTH: 28.07.40
PLACE OF BIRTH: Nicosia
MARITAL STATUS: Married to Dora, from Nicosia.
CHILDREN: Athina, Alex, Nico Andy, Dimi and Dimitra.
SCHOOLS/COLLEGE: Pancyprian Gymnasium, Harrow Technical, Central London University.
HOBBIES AND INTERESTS: Football (Arsenal supporter), amateur radio, DIY, computers and theatre.
PERSONAL PROFILE: Works at ICL as a Senior Support Specialist teaching younger engineers in maintenance of systems. Played football for various teams in Camden in the 60s. Started refereeing in 1970, joined Cypriot League in 1974 was member of management committee in various posts. General Secretary, referees association. London Football Association representative. 1st Cypriot on LFA Disciplinary Committee. General Secretary of Sunday Cup Competitions in LFA. Also was an actor in Theatro Technis.

JOANNA CONSTANTINIDES
Certified Microsoft Engineer

DATE OF BIRTH: 27.07.74
PLACE OF BIRTH: Limassol.
MARITAL STATUS: Single
SCHOOLS/COLLEGE: Latymer School, Edmonton; University of Staffordshire.
ACADEMIC QUALIFICATIONS: BSc Honours in Business Decision Analysis.
PROFESSIONAL QUALIFICATIONS: Microsoft Certified Engineer.
HOBBIES AND INTERESTS: Reading, cooking, walking and playing the guitar.
PERSONAL PROFILE: Created a web page for the Greek Cypriot Community, "Seekagreek..com".

SUSIE CONSTANTINIDES
Race Equality Officer

DATE OF BIRTH: 07.06.40
PLACE OF BIRTH: England. Father, Charles Constantinides, a policeman, from Tseri, Nicosia; Mother, Diana Constantinides from Greece.
MARITAL STATUS: Single
SCHOOLS/COLLEGE: North Harringey Junior School Hornsey High School (Grammar), Hendon College of Technology, Sorbonne University, Paris, Hillcroft College, Middlesex University, University of North London.
QUALIFICATIONS: Royal Society of Arts, Liaison Officers Diploma, Certificate in Qualified Social Work, PhD Reseacher, University of North London.
MEMBERSHIPS: Chair: Cypriot Community Centre (Haringey Cypriot Organisations), Chair: Cypriot Womens League (England), Member of the Secretariat and the Executive Council National Federation of Cypriots in Great Britain.
HONOURS/AWARDS: One of the Women of the Year nominated at ceremony by Smithkline Beecham in 1992 and 1993. Two awards from Haringey Council and Haringey Woman of the Year 1997 and 2001.
HOBBIES AND INTERESTS: History, language & communication, theatre, music, art, squash, archaeology and sociology.
PERSONAL PROFILE: Worked on Education and Equality issues. 1972 appointed Liaison Officer, Cypriot Community for the London Borough of Haringey. Spent a year researching the needs of the Cypriot Community (Greek and Turkish), especially in the areas of Education, Social Services and Housing. 1974 was lead officer in co-ordinating services to receive and liaise with the 11000 Cypriot refugees who came to Haringey. In 1986, became Race Equality Officer, Social Services. 1990 Principal Race Equality Officer of Haringey, over all services, co-ordinating the work of a team of Race Equality Officers as member of the Chief Executive's Team and Service. Has lectured at colleges, universities and to professional groups. Has published, eg "Cypriots in Haringey"; Written/ contributed papers for conference, seminars, professional publications, e.g British Journal of Guidance & Counselling. At present, working with the Cypriot elderly and disabled at the Cypriot Community Centre, Wood Green.

TONY CONSTANTINIDES
Businessman

DATE OF BIRTH: 27.11.63
PLACE OF BIRTH: London. Parents from Perapedhi and Pelendri.
MARITAL STATUS: Married to Eleni.
CHILDREN: Charlie.
SCHOOLS/COLLEGE: Salisbury School, Middlesex University.
ACADEMIC QUALIFICATIONS: BSc (Honours) in Eletronics.
HOBBIES AND INTERESTS: Soccer and motor racing.
PERSONAL PROFILE: Played for New Salamis Anorthosis and the Cypriot League team in the UK. Owns Excell IT Telecommunications Recruitment and Training Consultancy in London and globally all over the world, supplying contract and permanent engineers to all the large telecom industries.

THEO CONSTANTINIDES
Construction Cost Consultant

DATE OF BIRTH: 18.06.71
PLACE OF BIRTH: Birmingham, UK. Father from Pera Pedhi, Cyprus; Mother from Paleomylos, Cyprus.
MARITAL STATUS: Living with partner Dr Tanya Alan, from London.
SCHOOLS/COLLEGE: Latymer School, Edmonton, University of Salford, University of Salerno, Italy.
ACADEMIC QUALIFICATIONS: BSc (Honours) Quantity Surveying, PGD Informatics.
PROFESSIONAL QUALIFICATIONS: MRICS (Royal Institution of Chartered Surveyors.
HOBBIES AND INTERESTS: Football, playing and watching, travel, teaching Greek & Cypriot dancing.
PERSONAL PROFILE: Construction Cost Consultant.

ACHILLEAS CONSTANTINOU
Businessman

DATE OF BIRTH: 21.04.48
PLACE OF BIRTH: Platres
MARITAL STATUS: Married to Androulla.
CHILDREN: Three sons, one daughter.
SCHOOLS/COLLEGE: Arnos Secondary School, Waltham Forest Technical College, Kings College, London University.
ACADEMIC QUALIFICATIONS: LLB (Honours) He was awarded the shield of Haringey for the services to the borough in 1996.
HONOURS/AWARDS: Was awarded the Shield of Haringey for the services to the Borough.
HOBBIES AND INTERESTS: Tennis, swimming, chess, backgammon and collectors cars.
PERSONAL PROFILE: With his late brother Aristos, founded Ariella Fashions Ltd in the Sixties. First had a chain of retail shops in such locations as Carnaby Street, Oxford Street and Duke Street in London. The company now has a wholesale design and manufacturing business. In 1992, Ariella was honoured by a visit from the Princess Royal to its Wood Green headquarters in celebration of its 25th anniversary. It won two 'Woman Fashion Awards' in 1985 the British Apparel Export Award in 1996 and the Queens Award for Export Achievement in 1998. In his 32 year career, Mr Constantinou has served the fashion industry on numerous committees. He was a founder member of the Fashion Industry Action Group, which led to the formation of the British Fashion Council (BFC), and served on numerous Advisory Boards of London Fashion Exhibitions. He is a founder member and current director of the British Fashion Council and the Chairman of the BFC Mainstream Committee. He is also appointed to the Board of Management of the British Knitting and Clothing Export Council (UK Fashion Exports) and Founder and Chairman of the British Fashion & Design Protecion Association (FDPA) which was instrumental in changing UK case law to afford copyright protection to fashion design. Mr Constantinou has also appeared on numerous national television and radio programmes on ITV, BBC & CNN discussing fashion topics, and is the 'Fashion Guru' for LGR (London Greek Radio). Books: *Memorandum on the Law of Copyright, Design Protection* (contributor.)

Address: Ariella Fashions Ltd, Aristos House, 25 Watsons Road, Wood Green, London N22 7TZ
Tel: 0044 (0) 20 8888 1213
Fax: 0044 (0) 20 8889 8736
Email: fashion@ariella.co.uk
Website: ariella.co.uk

ANDREA CONSTANTINOU (Georgiou)
Journalist

DATE OF BIRTH: 09.06.82
PLACE OF BIRTH: London. Mother born in Larnaca.
MARITAL STATUS: Married to George Georgiou, a journalist born in Poland but raised in Ormidia, Cyprus.
SCHOOLS/COLLEGE: Mount Carmel R.C. Girls School, City & Islington College.
ACADEMIC QUALIFICATIONS: 11 GCSEs, 3 A Levels including Media Studies and Modern Greek.
HONOURS/AWARDS: Given best presenter and most hard worker awards at the Cyprus Wine Festival 1999.
HOBBIES AND INTERESTS: Reading magazines/newspapers, music and shopping.
PERSONAL PROFILE: English Section journalist for *Parikiaki* (the Grapevine column). Also had a column entitled 'The Rumour Mill' in Cypria in Britain magazine, and has reported the news in English on London Greek Radio. Presented The Entertainment programme at Parikiaki's Cyprus Wine Festival at Alexandra Palace in 1999. Was involved in a student exchange programme between Greek & Turkish Cypriot youths in Cyprus, which was organised by EKON in September 1999.
Email: AndreaConstantinou@hotmail.com

COSTAS CONSTANTINOU
Managing Director of Kate Kuba Shoes

DATE OF BIRTH: 09.11.68
PLACE OF BIRTH: London. Father from Pervolia. Mother from Famagusta.
MARITAL STATUS: Married to Katerina, born in London. (Father from Patriki. Mother from Limassol).
CHILDREN: Two children, Marina and Andrew.
SCHOOLS/COLLEGE: Southgate School.
HONOURS/AWARDS: 5 times winner UK footwear awards.
HOBBIES AND INTERESTS: Football and music.
PERSONAL PROFILE: Managing Director of Kate Kuba Shoes, shops in central London and suburbs.

FRIXOS CONSTANTINOU
Film and TV Producer

DATE OF BIRTH: 31.10.28
PLACE OF BIRTH: Lapithos, Kyrenia Distr.
MARITAL STATUS: Married to Ikouko, from Japan.
CHILDREN: Eroula and Alexander, both postgraduate students; Daphne, student.
SCHOOLS/COLLEGE: Lapithos Gymnasium.
MEMBERSHIPS: Member of the British Academy.
HONOURS/AWARDS: First T.V prize for Educational series, 1997.
HOBBIES AND INTERESTS: Writing and travelling
PERSONAL PROFILE: Film Producer. Work includes eight educational TV series, seven feature films, 15 documentaries, and ten animation series for children. Distributor of international films for other producers. Organised Greek film shows in London fom 1965 to 1970, in partnership with Paul Yiannakas. Also arranged the first overseas concert of Mikis Theodorakis with Maria Farantouri in 1966 at the then famous Saville Theatre in London. From 1965-1970, Frixos Constantine and Paul Yiannakas presented in London many live shows from Greece and Cyprus.

GEORGE CONSTANTINOU
(secular name)
ATHENAGORAS CONSTANTINOU
(ecclesiastical name)
Senior Clergyman

DATE OF BIRTH: 14.12.48
PLACE OF BIRTH: Anaphotia, Larnaca.
MARITAL STATUS: Celibate
ACADEMIC QUALIFICATIONS: B.D in Theology, Kings College, University of London, Degree in Theology from Athens University, Cambridge Diploma of English Studies.
PROFESSIONAL QUALIFICATIONS: Archimandrite. Also a trained Teacher 1970-1972 at Thomas Huxley College of Education.
HOBBIES AND INTERESTS: A Linguist, a Philologist, a Polyglot and a Polymath.
PERSONAL PROFILE: Senior Clergyman of the Greek Orthodox Church. A Greek Language Teacher since 1969.

JASON CONSTANTINOU
Surgeon

DATE OF BIRTH: 14.01.72
PLACE OF BIRTH: London. Parents from Famagusta.
MARITAL STATUS: Partner Penny Brown, a H.R.Officer, from Bedford.
CHILDREN: Thomas
SCHOOLS/COLLEGE: University College, London, Medical School.
ACADEMIC QUALIFICATIONS: MB BS BSc MRCS.
MEMBERSHIPS: British Medical Association, Medical Protection Society, Royal College of Surgeons.
HONOURS/AWARDS: A number of awards at university.
HOBBIES AND INTERESTS: Tennis and travelling.
PERSONAL PROFILE: Surgeon.

MARIA CONSTANTINIDOU
General Practitioner

DATE OF BIRTH: 25.09.45
PLACE OF BIRTH: Nicosia.
MARITAL STATUS: Married to Derck Essen, a Finance & Microsoft Consultant from Buckinghamshire.
CHILDREN: Tara, Oxford graduate; Michael, student of architecture at Cambridge.
SCHOOLS/COLLEGE: Gymnasium, Nicosia.
ACADEMIC QUALIFICATIONS: BSc.
PROFESSIONAL QUALIFICATIONS: MBBS, DCH.
MEMBERSHIPS: Member of the Royal College of Physicians.
HOBBIES AND INTERESTS: Student at Birkbeck College, part- time, university degree (BA) in Spainish & Latin Amercian studies.
PERSONAL PROFILE: General Practitioner.

MARIO CONSTANTINOU
Actor

DATE OF BIRTH: 05.06.64
PLACE OF BIRTH: England. Father from Paphos; Mother from Exomedothi.
MARITAL STATUS: Single
SCHOOLS/COLLEGE: Chingford Senior High School.
ACADEMIC QUALIFICATIONS: O Levels.
MEMBERSHIPS: Equity, Thalassaemia Society.
HOBBIES AND INTERESTS: Football and promoting Club Nights.
PERSONAL PROFILE: Actor, and jewellery manufacture. Played semi-professional football. Played for Venus in Cypriot football league. Acted in various theatre productions - *A Taste of Honey*; *Blind Faith*-Video. Films include *Swag*; and commercials Clairol 3-in-1 and *Times* Newspaper.

STELIOS CONSTANTINOU
Architect

DATE OF BIRTH: 22.02.41
PLACE OF BIRTH: Arsos Village, Limassol.
MARITAL STATUS: Married to Despina (Yenia) Constantinou, from Marathovounos Village Famagusta.
CHILDREN: Stella Maria and Alexia Renata, both at university; Nikolas Christian, at school.
SCHOOLS/COLLEGE: Nicosia Technical Institute, Cyprus, Thames Polytechnic, London.
QUALIFICATIONS: Diploma in Architecture and a certificate in Professional Studies.
MEMBERSHIPS: RIBA, Royal Institute of British Architects.
HOBBIES AND INTERESTS: Music, plays three musical instruments, paints water colours, woodwork and model making.
PERSONAL PROFILE: Practicing Architect, own practice for last 30 years. Architect for the new buildings of The Holy Cross & St Michael Church Hall, Golders Green., and St Constantine & St Helens Church, Croydon - a new church hall and repairs to Grade II listed church.

AMILIOS COSTA
Chartered Accountant

DATE OF BIRTH: 21.10.68
PLACE OF BIRTH: London.
Parents from Vasa Kilaniou, Limassol, Kalo Horio, Larnaca.
MARITAL STATUS: Married to Loulla, a Lettings Negotiator.
SCHOOLS/COLLEGE: Ashmole School, London School of Economics.
ACADEMIC QUALIFICATIONS: BSc (Honours) Economics. FCA.
PROFESSIONAL QUALIFICATIONS: Chartered Accountant.
HOBBIES AND INTERESTS: Watching and playing football, keeping fit and golf.
PERSONAL PROFILE: Partner in a Chartered Accountancy firm.

Postal address: Avco House, 6 Albert Road, Barnet, Herts EN4 9SH
Email: moss@kelpart.co.uk

ANDREW COSTA
Architect

DATE OF BIRTH: 17.02.67
PLACE OF BIRTH: London. Father from Kato Deftera; Mother from Vouno (nr Kyrenia).
MARITAL STATUS: Married to Venetia, an Architect, from the Isle of Wight.
SCHOOLS/COLLEGE: Ambler Primary, Highbury Grove School Secondary, University of Westminster, University of Kingston
ACADEMIC QUALIFICATIONS: BA (Honours) in Architecture, Diploma in Architecture.
MEMBERSHIPS: RIBA.
HOBBIES AND INTERESTS: Travel, music, sport and sculpture.
PERSONAL PROFILE: Architect.

ANTONY DANIEL COSTA
Singer with pop group Blue

DATE OF BIRTH: 23.06.81
PLACE OF BIRTH: UK. Grandparents from Famagusta and Morphou.
MARITAL STATUS: Single
SCHOOLS/COLLEGE: Hendon School.
ACADEMIC QUALIFICATIONS: Drama and Greek GCSE (A) and (B).
HONOURS/AWARDS: Brit Award 2002 for Best Newcomer.
HOBBIES AND INTERESTS: Football, singing, comedy and socialising.
PERSONAL PROFILE: Young recording artist signed to Virgin. Debut single *All Rise* entered the UK chart at No. 4, the second single *Too Close* went to No. 1. The band's first album *All Rise* went on to spawn three more singles including two No 1's. Second album, *One Love* went to the top of album charts. Did duet with Elton John

COSTAS COSTA
T.V. Personality

DATE OF BIRTH: 13.06.68
PLACE OF BIRTH: London. Father from Iko Marathasas; Mother from Ayios Sergios, Famagusta.
MARITAL STATUS: Single
SCHOOLS/COLLEGE: St Mark's Secondary School, Hammersmith and West London College, University of Westminster.
ACADEMIC QUALIFICATIONS: BA (Honours) Business Studies.
HOBBIES AND INTERESTS: Learning languages and travelling.
PERSONAL PROFILE: Comedy magician/TV Personality, has had two TV series in Cyprus, *Costas Costa Stis Okto* (Sigma TV) sept 96 to Jan 98, *Costas Costa Show* (PIK), Jan 00 to Jun 01.
Performs regularly in London, New York and Cyprus.

COSTAS CHARALAMBOS COSTA
Charity Work

DATE OF BIRTH: 05.04.61
PLACE OF BIRTH: London. Father Kato Deftera, Mother Vouno.
MARITAL STATUS: Single
SCHOOLS/COLLEGE: Highbury Grove.
HOBBIES AND INTERESTS: Travel, photography and swimming.
PERSONAL PROFILE: Director/Producer Icarus Productions. Was executive secretary for aid for Cyprus EAK for several years. Vice President of the Support Association of Northern Epirus organised the christening of 38 children from Northern Epirus. Assisted in building hospital in Northern Epirus and helped obtain medicine from the Wellcome Trust for their hospital.

GEORGE COSTA
Businessman

DATE OF BIRTH: 07.11.63
PLACE OF BIRTH: Pano Zodhia, Cyprus.
MARITAL STATUS: Married to Egli (née Gabrielidou), a Montessori nursery school teacher, from Lefkara, Cyprus.
CHILDREN: Andrew Thomas, attends Lochinvar School for Boys, and Elena Marie who attends Stormont School for Girls.
ACADEMIC QUALIFICATIONS: 13 O Levels and 4 A Levels. BSc (Honours) from UMIST in Textiles Economics and Management.
PROFESSIONAL QUALIFICATIONS: Business Growth Development, Cranfield School of Management.
MEMBERSHIPS: Institute of Directors, David Lloyd Club.
HONOURS/AWARD Small Business Growth of the Year Award for Export Achievement; Semi-Finalist in Ernst & Young Entrepreneur of the Year.
HOBBIES AND INTERESTS: Rowing, circuit training, cycling, boxing and Olympic Trap Shooting.
PERSONAL PROFILE: MD of Performance Textile Manufacturer.

GEORGIA COSTA
Charity Worker

DATE OF BIRTH: 21.07.68
PLACE OF BIRTH: Famagusta
MARITAL STATUS: Married to Donstan Mwangota, an Accounts Technician, from Tanzania.
CHILDREN: Matthew
SCHOOLS/COLLEGE: Fortismere School, Dean College of London, University Of East London.
ACADEMIC QUALIFICATIONS: BSc (Honours) MSc
HOBBIES AND INTERESTS: Travel.
PERSONAL PROFILE: Helps victims of torture & refugee children, who do not have parents/family in UK.

COSTAS COSTA A LONDON-BORN GREEK CYPRIOT WHO BECAME A TV PERSONALITY IN CYPRUS

LARA COSTA
Actress

PLACE OF BIRTH: London. Grandfather, Costa Sofocleaus (Halouvas), born in Analyonta; Grandmother, Maria Lazarou, born Larnaca.
MARITAL STATUS: Single
SCHOOLS/COLLEGE: London Studio Centre, Elmhurst Ballet School, Royal Ballet School.
ACADEMIC QUALIFICATIONS: 8 GCSEs.
MEMBERSHIPS: Equity.
HONOURS/AWARDS: Graduated with distinction, 1996 won most outstanding performer of year.
HOBBIES AND INTERESTS: Reading, travel, ski-ing and anything thats a challenge.
PERSONAL PROFILE: Actress. Has appeared in theatre in *Bombay Dreams*, *Saturday Night Fever*. Appeared on TV in *Smith & Jones*, *Bliss*, *Crimewatch*. TV commercials, such as *Evening Standard* and Motown.

PHILIPPOS COSTA
Cypriot Football League

DATE OF BIRTH: 15.08.40
PLACE OF BIRTH: Peristerona (Morphou).
MARITAL STATUS: Married to Eleni, a Dressmaker from Koma Tou Yialou and Strovolos, Nicosia.
CHILDREN: Costas, Aircraft Mechanic; Nicola, Reception Manager.
SCHOOLS/COLLEGE: Peristorena School.
PROFESSIONAL QUAILFICATIONS: Master Carpenter.
HOBBIES AND INTERESTS: Football within the Greek Cypriot Community (KOPA).
PERSONAL PROFILE: Carpenter/Shopfitter. Member of KOPA Cypriot Football Association for over 20 years covering many roles within.

DR ZACHARIAS COSTA
Medical Private Practice

DATE OF BIRTH: 20.02.25
PLACE OF BIRTH: Kondea
MARITAL STATUS: Married to Anastasia from Akhna.
CHILDREN: Costas, Christos, Anna, Charalambous and Georgia.
SCHOOLS/COLLEGE: Amercian Academy, Larnaca, Lille and Bordeaux (France) Universities.
ACADEMIC QUALIFICATIONS: MD, F.R.C.O.G., LRCP, MRCS, DIPVEN, MRCGP, LAH Dip, BA (Honours), Philosophy, D.T.M (France) .
HOBBIES AND INTERESTS: Studying Law with the Open University, writing books, learning languages.
PERSONAL PROFILE: In Medical Private Practice in North London. Was responsible for the eradication of the killer common disease in Cyprus called Hydatid (Echinoculus), about which he co-operated with the French Professors Jean Jean Biquet, Debroque and Gabren. Dr. Costa's first wife, Eleni, died of this disease at the age of 28.

DR ALAN C.F. CROSS
Doctor

DATE OF BIRTH: 12.02.74
PLACE OF BIRTH: London. Mother Greek Cypriot.
MARITAL STATUS: Single
SCHOOLS/COLLEGE: Chigwell School for Boys, U C L Medical School.
ACADEMIC QUALIFICATIONS: A Level Biology, Chemistry, Maths, General studies.
PROFESSIONAL QUALIFICATIONS: Medical Doctor MBBS.
MEMBERSHIPS: G.M.C. (General Medical Council).
HOBBIES AND INTERESTS: Music, sport, drama and travel.
PERSONAL PROFILE: Doctor, specialising in Psychiatry, East London Group.

ANDREW DANTIS
Tennis Coach

DATE OF BIRTH: 19.08.61
PLACE OF BIRTH: London. Father from Yialousa; Mother from Vothilaka.
MARITAL STATUS: To Maria Kyprianou, a Housewife, British Cypriot.
CHILDREN: Leon, at St. Columbus College; Danielle, at Queenswood School.
SCHOOLS/COLLEGE: Minchenden Comprehensive & North London Polytechnic.
ACADEMIC QUALIFICATIONS: 6 O Levels, 3 A Levels BA History.
MEMBERSHIPS: USPTR - United States Professional Tennis Registry, Cypriot Golf Society, Fore Golf Society.
HOBBIES AND INTERESTS: Travelling, walking, tennis and golf.
PERSONAL PROFILE: In Business for 15 years - Ran one Deli and two Sandwich shops, (from 1983-2000). 1992-94 was employed by Enfield FC. Part-time Tennis Coaching since 1993. Full Tennis coaching since Sept 2000.

STELIOS DAMIANOU
General Manager KEO UK

PLACE OF BIRTH: Ayios Theodoros, Larnaca, Cyprus.
MARITAL STATUS: Married to Beba, from Ayios Theodoros, Larnaca.
CHILDREN: Akis, MSC, M PHIL Biochemistry Biology Food Technology, Senior Food Technologist, M&S, Tony, Student, George, MSc Biochemisty, Molecular Biology.
PERSONAL PROFILE: General Manager of KEO UK.

DEMETRIOS DAVID
Former Chairman of Omonia FC UK

DATE OF BIRTH: 20.09.37
PLACE OF BIRTH: Pano Deftera Nicosia, Cyprus.
MARITAL STATUS: Married to Chrisoulla Eleftheriou, a Machinist/Hairdresser, from Pano Deftera.
CHILDREN: Eroulla, Company Director; Helen, Beautician; Rita Christina, Journalist.
SCHOOLS/COLLEGE: Elementary School Cyprus.
MEMBERSHIPS: AKEL, Omonia FC (London) Deftera Association (London).
HOBBIES AND INTERESTS: All sports, especially football; Cypriot politics and travelling.
PERSONAL PROFILE: Own Business as Clothing Manufacturer for 35 years, helped train unskilled people in clothing. Former Chairman Omonia FC (London). Chairman Deftera Association (London)

RITA CHRISTINA DAVID
News Reporter

DATE OF BIRTH: 12.01.74
PLACE OF BIRTH: London. Parents from Deftera, Cyprus.
MARITAL STATUS: Single
SCHOOLS/COLLEGE: Christ Church CE School, North Finchley, Southgate College, University of Sussex, Harlow College (For Post Graduate)
ACADEMIC QUALIFICATIONS: BA Honours History, University of Sussex. NCTS Post Graduate Journalism Diploma Assoc Board Royal Schools of Music (ABRSM).
HONOURS/AWARDS: Ted Bottomly Award, Newspaper Journalism, 1998. Grade 8 Piano.
HOBBIES AND INTERESTS: Watersports an literature, (fiction & non).
PERSONAL PROFILE: Current Job: News Reporter, *Retail Week Magazine*, previously Reporter on the *Enfield Gazette + Advertiser*. Contributor to *Parikiaki*. Also taught Piano & hosted a local Radio News Programme.(Radio North NID).

ZACH DAY
Actor

DATE OF BIRTH: 07.01.69
PLACE OF BIRTH: London. Mother from Rizokarpasso.
MARITAL STATUS: Single
SCHOOLS/COLLEGE: Leeds University.
ACADEMIC QUALIFICATIONS: BA Honours English, MA Theatre Studies.
MEMBERSHIPS: Equity.
HONOURS/AWARDS: Winner of several awards, National & International for Poetry.
PERSONAL PROFILE: Actor and Poet. Has appeared in Films and TV, including *Sammie & Rosie Get Laid*, and at the Narcissus Theatre in *Macbeth, Romeo & Juliet*.

GEORGINA DEMETRI
Teacher

DATE OF BIRTH: 21.07.67
PLACE OF BIRTH: London. Father from Exometochi; Mother from Astromeriti.
MARITAL STATUS: Married to John, London. (parents from Yialoussa)
CHILDREN: Two daughters.
SCHOOLS/COLLEGE: High Cross Tottenham, Middlesex Polytechnic.
ACADEMIC QUALIFICATIONS: B.Ed Honours
HOBBIES AND INTERESTS: Dancing, karaoke and interior design.
PERSONAL PROFILE: Teacher, was at Woodland's Park Junior School, Park View Academy Secondary School, Now at Lea Valley Primary School. Involved with lobby for Cyprus.

ALEXIS DEMETRIADES
English Champion Wrestler

DATE OF BIRTH: 06.03.79
PLACE OF BIRTH: London Parents from Morphou, Cyprus.
MARITAL STATUS: Single
SCHOOLS/COLLEGE: Hampstead Comprehensive.
HOBBIES AND INTERESTS: Cinema and travel.
PERSONAL PROFILE: Wrestler. Top athlete in the 74kg category in Freestyle Wrestling (an Olympic Sport) in England. Won the English Senior Championship for his weight. His coaches are confident that he can make the huge leap and qualify for the Olympics.

ANASTASIOS DEMETRIADES
Banking

DATE OF BIRTH: 24.5.61
PLACE OF BIRTH: Famagusta.
MARITAL STATUS: Married to Louz Marina, from Colombia.
SCHOOLS/COLLEGE: 1st Gymnasium Famgusta, Aylestone High School, University of Essex,
ACADEMIC QUALIFICATIONS: BA Honours
HOBBIES AND INTERESTS: Photography, cycling, swimming, and travelling.
PERSONAL PROFILE: Involved with the Birmingham Estia. Assistant Manager Cyprus Popular Bank Birmingham Branch

ANTONIOS COSTA DEMETRIADES
President of Larnaca Assoc in UK

DATE OF BIRTH: 18.04.36
PLACE OF BIRTH: Larnaca, Cyprus.
MARITAL STATUS: Married to Nora Palmiri, a Housewife, from Famagusta.
CHILDREN: Constantinos, Civil Engineer; Kyriacos, Car Mechanic.
SCHOOLS/COLLEGE: Studied in Cyprus at the Pancyprian Lyceum, Larnaca.
QUALIFICATIONS: Various courses in Accountancy, Shipping and Management. Also Official Trainer of the Cyprus Productivity Centre in TWI (training with Industry) in subjects of Supervision "Human Relations", Method Improvement and instruction techniques.
PERSONAL PROFILE: President of Larnaca Association in Great Britain, Member of Executive Committee of Greek Cypriot Brotherhood for Several years. Now retired.

PANICOS DEMETRIADES
University Lecturer

DATE OF BIRTH: 09.01.59
PLACE OF BIRTH: Limassol
MARITAL STATUS: Married to Svetlana Andrianova, a Lecturer in Economics, from Moscow.
CHILDREN: Polyvios, at school in Nicosia.
SCHOOLS/COLLEGE: Lanition, University of Essex and University of Cambridge.
ACADEMIC QUALIFICATIONS: PhD, MA, BA.
MEMBERSHIPS: Econometric Society.
PERSONAL PROFILE: Professor of Financial Economics, University of Leicester.

ALEXIA DEMETRIOU
Actress

DATE OF BIRTH: 25.11.81
PLACE OF BIRTH: UK.
Father from Nicosia, Cyprus; Mother from Larnaca, Ayios Theodoros, Cyprus.
MARITAL STATUS: Single
SCHOOLS/COLLEGE: Coombe Girls School New Malden, Surrey, Esher College.
ACADEMIC QUALIFICATIONS: 9 GCSEs (C+) A Levels Sociology, Theatre Studies and History. (BCC)
MEMBERSHIPS: CIM Certificate & Member of Chartered Institute of Marketing, also been Millennium Volunteer and have a 200 Voluntary Service Award.
HOBBIES AND INTERESTS: Dancing, socialising with friends, yoga, travelling and studying Psychology.
PERSONAL PROFILE: Fundraiser for children's charity, Barnardo's. Goes to schools to tell children about the work Barnado's does. Also goes to companies to manage fundraising events. From the ages of 11-14, played the part of Janine Butcher in *East Enders*.

ANDREAS DEMETRIOU
Rally Driver/ Company Director

DATE OF BIRTH: 25.03.64
PLACE OF BIRTH: London Parents from Paphos.
MARITAL STATUS: Married to Sue, from Ireland.
CHILDREN: Christopher and Anthony.
SCHOOLS/COLLEGE: Arnos Grove Secondary.
HOBBIES AND INTERESTS: Motor sport.
PERSONAL PROFILE: Company Director of a mobile phone company. Andreas is a motor sports driver and has won races at the Caterham R400 Championships in 2003 and 2004.

**ALEXIA DEMETRIOU
PLAYED THE PART OF
JANINE BUTCHER IN
EAST ENDERS FROM THE
AGES OF 11-14**

AVRAAM DEMETRIOU
Dental Surgeon

DATE OF BIRTH: 31.5.51
PLACE OF BIRTH: Limnia Famagusta.
MARITAL STATUS: Married to Myroulla, an Office Manager, from London (parents from Agios Sergios and Ardana).
CHILDREN: Andreas, Matthew and Christos.
SCHOOLS/COLLEGE: Famagusta Gymnasium, Tollington Park Sec. School, Tottenham Technical College, University College Hospital, Dental School.
PROFESSIONAL QUALIFICATIONS: BDS (Bachelor of Dental Surgery).
MEMBERSHIPS: Licenciate of Dental Surgeon LDS. RCS Royal College of Surgeons, England. Mellon in Limnia.
HOBBIES AND INTERESTS: Producing News Letter for Limnia - To Mellon, reading, writing and poetry.
PERSONAL PROFILE: Dental Surgeon work mainly with Cypriot Community. (Greek & Turkish). Fundraiser for UK Thalassaemisa Society.

DANIELLE DEMETRIOU
News Reporter

DATE OF BIRTH: 22.12.74
PLACE OF BIRTH: Sevenoaks, Kent. Father from Nicosia, Cyprus.
MARITAL STATUS: Single
SCHOOLS/COLLEGE: King's School, Canterbury, Trinity College, Dublin.
ACADEMIC QUALIFICATIONS: BA Honours French & Italian Postgrad Journalism Diploma
PERSONAL PROFILE: Currently working as a News Reporter at the *Evening Standard*. Formerly worked at *Daily & Sunday Telegraph*.

DEMETRI DEMETRIOU
Actor

DATE OF BIRTH: 15.6.73
PLACE OF BIRTH: Nicosia, Cyprus
MARITAL STATUS: Single
SCHOOLS/COLLEGE: King's College (University of London). Drama Centre London.
ACADEMIC QUALIFICATIONS: Law and Drama degrees.
HOBBIES AND INTERESTS: Reading, theatre, cinema, and swimming.
PERSONAL PROFILE: Now an actor. Appearances have included the film *Sea Wolf* and the TV programme *The Way We Live Now*.

DIMITRIOS (Jim) DEMETRIOU
Former President of Student Union

DATE OF BIRTH: 14.01.53
PLACE OF BIRTH: Larnaca
MARITAL STATUS: Married to Elpida (Nethi), currently working as Teaching Assistant for local Primary School, from Morphou,
CHILDREN: Andreas and Elena, both at Rushcroft school.
SCHOOLS/COLLEGE: Creighton School, Muswell Hill, Tottenham College of Technology 1973-76. West London College of Technology 1976-79. Polytechnic of Central London 1979-80.
PROFESSIONAL QUALIFICATIONS: Ordinary National Diploma in Building Construction, Higher National Diploma in Building Construction, Diploma in Building Management.
MEMBERSHIPS: Member of Chartered Institute of Building (MCIOB), Member of Association of Planning Supervisors (MAPS).
HOBBIES AND INTERESTS: My family, reunification of Cyprus, foreign affairs, cinema and eating out.
PERSONAL PROFILE: Currently employed as Contract Manager with a building contractor. President of Student Union at Tottenham College 1973-4 Treasurer of Cypriot Society at Tottenham College 1974-5. Active member of Lobby for Cyprus.

DIMITRIS DEMETRIOU
Former Mayor of Epping

DATE OF BIRTH: 20.06.49
PLACE OF BIRTH: Labathos
MARITAL STATUS: Married to Vasoulla, from Labathos.
CHILDREN: George, Maria & Katerina.
SCHOOLS/COLLEGE: Tricomo Gymnasium, Hotel School in Nicosia, West Ham College, North East London Polytechnic.
ACADEMIC QUALIFICATIONS: Diploma of Higher Education.
PROFESSIONAL QUALIFICATIONS: Qualified as a teacher.
HOBBIES AND INTERESTS: Business and gardening
PERSONAL PROFILE: Worked one and a half years as a teacher in Newham, opened a fish and Chip Shop and several restaurants, notably *Abbey Taverna* in Waltham Cross, and *Thatched House* in Epping. Twelve years Councillor in Epping and Waltham Abbey, Mayor Epping 1992-93, was chairman of the Planning Committee of Epping. President of Walthham Abbey Football Club in the Vauxhall League and Governor of St. Johns School in Epping.

GEORGE DEMETRIOU
DJ

DATE OF BIRTH: 01.09.76
PLACE OF BIRTH: London. Father Jimmy Demetriou, ex-Mayor of Epping.
MARITAL STATUS: Single
SCHOOLS/COLLEGE: St Johns Epping, Middlesex University.
PROFESSIONAL QUALIFICATIONS: Bsc in Hotel and Business Management.
HOBBIES AND INTERESTS: Tennis and Shopping.
PERSONAL PROFILE: Whilst at College did DJ part-time, won London DJ of the year 1996. Final held at Epping Country Club. Won £1000 and became a resident DJ at the club. Now into Music Production, had top 20 hit in British National Charts under name *Tru-faith*, the song was called 'Freak Like Me'. Also a DJ at LGR.

MADELEINE DEMETRIOU
University Lecturer

DATE OF BIRTH: 03.03.69
PLACE OF BIRTH: Nicosia
MARITAL STATUS: Single
SCHOOLS/COLLEGE: University of East Anglia, Bristol University, University of Kent.
QUALIFICATIONS: BA in Economic & Social Studies; MSc in Domestic Politics and Foreign Policy; PhD Graduate School of Politics & International Relations.
HOBBIES AND INTERESTS: Yoga, drama, Cypriot Women's Bi-Communal Group, Domestic Violence Niteline.
PERSONAL PROFILE: Lecturer in European Studies at University of Kent. Formerly Political researcher in Cyprus, reporter for *Cyprus Mail*, and has written several publications.

MICHAEL DEMETRIOU
Former Chairman of Carrera FC

DATE OF BIRTH: 01.08.31
PLACE OF BIRTH: Morphou
MARITAL STATUS: Married to Christine, a Dress Designer (Father from Ayios Andronicos; Mother from Ayia Varvara).
CHILDREN: Theodoros, Co. Director Euro Med Travel; Dinos, Film Producer; Marios, Managing Director Euro Med Travel; Andreas, Director Euro Med Travel and Actor.
SCHOOLS/COLLEGE: English School, Morphou Shoreditch College of Tailoring & Cutting.
MEMBERSHIPS: Morphou District Association DEKO UK.
HOBBIES AND INTERESTS: Football.
PERSONAL PROFILE: Was Secretary of Athletic Section of Greek Cypriot Botherhood for several years, played football with their team. Chairman of Carrera's football Club for eight years.

MARIO DEMETRIOU
Secretary of Twelve Apostles Greek Orthodox Church

DATE OF BIRTH: 05.05 68
PLACE OF BIRTH: London. Father from Morphou, Ayios Andronicos; Mother, London, Ayia Varvara.
MARITAL STATUS: Single
SCHOOLS/COLLEGE: Whittingham, Muswell Hill, Jnr; Friern Barnet Grammar, Hellenic College of London, Secondary.
ACADEMIC QUALIFICATIONS: 8 O Levels.
PROFESSIONAL QUALIFICATIONS: British Airways Basic, Level 1 & 2, Associate of Institute of Travel & Tourism.
HOBBIES AND INTERESTS: Tennis, theatre, travelling and religion.
PERSONAL PROFILE: Secretary of the Greek Orthodox Church of the Twelve Apostles, Hertfordshire, Member of the Committee for the Morphou District Association & a Founder of Support Association of Northern Epirus. Was on hunger strike for one week, just after Tassos Isaac & Solomos Solomou were murdered by the Turkish Army in Cyprus.

PANAYIOTIS (Peter) DEMETRIOU
Funeral Director

DATE OF BIRTH: 24.04.68
PLACE OF BIRTH: London. Parents from Pomos Paphos and Ayios Sergios (Famagusta).
MARITAL STATUS: Single
SCHOOLS/COLLEGE: Michenden School.
HOBBIES AND INTERESTS: Travel and shooting.
PERSONAL PROFILE: Owner of Demetriou & English Funeral Directors, based in Myddleton Rd, N.22.

SOULLA DEMETRIOU
Accountant

DATE OF BIRTH: 13.06.74
PLACE OF BIRTH: Nicosia, Cyprus
MARITAL STATUS: Single
SCHOOLS/COLLEGE: University of East Anglia.
QUALIFICATIONS: BEC ACA.
MEMBERSHIPS: Institute of Chartered Accountants in England and Wales.
PERSONAL PROFILE: Tax Supervisor.

THEODOROS (Doros) DEMETRIOU
Football

DATE OF BIRTH: 03.09.43
PLACE OF BIRTH: Mandres Famagusta, Cyprus.
MARITAL STATUS: Married to Margarita Anastasiou, a Childminder, from Livadia, Larnaca.
CHILDREN: Anastasios Demetriou, Branch Manager (Electrical Goods); Martha Lewis, Entertainer.
SCHOOLS/COLLEGE: Elementary School.
PROFESSIONAL QUALIFICATIONS: Financial Adviser.
MEMBERSHIPS: I.Q.A with Laurencian Life.
HOBBIES AND INTERESTS: Football.
PERSONAL PROFILE: Served as Head of Advertising with *Eleftheria* Newspaper. Referee in Greek League UK. Member of Anorthosis Football Committee UK.

TONY DEMETRIOU
Parikiaki Newspaper

DATE OF BIRTH: 10.07.78
PLACE OF BIRTH: London. Father from Nicosia; Mother, from Ayios Sergios, Famagusta.
MARITAL STATUS: Single
SCHOOLS/COLLEGE: Hadley Wood Primary School, Chancellors Secondary School, Oaklands College, London. Guildhall University, London.
ACADEMIC QUALIFICATIONS: 9 GCSEs BTEC Higher Diploma in Media, BA Honours Media Communications.
PROFESSIONAL QUALIFICATIONS: Qualified Journalist, Sports Reporter.
HOBBIES AND INTERESTS: Football (Arsenal Fan) music, travelling, going out: bars, clubs, restaurants
PERSONAL PROFILE: Served as *Parikiaki* English Page Contributor.

ELENI DIAKOU
Social Worker

DATE OF BIRTH: 22.03.47
PLACE OF BIRTH: Komi Kebir, Famagusta.
MARITAL STATUS: Married to David McCulloch, Scottish Environmental Health Manager.
CHILDREN: Androulla, GP; Adrian, Websites Specialist.
SCHOOLS/COLLEGE: Girls Classical Gymnasium Famagusta.
ACADEMIC QUALIFICATIONS: BA Social Studies and Politics.
PROFESSIONAL QUALIFICATIONS: DIPSW & Diploma in Management & PSW.
MEMBERSHIPS: BASW
HOBBIES AND INTERESTS: Walking, reading, visiting other countries and travelling.
PERSONAL PROFILE: Manager in Social Work. Lead in local, patchwork. Co-author of books on community social work and access to advice services. Amateur actress; set up Cypriot Day Centre in Islington, ex-Director of Theatro Technis.

MARY DOWSON (née KOUMI)
Teacher

DATE OF BIRTH: 30.05.54
PLACE OF BIRTH: London. Father Sykhari; Mother Pano Dikomo.
MARITAL STATUS: Married to Les Dowson, a Management Consultant.
CHILDREN: Katerina and Alexandra.
SCHOOLS/COLLEGE: Dame Alice Owen's Girls' School, Loughborough College of Education.
ACADEMIC QUALIFICATIONS: 5 O Levels, 2 A Levels, Certificate of Education, B.Ed Honours (2:1)
HOBBIES AND INTERESTS: Swimming, drama and community activities.
PERSONAL PROFILE: Teacher - Primary School since 1978, specialising in Special Needs. Voluntary Work: Successfully campaigned to raise funds from Haringey Council & Lottery Commission to build purpose built playgroup in local area.

Email: mary.dowson@btopenworld.com

PETER DROUSSIOTIS
Politics/Corporate Finance

DATE OF BIRTH: 21.09.60
PLACE OF BIRTH: Pera Chorion Nissou, Nicosia.
MARITAL STATUS: Married to Carolyn Burdin, a Teacher, from Yorkshire.
CHILDREN: Isabella, Alexandra and Theodora.
SCHOOLS/COLLEGE: Terra Santa College Cyprus, Alexandra Park School London, University of Birmingham, Bar School London.
ACADEMIC QUALIFICATIONS: LL B (Law & Politics)
PROFESSIONAL QUALIFICATIONS: Barrister-at-Law of the Middle Temple.
MEMBERSHIPS: The Labour Party, Society of Labour Lawyers, Episteme, The Fabian Society, European Movement, Liberty.
HOBBIES AND INTERESTS: Family, politics & current affairs, people, the countryside, history, I.T, astronomy and travelling.
PERSONAL PROFILE: Former Haringey Council Executive member. President of Episteme. Chair of corporate & finance group of the Society of Labour Lawyers. Member of Executive of Federation of Cypriots in GB and member of Central Council of World Federation of overseas Cypriots (POMAK). Acting Chair Labour Cypriot Society. Patron Whittington Hospital Thalassaemia Appeal. Chairman PGD Strategy, a corporate finance firm.
Email: peter.droussiotis@pgdstrategy.com

DEMETRIOS ECONOMIDES
Obstetrician & Gynaecologist

DATE OF BIRTH: 14.10.56
PLACE OF BIRTH: London. Parents from Lefkonico, Famagusta.
MARITAL STATUS: Married to Daphne Christie, a Scientific Editor, Wellcome History of Medicine, of the Stakis family from Kato Drys.
CHILDREN: Margarita and Alexandra.
SCHOOLS/COLLEGE: The English School, Nicosia; Charing Cross Medical School, London.
ACEDEMIC QUALIFICATIONS: MBBS, MD.
PROFESSIONAL QUALIFICATIONS: FRCOG.
MEMBERSHIPS : Royal Society of Medicine, Hellenic Medical Society.
HOBBIES AND INTERESTS: Travel, photography and shooting.
PERSONAL PROFILE: Consultant & senior lecturer obstetrician & gynaecologist, Royal Free Hopsital.

HERACLIS A ECONOMIDES
Investment Bank Director

DATE OF BIRTH: 18.03.61
PLACE OF BIRTH: Famagusta, Cyprus.
MARITAL STATUS: Married
CHILDREN: One daughter.
SCHOOLS/COLLEGE: English School in Nicosia; Archbishop Tennysons Grammar School, Kennington; Brasenose College, Oxford University.
ACADEMIC QUALIFICATIONS: BA in Philosophy, Politics, and Economics.
PROFESSIONAL QUALIFICATIONS: Chartered Accountant.
HOBBIES AND INTERESTS: Tennis, opera and travel.
PERSONAL PROFILE: First worked with Coopers and Lybrand, now with HSBC, Managing Director Equity Capital Markets.

HERACLES ECONOMIDES
Chartered Architect

DATE OF BIRTH: 03.02.46
PLACE OF BIRTH: Famagusta.
MARITAL STATUS: Married to Beba, from Macedonia.
CHILDREN: Mark, an Investment Banker; Jason, a Stockbroker.
SCHOOLS/COLLEGE: Praktiko of the 1st Gymnasium for Boys, Famagusta; University of North London.
PROFESSIONAL QUALIFICATIONS: Dip in Architecture, Chartered Architect Part III exams.
MEMBERSHIPS: Royal Institute of British Architects (RIBA).
HOBBIES AND INTERESTS: Badminton, travelling, Byzantine music and classical ballet.
PERSONAL PROFILE: Former Chairman of High Barnet Greek School, Membership Secretary of the Famagusta Association, member of St Katherines Church in Whetstone. Has practised architecture since 1973, the first 17 years in a large architect's office, first year as a contracts manager in Nigeria. Has had his own private practice since 1990.

NITSA ECONOMIDOU
Therapist

DATE OF BIRTH: 10.6.47
PLACE OF BIRTH: Limassol
MARITAL STATUS: Married to Paul Millns, a musician, composer, singer, from UK.
CHILDREN: Nina; Sophie; Andreas.
SCHOOLS/COLLEGE: Lanition Gymnasium, Limassol; Kingston University, London, Trent University, Nottingham.
ACADEMIC QUALIFICATIONS: BSc Sociology.
PROFESSIONAL QUALIFICATIONS: COSW Postgraduate social work, Dip Psychosynthesis, Dip Supervision.
MEMBERSHIPS: UK Council of Psychotherapy.
PERSONAL PROFILE: Therapist, Counsellor and supervisior in the helping professions. Parent-child, couple relationship issues specialisation.

DR GEORGE JOHN EFSTATHIADES
Served as Honorary Commissioner for the Republic of Cyprus in Birmingham

DATE OF BIRTH: 23.03.39
PLACE OF BIRTH: Kato-Drys.
MARITAL STATUS: Married to Antigone (Loizides), a Company Director, from Nicosia, Cyprus.
CHILDREN: John, Consultant Engineer; Marios, Insurance Office Manager; Helena, Flight Attendant.
SCHOOLS/COLLEGE: Kato Drys Primary; Pancyprian Gymnasium, Nicosia; University of Birmingham.
ACADEMIC QUALIFICATIONS: BSc, PhD (Mechanical Engineering).
PERSONAL PROFILE: Chief Engineer, Hellenic Mining Corporation Cyprus 1966-67. University Lecturer since 1967. Founder & Managing Director of Zet Insurances Services Ltd since 1977. Chairman of "Justice of Cyprus - Birmingham" 1974, Chairman of Church committee of the Greek Orthodox Church of St Andrew and Dormitor of Theotokos - Birmingham 1980-81. Honorary Commissioner for the Republic of Cyprus in Birmingham since 1981-2004.

GEORGE PETROS EFSTATHIOU
Professor of Astrophysics

DATE OF BIRTH: 02.09.55
PLACE OF BIRTH: London. Parents from Achna, Cyprus.
MARITAL STATUS: Married to Yvonne Nobis, Professor of Astrophysics, University of Cambridge, from Bourne-mouth, Dorset.
CHILDREN: Zoe Jane and Peter Lewis.
SCHOOLS/COLLEGE: Somerset School, Tottenham London; Keble College, University of Oxford; Durham University.
ACEDEMIC QUALIFICATIONS: BA (1976), PhD (1979).
MEMBERSHIPS: Fellow of Royal Society, Fellow of Institute of Physics, Fellow of Royal Astronomical Society.
HONOURS/AWARDS: Maxwell medal & prize Institute of Physics 1990, Bodassaki prize for Astrophysics 1994, Bappu Medal, Astronomical Society of India 1988, Robinson prize for Cosmology, Univ Newcastle 1997.
HOBBIES AND INTERESTS: Running and playing guitar.
PERSONAL PROFILE: Junior research fellow 1980-84, Senior research fellow, 1984-88 Kings College Cambridge; Assistant director of research, Institute of Astronomy, Cambridge.
Savilian Prof of Astronomy, Univ of Oxford (1988-1997), Head of Astrophysics (1988-1994), Professor of Astrophysics University of Cambridge (1997-present).

SOPHIA EFSTATHIOU
Teacher

DATE OF BIRTH: 07.10.68
PLACE OF BIRTH: London. Parents from Nicosia
MARITAL STATUS: Single
SCHOOLS/COLLEGE: Oakthorpe School, Warwick University Aberystwyth.
ACADEMIC QUALIFICATIONS: BSc Sociology. PGCE.
HOBBIES AND INTERESTS: Travelling and cinema.
PERSONAL PROFILE: Teacher at Earlsmead Primary School.

STATHI EFSTATHIOU
University Lecturer

DATE OF BIRTH: 15.10.60
PLACE OF BIRTH: London. Parents from Achna.
MARITAL STATUS: Married to Caroline, a Computer Programmer, from Cheshire.
CHILDREN: Claudia Mary and James.
SCHOOLS/COLLEGE: Southgate Comprehensive; Leeds University (undergraduate), Cambridge University (postgraduate).
ACADEMIC QUALIFICATIONS: BSc Microbiology, PhD Virology.
MEMBERSHIPS: Society of General Microbiology.
HOBBIES AND INTERESTS: Music and guitar.
PERSONAL PROFILE: Senior Lecturer, Dept of Pathology Cambridge University. Research area - virus pathogenesis and gene therapy. Editorial Journal of Genereal Virology (1995-2000), Member of the Virus Group Committee of the Society of General Microbiology. Member of the European Society of Gene Therapy Meetings Organising Committee. Member of the SGM Herpesvirus Workshop Committee (1989-1991).

TASSOS EFSTATHIOU
Architect

DATE OF BIRTH: 24.04.55
PLACE OF BIRTH: London
MARITAL STATUS: Married to Gillian, from Southend.
CHILDREN: Andreas, Joseph and Alexandra.
SCHOOLS/COLLEGE: Henry Thornton School, Southbank Polytechnic.
ACaDEMIC QUALIFICATIONS: 5 GCEs, 2 A Levels, OND Building; BA, MA Architecture.

HOBBIES AND INTERESTS: Golf, Bridge, eating out and music.

PERSONAL PROFILE: Architect, Director of Building Company, Chairman of under-13s football team, on committee of parents for scouts in Southgate 6th group.

ANDROULLA EFSTRATIOU
Medical Researcher

DATE OF BIRTH: 03.07.60
PLACE OF BIRTH: London. Parents from Famagusta and Larnaca.
MARITAL STATUS: Single
SCHOOLS/COLLEGE: St Joseph's Convent Grammar School, City University London.
ACADEMIC QUALIFICATIONS: BSc, PhD.
PROFESSIONAL QUALIFICA-TIONS: SRCS, MRCPath

MEMBERSHIPS: Royal College of Pathologists, American Society for Microbiology, Hellenic Medical Society.
HONOURS/AWARDS: Louis Pasteur Medal for Distinction in Infectious Diseases.
HOBBIES AND INTERESTS: Gardening, art and travel.
PERSONAL PROFILE: Head of WHO Collaborating Centre for Reference and Research on Diptheria and Streptococcal Infections, Health Protection Agency London. Consultant for Cyprus Ministry of Health, and Consultant for World Health Organisation and European Commission. Member of numerous medical advisory committees, Co-ordinator of three European Commission funded programmes on infectious diseases. Co-ordinator European Working Group on Diptheria, Editorial Board - Medical Journals.

Email: androulla.efstratiou@hpa.org.uk

STRATOS EFSTRATIOU
Dentist

DATE OF BIRTH: 04.09.67
PLACE OF BIRTH: Johannesburg, South Africa. Father from Peristerona, Paphos; Mother from Nicosia.
MARITAL STATUS: Married to Chrisoula Nicolopoulou, a Dentist, also from Johannesburg (parents from Peloponiso).
CHILDREN: Nicholas and Angela.

SCHOOLS/COLLEGE: University of Witwatersrand, SA.
PROFESSIONAL QUALIFICATIONS: BDS (Bachelor of Dental Surgery).
HOBBIES AND INTERESTS: Golf and squash.
PERSONAL PROFILE: Dentist, private practitioner and owner of a six surgery practice.

DR CHRIS EFTHYMIOU
Doctor

DATE OF BIRTH: 11.12.73
PLACE OF BIRTH: Famagusta.
MARITAL STATUS: Single
SCHOOLS/COLLEGE: Ewell Castle School, Surrey; St Bartholomews Medical School; University of London, Royal College of Surgeons.
QUALIFICATIONS: MBBS, BSc (Honours) Physiology, MRCS.
PERSONAL PROFILE: Cardiothoracic Surgeon trainee at UCH London, now completeing PhD. Formula One doctor at Monaco and the British Grand Prix.

COSTAS EFTHYMIOU
Schools and Community (Deceased)

DATE OF BIRTH: 23.09.23
PLACE OF BIRTH: Tseri, Nicosia.
CHILDREN: Andreas and Christalla, from first marriage; Lakis, from second marriage.
SCHOOLS/COLLEGE: Elementary school in Cyprus.
MEMBERSHIPS: Akel.
HOBBIES AND INTERESTS: Politics.
PERSONAL PROFILE: Fought with the Army in the Second World War in the Middle East and Italy. Was Secretary of the Greek Parents Association. Chairman of the Cypriot Elderly Organisation in Enfield.

Address: 36 Canada Avenue, London N18 1AS.

IOANNIS EFTHYMIOU
Chief Exec Association of Greek Cypriot Travel Agents, UK

DATE OF BIRTH: 09.01.46
PLACE OF BIRTH: Morphou.
MARITAL STATUS: Divorced
SCHOOLS/COLLEGE: Greek Gymnasium, Morphou.
HOBBIES AND INTERESTS: Reading, writing, cinema and travel.
PERSONAL PROFILE: Chief Executive AGTA (UK), now generally regarded as the mouthpiece for Greek Cypriot specialist travel agents and tour operators in the UK, the number one market for Cyprus. tourism.

PAVLINA EFTHYMIOU
Treasurer of Greek School, Sheffield

DATE OF BIRTH: 09.06.61
PLACE OF BIRTH: Aradippou.
MARITAL STATUS: Divorced
CHILDREN: Margarita, Sophia, Elena and Maria.
SCHOOLS/COLLEGE: Ayios Georghios High School, Larnaca; Stafford College of further education, England.
ACADEMIC QUALIFICATIONS: 'O' Levels, 4 A Levels, City & Guilds Certificate.
MEMBERSHIPS: SCAIS (Sheffield Community Access & Interpreting Service).
HOBBIES AND INTERESTS: Music, dance, cinema and work!
PERSONAL PROFILE: Fish & chip shop proprietor, member of women's committee in church, Treasurer, Teacher (Assistant), Secretary of Greek School of Sheffield.

Address: 33 Station Rd, Chapel Town, Sheffield S35 2XE

PETROS EFTYCHIOU
High Commissioner for the Republic of Cyprus in the UK

DATE OF BIRTH: 25.10.50
PLACE OF BIRTH: Nicosia, parents from Tricomo.
MARITAL STATUS: Married
CHILDREN: Two daughters
SCHOOLS/COLLEGE: 1969, The English School Nicosia, 1975 American University of Beirut
QUALIFICATIONS: A.I.D Scholar, B.A Political Science/Public Administration
HOBBIES AND INTERESTS: Sports, Football- Played for Apoel in Cyprus.
PERSONAL PROFILE: Between the years of 1975-1977 Eftychiou worked in the private sector with a group of British and Greek business consultants in Athens and participted as a researcher in writing a book on investment prospects in the Eastern Mediterranean. He then worked as an administrative Officer for the Ministry of Finance in Nicosia until 1979, when he joined the Ministry of Foreign Affairs as Second Secretary.
In 1984, he worked in Brussels as a Secretary for the Permanent Mission of Cyprus (and Embassy to Benelux countries) Three years later he took the position of Secretary/Counsellor, Deputy Head of the EEC Department, Ministry of Foreign Affairs, Nicosia. For a temporary period of five months, Eftychiou acted as Acting High Commissioner of Cyprus, Canberra. Later on that year, in New York, he took on the role of Deputy Counsellor, a permanent position, representing Cyprus to the UN.
In 1993 he was elected Minister of Plenipotentiary, Chief of Cabinet of the Minister of Foreign Affairs, Nicosia. In 1994 and then again in 2000, Eftychiou worked as the Ambassador of Cyprus to the State of Israel. Between these years he was the permanent representative at the UN office in Geneva, the W.T.O and other international organisations in Geneva. (In 1998 he was elected and served for a year as vice president of the Economic Commission for Europe) In 2003, he established himself as the Director of E.U Affairs for the Ministry of Foreign Affairs, Nicosia. In the absence of the Permanent Secretary, Eftychiou assumes the duties of Acting Permanent Secretary of the Ministry of Foreign Affairs.
Nevertheless, in 2004 he was appointed High Commissioner for Cyprus in the UK.

MRS ZACK ELEFTHERIADOU
Psychologist & Psychotherapist

DATE OF BIRTH: 29.09.66
PLACE OF BIRTH: Famagusta.
MARITAL STATUS: Married to Paul Clarke, IT Director at 'Common Purpose'.
CHILDREN: Jake and Alexandros.
SCHOOLS/COLLEGE: Dover College, Richmond College, University of London, Regents' College
QUALIFICATIONS: BA Psychology, MSc Child Development, MA in the Psychology of Psychotherapy and Counselling.
HONOURS/AWARDS: BA award - received Social Sciences prize, MSc - Thesis A (distinction).
HOBBIES AND INTERESTS: Gardening, music, writing
PERSONAL PROFILE: Psychologist and psychotherapist with private practice in North London. Also works at the medical foundation for the care of victims of torture. Has had several works published.

ANDREAS ELEFTHERIOU
President Greek Church Torquay

DATE OF BIRTH: 12.4.35
PLACE OF BIRTH: Piyi, Famagusta
MARITAL STATUS: Married to Eleni Constandinou from Ayios Athanasios, Limassol
SCHOOLS/COLLEGE: Piyi - Lefkoniko High
PROFESSIONAL QUALIFICATIONS: Restaurateur
PERSONAL PROFILE: President of the Greek Church in Torquay for five years.

SAPPHIRE ELIA
Actress

DATE OF BIRTH: 15.04.87
PLACE OF BIRTH: UK.
Maternal grandparents from Lapithos, paternal grandparents from Larnaca and Akanthou.
MARITAL STATUS: Single
SCHOOLS/COLLEGE: Sylvia Young Theatre School since the age of eight.
ACADEMIC QUALIFICATIONS: Honours in LAMDA acting exam.
HOBBIES AND INTERESTS: Singing, dancing and skiing.
PERSONAL PROFILE: Sapphire has performed for the Princess Royal. Filmed in American Space Camp. Performed in choir for Lady Rattlings Charity Ball, and performed many times at the Royal Albert Hall. Played Cossette in *Les Miserables* on the London stage, and appeared on TV in comedy awards and *Fun Song Factory*.

ANDREAS ELIADES
Founder member of Lefkara Assoc of GB

DATE OF BIRTH: 01.12.44
PLACE OF BIRTH: Pano Lefkara.
MARITAL STATUS: Married to Ephtihoula, an administrator at Greek and Greek Cypriot community of Enfield, from Pano Lefkara.
CHILDREN: George, IT support engineer; Nico, runs business in Canada; Zoe and Joanna, university graduates.
SCHOOLS/COLLEGE: Lefkara Gymnasio.
PROFESSIONAL QUALIFICATIONS: Cutter, ladies' clothing.
HOBBIES AND INTERESTS: Gardening, socialising and DIY
PERSONAL PROFILE: Established with other members of the Greek community the Southgate Greek School. Founder member of Lefkara Association of Great Britain.

EPHTIHOULA ELIADES (LOULA)
Schools & Community

DATE OF BIRTH: 21.07.49
PLACE OF BIRTH: London.
Parents from Pano Lefkara.
MARITAL STATUS: Married to Andreas from Pano Lefkara.
CHILDREN: George, Nicholas, Zoe and Joanna.
SCHOOLS/COLLEGE: Holland Park Comprehensive, Southgate College.
ACEDEMIC QUALIFICATIONS: RSAs & GCEs in various subjects, also NVQ.
PROFESSIONAL QUALIFICATIONS: Currently studying HNC in Business.
HOBBIES AND INTERESTS: Gym, volunteer work and socialising.
PERSONAL PROFILE: Founder member Southgate Greek School/Lefkara Assoc of GB.

GEORGE ELIADES
Civil Engineer

DATE OF BIRTH: 30.03.71
PLACE OF BIRTH: London.
Parents from Lefkara, Larnaca.
MARITAL STATUS: Single
SCHOOLS/COLLEGE: Walker School, Southgate; Broomfield School, Southgate University of Herts.
QUALIFICATIONS: 8 O Levels, 3 A Levels, B.Eng (Honours) Civil Engineering, Microsoft Certified System Engineer
HOBBIES AND INTERESTS: Clubbing, football, MG Owners Club.
PERSONAL PROFILE: Worked in Civil Engineering in Saudi Arabia for five years, now IT Systems Engineer for Sun Microsystems plc.

NICHOLAS ANDREAS ELIADES
Businessman

DATE OF BIRTH: 29.03.73
PLACE OF BIRTH: London.
Parents from Pano Lefkara.
MARITAL STATUS: Single
SCHOOLS/COLLEGE: Southgate School, Sussex University.
QUALIFICATIONS: BA Honours Economics with Economics, History, five years management.
HOBBIES AND INTERESTS: Football and table tennis.
PERSONAL PROFILE: Owner of ANC Worldwide Ltd "Advertising New Concepts" upmarketing in Canada.

PANOS ELIADES
Accountant/Sports Promoter

DATE OF BIRTH: 24.04.51
PLACE OF BIRTH: London.
Parents from Livadia who had the Shaftesbury Restaurant in London's West End.
MARITAL STATUS: Married to Angela.
CHILDREN: Christian has a degree in Ecomonics from LSE; Eleonora is studying economics at LSE.
SCHOOLS/COLLEGE: Tollington Grammar, Loughborough University.
PROFESSIONAL QUALIFICATIONS: Chartered Accountant.
HOBBIES AND INTERESTS: Football, (Spurs supporter).
PERSONAL PROFILE: First worked at Stoy and Hayward specialising in insolvency. In 1980 formed own practice Panos Eliades & Co Chartered Accountants, specialising in liquidations. In 1991 bought contract of the boxer Lennox Lewis to manage and promote him. Director of Panix Promotions.

ANTHONY CONSTANTINOU IOANNOU ELIAKIS
Poet

DATE OF BIRTH: 01.02.30
PLACE OF BIRTH: Anaphotia, Larnaca.
MARITAL STATUS: Single
SCHOOLS/COLLEGE: Pancyprian Commercial Lyceum, Larnaca; Grays Inn, London.
HOBBIES AND INTERESTS: Swimming, shooting and gambling.

PERSONAL PROFILE: Former entrepreneur. Wrote and published a collection of poetry in Famagusta. LGR Radio contributor.

DR C.P. ELLINAS
Civil and Structural Engineer

DATE OF BIRTH: 18.09.49
PLACE OF BIRTH: Engomi, Famagusta.
MARITAL STATUS: Single
CHILDREN: Olympia
SCHOOLS/COLLEGE: University College London.
ACADEMIC QUALIFICATIONS: BSc (Honours), PhD.
MEMBERSHIPS: Fellow of Institute of Civil Engineers.

PERSONAL PROFILE: Civil and Structural Engineer, Managing Director of Oil & Gas Energy at Mott McDonald Group. Has written many publications, both books and magazine contributions.

MICHAEL S ELLINAS
Managing Director of Eleftheria Newspaper

DATE OF BIRTH: 09.04.57
PLACE OF BIRTH: Pafos (Houlou).
MARITAL STATUS: Married to Elissa Xenophontos, born in Pafos, Secondary School Teacher.
CHILDREN: Stavros, Secondary School.
SCHOOLS/COLLEGE: Lanition Gymnasium, Limassol.

ACADEMIC QUALIFICATIONS: Law Degree (BA), University of Athens (Law Dept.).
HOBBIES AND INTERESTS: Greek Dancing.
PERSONAL PROFILE: Currently, Managing Director of weekly Greek Newspaper, Eleftheria. Also, headmaster of independent Greek Community Schools of Barnet (Manor Hill & Finchley). President of the Democratic Party of Cypriots in England (DEKO).
Vice Chairman of the National Federation of Cypriots in the UK.

PETER EPAMINONDAS
Deacon & Solicitor

DATE OF BIRTH: 27.01.62
PLACE OF BIRTH: Larnaca.
MARITAL STATUS: Married to Kyriacou, a Housewife, from Alethrico.
CHILDREN: George and Melanie.
SCHOOLS/COLLEGE: Wolverhampton University, University of London King's College.

ACADEMIC QUALIFICATIONS: LL.B (Honours), LL.M.
PROFESSIONAL QUALIFICATIONS: Law Society final exams.
MEMBERSHIPS: Law Society.
HOBBIES AND INTERESTS: Religion.
PERSONAL PROFILE: Solicitor, qualified 1990. Currently Associate in the firm of Robinsons Solicitors, Derby. Deacon of the Greek Orthodox Church, Archdiocese of Thyateira and Great Britain. Ordained 23.1.00. Church name: Father Aimilianos.

AGAMEMNON A EPENETOS
Doctor/Scientist

DATE OF BIRTH: 15.10.49
PLACE OF BIRTH: Nicosia
MARITAL STATUS: Married to Panayiota.
CHILDREN: Antoni and Kristina.
SCHOOLS/COLLEGE: Famagusta 1st Gymnasium, Glasgow University.
QUALIFICATIONS: MB.chB, FRCP, PhD.
MEMBERSHIPS: Many medical societies.
HONOURS/AWARDS: Doctor of the Year Award.
HOBBIES AND INTERESTS: Starting Biotec Companies.
PERSONAL PROFILE: Doctor (medical), Scientist, Company Director.

DR SPIROS EPISKOPOU
Former General Manager of Cyprus Popular Bank UK

DATE OF BIRTH: 27.01.59
PLACE OF BIRTH: Paphos.
MARITAL STATUS: Married to Dianne from Wales.
CHILDREN: Stefan and Erik
SCHOOLS/COLLEGE: English School Nicosia, University of East Anglia.
ACADEMIC QUALIFICATIONS: BA Honours Economics, PhD in Industrial Economics.
HOBBIES AND INTERESTS: Motor racing, swimming and walking.
PERSONAL PROFILE: Joined Popular Bank in 1988 as a Credit Analyst and worked up to General Manager of UK Popular Bank, now returned to Cyprus. Was also Director of the Cyprus/British Chamber of Commerce and Industry.

AKIS ERACLEOUS
Co-Founder, London Greek Radio

DATE OF BIRTH: 26.12.52
PLACE OF BIRTH: Famagusta
MARITAL STATUS: Married to Julietta, a Housewife, from London.
CHILDREN: Emilios, Eva and Markos.
SCHOOLS/COLLEGE: Islington Green School, London.
QUALIFICATIONS: 6 grade 1 CSEs, 1 A Level Art. Certificate of Hotel and Catering Management.
MEMBERSHIPS: Equity.
HOBBIES AND INTERESTS: Football, Arsenal supporter. Watching a good movie or listening to a good album. Cycling and swimming
PERSONAL PROFILE: Original founder of Kiss FM, a London based dance music radio station. Co-founded London Greek Radio in 1983, and was appointed General Manager in 1989 when the station obtained its legal licence. Currently owns a highly successful independent record label, Nice 'N' Ripe Records, and still presents his own show on LGR every weekday between 10am and 1pm.

PETROS PAVLOU EROTOCRITOU
Doctor

DATE OF BIRTH: 31.12.44
PLACE OF BIRTH: Limassol.
MARITAL STATUS: Married to Sarah, a practice nurse, from England.
CHILDREN: Paul, at medical school.
SCHOOLS/COLLEGE: Lanition Gymnasium, Limassol.
QUALIFICATIONS: MD, SIM 1973 Athens Medical School, Athens University 1980 SIM.
MEMBERSHIPS: GMC, MDU, BMA London.
HONOURS/AWARDS: 1990 Aviation Medicine.
HOBBIES AND INTERESTS: Game shooting, DIY, gardening, olive oil production and wine growing.
PERSONAL PROFILE: After qualifying, worked in hospitals until 1982 then entered general practice. Currently general practitioner. Regular attender of local Greek Orthodox church.

CHRIS KRITOS EROTOKRITOU
Manager, Enfield Jets Basketball team

DATE OF BIRTH: 06.04.62
PLACE OF BIRTH: London. Father from Trahoni.
MARITAL STATUS: Married to Elena from Famagusta.
CHILDREN: Twins, Androulla and Constantinos.
SCHOOLS/COLLEGE: Drayton Comprehensive, University of Southampton.
QUALIFICATIONS: Electronic Engineering degree. (BSc Honours). Also took a Radio Operator's course at the Merchant Navy College, Kent.
HOBBIES AND INTERESTS: Watching his children grow up and supporting them in all their endeavours.
PERSONAL PROFILE: Works for Cellnet. Played rugby for the Merchant Navy, Saracens, then Haringey. Manages and coaches Enfield Jets Basketball Club for 12-18 year olds, who have won several cups and leagues and are soon to have national status. Chairman of basketball development for the North District, comprising of the boroughs of Enfield, Haringey, Hackney and Barnet. Head coach for the London Active Partnership Scheme, designed to encourage youngsters to participate in sport. Member of the Enfield Youth Advisory Association. Also promotes Greek concerts in the UK.

TASOS EROTOKRITOU
Politics and Community work

DATE OF BIRTH: 11.09.34
PLACE OF BIRTH: Chloraka, Paphos.
MARITAL STATUS: Separated.
CHILDREN: Yianni, Law graduate from Cardiff University; Erotokritos, Engineer; and daughter Maria.
SCHOOLS/COLLEGE: Chloraka Elementary.
MEMBERSHIPS: Union of Tailors, Islington Cypriot Association and AKEL.
HOBBIES AND INTERESTS: Birds (has large aviary).
PERSONAL PROFILE: Former Secretary of AKEL Islington and in the Secretariat of AKEL UK. Former member of OESEKA Committee, and formerly on the committee of the Islington Cypriot Association. Committee member of EKA.

ANDROULLA EROTOKRITOU
Actress

DATE OF BIRTH: 12.01.87
PLACE OF BIRTH: London (twin with a brother). Parents from Nicosia and Famagusta.
MARITAL STATUS: Single
SCHOOLS/COLLEGE: Chesterfield Junior School, Bishop Stortford Secondary, Sylvia Young Theatre School.
HOBBIES AND INTERESTS: Swimming, reading, travel and shopping.
PERSONAL PROFILE: Actress, dancer, singer. Choreographer at both junior and secondary school productions. Performed in the *Night of 1000 Voices* at the Royal Albert Hall 1999 & 2000. Michael Jackson's album launch at London's Hippodrome 1998, solo spot. TV appearances on Nickleodeon and ITV's *Diggit*, and Queen Mother's 100th birthday celebrations.

ELEFTHERIOS EUGENIOU
Former Secretary of Greek Cypriot Brotherhood

DATE OF BIRTH: 02.02.31
PLACE OF BIRTH: Pyrgos, Limassol.
MARITAL STATUS: Married.
CHILDREN: Six.
HONOURS/AWARDS: Honoured by the Greek Orthodox Church in Great Britain for services to the Community.
PERSONAL PROFILE: Managing Director of group of companies. Was Secretary of Greek Cypriot Brotherhood and former Chairman of the Greek Cypriot Community Association in Hendon.

GEORGE EUGENIOU
Actor and Founder of Theatro Technis

DATE OF BIRTH: 14.06.31
PLACE OF BIRTH: Limassol.
MARITAL STATUS: Married to Maroulla
CHILDREN: Aris
SCHOOLS/COLLEGE: Open University.
ACADEMIC QUALIFICATIONS: BA in Arts.
MEMBERSHIPS: Equity
HOBBIES AND INTERESTS: Writing plays and directing.
PERSONAL PROFILE: Formed Theatro Technis in 1957 in Camden Town. Actors that went through the Theatro were Peter Polycarpou, Demetris Andrea, Anna Savva and George Savvides. Appeared in films Moonlight with Dirk Bogarde, Riviera Touch with Morecombe and Wise, and Hungry Hill with Robert Mitchum.

DESPINA EVANGELOU
Teacher

DATE OF BIRTH: 10.08.61
PLACE OF BIRTH: London. Father Andreas, from Nicosia; Mother Penelope, from Millikouri, (sister of the late Father Leondios from St John the Baptist, Haringey).
MARITAL STATUS: Married to Evangelo, born in UK, parents from Mazoto and Psematismeno.
CHILDREN: Andria, Rina, and Kyriako.
SCHOOLS/COLLEGE: St Marthas Convent, Southgate College, St Marys Twickenham Teaching College.
ACADEMIC QUALIFICATIONS: B.Ed Honours
HOBBIES AND INTERESTS: Travelling and reading.
PERSONAL PROFILE: Teacher. Taught at Cuckoo Hall School in Edmonton, Firs Farm Primary School in Palmers Green. Treasurer at Queenswell Greek School.

STELIOS EVANGELOU
Chairman of Kalogrea Association

DATE OF BIRTH: 20.12.39
PLACE OF BIRTH: Kalogrea
MARITAL STATUS: Widower, was married to Beatrice from Ireland.
CHILDREN: Nicos, Graduate in Economics, works in insurance; and Angela, Maths graduate, working for Morgan Stanley UK.
SCHOOLS/COLLEGE: Kyrenia Gymnasium.
PROFESSIONAL QUALIFICATIONS: Chartered Certified Accountant.
MEMBERSHIPS: Member of the Securities Institute and the British Institute of Management.
HOBBIES AND INTERESTS: Swimming, football, reading, stock market and travelling.
PERSONAL PROFILE: Joined Bank of Cyprus in 1974 as assistant chief accountant, later became chief accountant and financial controller. Dec 1998, Head of Treasury and Private Banking until Dec 1999. Now senior financial consultant. Chairman of Kalogrea Association. Chairman of St Raphael Greek Orthodox Church in Sutton, Surrey. Chairman of the Sutton Greek Language School and former Treasurer of Tooting Greek School

HELEN EVANS
Head Teacher

DATE OF BIRTH: 18.05.54
PLACE OF BIRTH: London. Father from Agios Sergios; Mother from Ardana.
MARITAL STATUS: Divorced
CHILDREN: Joanna, Thomas and Alexa.
SCHOOLS/COLLEGE: Tollington Park, Westminster College, Battersea Teachers College.
PROFESSIONAL QUALIFICATIONS: Cert Ed.
MEMBERSHIPS: NAHT.
HOBBIES AND INTERESTS: Theatre and reading.
PERSONAL PROFILE: Head teacher. Maths LEA leader.

KYRIAKOS NICOS FALEKKOS
Dental Surgeon

DATE OF BIRTH: 26.05.60
PLACE OF BIRTH: Johannesburg, South Africa. Grandparents from Kaimakli Nicosia.
MARITAL STATUS: Single
SCHOOLS/COLLEGE: Marian College, Johannesburg.
ACADEMIC QUALIFICATIONS: Matriculation Certificate.
PROFESSIONAL QUALIFICATIONS: Bachelor of Dental Science.
MEMBERSHIPS: British Dental Health Foundation - Confederation of Dental employers, General Dental Practioners Association .
HONOURS/AWARDS: Vocational Training Trainer (Dental).
HOBBIES AND INTERESTS: Photography, computer graphics and music.
PERSONAL PROFILE: Dentist, Practice Owner, Appointed Trainer of Newly Qualified Dentists.

NICK FIACA
Journalist

DATE OF BIRTH: 05.07.66
PLACE OF BIRTH: London. Father, Andreas from Tripimeni, had Fiaca Dress Co. Mother, Angela from Agios Amvrosios.
MARITAL STATUS: Single
SCHOOLS/COLLEGE: Queen Elizabeth Boys School, Southampton University, Journalist Course at Harlow College.
HOBBIES AND INTERESTS: Football, (West Ham), music and travelling.
PERSONAL PROFILE: Journalist started work for Thomson Regional Newspapers at Luton. Wrote Sport and Newspages for Harlow & Epping - 1993 Turned Freelance and now does work for *News of the World*, *News of the World Magazine*, *TV Quick*, *TV Choice*, *OK Magazine*, *Sky Magazine*, *90 mins* & *Shoot*.

SAVVAS FIACA
Solicitor

DATE OF BIRTH: 26.04.61
PLACE OF BIRTH: London. Father, Andreas from Tripimeni; Mother, Angela from Agios Amvrosios.
MARITAL STATUS: Married to Michelle from London.
CHILDREN: Luke and Elli.
SCHOOLS/COLLEGE: Queen Elizabeth Boys School, Warwick Univesity, Wolverhampton Law School.
ACADEMIC QUALIFICATIONS: LLB Law.
HOBBIES AND INTERESTS: Football, (Tottenham Supporter) and music.
PERSONAL PROFILE: A Solicitor, a Partner in B. D. Laddie in Westminster, Specializes in Property Litigation.

DINOS FLORENTZOU
Founder EDEK UK

DATE OF BIRTH: 11.02.42
PLACE OF BIRTH: Agros
MARITAL STATUS: Married to Theodoulla from Agros.
CHILDREN: One son, one daughter.
SCHOOLS/COLLEGE: Agros Elementary & High School. Borough Polytechnic now (South Bank University).
PROFESSIONAL QUALIFICATIONS: City & Guilds in Electrical Engineering.
HONOURS/AWARDS Honoured by EDEK 1986 for Services to the Party and to Cyprus.
HOBBIES AND INTERESTS: Travel, football, helping Youth & Community.
PERSONAL PROFILE: Had Electrical business from 1960-73, then from 1974 till now, had a Coach and Travel Co, called Dinos Travel. 1959-60 was a Committee Member of Union of Cypriot Students, was Chairman of Achillean FC that merged with Cosmos FC & then Chairman there. Has been Cypriot Football League's Management Committee for 12 years. In 1972, co-founded the Greek School at Streatham where he was Chairman until 1988. Chairman of Agros Association UK. Trustee of St. Nectarius Church at Battersea, now Chairman. Committee member of OESEKA 1973-74. Co-founded EDEK UK Political Party and was their first Chairman. Now member of Secretariat.

PETROS SERGHIO FLORIDES
Professor

DATE OF BIRTH: 16.02.37
PLACE OF BIRTH: Lapithos (Kyrenia) Cyprus.
MARITAL STATUS: Married to Despina (Christoforou), a Housewife, from Athens.
CHILDREN: Serghios, IT; Andros, an Economist; Constantinos, IT.
SCHOOLS/COLLEGE: Commercial Lyceum (Famagusta), Northern Polytechnic (now University of North London) & Royal Holloway College (University of London).
ACADEMIC QUALIFICATIONS: BSc (special Honour in Mathematics), Univ. of London; PhD, University of London; M.A. (Trinity College, Dublin).
MEMBERSHIPS: Fellow of the Royal Astronomical Society, Member of the Society of General Relativity & Gravitation, Senior Fellow of Trinity College, Dublin.
HOBBIES AND INTERESTS: Music and reading.
PERSONAL PROFILE: Associate Professor in Applied Mathematics, Trinity College, Dublin. Professor in

Applied Mathematics (Grade A) at the University of Crete (1984-88), Member of the Preparatory Committee for the Establishment of the University of Cyprus, Chairman of the Selection Committee for the appointment of the first members of staff in the Dept. of Mathematics and Statistics of the University of Cyprus.

Address: School of Mathematics, Hamilton Building, Trinity College, University of Dublin, Dublin 2, Ireland. Email: florides@maths.tcd.ei

SERGHIS PETROU FLORIDES
Founding Member of PEO in Cyprus

DATE OF BIRTH: 26.01.1903
PLACE OF BIRTH: Lapithos
MARITAL STATUS: Married to Panayiota - From Lapithos.
CHILDREN: Yiannakis, Musician; Costakis, Musician and Restaurateur; Andreas, Taxi Driver; Petros, Professor at Trintiy College Dublin; Nitsa, Housewife.
SCHOOLS/COLLEGE: Elementary School Lapithos.
MEMBERSHIPS: LELA AKEL Labour Party, Lapithos Association.
HONOURS/AWARDS Honoured with AKEL Veteran's Award.
HOBBIES AND INTERESTS: Poetry and music.
PERSONAL PROFILE: Was a builder, poet, active member of the Greek Parents Association. Former Chairman of Coppetts Wood Greek School, and a founding member of the Trade Union PEO in Cyprus

COSTAS FRANGESKIDES
Solicitor

DATE OF BIRTH: 16.10 67
PLACE OF BIRTH: London. Parents from Limnia Cyprus & Chios Greece
MARITAL STATUS: Married to Maria from London. A Solicitor whose parents are from Neo Livadhi Limassol & Paphos
CHILDREN: Two sons
SCHOOLS/COLLEGE: St. Christophers Junior School, John Lyon Secondary School. University of Essex, College of Law Guildford.
ACADEMIC QUALIFICATIONS: BA (Hons) Dip of Law
MEMBERSHIPS: Law Society.
HOBBIES AND INTERESTS: Reading, films, tennis, soccer and current affairs.
PERSONAL PROFILE: Senior Solicitor in Insurance and Reinsurance Litigation with City Law firm Holman Fenwick & Willan. Treasurer of Anglo Cypriot Lawyers Association. Active member of Lobby for Cyprus.

MARIA NICOLA FRANGESKIDES
Solicitor

DATE OF BIRTH: 02.01.67
PLACE OF BIRTH: London. Parents from Neo Livadhi, Limassol and Paphos.
MARITAL STATUS: Married To Costas, a Solicitor born in London. (parents from Limnia, Cyprus and Chios Greece).
CHILDREN: Two sons.
SCHOOLS/COLLEGE: Whittingham Junior School, Henrietta Barnett, UCL London, College of Law (Chancery Lane).
ACADEMIC QUALIFICATIONS: LLB (Honours).
MEMBERSHIPS: Law Society, London Maritime Arbitrators Association, London Court of International Arbitration.
HOBBIES AND INTERESTS: Swimming, theatre and dancing.
PERSONAL PROFILE: A Solicitor, a Partner & Head of Commercial litigation at London Offices of a large US firm Coudert Bros, Chairwoman of Anglo Cypriot Lawyers Association, Member of Lobby for Cyprus.

BELINDA FRIXOU
Solicitor

DATE OF BIRTH: 07.07.55
PLACE OF BIRTH: Varosi, Famagusta, Cyprus, (Parents from Yialousa).
MARITAL STATUS: Separated
CHILDREN: Christian, at school.
SCHOOLS/COLLEGE: Liverpool Institute, London School of Economics.
ACADEMIC QUALIFICATIONS: LLB Law.
PROFESSIONAL QUALIFICATIONS: Solicitor.
MEMBERSHIPS: Law Society.
HOBBIES AND INTERESTS: Travelling, theatre and music.
PERSONAL PROFILE: Senior Partner of a firm of Lawyers in Kingsway. Trustee of Radiomarathon (For children with special needs).

MICHAEL GABRIEL (Gavrilatsou)
Chairman of Kato Drys Association UK

DATE OF BIRTH: 15.10.60
PLACE OF BIRTH: Coventry.
Parents Harry and Stella from
Kato Drys.
MARITAL STATUS: Married to
Mary from Kato Drys.
SCHOOLS/COLLEGE: Hearsall
Secondary School, Coventry;
Tilehill College, Coventry;
Lancaster University.
ACADEMIC QUALIFICATIONS:
BA Honours in International
Politics, also Chartered Institute of Bankers Exams
(ACIB).
HOBBIES AND INTERESTS: Football (Coventry fan),
history of Greece and Cyprus and playing drums.
PERSONAL PROFILE: Bank of Cyprus Corporate
Manager in Birmingham. Chairman of Kato Drys
Association. Member of Action for Cyprus. Member
of Hellenic Association of Cyprus. Active in
community affairs, and provided assistance in the
compilation of *The Cypriot Who's Who*.

ELENA GABRILATSOU
2nd Assistant Director for the Comedy
Drama Dept at Granada TV

DATE OF BIRTH: 08.08.76
PLACE OF BIRTH: Bury,
Manchester. Parents from Kato
Drys and Skarinou.
MARITAL STATUS: Single
SCHOOLS/COLLEGE: Bury
Grammar School Girls,
Manchester Met University.
ACADEMIC QUALIFICATIONS:
BA (Honours) Creative Arts
Music and Drama.
HOBBIES AND INTERESTS: Watching films and playing
piano.
PERSONAL PROFILE: 2nd Assistant Director for the
Comedy Drama Dept at Granada TV. Productions
include *Cold Feet* and the *Royle Family*. Currently
working on a new drama called *Donovan*.

PANAYIOTIS GALANIS
Sales Manager North London Weekly Post

DATE OF BIRTH: 20.12.62
PLACE OF BIRTH: Achna.
Father from Athens; Mother
from Paralimni.
MARITAL STATUS: Divorced
CHILDREN: Georgina.
SCHOOLS/COLLEGE:
Abbeywood Secondary School,
Woolwich College.
ACADEMIC QUALIFICATIONS:
O Levels: Maths, English,
Physics, Chemistry and Greek.
PROFESSIONAL QUALIFICATIONS: City & Guilds 747
Computing, First Aid Course.
HONOURS/AWARDS: Awarded best supplement for
2001 out of 44 newspapers by *Daily Independent* and
Independent On Sunday for the *It's All Greek To Me*
supplement that was produced by Panayiotis.
HOBBIES AND INTERESTS: Judo, martial arts and Greek
music.
PERSONAL PROFILE: Was Senior Advertising Advisor
at Independant newspapers (Regionals) Ltd. Now Sales
Manager at North London Weekly Post

CATIA GALATARIOTOU
Psychoanalyst

DATE OF BIRTH: 30.01.55
PLACE OF BIRTH: Limassol.
MARITAL STATUS: Divorced
CHILDREN: Alfred and Anna.
SCHOOLS/COLLEGE: Limassol
Gymnasium, Middlesex
Polytechnic, Inns Of Court,
Centre for Byzantine, Ottoman
and Modern Greek Studies,
University of Birmingham,
British Institute Of
Psychoanalyst.
ACADEMIC QUALIFICATIONS: BA (Honours) in
Humanities, phD in Byzantine Studies.
PROFESSIONAL QUALIFICATIONS: Barrister at Law
London.
MEMBERSHIPS: Member Of Cyprus Bar, Member of
British Psychoanalytical Society.
HOBBIES AND INTERESTS: My children, art, theatre,
travelling and food & wine.
PERSONAL PROFILE: Worked as Lawyer in Cyprus.
Worked as a NHS Psychotherapist at various hospitals.
Currently a Psychoanalyst in private practice and a
Teacher of Psychanalytic theory at University College
London.

COSTAS GAVRIEL
Co Founder of the Midlands Golf Society

DATE OF BIRTH: 09.06.52
PLACE OF BIRTH: Akrounda, Limassol.
MARITAL STATUS: Married to Androulla, a Business Partner (Mensa Member), from Nicosia.
CHILDREN: Panicos, (BEng Honours), Manager of Theo's Food Co; Rebecca Nicole, at University of Wolverhampton.
SCHOOLS/COLLEGE: Lanition School, Limassol, Alliance Francais, Paris.
MEMBERSHIPS: Greek Cypriot Golf Society, Midlands, Chairman for five years.
HOBBIES AND INTERESTS: Golf, football, travel, theatre and music.
PERSONAL PROFILE: Self-employed shop proprietor, one of the Founders of Midlands Golf Society. Organiser of Radio Marathon Golf Day in Midlands and various local charity events. Assisted in founding and playing (1970) Kypros F.C. Midlands.

Address: 96 Codsall Rd, Tettenhall, Wolverhampton WV6 9QP

ANDREAS GAVRIELIDES
Active Member of Cypriot Community UK

DATE OF BIRTH: 09.10.39
PLACE OF BIRTH: Nicosia.
MARITAL STATUS: Married to Antigoni, born in Rizokarpasso.
CHILDREN: Stala, BA (Honours), MA Int Relations; Patapios, at college.
SCHOOLS/COLLEGE: Pancyprian Gymnasium, Nicosia, Norwood Technical College, London, University Of London.
ACADEMIC QUALIFICATIONS: 3 A Level, 4 GCE O Level BSc Electrical Engineering, B.Sc Special Maths.
MEMBERSHIPS: Greek-Kurdish Solidarity Committee in UK, founding member 1991, Acting Secretary 1991-2001, Association Rizokarpasso.
HOBBIES AND INTERESTS: Current affairs and politics, theatre, classical music, opera, reading, travelling and voluntary community work.
PERSONAL PROFILE: Active Member of Cypriot Community UK. Former Director of Kypros Holidays in Cyprus and UK. Active member of Theatro Technis.

STALA M GAVRIELIDES
Researcher in Economics and Political Science

DATE OF BIRTH: 22.07.68
PLACE OF BIRTH: London. Father, Andreas from Nicosia; Mother, Antigoni from Rizokarpasso.
MARITAL STATUS: Single
SCHOOLS/COLLEGE: Mount Allison University, New Brunswick, Canada, McGill University, Montreal, Canada.
ACADEMIC QUALIFICATIONS: BA Economics & Political Science, MA International Relations.
PERSONAL PROFILE: Researcher in Economics & Political Science in various universities in Canada. Researcher for Lord Avebury a Parliamentary Human Rights Group in UK.

DR THEKLI MARIA GEE (née KAKOULLIS)
Specialist Registrar, Medical Microbiology

DATE OF BIRTH: 29.05.72
PLACE OF BIRTH: Birmingham, UK. Father, Michael Kakoullis from Pyla, Larnaca; Mother, Soula (née Sergi) from Limnia, near Famagusta.
MARITAL STATUS: Married to Dr Bruce Colin Gee, a Dermatologist, born in Manchester.
SCHOOLS/COLLEGE: Blue Coat School, Holy Child School, King Edward VI High School for Girls, Birmingham University 1990-1996.
ACADEMIC QUALIFICATIONS: BSc Honours (1st class) Medical Biochemistry, 1993 at Birmingham University, MBChB with honours Medicine, 1996 at Medical School.
PROFESSIONAL QUALIFICATIONS: MRCP (UK) Member of the Royal College of Physicians, Trainee member of the Royal College of Pathologists.
MEMBERSHIPS: British Medical Association, British Society of Antimicrobial Infection Agents and Chemotherapy, UK Hospital Infection Society. Member of the National Trust.
HONOURS/AWARDS: Duke of Edinburgh's Award-Bronze, Silver & Gold, John Skirrow-Wright Memorial Prize 1990.
HOBBIES AND INTERESTS: Hiking, skiing, aerobic and fitness training, swimming, tennis, badminton, theatre, photography, art, and travel.
PERSONAL PROFILE: Specialist Registrar in Medical Microbiology. Currently working as registrar at the University Hospital, Queen's Medical Centre in Nottingham

ALEXIOS GENNARIS
IT Skills Trainer and Needs Assessor for North London Regional Access Centre

DATE OF BIRTH: 16.11.66
PLACE OF BIRTH: London. Father from Limassol; Mother from Ayios Theodoros, Pitsillia.
MARITAL STATUS: Married to Frosoulla (née Kofteros)a Housewife, from London.
CHILDREN: Chrysostomos, Michalis and Marina, all at school
SCHOOLS/COLLEGE: Martin Primary School, Christ Church C of E Secondary School, Woodhouse 6th Form College.
ACADEMIC QUALIFICATIONS: A Level Business Studies.
HOBBIES AND INTERESTS: Jiu Jitsu, keep fit, art, music, escapology, fire eating and magic.
PERSONAL PROFILE: An IT Skills Trainer and Needs Assessor for the North London Regional Access Centre. Teaches university students with dyslexia, dyspraxia, mental health issues, visual impairment and physical disabilties. Also evaluates specialised software and equipment.

ANREAS GEORGALLI
Professional Tribute Artist

DATE OF BIRTH: 10.12.68
PLACE OF BIRTH: Glasgow, Scotland. Father from Ayios Serghios Famagusta, Cyprus; Mother from Naples, Italy.
MARITAL STATUS: Married to Thalia Nicolaidou, a Housewife, (niece of Nicos Nicolaides, founder of Radio Pafos, who first broadcast the news that Makarious was alive, in 1974), from Pafos, Cyprus.
CHILDREN: George and Anthea, school age.
SCHOOLS/COLLEGE: Tottenham County School, Middlesex University.
ACADEMIC QUALIFICATIONS: Postgraduate in Environmental Studies.
PROFESSIONAL QUALIFICATIONS: City and Guilds in Horticulture.
MEMBERSHIPS: Dean Martin Association and Centre for Alternative Technology.
HOBBIES AND INTERESTS: Singing, gardening, travelling, human evolution, culture and mythology.
PERSONAL PROFILE: Professional tribute artist, Previously a landscape gardener. Appeared on *Stars in Their Eyes*, November 2000 as Dean Martin.

CHRIS GEORGALLIS
Pharmacist

DATE OF BIRTH: 25.10.57
PLACE OF BIRTH: Nicosia
MARITAL STATUS: Single
SCHOOLS/COLLEGE: Ackland Burghley, Chelsea College, University of London, School of Pharmacy.
QUALIFICATIONS: Degree in Pharmacy, Registered Pharmaceutical Chemist.
MEMBERSHIPS: Member of Royal Pharmaceutical Society of Great Britain, Member of Cyprus Study Circle.
HOBBIES AND INTERESTS: Sport, Philately of Cyprus and photography
PERSONAL PROFILE: Been a Pharmacist for 19 years and worked within the hospital clinical areas. Worked for the Royal Free Hospital NHS Trust.

SAVVAKIS ANDREOU GEORGALLIS
Former Editor of Haravgi in Cyprus/Co-Founder of Omonia FC in London

DATE OF BIRTH: 24.10.30
PLACE OF BIRTH: Marathovounos Village, Famagusta.
MARITAL STATUS: Married to Margarita, a Housewife, from Ayios Georgios Spathariko Famagusta.
CHILDREN: Andrea, Housewife; Liza has Economics Degree, Estate Agent.
SCHOOLS/COLLEGE: London University and Lincolns Inn.
QUALIFICATIONS: MA and Barrister At Law.
HOBBIES AND INTERESTS: Sports.
PERSONAL PROFILE: Member of committee for Omonia Football Club Nicosia. One of the Founders of Omonia Football Club London. Editor of Haravgi Newspaper from its birth in 1955 to 1969, when he came to U.K.
Member of the Committee of the Youth Organisation (EDON).

REV. CHRYSOSTOMOS GEORGHIOU
Priest

DATE OF BIRTH: 13.12.30
PLACE OF BIRTH: Nicosia.
MARITAL STATUS: Married to Constandia Georghiou from Cyprus.
CHILDREN: One daughter and two sons, all married and have children.
SCHOOLS/COLLEGE: Pancyprian Gymnasium, Commercial Lyceum, Larnaca.
PROFESSIONAL QUALIFICATIONS: Electrician, Priest
PERSONAL PROFILE: Formerly an Electrician and now a Priest in Great Yarmouth.

LIZA GEORGHIADES
Teacher

DATE OF BIRTH: 29.05.50
PLACE OF BIRTH: Nicosia. Grandparents from Kyrenia.
MARITAL STATUS: Married to Myles Gibbons, a Teacher, from Ireland.
CHILDREN: David and Paul, both at school; Caroline, Vaughan and Rebecca from previous marriage.
SCHOOLS/COLLEGE: The English School, Nicosia, Bradford University.
ACADEMIC QUALIFICATIONS: 6 O Levels, 3 A Levels, BA (Honours) at Open University.
PROFESSIONAL QUALIFICATIONS: BSc (Honours) Literature and Politics, PGCE (Post Graduate Certificate of Education).
HOBBIES AND INTERESTS: Reading, swimming and theatre.
PERSONAL PROFILE: Teacher of English/Drama, English as an additional language. Teacher of Special Needs.

MARIOS C. GEORGHIADES
Accountant

DATE OF BIRTH: 06.09.66
PLACE OF BIRTH: Nicosia
MARITAL STATUS: Married to Maria, Customer Service Rep with HSBC Bank Plc, from London.
CHILDREN: Daniel and Harry.
SCHOOLS/COLLEGE: Kykkos A, Lyceum, Nicosia, Luton College of Higher Education, Luton, Bedfordshire, Accountancy Tutors/EW School of Accountancy, BPP Professional Training School.
PROFESSIONAL QUALIFICATIONS: Fellow member of The Association of Chartered Certified Accountants (ACCA), Associate member of The Association of Accounting Technicians (AAT).
MEMBERSHIPS: Member of the Association of Martial Arts (AMA) and Member of the British Council for Chinese Martial Arts (BCCMA).
HONOURS/AWARDS: Chief Instructor of International Shaolin (Kung Fu) academy. Appointed as a Chairman of International Shaolin (Kung FU) academy-Cyprus branch.
HOBBIES AND INTERESTS: Martial arts and music (Djing).
PERSONAL PROFILE: Former Assistant to Trade Counsellor, Cyprus High Commission, London, Chief Accountant-Cyprus Tourism Organisation, London. Currently employed at Alexander Johnson & Co. a firm of Chartered Certified Accountants and Registered Auditors, as Audit Manager. Active committee member of "The Association Of Cypriot Qualified Accountants in the UK". School Governor at Tottenhall Infants School - Chairman of the Finance Committee. Hosts martial arts tournaments and competitions in the UK and abroad for the International Shaolin Kung Fu Academy.

GEORGE GEORGHIOU
Actor

DATE OF BIRTH: 11.11.48
PLACE OF BIRTH: Frenaros.
MARITAL STATUS: Divorced
CHILDREN: One daughter.
SCHOOLS/COLLEGE: St Michaels in Camden, Kynaston Secondary, Kingsway College, Pheldene Stage School.
HOBBIES AND INTERESTS: Painting and making model boats.

PERSONAL PROFILE: Actor, TV work in Mind your Language, Dr In The House, Dr At Sea, Please Sir Films, Home Sweet Honeycomb with Michael Crawford. Theatre work, Zigger Zagger at Strand Theatre. Was Manager of Wyndham Picadilly and Criterion Theatres.

HELEN GEORGHIOU
Teacher

DATE OF BIRTH: 01.11.52
PLACE OF BIRTH: London. Parents from Akanthou, Famagusta.
MARITAL STATUS: Married to Father Ierotheos, a Greek Orthodox Priest, from Akanthou.
CHILDREN: Sotos, at Anglia University; Neofi, 6th Form at school; Skevi, at school.
SCHOOLS/COLLEGE: St Gabriels Teacher Training College, qualified in 1975.
HOBBIES AND INTERESTS: Reading, cooking and world affairs.
PERSONAL PROFILE: Teacher

DR MARIA GEORGHIOU
Doctor

DATE OF BIRTH: 16.08.73
PLACE OF BIRTH: Nicosia. Father from Ayios Pavlos, Nicosia; Mother from Katokopia, Morphou.
MARITAL STATUS: Single
SCHOOLS/COLLEGE: University College, London (UCL), Guys, Kings and St Thomas School of Medicine (GKT), London.
ACADEMIC QUALIFICATIONS: MBBS (medicine), GKT, BSc (Hons) Physiology, UCL.
PROFESSIONAL QUALIFICATIONS: MBBS Medicine
MEMBERSHIPS: British Medical Association, Anthony Nolan Bone Marrow Trust. Member St Sofia Cathedral Choir

HONOURS/AWARDS: University of London Full Colours for Volleyball, Travel Scholarship to the Amazon Region of Peru.
HOBBIES AND INTERESTS: Travelling, South America, Asia, scuba diving, Latin American dance, painting and National League Volley Ball.
PERSONAL PROFILE: As a student was a member of Lobby for Cyprus. Whilst at university was elected President of the UCL Cypriot Society and later the Hellenic Society of Guys and St. Thomas's School of Medicine. Currently working in Accident & Emergency in London, and planning to pursue a career in anaesthetics.

Email: mariageorghiou@hotmail.com

NICOLAS GEORGIADES
President of United Cypriot Youth Organisation and Member of the AKEL Secretariat

DATE OF BIRTH: 17.08.71
PLACE OF BIRTH: Nicosia.
MARITAL STATUS: Single
SCHOOLS/COLLEGE: Archbishop Makarios Lyceum, Nicosia, Essex University, City Business School.
ACADEMIC QUALIFICATIONS: BA, Accounting and Financial Management.
PROFESSIONAL QUALIFICATIONS: MSc, Internal Audit & Management, Practitioner Member of Internal Auditors UK.
MEMBERSHIPS: Institute of Internal Auditors UK, British Rumanian Chamber of Commerce
HONOURS/AWARDS: Supplier of the Year award, from a main High St Fashion retailer.
HOBBIES AND INTERESTS: Politics and sport.
PERSONAL PROFILE: Chief Operations Officer for a group of companies (one in Cyprus, one in UK and three in Romania). President of United Cypriot Youth Organisation. Ex Vice President of the National Federation of Cypriot Students in the UK. Member of the Secretariat of AKEL UK. Member of the Executive Committee of Episteme, and former member of the Executive of the National Federation of Cypriots.

ELIKKOS GEORGIADES
Barrister

DATE OF BIRTH: 21.06.53
PLACE OF BIRTH: Engomi, Nicosia.
MARITAL STATUS: Divorced
CHILDREN: Tiffany.
SCHOOLS/COLLEGE: English School, Nicosia.
PROFESSIONAL QUALIFICA-TIONS: LNCP: Licentiate Member of National Council Of Psychotherapists.
HOBBIES AND INTERESTS: Music and socialising.
PERSONAL PROFILE: Joined Scotland Yard as an Executive Officer, whilst there studied Law externally, took a degree in Law, then became a Barrister. In 1994 set up Chambers by himself as a Sole Practitioner at Bromley Chambers. Studied Graphology which is a scientific analysis of personality from handwriting. Qualified Psychotherapist and Hypnotherapist.

STEVE GEORGIADES
Businessman

DATE OF BIRTH: 25.12.55
PLACE OF BIRTH: Nicosia
MARITAL STATUS: Married to Bronya from Northumberland, Director of A.C. Georgiades Ltd.
CHILDREN: Katrina and Christopher, both at school.
SCHOOLS/COLLEGE: Creighton Comprehensive, Muswell Hill, London.
MEMBERSHIPS: Hazelwood Tennis Club, CPSA and BASC, TR6 Owners Club.
HOBBIES AND INTERESTS: Shooting, football and tennis.
PERSONAL PROFILE: Moved to London from Cyprus with parents in 1962. Father (Christo Georgios Georgiades) originally from Nicosia, deceased 1980, mother Virginia Georgiades (Florides) originally from Aradippou, now living in Limassol. Started own business at 20 years old as a consultant and supplier of edible oil. Eventually moved into soft drinks market supplying fast food distribution in GB. Currently Managing Director of A C Georgiades Ltd. Total turnover of the year end 2000 was £12 million. Offices based in Essex and Northumberland. Now resides in Morpeth, Northumberland with family and commutes to London on a regular basis

ACHILLEAS GEORGIOU
Enfield Councillor

DATE OF BIRTH: 19.09.57
PLACE OF BIRTH: Nicosia
MARITAL STATUS: Married
CHILDREN: Two sons.
SCHOOLS/COLLEGE: London School Of Economics, University Of Bath.
ACADEMIC QUALIFICATIONS: BA (Honours), DIP Econ, M.sc.
HOBBIES AND INTERESTS: Football and cycling.
PERSONAL PROFILE: Communications (Media/Public Relations), Councillor Of Enfield.

ALEXANDRA GEORGIOU
Arts & Textiles Teacher

DATE OF BIRTH: 30.10.58
PLACE OF BIRTH: Famagusta. Father from Paphos, Mother from Limassol.
MARITAL STATUS: Divorced
CHILDREN: Dimitri.
SCHOOLS/COLLEGE: Carlton Infants, Kentish Town; Summerside Infants, North Finchley; College for the Distributive Trades, London; Middlesex University, Herts; Chelsea College of Art, London; Institute of Education, London.
QUALIFICATIONS: Foundation Certificate in Art & Design; British Display Society Advanced Level Diploma; BA (Honours) in Fine Art; PGCE in Art & Design.
MEMBERSHIPS: NSEAD Union.
HONOURS/AWARDS: Won prize for Best Display in UK (1981) and Royal Wedding Presents at St James Palace.
HOBBIES AND INTERESTS: Visiting art exhibitions, photography and cinema.
PERSONAL PROFILE: Worked in display and exhibitions until 1991 before returning to Higher Education. Arts Co-ordinator for the Greek Cypriot Brotherhood.

Email: AlexGeorgiou1234@aol.com

ANDY (Andreas) GEORGIOU
Architect, Owner of Starsky & Hutch Clubs

DATE OF BIRTH: 05.09.62
PLACE OF BIRTH: Greenwich, London. Father Georgos from Psematismenos.
MARITAL STATUS: Single
SCHOOLS/COLLEGE: St Mary's Infants, Lewisham, Kidbrooke Park Junior, Eltham, Christ's College, Blackheath, Winton School, Croydon, Kingston Polytechnic, Kingston.
ACADEMIC QUALIFICATIONS: 14 O levels, 3 A levels (English Literature, Art and History of Art).
PROFESSIONAL QUALIFICATIONS: BA (Honours) Architecture, R.I.B.A. Parts 1 & 2
MEMBERSHIPS: Board of Governors, Winton School, Croydon since 1995.
HOBBIES AND INTERESTS: Producing music, photography, athletics, travelling, football, squash and most other sports.
PERSONAL PROFILE: Founder Member of London Greek Youth Association. Founder & Owner of Starsky & Hutch Nightclubs worldwide.

ANDREAS GEORGIOU
Chairman of St Lukes Greek Orthodox Church in Glasgow

DATE OF BIRTH: 10.05.37
PLACE OF BIRTH: Kato Zodia, Morphou.
MARITAL STATUS: Married to Niki, from Famagusta.
CHILDREN: Demetrios, Georgios, Mary and Kaladea.
SCHOOLS/COLLEGE: Greek Gymasium, Morphou.
HOBBIES AND INTERESTS: Football, (Glasgow Rangers Fan).
PERSONAL PROFILE: In 1958 worked for four years with Classic Cinemas in London. Then from 1962 worked with Reo Stakis PLC. Chairman of St Lukes Greek Orthodox Church in Glasgow. Member of Scottish Hellenic Society.

ANTONIS KYRIAKOS GEORGIOU
Author and Researcher

DATE OF BIRTH: 14.12.67
PLACE OF BIRTH: London. Father, Kyriakos from Kalopsida; Mother, Elizabeth from Asha.
MARITAL STATUS: Married to Anna Maria Paraskeva from London, (parents from Ayia Triada and Athienou).
CHILDREN: Athena.
SCHOOLS/COLLEGE: Southgate School, University of Gothenburg.
MEMBERSHIPS: Kalopsida Association, Vatili Association, Lobby for Cyprus.
HOBBIES AND INTERESTS: Travel.
PERSONAL PROFILE: Formed the 1st research centre for occupied towns and villages of Cyprus. Published the book *The Living Past Of Kalopsida*

CHRIS GEORGIOU (Deceased)
Former Chair of AEL FC & Fisher Athletic. Secretary of Kisos Political Party UK

DATE OF BIRTH: 13.01.44
PLACE OF BIRTH: Famagusta.
MARITAL STATUS: Divorced
CHILDREN: Paul, Estate Agent.
PROFESSIONAL QUALIFICATIONS: F.N.A.E.A. Federation National Association Of Estate Agents, was Treasurer.
HOBBIES AND INTERESTS: Football and politics.
PERSONAL PROFILE: Although Chris had two kidney transplants, two plastic hips, four heart by-passes, and thyroid gland removed, he remained smiling and very active. Had an Estate Agency Hornsey Agencies. Was Director at Barnet FC. General Secretary of Kisos Political Party UK. Was chairman of AEL football club in KOPA won several championships and cups and LFA Runners Up. Was Chairman of Fisher Athletic who play in premier division of the Dr Martens League. Chris did a lot of charity work for Thallasaemia and kidney research.

COSTAS MODESTOU GEORGIOU
Chairman of Enfield Business Assoc

DATE OF BIRTH: 12.02.48
PLACE OF BIRTH: Vasilli.
MARITAL STATUS: Married to Angela from Rizokarpasso.
CHILDREN: Katerina, at Derby University; Andrew, at Norwich University.
SCHOOLS/COLLEGE: Eastbourne College of Further Education, Bournemouth College of Technology.
HOBBIES AND INTERESTS: Walking and politics.
PERSONAL PROFILE: Teacher at Bournemouth College. Then worked at Metal Box as a Setter Engineer, where he was Chairman of TGWU section at Metal Box. Had a shoe repair shop in Palmers Green, now a Property Developer. Served as Chairman of Leonarisso-Vaslli Association for five years. Chairman of Green Lanes Business Association for last five years. Now Chairman of Enfield Business Association. Member of Lobby for Cyprus.

ELPIDA GEORGIOU
Primary School Teacher

DATE OF BIRTH: 16.03.65
PLACE OF BIRTH: London. Father from Arakapas, Limassol; Mother from Yialousa.
MARITAL STATUS: Married to Alkis, from Asha, Cyprus.
CHILDREN: Melios and Sotiri.
SCHOOLS/COLLEGE: South Haringey Infants and Juniors, Cromer Road Primary, East Barnet Secondary, University North London.
PROFESSIONAL QUALIFICATIONS: BEd Honours (First Class).
HOBBIES AND INTERESTS: Yoga, reflexology, aromatherapy and gardening.
PERSONAL PROFILE: Primary School Teacher in Haringey for 14 years.

GEORGE GEORGIOU
Solicitor

DATE OF BIRTH: 08.11.58
PLACE OF BIRTH: London. Parents from Vothilakas and Ayios Andronicos.
MARITAL STATUS: Married to Andrea from Ayios Andronicos; Karpassia.
CHILDREN: Three daughters.
SCHOOLS/COLLEGE: Sir William Collins School, Kingsway College, Middlesex University, Guildford Law School.
ACADEMIC QUALIFICATIONS: BA Honours Law.
HOBBIES AND INTERESTS: Football, (Arsenal Fan).
PERSONAL PROFILE: Solicitor, Partner in Georgiou Nicholas Solicitors. Former Chairman of Monken Hadley Conservative Association.

GEORGE GEORGIOU
Actor and Co-Producer

DATE OF BIRTH: 27.05.78
PLACE OF BIRTH: London. Parents from Dhali.
MARITAL STATUS: Single
SCHOOLS/COLLEGE: Drama Centre, London.
ACADEMIC QUALIFICATIONS Degree B(A) Acting.
MEMBERSHIPS: Equity.
HOBBIES AND INTERESTS: Dance, theatre, films, yoga and travelling.
PERSONAL PROFILE: Actor and Co-Producer of Kiss & Tell Theatre Company. Work includes commercials, theatre and film. Theatre company is to provide chances for ethnic actors to showcase their talents.

GEORGE GEORGIOU
Chairman of Greek Orthodox Church in Croydon

DATE OF BIRTH: 26.01.40
PLACE OF BIRTH: Psematismenos, Larnaca.
MARITAL STATUS: Married to Sonia from Vokolida.
CHILDREN: Andrew, Owner of Starsky & Hutch Clubs; Christos, Graphic Designer; Panayiotis, in Banking; Loukia, in Marketing.
HOBBIES AND INTERESTS: Shooting and socialising.
PERSONAL PROFILE: Damp Proofing and Building Contractor. Served as Chairman Of Greek Orthodox Church in Croydon. Member of Vokolida Village

GEORGE A. GEORGIOU
Journalist

DATE OF BIRTH: 17.08.73
PLACE OF BIRTH: Poland. Father from Ormidia, Cyprus; Mother from Poland.
MARITAL STATUS: Married to Andrea Constantinou, who works for *Parikiaki* Greek Cypriot newspaper as a journalist, born in England.
SCHOOLS/COLLEGE: Makarios III Lyceum in Larnaca and the Europa College for Journalists in Nicosia.
ACADEMIC QUALIFICATIONS: Diploma in Journalism and Public Relations.
MEMBERSHIPS: Secretary of Omonia F.C in London and KOPA (Cypriot football league in London).
HONOURS/AWARDS: Award for services as district secretary of the Edon Youth Organisation in Cyprus.
HOBBIES AND INTERESTS: Football, reading, history, politics and philosophy.
PERSONAL PROFILE: Journalist. Has worked for Haravgi, Radio Astra, Parikiaki, Hellenic TV, Cypria in Britain. Formerly editor at Parikiaki and Cypria in Britain. Currently working at Varosi Lettings and Estates. Has travelled to Cuba for the International Festival of Youth & Students, to Palestine for an interview with Saeb Eracat (chief Palestinian negotiator), to Luxembourg, Russia and Ireland for work purposes, and has attended conferences in the occupied area of Cyprus.

GEORGE ANDREW GEORGIOU
Teacher

DATE OF BIRTH: 05.01.57
PLACE OF BIRTH: London. Father from Koma Tou Yialou; Mother from Vasili.
MARITAL STATUS: Married to Androulla (Antoniou), a classroom assistant from Lythrothondas.
CHILDREN: Stella, Andrew, Stacey, all at school.
SCHOOLS/COLLEGE: Minchenden Secondary School, London College Of Music, Middlesex Polytechnic, North London University.
ACADEMIC QUALIFICATIONS: A.L.C.M, G.L.C.M, Cert. ED., B.E.D.Hon, L.L.C.M. T.D.
HONOURS/AWARDS: B.ED. Honours
HOBBIES AND INTERESTS: Music and sport
PERSONAL PROFILE: Music Teacher. Has helped charities such as Great Ormond St, Wishing Well Appeal, Hearing Dogs, Thallassaemia Society. Runs a recording studio at Lea Valley Primary School, recording children's compositions and helping them to compose.

GEORGE DEMOSTHENES GEORGIOU
Lecturer in Accountancy University Of Aberdeen

PLACE OF BIRTH: Nicosia.
MARITAL STATUS: Married.
CHILDREN: Marina.
ACADEMIC QUALIFICATIONS: BS, MAcc, Ph.D
PROFESSIONAL QUALIFICATIONS: US Certified Public Accountant (CPA).
PERSONAL PROFILE: Lecturer in Accountancy, University of Aberdeen.

GEORGIA CLARKE/GEORGIOU
Actress

DATE OF BIRTH: 01.08.57
PLACE OF BIRTH: London. Parents from Limassol and Asha.
MARITAL STATUS: Married to Barry Wickens, a musician.
CHILDREN: Nicholas and Michael.
SCHOOLS/COLLEGE: Willesden High School, East 15, Acting School, Debdon Essex.
ACADEMIC QUALIFICATIONS: Acting Diploma.
PROFESSIONAL QUALIFICATIONS: TEFEL teacher.
MEMBERSHIPS: Equity, A.I.
HOBBIES AND INTERESTS: Reading, walking, cinema and theatre.
PERSONAL PROFILE: Actress with Theatro Technis. Has appeared with The Natural Theatre on tour, on TV in Capital City, and in films The Nutcracker, Leave To Remain, and Eleni.

FATHER IOANNIS GEORGIOU
Priest

DATE OF BIRTH: 31.04.31
PLACE OF BIRTH: Dromolaxia, Larnaca.
MARITAL STATUS: Married to Theofanou from Ayios Elias.
CHILDREN: One son, one daughter and seven grandchildren.
SCHOOLS/COLLEGE: Dromolaxia Elementary School.
HOBBIES AND INTERESTS: Gardening and reading.
PERSONAL PROFILE: Priest at St Lazarus and St Andrews Church in Forest Gate, London.

KAY GEORGIOU
Solicitor

DATE OF BIRTH: 02.06.61
PLACE OF BIRTH: London. Parents from Aradipou and Ardana.
MARITAL STATUS: Single
SCHOOLS/COLLEGE: Hornsey High, London University, Lancaster Gate Law School.
ACADEMIC QUALIFICATIONS: BA Honours History and Politics.
HOBBIES AND INTERESTS: Theatre, opera and cinema.
PERSONAL PROFILE: Solicitor, own practice specialising in Family Law.

KYRIAKOS SPIROS GEORGIOU
Served as Vice Chairman and Registration Secretary of the Cypriot Football League UK

DATE OF BIRTH: 20.02.37
PLACE OF BIRTH: Komi Kebir.
MARITAL STATUS: Married to Panayiota from Morphou
CHILDREN: Spiros.
SCHOOLS/COLLEGE: Pitmans, accounts.
HOBBIES AND INTERESTS: Football, (Arsenal supporter).
PERSONAL PROFILE: Former member of Greek Parents Association. Former Chairman Komi Kebir Association. Served as Vice-Chairman and Registration Secretary of the Cypriot Football League, UK.

MYRIA GEORGIOU
Lecturer

DATE OF BIRTH: 15.08.71
PLACE OF BIRTH: Nicosia.
MARITAL STATUS: Married.
SCHOOLS/COLLEGE: Panteion University, Athens, Boston University, Boston, Massachusetts, London School of Economics and Political Science (LSE).
ACADEMIC QUALIFICATIONS: BA Sociology, MSc Journalism, PhD Media & Communication.
MEMBERSHIPS: British Sociological Association, National Union Of Journalists, Athens Association Of Journalists.
HOBBIES AND INTERESTS: Travel, languages, theatre, film and reading.
PERSONAL PROFILE: Since January 2001 has been working as a Reasearch Fellow at the London School of Economics and Political Science (LSE). Specific area of study is minority media and currently working on a European research project aiming at mapping diasporic media production in the EU. In January 2001 completed PhD Doctoral reasearch focused on the role of ethnic media in the construction of Greek Cypriot identities in North London. Previously a journalist. Between 1989 and 1996 worked as a journalist in Athens, first for the Daily Avgi and then for Eleftherotypia, also appointed as a correspondent for CBC's Radio 3 and then for Astra. Moved to London, and between 1997 and 2000 worked as a journalist and presenter for the Greek Section of BBC World Service. Now lecturer at Leeds University.

NEOCLIS GEORGIOU
Chairman of KLN Football Club

DATE OF BIRTH: 10.11.39
PLACE OF BIRTH: Omodhos.
MARITAL STATUS: Married to Louise from New Zealand.
CHILDREN: Mario, Christina and Sophia.
SCHOOLS/COLLEGE: Larnaca Lyceum.
HOBBIES AND INTERESTS: Football.
PERSONAL PROFILE: Motor Mechanic by trade. Played football for ALKI in Cyprus at 17 years old. Played in UK for KLN for 20 years, then committee member, now Chairman

PETER GEORGIOU
International Fencing Champion

DATE OF BIRTH: 10.04.52
PLACE OF BIRTH: Wales.
Father from Pano Lakatamia;
Mother from Leonariso.
MARITAL STATUS: Divorced
CHILDREN: Melitsa,
Hairdresser; Louis Andreas,
Hairdresser; Alexander Peter,
Plant Driver.
ACADEMIC QUALIFICATIONS:
City & Guilds Certificate in
Hairdressing, City & Guild
Youth Trainers Award.
PERSONAL PROFILE: Hairdresser. Established the
Newport Clinic of Trichology and Dermocosmetology.
Was President of the National Hairdressers Federation
Welsh area. Represented Wales on the National
Executive Council, National Hairdressers Federation.
In 1997 opened consultancy room at St Josephs Private
Hospital South Wales. 2003 Vice-President, British
Biosthetic Society. Was Welsh School Fencing
Champion in 1966. 1968 represented Wales at the
National Schoolboy Championships. 1968 received
Silver Award fom British Amateur Fencing Association.
1971 represented Wales at the British Quadrangular
Tournament. 1972 represented Wales at the International
Tournament, Denmark. 1972 winner Welsh Men's
Team Championships.

Email: Peter@hairlosswales.co.uk

PETROS GEORGIOU
Sercretary of Acheritou Football Club

DATE OF BIRTH: 22.03.51
PLACE OF BIRTH: Acheritou
MARITAL STATUS: Married to
Stavroulla, a Housewife, from
Frennaros.
CHILDREN: George, Electrician;
Theodora, at Barnet High
School.
SCHOOLS/COLLEGE:
Paddington College for
Electrical Installation.
HOBBIES AND INTERESTS: Football.
PERSONAL PROFILE: Owns Electrical Wholesale
Business. Secretary of Acheritou Football Club.

VASOS GEORGIOU
Accountant

DATE OF BIRTH: 27.12.56
PLACE OF BIRTH: Birmingham.
Parents from Xylophagou.
MARITAL STATUS: Married to
Kika.
CHILDREN: Four children.
SCHOOLS/COLLEGE: Copeland
School, Wembley, Central
London Polytechnic.
ACADEMIC QUALIFICATIONS:
ACCA.
HOBBIES AND INTERESTS:
Football, badminton and travel.
PERSONAL PROFILE: Accountant, Partner in Anthony
Lawson, Southgate.

NIKI GELSTHORPE
Chairwoman of the Philiptochos Of The
Folkestone Greek Orthodox Church

DATE OF BIRTH: 25.09.43
PLACE OF BIRTH: Petra Soleas
MARITAL STATUS: Married to
Peter, from Yorkshire.
CHILDREN: One daughter, two
sons.
SCHOOLS/COLLEGE: Solea
Grammar School, Mander
College, Bedford.
HOBBIES AND INTERESTS:
Flowers and cooking
PERSONAL PROFILE: Worked in Accountantcy for 25
years. Chairwoman of the Philoptochos of the
Folkestone Greek Orthodox Church.

CRISPIN GERMANOS
Teacher

DATE OF BIRTH: 12.03.74
PLACE OF BIRTH: London. Father from Kyrenia; Mother
from London.
MARITAL STATUS: Single
SCHOOLS/COLLEGE: English School, Nicosia, London
University, Reading University.
ACADEMIC QUALIFICATIONS: BA History, MA History.
HOBBIES AND INTERESTS: Football, reading and travel.
PERSONAL PROFILE: History Teacher at William Ellis
School.

GEORGE LOIZOU GEROLEMOU
Restaurateur and Author

DATE OF BIRTH: 26.1.1913
PLACE OF BIRTH: Cyprus
MARITAL STATUS: Married to Ivy Victoria Cooper, a Housewife, from Didcot near Oxford.
CHILDREN: Georgina, Assistant Manageress; twins Nicholas, semi-retired and Louis, restaurateur.
SCHOOLS/COLLEGES: Elementary.
MEMBERSHIPS: Labour Party (50 years), Cyprus Brotherhood, RAF Association.
HONOURS/AWARDS: The National Federation of Cypriots in Great Britain awarded to George Gerolemou on June 3rd 1993, at the Theatro Technis, a silver tray as an indication of gratitude and love for his services to the community, and his long struggle for justice and freedom in Cyprus.
PERSONAL PROFILE: Successful restaurateur. Has published two books, *A Cypriot Airman Without Wings* (in English) and *Adventures of a Cypriot Emigrant* (Peripeties Kypriou Metanasty in Greek).

ENTRANTS IN GREEK CYPRIOTS IN THE UK HAVE BEEN NOMINATED FOR THEIR ACHIEVEMENTS AND CONTRIBUTIONS. YOU CAN NOMINATE SOMEONE OR YOURSELF WHO DESERVES TO BE IN THE BOOK. ENTRIES ARE FREE. SEND IN YOUR NOMINATIONS, INCLUDING NAME, CONTACT ADDRESS, TELEPHONE NUMBER AND EMAIL TO GREEK CYPRIOTS IN THE UK 111 ST THOMAS'S ROAD LONDON N4 2QJ TELEPHONE 020 7503 3498 EMAIL cypriotwhoswho@aol.com

---

FILIOS A GRAMMENOPOULOS
Council Member Hellenic Community Trust

DATE OF BIRTH: 05.06.23
PLACE OF BIRTH: Larnaca.
MARITAL STATUS: Married to Nitsa, in 1945, from Larnaca.
CHILDREN: Mary Bromley, Art Historian; Anthony, Architect.
SCHOOLS/COLLEGE: Graduate Pancyprian Commercial Lyceum Larnaca, Graduate American Academy, Larnaca.
ACADEMIC QUALIFICATIONS: BA, London.
MEMBERSHIPS: The Hellenic Centre, London (Life Member).
HONOURS/AWARDS: Order of St Mark (1st class) Patriarchate of Alexandria.
HOBBIES AND INTERESTS: Anthropology, history and evolutionary matters.
PERSONAL PROFILE: Businessman & Director of companies. Nairobi, Kenya (1948-1972). President Rotary Club of Nairobi (1976-1977). Chairman Kenya Motor Vehicle Importers Assocn (1967-70). Hon. Consul Of Cyprus, Kenya 1968-1974. High Commissioner for Cyprus (1974-1984) resident in Nairobi, Kenya and accredited concurrently to Uganda, Tanzania, Zambia, Mozambique, Seychelles and Sultanate of Oman. Permanent Representative of Cyprus to U.N . Environment Programme (UNEP). Permanent Representative of Cyprus to U.N. Human Settlements Organisation (habitat) 1977-1984). Retired to United Kingdom - June 1985. Founder member of the Hellenic Centre, London and it's first Chairman of the Executive Board 1991-1993. Council Member Hellenic Community Trust (1991 to date).

CHRISTOPHER GRECO
Actor/Producer

DATE OF BIRTH: 17.02.65
PLACE OF BIRTH: Achna.
MARITAL STATUS: Married to Maria Odysseos, a reservation Clerk at Cyprus Airways, from Nicosia.
CHILDREN: Katerina, at Winchmore Secondary School; George, at Highfield Primary School; Elli
SCHOOLS/COLLEGE: Pancyprian Lyceum (Larnaca), Mountview Theatre School, London; International School of Acting.
PROFESSIONAL QUALIFICATIONS: Performing Arts Diploma.
MEMBERSHIPS: Equity.
HOBBIES AND INTERESTS: Poetry, art and photography.
PERSONAL PROFILE: Actor, Producer. Member of EAK (Aid for Cyprus Charity Organisation).

GEORGE GREGORIOU ('Kokis')
Music Presenter and Newsreader at LGR

DATE OF BIRTH: 13.12.54
PLACE OF BIRTH: Ayios Theodoros, Famagusta.
MARITAL STATUS: Married to Christalla from London (parents from Acheritou and Famagusta).
CHILDREN: Gregory and Stella.
SCHOOLS/COLLEGE: Gymnasium of Tricomo.
MEMBERSHIPS: Member of Equity, appeared on TV commercials, such as Texaco Oil and Smirnoff Vodka.
HONOURS/AWARDS: Diploma in Music Presentation and News Casting.
HOBBIES AND INTERESTS: Music, travel, sports and reading.
PERSONAL PROFILE: Director and Share Holder of LGR. Programme controller, Newsreader, Music Presenter at LGR, and producer, singer and member of the Venus Band. Appeared on New Generation Game with Jim Davidson, representing Cyprus and Greece on live TV, in the Eurovision Song Contest (sort of!) and appeared on breakfast TV's morning show. Produced 4 CDs: Ellinika Laika Tragoudia (Vols 1 and 2), Varosi Mou and To Horio Mou. Appeared on Cyprus TV, has sung with Greek singers such as Nicos Xanthopoullos and Demitris Kontolazos.

PANIKOS GREGORIOU
Secretary of Oeseka

DATE OF BIRTH: 15.08.51
PLACE OF BIRTH: Tricomo.
MARITAL STATUS: Married to Elizabeth, a Secretary, from Norway.
CHILDREN: Helen, Florist; Kate, Fashion Designer.
SCHOOLS/COLLEGE: Economic Lyceum of Tricomo, Kensington College.
ACADEMIC QUALIFICATIONS: HND Business Studies and Accountancy.
HOBBIES AND INTERESTS: Football.
PERSONAL PROFILE: Accountant. Treasurer of North London Greek Educational Association and Secretary of Oeseka (Federation of Educational Associations of Greek Cypriots in England).

ARCHBISHOP GREGORIOS OF THYATEIRA & GREAT BRITAIN (Nee Gregorios Theocharous Hadjittofi)
Archbishop of Thyateira and Great Britain

DATE OF BIRTH: 28.10.28
PLACE OF BIRTH: Marathovounos, Famagusta.
SCHOOLS/COLLEGE: Lefkonikon High School, Pan-Cyprian Gymnasium, Theology University of Athens (1958).
QUALIFICATIONS: Chancellor of the Archdiocese of Thyateira & Great Britain 1965-1979; Honorary Doctorate, University of North London.
HOBBIES AND INTERESTS: Poetry, history, gardening and farming.
PERSONAL PROFILE: Deacon, 24.06.53; Priest 19.04.59, Bishop 12,12 1970, consecrated as Bishop of Tropaiou. Elected Archbishop of Thyateira & Great Britain 16.04.88. Orthodox President of the Anglian & Eastern Churches Association, and the Fellowship of St Alban & St Sergius; Co-President of the Society of St John Chrysostomos, and the Council of Christians & Jews.

YIANNIS GRIVAS
Actor/Poet

DATE OF BIRTH: 10.09.48
PLACE OF BIRTH: Klirou, Nicosia
MARITAL STATUS: Married to Marikou from Ayios Andronicos, Karpassi.
CHILDREN: Four sons, one daughter
SCHOOLS/COLLEGE: Pancyprian Gymnasium.
MEMBERSHIPS: Equity.
HONOURS/AWARDS: Honoured by Black Cab Association for raising money for handicapped children.
HOBBIES AND INTERESTS: Acting, football, Man Utd Fan.
PERSONAL PROFILE: As an actor, has appeared on TV in Into The Blue, a BT commercial. A DJ with LGR, and has written songs with Hajimike. Also involved with Thea Theatrical Group.

DR CHRISTOS HADJICHARITOU
General Practitioner

DATE OF BIRTH: 30.09.46
PLACE OF BIRTH: Pallouriotisa, Nicosia.
MARITAL STATUS: Married to Leila, from England (parents from Poland).
CHILDREN: Elias, in Management & Administration; Barbara Anna, Student.
SCHOOLS/COLLEGE: Pancyprian Gymnasium Nicosia, University of Athens.
ACADEMIC QUALIFICATIONS: MD (Athens) 1971, LRCP. MRCG (London) 1979.
HOBBIES AND INTERESTS: Charity Work.
PERSONAL PROFILE: GP in Wakefield since 1982. Honorary Commissioner for the Republic of Cyprus in Leeds since 1990. Involved with Greek Orthodox Church and Community in Leeds.

Home address: 16 Falkland Mount, Moortown, Leeds LS17 6JG

ANASTASIOS HADJIHANNAS
Ex-Chairman of Association of Cypriot Maronites

DATE OF BIRTH: 17.01.46
PLACE OF BIRTH: Ayia Marina Skyllouras, Nicosia.
MARITAL STATUS: Married to Liza from Cyprus.
CHILDREN: Joseph, John, Helen and Mariana.
ACADEMIC QUALIFICATIONS: Degree in Electrical Engineering.
MEMBERSHIPS: Member of Hiceic.
HOBBIES AND INTERESTS: Football, politics and clubs.
PERSONAL PROFILE: Ex-Chairman of Association of Cypriot Maronites, Member of the Committee of EFEKA.

GREGORY CHRISTODOULOU HADJIKYRIACOU
Accountant

DATE OF BIRTH: 27.01.58
PLACE OF BIRTH: Cyprus. Parents from Marathovouno.
MARITAL STATUS: Married to Marica Michael Hannides from Southampton.
CHILDREN: Haralambia, Christodoulos at school.
SCHOOLS/COLLEGE: Kilburn Polytechnic.
PROFESSIONAL QUALIFICATIONS: Chartered Certified Accountant.
HOBBIES AND INTERESTS: Travel.
PERSONAL PROFILE: Accountant.

ANDREAS HADJIMAMAS
Chartered Surveyor

DATE OF BIRTH: 22.10.34
PLACE OF BIRTH: Peristerona, Nicosia.
MARITAL STATUS: Married to Nursing Sister from Cyprus.
CHILDREN: Alex, Bank of Cyprus Employee; Sylvia, University Student.
SCHOOLS/COLLEGE: Pancyprian Gymnasium.
ACADEMIC QUALIFICATIONS: Chartered Surveyor.
MEMBERSHIPS: Royal Institute of Chartered Surveyors (FRICS).
HOBBIES AND INTERESTS: Swimming and tennis.
PERSONAL PROFILE: Secretary/Treasurer of Church Committee, St Cosmas and St Damian Church.

GEORGE HADJIMATHEOU
Professor, London Metropolitan University

DATE OF BIRTH: 12.06.43
PLACE OF BIRTH: Aradippou, Larnaca.
MARITAL STATUS: Married to Helen Suddards, an IT Consultant, from Britain.
CHILDREN: Chloe, BA English & Philosophy; Katerina, BA English & Philosophy.
SCHOOLS/COLLEGE: Pancyprian Lyceum, Larnaca, Pedagogical Academy, Nicosia, ASOEE, Athens; LSE, London University.
ACADEMIC QUALIFICATIONS: BA Econ; MSc Econ, MSc Econometrics, PhD.
MEMBERSHIPS: Royal Economic Society; American Economic Association.
HOBBIES AND INTERESTS: Walking, skiing, theatre and poetry.
PERSONAL PROFILE: Professor of Economics, Head of Economics, Finance and International Business Department, London Metropolitan University.

ANDROULA HADJIMICHAEL
Lecturer

DATE OF BIRTH: 13.03.48
PLACE OF BIRTH: Yialousa.
MARITAL STATUS: Married to Sotiris, an Engineer, from Vasili.
CHILDREN: Yiannis, in Computing; Marios, in Sales.
SCHOOLS/COLLEGE: Greek Gymnasium (Yialousa), Greek Educational Institute G/B. UL Institute of Education.
ACADEMIC QUALIFICATIONS: Dip Ed. MA in Education.
PROFESSIONAL QUALIFICATIONS: Lecturer in ESOL.
MEMBERSHIPS: NATFHE.
HOBBIES AND INTERESTS: Reading and writing poetry.
PERSONAL PROFILE: Lecturer & Coordinator in ESOL (City and Islington College). Teacher of the Greek Language and Culture at the Greek Supplementary Schools in GB.

THEOPHANIS (Fanos) COSTA HADJI-MICHAEL
Charity Worker

DATE OF BIRTH: 27.07.28
PLACE OF BIRTH: Larnaca.
MARITAL STATUS: Married to Myroulla Kyriakou (Komi Kebir).
CHILDREN: Rebecca and Constantinos, both married.
SCHOOLS/COLLEGE: Larnaca Commercial Lyceum.
ACADEMIC QUALIFICATIONS: Graduate of above School with Ordinary/Distinction in English).
MEMBERSHIPS: Committee. Larnaca Association, Atoma Me Eidikes Ananges. Greek & Cypriot Cultural & Educational Youth & Legal Centre.
HOBBIES AND INTERESTS: Voluntary Work.
PERSONAL PROFILE: Charity (Cancer Research), Help Hammer Cancer Fund Raising Organiser
Various Occupations, for the last 16 years Travel Agency Employee.

MIROULLA HADJIMICHAEL
Charity Worker

PLACE OF BIRTH: Komi Kebir.
MARITAL STATUS: Married to Theophanis (Fanos) Hadjimichael.
CHILDREN: Rebecca, Constantinos, both married.
SCHOOLS/COLLEGE: Elementary.
PERSONAL PROFILE: Hammer, Cancer Fund Raising Organiser.

DIMITRI J. HADJIMINAS
Breast & Endocrine Surgeon

DATE OF BIRTH: 26.10.61
PLACE OF BIRTH: Athens.
Father, Yiannis from Kyrenia.
MARITAL STATUS: Married to Catherine Louise, a Private Practice Manager, from England.
CHILDREN: Steven and Alexandra, at school.
SCHOOLS/COLLEGE: Athens Medical School.
QUALIFICATIONS: MBBS, MD MPhil. FRCS (Eng), FRCS (Ed), FRCS (Gen Surg).
HOBBIES AND INTERESTS: Tennis.
PERSONAL PROFILE: Breast & Endocrine Surgeon, Director of St. Mary's Breast Unit, Honorary Senior Lecturer, Chairman Harley St. Clinic Breast Unit.

Address: 88 Harley St, London W1G 7HR
Tel: 020 8421 1274.
Email address: dhadjiminas@breastsurgeon.co.uk.

EVA HADJINICOLA
Head Teacher

DATE OF BIRTH: 5.2.50
PLACE OF BIRTH: London. Parents from Komi Kebir, Cyprus.
MARITAL STATUS: Divorced
CHILDREN: Ntinos, BA Honours, Graphic Design; Christopher, Foundation Course.
SCHOOLS/COLLEGE: Shelbourne School, Holloway London; Middlesex College; Sheffield University.
ACADEMIC QUALIFICATIONS: Cert.Ed, Dip.Ed, M.Ed.
HOBBIES AND INTERESTS: Reading and swimming.
PERSONAL PROFILE: Headteacher, Private English Primary School in Cyprus as of September 2001.

MARILENA LOIZIDOU HADJINICOLAOU
Senior Lecturer in Surgical Oncology at UCL

PLACE OF BIRTH: Nicosia
MARITAL STATUS: Married to John, Chartered Accountant, from Famagusta.
CHILDREN: Leonidas.
SCHOOLS/COLLEGE: Kykko Gymnasium for Girls Nicosia (Secondary School), English School, Nicosia (Part-time, Secondary School), McMaster University, Ontario, Canada, Southampton University, UK.

ACADEMIC QUALIFICATIONS: BSc, MSc, PhD.
MEMBERSHIPS: Institute of Learning & Teaching British Association of Surgical Oncology, Society of Academic & Research Surgery, Hellenic Medical Society.
HOBBIES AND INTERESTS: Scuba-diving and piano.
PERSONAL PROFILE: Non-clinical Senior Lecturer in surgical oncology (UCL) University College, London.

DR MARIOS HADJINICOLAOU
University Lecturer

PLACE OF BIRTH: Nicosia
MARITAL STATUS: Married to Leila, from Tunisia.
CHILDREN: Gregory and Iosif
SCHOOLS/COLLEGE: The English School, Nicosia.
ACADEMIC QUALIFICATIONS: BSc (Honours), MSc, PhD.
PROFESSIONAL QUALIFICATIONS: C.Eng
MEMBERSHIPS: Miee, Mieee.
HOBBIES AND INTERESTS: Classical Music.
PERSONAL PROFILE: Lecturer, Dept. Electronic & Computer Engineering, Brunel University.

PANAYIOTIS HADJI-PANAYI
Former Chairman of Rizokarpasso Association

DATE OF BIRTH: 08.09.34
PLACE OF BIRTH: Rizokarpasso, Famagusta.
MARITAL STATUS: Married to Andriana, a Dental Surgeon from Rizokarpasso.
CHILDREN: Demetri, Medical Doctor; Christian, Multi-Media Consultant.
SCHOOLS/COLLEGE: Rizokarpasso High School, Birmingham College of Commerce, Fircroft College, Birmingham. University of Leicester, Birkbeck College, London.
ACADEMIC QUALIFICATIONS: Dip. in Bus. Admin. Dip in Soc. Science. BA (Hon) SOC Sc. Dr. of Phil. (Unfinished).
HOBBIES AND INTERESTS: Reading, National & International Affairs, Community Affairs, Travel, History, Cyprus.
PERSONAL PROFILE: Association of Rizokarpasso, (Honarary Chairman), Greek Cypriot Brotherhood, Cypriot Forum for Labour, Federation of Cypriots in Britain - Member of the Executive & Secretariat for over 20 yrs.

ANDRIANA HADJI-PANAYI
Dental Surgeon

DATE OF BIRTH: 11.09.44
PLACE OF BIRTH: Rizokarpasso, Famagusta.
MARITAL STATUS: Married to Panayiotis, from Rizokarpasso, Financial Advisor
CHILDREN: Demetri, Medical Doctor; Christian, Multi Media Consultant.
SCHOOLS/COLLEGE: University of Sydney, Australia, Birkbeck College, University of Kent.
ACADEMIC QUALIFICATIONS: Batchelor of Dental Surgery, Diploma in International Studies, Master in International Relations.
PROFESSIONAL QUALIFICATIONS: Dental Surgeon.
MEMBERSHIPS: British Dental Association, British Dental Health Foundation, Greek Cypriot Brotherhood, Association of Rizokarpasso, Cypriot Forum for Labour, Hellenic Society of Professional People & Scientists in Great Britain.
HOBBIES AND INTERESTS: Art, music, theatre, opera, travel, current affairs & international & domestic politics.
PERSONAL PROFILE: Practicing Dental Surgeon for 32 years.

CHRISTIAN HADJI-PANAYI
Project Manager

DATE OF BIRTH: 04.03.75
PLACE OF BIRTH: Luton, Bedfordshire, UK. Parents from Rizokarpasso, Famagusta.
SCHOOLS/COLLEGE: Haberdashers, University College, London. Sussex University.
ACADEMIC QUALIFICATIONS: BA Honours, History, MA Multi-Media & IT.
PROFESSIONAL QUALIFICATIONS: Consultant in Multi-Media.
HOBBIES AND INTERESTS: Piano, guitar, swimming, canoeing, skiing and travelling.
PERSONAL PROFILE: Practicing as a Project Manager Multi-Media Consultant in the City.

DR DEMETRI HADJI-PANAYI
Doctor

DATE OF BIRTH: 19.05.73
PLACE OF BIRTH: Luton, Bedfordshire, UK. Parents from Rizokarpasso, Famagusta.
MARITAL STATUS: Single
SCHOOLS/COLLEGE: Haberdashers, St. Mary's Medical School, Imperial College, London.
ACADEMIC QUALIFICATIONS: BSc Physiology. MBBS.
PROFESSIONAL QUALIFICATIONS: Medical Doctor.
MEMBERSHIPS: British Medical Association, General Medical Council.
HOBBIES AND INTERESTS: Tennis, golf, skiing, swimming, reading & writing.
PERSONAL PROFILE: Practising Medical Practitioner, specialising in Gynaecology & presently conducting Research at the Royal Free Hospital in London.

ANDROULLA HADJISIMOU
Childcare Lawyer

DATE OF BIRTH: 15.12.73
PLACE OF BIRTH: London. Father from Akanthou, Mother from Patriki
MARITAL STATUS: Single
SCHOOLS/COLLEGE: Waverley Secondary School, Croydon College, Keele University, Inns of Court School of Law, London, College of Law, London, Kings College (University of London).
ACADEMIC QUALIFICATIONS: LLB (Honours), Law & History.
PROFESSIONAL QUALIFICATIONS: Solicitor.
MEMBERSHIPS: National Children's Bureau and Amnesty International.
HOBBIES AND INTERESTS: Keep fit.
PERSONAL PROFILE: Currently working for the London Borough of Greenwich's Social Services Legal Department.

MICHELLE SOTIRIS HADJISIMOU
Solicitor

DATE OF BIRTH: 24.08.77
PLACE OF BIRTH: London. Parents from Akanthou and Patriki.
MARITAL STATUS: Single
SCHOOLS/COLLEGE: Waverley School, Dulwich/London, Selhurst College, Croydon, Keele University, Keele/Staffordshire.
ACADEMIC QUALIFICATIONS: LLB Joint Honours, Law and Politics.
PROFESSIONAL QUALIFICATIONS: Legal Practice Course.
MEMBERSHIPS: Law Society
HOBBIES AND INTERESTS: Football, reading, and aerobics.
PERSONAL PROFILE: Solicitor (Conveyancer)

SOTERIS ANTONIOU HADJISOTERIOU
Writer and Poet

DATE OF BIRTH: 12.12.45
PLACE OF BIRTH: Komi Kebir, Famagusta.
MARITAL STATUS: Married to Julita B., a Teacher, from the Philippines.
SCHOOLS/COLLEGE: Ellinicon Emporicon Gymnasium, Tricomou.
ACADEMIC QUALIFICATIONS: Cypriot GCSE Level.
HOBBIES AND INTERESTS: Reading, walking and travelling.
PERSONAL PROFILE: Writer and poet who has published a collection of poems in Greek, *Ta Apanta* (Cyprus 1997), and a compilation of prose and verse entitled *Philippines: Journey to a Dream*.

GEORGE HAJIFANIS
Architect and Community Worker

DATE OF BIRTH: 25.02.37
PLACE OF BIRTH: Larnaca.
MARITAL STATUS: Married to Eleni Sozou.
CHILDREN: Two daughters.
SCHOOLS/COLLEGE: Studied Architecture, University of London. University of Westminster, University of Essex.
MEMBERSHIPS: Member of the Royal Institute of British Architects and the Royal Society of Arts.

HOBBIES AND INTERESTS: Books, arts, topography, Greek affairs and tennis.

PERSONAL PROFILE: Board of Governors of the Metropolitan University. Founding member and president of the Union of Cypriot Students. General Secretary of the Cyprus Relief Fund. Founding member of National Federation of Cypriots in GB and General Secretary for years. Has Architectural practice that deals with local Authorities and private individuals & companies in England, Cyprus, Greece, Malta, Nigeria & Rumania.

STELIOS HAJI-IOANNOU
Businessman

DATE OF BIRTH: 14.02.67
PLACE OF BIRTH: Glyfada, Greece. Father from Pedhoula; Mother from Limassol.
MARITAL STATUS: Single
SCHOOLS/COLLEGE: Doukas High School Athens, London School of Economics, City University.
ACADEMIC QUALIFICATIONS: BSc Economics; MSc Shipping Trade & Finance.
MEMBERSHIPS: Doukas High School Athens, London School of Economics, City University.
HOBBIES AND INTERESTS: Sport and travel.
PERSONAL PROFILE: Founder, ex-Chairman and shareholder of Easy Jet Airlines; owner of Easy Internet Cafes, Easy Car Hire. Founding Chairman of Cymera, the Cyprus Marine Environment Protection Association.

REV. FOKAS HAJILOIZIS
Reverend

DATE OF BIRTH: 22.06.54
PLACE OF BIRTH: Cyprus, Famagusta - Peristeronopiyi.
MARITAL STATUS: Married to Zooulla.
CHILDREN: Constantinos, Stella, Marios and Kiriaki.
SCHOOLS/COLLEGE: Gymnasium, Famagusta.
PROFESSIONAL QUALIFICATIONS: Reverend.
HOBBIES AND INTERESTS: Football and swimming.
PERSONAL PROFILE: Reverend for Mansfield Sheffield & District Greek Orthodox Church.

ANDREAS ANTONIOU HAJIMICHAEL
President of the Greek Community in Margate

DATE OF BIRTH: 23.06.37
PLACE OF BIRTH: Aradippou Larnaca.
MARITAL STATUS: Married to Elli Louca Theodoulou, a Housewife, from Aradippou.
CHILDREN: Tony Michael, Building Surveyor; George Michael, Teacher - American Academy, in Cyprus; Theodora Michael, at Westminster University.
SCHOOLS/COLLEGE: American Academy - Cyprus, Balham & Tooting College of Commerce - London.
PROFESSIONAL QUALIFICATIONS: Certified Accountant.
PERSONAL PROFILE: Restaurateur - Business in Margate since 1962, casino owner for 15 years - Property Developer - Secretary from the beginning of the formation of the Greek Community in Margate for 15 years & president for the last three years.

HAJIMIKE aka MIKE HAJIMICHAEL
DJ, Musician, Journalist

DATE OF BIRTH: 24.04.60
PLACE OF BIRTH: Nicosia. Parents from Marathovouno & Lefkoniko.
MARITAL STATUS: Married.
CHILDREN: One child.
SCHOOLS/COLLEGE: William Pitt Junior High, Sir George Monoux, Waltham Forest, College, Essex University, Birmingham University.
ACADEMIC QUALIFICATIONS: BA Gov & Sociology, MA Literature, PhD Cultural Studies, Thesis on British Cypriots.
PERSONAL PROFILE: DJ, Musician, Freelance Journalist, worked for Cyprus Weekly, Cyprus Mail, Parikiaki. TV Presenter Radio Show host Sigma TV, Radio Proto CYBC, Produced three CDLPS. Currently employed full-time at Intercollege Cyprus.

MARIOS HAJIPANAYI
Actor/Athletics

DATE OF BIRTH: 16.08.62
PLACE OF BIRTH: London. Parents from Larnaca and Psematismeno.
MARITAL STATUS: Married.
CHILDREN: Constandia.
SCHOOLS/COLLEGE: Wood Green School, Barnet College.
ACADEMIC QUALIFICATIONS: BEC General Diploma.
HOBBIES AND INTERESTS: Athletics.
PERSONAL PROFILE: Worked as Care Manager & Assistant Social worker for London Borough of Haringey. Competed in the Hammer Event for Haringey Athletics Club and the Counties of Essex and Middx under 19s. Was Haringey Athletic Coach for Shot Putt, Hammer, Javelin and Discus. Team Manager and Head Coach for England National Athletics Squad for people with learning difficulties. Also an actor: has appeared in *Bridget Jones's Diary*, on TV in *The Bill*; on stage in *Cinderella* and Old Time Musical; been in TV Commercials for British Telecom, Ericsson.

HARRY HAJIPAPAS
Managing Director of Cyplon Travel

DATE OF BIRTH: 21.07.58
PLACE OF BIRTH: Kenya. Father from Trimiklini, Cyprus; Mother born in Tanzania of Cypriot parents.
MARITAL STATUS: Married to Debra Bennett, a Housewife, from London.
CHILDREN: Christos and Voula, at school.
SCHOOLS/COLLEGE: Creighton School Muswell Hill, London School of Economics.
ACADEMIC QUALIFICATIONS: 8 O Levels, 3 A Levels, BSc (Econ), MBA (Marketing) MINSTM, Diploma (Inst. Of Marketing) MRS (Dip).
MEMBERSHIPS: Chelsea Football Club; Council Member of AGTA (The Assoc. of Greek Travel Agents).
HOBBIES AND INTERESTS: Reading, theatre, cinema and football.
PERSONAL PROFILE: Set up Taiwan Christmas Decorations Trade Centre in 1982. 1985 joined family business - Cyplon Travel - that specialises in different facets of the travel industry, eg tour operation to Cyprus, Greece & Dubai as well as Retail/Wholesale/Business & Groups and Incentives. Established ten-year relationship with Chairman of Chelsea Football Club, Ken Bates, and set up travel agency for players, staff & supporters. Organised several trips to Europe taking thousands of supporters to watch Chelsea matches.

ZACHARIA (Sugar) HAJISHACALLI
Musician

DATE OF BIRTH: 08.07.54
PLACE OF BIRTH: London. Father from Yialousa; Mother from Leonarisso.
MARITAL STATUS: Married to Androulla, a Housewife, from Livadhia, Larnaca.
CHILDREN: Georgina, BA Honours, Fashion, Surrey Institute of Art and Design; Barbara, HND in Business, Barnet College.
SCHOOLS/COLLEGE: Highbury Grove Secondary, Tottenham Technical College.
ACADEMIC QUALIFICATIONS: 5 O Levels, BTech Electronics.
PROFESSIONAL QUALIFICATIONS: Sound Engineer.
MEMBERSHIPS: PRS - MCPS - BASCA.
HOBBIES AND INTERESTS: Music, Writing, Esoteric Mysticism, Star Trek, Family
PERSONAL PROFILE: In the Greek band Spartacus. Produces songs, set up studio specialising in ethnic music. Has produced over 300 songs and 20 albums; writes music for documentaries, films, adverts, and corporate jingles. Recorded & toured with "Boy George" Band "Jesus Loves You". Recorded & wrote Ancient Greek music for film The Odessey. Played Santouri in film The Saint. Instruments played: bouzouki, baglamas, tzouras, santouri, pithkiavlin, percussion keyboards

CONSTANTINOS ARGYROU HAJIVASSILLOU
Surgeon

DATE OF BIRTH: 27.04.61
PLACE OF BIRTH: Cyprus
MARITAL STATUS: Married
CHILDREN: Two daughters.
SCHOOLS/COLLEGE: Kykko Gymnasium, Nicosia. Edinburgh University.
ACADEMIC QUALIFICATIONS: BSc (Honours) Physiology. MB CHB, FRCS, MD.
PERSONAL PROFILE: Consultant Paediatric, Neo Natal Surgeon, Lecturer at University of Glasgow, Designed Medical & Surgical devices.

DR SOTIRIS HAMILOS
Dental Surgeon

DATE OF BIRTH: 20.03.45
PLACE OF BIRTH: Gypsos
MARITAL STATUS: Married to Diana from UK.
CHILDREN: Marcos, a Banker; Michael, IT Expert; Anna, Planner.
SCHOOLS/COLLEGE: Lefkoniko Gynasium, Kingston College, London University.
PROFESSIONAL QUALIFICATIONS: Dentist.
HOBBIES AND INTERESTS: Photography, Bridge, gardening and travelling.
PERSONAL PROFILE: Has Dental practice in Croydon. Chairman of GYPSOS friendly Association.

YIANOULLA HANNA
Justices Clerk Secretary

DATE OF BIRTH: 30.01.46
PLACE OF BIRTH: Nicosia.
MARITAL STATUS: Divorced
CHILDREN: Nick and Christina, both work in Education.
SCHOOLS/COLLEGE: Komi Kebir Elementary, Pancyprian Gymnasium, Nicosia, College for Further Education.
MEMBERSHIPS: Association of Police & Court Interpreters; Arachne, a Greek Cypriot Women's Organzisation.
HOBBIES AND INTERESTS: Eating out, concerts and travel.
PERSONAL PROFILE: Justices Clerk Secretary at Highbury Corner Magistrates Court. Worked in the Court's Service since 1973. Responsible for organising District Judges & Justices of the Peace sittings amongst other duties. Interpreter for the Courts' Service and Police Stations.

Email address: translations@jhanna.eslife.co.uk

JOHN MICHAEL HANNIDES
Councillor

DATE OF BIRTH: 25.11.63
PLACE OF BIRTH: Southampton. Parents from Koma-Tou-Yialou.
MARITAL STATUS: Married to Athanasia, London, Bank Official.
CHILDREN: Michael John, toddler.
SCHOOLS/COLLEGE: Richard Taunton College/ University of Wolverhampton.
ACADEMIC QUALIFICATIONS: Honours Degree.
MEMBERSHIPS: Member of the Employment Consultants Institute.
HOBBIES AND INTERESTS: Sport,cinema and current affairs.
PERSONAL PROFILE: Recruitment Consultant. Elected Local Councillor - Southampton City Council since 1994.

NICHOLAS MICHAEL HANNIDES
Solicitor

DATE OF BIRTH: 05.11.58
PLACE OF BIRTH: Southhampton. Parents Koma-Tou-Yialou.
MARITAL STATUS: Married to Denise, a Housewife, from England.
CHILDREN: Nicholas, at secondary school; Marika, Michael and Haralambia at junior School.
SCHOOLS/COLLEGE: Shirley Junior School/Bellemoor Secondary/Richard Tauntons College - Southampton. Cardiff University.
ACADEMIC QUALIFICATIONS: 10 O Levels, 5 A Levels, LLB.
PROFESSIONAL QUALIFICATIONS: Law Finals.
MEMBERSHIPS: Law Society.
HOBBIES AND INTERESTS: Sports, mainly football - Runs Son's Team, Church/Community Affairs.
PERSONAL PROFILE: Solicitor (since 1984). Represents most of Cypriot community in Southampton. President of Greek Orthodox Church community of St. Nicolas, Southampton (last four years) Major fund raising activities. Father - "George" Hannides. (First Cypriot resident in Southampton)

KATIA DAVID-HARMANDA
Elected Councillor, Magistrate, Broadcaster

DATE OF BIRTH: 04.02.67
PLACE OF BIRTH: London. Parents from Kozani, Greece and Ayios Andronicos, Cyprus.
MARITAL STATUS: Married to Chris Harmanda from Acheritou, Cyprus.
CHILDREN: Lucy and Eleni (Hellenic College, London).
SCHOOLS/COLLEGES: Hellenic College of London.
ACADEMIC QUALIFICATIONS: BSc, MBA.
HOBBIES AND INTERESTS: Photography.
PERSONAL PROFILE: Broadcaster, trained Solicitor, Magistrate, Elected Councillor and Cabinet Member, London Borough of Barnet. Ex-Chairman of the Independent Greek Schools UK. School Governor at Manor Hill and Queen Elizabeth Girls School in Barnet. Chairwoman Barnet area Planning, Director Arts depot. Finchley General Secretary of all elected Greeks abroad. (Part of the Foreign Ministry in Greece)

TAKIS HARMANDA
Director & a Co Founder of London Greek Radio

DATE OF BIRTH: 12.01.59
PLACE OF BIRTH: Acheritou.
MARITAL STATUS: Married to Katia Harmanda, Councillor in Barnet Council.
CHILDREN: Two daughters.
SCHOOLS/COLLEGE: Holloway School, Dean College.
ACADEMIC QUALIFICATIONS: Bsc in Marketing.
HOBBIES AND INTERESTS: Football, boxing and travel.
PERSONAL PROFILE: Saw need of Greek Radio Station and Co founded London Greek Radio 1983. Director Shareholder & Company Secretary of LGR. Among the founders of Acheritou Assoc. Vice Chair of Hadley Wood Conservative Assoc. Known for his wide Charity work.

NICHOLAS DEMOS HARRIS
Headmaster

DATE OF BIRTH: 02.11.44
PLACE OF BIRTH: Famagusta.
MARITAL STATUS: Married to Christine, a Teacher, from the UK.
CHILDREN: Elena Christina, Graduated 2001 from The London Institute (London College of Fashion).
SCHOOLS/COLLEGE: Haverstock School, Chalk Farm, London. British Institute (Sorbonne, Paris), Manresa House, Battersea College of Education, Roehampton. Institute of Education, London University.
ACADEMIC QUALIFICATIONS: Certificate of Education, Batchelor of Education.
PROFESSIONAL QUALIFICATIONS: QTS (Qualified teacher status, Headmaster from 1979 Argyll Primary School. Gospel Oak Primary School.
MEMBERSHIPS: National Union of Teachers - Teachers' Benevolent Fund - NAHT (National association of Headteachers).
HOBBIES AND INTERESTS: Reading (particularly travel & biographies), Greek culture, history and religion, football, wildlife conservation and gardening.
PERSONAL PROFILE: President of Greek Orthodox Community of St. Athanasios, Cambridge from 1990 to date. Sec. of Consultative Committee of Head Teachers (Camden - Westminster, Inner London Education Authority) Local treasurer NUT Islington Assoc. 1983-90

DEMIS HASSABIS
Chess Master, Mind Sports Olympiad Champion, Computer Games Designer

DATE OF BIRTH: 27.07.76
PLACE OF BIRTH: London. Grandparents from Famagusta.
SCHOOLS/COLLEGE: Cambridge University.
ACADEMIC QUALIFICATIONS: Double First, BA Honours, Computer Science.
HONOURS/AWARDS: Chess Master, four times Mind Sports Olympiad Champion.
HOBBIES AND INTERESTS: Games: Chess, Diplomacy.
PERSONAL PROFILE: Chairman & Chief Executive Officer and Creative Director of Elixir.
Broke into industry age 17 when co-created Theme Park with Peter Molyneux at Bullfrog. Taught himself to play chess at four years old, became chess Master at twelve and was highest ranked player of his age in the world. Won over 20 medals in total at the 1998/99/2000 Mind Sports Olympiads, including prestigious

overall title, The Pentamind World Championship on all three occasions. For these was awarded the title of international Grand Master. Elixir Studios was founded by Demis in 1998, a successful computer games company that employs over 60 people at their offices in Camden, London.

Address: Elixir Studios Ltd, 4th Floor, the Forum, 74-80 Camden St, London NW1 2LL
Email: info@elixir-studios.co.uk

Dr REBECCA HATJIOSIF
Doctor

DATE OF BIRTH: 20.09.55
PLACE OF BIRTH: Nottingham, England. Father from Strovolos, Nicosia; Mother from Davlos.
CHILDREN: Andreas Evangelos and Maria Josephina, at school.
SCHOOLS/COLLEGE: Loughborough Girls High School, Leeds University.
QUALIFICATIONS: 9 GCSEs, 3 A Levels

MBCHB. DRC0G. FPC (Bachelor of Medicine & Surgery Diploma of Obstetrics & Gynaecology, Family Planning Cert).
MEMBERSHIPS: British Medical Assoc., Hellenic Medical Soc. Referral Advisor to Haringey Primary Care Trust.
HOBBIES AND INTERESTS: Reading, golf, travel, art theatre and music.
PERSONAL PROFILE: General Practitioner, Muswell Hill, Member of Ladies Committee - Cypriot Estia.

ANDREE HAVA
Events Information Adviser

DATE OF BIRTH: 24.10.51
PLACE OF BIRTH: London. Father from Limassol; Mother from Vassa.
MARITAL STATUS: Married to Andrea from Athienou.
CHILDREN: Evi, Solicitor; Marisa, Project Appraisal & Monitoring Officer, Urban Regeneration; Natasha, studying Human Genetics at UCL.
SCHOOLS/COLLEGE: Hornsey School for Girls.
ACADEMIC QUALIFICATIONS: 6 GCE O Levels.
MEMBERSHIPS: Minority Business Network.
HOBBIES AND INTERESTS: Antiques, fitness training, travel, music and theatre.
PERSONAL PROFILE: Information Adviser (events), Business Link Hertfordshire.

CONSTANTINOS KAMEL HAWA
Philanthropist

DATE OF BIRTH: 15.11.33
PLACE OF BIRTH: Kato Polemidhia.
MARITAL STATUS: Married to Androulla, a Housewife, from Limassol.
CHILDREN: Stelios, Fashion Designer; Zoe, Teaching Assistant.
SCHOOLS/COLLEGE: Commercial Academy of Cyprus.
HONOURS/AWARDS: Award from Archbishop & President of Cyprus Makarios III Re-Charitable Donations.
HOBBIES AND INTERESTS: Football.
PERSONAL PROFILE: Member of Cyprus Brotherhood.

STELIOS HAWA
Designer

DATE OF BIRTH: 05.12.59
PLACE OF BIRTH: Limassol.
MARITAL STATUS: Single.
SCHOOLS/COLLEGE: Creighton School, London College of Fashion, Kingston Polytechnic.
ACADEMIC QUALIFICATIONS: BA Honours in Fashion, London Diploma in Fashion.
HOBBIES AND INTERESTS: Collecting antiques and travel.
PERSONAL PROFILE: Shop in Knightsbridge to produce ready to wear collection. Also Dress agency where ladies buy and then bring back to resell. Has famous clients.

CHESS MASTER, DEMIS HASSABIS, ALSO FOUR TIMES MIND SPORTS OLYMPIAD CHAMPION AND CO-CREATOR OF THE COMPUTER GAME 'THEME PARK'

LUCY HAYCOCK
Served as Mayor of Scarborough

DATE OF BIRTH: 08.05.43
PLACE OF BIRTH: Famagusta.
MARITAL STATUS: Married to Ted Haycock.
CHILDREN: Elaine, Doctor lecturing in Scotland; Solette, Marketing Consultant; Nicholas.
SCHOOLS/COLLEGE: Attended College in Cyprus to GCSE level.
HOBBIES AND INTERESTS: Flower arranging, cooking and community work.
PERSONAL PROFILE: Borough Councillor for 18 yrs. Mayor 2001-2002 Scarborough Borough Council.

GEORGIA HAYHOE
President of the Greek School Committee in Northampton

DATE OF BIRTH: 14.08.62
PLACE OF BIRTH: Nicosia.
MARITAL STATUS: Married to Mark Hayhoe, a Regional Investment Manager, from Bristol, UK.
CHILDREN: Francesca and Anthony, at school.
SCHOOLS/COLLEGE: HTI Nicosia 1980-83 High School 1974-80.
ACADEMIC QUALIFICATIONS: HND Civil Engineering.
HOBBIES AND INTERESTS: Painting, learning Spanish, keeping fit, working at Northampton Greek School.
PERSONAL PROFILE: President of the Greek School Committee in Northampton.

Address: 62 Weggs Farm Road, Duston, Northampton, NN5 6HD

THREE FEMALE COUNCILLORS IN THE 'H' SECTION ALONE! KATIA HARMANDA, LUCY HAYCOCK AND IRINI GERMANICOS HENDERSON

IRINI GERMANACOS HENDERSON
Councillor and Cabinet Member

DATE OF BIRTH: 14.03.42
PLACE OF BIRTH: Limassol.
MARITAL STATUS: Married to Euan Scott Henderson, Professor of IET - Open University.
CHILDREN: Christopher, Senior Manager, Boots UK; Anna, Section Manager, Milton Keynes College of FE.
SCHOOLS/COLLEGE: Pancyprian Gymnasium, Guys Hospital School of Physiotherapy, Open University.
ACADEMIC QUALIFICATIONS: Diploma in Physiotherapy, BA - Open University.
PROFESSIONAL QUALIFICATIONS: Chartered Physiotherapist, State Registered Physiotherapist.
MEMBERSHIPS: Justice of the Peace, also a Liberal Democrat Councillor for Newport Pagnell.
HOBBIES AND INTERESTS: Opera, reading, theatre, gardening and family.
PERSONAL PROFILE: Leader of the Opposition Newport Pagnell Council. Now cabinet member for Liberal Democrats administration running Milton Keynes Council. Chair of Age Concern Milton Keynes for many years. Member of many local Community groups, School Governor etc..

TONY HJIHANNAS
Former Champion Wrestler

DATE OF BIRTH: 03.02.41
PLACE OF BIRTH: Ayia Marina Skyloura, Nicosia.
MARITAL STATUS: Married to Suzanna from Ayia Marina.
CHILDREN: Joseph, Andrew and Marina, who is a Solicitor.
HOBBIES AND INTERESTS: Shooting.
PERSONAL PROFILE: DHKO Committee Member in UK. Worked as a Mechanic then Dress Manufacturer. Was a Wrestling Professional until 1990, regular on TV; Middle East Champion, Middleweight World Champion. Was Walker and Southgate Greek School Chairman, and one of the founders & Chairman of the Maronites Assoc. in UK.

CONSTANTIA HAJIPANAYI
Community Schools Activist

DATE OF BIRTH: 02.10.26
PLACE OF BIRTH: Psematismenos.
MARITAL STATUS: Widow, was married to Spyros Hjipanayi from Larnaca.
CHILDREN: George, Christos and Marios.
SCHOOLS/COLLEGE: Psematismenos Elementary.
HOBBIES AND INTERESTS: Reading.
PERSONAL PROFILE: Was a Manageress in Dress Factory. 1960 became involved in Greek Schools. Founder Member of OESEKA. Chairwoman of North London Cypriot Assoc. Member of National Federation of Cypriots Executive Committee.

Dr. PANTELLIS HAJI-YIANNAKIS
Consultant Oncologist

DATE OF BIRTH: 13.12.67
PLACE OF BIRTH: Nicosia.
MARITAL STATUS: Married to Jane, a Psychologist, from England.
CHILDREN: George
SCHOOLS/COLLEGE: English School Nicosia, University of Nottingham.
ACADEMIC QUALIFICATIONS: Bmed sci, BM, BS, MRCP, FRCR.
PROFESSIONAL QUALIFICATIONS: Specialist in Oncology.
HOBBIES AND INTERESTS: Tennis, gym and travelling.
PERSONAL PROFILE: Consultant Oncologist at Derriford Hospital, Plymouth.

APHRODITE HUBBARD
Nurse & Community Worker

DATE OF BIRTH: 30.03.36
PLACE OF BIRTH: Tricomo.
MARITAL STATUS: Married to Michael Hubbard, a Geologist, from England.
CHILDREN: Andrew, Classical Pianist; Alexandra, History Teacher.
SCHOOLS/COLLEGE: Greek Gymnasium Famagusta.
ACADEMIC QUALIFICATIONS: Cyprus Cert in English.
PROFESSIONAL QUALIFICATIONS: SRN (State Registered Nurse).
MEMBERSHIPS: RCN (Royal College of Nursing).

HONOURS/AWARDS: Diploma of Care of the Elderly Bedford Hospital.
HOBBIES AND INTERESTS: Reading, gardening, cooking, also promoting role of women Greek Church.
PERSONAL PROFILE: Worked for 42 years as a Nurse. Last 17 years as Community Nurse in baby clinics. Actively involved in Immunisation Programmes & in School Nursing. While a Community Nurse worked for a Group Practice of GPs involved in assessing the needs of the elderly. Works with the community at St Mamas Greek Orthodox Church in Bedford.

ALEXANDRA HUBBARD
Teacher

DATE OF BIRTH: 08.09.75
PLACE OF BIRTH: Bedford. Mother from Tricomo.
MARITAL STATUS: Single
SCHOOLS/COLLEGE: Wooton Upper School, Aberystwyth University.
ACADEMIC QUALIFICATIONS: 2:1 Degree in History (BA Honours).
PROFESSIONAL QUALIFICATIONS: PGCE Secondary.
HOBBIES AND INTERESTS: Singing, travelling and reading.
PERSONAL PROFILE: Teacher in History.

ANDREW HUBBARD
Classical Pianist

DATE OF BIRTH: 19.04.66
PLACE OF BIRTH: Tricomo, near Famagusta.
MARITAL STATUS: Single
SCHOOLS/COLLEGE: Bedford School, The Royal Academy of Music London.
ACADEMIC QUALIFICATIONS: 9 O Levels, 3 A Levels, GRSM Honours.
PROFESSIONAL QUALIFICATIONS: LRAM.
MEMBERSHIPS: Musicians Union.
HONOURS/AWARDS: Harry Fargeon Prize.
HOBBIES AND INTERESTS: Cookery, travel, cats, the arts.
PERSONAL PROFILE: Classical Pianist and Musician. Gives regular performances all over Europe.

MICHAEL STAVROU IACOVOU
Accountant, Treasurer of the Hellenic Community Trust

DATE OF BIRTH: 26.07.34
PLACE OF BIRTH: Larnaca.
MARITAL STATUS: Married to Patricia (née McDermott), part-time costumier, from Sevenoaks.
CHILDREN: Paul Christian and Martin Andrew.
SCHOOLS/COLLEGE: Elementary school, Larnaca, Commercial Lyceum Larnaca.
PROFESSIONAL QUALIFICATIONS: Fellow of the Institute of Chartered Accountants in England & Wales (FCA), Member of the British Institute of Management (MBIM).
MEMBERSHIPS: Association of Cypriot Qualified Accountants in the UK (founding member and former chairman); Cypriot Estia of London (Secretary); The Hellenic Centre (founding member).
HOBBIES AND INTERESTS: Reading, drawing/painting, gardening, backgammon and friendly card games.
PERSONAL PROFILE: Principal M.S. Iacovou & Co Chartered Accountants. Treasurer of Hellenic Community Trust since its establishment in 1993/4.

AKIS NEOKLIS IOANNIDES
Chairman of St Eleftherius Church in Leyton

DATE OF BIRTH: 23.08.39
PLACE OF BIRTH: Pedhoula.
MARITAL STATUS: Married to Maroulla from Larnaca.
CHILDREN: Yiannis, George and Evangelos.
SCHOOLS/COLLEGE: Pedhoula Gymnasium; College of Aeronautical and Automobile Engineering, London.
HOBBIES AND INTERESTS: Helping the community, family life and travel.
PERSONAL PROFILE: Owner of a manufacturing company producing edible food carriers supplying restaurants and hotels, based in Ponders End, Middlesex. Chairman of St Eleftherious Church in Leyton. Trustee of St Nicholas Educational Trust. General Secretary of the Association of Greek Orthodox Communities of GB.

REV. A. IOANNIDES
Priest

DATE OF BIRTH: 28.02.26
PLACE OF BIRTH: Famagusta.
SCHOOLS/COLLEGE: Greek School.
HOBBIES AND INTERESTS: Greek Church.
PERSONAL PROFILE: Priest of the Greek Orthodox Church of the Holy Trinity, Brighton.

COSTAS IOANNIDES
University Lecturer

DATE OF BIRTH: 10.02.48
PLACE OF BIRTH: Nicosia.
MARITAL STATUS: Married to Cleopatra Stavropoulos, a Sales Assistant, from Greece
CHILDREN: Alexandros, at university; Marios Omiros, at college; Anna Fotini, at school.
SCHOOLS/COLLEGE: Pancyprian Gymnasium, Dudley Technical College, University of Liverpool, University of Surrey.
ACADEMIC QUALIFICATIONS: BSc, PhD, DSc.
HONOURS/AWARDS: American Association for Cancer Research - recognition of work in the field of cancer.
HOBBIES AND INTERESTS: Music and theatre
PERSONAL PROFILE: Published more than 250 papers in scientific journals. Edited eight scientific books. University Lecturer.

KIKI OLYMPIOS-IOANNIDES
General Secretary of the Democratic Party in the UK

DATE OF BIRTH: 23.09.55
PLACE OF BIRTH: Nicosia.
CHILDREN: Constantine Ioannides, BSc Politics with Economics, MSc, London School of Economics; Miltiades Ioannides, BSc Chemistry & Management Kings College London; Elena Ioannides, LLB University College London, LLM, London School of Economics.
SCHOOLS/COLLEGE: The American Academy, Nicosia.
ACADEMIC QUALIFICATIONS: BSc Honours in Politics/International Relations (Open University). Currently studying for an MBA.
HOBBIES AND INTERESTS: Politics.
PERSONAL PROFILE: Currently General Secretary of the Democratic Party in the UK and also a member of the Executive of the National Federation of Cypriots in Great Britain. After bringing up children to school age, Kiki started working for the Open University in Milton Keynes in 1988. Currently Programme Manager for the United States Open University and the Arab Open University.

ANDREAS IOANNOU
Treasurer Pentayia Association; Owner of Aroma Patisserie

DATE OF BIRTH: 03.08.51
PLACE OF BIRTH: Pentayia.
MARITAL STATUS: Married to Maria (née Kyriacou), a Pastry Chef, born in London.
CHILDREN: Angela, at Kings College, University of London and Anna, at school.
SCHOOLS/COLLEGE: Borehamwood College.
ACADEMIC QUALIFICATIONS: 11 O levels and Diploma in Computer Engineering.
PROFESSIONAL QUALIFICATIONS: Food Hygiene Certificate.
MEMBERSHIPS: Pentayia Association.
HOBBIES AND INTERESTS: Travelling and football.
PERSONAL PROFILE: Owner of Aroma Patisserie and Treasurer of the Pentayia Association.

ANDREAS ELIA IOANNOU
Accountant

DATE OF BIRTH: 06.10.50
PLACE OF BIRTH: Neo Chorion Kythreas, Nicosia.
MARITAL STATUS: Married to Dimitra from Gastria Famagusta.
CHILDREN: Eliana, Solicitor; Ioannis, studying medicine at UCL; Christiana at University.
SCHOOLS/COLLEGE: Pancyprian Gymnasium.
PROFESSIONAL QUALIFICATIONS: Chartered Accountant.
HOBBIES AND INTERESTS: Shooting, Tottenham Football Club.
PERSONAL PROFILE: Partner Ioannou & Co Accountants. Director of Intersky Holidays Chairman of St John the Baptist Greek School. On the committee of EFEPE.

CONSTANTINOS ELIA IOANNOU
Accountant

DATE OF BIRTH: 21.06.56
PLACE OF BIRTH: Neon Chorion Kythreas, Nicosia.
MARITAL STATUS: Married to Florentia (née Savva), a Biochemist, from Achna, Famagusta.
CHILDREN: Christina, Marina, Elias, Elina, all at school.
SCHOOLS/COLLEGE: Technical School of Nicosia, Kingsway College for Further Education, North London University.
ACADEMIC QUALIFICATIONS: Foundation course in Accountancy.
PROFESSIONAL QUALIFICATIONS: Chartered Accountant (FCA).
MEMBERSHIPS: Fellow of Institute of Chartered Accountants in England & Wales. Committee member of North London Society of Chartered Accountants - Chairman 1998-2000. Vice President of London Society of Chartered Accnts.
HOBBIES AND INTERESTS: Reading, walking, cinema, golf, nature watch and travelling.
PERSONAL PROFILE: Partner in Ioannou & Co, and Director of several companies.
Governor of All Saints Primary (CofE) School in Whetstone. Governor of St. John the Baptist Greek School. Treasurer of St. John the Baptist Church in London N8.

CONSTANTINOS S. IOANNOU
Principal Lecturer in Structures & Design

DATE OF BIRTH: 23.02.49
PLACE OF BIRTH: Yerolakos, Nicosia.
MARITAL STATUS: Married to Stella (née Yiangou Kyriakou), a Biochemist, from Famagusta.
CHILDREN: Savvas, Microbiologist; Christos, studying Ecology at UCL; Elena, studying medicine at Kings College.
SCHOOLS/COLLEGE: Willesden College of Technology; Queen Mary College, Imperial College, Univ of London.
ACADEMIC QUALIFICATIONS: B.Sc (Eng), M.Sc (Structr.Eng), DIC (Diploma of Imperial College).
HOBBIES AND INTERESTS: Philatelism, history, classical music, aviation and traditional Greek music.
PERSONAL PROFILE: Principal Lecturer in Structures and Design at University of East London.

Email: c.s.ioannou@ael.ac.uk

DEMETRA (YIAKOUMI) IOANNOU
Director of Haringey Racial Equality Council

DATE OF BIRTH: 12.12.62
PLACE OF BIRTH: London. Father, Andreas Yiakoumi from Komi Kebir; Mother, Loukia from Eftakomi.
MARITAL STATUS: Divorced
CHILDREN: Lucy and Mario.
SCHOOLS/COLLEGE: High Cross Tottenham, CRE Post entry training at Liverpool University.
HOBBIES AND INTERESTS: Football, (Tottenham fan) and most sports.
PERSONAL PROFILE: Director of Haringey Racial Equality Council.

DESPOULLA IOANNOU
Teacher

DATE OF BIRTH: 02.06.78
PLACE OF BIRTH: London. Father from Komi Kebir; Mother from Paralimni.
MARITAL STATUS: Single
SCHOOLS/COLLEGE: Aylward Secondary School, Middlesex University.
ACADEMIC QUALIFICATIONS: BA Honours Art Practice & the Community with Social Policy (First Class Honours); PGCE Art and Design.
HOBBIES AND INTERESTS: Art, travel, health & fitness, music.
PERSONAL PROFILE: Full time teacher and Head of Art and Design (and Textiles), Seven Kings High School. Has worked with young people in the community within the Youth Services and the Social Services.

Email address: despoullaioannou@hotmail.com

JOHN IOANNOU
Actor

DATE OF BIRTH: 27.05.49
PLACE OF BIRTH: Nicosia.
MARITAL STATUS: Single
SCHOOLS/COLLEGE: Alfred Prichard Primary School, City of Bath Boys School, Webber-Douglas Acadamy of Dramatic Art.
ACADEMIC QUALIFICATIONS: A Level Spanish and French.
PROFESSIONAL QUALIFICATIONS: Webber-Douglas Academy of Dramatic Art Diploma.
MEMBERSHIPS: Equity.
HONOURS/AWARDS: Watson Trophy for Solo Acting. The de Reyes Memorial Trophy for Verse Speaking (Bath Mid Somerset Festival).
HOBBIES AND INTERESTS: Reading, individuation
PERSONAL PROFILE: Actor. Played Bartholomew in Franco Zeffirelli's *Jesus of Nazereth*. Only white actor to play Zachariah in Athol Fugard's *The Blood Knot*, for Temba Theatre Co. Was on the Board of Temba Theatre Co. for some 15 years until it closed. Played on TV in *The Bill* and *London's Burning*.

JOHN IOANNOU
Businessman

DATE OF BIRTH: 15.02.61
PLACE OF BIRTH: Nicosia
MARITAL STATUS: Married to Anna (née Papandreou), from Akaki .
CHILDREN: Three children,
SCHOOLS/COLLEGE: American Academy Larnaca, St Marys in Hendon, Barnet college, South Bank Univ.
ACADEMIC QUALIFICATIONS: BSc Honours Electronics, MSc Information Technology.
MEMBERSHIPS: Institute of Electrical & Electronic Engineers.
HONOURS/AWARDS: 2000 award, Deloitte Touche.
HOBBIES AND INTERESTS: Basketball, football, squash and music.
PERSONAL PROFILE: Founder AJP Computers PLC, also own property investment co AJP Investments Ltd, (specialising in serviced office accommodation). AJP Computers won best subnotebook of the year 2002 Award from PC Advisor. Was voted one of the fastest 50 growing IT Companies by Deloitte Touche. Won award for notebooks at the PC Direct Hits Awards (1992, 98, 99 & 2000), also Special Achievement Award for Business 1997. AJP were first to launch an Intel Pentium 200 MH2 Notebook in the UK. Leaders in flatscreen technology. Directors of AJP were semi-finalists in the Entrepreneeur of the Year Awards 2000 from Ernst & Young.

KOULLA IOANNOU
Community Worker

DATE OF BIRTH: 08.12.52
PLACE OF BIRTH: London, father from Chirokitia, Mother from Lefkara.
MARITAL STATUS: Widow
CHILDREN: John, Andrew, Harry, all in full time employment.
SCHOOLS/COLLEGE: Alperton High School Wembley.
ACADEMIC QUALIFICATIONS: O and A levels. Diploma in Sociology. Various community work certificates.
HOBBIES AND INTERESTS: Family, art, history and gardening.
PERSONAL PROFILE: Community Worker. At present manager of Camden Cypriot Womens Organisation. Served on Parent Committees and on Governing bodies of two schools in South London and remains on the advisory body of Wandsworth Education Committee.

KYRIAKOS IOANNOU
Teacher & Chairman of Trypimeni Association

DATE OF BIRTH: 13.09.36
PLACE OF BIRTH: Tripimeni, Famagusta.
MARITAL STATUS: Married to Flori born in London, (parents from Eptakomi).
CHILDREN: John, Tony, Loulla.
SCHOOLS/COLLEGE: English School Nicosia, Morphou Teacher Training College.
HOBBIES AND INTERESTS: Shooting and gardening.
PERSONAL PROFILE: Teacher in Cyprus for 19 yeras. Came to England in 1975, was relief teacher at Mandeville Secondary in Edmonton, then two years in Civil Service. Teaches Greek in Greek Schools in London. In 1988 became a supply teacher for primary schools, and from 1993 teacher at Lea Valley Primary School. Chairman of Trypimeni Association.

MARIA IOANNOU
Teacher

DATE OF BIRTH: 10.05.76
PLACE OF BIRTH: UK.
Father from Komi Kebi; Mother from Paralimni.
MARITAL STATUS: Single
SCHOOLS/COLLEGE: Aylward School, Middlesex University, University of Kent at Canterbury, University of North London.
ACADEMIC QUALIFICATIONS: Foundation course in Art and Design. Sociology BA with Honours. Primary PGCE.
PERSONAL PROFILE: Currently an infant school teacher.

Mr. P. IOANNOU
President of Greek School in Great Yarmouth

DATE OF BIRTH: 01.06.61
PLACE OF BIRTH: Milia
MARITAL STATUS: Married to Maria Georgiou, a hairdresser, from Eptakomi.
CHILDREN: Fortina and Joanna
SCHOOLS/COLLEGE: Milia, Cyprus.
HOBBIES AND INTERESTS: Family, garden and business.
PERSONAL PROFILE: In partnership with wife at restaurant. President Greek School, Treasurer Greek Church, Member of Greek Community Committee in Gt. Yarmouth.

PETER IOANNOU
Businessman

DATE OF BIRTH: 15.02.61
PLACE OF BIRTH: Nicosia
MARITAL STATUS: Married to Yiota (née Kokkinis), from Athienou.
CHILDREN: Three children.
SCHOOLS/COLLEGE: American Academy Larnaca; St Marys Hendon, Barnet College, South Bank University.
ACADEMIC QUALIFICATIONS: BSc Honours Electronics, MSc Information Technology.
HONOURS/AWARDS: 2000 award, Deloitte Touche.
MEMBERSHIPS: Member of Institute of Electrical & Electronic Engineers.
HOBBIES AND INTERESTS: Reading, football and family.
PERSONAL PROFILE: Founder AJP Computers PLC with brother John, also own property investment co AJP Investments Ltd, (specialising in serviced office accommodation). AJP Computers won best subnotebook of the year 2002 Award from PC Advisor. Was voted one of the fastest 50 growing IT Co's by Deloitte Touche. Won award for notebooks at the PC Direct Hits Awards (1992, 98, 99 & 2000), also Special Achievement Award for Business 1997. AJP were first to launch an Intel Pentium 200 MH2 Notebook in the UK. Leaders in flatscreen technology. Directors of AJP were semi-finalists in the Entrepreneur of the Year Awards 2000 from Ernst & Young.

SAVVAS IOANNOU
Businessman & Community Work

DATE OF BIRTH: 22.10.58
PLACE OF BIRTH: Nicosia.
MARITAL STATUS: Married to Evanthia, a Director.
CHILDREN: Louise, at college; Yiannos, at Brunel University.
SCHOOLS/COLLEGE: Grammar School, Nicosia.
HONOURS/AWARDS: Halfords Award for 'Best UK Supplier', Harrow & Brent 'Best Enterprise'.
HOBBIES AND INTERESTS: Regular exercising and International politics.
PERSONAL PROFILE: Managing Chairman of COSMOS group of Companies Ltd. Committee Member of Kingsbury Greek School, and the United Greek Cypriot Aid Organisation.

VASOS ELIA IOANNOU
Accountant

DATE OF BIRTH: 11.01.49
PLACE OF BIRTH: Neon Chorion Kythreas, Nicosia.
MARITAL STATUS: Married to Kika from Agios Andronicos.
CHILDREN: Andreas, Elias, Socrates and Elena.
SCHOOLS/COLLEGE: Pancyprian Gymnasium, Nicosia.
PROFESSIONAL QUALIFICATIONS: Chartered Accountant.
HOBBIES AND INTERESTS: Shooting, Arsenal supporter.
PERSONAL PROFILE: Partner in Ioannou & Co. Chartered Accountants. Director of Intersky Holidays. Director in Investment Property Co. One of the founders of the Cypriot Qualified Accountants Association in UK and was Chairman for two years. Former member of the Queenswell Greek School Committee

GEORGE JACKOS
Actor

DATE OF BIRTH: 25.11.57
PLACE OF BIRTH: Limassol.
MARITAL STATUS: Single
COLLEGE: Haverstock School, E15 Drama School.
HOBBIES AND INTERESTS: Films.
PERSONAL PROFILE: Appeared on TV in *One Last Chance*, *Soldier Soldier*, *The Bill*, *Coronation Street*, *Grafters*, *Sunburn*, *Fools Gold*, *Emmerdale*, *Making Out*, *Professional*, *Bugs*. Films include *Indiana Jones*, *Navy Seals*, *Essex Boys*.

CHRYSI YIANNI JACOB (née KOUSSERTARI)
Senior Lecturer at St Martins School Of Art

DATE OF BIRTH: 14.11.43
PLACE OF BIRTH: Yialousa.
MARITAL STATUS: Married to Christopher Jacob, Computer Manager working at Middlesex University.
CHILDREN: Two daughters, one granddaughter.
SCHOOLS/COLLEGE: Christopher Hutton Primary School, Shoreditch Comprehensive School, St Martins School of Art.
ACADEMIC QUALIFICATIONS: National Diploma in Dress Design.
HOBBIES AND INTERESTS: Walking, swimming, travel and collecting coins.
PERSONAL PROFILE: Senior Lecturer at St Martins School of Art. Responsible for the four year BA Fashion Design and Marketing course. In addition teaches on the Menswear course and has taught many famous students such as Katherine Hamnett, John Galliano and Sade who is now a Jazz singer.

DR STELIOS CONSTANTINOU JOANNIDES
Doctor-Gerontology, Geriatrics

DATE OF BIRTH: 23.01.46
PLACE OF BIRTH: Kaimakli
MARITAL STATUS: Married to Veronica Donnelly from Ireland.
CHILDREN: Costas, Lecturer at University of Hertfordshire; Stavros, Advisor on tissue viability at Huntleigh Healthcare, and Titania, Cambridge graduate and teacher at Hartlington School, Bedfordshire.
SCHOOLS/COLLEGE: Pancyprian Gymnasium Nicosia, UCL London, Bristol Royal Infirmary, Watford General, Great Ormond Street Hospital, Surrey, Herts & Leeds Universities.
QUALIFICATIONS: MBCHA Cert Ed (Leeds); MPhil (Surrey); PhD (Reading); DTMed (UCL).
MEMBERSHIPS: Fellow of the Royal Society of Health; Member of Archaeology Society, Herts.
HONOURS/AWARDS: Winner of the Villis Award (University of Surrey). Centenary Red Cross - Republic of Bulgaria.
HOBBIES AND INTERESTS: Reading, antiques, history, backgammon and photography.
PERSONAL PROFILE: Has written books, articles and essays in many medical magazines. Founder member and Secretary of Kaimakli Association.

COSTAS ANDREOU JOANNOU
Accountancy, Shipping and General Insurance

DATE OF BIRTH: 22.02.56
PLACE OF BIRTH: Agios Epiktitos.
MARITAL STATUS: Married to Elenitsa from Famagusta.
CHILDREN: Andrea, studying English at Queen Marys University London and Panayiota, studying for A Levels.
SCHOOLS/COLLEGE: Kyrenia Gymnasium, Tottenham College of Technology, London School of Economics.
ACADEMIC QUALIFICATIONS: BSc Honours in Management Science.
PROFESSIONAL QUALIFICATIONS: Chartered Certified Accountant.
MEMBERSHIPS: Baltic Exchange and Cypriot Brotherhood.
HOBBIES AND INTERESTS: Swimming, writing, reading, golf and walking.
PERSONAL PROFILE: Vice Chairman and Co Founder of the audit and accountancy firm KOUNNIS AND PARTNERS PLC.
Chairman and Co Founder of CYSTAR Insurance Services Ltd and Group Chairman and founder of Cystar Group Ltd involved in shipping and financial. Executive member of Democratic Rally in UK.

KYRIACOULLA JOANNOU
Makeup Artist

DATE OF BIRTH: 12.05.79
PLACE OF BIRTH: Manchester. Father from Kalopsida; Mother from London
(parents from Komi Kebir and Lefkoniko).
MARITAL STATUS: Single
SCHOOLS/COLLEGE: Hesketh Fletcher, Salford College (Worsley Campus).
QUALIFICATIONS: NVQ Level 2; One year theatrical makeup, hair and beauty.
HOBBIES AND INTERESTS: Music, art and gym.
PERSONAL PROFILE: Makeup artist for four years, photographic work, TV, magazines, newspapers, adverts, corporate videos. Helped out on *Cold Feet, Bloody Foreigners, Rifts*. Has done work for agencies in Manchester, such as PHA, Boss and Model Plan.

CHRIS JOSEPH
Businessman

DATE OF BIRTH: 31.08.45
PLACE OF BIRTH: Larnaca.
MARITAL STATUS: Married to Maria.
CHILDREN: Eleanor, Desi, Andrew and Bobbie.
SCHOOLS/COLLEGE: St Georges, Larnaca.
MEMBERSHIPS: Thalassaemia Society UK.
HONOURS/ADWARDS: From various charities .
HOBBIES AND INTERESTS: Gym, travelling and socialising.
PERSONAL PROFILE: Fashion, properties, hotels. Helped many organisations along with his brother Costas.

MARIA JOSEPH
President of Hadley Wood Cockfosters Conservatives

DATE OF BIRTH: 06.03.47
PLACE OF BIRTH: Agios Amvrosios Kyrenia.
MARITAL STATUS: Married to Chris, a Hotelier, from Larnaca.
CHILDREN: Eleanor, Desi, Andrew and Bobbie.
SCHOOLS/COLLEGE: Barnsbury Central.
MEMBERSHIPS: Conservative Party, Thalassaemia Society, Greek Women's Philanthropic Society, St Katherines Church.
HOBBIES AND INTERESTS: Politics, charities, travelling and grandchildren.
PERSONAL PROFILE: Studied and worked in hairdressing then fashion. Chaired Conservatives in Hadleywood/Cockfosters. Currently president. Maria helps many organisations and charities.

ENTRANTS IN GREEK CYPRIOTS IN THE UK HAVE BEEN NOMINATED FOR THEIR ACHIEVEMENTS AND CONTRIBUTIONS. YOU CAN NOMINATE SOMEONE OR YOURSELF WHO DESERVES TO BE IN THE BOOK. ENTRIES ARE FREE. SEND IN YOUR NOMINATIONS, INCLUDING NAME, CONTACT ADDRESS, TELEPHONE NUMBER AND EMAIL TO GREEK CYPRIOTS IN THE UK 111 ST THOMAS'S ROAD LONDON N4 2QJ TELEPHONE 020 7503 3498 EMAIL cypriotwhoswho@aol.com

ANDREAS S. KACOURIS
Ambassador for the Republic of Cyprus to Ireland

DATE OF BIRTH: 21.07.60
PLACE OF BIRTH: London. Parents from Famagusta.
MARITAL STATUS: Married to Kareen.
CHILDREN: Stephen Matthew and Andreana.
S C H O O L S / C O L L E G E: Buckingham College for Boys, Lancaster University, Carlton University, Ottowa in Canada.
QUALIFICATIONS: BA (Honours) in Politics; MA (International Affairs).
HOBBIES AND INTERESTS: Current affairs.
PERSONAL PROFILE: Ministry of Foreign Affairs for the Republic of Cyprus since 1984; currently Ambassador for the Republic of Cyprus to Ireland.

CHRISTODOULUS S. KACOURIS (Lakis)
Accountant

DATE OF BIRTH: 10.01.73
PLACE OF BIRTH: London. Parents from Famagusta.
MARITAL STATUS: Single.
SCHOOLS/COLLEGE: Merchant Taylor's School; Queen Mary & Westfield, University of London; Lancaster University.
ACADEMIC QUALIFICATIONS: GCSEs/A Levels/ BSc (Honours) Mathematical Sciences/ MBA.
PROFESSIONAL QUALIFICATIONS: Chartered Management Accountant.
MEMBERSHIPS: FCMA (Fellow of Chartered institute of Management Accountants).
HOBBIES AND INTERESTS: Sport (Especially Rugby)
PERSONAL PROFILE: Financial Controller at City Bank. Treasurer/player of London Nigerians Rugby Union Club.

HELEN KACOURIS
Deputy HeadTeacher of Secondary School

DATE OF BIRTH: 16.04.63
PLACE OF BIRTH: London. Parents from Famagusta.
S C H O O L S / C O L L E G E: Peterborough St Margarets School for Girls; Hughes Hall, Cambridge Univerity.
ACADEMIC QUALIFICATIONS: GCEs, O Levels, A Levels, BA (Honours), English/Education.
HOBBIES AND INTERESTS: Sport, travel, theatre and singing.
PERSONAL PROFILE: Secondary School Deputy Headteacher.

ZOE KAKOLYRIS
Artist

DATE OF BIRTH: 16.12.76
PLACE OF BIRTH: London. Father, Panayiotis, owner of Bevelynn food products, from Athens. Mother, Artemis, from Nicosia.
MARITAL STATUS: Single
SCHOOL/COLLEGE: Sir Winston Churchill School for the Deaf in Brighton.
ACADEMIC QUALIFICATIONS: 1 GCSE, Maths
MEMBERSHIPS: Royal National Institute for the Deaf.
HONOURS/AWARDS: Invited to Buckingham Palace by Princess Anne where the National Autistic Society presented to the Princess Royal 'On the Slopes' picture painted by Zoe in recognition of her work with the society.
PERSONAL PROFILE: As a result of strong antibiotics given for strong colds when Zoe was six months old she became deaf although it was not until two and a half years later that the deafness was properly diagnosed. It was not until Zoe was twenty four that the Asperger Syndrome she also suffers from was recognised. Zoe produces extraordinary artwork, full of humour and vitality.

ZOE KAKOLYRIS WHO IS DEAF WAS INVITED TO BUCKINGHAM PALACE BY PRINCESS ANNE WHERE THE NATIONAL AUTISTIC SOCIETY PRESENTED TO THE PRINCESS ROYAL 'ON THE SLOPES' A PICTURE PAINTED BY ZOE IN RECOGNITION OF HER WORK WITH THE SOCIETY

KYRIAKOS KAKKO
Former Chairman Komi Kebir
Association

DATE OF BIRTH: 25.03.28
PLACE OF BIRTH: Komi Kebir.
MARITAL STATUS: Widower.
CHILDREN: Two daughters, one grandson.
HOBBIES AND INTERESTS: Sport and politics.
PERSONAL PROFILE: Came to England in 1955; worked as a Dress Manufacturer, then as a Carpenter. Former Chairman of the Komi Kebir Association and their representative to National Federation of Cypriots in the UK, for 25 years. Still actively involved in the work of the Komi Kebir Association.

MICHAEL KAKOULLIS
Optometrist

DATE OF BIRTH: 26.11.43
PLACE OF BIRTH: Pyla Village, Larnaca.
MARITAL STATUS: Married to Soula (née Seridou), a non-practising Physiotherapist, from Limnia Village, Famagusta.
CHILDREN: Dr Thekli Gee, Registrar in Medical Microbiology (infectious diseases); Miss Irene Kakoullis, university graduate; Dr Alexander Kakoullis, Junior Doctor.
SCHOOLS/COLLEGE: Primary School of Pyla, American Academy, Larnaca, Aston College, Birmingham, Aston University.
ACADEMIC QUALIFICATIONS: BSc Honours in Optometry and Vision Sciences.
PROFESSIONAL QUALIFICATIONS: FBOA, FDMC, DCLP.
MEMBERSHIPS: Michael works with his brother Costa in their family group of practices and as a part time tutor/lecturer to the final year students of Aston University, Vision Sciences Department.

AGATHA KALISPERAS
Director of the Hellenic Centre

DATE OF BIRTH: 06.04.46
PLACE OF BIRTH: Nicosia.
MARITAL STATUS: Divorced
CHILDREN: Costas, an Investment Banker; Leandros, an Investment Banker.
SCHOOLS/COLLEGE: Pancyprian Gymnasium, Nicosia, London University, Surrey University.
ACADEMIC QUALIFICATIONS: BSc (Honours) Psychology, MSc Tourism Management.
MEMBERSHIPS: Institute of Personnel Management.
HOBBIES AND INTERESTS: Opera, theatre, travel and Bridge.
PERSONAL PROFILE: Director of The Hellenic Centre for four years Jan 1997-Jan 2001. Reappointed as Director in April 2003. Justice of the Peace since 1994. School Governor since 2002.

Email: director@helleniccentre.org.

ANDREAS NICOLAS KALISPEARAS
President of North London Greek
Educational Association

DATE OF BIRTH: 18.02.39
PLACE OF BIRTH: Leonarisso, Famagusta.
MARITAL STATUS: Married to Maroulla Costa Michael, a Housewife/Teacher of Greek language in the community schools, from Ayios Elias, Famagusta.
CHILDREN: Militsa, Stevi, Nicholas.
SCHOOLS/COLLEGE: Rizokarpasso Greek Gym-nasium, Laura College, Clapton E5.
ACADEMIC QUALIFICATIONS: Cyprus Certificate Of Education, English, Maths A & B and Geography, Certificate Grade Credit.
PROFESSIONAL QUALIFICATIONS: Bookeeping and Accountancy.
PERSONAL PROFILE: 1970-2000 owned own company making tents and caravan awnings. From 1995 has been working for Haringey Council in the social services department as an emergency response officer dealing with the elderly and special needs. In 1979 became a member of the North London Cypriot Association and Assistant Treasurer in 1980, running 10 Greek Community Schools in North London. In 1990 was elected President of the Association, which is now called the North London Greek Educational Association and is a registered charity. Through the Association he has become a board member of the Cypriot Community Centre, Vice-President of OESEKA, and also a member of EFEPE in Great Britain.

MARIO KALLI
Actor

DATE OF BIRTH: 24.02.66
PLACE OF BIRTH: London. Parents from Yialousa and Lefkoniko.
MARITAL STATUS: Married to Jenny. Father from Paphos.
CHILDREN: Natasha and Daniella.
SCHOOLS/COLLEGE: Bognor Regis Comprehensive School. Academy of Live and Recorded Arts.
PERSONAL PROFILE: Professional actor since 1987. Appeared in plays in the Sheffield Crucible, Edinburgh Theatre Royal. Appeared on TV in *The Bill, Lock Stock, Second Sight, Casualty*. In Commercial for W.H. Smith with Nicholas Lyndhurst.

MICHAEL KALLI
Footballer

DATE OF BIRTH: 24.06.80
PLACE OF BIRTH: London. Grandparents from Yialousa, Leonarisso
MARITAL STATUS: Single.
SCHOOLS/COLLEGE: St. Andrews, Ashmole, University of Luton.
ACADEMIC QUALIFICATIONS: BA Honours in Politics.
PROFESSIONAL QUALIFICATIONS: Eight caps for England University football team.
HOBBIES AND INTERESTS: Football Tottenham FC, Goalkeeper and socialising,
PERSONAL PROFILE: Plays football for Wingate Finchley FC, and has also played for Enfield FC. Has represented Britain against the National Game Eleven. Played for Watford, Portsmouth, Cambridge, Liverpool and Southend Youth.
Represented England Universities in the Great Britain Games in 2001.

GEORGE KALLIS
Musician

DATE OF BIRTH: 29.11.74
PLACE OF BIRTH: Nicosia.
MARITAL STATUS: Single
SCHOOLS/COLLEGE: Berkley College of Music (Boston), Royal College of Music (London).
QUALIFICATIONS: MMus in Composition for Screen, BMus in Composition, BMus in Film Scoring Composer/Songwriter/Producer PRS MCPS.
HOBBIES & INTERESTS: Music.
PERSONAL PROFILE: 2000 Scored the music for a production play *Iphigenia in Aulis*, London UK. Composed and arranged entry for the Eurovision Song Contest 1999.
Extensive experience in Computer Programming using MIDI and Hard Disk Recording.

GEORGE KALLIS
Chairman of St John the Baptist Greek Orthodox Church

DATE OF BIRTH: 13.03.29
PLACE OF BIRTH: Labathos.
MARITAL STATUS: Married to Maroulla.
CHILDREN: Jack, Antonis, both accountants in Cyprus, Panayiotis, a heart surgeon.
HOBBIES AND INTERESTS: Politics, Anorthosis FC.
PERSONAL PROFILE: .Involved with St. John the Baptist Greek Church Wightman Road, 18 years treasurer, then Chairman. Member of Labathos Association.

KIKIS KALLIS
Accountant

DATE OF BIRTH: 12.08.51
PLACE OF BIRTH: Lapathos.
MARITAL STATUS: Married to Eleni from Komi Kebir.
CHILDREN: Sophia and Tania.
SCHOOLS/COLLEGE: Tricomo Gymnasium.
QUALIFICATIONS: Certified Accountant.
MEMBERSHIPS: Cypriot Golf Society, Brocket Hall Golf Club, David Lloyds.
HOBBIES AND INTERESTS: Golf, tennis, shooting and travelling.
PERSONAL PROFILE: An Accountant, has own practice Kallis & Co, specialising in Insolvency, Office in Whetstone.

PANAYIOTIS KALLIS
Consultant Cardiac Surgeon

DATE OF BIRTH: 1959
PLACE OF BIRTH: Lapathos.
MARITAL STATUS: Married to Sophia, from London (parents from Karavas).
CHILDREN: Georgio.
SCHOOLS/COLLEGE: William Ellis School. University College Hospital, Medical School.
ACADEMIC QUALIFICATIONS: BSc (Honours) MB BS (Honours) FRCS MS.
MEMBERSHIPS: Fellow of the Royal College of Surgeons, British Cardiac Society.
HOBBIES AND INTERESTS: Tennis and golf.
PERSONAL PROFILE: Consultant Cardiac Surgeon at the Middlesex Hospital. Also based at 88 Harley St, London W1N 1AE Tel: 020 7255 1895

EVI KALODIKI
Research Fellow On Vascular Surgery

DATE OF BIRTH: 10.01.56
PLACE OF BIRTH: Nicosia.
MARITAL STATUS: Single
SCHOOLS/COLLEGE: Larnaca High School, University of Athens, Medical School, University of Athens, Imperial College, London..
ACADEMIC QUALIFICATIONS: 1979, Medical Graduation (Athens); 1982, MD Thesis "Honours", University Of Athens, 1984, BA English Literature, University of Athens, 1996, PhD Thesis, University Of London, 1997, DIC Diploma Of Imperial College.
PROFESSIONAL QUALIFICATIONS: Certificate in Vascular Surgery, Diploma of Specialisation in General Surgery.
MEMBERSHIPS: Surgical Research Society of GB and Ireland, European Society for Vascular Research, Hellenic Medical Society, UK, The Hellenic Society of Professional People & Scientists in GB (President), The Friends of the University of Cyprus. Trustee in theDiaspora Centre, The Hellenic Centre
HOBBIES AND INTERESTS: Reading, theatre and travelling.
PERSONAL PROFILE: Research Fellow on vascular surgery; involved in cultural (non-political) activities.

ALEXANDRA KALYMNIOS
Film Director

DATE OF BIRTH: 08.01.80
PLACE OF BIRTH: London. Father from Piraeus, Greece; Mother, from Nicosia, Cyprus.
MARITAL STATUS: Single
SCHOOL/COLLEGES: The Latymer School, Edmonton, London; Bournemouth University.
ACADEMIC QUALIFICATIONS: BA (Honours) Television and Video Production, 2:1, A Levels - Media Studies, English, Maths, Modern Greek, 11 GCSEs, RSM in music and RAD in dance.
PROFESSIONAL QUALIFICATIONS: BBC Training includes: Researching for TV, DSR500 Camera Course, DV XPress Editing Course, Drama Directing.
MEMBERSHIPS: Member of the British Academy of Television and Film (BAFTA).
HONOURS/AWARDS: Awarded funding for script *More than a Job's Worth* from Enfield Film Council. Best New Director Award, Greenwich Film Festival.
HOBBIES & INTERESTS: Travelling, music, art, dance, theatre, film, video, sport and physical training.
PERSONAL PROFILE: Television researcher at the BBC. Over the past six years directed and produced short films, professional corporate videos, written and directed for the Children's BBC programme *Stitch Up*. Completed director training programme in Children's BBC Drama.

MARIA KALYMNIOS (née TSIANIDOU)
Teacher

DATE OF BIRTH: 23.01.51
PLACE OF BIRTH: Kaimakli, Nicosia.
MARITAL STATUS: Married to Dr. D Kalymnios, a Physicist - Scientist, Lecturer at London Metropolitan University, from Greece.
CHILDREN: Triada, Lawyer; Harilaos, first class degree in Physics and Astrophysics; Alexandra, TV/Video producer.
SCHOOLS/COLLEGE: Primary School Cyprus, Tollington Park Secondary, Hull University.
QUALIFICATIONS: Master of Arts in Education, University of London) Certificate in Education - University of Hull. Diploma in Education, University of London.
HOBBIES AND INTERESTS: Arts, music, sport and travel.
PERSONAL PROFILE: Teacher in mainstream schools, Advisory and Support Teacher, Co-ordinator of Primary and Secondary Schools (Head of Bilingual & Home-School project in Barnet - Helped & taught for 25 years on a voluntary basis at the Greek Community Schools in North London. Secretary of the North London Greek Educational Association (voluntary).

Email address: Mary@woodlandway.u-net.com

TRIADA KALYMNIOS
Law & Music

DATE OF BIRTH: 10.04.75
PLACE OF BIRTH: Beverley, Yorkshire, England. Father from Greece; Mother from Kaimakli Nicosia.
MARITAL STATUS: Single
SCHOOLS/COLLEGE: Belmont Junior school, London; Latymer Secondary School; University of Sussex (plus one year Law School in London).
QUALIFICATIONS: Bachelor of Law with Honours LLB European Commercial Law with French. Diploma de Droit Francais; Law Society BAC 1 + 11 - Russian.
HONOURS/AWARDS: Grade V in violin and piano; Grade III in flute.
HOBBIES AND INTERESTS: Scuba diving, sailing, snowboarding and music. Travelled extensively (one year travelling around the world) including USA, Asia, Australia and Europe.
PERSONAL PROFILE: Works in West End law firm and writes for various legal publications.

COSTAS KALYVIDES
Solicitor

DATE OF BIRTH: 05.06.58
PLACE OF BIRTH: London. Father from Kyrenia; Mother from Larnaca.
MARITAL STATUS: Married to Maria (née Gabriel), a Legal Executive, born in London of Greek Cypriot parents.
CHILDREN: Emilios Costi and Efthymia.
SCHOOLS/COLLEGE: Norfolk House Prep School North London; Langley School, Norfolk; Staffordshire University; Chester College of Law.
QUALIFICATIONS: Solicitor's finals and Law Degree BA (Honours) Law.
MEMBERSHIPS: Law Society,
HOBBIES AND INTERESTS: Opera and the arts.
PERSONAL PROFILE: Solicitor.

DR ANDREAS DEMETRI KANARIS
Honorary Commissioner for the Republic of Cyprus in Manchester

DATE OF BIRTH: 23.05.28
PLACE OF BIRTH: Piyi.
MARITAL STATUS: Married to Vivi from Greece.
CHILDREN: Antigoni, Demetris, Maria, Leonidas and Vera.
SCHOOLS/COLLEGE: Pancyprian Gymnasium, Manchester University.
ACADEMIC QUALIFICATIONS: BSc, PhD.
HOBBIES AND INTERESTS: Travel, reading and community affairs.
PERSONAL PROFILE: Instructor of Physics at Manchester University. Several research publications in physics journals. Honorary Commissioner for the Republic of Cyprus in Manchester since 1980. Former Chairman of Hellenic Brotherhood in Manchester and Greek Orthodox Community of Manchester.

MICHAEL KANIAS
Actor

DATE OF BIRTH: 18.03.66
PLACE OF BIRTH: London. Father from Yialousa; Mother from Tavros.
MARITAL STATUS: Single
SCHOOLS/COLLEGE: Winns Infant and Junior School, William McGuffie and Sir George Monoux School.
ACADEMIC QUALIFICATIONS: 4 GCE NVQ Level 3 in I.T.
MEMBERSHIPS: Equity.

PERSONAL PROFILE: Actor. Cameo in Fifth Element; Sooty show with Matthew Corbett. Photographic modelling. Also an events manager

COSTAS KAOUNIDES
Co Founder and First General Secretary of Omonia FC, Cyprus

DATE OF BIRTH: 06.08.24
PLACE OF BIRTH: Assia
MARITAL STATUS: Married to Beatrice, born in New York, Cypriot origin.
CHILDREN: Lakis, Lecturer at Queen Mary University; Carolina, Editor English section, *Parikiaki* Newspaper; Monica, Housewife.
SCHOOL/COLLEGE: English School, Nicosia.
MEMBERSHIPS: Executive Committee of Cypriot football league in England for several years.
PERSONAL PROFILE: Co founder and first General Secretary of Omonia FC, Cyprus. Also, co founder of Omonia Fc London and Honorary President.
Journalist for Haravgi, Cyprus, for several years and now journalist for Parikiaki Newspaper, London.

EVI PAPALOIZOU KAPLANIS
Former Associate Professor of Finance

DATE OF BIRTH: 30.12.58
PLACE OF BIRTH: Nicosia.
MARITAL STATUS: Married to Dr. Costas Kaplanis from Nicosia, ex-Investment Banker.
CHILDREN: One son, one daughter, both at school.
SCHOOLS/COLLEGE: London School of Economics, London Business School.
ACADEMIC QUALIFICATIONS: B.Sc (Econ), M.Sc, Ph.D (Lon).
HOBBIES AND INTERESTS: History of Art.
PERSONAL PROFILE: Former Associate Professor of Finance, London Business School, University of London.

MICHAEL KARAGEORGIS
Restaurateur

DATE OF BIRTH: 12.07.31
PLACE OF BIRTH: Lefkonico, Cyprus.
MARITAL STATUS: Married to Panayiota from Lefkonico.
CHILDREN: Miranda, Kyriakos, Ourania.
SCHOOLS/COLLEGE: High School at Lefkonico.
PROFESSIONAL QUALIFICATIONS: Caterer.
PERSONAL PROFILE: Co owner of Elyzee Restaurant in the West End.

ELLI KARAGEORGE
Treasurer of Greek School in Coventry

DATE OF BIRTH: 24.10.60
PLACE OF BIRTH: Coventry., Grandparents from Larnaca.
MARITAL STATUS: Married to Tasos Karageorge, a self-employed Fish Shop Owner, from Mazotos, Larnaca.
CHILDREN: Costas, Michael, Anna and Nicholas.
SCHOOLS/COLLEGE: Mazotos Elementary, American Academy, Larnaca; Leicester College.
HOBBIES AND INTERESTS: Art and design, Floristry, Music-Greek and English, Religion, Helping members at Greek School.
PERSONAL PROFILE: Housewife, mother and Shopworker with 20 members of staff. Served as member of Greek School Committee for over 10 years as Treasurer.

DR. COSTAS I. KARAGEORGHIS
University Lecturer

DATE OF BIRTH: 15.09.69
PLACE OF BIRTH: London. Parents from Anaphotia, Larnaca.
MARITAL STATUS: Married to Tina Suzanne, from Kent.
CHILDREN: Anastasia Elizabeth, Lucia Philomena, both at school.
SCHOOLS/COLLEGE: Langley Park School, Brunel University, United States Sports Academy (Daphne, Alabama)
ACADEMIC QUALIFICATIONS: PhD in Psychology; MSc in Sport Psychology; BA Honours in Sport Science and Music; certificates in clinical hypnotherapy and counselling.
PROFESSIONAL QUALIFICATIONS: UK Athletics Level three perfomances coach; Guildhall School of Music - Grade 8 Pianoforte, Grade 8 music theory; accredited sports psychologist.
MEMBERSHIPS: British Olympic Association Psychology Advisory Group.
HONOURS AND AWARDS: 1998 BASES Prize for Best Sport Psychology Presentation at Annual Conference. Awarded in excess of £200,000 in research funding as principal investigator.
HOBBIES AND INTERESTS: Athletics, music and international politics.
PERSONAL PROFILE: Senior Lecturer at Brunel University (2000 to present). Reviewer for five international academic journals. Secretary of Greek School at St Mary's Cathedral, Camberwell.

ODYSSEAS KARAGEORGIS
Chairman of Lefkonico Association

DATE OF BIRTH: 28.10.33
PLACE OF BIRTH: Lefkoniko.
MARITAL STATUS: Married to Jovanka.
CHILDREN: Kyriakos, Economics graduate from UCL; Alexander, studying Modern Languages at UCL; Christopher, at Westminster School.
SCHOOLS/COLLEGE: Lefkoniko High School; Famagusta Gymnasium; Battersea College of Advanced Technology (graduated in 1958) Affiliated to London University, later Surrey University.
ACADEMIC QUALIFICATIONS: Dip Electrical Engineering.
PROFESSIONAL QUALIFICATIONS: Chartered Electrical Engineer; MIEE.
HOBBIES AND INTERESTS: Reading, volleyball, athletics; Famagusta Gymnasium 400m record-holder.
PERSONAL PROFILE: First worked with GEC specializing in microwave equipment, then joined Research and Development Laboratories of STL (Standard Telephone Labs); and later on Fibre Optics at STL. Pioneered the automatic landings of aircraft, worked on classified and NASA Projects specializing on Aircraft Horn Aerials. 1971 offered the position of Chief Engineer in Cyta, Cyprus. Was a founder member of EFEKA, and Secretary of the Hellenic Society, University of London, 1956-58. Chairman of EFEKA 1958-60. Current Chairman of Lefkoniko Association UK, and first Chairman of the University of London Volleyball Association. Director of the renowned Greek restaurant Elyzee in London's West End.

HELEN KARAMALLAKIS
Teacher

DATE OF BIRTH: 20.03.62
PLACE OF BIRTH: London. Father from Nicosia, mother from Ora.
MARITAL STATUS: Married to Michael Davis, an English Science Teacher, for 9 years.
CHILDREN: Twins: Katerina and Christopher; Sophia.
SCHOOLS/COLLEGE: Winchmore School, London University, Chelsea College, Oxford University, Keble College.
ACADEMIC QUALIFICATIONS: 7 O Levels, 3 A Levels, BSc Biology.
PROFESSIONAL QUALIFICATIONS: PGCE Science Education.
HOBBIES AND INTERESTS: Film, music, cooking, eating out, gardening and the enviroment.
PERSONAL PROFILE: Teacher, previous posts at Manor Hill School, East Barnet; Queen Elizabeth Boys; then Winchmore School. Now teaches science to beauty therapy students at the London School of Fashion.

NICHOLAS KARANICHOLAS
Martial Arts Champion

DATE OF BIRTH: 26.10.86
PLACE OF BIRTH: London. Father from Kato Varosi; Mother from Limassol.
MARITAL STATUS: Single
SCHOOLS/COLLEGE: Loyola Prep School (Buck-hurst Hill Essex), Davenant Foundation Sports College.
ACADEMIC QUALIFICATIONS: GCSE in Greek when 14 years old, Bronze Prize in National (UK) Maths test at 13.
MEMBERSHIPS: Shikon UK, Squad member C.P.S.A.
HONOURS/AWARDS: Kumite-Fighting, Kata- Exhibition of Style. Won several awards, both National and Junior Championships for that style, most notably the 2000 World Championship at Glasgow, and the 2001 London Youth Games at Crystal Palace.
HOBBIES AND INTERESTS: Football, rugby, dance, shooting, drumming, drama and music.
PERSONAL PROFILE: Student studying for GCSEs. Teaches part time Karate. In 1998, selected to join Saracen Rugby Club (did not take up offer due to Karate commitments).

ELENI KARAOLI
Education Co-ordinator

DATE OF BIRTH: 28.09.50
PLACE OF BIRTH: Famagusta.
MARITAL STATUS: Married To Christaki an Office Manager at Big K Charcoal Merchants.
CHILDREN: Stylianos, BSc MSc, and Louis.
SCHOOLS/COLLEGE: Famagusta Girls Gymnasium, Alexandra Park.
PROFESSIONAL QUALIFICATIONS: BEd Teaching qualification.
MEMBERSHIPS: The Institute of Linguists, North London Schools Network.
HOBBIES AND INTERESTS: Theatre, Greek music and travel.
PERSONAL PROFILE: Examiner for the Institute of Linguists. Head of Greek at the centre of Bilingualism, Chair of Co-ordinating Committee for GCSE and A Level Greek. Teacher and Head Teacher of Finchley Independent Greek School 1994-1999. Monthly column in Eleftheria Newspaper Co-ordinator of European School Projects; International Links Officer.

ANDREAS CHRISTOU KARAOLIS
Executive Secretary of the National Federation of Cypriots and Greek Cypriot Brotherhood

DATE OF BIRTH: 20.12.39
PLACE OF BIRTH: Morphou, Cyprus.
MARITAL STATUS: Married to Mary Helen Karaolis (née Pallicaros) from Rizokarpasso, born in London. Headteacher at The Ravenscroft School.
CHILDREN: Christos, studying Law at Trinity College, Oxford; Gregory, studying Natural Sciences at Christ's College, Cambridge; George, studying A-Levels at Queen Elizabeth's School.
SCHOOL/COLLEGES: Greek Gymnasium of Morphou, Pedagogical Academy, Nicosia, Cyprus. Birbeck College, London.
QUALIFICATIONS: Diploma, Pedagogical Academy. BA Classical Greek, Birbeck College.
MEMBERSHIPS: Digenis Akritas, Morphou Football Club Greek Cypriot Brotherhood, Theatro Technis.
HOBBIES & INTERESTS: Politics, reading, football, chess and backgammon.
PERSONAL PROFILE: Executive Secretary, National Federation of Cypriots and Greek Cypriot Brotherhood, 1981 – present. Organised and participated in seminars and other functions to promote the just cause of Cyprus in the UK and Europe. Teacher at Manor Hill Greek School, 1991 – present. Initiated the twinning of Morphou with Barnet, 1995 Teacher at Baufoy School and South Bank Institute, 1974 – 1979. Hood Centre, Adult Educational Institute, 1976 – 1981. Headteacher-Coordinator, Greek Schools North London Cypriot Assn, 1972 – 1981. Teacher at Hendon Greek School, 1972 – 1981. Cyprus Educational Mission member, 1969 – 1972. General Secretary, Committee Development of Morphou, 1965 – 1969. Initiated Digenis Akritas' participation in the Cyprus football league, 1966.

MARY HELEN KARAOLIS HEADTEACHER OF RAVENSCROFT COMPREHENSIVE SCHOOL IN BARNET

LOUIS KARAOLIS
Athletics School and County Champion

DATE OF BIRTH: 05.08.83
PLACE OF BIRTH: Enfield, London. Father from Morphou. Mother from Famagusta.
MARITAL STATUS: Single
SCHOOLS/COLLEGE: Keeble Prep School, St Albans Secondary School, Woodhouse College, Premier Training and Development College.
ACADEMIC QUALIFICATIONS: 11 GCSEs A-B, 3 AS's
PROFESSIONAL QUALIFCATIONS: Studying for Diploma in Personal Training.
MEMBERSHIPS: Haringey & Enfield Athletics Club, Lloyds Fitness Club.
HONOURS/AWARDS: Silver medal in 4 x 400-metre relay in Cyprus Youth Games 2002.
HOBBIES AND INTERESTS: Basketball, tennis, reading and sports literature.
PERSONAL PROFILE: School and county champion in 200 and 400-metre running. Currently sports massage therapist.

MARY HELEN KARAOLIS (née PALLICAROS)
Head Teacher

DATE OF BIRTH: 04.05.47
PLACE OF BIRTH: London. Father, Gregory Pallicaros from Sisklypos; Mother, Andriana Hajiyiangou from Rizokarpasso.
MARITAL STATUS: Married to Andreas Karaolis, Executive Secretary of the National Federation of Cypriots and Executive Secretary of the Greek Cypriot Brotherhood, born in Morphou.
CHILDREN: Christos, Gregory, George, all attending Queen Elizabeth's Grammar School for Boys.
SCHOOLS/COLLEGE: Morpeth Comprehensive School, Head Girl & House Captain, University of London Institute of Education, London School of Economics University of London, London Leadership Centre.
PROFESSIONAL QUALIFICATIONS: Bachelor of Education, Master of Arts Degree, National Professional Qualification for Headship.
MEMBERSHIPS: Greek-Cypriot Brotherhood, National Association of Head Teachers, Amnesty International.
HOBBIES AND INTERESTS: Community affairs, reading, current affairs, walking, gardening, chess and backgammon.
PERSONAL PROFILE: Headteacher of Ravenscroft Comprehensive School; Member of Barnet LEA Asset Management Plan Steering Committee; Member of Barnet LEA SEN Consultative Committee; previously examiner for GCSE Economics and Business Studies; previously Parent-Governor on the governing body of Moss Hall Infant and Junior Schools.

PANAYIOTIS PANTELIS (PETER) KARATAOS
Psychologist

DATE OF BIRTH: 02.02.60
PLACE OF BIRTH: Manchester. Parents from Famagusta.
SCHOOLS/COLLEGE: University of Bradford: School of Psychology; University of Manchester: Faculty of Medicine.
ACADEMIC QUALIFICATIONS: B.Sc (Honours) Psychology; MSc Clinical Psychology.
PROFESSIONAL QUALIFICATIONS: C.Clin.Psychol.; AFBPS.
PERSONAL PROFILE: Consultant Clinical Psychologist & Head of Psychological Services, King Edward VII Hospital, Windsor. Consultant Clinical Psychologist & Head of Child and Adolescent Psychology, East Berkshire Healthcare NHS Trust. Consultant Clinical Psychologist, North London Nuffield Hospital. Director, Blackhill Healthcare Ltd.

COSTAS KARAVIAS
Businessman

DATE OF BIRTH: 31.07.55
PLACE OF BIRTH: Kyrenia
MARITAL STATUS: Married To Voulla from Nicosia.
CHILDREN: Nadia, Anthia, and Stephanos.
SCHOOLS/COLLEGE: Woodgreen School, Southgate College.
HOBBIES AND INTERESTS: Tennis, (Man Utd Fan).
PERSONAL PROFILE: Started own company called the WH Group, Manufacturer of Computer and furniture systems employing 120 people Sold the company in 1998, then bought it back in 2001. Sold the computer side and has the furniture systems side.

THOMAS ELIAS KARAVIS
Architect

DATE OF BIRTH: 20.11.55
PLACE OF BIRTH: Britain. Parents and Grandparents from Karavas, Kyrenia.
MARITAL STATUS: Married To Mareanthe. Father from Ayios Dometios, Nicosia; Mother from Lagoudera, Nicosia.
CHILDREN: Alexia, at Henrietta Barnet School; Sofia, at Our Lady of Lourdes School.
SCHOOLS/COLLEGE: Kykko Gymnasium, Nicosia The English School Nicosia; University of Westminster London. (formerly PCL).
QUALIFICATIONS: BA (Honours), Dip Arch, RIBA.
HONOURS/AWARDS: Winner of the Sir Bannister Fletcher best student thesis at final diploma year; winner of AD Best UK Design Project.
HOBBIES AND INTERESTS: Travel, photography, aviation, technology and reading.
PERSONAL PROFILE: Architect. Currently Project Architect on the Interamerican Headquarters in Athens.

ELLI KARAVOKYRI
Former Secretary of Cypriots Women's League

DATE OF BIRTH: 18.05.22
PLACE OF BIRTH: Famagusta.
MARITAL STATUS: Widow of Panayiotis Karavokyri, a Civil Servant, from Famagusta.
CHILDREN: Alkistis Christodoulou, 55, a Housewife.
SCHOOLS/COLLEGE: The Greek Gymnasium, Famagusta.
PROFESSIONAL QUALIFICATIONS: Social Security Advisor.
MEMBERSHIPS: AKEL, Cypriot Womens League.
HOBBIES AND INTERESTS: Politics.
PERSONAL PROFILE: Worked with the Camden Cypriot Womens Organisations, under L.B. of Camdens Social Sevices, for the needs of elderly people. Served as the Secretary of C.W.L., for twelve years. Served as a member of AKEL's London District Committee for 22 years.

CHRISTOS ANTONY KARAYIANNIS
President of Mandres Association

DATE OF BIRTH: 1.10.46.
PLACE OF BIRTH: Cyprus (Mandres)
MARITAL STATUS: Married to Carol, a Creche Assistant, from England.
CHILDREN: Antony, a Tube Driver; Lisa, a Business Systems Training Officer; Julie, IT Recruitment Consultant.
HOBBIES AND INTERESTS: Gardening, snooker and golf.
PERSONAL PROFILE: Builder and President of Mandres Village Association.

JOHN KARAYIANNIS
Architect

DATE OF BIRTH: 17.07.60
PLACE OF BIRTH: London. Father, Savvas, from Mandres, Cyprus; Mother, Vassiliki from Chirokitia, Cyprus.
MARITAL STATUS: Married To Sandra, (nee Bennett), a Physiotherapist, from the UK, of English descent.
CHILDREN: Sophia and Louisa
SCHOOLS/COLLEGE: Latymer Upper School, University of Westminster (formerly Polytechnic of Central London), University of Strathclyde.
QUALIFICATIONS: BA (Honours), Dip Arch, MSc, RIBA.
PERSONAL PROFILE: Architect, running a small practice.

Email: jk@mailbox.co.uk

PETROS KARAYIANNIS
Senior Reader in Molecular Virology, Imperial College of Science, London

DATE OF BIRTH: 31.07.51
PLACE OF BIRTH: Famagusta,
MARITAL STATUS: Married To Maria from Kyrenia.
CHILDREN: Nicholas, Stiliana and Georgios.
SCHOOLS/COLLEGE: 1st Gymnasium for Boys, Famagusta, Cyprus. Waltham Forest Technical College, University of Liverpool, Department of Microbiology.
ACADEMIC QUALIFICATIONS: BSc in Microbiology (1976) PhD in Microbiology (1980).
MEMBERSHIPS: Fellow of the Institute of Biomedical Sciences (FIBMS) 1987 - to present; Society for General Microbiology; European Association for the Study of the Liver; Fellow of the Royal College of Pathologists.
HOBBIES AND INTERESTS: Squash, swimming, gardening and stamp collecting.

PERSONAL PROFILE: Research work interests are concerned with the study of molecular biology of the hepatitis viruses. Petros leads a research team of five scientists, who are studying the mechanism of viral persistence (ie. Chronic infection) and how viruses avoid the host's immune response.

SAVVAS KARAYIANNIS
Chairman of Kingston Greek Orthodox Church

DATE OF BIRTH: 1926
PLACE OF BIRTH: Mandres - Famagusta.
MARITAL STATUS: Married To Vassiliki (Frangou), from Chirokitia.
CHILDREN: Akis, an Economist Banker; John, an Architect.
SCHOOLS/COLLEGE: Lefkonico High School, University of London Goldsmith College.
PROFESSIONAL QUALIFICATIONS: Teacher's Certificate.
PERSONAL PROFILE: Voluntary work and contribution for the advancement of political, Social Welfare and Educational aims of the Hellenic Community in the UK. Chairman of Kingston Greek Orthodox Church.

TASSOS GEORGIOU KARAYIANNIS
Professor of Engineering at South Bank University

DATE OF BIRTH: 24.01.57
PLACE OF BIRTH: Kato Zodhia.
MARITAL STATUS: Married to Elena Karayiannis, a Deputy Branch Manager, Cyprus Popular Bank, from Kato Zodhia.
CHILDREN: George
SCHOOLS/COLLEGE: The English School, Nicosia; City University, London; The University of Western Ontario, Canada.
ACADEMIC QUALIFICATIONS: BSC (Honours) Mechanical Engineering, phD Mechanical Engineering.
PROFESSIONAL QUALIFICATIONS: Chartered Engineer.
MEMBERSHIPS: Institute of Mechanical Engineers, The Institute of Refrigeration, Chartered Institution of Building Services Engineers
HONOURS\AWARDS: Archbishop Makarios III Scholarship 1978-1981 (to study at City University), Special University Scholarship, 1981-1985, University of Western Ontario, Canada
HOBBIES AND INTERESTS: Greek Literature and tennis.
PERSONAL PROFILE: Professor of Engineering, Head of Division of Environmental, Energy and Building Services Engineering South Bank University.

NICOLAS KARROUS
Chairman of the Lefkara Association

DATE OF BIRTH: 17.07.45
PLACE OF BIRTH: London. Parents from Lefkara.
MARITAL STATUS: Married to Elenitsa, a Dressmaker, from Kato Drys.
CHILDREN: Katerina, Hairdresser; Costandina, Secretary; Haralambos, Computer Technician.
SCHOOLS/COLLEGE: Ackland Burleigh in Tufnell Park, Barnet College.
QUALIFICATIONS: Mechanical Engineering, pattern & design. RSA Bookkeeping & Accounting.
PERSONAL PROFILE: Started in engineering then moved onto the fashion trade and ran his own business. Currently working as a self-employed bookkeeper. Chairman of the LEFKARA Assoc GB.

KYRIACOS GARY KARSA
Football

DATE OF BIRTH: 15.09.61
PLACE OF BIRTH: London. Father from Rizorkarpaso; Mother from Peristeropiyi.
MARITAL STATUS: Married to Bobbie, a Pre-school Teacher, (parents from Kontea).
CHILDREN: Rebecca and George, both at school.
SCHOOLS/COLLEGE: Highbury Grove Comprehensive School, 1972-1978, Southgate Technical College, Central College for Physical Recreation. College of North East London.
ACADEMIC QUALIFICATIONS: 5 O Levels, English Language, English Literature, Maths, Art, Modern Greek.
PROFESSIONAL QUALIFICATIONS: FA Advance. Coaching Licence UEFA 'A' Coaching Award.
MEMBERSHIPS: The Football Association Coaches Association.
HOBBIES AND INTERESTS: Football and sport development in general. Reading and writing.
PERSONAL PROFILE: Previously with Barnet FC and Charlton FC; now with Orient FC, in charge of the Youth Academy.

MICHAEL KASHIS
Head Teacher/Politics

DATE OF BIRTH: 16.07.40
PLACE OF BIRTH: Neochorio Kythrea, Cyprus.
MARITAL STATUS: Married to Maria, an ex-Consular Officer, from Cyprus.
CHILDREN: Kypros, Teacher; Costas, Bank Officer; Agathoclis, Solicitor.
SCHOOLS/COLLEGE: Elementary - Neochorio - Cyprus, Pancyprian Gymnasium - Nicosia Cyprus, Teachers' Training College Cyprus, University of Edinburgh.
QUALIFICATIONS: - Diploma, University of London - MA Phil. Teacher/Headteacher/Advisory Teacher, Chief Examiner - Greek Language, ULEAC.
MEMBERSHIPS: National Federation of Cypriots in UK.
HOBBIES AND INTERESTS: Literature, gardening, Byzantine music.
PERSONAL PROFILE: Secretary of POED (Teachers Trade Union, Cyprus) 1973-1980. Currently Secretary of EDEK UK.

FATHER IACOVOS KASINOS
Priest

DATE OF BIRTH: 10.06.40
PLACE OF BIRTH: Ypsonas Limassol.
MARITAL STATUS: Married to Irini from Lefkara.
CHILDREN: Two sons and one daughter.
SCHOOLS/COLLEGE: Limmasol Greek Gymnasium Lanition.
HOBBIES AND INTERESTS: Religion and gardening.
PERSONAL PROFILE: Started as Deacon at Liverpool then Theological school in Cyprus for one year. Later ordained Priest at Greek Orthodox Church of St. Nicolas, Liverpool.

Dr. GEORGE KASSIANOS
General Practitioner

DATE OF BIRTH: 30.09.48
PLACE OF BIRTH: Lyssi, Famagusta.
MARITAL STATUS: Married To Karen a nurse by profession, born in Canada by British Parents.
CHILDREN: Alexis, studying Medicine; Nicholas, doing A Levels; Julian, at school.
SCHOOLS/COLLEGE: Nicosia Gymnasium, Zographos Grammar, Athens. Lodz Medical Academy Poland 1968-74 with a scholarship from the International Union of Students (1967).
ACADEMIC QUALIFICATIONS: MD Honours, LRCS (Edin) FRCGP, MILT, DRCOG, LRCP (Edin).
MEMBERSHIPS: Member Primary Cave Cardio-vascular Society, Member of the British Hypertension Society.
HONOURS/AWARDS: Doctor of the year Award, British Migraine Association, 1st research prize Medical Academy LODZ.
HOBBIES AND INTERESTS: Reading, gardening and music.
PERSONAL PROFILE: General Practitioner Bracknell. Appeared on TV, *Watchdog*, *BBC News*, *Sky News*, Debates on BBC2. Appeared in the *Daily Telegraph*, *Independent*, written several books. Editor of *Audit General Practice Journal*. Hon Secretary British travel Health Association.

Email: gckassianos@btinternet.com

COSTAS KATSANTONIS
Professional Boxer

DATE OF BIRTH: 16.10.70
PLACE OF BIRTH: London. Father from Limassol, Cyprus; Mother from England (parents from Famagusta and Paralimni).
CHILDREN: Marcus and Elysia.
SCHOOLS/COLLEGE: Firs Farm Primary School, Winchmore Secondary School.
HONOURS/AWARDS: Twice Middlesex & Regional Area Junior Champion (amateur). British Southern Area Light Welter Champion (professional).
PERSONAL PROFILE: Professional Boxer.

CHRISTOS KATSIKIDES
Chairman of Greek School and Church in Battersea

DATE OF BIRTH: 21.11.21
PLACE OF BIRTH: Mandres.
MARITAL STATUS: Married To Koulla from Ayios Elias, Famagusta.
CHILDREN: Four sons, one daughter and nine grandchildren.
SCHOOLS/COLLEGE: Mandres Elementary.
HOBBIES AND INTERESTS: Reading.
PERSONAL PROFILE: Came to England in 1952 worked as a Tailor then opened dressmaking factory Reno Gowns until retirement. One of the founders of St. Nectarius Church in Battersea Chairman for 31 years. Also Chairman of Greek School at Battersea.

CHRISTINE KATSOURIS
Journalist

DATE OF BIRTH: 15.04.55
PLACE OF BIRTH: London. Father from Komi Kebir. Mother from Ireland.
MARITAL STATUS: Married to Neil Wilson, a Journalist, from the UK.
CHILDREN: Franklin Christopher John, at Primary School.
SCHOOLS/COLLEGE: London University (School of Oriental & African Studies).
ACADEMIC QUALIFICATIONS: MA (History), BA (History & Politics).
MEMBERSHIPS: Subscription to Amnesty International.
HOBBIES AND INTERESTS: Travel, cycling, swimming, reading, cinema, African issues.
PERSONAL PROFILE: Currently a Journalist covering Oil & Politics for Energy Intelligence GP Publishers. Formerly Speechwriter/Press Officer at World Bank, writer at UN, Former Risk Analyst at London Forfeiting Co. Former Writer at Middle East Economic Digest. Voluntary work: Rosendale Play Centre (for kids of working mothers).

PANIKOS KATSOURIS
Businessman

DATE OF BIRTH: 27.05.1950
PLACE OF BIRTH: Komi Kebir.
MARITAL STATUS: Married to Diana Armenian from Iran
CHILDREN: One son Alexander
SCHOOL/COLLEGE: Eftakomi Elementary, Famagusta Gymnasium and Southampton University
ACADEMIC QULIFICATIONS: BSc Economics
HOBBIES AND INTERESTS: Golf, Photography and Skiing.
PERSONAL PROFILE: In 1974 Panikos joined the family business Katsouris Brothers Ltd importers of Cypriot and Greek food products and with their Cypressa label they have expanded to become a household name within the Cypriot and UK community. He is a founding director of Katsouris Fresh Foods Ltd, Filo pastry Ltd and Wine and Mousaka Restaurants.

MARINA KATTIRTZI
Managing Business Director of Focus Training Centre

DATE OF BIRTH: 20.08 65
PLACE OF BIRTH: London. Father, Nick Savva, from Famagusta; Mother, Androulla, from Morphou.
CHILDREN: Andrea and Anastasia.
SCHOOLS/COLLEGE: Clissold Park School, College of North East London.
HOBBIES AND INTERESTS: Tennis.
PERSONAL PROFILE: Managing Business Director of Focus Training Centre, which tries to get people back into work e.g mothers and 14-16-year-olds. Funded by the European Centre Fund, Enfield Council and Jobcentre Plus.

ANDREW KAZAMIA IS BEST KNOWN FOR HIS EIGHT YEARS PLAYING THE LEADING ROLE OF NICK GEORGIADES IN ITV'S HIGHLY SUCCESSFUL LONDON'S BURNING

CHRISTOS KAVALLARES, MBE
Community Work & Race Relations

DATE OF BIRTH: 11.10.35
PLACE OF BIRTH: Lapithos, Cyprus.
MARITAL STATUS: Married To June Hedley, a Housewife, from Newcastle, UK.
CHILDREN: Kypros, Engineer; Christina, Stylist; Marios, Software Manager.
PROFESSIONAL QUALIFICATIONS: School Certificate, Intermediate Electronics.
MEMBERSHIPS: Electronics Engineering.
HONOURS/AWARDS: Gold Medal London Borough Haringey awarded Two Mayoral Cerificates of Merit. Haringey branch UNISON plaque awarded, Race Equality Council plaque awarded, Academy Club Shield awarded. MBE for work in Race Relations.
HOBBIES AND INTERESTS: Sailing, skiing, theatre and politics.
PERSONAL PROFILE: Self employed electronic engineer, retail manager, property management. Haringey Race Equality Council Chair (29 years in Honorary positions, Haringey Cypriot Organisation Vice Chair (15 years in honorary positions) Was Home Office Advisor for six years in race relations and community affairs.

ANDREW KAZAMIA
Actor

DATE OF BIRTH: 09.12.52
PLACE OF BIRTH: Famagusta
MARITAL STATUS: Married to Frances, a Theatre Designer.
CHILDREN: Dino and Alex, (at school.
SCHOOLS/COLLEGE: Wilsons School, Central School of Speech & Drama.
PERSONAL PROFILE: Since graduating from London's Central School of Speech & Drama, Andrew has enjoyed a high profile and varied career in the UK, successfully combining acting, writing and directing. As an actor, his theatre work includes stints at Manchester's Royal Exchange Theatre (*Hamlet, Sexual Perversity in Chicago,* the *Government Inspector*) and at The Warehouse (Heathcliffe in *Wuthering Heights*). On TV he has appeared in award winning series (*Inspector Morse, Widows*), but is best known for his eight years playing the leading role of Nick Georgiades in ITV's highly successful *London's Burning*. His directing work has encompassed numerous theatre productions including a double bill of his own one-act plays for The Royal Shakespeare Company as well as productions at Manchester's Royal Exchange.

His writing credits include original single films for both the BBC and Channel 4, as well as feature film adaptations of the novels *Cyril's Birthday* and *SuperTex* by Leon de Winter (currently in pre-production). Andrew's award-winning short film, *Gooseberries Don't Dance* (starring Ian Holm) was selected to launch the British Short Film Festival, as well as screenings in New York and Los Angeles as part of the British 'New Directors' programme.

PRODROMOS KENTEA
Involvement with Cypriot and Community Press Distribution

DATE OF BIRTH: 08.06.24
PLACE OF BIRTH: Ayios Elias, Famagusta.
MARITAL STATUS: Widower, married to Anna from Livadhia.
CHILDREN: Rena, Teacher; Kenteas, Fruit/Vegetable Wholesaler Supplier.
PERSONAL PROFILE: Involved with community work especially with Cypriot and community press distribution.

ELLENA KIKI
Picture Researcher for Newspaper and Magazines

DATE OF BIRTH: 02.04.73
PLACE OF BIRTH: London, parents from Eptakomi.
MARITAL STATUS: Single
SCHOOLS/COLLEGE: Great Yarmouth High School, Great Yarmouth College of Higher Education, Norwich School of Art, Cleveland College of Art, London College of Printing.
ACADEMIC QUALIFICATIONS: 9 GCSEs, 3 A Levels, BTEC in Art 7 Design, HND BTEC in Design Communications (advertising fashion & Editorial Photography).
PROFESSIONAL QUALIFICATIONS: Postgraduate Diploma in Photojournalism.
HONOURS/AWARDS: Winner of Portrait Photography Award in a competition arranged by Cosmopolitan Magazine in 1996.
HOBBIES AND INTERESTS: Photography, travel and art.
PERSONAL PROFILE: Freelance Picture Researcher at the *Times* and on various children's magazines at the BBC.

JOHN KIKI
Artist

DATE OF BIRTH: 09.05.43
PLACE OF BIRTH: Eptakomi, Famagusta.
MARITAL STATUS: Married To Mary from Eptakomi.
CHILDREN: Ellena, works for *The Times*; Antonia, works in the National Gallery.
SCHOOLS/COLLEGE: Camberwell Art College, Royal Academy Schools.
PERSONAL PROFILE: Artist.
Paintings in major collections inlude Chantry Bequest, National Gallery of Wales. The Saatchi collection Gallop Finland Siemens PLC.

CARY KIKIS
Champion Snooker Player

DATE OF BIRTH: 18.08.73
PLACE OF BIRTH: Great Yarmouth. Parents from Eptakomi and Limnia.
MARITAL STATUS: Single
SCHOOLS/COLLEGE: Caister High.
PERSONAL PROFILE: Played snooker from the age of twelve. Turned professional at 17 played against Ronnie O'Sullivan, Mark Williams. Breaking into top 100 players in the World. Had to give up Snooker at the age of 19 because diagnosed with ME - now cured. Has own health business called KIKI Ltd based in Great Yarmouth specialising in mail order nutritional products.

MARO KIKIS
Community Work

DATE OF BIRTH: 15.06.53
PLACE OF BIRTH: Limnia, Cyprus.
MARITAL STATUS: Married To Paul Kikis, London Restauranteur.
CHILDREN: Kyriacos, Nutritionist; Georgina, Sales Executive.
SCHOOLS/COLLEGE: Limnia Secondary.
HOBBIES AND INTERESTS: Swimming and reading.
PERSONAL PROFILE: Restaurant Owner, Chairwoman of Philoptohos for eight years at Great Yarmouth.

THEOUDOU KIKKILOU
Former Chairwoman of the Leonarisso/ Vasilli Association

DATE OF BIRTH: 01.11.36
PLACE OF BIRTH: Leonarisso.
MARITAL STATUS: Married To Petros from Famagusta.
CHILDREN: Maria and Katerina
EDUCATION: Elementary School, Leonarisso; Gymnasium of Famagusta.
HOBBIES AND INTERESTS: Helping people.
PERSONAL PROFILE: Came to England in 1974. One of the founders and chairwoman of the Leonarisso Vasilli Association for 9 years.

FATHER NIKIFOROS KIKKOTIS
Priest (Deceased)

DATE OF BIRTH: 18.04.30
PLACE OF BIRTH: Galata.
MARITAL STATUS: Single
SCHOOLS/COLLEGE: Galata Elementary School, Pancyprian Gymnasium, Nicosia, Studied Theology at Athens University.
HOBBIES AND INTERESTS: Reading.
PERSONAL PROFILE: Started as Deacon. Ordained as Priest in 1966 at All Saints Church, Camden Town and served as Priest there.

MARINA KILIKITAS
Solicitor

DATE OF BIRTH: 17.07.76
PLACE OF BIRTH: London. , Father from Achna; Mother from Styllous.
MARITAL STATUS: Single
SCHOOLS/COLLEGE: Southgate School, University of Southampton, College of Law London.
ACADEMIC QUALIFICATIONS: LLB Honours.
PROFESSIONAL QUALIFICATIONS: Solicitor.
HOBBIES AND INTERESTS: Swimming, running, cooking and music.
PERSONAL PROFILE Works at Holborn College Of Law, Distance learning Sales Leader. Voluntary work for the Howard League for Penal Reform. Advisor for the Citizenship and Crime Project to educate groups of teenagers on the Criminal Justice System. Commitee member of St Helens Ladies Association, organizing fundraising events. Captain Southgate School Athletics Team 1991-1993.

GEORGE KILLIKITAS
Football

DATE OF BIRTH: 24.08.50
PLACE OF BIRTH: England, Parents from Achna.
MARITAL STATUS: Married
CHILDREN: Anastasia and Panayiota.
SCHOOLS/COLLEGE: St Mary Magdalenes School. Barnsbury Boys.
HOBBIES AND INTERESTS: Football, (Arsenal Fan).
PERSONAL PROFILE: Co Founder of Achna FC. Keen member of Achna Association, Secretary & Director of Haringey Football Club.

HELEN CHIMONAS KIRTSIDES
Teacher

DATE OF BIRTH: 13.08.74
PLACE OF BIRTH: London. Father Andreas Chimonas (OESEKA Chairman)from Xylotympou; Mother from Xylofaghou.
MARITAL STATUS: Married to Tasos Kirtsides, a Banker.
SCHOOLS/COLLEGE: Winchmore School, Middlesex University.
ACADEMIC QUALIFICATIONS: BA.Ed Art Honours.
HOBBIES AND INTERESTS: Dancing, music and socialising.
PERSONAL PROFILE: Teacher at Grange Park Primary School. Teaches Greek Dancing at Hazelwood Youth Club. Member of Datcha Dance Group.

CHARILAOS KITROMILIDES
Teacher, Social Worker

DATE OF BIRTH: 27.08.16
PLACE OF BIRTH: Nicosia.
MARITAL STATUS: Widower (was married to Julia).
CHILDREN: Yiannis, University Lecturer; Nadia, Self Employed.
SCHOOLS/COLLEGE: Pancyprian Gymnasium, Didaskalio, Morphou Teachers College, Westminster College.
ACADEMIC QUALIFICATIONS: Teacher's Certificate, Social Science.
HONOURS AND AWARDS: Haringey Shield and Cross from Archdiocese of Thyateira and GB.
PROFESSIONAL QUALIFICATIONS: Teacher, Social Worker.
HOBBIES AND INTERESTS: Gardening, walking and reading.
PERSONAL PROFILE: One of the founders of the Academy Social Club, Parents Guidance Centre, Oak Leaf Club.

K GREEK CYPRIOTS in the UK

ALEXANDER KLEANTHOUS
Solicitor

DATE OF BIRTH: 10.07.65
PLACE OF BIRTH: Newcastle. Father from Limassol.
MARITAL STATUS: Single
SCHOOLS/COLLEGE: Merchant Taylors School Northwood, Brasenose College Oxford.
ACADEMIC QUALIFICATIONS: BA Oxford.
PROFESSIONAL QUALIFICATIONS: Solicitor.
MEMBERSHIPS: Law Society.
HOBBIES AND INTERESTS: Military History.
PERSONAL PROFILE: Director of Knowledge Management, Baker & McKenzie, London.

ANDREAS KLEANTHOUS
President of Philia Association

DATE OF BIRTH: 08.07.42
PLACE OF BIRTH: Philia, Morphou, Nicosia.
MARITAL STATUS: Married To Sotiroulla, born in London, (Father from Eptakomi, Mother from Komi Kebir).
CHILDREN: Helen, married with two children; Olivia, married with one child; Areti, 2nd year at Brunel University; Chris, 3rd year at Barnet College.
SCHOOLS/COLLEGE: Completed 6th Form High School in Nicosia.
PROFESSIONAL QUALIFICATIONS: Telecom Technician's course, Southgate College.
HOBBIES AND INTERESTS: Shooting, gardening and DIY.
PERSONAL PROFILE: Was Manager with BT for many years. Parent Governor with Broomfield School for four years. President of Philia Association.

ANTHONY KLEANTHOUS BECAME THE YOUNGEST FOOTBALL LEAGUE CHAIRMAN AND OWNER OF BARNET FC AGED 28

ANTHONY KLEANTHOUS
Chairman of Barnet FC

DATE OF BIRTH: 26.11.66
PLACE OF BIRTH: London. Father, Andreas, from Limassol; Mother, Anna, from Rizokarpasso.
SCHOOLS/COLLEGE: St Aloyisius, Hornsey.
PERSONAL PROFILE: At the age of 20 was youngest licensee to operate a Shell petrol station. The founder of NAG Telecom, which became the second largest mobile phone retailer in the UK while he was a chief executive. Tony is the second biggest shareholder in the retail group called Chancerealm which owns Rymans the Stationers and Partners, the stationers. Also a shareholder in Contessa Lingerie.
At 28 became the youngest football league chairman and owner of Barnet FC. At 32 became chairman of Service Direct PLC where he merged Samsung Telecom UK with Zoo Internet Enterprize to becom the largest independent suppliers and maintainers of telephone systems in the UK. Recently appointed Chairman of Triton Europe who are one of the largest manufacturers in the world, manufacturing media products in the Far East.

COSTAS PHOTIOS KLEANTHOUS
Businessman

DATE OF BIRTH: 15.06.38
PLACE OF BIRTH: Limassol. Emigrated to England in 1952.
MARITAL STATUS: Married To Valerie Anne, a Solicitor & Family Mediator, from Newcastle-upon Tyne.
CHILDREN: Alexander Photios, Solicitor; Anthony Christopher, Global and Ecommerce Business Manager for a major pharmaceutical company.
SCHOOLS/COLLEGE: Lanition Gymnasium, Limassol; Hackney Downs Grammar School, London; Sir John Cass College (now Guildhall University).
ACADEMIC QUALIFICATIONS: BSc (special) Mathematics.
HOBBIES AND INTERESTS: Antiques, history, the environment and music - Classical and Jazz.
PERSONAL PROFILE: Has antiques business with brother Chris in Portobello Road. Chairman of Portobello Antiques Dealers and Director of the National Association of Art & Antique Dealers. Has served as Vice-Chairman of the Greek Cypriot Brotherhood for over ten years. Co-founder and Trustee of the Hellenic Centre, London. In Cyprus, Chairman of the Luona Foundation for the Regeneration of the Cypriot Countryside and the Cyprus Conservation Foundation.

KLEANTHIS LOUCAS KLEANTHOUS
Eye Surgeon

DATE OF BIRTH: 21.05.58
PLACE OF BIRTH: London. Father, Louca from Nikita Morphou; Mother, Rubina from Rizokarpasso.
MARITAL STATUS: Single
SCHOOLS/COLLEGE: Emanuel School in Battersea, London Hospital Medical College.
QUALIFICATIONS: MBBS.
MEMBERSHIPS: Fellow of the Royal College of Surgeons, Fellow of the Royal College of Opthalmologists.
HOBBIES AND INTERESTS: Target shooting and Greek Antiquities.
PERSONAL PROFILE: Eye Surgeon, now based in the Channel Islands. Did Charity Work in Nepal on a Cataract Camp.

LAMBROS KLEANTHOUS
Treasurer KLN Football Club

DATE OF BIRTH: 27.04.48
PLACE OF BIRTH: Kampia, Nicosia.
MARITAL STATUS: Married to Georgia from Paphos.
CHILDREN: Andrew and Maria.
SCHOOLS/COLLEGE: Samuel Economic School, Nicosia.
HOBBIES AND INTERESTS: Golf and football.
PERSONAL PROFILE: 1963 came to England, was waiter in Ivy Restaurant, then car body repairer, then opened Dress Manufacturing Business called Lella Brothers, with brother Klitos and Eleni Constantinou. Now major supplier to *New Look* and other companies. Involved with KLN Youth Club as a committee member. Treasurer for several years. Was also a member of Queenswell Greek School Committee.

NIKIFOROS (NICK) KLEANTHOUS
Businessman

DATE OF BIRTH: 09.02.51
PLACE OF BIRTH: Paleomylos Troodos.
MARITAL STATUS: Widower
CHILDREN: Zoe, BSc in Psychology; Natasha, at Sheffield University studying for an MA in Journalism.
SCHOOLS/COLLEGE: Clissold Park School.
HOBBIES AND INTERESTS: Golf, shooting and music.
PERSONAL PROFILE: Was in the Garment Industry from 1970. Formed the company called KACY Ltd, women's tailoring manufacturers. It grew into a substantial size, employing 30 people and subcontracting to companies employing several hundred people. In 1993, received the Queen's Award for export achievement. The company ceased trading in 1997 when Nick retired; it still exists, though its only activity is to rent out its properties.

Email: nick.k@dsl.pipex.com

TAKIS KLEANTHOUS
Football

DATE OF BIRTH: 28.07.50
PLACE OF BIRTH: Kampia, Nicosia.
MARITAL STATUS: Married to Vivian.
CHILDREN: Alex, in Business; Melina, at University.
SCHOOLS/COLLEGE: Friern Barnet County School.
MEMBERSHIPS: Cypriot Golf Society.
HOBBIES AND INTERESTS: Golf and football (Tottenham Fan).
PERSONAL PROFILE: Former Secretary of KLN Football Club and Results Secretary of Cypriot Football league in UK. Owner of Big K Charcoal Merchants with premises in North London and Kings Lynn. Suppliers to *Waitrose*, *John Lewis*, *Homebase*, Petrol Stations and Restaurants.

AMBASSADOR MYRNA Y KLEOPAS
High Commisioner for the Republic of Cyprus in the UK

DATE OF BIRTH: 23.08.44
PLACE OF BIRTH: Nicosia.
MARITAL STATUS: Married to Yiangos P Kleopas.
CHILDREN: Kleopas, Sophia and one grandson.
SCHOOLS/COLLEGE: Studied Law at Grays Inn, London.
HOBBIES AND INTERESTS: Reading, the arts, swimming, walking.

PERSONAL PROFILE: 1971-1977, Practised law in Cyprus. 1977-1979. Served as Legal Advisor on Human Rights to the Ministry of Foreign Affairs. Also served to the Political Affairs Division of the Ministry dealing with human rights. April 1979, entered permanently the Minstry of Foreign Affairs. 1979-1980, served in the Political Affairs Division of the Ministry of Foreign Affairs. April 1980-1986, served as Counsellor at the Cyprus High Commission, London. 1981, also appointed Consul-General at the Cyprus High Commission, London. Aug 1986-1990, served in the Political Affairs Division of the Ministry of Foreign Affairs, dealing with international Organisations, bilateral relations, womens affairs, human rights, Commonwealth and Non-Aligned affairs. 1988, also appointed representative of the Ministry of Foreign Affairs to the Central Agency for Women's Rights of the Republic of Cyprus. 1989, Deputy Director of the Political Affairs Division of the Ministry of Foreign Affairs. 1989, Appointed Cyprus Representative to the UN Commission for the Status of Women. Oct 1990-1993, served as Director of the Office of the Permanent Secretary of the Ministry of Foreign Affairs. Nov 1993-Oct 1996, Appointed Ambassador to China with parallel accredition to Japan, Pakistan, Mongolia and the Phillipines. Nov 1996-1997, Appointed Director of the Political Affairs Division (Cyprus Question) of the Minstry of Foreign Affairs. Dec1997, Appointed Ambassador to Italy with parallel accreditation to Switzerland, Malta and San Marino. July 2000, appointed High Commissioner to the UK, Participated in several international conferences and meetings, including the Commomwealth Heads of Government meetings in Kuala Lumpur 1989, Harare 1991, Nicosia 1993 and Edinburgh 1997. Speaks Greek, English and French.

GEORGE KLOKKOS
Accountant

DATE OF BIRTH: 09.10.53
PLACE OF BIRTH: London. Parents from Lefkoniko.
MARITAL STATUS: Married to Spyroulla, (father was from Yiallousa and mother from Avgorou).
CHILDREN: Michael, studying Graphical Communication at Chelsea Art College; Louisa, taking A Levels.

SCHOOLS/COLLEGE: Park Lane Primary; Wembley Country Grammar, and Essex University.
ACADEMIC QUALIFICATIONS: BA (Econ) A.C.A.
MEMBERSHIPS: Member of the Institute of Chartered Accountants in England & Wales.
PERSONAL PROFILE: 1984 was appointed Financial Director of Robyn of Derby Group, two years later Financial Director of Surecom Ltd. In 1990 was appointed Main Board Director with Centurion Press Group. Now involved in a trade publishing and exhibitions company.

MARIA KOKOTSI
Teacher

DATE OF BIRTH: 08.10.66
PLACE OF BIRTH: London. Father from Mykonos, Mother from Rizokarpasso.
MARITAL STATUS: Married to Stelios, a Banker from Morphou.
CHILDREN: Christos and Aristodelis.
SCHOOLS/COLLEGE: King Edward VI in Lincolnshire; Hatfield University.
ACADEMIC QUALIFICATIONS: B.Ed.
HOBBIES AND INTERESTS: Looking after kids.
PERSONAL PROFILE: Taught at St Francis de Sales and Crowland Primary School. Now at Lea Valley Primary School.

CHRISTAKIS IOANNOU KOLIAS
Poet

DATE OF BIRTH: 21.06.29
PLACE OF BIRTH: Pano Platres Limassol.
MARITAL STATUS: Married to Demetra Kolias from Limassol.
CHILDREN: Androulla, a Hairdresser; George, a Sales Rep in men's clothing.
SCHOOLS/COLLEGE: Technical School, Limassol.
PROFESSIONAL QUALIFICA-TIONS: Car Mechanical Engineer.
HOBBIES AND INTERESTS: Poetry.
PERSONAL PROFILE: Motor Mechanic, poet. Has helped many and various charity organisations.

MARIOS KOMBOU
Actor

DATE OF BIRTH: 27.02.65
PLACE OF BIRTH: East End of London. Father born in Pentayia, raised in Famagusta; Mother from Rizokarpasso.
MARITAL STATUS: Single
SCHOOLS/COLLEGE: Rhodes Avenue Junior School, Alexandra Park Secondary School (Muswell Hill), Waltham Forest College, Alan International Hairdressing Academy, ALRA (Academy of Live and Recorded Arts), Drama School.
PROFESSIONAL QUALIFICATIONS: O & A Levels, Hairdressing Diploma, three year Acting and Musical Theatre Degree. Only UK Elvis Presley Tribute Act to have been officially endorsed by Elvis's first cousin, Donna Presley
HOBBIES AND INTERESTS: Football (Salamina & Cypriot Football League, representative Goalkeeper for many years), golf, skiing and music.
PERSONAL PROFILE: Actor and singer. Voted in the Top 5 Elvis Tribute Artists in the world at the *Images of Elvis Contest*, Memphis, USA 2000/2001. Just finshed filming a TV series (playing the part of a soccer coach) for The United Nations, to promote good fellowship between Greeks & Turks, to be aired in December on RIK TV. Mario won the leading role in *Jailhouse Rock* at the Picadilly Theatre, London, in 2004.

ANDREAS DEMETRIOU KOMIATIS
Management and Business Consultant

DATE OF BIRTH: 15.10.41
PLACE OF BIRTH: Kato Varosha.
MARITAL STATUS: Married to Elizabeth from Portsmouth.
CHILDREN: Antonina, a Lab Technician; Zoe, an Environmentalist; Marianna, a Beauty Therapist; Alexandros, at college.
SCHOOLS/COLLEGE: Bradford University.
HOBBIES AND INTERESTS: Clay pigeon shooting, gardening, cooking and Byzantine music.
PERSONAL PROFILE: Management and Business Consultant, has a company called Manufacturing Management Support Ltd (MMS Ltd). Head of Hellenic School, Shropshire, teaching Greek.

CHARALAMBOS KOMODROMOS
Author of the book *Yialousa Through the Ages 9* (Deceased)

DATE OF BIRTH: 28.06.38
PLACE OF BIRTH: Yialousa.
MARITAL STATUS: Married to Laoura from Yialousa.
CHILDREN: Loula, Elli, Petrina.
SCHOOLS/COLLEGE: Westminster College & Regent Polytechnic.
ACADEMIC QUALIFICATIONS: Business Management.
HOBBIES AND INTERESTS: History and ornithology
PERSONAL PROFILE: Author of the book *Yialousa Through The Ages*.

MICHAEL JOHN KONIOTES
Chartered Engineer

DATE OF BIRTH: 12.06.35
PLACE OF BIRTH: London. Father from Konia Paphos.
MARITAL STATUS: Married to Audrey, a Housewife, born in London.
CHILDREN: Andrew, Project Manager with a major construction company; Jacqueline, Account Support Manager.
SCHOOLS/COLLEGE: Belmont Secondary Modern School; Enfield Technical School; Enfield Technical College.
ACADEMIC QUALIFICATIONS: Civil Engineering Parts 1 and 2 of the Institution of Civil Engineers Examinations.
PROFESSIONAL QUALIFICATIONS: C Eng Chartered Engineer, FICE Fellow of the Institution of Civil Engineers, FIHT Fellow of the Institution of Highways and Transportation.
HOBBIES AND INTERESTS: Gardening and DIY.
PERSONAL PROFILE: After qualification in 1958, spent two years National Service in the Royal Engineers working in the UK on their railway and ports. Then returned to work in the Bridge Office of the Chief Engineers Department of the Midland Railway. Employed on the redesign of bridges. After four years as a bridge design engineer, he was promoted to the position of Senior Bridge Engineer responsible for the design of all bridges in Surrey on the M25, M3, Esher Bypass and Gatwick Link. In 1984, was employed by WS Atkins and took on the post of highway advisor to the Government of Sri Lanka.

LEON ALFRED KONIOTES
Quantity Surveryor

DATE OF BIRTH: 19.12.29
PLACE OF BIRTH: London, England. Parents from Konia Paphos.
MARITAL STATUS: Married to Brenda, a Housewife.
CHILDREN: Helen Griffin, Private Secretary & Word Processing Specialist; Alex, has restaurant in Paphos.
SCHOOLS/COLLEGE: Hertford Grammar school (Now Richard Hale School); Tottenham County School; South West Essex Technical College.
ACADEMIC QUALIFICATIONS: Matriculation 9 subjects.
PROFESSIONAL QUALIFICATIONS: FRICS-Chartered Quantity Surveyor Qualified 1953.
MEMBERSHIPS: Old Scholars Association of Richard Hale School Hertford.
HOBBIES AND INTERESTS: Family, family history research, DIY and gardening.
PERSONAL PROFILE: After qualifications, two years National Service, Engineers Construction Division. Started work with The Wood & Weir Partnership" Chartered Quantity surveyors 1950 as Junior Surveyor, stayed with firm 42 years rising to Senior Partner. Was Consultant on all types of construction projects, including schools, offices, hotels, etc.

PETER NICANDROS KONIOTES
Snooker Referee

DATE OF BIRTH: 19.04.33
PLACE OF BIRTH: Tottenham, London. Father Leandros Koniotes from Konia Paphos.
MARITAL STATUS: Married to Iris Joyce, née Blake, a Hairdresser's Assistant and Receptionist, from Tottenham.
CHILDREN: Tina Maroulla, a Production Co-ordinator in the photographic Industry; Anita Melanie, a full-time mother.
SCHOOLS/COLLEGE: Tottenham County School, Pitmans College.
ACADEMIC QUALIFICATIONS: RSA Advanced Bookkeeping, Shorthand & Typing, Business studies. GCSE Modern Greek 1997.
PROFESSIONAL QUALIFICATIONS: Professional Snooker Referee, Grade 1 Examiner.
MEMBERSHIPS: Various Local Clubs and Snooker Associations.
HOBBIES AND INTERESTS: Snooker, quizzes, DIY, fitness and antiques.
PERSONAL PROFILE: Owner of two Snooker Clubs, active snooker Referee at many TV Tournaments 1975/ 92. Now retired after heart problems and by-pass surgery. Helped local Advocacy Group. Raised money for Cancer Research by swimming.

ENTRANTS IN GREEK CYPRIOTS IN THE UK HAVE BEEN NOMINATED FOR THEIR ACHIEVEMENTS AND CONTRIBUTIONS. YOU CAN NOMINATE SOMEONE OR YOURSELF WHO DESERVES TO BE IN THE BOOK. ENTRIES ARE FREE. SEND IN YOUR NOMINATIONS, INCLUDING NAME, CONTACT ADDRESS, TELEPHONE NUMBER AND EMAIL TO GREEK CYPRIOTS IN THE UK 111 ST THOMAS'S ROAD LONDON N4 2QJ TELEPHONE 020 7503 3498 EMAIL cypriotwhoswho@aol.com

PHILLIP ROY KONIOTES
Business and Charity Work

DATE OF BIRTH: 13.05.49
PLACE OF BIRTH: London. Father from Konia Paphos.
MARITAL STATUS: Married to Linda Valerie (née King), Personal Assistant.
SCHOOLS/COLLEGE: Belmont Secondary Modern, Tottenham County, Tottenham Technical College.
ACADEMIC QUALIFICATIONS: 4 GCE A Levels.
PROFESSIONAL QUALIFICATIONS: HND & Endorsements Structural Engineering.
HOBBIES AND INTERESTS: Scuba diving, cycling, travel to Polar regions.
PERSONAL PROFILE: Director of Normanshire Building Co Ltd. Owner of office buildings. Support Cystic Fibrosis Trust. Built the largest tricycle in the world, 24 seats, to raise money for charity, in Guinness Book Of Records 1998.
Gives talks on Artic dog sledding, scuba diving and travel.

SOTOS KONTOYIANI
Football

DATE OF BIRTH: 06.08.50
PLACE OF BIRTH: Famagusta.
MARITAL STATUS: Married to Ria, a hairdresser, from Larnaca.
CHILDREN: Kyriaki, Beauty Therapist Lecturer; Zino, Motor Engineer.
SCHOOLS/COLLEGE: Croydon College, Croydon Surrey.
PROFESSIONAL QUALIFICATIONS: City & Guilds Motor Vehicle Engineer.
PERSONAL PROFILE: Sports Football Community Organiser. Secretary of Cosmos '90 FC for last 15 years.

MARIA KORIPAS (Aghababaie)
Opera Performer

DATE OF BIRTH: 08.09.57
PLACE OF BIRTH: London. Father from Koma Tou Yialou; Mother from Rizokarpasso.
MARITAL STATUS: Married to Hassan Aghababaie from Iran, a trained Sculptor/Fine Artist, practising Interior Designer.
CHILDREN: Arian and Nikian.
SCHOOLS/COLLEGE: Star Cross School, Laban Centre London. Studied Dance & Theatre.
PERSONAL PROFILE: Since 1984 performed in over 20 major productions with the English National Opera as dancer and actress. Also danced in Parsifal (Royal Opera) and Le Boheme (Royal Albert Hall). Her work for the BBC includes WOZZEC with the English National Opera. Wives and Daughters and the film Verdi with the English National Opera. Her Operatic roles include Papagena in Magic Flute. Fibrilla in TURCO in Italia (Stately Homes Music Festival). Spirit in Pillow Song (Purcell Room SouthBank. She has given world premiers of Works written for her, EI Tigre by Ben Bartlett (Donmar Warehouse, Covent Garden Opera Festival), The Conference of the Birds by Dirk Campbell (The Place Theatre). Stella in the Tales Of Hoffman (Royal Opera). Since 1989 she has been producing choreographic works for opera and teaching movement and dance to opera singers. In 1998 Maria created the Performance Studies Dance Programme for Birkbeck College, Univesity Of London and continues her work as educator and director of these courses.

CHAS K. KOSHI
Singer/Songwriter/Producer

DATE OF BIRTH: 03.02.62
PLACE OF BIRTH: London. Parents from Nicosia.
MARITAL STATUS: Married to Maria, a Housewife, from Birmingham.
CHILDREN: Sophia, Christopher and Theo (at school).
SCHOOLS/COLLEGE: Royal Trinity Music College, Haringey Junior School Stationers Company School, Gregoriou Grammar School, Cyprus, Tottenham Technical College.
ACADEMIC QUALIFICATIONS: A Levels in Art and Technical Drawing/Pianoforte Grades, 1,2 3,4,5.
MEMBERSHIPS: PRS, MCPs, Pamra Musician's Union.
HOBBIES AND INTERESTS: Life and family.
PERSONAL PROFILE: Musical Pop Producer/Songwriter, achieved to set up, also plays in the Greek Cypriot band Spartacus. Has also represented Cyprus in the Eurovision Song Contest.

PETER KOSTA (Panayiotis Kosta Vardakis - legal name)
Actor

DATE OF BIRTH: 22.03.49
PLACE OF BIRTH: Avgorou, Famagusta.
MARITAL STATUS: Single
SCHOOLS/COLLEGE: Hengrove School, Bristol, Filton High School, Bristol, The Rose Bruford College of Speech and Drama, London.
ACADEMIC QUALIFICATIONS: Rose Bruford College Diploma (RBC Dip).
MEMBERSHIPS: British Actors Equity, Directors Guild of G.B, Green Room Club, Players Theatre Club, Cyprus Actors Union.
HOBBIES AND INTERESTS: Cinema, travel and food.
PERSONAL PROFILE: Actor and Director. Member of Equity Council, Save London Theatres Campaign, International Campaign for Artists' Freedom. Has appeared on TV in *Sunburn, Family, One Last Chance*.

MARIA KORIPAS OPERA DANCER AND ACTRESS IN OVER 20 MAJOR PRODUCTIONS WITH THE ENGLISH NATIONAL OPERA

NICOS KOTSIAMANIS
Sculptor

DATE OF BIRTH: 29.07.46
PLACE OF BIRTH: Morphou
MARITAL STATUS: Married to Veronica.
CHILDREN: Charalambous, BSc Computer Science; Alexandros, at University.
SCHOOLS/COLLEGE: East Ham Polytechnic, Byam Show School of Art.
ACADEMIC QUALIFICATIONS: Dip in Art & Design; LDN Certificate in Art; Postgraduate in Art.
HONOURS/AWARDS: Gold Cross of Thyateira.
MEMBERSHIPS: Royal Society of British Sculptors.
HOBBIES AND INTERESTS: Theatre, politics and athletics.
PERSONAL PROFILE: President of the Morphou District Association. Former Secretary to the National Federation of Cypriots, former member of the Secretariat. Sculptor and painter. Had exhibitions in Cyprus, London, Athens, USA, Mansfield. Notable works include a colossal bronze statue of Archbishop Makarios for the precinct of Archbishops Palace, Nicosia. Also statues of other leading figures all over the world, including the President Kennedy Statue for the Kennedy Centre in Boston, to commemorate 40 years since his death. Press articles in *The Sunday Times, The Observer,* also TV BBC Midland.

KLEANTHIS GEORGIOU KOTSIOFIDES
Artist

DATE OF BIRTH: 04.11.39
PLACE OF BIRTH: Larnaca.
MARITAL STATUS: Married to Christina, a Housewife, born in Alexandria, Egypt.
CHILDREN: George, a Freelance Journalist; John, Assistant Manager in a retail business.
SCHOOLS/COLLEGE: Commercial Lyceum of Pedhoulas and Anotati Emporiki, Athens.
PERSONAL PROFILE: Worked for the Bank of Cyprus (London) Ltd from 1961. From 1974 to 1996 was the Manager of the main branch at Charlotte Street. Retired from the Bank in 1999 from the position of Senior Regional Business Development Manager. Wrote a specialist Glossary of Business Terms (English-Greek, Greek English) Dictionary- published by Peter Collin Publishing. Wrote a Dictionary of Cypriot Dialect translated into a spoken Greek and English - to be published. Group Art exhibition at Gallery K and shortlisted for the Bank Of Cyprus Art Award 1993.

Joint painting exhibition with Renos Lavithis *Thalassina-Images from the Islands* at the Hellenic Centre (September 2001) and hellenic scenes and images (March 2003).

Website: www.greekfineart.co.uk

CONSTANTINA KOULLA
Creative Director at Eve Magazine

DATE OF BIRTH: 01.10.69
PLACE OF BIRTH: London. Father from Rizokarpasso; Mother from Gerani.
MARITAL STATUS: Single
SCHOOLS/COLLEGE: Southall School for Girls, Woodhouse Sixth Form College, Middlesex University.
ACADEMIC QUALIFICATIONS: 9 O Levels, 3 A Levels
PROFESSIONAL QUALIFICATIONS: BA (Honours) Graphic Design.
HOBBIES AND INTERESTS: Music and travel
PERSONAL PROFILE: Creative Director at Eve Magazine, BBC Worldwide.

email: dina.koulla@bbc.co.uk

JOHN KOULOUMBRIDES
Former Secretary of St Katherines Church in Barnet

DATE OF BIRTH: 19.03.39
PLACE OF BIRTH: Gerani, Famagusta.
MARITAL STATUS: Married to Christine Georgiou, a retired Secretary, from Davlos Famagusta.
CHILDREN: Eva, Teacher; Andrew, National Director of CMG Plc.
SCHOOLS/COLLEGE: Hellenic Gymnasium of Famagusta, University of Athens, Balham & Tooting College For Commerce.
PROFESSIONAL QUALIFICATIONS: Travel & Tourism BA Courses Diploma A.
MEMBERSHIPS: Democratic Rally UK, Association Greek Orthodox Communties in Great Britain, Conservative Party UK.
HONOURS/AWARDS: From Democratic Rally UK.
HOBBIES AND INTERESTS: Gardening, communities and general affairs.
PERSONAL PROFILE: Travel Consultant. Former secretary of the Greek Orthodox Community of St Katherine, Barnet.

JASON KOUMAS
Professional Footballer

DATE OF BIRTH: 25.09.79
PLACE OF BIRTH: Wrexham. Parents from Paralimni.
MARITAL STATUS: Single
SCHOOLS/COLLEGE: Mosslands School.
ACADEMIC QUALIFICATIONS: 6 GCSEs.
PROFESSIONAL QUALIFICATIONS: Professional Footballer.
MEMBERSHIPS: P.F.A Professional Football Association.
HONOURS/AWARDS: Echo Player of the Year, Tranmere Player of the Year and Top Goal Scorer.
HOBBIES AND INTERESTS: Snooker and golf.
PERSONAL PROFILE: Welsh International, now playing for West Bromwich Albion. Transferred from Tranmere Rovers, reportedly for £2 million. Does charity work for children's hospitals.

JOSEF KOUMBAS
Artist

DATE OF BIRTH: 08.11.44
PLACE OF BIRTH: London. Father from Rizokarpasso.
SCHOOLS/COLLEGE: Gifford St Secondary School, Central St. Martins.
ACADEMIC QUALIFICATIONS: BA Honours in Critical Fine Art.
HOBBIES AND INTERESTS: Travel.
PERSONAL PROFILE: Started Cuba Arts fund on his initiative to raise funds for Cuban Artists. Had his own band in the 1970s, played and recorded in those days with Dave Stewart before Eurythmics. Appeared in films *Merlin*, *Shakespeare in Love*, *Gladiator*. As an artist, produced stone slabs based on a panel cast from one of the original Parthenon frieze slabs, displayed at Wood Green shopping centre and St. Martins Art College.

NINOS KOUMETTOU
Accountant/Schools

DATE OF BIRTH: 04.10.52
PLACE OF BIRTH: Kormakitis, near Kyrenia.
MARITAL STATUS: Married to Aliki.
CHILDREN: Yiannis, Marita and Vasilia.
SCHOOLS/COLLEGE: English School, Nicosia.
PROFESSIONAL QUALIFICATIONS: Chartered Accountant FCA.
HOBBIES AND INTERESTS: Shooting, swimming and football.
PERSONAL PROFILE: Chairman of Independent Greek Schools of London. Former Chairman of Union of Independent Maronites in UK. Treasurer and Executive Member of the National Federation of Cypriots in UK. Founder member of the Association of Cypriot Qualified Accountants.

MAGGIE (MARGARET) KOUMI
Former Editor, Hello! Magazine

DATE OF BIRTH: 15.07.42
PLACE OF BIRTH: London, England. Father from Kilanemos (Deceased); Mother from Koma Tou Yialou.
MARITAL STATUS: Married To Ramon Sola, an Artist, from Barcelona, Spain.
SCHOOLS/COLLEGE: Buckingham Gate, Victoria, London SW1.
ACADEMIC QUALIFICATIONS: GCEs in English Language, Literature, French, Shorthand and typing.
PROFESSIONAL QUALIFICATIONS: On-the-job training.
HONOURS/AWARDS: None personally, but Media Awards for Magazine.
HOBBIES AND INTERESTS: Reading (and tidying up!)
PERSONAL PROFILE: Former Editor of *Hello* Magazine (currently Consultant Editor at *Hello*).
Previous Positions: Editor *19* Magazine. Managing Editor: *Practical Parenting*, *Practical Health*.

GEORGE KOUNIS

Member of the Board of Directors of the Institute for Orthodox Christian Studies, Cambridge

DATE OF BIRTH: 22.10.52
PLACE OF BIRTH: Cairo, Egypt. Father born in Peyia, Paphos.
MARITAL STATUS: Married to Maria, a Housewife, from Petra Soleas.
CHILDREN: Two daughters are married with children; one son is a Macro-Economist with Fortis Investment Bank in Amsterdam. Youngest daughter studying Law at Warwick University.
SCHOOLS/COLLEGE: Birkbeck College, University of London.
ACADEMIC QUALIFICATIONS: M.A. (Dogmatology) with Distinction.
HONOURS\AWARDS: Elfreda Mayes Memorial Prize 98.
HOBBIES AND INTERESTS: Studying and being of service to the community.
PERSONAL PROFILE: Managing Director of BESPOKE a company which writes tailor made business software. Member of the board of Directors of the Institute for Orthodox Christian Studies, Cambridge.

NICHOLAS KOUNIS

Macro Economist

DATE OF BIRTH: 28.06.76
PLACE OF BIRTH: London. Parents from Paphos.
MARITAL STATUS: Engaged to Dorien Buckers who is a 'New Economy' policy analyst with a Government Ministry in Netherlands.
SCHOOLS/COLLEGE: London Guildhall University, Durham University.
ACADEMIC QUALIFICATIONS: BA (Honours) in Economics, MSc in Corporate and International Finance.
HOBBIES AND INTERESTS: Football, cycling and politics.
PERSONAL PROFILE: Macro-Economist with Fortis Investment Bank in Amsterdam advising on UK and Swedish economic performance as relating to financial markets and securities. Previously with H.M. Treasury on UK Macroeconomic and Fiscal Policy and on UK economic policy towards Russia & Ukraine.

DEMETRIOUS KOUNNIS

Accountant

DATE OF BIRTH: 30.06.39
PLACE OF BIRTH: Kalopsida, Famagusta.
MARITAL STATUS: Married to Evelyn from Isle of Wight.
CHILDREN: Gary and Constandinos.
SCHOOLS/COLLEGE: Famagusta Gymnasium, Chiswick College.
HONOURS/AWARDS: Fellow of the International Accountants, Fellow of the Authorised and Public Accountants.
HOBBIES AND INTERESTS: Swimming and business.
PERSONAL PROFILE: Started Kounnis Freeman Accountants in 1961. Chairman now in Kounnis and Partners PLLC. Formed Kounnis Brokers in 1970 and owns Kounnis Group PLC Property Co.

PANAYIOTIS KOUNNIS

Former General Manager at Laiki Bank in UK

DATE OF BIRTH: 30.04.56
PLACE OF BIRTH: Kalopsida, Famagusta.
MARITAL STATUS: Married to Eleni G Tappa, a High School Teacher, from Prastio, Famagusta.
CHILDREN: Constantinos, at Cambridge University studying Economics; Dora, at Secondary School; Christina, at Secondary School.
SCHOOLS/COLLEGE: B'Gymnasium, Famagusta.
ACADEMIC QUALIFICATIONS: Athens Graduate School of Economics and Business, Post-Graduate diploma in Management (MIM).
PROFESSIONAL QUALIFICATIONS: Chartered Association of Chartered Accountants (ACCA).
HOBBIES AND INTERESTS: Music, dancing, drawing and painting.
PERSONAL PROFILE: Former General Manager of Laiki Bank in UK.

NICK KOUNOUPIAS
Solicitor

DATE OF BIRTH: 01.01.63
PLACE OF BIRTH: London. Father from Klirou; Mother from Akanthou.
MARITAL STATUS: Single
CHILDREN: Sophia and Alexander.
SCHOOLS/COLLEGE: St Pauls School, London, Queen Mary College, London University.
ACADEMIC QULIFICATIONS: LLB (Honours).
PROFESSIONAL QUALIFICATIONS: Solicitor.
MEMBERSHIPS: Law Society, Lobby For Cyprus, Amnesty International.
HOBBIES: Music, European literature and Human Rights.
PERSONAL PROFILE: Solicitor specialising in copyright law and regarded as one of the leading practitioners in Europe in this field. Lectures widely in this field and has written several articles. Presently employed by the MCPS/PRS Music Alliance as the head of litigation and anti-piracy operations. These bodies are music industry collecting societies responsible for the collection of royalties on behalf of songwriters and music publishers whenever their songs are exploited. In the past he has represented the Autocephalous Church of Cyprus in its worldwide litigation to recover stolen religious artefacts, including mosaics and icons, originally stolen from churches and monasteries in the occupied area. In 1993 joined the Lobby for Cyprus and was its executive co-ordinator from 1995 to 1997 and is now the honorary co-ordinator.

CHRISTOS KOUPPARIS
Accountant, Ex-Chairman of EKEKA

DATE OF BIRTH: 14.02.26
PLACE OF BIRTH: Lefkoniko.
MARITAL STATUS: Married to Elizabeth from Achna.
CHILDREN: Eroulla, Interior Designer; Katie, Computer Operator.
SCHOOLS/COLLEGE: Lefkoniko High School; Foulks Lynch, Tooting Broadway College, London.
PROFESSIONAL QUALIFICATIONS: Chartered Certified Accountant.
MEMBERSHIPS: British Institute of Management, Certified and Corporate Accountants.
HOBBIES AND INTERESTS: Reading and studying, Cypriot Community Problems.
PERSONAL PROFILE: Accountant - had practice in London for 30 years. Lecturer in London on Taxation and Auditing. Founding member and ex Chairman of EKEKA. General Secretary of the National Cypriot Committee 1952-1959. Chairman of the Repatriated Cypriots 1991-1996 in Cyprus. Published a book - *50 Years of Contribution for the Cypriot Cause.*

DR LUKE KOUPPARIS
Doctor of Medicine

DATE OF BIRTH: 05.01.71
PLACE OF BIRTH: London. Parents (Lefkonico).
MARITAL STATUS: Single
SCHOOLS/COLLEGE: St. Bartholomews Hospital Medical School.
PROFESSIONAL QUALIFICATIONS: BSc MBBS FRCA, DFFP, MRCGP.
HOBBIES AND INTERESTS: IT - developed websites at www. uk practice.net and www.frca.co.uk
PERSONAL PROFILE: General Practitioner.

SIMON KOUPPARIS
Architect

DATE OF BIRTH: 23.03.41
PLACE OF BIRTH: Lefkoniko
MARITAL STATUS: Married to Linda from London.
CHILDREN: Luke, Anaesthetist; Anthony, Surgeon.
SCHOOLS/COLLEGE: High School Lefkoniko, University of North London.
QUALIFICATIONS: BSc (Honours) Dip.Arch (UNL).
MEMBERSHIPS: Royal Institute of British Architects (RIBA).
HOBBIES AND INTERESTS: Golf, swimming, walking, reading and politics.
PERSONAL PROFILE: Architect with own practice called Koupparis Associates in Kentish Town. Secretary of Lefkoniko Association, and in the Executive Committee of the National Federation of Cypriots. Also Vice-Chairman of the Democratic Rally in UK.

KYRIAKOS KOUREAS
Footballer

DATE OF BIRTH: 06.09.47
PLACE OF BIRTH: Famagusta. Father from Yialloussa; Mother from Limassol.
CHILDREN: One son
SCHOOLS/COLLEGE: Famagusta Gymnasium.
HONOURS/AWARDS: 36 International Caps for Cyprus.
HOBBIES AND INTERESTS: Football, basketball and swimming.
PERSONAL PROFILE: Footballer, played for New Salamis in Cyprus Ethnikos and Olympiakos in Greece. Also represented American All Stars. Youngest player to represent Cyprus, played in European Cup Games, played in UEFA against Spurs in the Cypriot Football League in UK, managed the League team, New Salamis and Anorthosis.

MARIOS KOUSOULOU
Politics

DATE OF BIRTH: 10.10.52
PLACE OF BIRTH: Lefkoniko.
MARITAL STATUS: Married to Janet, a College Lecturer in IT and Business Studies, from Enfield.
CHILDREN: Stuart, Retail Deputy Manager; Emma, doing a Masters Degree in Politics and International Affairs at Keele University.
SCHOOLS/COLLEGE: St Davids Hornsey, Tottenham College of Technology, University of North London.
ACADEMIC QUALIFICATIONS: LLB (Honours) and degree in Building.
PROFESSIONAL QUALIFICATIONS: M.C.I.O.B. Institute of Builders, M.I.C.W Institute of Clerk of Works.
HONOURS/AWARDS: Justice of the Peace - Magistrate since 1990.
HOBBIES AND INTERESTS: Squash player.
PERSONAL PROFILE: Chief Clerk of Works, Haringey Council. Labour Councillor for 4 years and Labour Group leader for one year. Constituency Chairman for two years, Press Officer for four years.

CHRISTOS KOUTSOFTAS
Chairman of Aradippou Association

DATE OF BIRTH: 11.8.60
PLACE OF BIRTH: Aradippou, Cyprus.
MARITAL STATUS: Married
CHILDREN: Andrea and Demetris.
SCHOOLS/COLLEGE: Makarios III Secondary School, Larnaca, Cyprus.
ACADEMIC QUALIFICATIONS: Graduate of Classical Studies (was awarded a University Scholarship).
MEMBERSHIPS: President of Aradippou Association UK, a member of the Board of The Cypriot Community Centre.
HOBBIES AND INTERESTS: Reading travelling, sport and socialising.
PERSONAL PROFILE: Arrived in UK in 1986 Manager at Jentone Ltd. Involved with Aradippou Association UK since established, now President. Also responsible for a memorial service for Cypriot war heroes, which is conducted in August every year.

IOANNIS-METAXAS MENICOU KOUVAROS
Honorary President, Limnia Association

DATE OF BIRTH: 11.02.41
PLACE OF BIRTH: Limnia.
MARITAL STATUS: Married to Victoria, a Greek School Teacher, from Gypsos.
CHILDREN: Menicos, a graduate in Economics & Politics, working at Pricewaterhouse Coopers; Elena, Student.
SCHOOLS/COLLEGE: Famagusta Gymnasium, Kingsway College, Hackney College, Elephant & Castle College.
HONOURS/AWARDS: From Democratic Rally for long service to the party.
HOBBIES AND INTERESTS: Football, swimming and politics.
PERSONAL PROFILE: Owns Fish Bar & Kebab House. Secretary for press and information DESY UK. Limnia Association. Co-founder, President and Honorary President, Member of the Secretariat of the National Federation of Cyprus, 1999-2001.

Address: 5 Greenheys Drive, London E18 2HA.

MENICOS IOANNIS KOUVAROS
Accountant & Youth Organisations

DATE OF BIRTH: 29.03.78
PLACE OF BIRTH: London.
Parents from Limnia and Gypsou.
MARITAL STATUS: Single
SCHOOLS/COLLEGE: London School of Economics & Political Science, Queen Mary College, Ilford County High Grammar School, Forest School.
ACADEMIC QUALIFICATIONS: Management M.Sc (graduated with Merit); Economics & Politics B.Sc (1st class Honours); A levels in Maths, Physics, History, Modern Greek.
MEMBERSHIPS: Institute of Chartered Accountants, Scotland.
HOBBIES AND INTERESTS: Current affairs, Impressionist and post-impressionist art, tennis and long distance running.
PERSONAL PROFILE: Associate at Pricewaterhouse Coopers- Banking & Capital Markets, Assurance & Business Advisory Services. Community involvement: World Federation of Overseas Cypriot Youth-President, 2002. National Federation of Cypriot Youth-Founding Member, 1999. National Fed of Cypriots-Secretariat Member, 1999-2001.Gypsos Friendly Association-Youth Sec, 1997-1999. Limnia Association (SLAA) -Youth Sec, 1996 to 2003.

PHOTOS KOUZOUPIS
Politics & Community Work

DATE OF BIRTH: 14.05.54
PLACE OF BIRTH: Famagusta Parents from Paphos.
MARITAL STATUS: Married To Chrisanthi.
CHILDREN: Three sons and three daughters
SCHOOLS/COLLEGE: 1st Gymnasium, Famagusta. Willesden College. University College London.
ACADEMIC QUALIFICATIONS: BSc in Architecture.
HOBBIES AND INTERESTS: Reading, music and football.
PERSONAL PROFILE: Former Secretary of OESEKA, Organiser Secretary of Akel, Member of the Secretariat of the National Federation of Cypriots UK. Chairman of Hazelwood Greek School. Member of the Executive Committee of the Greek Parents Association. Executive Member of the Enfield Cypriot Association

ALKIS KRITIKOS
Actor

PLACE OF BIRTH: Limassol.
MARITAL STATUS: Single
SCHOOLS/COLLEGE: Lanition Gymnasium Limassol, Isleworth Polytechnic, Drama School Delyon in Richmond.
MEMBERSHIPS: Equity & Directors Guild of GB.
HOBBIES AND INTERESTS: Music.
PERSONAL PROFILE: Actor, Director at Several Theatres all over the UK. Appeared on TV in *The Cuckoo Waltz* with Diane Keen, and *The Adventures of Sherlock Holmes* with Jeremy Brett. Also appeared in *Connie* with Stephanie Beacham, and in the James Bond film *For Your Eyes Only* with Roger Moore.

ANDREW KROKOU
Councillor

DATE OF BIRTH: 28.10.47
PLACE OF BIRTH: Camden. Parents from Eptakomi.
MARITAL STATUS: Married to Angela Greatley (former leader of Haringey Council), Fellow in Mental Health, Kings Fund. Now working at Sainsbury's Centre for Mental Health (Director of Policy).
CHILDREN: Thomas, Manager with Browns Bar/Rest Chain; Katherine, student, Newcastle University.
SCHOOLS/COLLEGE: Newcastle University, London University.
ACADEMIC QUALIFICATIONS: B.A., M.A.(Urban Education).
PROFESSIONAL QUALIFICATIONS: P.G.C.E.
MEMBERSHIPS: Trustee Tottenham Grammar School Foundation.
HOBBIES AND INTERESTS: Opera, reading and Tottenham Hotspur.
PERSONAL PROFILE: Teacher, responsible for Timetabling and Business Studies. Member Haringey Council 1971-1978, Chair of Finance Committee, re-elected May 2002, Chair of Alexandra Palace and Park Board.

ANDREAS KTORI
Restaurateur

DATE OF BIRTH: 10.10.42
PLACE OF BIRTH: Rizokarpasso, Famagusta.
MARITAL STATUS: Widower; was married to Amalia Ktori from Rizokarpasso, Famagusta.
CHILDREN: Nicholas, Chartered Accountant; Demetrios, Statistician; Anna, Market Research.
SCHOOLS/COLLEGE: Rizokarpasso High School.
MEMBERSHIPS: Moseley Golf Club, Cypriot Golf Society, London, Greek Cypriot and French Golf Society, Midlands.
HOBBIES AND INTERESTS: Golf.
PERSONAL PROFILE: Restaurateur. Charity work for St Mary's Hospice Birmingham, charity work for Radiomarathon.

NICHOLAS KTORI
Accountant

DATE OF BIRTH: 23.04.67
PLACE OF BIRTH: London. Parents from Rizokarpaso.
MARITAL STATUS: Married to Sarah from Birmingham a Chartered Accountant.
SCHOOLS/COLLEGE: K.E.VI Camphill Boys, Birmingham, Sheffield University.
ACADEMIC QUALIFICATIONS: BA (Honours) Economics and Statistics.
PROFESSIONAL QUALIFICATIONS: Chartered Accountant.
HOBBIES AND INTERESTS: Football, current affairs and travel.
PERSONAL PROFILE: Assistant Director in Corporate Finance at Ernst & Young, Birmingham. Specialising in Private Equity Transactions.

DR JAKOVOS A. KYPRI
International Affairs

DATE OF BIRTH: 08.06.71
PLACE OF BIRTH: London. Parents from Famagusta.
MARITAL STATUS: Single
SCHOOLS/COLLEGE: Cambridge University (Pembroke College), University Libre De Bruxelles, (Belgium), London School of Economics, and University of Kingston Upon Hull.
ACADEMIC QUALIFICATIONS: Doctorate in Political Science; Masters in Security & Strategy; Bachelors in Politics & Political History.
PROFESSIONAL QUALIFICATIONS: CIMA Exemptions (Accounting).
MEMBERSHIPS: International Institute for Strategic Studies (IISS), Royal Institute for International Affairs (RIIA).
HOBBIES AND INTERESTS: Skiing, clay pigeon shooting and travelling.
PERSONAL PROFILE: Senior Associate at Eurasia Group focusing on Middle East and North Africa. His research interests include Mediterranean Politics Europe's Security Defense Initiative (ESDI), NATO-EU relations, defence and force structures, CBM's and human rights issues.

KYPROS KYPRI
Accountant

DATE OF BIRTH: 15.04.47
PLACE OF BIRTH: Achna
MARITAL STATUS: Married to Despina Sophocleous, a Secretary and Housewife, from Pyla, Larnaca.
CHILDREN: Anna, Teacher; Elena and Gregory, both at school.
SCHOOLS/COLLEGE: Selhurst Grammar, City of Westminster College, Accountancy Department.
ACADEMIC QUALIFICATIONS: 6 O Levels, 3 A Levels
PROFESSIONAL QUALIFICATIONS: FCCA.
MEMBERSHIPS: Chartered Association of Certified Accountants, Greek Association for Language Enhancement.
HOBBIES AND INTERESTS: Gardening, all sports particularly athletics and gymnastics. Interests in education.
PERSONAL PROFILE: Qualified 1978. Own Accountancy Practice since 1980. Member of group which set up St Cyprian School, where he is a Governor.

THEO KYPRI
Former British Trampoline Champion

PLACE OF BIRTH: London. Father from Ormidhia; Mother from Palekythron.
MARITAL STATUS: Single
SCHOOLS/COLLEGE: Highbury Grove.
ACADEMIC QUALIFICATIONS: 2 O levels, 2 CSEs
MEMBERSHIPS: Member of Register of British Stunt Performers.
HONOURS/AWARDS: Winner of Sports Personality of the Year Award in Islington.
HOBBIES AND INTERESTS: Reading, backgammon, guitar and music.
PERSONAL PROFILE: Former British Trampoline Champion 8th in the World Championships. Holder of ten national titles. Disc Jockey for LGR's New Generation Show. Writer of a weekly sports column in Parikiaki. Represented Cyprus at the 1999 World Trampoline Championships. Professional Stunt Performer in The Film & TV Industry for five years, credits include: *Tomb Raider*, *Mortal Kombat*, *102 Dalmations*, *Harry Potter*, *The Mummy Returns*, *Dungeons & Dragons*, *Spy Game*, *Band Of Brothers*, *Highlander 4* and *Entrapment*.

AKIS KYPRIANOU
Businessman

DATE OF BIRTH: 15.01.60
PLACE OF BIRTH: Nicosia.
MARITAL STATUS: Married to Karen, a Housewife, from Manchester.
CHILDREN: Olivia, Ioannis and Amelia, all at school.
SCHOOLS/COLLEGE: University of North London.
ACADEMIC QUALIFICATIONS: HND in Business Studies.
MEMBERSHIPS: ITT Institute of Directors.
HOBBIES AND INTERESTS: Football, gardening and travelling.
PERSONAL PROFILE: Head of Tour Operating, Division of Libra Holidays.

ERMIS KYPRIANOU
Hotelier

DATE OF BIRTH: 14.05.39
PLACE OF BIRTH: Dhali Village, Nicosia.
MARITAL STATUS: Married to Maria from Rizokarpaso, Famagusta.
CHILDREN: Nicos, Helen and Cypriella, all Company Directors.
SCHOOLS/COLLEGE: Emporikon Lykeion, Nicosia.
ACADEMIC QUALIFICATIONS: Fellow Hotel & Catering Institute.
PROFESSIONAL QUALIFICATIONS: MHCI, FHCIT B.
MEMBERSHIPS: Institute of Directors, Confederation of British Industry, Essex Chamber of Commerce.
HOBBIES AND INTERESTS: Reading and religious studies.
PERSONAL PROFILE: Serving Trustee in a number of Churches. Hon. President St George's Church Gants Hill, Ilford. Owner of Heybridge Hotel, Essex for a number of years.

KYPROS KYPRIANOU
Accountant

DATE OF BIRTH: 28.09.54
PLACE OF BIRTH: London. Father from Dikomo, Kyrenia; Mother from Lythrodontas, Nicosia.
MARITAL STATUS: Married to Nasrin (Anastasia), a Chartered Accountant, from Tanzania.
CHILDREN: Harry and Marios, at school.
SCHOOLS/COLLEGE: Merrywood Grammar School, Bristol. North London University.
PROFESSIONAL QUALIFICATIONS: BA (Honours) Accounting.
MEMBERSHIPS: Member of the Institute of Chartered Accountants in England and Wales.
HOBBIES AND INTERESTS: Theatre and music
PERSONAL PROFILE: Accountant. Chairman of the ACQA 2002.

KYPROS KYPRIANOU
Football

PLACE OF BIRTH: London parents from Kornos
MARITAL STATUS: Married
CHILDREN: Three sons
SCHOOL/COLLEGE: Alexandra Park, City University London.
ACADEMIC QUALIFICATIONS: BSc in Acturial Science. ACIB (Qualified Banker)
HOBBIES AND INTERESTS: Football, especially watching his sons play.
PERSONAL PROFILE: Played Football in the Cypriot League UK. Played and captained Omonia and the League team. Also played for AEL and New Salamis. Vice Chairman of Omonia Youth Football Club.
Former Bank of Cyprus (UK) Departmental Head of Corporate Banking. Now Commercial Director for Ryman, La Senza, Contessa and Partners.

LOUKIS KYPRIANOU
Magician

DATE OF BIRTH: 15.05.31
PLACE OF BIRTH: Analiondas Nicosia.
MARITAL STATUS: Married to Sophie Antoni Arkoulli, from Alexandria, Egypt.
CHILDREN: Antony, Contract Manager Libra Holiday Group; Kypro, 43, Director "KYP Driving School"; Ted, Director Consultant "Essential Safety Products".
SCHOOLS/COLLEGE: Commercial School of Samuel.
ACADEMIC QUALIFICATIONS: O and A Levels in English.
PROFESSIONAL QUALIFICATIONS: Accountant, Magician Illusionist.
MEMBERSHIPS: The Magic Circle of England The International Brotherhood of Magicians.
HONOURS/AWARDS: Honourable Citizen of St Pancras.
HOBBIES AND INTERESTS: Football.
PERSONAL PROFILE: Magician, Member and co-Founder of St Andrews Greek Church and School and of St Michael Church and School of Hendon. General Secretary of Cyprus Brotherhood Association in the 60s. Involved with Greek Cypriot Football League with club Anemos, and was also a member of the Committee of the Greek Cypriot Football League in the UK.

ANDREW KYRIACOU
Secretary of SOLEA Association in UK

DATE OF BIRTH: 26.10.58
PLACE OF BIRTH: London. Parents from Petra, Soleas and Skarinou, Larnaca.
MARITAL STATUS: Married to Ekaterini, an Optometrist, from Ktima.
CHILDREN: Demetrios, Marios and Sotirios.
SCHOOLS/COLLEGE: The English School, Nicosia, Finchley Manor Hill, Barnet College, Aston University.
ACADEMIC QUALIFICATIONS: BSc, MSc Chemical Engineering.
MEMBERSHIPS: MichE.
HOBBIES AND INTERESTS: Collects antiquarian books about Cyprus, and Byzantine music.
PERSONAL PROFILE: Senior Engineering Specialist with Bechtel, Secretary of Solea Association in the UK.

ANDREW KYRIACOU
Pop Artist

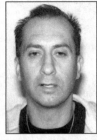

DATE OF BIRTH: 18.04.58
PLACE OF BIRTH: London. Father from Asha, mother from Rizokarpaso.
MARITAL STATUS: Divorced
CHILDREN: Stephanie and Natalie.
SCHOOLS/COLLEGE: William Foster School.
ACADEMIC QUALIFICATIONS: O Levels and CSEs.
HONOURS/AWARDS: Gold & Silver Discs for Record Sales, including no 1's.
HOBBIES AND INTERESTS: Arsenal Season Ticket Holder, Reading, Current Affairs, playing with his children, Films & Music
PERSONAL PROFILE: Drummer & Vocalist for 80s' pop band *Modern Romance*. Currently Gigging with new line-up of Modern Romance. Session work includes: Boy George, Angie Gold, John Themis, Craig McGlaughlin, David Austin, also a drummer with the Spartacus.

Email address: creativerom007@aol.com.

EKATERINI KYRIACOU
Optometrist

DATE OF BIRTH: 31.03.63
PLACE OF BIRTH: Ktima.
MARITAL STATUS: Married to Andrew Kyriacou, a Chemical Engineer from London(father from Petra, Mother from Skarinou).
CHILDREN: Demetrios, Marios, both at school and Sotirios.
SCHOOLS/COLLEGE: Rokesly Junior School, Hornsey High School For Girls, City University.
ACADEMIC QUALIFICATIONS: BSc.
PROFESSIONAL QUALIFICATIONS: MC Optom.
MEMBERSHIPS: Member of the British College of Optometry.
HOBBIES AND INTERESTS: Swimming and walking
PERSONAL PROFILE: Optometrist, Specsavers Opticians

GEORGE KYRIACOU
Founder of Gallery K

DATE OF BIRTH: 13.03.40
PLACE OF BIRTH: Exo-Metochi, Nicosia.
MARITAL STATUS: Married to Maria (Ritsa) Economidou, an Art Gallery Director, from Kakopetria.
CHILDREN: Panikos , Diplomat; Andreas, Marine Inspector; Lefkos, Architect; Eleni, Studying Architecture.
SCHOOLS/COLLEGE: English School, Teachers Training College 1957-1959, Chelsea School Of Art 1961-1964, Sorbonne, Paris 1971-1972, Polytehnic Of Central London 1976-1977- DALA (Diploma in Arts & Leisure Administration).
PROFESSIONAL QUALIFICATIONS: Teacher, Sculptor, Art Administrator.
MEMBERSHIPS: Hellenic Centre (Steering Committee, Chairman 1988-1992), Member Of The Council Of The Hellenic Community Trust.
HONOURS/AWARDS: Awarded first prize in the competitions for the Monuments To The Uknown Policeman (1969) and To Gregoris P. Auxentiou (1972).
HOBBIES AND INTERESTS: Art collecting including studio ceramics.
PERSONAL PROFILE: Participated in the Liberation Of Cyprus against British Colonial Rule 1955-1959, arrested and detained as political prisoner No 1533. In 1975 initiated with a small group of friends The Founding Of The Opposition Political Party Of The Democratic Rally. He was honoured in December 2001 by the party as one of its founding fathers. Worked from 1964-1978 as an Art Teacher in secondary education and from 1969-1978 worked as a Cultural Officer mainly responsible for the visual arts at the ministry of education and culture. Director of Gallery K in Hampstead.

JOHN KYRIAKOU
Footballer

DATE OF BIRTH: 10.09.87
PLACE OF BIRTH: London. Parents from London. Grandparents from Gerani and Agia Varvara Nicosia.
MARITAL STATUS: Single
SCHOOL/COLLEGE: Burleigh and Goffs Oak Cheshunt.
HOBBIES AND INTERESTS: Snooker, computers and music.
PERSONAL PROFILE: Footballer, right back, in his 1st Year at Tottenham Football Club Academy. Represented Middlesex at District Level.

KYRIAKOS KYRIACOU
Solicitor

DATE OF BIRTH: 07.01.69
PLACE OF BIRTH: London. Parents from Nikitari, Nicosia.
MARITAL STATUS: Married to Maria, a Teacher.
SCHOOLS/COLLEGE: Riverston School, Erith College, University of London.
QUALIFICATIONS: LL.B (Honours) Solicitor.
MEMBERSHIPS: Commonwealth Lawyers Association.
HOBBIES AND INTERESTS: Writing fiction and poetry.
PERSONAL PROFILE: Partner in Langshaw Kyriacou Solicitors. Has had a number of High Profile cases reported in the Press, including *The Times, Evening Standard, Private Eye*. Also interviewed for *Business Monthly* and *Law Society Gazette* re: Lawyer in the news.

KRYSTAL KYRIACOU
Actress

DATE OF BIRTH: 13.01.65
PLACE OF BIRTH: London. Father from Skarinou near Larnaca; Mother from Styllous near Famagusta.
MARITAL STATUS: Single.
SCHOOLS/COLLEGE: Peterborough and St Margaret's, St Dominic's Sixth Form, West London Inst. in Twickenham.
ACADEMIC QUALIFICATIONS: 8 O Levels; 2 A Levels; B.EP(Honours).
PROFESSIONAL QUALIFICATIONS: Natural Health Therapy Diploma.
HOBBIES AND INTERESTS: Piano playing, theatre, nutrition and yoga.
PERSONAL PROFILE: Actress and Drama/Dance Teacher.

RITSA KYRIACOU
Founder of Gallery K

PLACE OF BIRTH: Kakopetria.
MARITAL STATUS: Married to George Kyriacou, a Sculptor from Exo Metochi.
CHILDREN: Lefkos who has a degree in Architecture working in New York, Eleni studying Architecture in UCL.
ACADEMIC QUALIFICATIONS: Dip in Modern Art, DIP in fine Decorative Art.
HOBBIES AND INTERESTS: Reading and travelling.
PERSONAL PROFILE: 1969 came to England. One of the founding members of The Hellenic Centre, member of the Hellenic Community Trust, Member of the Womens Committee of Estia. Was curator of exhibitions at the Hellenic Centre. Formed K Antiques and Fine Art Ltd 20 years ago, and Gallery K eleven years ago in Hampstead and in Cyprus. Published 52 books about Art.

SOPHIA KYRIACOU
Broadcast Graphic Designer

DATE OF BIRTH: 12.03.69
PLACE OF BIRTH: London. Father from Flasou; Mother from Livadhia.
MARITAL STATUS: Single
SCHOOLS/COLLEGE: Skinners Company's School For Girls, Camberwell College of Art, Central St Martins College of Art & Design.
ACADEMIC QUALIFICATIONS: 5 O Levels, 2 A Levels, Foundation course in Art & Design, BA (1st Class Honours) in Graphic Design, MA in Communication Design.
HONOURS/AWARDS: High Commendation in 1993 by the Royal Society of Arts for my short animated film *A Different Point Of View* which was screened in both the National Film Theatre and the I.C.A in London, followed by an exhibition of the film and the storyboard at the Design Museum.
HOBBIES AND INTERESTS: Music, guitar, bouzouki, singing (in particular Soul). Produces own dance music. Relaxes by playing squash and socialising.
PERSONAL PROFILE: Broadcast Graphic Designer for the BBC. Programmes to date include *10 o'clock News, Weekend Watchdog, Healthcheck, World Liquid News*. Designed opening titles for both daytime and primetime TV, and redesigned the entire *Liquid News* Programme on BBC3. Other titles include *The Teaching Awards, In Stephen's Name* (Black Britain Special), *Flying Gardener, Money Programme Special, Crimewatch Daily, Mean Streets,* **Ever Wondered About Food?** and, recently, *Tomorrow's World Roadshow.*

ALEC KYRIAKIDES
Microbiologist

DATE OF BIRTH: 29.01.65
PLACE OF BIRTH: South Shields, County Durham. Father and Grandparents from Pano Deftera.
MARITAL STATUS: Married to Susan, a Teaching Assistant, from Southend-on-Sea.
CHILDREN: Amelia and Oliver.
SCHOOLS/COLLEGE: Shoeburyness Comprehensive School, Surrey University.
ACADEMIC QUALIFICATIONS: BSc (Honours) Microbiology.
MEMBERSHIPS: Member of the Institute of Food Science and Technology (MIFST).
HOBBIES AND INTERESTS: Book writing, football and decorating.
PERSONAL PROFILE: Head of Product Safety for Sainsbury's Supermarkets Ltd, Member of the Advisor Committee on the Microbiological Safety of Food (ACMSF), Author of books on E. coli, Listeria, Salmonella and Clostridium Botulinum.

CHARALAMBOS KYRIAKIDES
Church

DATE OF BIRTH: 22.01.29
PLACE OF BIRTH: Myrtou. Kyrenia.
MARITAL STATUS: Married to Hariklia from Nicosia.
CHILDREN: Andrew, Accountant; George, Aeronautical Engineer; Maria, at University studying to be a Teacher. Also lost his son Stephanos in 1999.
SCHOOLS/COLLEGE: Commercial Samuel College Nicosia. City of London College.
PROFESSIONAL QUALIFICATIONS: Accountant.
HONOURS/AWARDS: Gold Cross of Thyateira.
HOBBIES AND INTERESTS: Football and backgammon.
PERSONAL PROFILE: One of the founders and trustee of St. John the Baptist Church in Wightman Rd. Served as President, Secretary and Treasurer of Greek Orthodox Communities in Great Britain.

COSTAS KYRIAKIDES
Secretary of KLN Football Club

DATE OF BIRTH: 19.03.48
PLACE OF BIRTH: Nicosia
MARITAL STATUS: Divorced
CHILDREN: Marianne, Royal Bank of Scotland; Christopher, College; Philippos, Alexandros and Michael, at School.
SCHOOLS/COLLEGE: Technical Institute, Southgate Technical College.
ACADEMIC QUALIFICATIONS: City Guilds, Mech Technician.
MEMBERSHIPS: Cyprus Youth (KLN) FC.
HOBBIES AND INTERESTS: Football-coaching.
PROFESSIONAL QUALIFICATIONS: Precision Engineer (CNC). FA coaching Certificate. FA Football Team Management Certificate. LFA Referee's Certificate.
PERSONAL PROFILE: Currently Honourable Secretary of Cyprus Youth (KLN) FC (Ten years) and KOPA's Referee's Secretary.

JASON KYRIAKIDES aka Jason Kaye
Disc Jockey

DATE OF BIRTH: 19.02.69
PLACE OF BIRTH: London. Grandparents from Limassol.
MARITAL STATUS: Single.
SCHOOLS/COLLEGE: Southgate School, Cockfosters, London.
ACADEMIC QUALIFICATIONS: 6 O Levels.
HONOURS/AWARDS: Awards of Recognition 2000, Camden Palace, Top Tune 2001 for Boo-Sticky Feat. Ms Dynamite- Morgan's Spiced UK Garage Awards 2001.
HOBBIES AND INTERESTS: Watching and playing football.
PERSONAL PROFILE: Jason Kaye is a well respected club DJ and promoter. With over ten years experience, he has pioneered the UK dance music sound. Recently quoted as being Prince William's favourite DJ. As co-promoter of Garage Nation, one of the most successful Garage club nights, he has promoted over 30 annual club nights in the UK, and a CD compilation series produced by Sony Music. Jason has also taken the Garage sound to the European market with regular nights in Ayia Napa, Ibiza, Germany and Switzerland. Jason also co-owns Social Circles, an indie record label that promotes and produces UK Dance Music. The highly acclaimed track 'BOO' reached No 12 in the UK charts in June 2001.

JOHN KYRIAKIDES
Trustee of Radio Marathon, Director LGR

DATE OF BIRTH: 13.06.44
PLACE OF BIRTH: Famagusta.
MARITAL STATUS: Married to Helen, a Housewife, UK Cypriot..
CHILDREN: Pamela, Lisa and Alexander, all at school.
SCHOOLS/COLLEGE: Lyceum in Famagusta, Norwood Technical College, London.
ACADEMIC QUALIFICATIONS: Certificate in Radiotelegraphy, Certificate in Telecoms & Electronics.
PROFESSIONAL QUALIFICATIONS: Electronics.
MEMBERSHIPS: Federation of Small Business.
HONOURS/AWARDS: 1st Class Marine Prize in Radio Telegraphy.
HOBBIES AND INTERESTS: Gardening, radio, and electronics telecoms.
PERSONAL PROFILE: Property Developer. Chairman of SAEA; Society of Children with Special Needs. Ex-Chairman of first Multi -ethnic Radio Station in Britain (Spectrum Radio). Director of London Greek Radio. Trustee of Radio Marathon Body. Ex Governor of Hawkswood School for Deaf Children. Also publisher of the Greek Directory.

ROBERT KYRIAKIDES
Solicitor

DATE OF BIRTH: 24.07.49
PLACE OF BIRTH: London. Grandparents from Kato Amiandos.
MARITAL STATUS: Married to Patricia Johnson, a State Registered Nurse.
CHILDREN: Matthew, at college; Richard, at school.
SCHOOLS/COLLEGE: George Greens Grammar School, London E14, Manchester University, Liverpool College of Law.
ACADEMIC QUALIFICATIONS: LLB (Honours), T E P.
PROFESSIONAL QUALIFICATIONS: Solicitor.
MEMBERSHIPS: Cypriot Golf Society, Cowbridge Cricket Club, South Herts Golf Club, Society Of Trust & Estate Practitioners, The Law Society, International Solar Energy Society.
HONOURS/AWARDS: ILEA Modern Languages Scholarship 1966, WH Rhodes Educational Trust (Canada) 1967.
HOBBIES AND INTERESTS: Golf, cricket and writing.
PERSONAL PROFILE: Foundation Governor George Green's School, Solicitor and Senior Partner, Kyriakides & Braier, Chief Executive Genersys plc. Author of the books *Master Conman* (Head Press) and *A Concise Guide to Energy in the United Kingdom*.

COSTAS KYRIAKOU
Chairman of the St John Greek Orthodox Church in Hackney

DATE OF BIRTH: 20.06.22
PLACE OF BIRTH: Komi Kebir.
MARITAL STATUS: Married to Ioanna, from Patriki.
CHILDREN: John, Civil Engineer; Varnava, Engineer; Kaliopi, Housewife. Six grandchildren and three great grandchildren.
HOBBIES & INTERESTS: Gardening and playing the violin.
PERSONAL PROFILE: Worked as a Mechanic, now retired. Chairman of the St John Greek Orthodox Church in Hackney.

KYRIAKOS KYRIAKOU
Designer

DATE OF BIRTH: 18.12.72
PLACE OF BIRTH: London. Father from Pachna; Mother from Agios Loucas, Famagusta.
MARITAL STATUS: Single
SCHOOLS/COLLEGE: St. Davids & St. Katherines School Hornsey - Southgate College.
PERSONAL PROFILE: Ladies Wear Designer. Celebrity clients: Victoria Beckham, Tracy Shaw, Amanda Holden. Specialist in Corsetry. Seven years in business the Company is called Kyri.

MARIOS KYRIAZIS
Anti-Ageing Physician and Author

DATE OF BIRTH: 11.03.56
PLACE OF BIRTH: Larnaca
MARITAL STATUS: Married to Stella from London.
CHILDREN: Neoclis, at school.
SCHOOLS/COLLEGE: Larnaca Gymnasium, University of Rome, University of London.
ACADEMIC QUALIFICATIONS: MD, MSc, BA, CBiol.
PROFESSIONAL QUALIFICATIONS: Diploma in Geriatric Medicine.
MEMBERSHIPS: Member of the Institute of Biology.
HOBBIES AND INTERESTS: Medical History.
PERSONAL PROFILE: Founder of the British Longevity Society. Anti-Ageing Physician and Author

ANDREAS KYRRIS
Former Secretary of Greek Basketball Team

DATE OF BIRTH: 29.03.80
PLACE OF BIRTH: King's Lynn, Norfolk. Father from Gypsos; Mother from Piyi.
MARITAL STATUS: Single
SCHOOLS/COLLEGE: Nottingham High School For Boys, Fitzwilliam College, Cambridge Medical Student.
QUALIFICATIONS GCSE: 7 A*, 3A, 1B, A Levels, 5A, 1C.
PROFESSIONAL QUALIFICATIONS: BA Medical Sci.
MEMBERSHIPS: CCC Cambridge Campaign for Cyprus.
HOBBIES AND INTERESTS: Byzantine music, classical singing, playing the piano, violin, poetry, performing in Medics Review, appears on TV (Local) and University Radio.
PERSONAL PROFILE: Whilst at school was a secretary of the Greek Basketball Team, that was sponsored by Sainsbury Cola.

DEMETRA KYRRIS
Chair of Greek School in Nottingham

DATE OF BIRTH: 07.07.59
PLACE OF BIRTH: Nicosia
MARITAL STATUS: Married to Hector, a Caterer, from Gypsos.
CHILDREN: Andreas Kyrris; at Cambridge University, Katerina Kyrris, still at school.
SCHOOLS/COLLEGE: School Higher Education in Larnaca, Clarendon College, Peoples College, Nottingham.
ACADEMIC QUALIFICATIONS: BTEC in Leisure Studies, RSA Exercise to Music, Beauty Care and Personality, IT, RsA Computer Courses.
PROFESSIONAL QUALIFICATIONS: Administration and Management.
HOBBIES AND INTERESTS: Keeping fit and reading
PERSONAL PROFILE: Volunteer translator at the Hospital for mainly Greeks from the mainland. For the last ten years has been a member of Nottingham Greek Community. Served as Chairwoman of Philoptochos for two years. Chairwoman of Parents Association. Also for ten years Chairwoman of the Greek School.

MARIOS PAMBOS LAMBIS
Barrister

DATE OF BIRTH: 18.11.64
PLACE OF BIRTH: Islington, London. Father from Ayia Fyla, Limassol; Mother from Polemidhia, Limassol.
MARITAL STATUS: Single
SCHOOLS/COLLEGES: International School of London; Sussex University; City University.
ACADEMIC QUALIFICATIONS: BA (Honours); Diploma in Law.
PROFESSIONAL QUALIFICATIONS: Bar Vocational Course.
MEMBERSHIPS: Middle Temple, Liberty, Amnesty International, Anglo-Cypriot Lawyers Association; European Lawyers Association.
HOBBIES AND INTERESTS: Cinema, swimming and travel.
PERSONAL PROFILE: Barrister of ten years calling, specialising in criminal cases. Has been involved in high profile cases such as the Iraqi hijacking, appeals involving human rights and matters of disclosure.

PHOTIS LAMBRIANIDES
Chairman of Kalavassos Village Association UK

DATE OF BIRTH: 27.09.50
PLACE OF BIRTH: Kalavassos
MARITAL STATUS: Married to Georgina from London. (parents from Kalavassos and Dochni).
CHILDREN: Apostolos and Elena.
SCHOOLS/COLLEGES: American Academy, Larnaca; University of Wales.
ACADEMIC QUALIFICATIONS: BSc (Honours) Economics.
PROFESSIONAL QUALIFICATIONS: Professional Certified Accountant.
HOBBIES AND INTERESTS: Travelling, walking, hiking, tennis and gardening.
PERSONAL PROFILE: Commercial Director of Olympic Holidays, major tour operator for Greece and Cyprus. Chairman of Kalavassos Village Association UK. Was on the committee of Moss Hall Greek School.

CHRISTOFIS LAMBROU
Former Vice Chairman OESEKA

DATE OF BIRTH: 23.09.34
PLACE OF BIRTH: Achna
MARITAL STATUS: Married
CHILDREN: Four sons, one daughter.
MEMBERSHIPS: AKEL
HOBBIES AND INTERESTS: Politics and football.
PERSONAL PROFILE: Vice Chairman of Greek Parents' Association; Secretary OESEKA for eight years; Vice Chairman OESEKA for four years.

LAMBROS LAMBROU
Solicitor/Journalist

DATE OF BIRTH: 07.04.64
PLACE OF BIRTH: London. Parents from Achna and Kontea.
MARITAL STATUS: Married to Nadia from England.
CHILDREN: Two daughters
SCHOOLS/COLLEGES: City University; Wolsey Hall, Oxford; Greenwich University.
ACADEMIC QUALIFICATIONS: BA (Honours) Sociology; MA in Communications Policy.
PROFESSIONAL QUALIFICATIONS: Solicitor.
HOBBIES AND INTERESTS: Golf, following Arsenal
PERSONAL PROFILE: Former editor of the English Section of *Parikiaki* newspaper. Was London correspondent for *Cyprus Weekly*, and currently writes articles in the Arsenal Football Programme. Now a Solicitor and Partner with YVA Solicitors.

RENOS G LAVITHIS
Artist/Designer

DATE OF BIRTH: 25.10.44
PLACE OF BIRTH: Paphos, Cyprus
MARITAL STATUS: Married to Anna S Lavithis, works in theatre and poetry, from Manchester.
CHILDREN: Niki, Theatre & Dance Director/Co-ordinator.
SCHOOLS/COLLEGES: Gymnasium of Paphos); Ealing School of Art; London College of Printing.
ACADEMIC QUALIFICATIONS: Degree in Graphic Design; postgraduate course in Typographic Design.
HOBBIES AND INTERESTS: Stamp collecting, photography, writing and travelling.
PERSONAL PROFILE: Created and runs a design/advertising/publishing company, working for the *Daily Mail* from 1974 till retirement. Major occupation now is painting, including Greek themes and images.
Web address: www.greekfineart.co.uk
email: lavithis@hotmail.com

CHRISTO LAZARI
Businessman

DATE OF BIRTH: 20.05.46
PLACE OF BIRTH: Dhora, Limassol, Cyprus.
MARITAL STATUS: Married to Maria, a Company Director, from Dhora.
CHILDREN: Leonidas, BA Honours, Economics; Nicholas, BA Honours, Economics; MA Property Law & Valuation; Andrie, LLB Honours; MA Property Law & Valuation.
HOBBIES AND INTERESTS: Reading.
PERSONAL PROFILE: Owner of a dress manufacturing and property company. Member of the Radiomarathon *Children in Need* Committee.

ATHANASIS LAZARIDES
Honorary Commissioner for the Republic of Cyprus for Bristol

DATE OF BIRTH: 19.12.61
PLACE OF BIRTH: Bristol. Father from Rizokarpasso; Mother from Trikomo.
MARITAL STATUS: Married to Natalie Scott.
CHILDREN: Pavlos and Konstantino, both studying in Nicosia, Cyprus.
SCHOOLS/COLLEGES: Henbury School, Bristol; Birmingham Polytechnic.
ACADEMIC QUALIFICATIONS: BA Honours Business Studies.
MEMBERSHIPS: Member of the Federation of Recruitment & Employment Services.
HOBBIES AND INTERESTS: Travel.
PERSONAL PROFILE: UK Business Development Director for Randstad Employment Bureau, the third largest employment business in the world. Honorary Commissioner for the Republic of Cyprus for Bristol, South West and South Wales. President of the Greek Orthodox Community of Bristol.

STEPHEN LAZARIDES
Photographer

DATE OF BIRTH: 03.09.69
PLACE OF BIRTH: Bristol. Father from Famagusta; Mother English.
MARITAL STATUS: Long-term partner, Susana Vazquez-Liston, Spanish Fashion Designer.
SCHOOLS/COLLEGES: Brimsham Green School, Yate; Bristol Filton Technical. College; Newcastle Polytechnic
ACADEMIC QUALIFICATIONS: BA Honours Media Studies.
HOBBIES AND INTERESTS: Loud music, collecting books and graffitti.
PERSONAL PROFILE: Founder of PYMCA., a photo-library of British youth culture. Photo-editor of several magazines.

DEMETRIS LAZAROU
Former Organizing Secretary of AKEL

DATE OF BIRTH: 05.10.54
PLACE OF BIRTH: Marathovounos, Cyprus.
MARITAL STATUS: Married to Eleftheria, a Housewife, born in London.
CHILDREN: Miranda, nursery nurse; Lefteris, recruitment officer.
SCHOOLS/COLLEGES: Technical School, Famagusta; Hendon College, London; University of London.
ACADEMIC QUALIFICATIONS: Diploma in Community Studies.
PROFESSIONAL QUALIFICATIONS: In Youth Work.
MEMBERSHIPS: Various Cypriot organisations; political and professional organisations.
HOBBIES AND INTERESTS: Football and politics.
PERSONAL PROFILE: From 1999, has worked as a letting agent. 1982-90: General Secretary of Ekon; 1991-99: Organising Secretary of AKEL in Great Britain. 1990-2000: Member of Central Committee of AKEL (Cyprus).

TONY LAZAROU
Chairman of Enfield FC

DATE OF BIRTH: 04.04.56
PLACE OF BIRTH: UK. Father from Kaimakli; Mother from Yialloussa.
MARITAL STATUS: Single
SCHOOLS/COLLEGES: Tollington Park School, Winchmore Hill; Turnford College.
HOBBIES AND INTERESTS: Football and reading.
PERSONAL PROFILE: Worked for Adam Kennedy, becoming their Managing Director. Chairman of Enfield Football Club.

MAKIS LAZOS
Poet

DATE OF BIRTH: 15.02.45
PLACE OF BIRTH: Achna, Famagusta, Cyprus.
MARITAL STATUS: Married to Myrofora, a hairdresser from Prastio, Famagusta.
CHILDREN: Jason and George Lazou, both hairdressers.
SCHOOLS/COLLEGES: Ekonomikon Gymnasium, Famagusta; Morley School of English, London; Sir John Cass

School of Art, London.

ACADEMIC QUALIFICATIONS: High school diploma.

PROFESSIONAL QUALIFICATIONS: From the Morris School of Hairdressing.

MEMBERSHIPS: Achna Association and LELA – Poets' and Artists' Association.

HONOURS/AWARDS: Four first prizes for hairdressing, out of six competitions entered in the 60s.

HOBBIES AND INTERESTS: Literature, poetry, painting, acting, writing and dancing.

PERSONAL PROFILE: Has published a book of poetry, *Visions of an Immigrant*, and composed four stage productions: *Tears of Famagusta*, *Swans of Kyrenia*, *Achna Perimene Mas* and *Cyclamens of Karpasia*. Wrote and produced the CD *Achna Perimene Mas*, and held a one-man art exhibition in the year 2000.

CHRISTOFOROS LAZOU
Scientific Research

DATE OF BIRTH: 10.05.42
PLACE OF BIRTH: Achna.
MARITAL STATUS: Married to Elizabeth Yeats.
CHILDREN: Two sons
SCHOOLS/COLLEGES: Technical Polytechnic, Nicosia; University of London.
ACADEMIC QUALIFICATIONS: BSc in Mathematics & Physics.
PERSONAL PROFILE: University career of over 20 years in leading edge computing, providing technical services for large-scale applications in cosmology, climate, aerospace, medicine and many other fields of scientific research. Currently runs HiPerCom Ltd, specialising in high-performance computing. Has written widely in scientific/technical journals and is best known for his book *Supercomputers and their Use*, published in three editions by Oxford University Press.

GEORGE LEFTERI
Financial Director, London Greek Radio and Venus & Co

DATE OF BIRTH: 05.12.52
PLACE OF BIRTH: Famagusta. Father from Tricomo; Mother from Labathos.
MARITAL STATUS: Married to Paraskevi Evangelou from Labathos.
CHILDREN: Two sons, one daughter.
SCHOOLS/COLLEGES: First and Second Gymnasium, Famagusta; Hammersmith & West London College; Middlesex University.
ACADEMIC QUALIFICATIONS: HND and Post-Graduate in Business Studies.
PROFESSIONAL QUALIFICATIONS: Fellow of the Financial Accountants.
HOBBIES AND INTERESTS: Travel, swimming, pool and snooker.

PERSONAL PROFILE: Financial Director of London Greek Radio. Financial Director of Venus & Co. Director of Eurovenus Ltd. Former Chairman of Anorthosis FC, and former Governor of Tottenhall School. Chairman of Walker School PTA. Member of the Executive Committee DYSY UK.

LEONIDAS LEONIDOU
Chairman of EKEKA

DATE OF BIRTH: 13.10.47
PLACE OF BIRTH: Ayios Theodoros, Famagusta.
MARITAL STATUS: Married to Anne-Marie from London (parents from Constantinople).
CHILDREN: Four sons.
SCHOOLS/COLLEGES: Famagusta Gymnasium; Athens University; University of Wales (Institute of Science and Technology, Cardiff).
ACADEMIC QUALIFICATIONS: Degree in Physics; MSc in Electronics and computing.
HOBBIES AND INTERESTS: Writing and research.
PERSONAL PROFILE: Worked as a senior manager in BT. Founder of the Internet Portal Group of websites for the Greek Cypriot community called Nostos.com. Author of the book *Ayios Theodoros Karpasias*, and of the biography of General Grivas (2 volumes). Chairman of EKEKA, the federation of Cypriot refugees in the UK. Chairman of Ayios Theodoros Association UK. Teaches Greek at several Greek schools. During the Cypriot revolt against British rule, he was a pupil in his village's primary school and, with his mother seriously ill in hospital and his father a political prisoner, he wrote a letter to the Cyprus Governor, Sir Hugh Foot, pleading for the release of his father. The letter received wide media publicity.

KRISTIAN LEONTIOU
Singer/ Songwriter

DATE OF BIRTH: 02.82
PLACE OF BIRTH: London. Father, Leonti from Agios Andronicos Karpassi; Mother Paraskevoulla from Agio Amvrosio.
MARITAL STATUS: Single
SCHOOLS/COLLEGE: Hatch End School.
HOBBIES AND INTERESTS: Karate, bikes and snooker.

PERSONAL PROFILE: Kristian is black belt in Karate. Played snooker and rode bikes to a semi professional level. Went to South London, played his demo to a management company who then declined him. As he was leaving he bumped into Mike Sault of Warner Chappell (publishers of Dido and Artful Dodger) who heard Kristians song through the office wall and realised that the youngster had one of the best voices he had ever heard.

Recorded the single *Story of my Life* and the album *Someday Soon*, that have both gone into the charts

DR ANDREAS NICOLAOU LESTAS
Haematologist

DATE OF BIRTH: 16.09.31
PLACE OF BIRTH: Pano Zodia.
MARITAL STATUS: Married to Agni from Paphos.
CHILDREN: Nicholas, Elli and Marina.
SCHOOLS/COLLEGES: Lykeion, Paphos; Athens University; London University.
ACADEMIC QUALIFICATIONS: BSc in Special Chemistry; PhD in Medicine.
MEMBERSHIPS: Fellow of the Royal Society of Chemistry; Member of the British Society of Haematology.
HOBBIES AND INTERESTS: Travel.
PERSONAL PROFILE: Worked in Kings College Hospital for 34 years – now retired.

ANASTASIOS PAUL LEVENTIS OBE
Chairman of the AG Leventis Foundation

DATE OF BIRTH: 19.05.41
PLACE OF BIRTH: Ghana.
MARITAL STATUS: Married
CHILDREN: Three.
SCHOOLS/COLLEGES: In England and France.
HONOURS/AWARDS: Honoured with the award of Commander of the order of the British Empire in the Queen's Birthday Honours List of 2004. Also honoured with the award of order of Madarski Konnik by the President of Bulgaria in 2004. He was appointed Officer of Order of the Federal Republic, Nigeria in 2002.
PERSONAL PROFILE: After completing his education, he joined the Leventis Group in Nigeria where he became involved in all aspects of its operations.
He is now on the Board of Directors on Leventis Group Companies in Nigeria and is also a Director of Leventis Group International Companies which have investments worldwide. He supervises Leventis group activities in Nigeria. A P Leventis is Chairman of the A G Leventis Foundation.
As well as his business interests, A P Leventis has been involved in international activities which encourage sustainable models of development and, in this capacity, he is: a Founder Trustee of the Nigerian Conservation Foundation; Honorary Vice-President of BirdLife International; a Fellow of the Royal Geographical Society; until recently, for seven years, a member of the Board of Trustees of the Brazilian Atlantic Rainforest Trust.
In his personal capacity, he has supported biodiversity conservation in many countries and encouraged research and education in this field.
A P Leventis was accredited Honorary Commissioner for the Republic of Cyprus to Nigeria by the Government of the Republic of Cyprus on 04 April 1990.

CONSTANTINE LEVENTIS
Chairman of the Trustees of the AG Leventis Foundation (Deceased)

DATE OF BIRTH: 19.04.38
PLACE OF BIRTH: Larnaca.
MARITAL STATUS: Married Edmée in 1970.
CHILDREN: Anastasis, Businessman; Louisa, Administrator; George, Student at Oxford University.
SCHOOLS/COLLEGES: Harrow School and Clare College, Cambridge.
ACADEMIC QUALIFICATIONS: MA in Classics.
MEMBERSHIPS: Numerous organisations.
HONOURS/AWARDS: Honorary Doctorate from the University of Ghana; Honorary Fellowships from the University of North London and Royal Holloway College, London; Taxiarchis tou Tagmatos tou Foinika, Hellenic Republic; Commandeur de l'Ordre des Arts et des Lettres, French Republic; Archon Orphanotrophos, Oecumenical Patriarchate; Archon of the Patriarchate of Alexandria.
PERSONAL PROFILE: Was Company Director. Chairman of the Trustees of the AG Leventis Foundation. From 1979, Ambassador and Permanent Delegate of Cyprus to UNESCO. Member of the Council of the University of Cyprus. Member of the Board of the Bank of Cyprus. Member of the Council of Europa Nostra.

EDMEE LEVENTIS (née VASSILIADES)
Former Chairwoman of the Board of Governors, Hellenic College

DATE OF BIRTH: 20.02.45
PLACE OF BIRTH: Paphos.
MARITAL STATUS: Married to Constantine Leventis.
CHILDREN: Anastasis, Businessman; Louisa, Administrator; George, Student at Oxford University.
SCHOOLS/COLLEGES: Pancyprian Gymnasium (Phaneromeni), Nicosia; University of Rome, La Sapienza.
ACADEMIC QUALIFICATIONS: MA in Political Science.
MEMBERSHIPS: Anglo-Hellenic League; Caryatids, British Museum; Cypriot Estia of London; Greek Cypriot Brotherhood; Hellenic Centre; Hellenic Foundation; Lykion ton Hellinidon (London Lyceum of Greek Women); Hellenic Society of Professional People and Scientists in Great Britain; Royal Academy.

PERSONAL PROFILE: Full-time voluntary worker. Former Chair and present Member of the Board of Governors of the Hellenic College. Former Chairwoman of the Executive Board of the Hellenic Centre and present Member of the Hellenic Community Trust. Member of the Board of the Anglo-Hellenic League. Member of the Board of the Hellenic Foundation.

MARTHA LEWIS
Singer/Actress

DATE OF BIRTH: 20.06.62
PLACE OF BIRTH: London. Parents from Larnaca and Famagusta.
MARITAL STATUS: Single
SCHOOLS/COLLEGES: Middlesex University.
ACADEMIC QUALIFICATIONS: BA Honours in Performing Arts.
PERSONAL PROFILE: Actress, vocalist, composer. Part of the creative partnership Martha & Eve, who have a number of TV, radio and theatre shows to their credit. They have released their third album, and recent performances include various festivals throughout Europe. Martha composes, arranges and performs work for the nine-piece orchestra Cafe Aman, and has also written and composed work for film and TV. She has appeared on TV in *Daytime Live*, *Birds of a Feather*, *Mid-life*, *Edinburgh Nights*, *Middlemarch* and other programmes.

BAMBOS LIASIDES
Businessman

DATE OF BIRTH: 22.10.55
PLACE OF BIRTH: London. Parents from Labathos and Komi Kebir.
MARITAL STATUS: Separated
CHILDREN: Charlie and Isabelle.
SCHOOLS/COLLEGES: Dame Alice Owens; Marketing Centre for Business Studies.
PROFESSIONAL QUALIFICATIONS: Certificate and Diploma in Marketing.
MEMBERSHIPS: Member of the Chartered Institute of Marketing.
HOBBIES AND INTERESTS: Ancient history and food.
PERSONAL PROFILE: Founded Brainstorm Computer Solutions in 1982, specializing in the field of communication and information management. Initiated and completed Advanced projects with BT, the British Government and the European Commission. Developed and launched first range of mobile text services in Europe with Vodafone, Cellnet and One2One.

ANDREAS D. LIVERAS
Businessman

DATE OF BIRTH: 01.04.35
PLACE OF BIRTH: Anayia, Nicosia.
MARITAL STATUS: Married to Anna Erotokritou from Ergates, Nicosia.
CHILDREN: Mary, Sophia, Dion and Krita.
MEMBERSHIPS: Monaco Yacht Club; Mediterranean Yacht Brokers Association.
HONOURS/AWARDS: Awarded the Medaille de la Paix et de la Reconciliation (1999) by HM King Kigeli V, for assisting the cause of Rwandan refugees who were victims of genocide. Awarded the Adwa Centenary Medal (1999) by HRH Prince Haile-Selasse, for supporting the Crown Prince and providing educational scholarships to Ethiopian youths. Received an award for *Outstanding Management of Leading Charter Yachts* in 1998, from Volvo Yacht Capital. Awarded *Best Refit Yacht* in 1992 by Showboat International.
HOBBIES AND INTERESTS: Tennis, and water- and snow-skiing. Keen pilot.
PERSONAL PROFILE: Andreas arrived in England in 1963, and started work as a salesman for a patisserie in London. Within five years, he had bought the company, and 15 years later it was the leading manufacturer of quality frozen gateaux in the UK. He sold the business to Grand Met in a multi-million pound deal, then, in 1986, he founded Liveras Yachts, a company that owns and charters luxury super yachts.

BARBARA HEBE LLOYD (née Loukianos)
Teacher

DATE OF BIRTH: 30.12.57
PLACE OF BIRTH: London. Father from Ayia Trias, Yialloussa, Karpasia; Mother from Ayios Theodoros, Karpasia.
MARITAL STATUS: Married to Alan Lloyd, a Teacher and Artist, from England.
CHILDREN: Adam and Chloe, both at Overton Grange School, Sutton, Surrey.
SCHOOLS/COLLEGES: Bexleyheath School; Portsmouth University; Institut d'Etudes Politiques – University of Strasbourg.
ACADEMIC QUALIFICATIONS: O Levels, A Levels, BA Honours in French Studies.
PROFESSIONAL QUALIFICATIONS: PGCE in Modern Foreign Languages (Secondary Education).

HOBBIES AND INTERESTS: Enjoys sport: tennis, skiing, football, swimming. Cooking, travel, music, reading and activities with the family.

PERSONAL PROFILE: Secondary school teacher of French and Spanish. Formerly employed as a PA to Eurotunnel Directors. Part of the team which won the bid to build the Channel Link in 1986.

NICK 'POWER' LOIZIDES
Pioneer of the Ayia Napa Club Scene

DATE OF BIRTH: 23.05.59
PLACE OF BIRTH: London. Father, Michalakis Koutroullis, from Nicosia; Mother, Chrystalla Partou, from Asha, Famagusta.
MARITAL STATUS: Married to Kou Hajimichael, a Housewife, from Edmonton.
CHILDREN: Michelle; Dion; Angela Meryl; Kiah and Mike.
SCHOOLS/COLLEGES: Seven Sisters Infants & Junior School; St Davids C of E Secondary School; Tottenham College of Technology.
HOBBIES AND INTERESTS: Body-building, boxing and music production.
PERSONAL PROFILE: Businessman in the entertainment industry. Pioneer of the Ayia Napa clubscene, and the person who kicked-started Ayia Napa's current popularity. Former owner of the now defunct Music Power Group of record stores in London. Former radio presenter with London *Kiss 100 FM*, and several other pirate radio stations.

ANDREAS LOIZOU
Director, Financial Times Knowledge

DATE OF BIRTH: 13.12.64
PLACE OF BIRTH: London. Father's family from Ayia Trias, Yialoussa, Cyprus; Mother's family from Zurich, Switzerland.
MARITAL STATUS: Married to Monica Hernanz from Madrid, Spain.
SCHOOLS/COLLEGES: Chatham House Grammar School, Ramsgate, Kent; University of Leeds; London Institute.
ACADEMIC QUALIFICATIONS: BA (First Class Honours) in English; MA in Media Strategy.
PROFESSIONAL QUALIFICATIONS: Chartered Accountant.
PERSONAL PROFILE: Director, Financial Times Knowledge.

ANDROS LOIZOU
University Lecturer

DATE OF BIRTH: 02.06.41
PLACE OF BIRTH: London. Father from Komi Kebir; Mother from Koma tou Yialou.
MARITAL STATUS: Married to Moira Anne Mercer, a trained teacher, hypnotherapist and counsellor, from Bolton, Lancashire, who is of Anglo-Irish descent.
CHILDREN: Sophia, Student of Creative Music Technology; Stavros, Student of Fine Art; Nicholas, Computing Student.
SCHOOLS/COLLEGES: Bedford School, Bedford (1951-9); University College London (1961-8, as undergraduate and postgraduate); London School of Economics (1983-4).
ACADEMIC QUALIFICATIONS: BA Honours, MSc (Econ), PhD.
MEMBERSHIPS: Society for Greek Political Thought.
HOBBIES AND INTERESTS: Music: plays piano and sings for a choral society. Has a keen interest in politics and current affairs.
PERSONAL PROFILE: Andros Loizou teaches philosophy at the Centre for Professional Ethics, University of Central Lancashire, where he holds the post of Reader in Metaphysics. His main publications to date are: two books on the nature of time, an edited collection of papers on Greek ethical and political thought, and some papers on Plato's *Republic*.

CHRISTINA LOIZOU
Psychiatric Nurse

DATE OF BIRTH: 21.01.63
PLACE OF BIRTH: London. Father from Ayia Trias, Yialoussa; Mother from Zurich, Switzerland.
MARITAL STATUS: Single
SCHOOLS/COLLEGES: Lausanne County Secondary; Margate Thanet Technical College; Christ Church University, Canterbury.
ACADEMIC QUALIFICATIONS: BA Honours History and Applied Social Sciences.
PROFESSIONAL QUALIFICATIONS: Enrolled Nurse General; Registered Mental Nurse.
HOBBIES AND INTERESTS: Swimming, travel, theatre and cinema.
PERSONAL PROFILE: Works as a Psychiatric Nurse and has looked after the elderly mentally ill for many years.

PROFESSOR GEORGHIOS LOIZOU
Professor in Computer Science

DATE OF BIRTH: 07.04.57
PLACE OF BIRTH: Livadhia, Larnaca, Cyprus.
MARITAL STATUS: Married to Diane, an HR Manager, from London.
CHILDREN: Suzanne, Finance Manager; Melanie, Deputy Director, Sales & Marketing; Michael, Accountant.
SCHOOLS/COLLEGES: Elementary School, Livadhia, Larnaca, Cyprus; Pancyprian Commercial Lyceum, Larnaca, Cyprus; Teacher Training College, Morphou, Cyprus; University of London.
ACADEMIC QUALIFICATIONS: BA Mathematics (1st Class Honours); Postgraduate Diploma in Numerical Analysis; PhD in Computation Methods.
MEMBERSHIPS: British Computer Society; IEEE Computer Society.
HOBBIES AND INTERESTS: Ancient history, politics, travel and theatre.
PERSONAL PROFILE: Professor and Head of School of Computer Science & Information Systems at Birkbeck College, University of London. Author of *A Guided Tour of Relational Databases and Beyond.*

KATHERINA MARIA LOIZOU
Director of Sheffield International Documentary Festival

DATE OF BIRTH: 07.03.61
PLACE OF BIRTH: London. Father from Ayia Trias, Yialoussa; Mother from Zurich, Switzerland.
MARITAL STATUS: Single
CHILDREN: Alexander.
SCHOOLS/COLLEGES: London College of Printing; University College, London; Clarendon House Grammar School, Ramsgate.
ACADEMIC QUALIFICATIONS: MA in Documentary; BA (Honours) Geography; 9 O Levels, 3 A Levels
MEMBERSHIPS: Royal Television Society; Women in Film and Media.
PERSONAL PROFILE: Director since 1996 of Sheffield International Documentary Festival, one of the UK's premier media events.

LINDA LOIZOU
Actress

DATE OF BIRTH: 31.05.56
PLACE OF BIRTH: London. Parents from Paphos and England.
MARITAL STATUS: Single
SCHOOLS/COLLEGES: North London Academy of Speech and Drama; Chickenshed Theatre Co.
ACADEMIC QUALIFICATIONS: BTech in Performing Arts.
MEMBERSHIPS: Equity.
HOBBIES AND INTERESTS: Learning languages; computers.
PERSONAL PROFILE: Actress, singer and dancer. TV credits include *The Satirist and Two Deaths*; theatre roles include *Aladdin* and *Cinderella*. Linda has been put forward for a part in the third *Silence of the Lambs* film in Hollywood.

LOUIS LOIZOU
Chairman, Twelve Apostles Church, Hertfordshire

DATE OF BIRTH: 11.01.46
PLACE OF BIRTH: Komi Kebir.
MARITAL STATUS: Married to Liz from Kiti.
CHILDREN: Flora, French teacher; Zoe, Production Manager for ITN; Chris, a graduate.
SCHOOLS/COLLEGES: Holloway School; University of Wales.
ACADEMIC QUALIFICATIONS: BA Economics and History.
HOBBIES AND INTERESTS: Opera, skiing and football (Spurs and Barnet fan).
PERSONAL PROFILE: Chairman of the Twelve Apostles Church in Hertfordshire. Member of the Welwyn Hatfield Ethnic Minorities Committee, Cambridge Orthodox Institute and Hertfordshire Black and Ethnic Minorities Committee.. Played for London Schoolboys Basketball.

SOZOS LOIZOU
Principal Clinical Scientist in Rheumatology

DATE OF BIRTH: 01.05.42
PLACE OF BIRTH: Larnaca.
MARITAL STATUS: Single
SCHOOLS/COLLEGES: Stoneham Grammar, Reading; Kings College London; Royal Postgraduate Medical School.
ACADEMIC QUALIFICATIONS: BSc, MSc, PhD, DMS.
HONOURS/AWARDS: Invitation to the Buckingham Palace Garden Party by HM the Queen, in recognition of his services to British science and to the Royal Postgraduate Medical School.
HOBBIES AND INTERESTS: Reading, theatre, art, walking and swimming.
PERSONAL PROFILE: Principal Clinical Scientist in Rheumatology at Imperial College of Medicine, Hammersmith Hospital. Has published several scientific papers. Was invited as a visiting scientist by the World Health Organisation Immunology Laboratories in Venezuela. In September 1999, he undertook a lecture tour in South Africa. In March 2000, he was Visiting Professor to the Italian Institute of Medical research in Milan.

STAVROS LOIZOU
Managing Director, Lewis Charles Securities

DATE OF BIRTH: 10.10.64
PLACE OF BIRTH: London. Father from Larnaca; Mother from Limassol.
MARITAL STATUS: Married to Joanne Allen, a Housewife from London.
CHILDREN: Jessica Sophia and Sophia Isabella.
SCHOOLS/COLLEGES: Highgate School; City University Business School.
ACADEMIC QUALIFICATIONS: 10 O Levels, 3 A Levels; BSc (Honours) Banking & International Finance.
PROFESSIONAL QUALIFICATIONS: NASD Series 3/7, UK Registered Rep.
HOBBIES AND INTERESTS: Sport and travel.
PERSONAL PROFILE: Managing Director of Lewis Charles Securities (private client stockbrokers). Formerly Managing Director of SFS stockbrokers. Previously Manager of Strategic Trading Group at Fuji Bank Limited (London).

Address: 47 Chiswell Street, London EC1 Y4UP

THOMAS LOIZOU
Football Manager

DATE OF BIRTH: 09.06.60
PLACE OF BIRTH: UK. Father from Tavros; Mother from Larnaca.
MARITAL STATUS: Divorced
CHILDREN: Gina; Stella; Andrew.
SCHOOLS/COLLEGES: Chase Boys' School.
PROFESSIONAL QUALIFICATIONS: The FA Advanced Coaching Licence UEFA A Award.
MEMBERSHIPS: FA Coaches Association.
HOBBIES AND INTERESTS: Shooting and playing the saxophone.
PERSONAL PROFILE: Soccer Manager (full-time), formerly, Enfield, Cheshunt and Cypriot Football League Manager.

ZOE MORRIS (neé LOIZOU)
Head of Production, ITN Factual

DATE OF BIRTH: 22.04.76
PLACE OF BIRTH: London. Father, Louis, from Komi Kebir; Mother, Liz, from Kiti.
MARITAL STATUS: Married to James Morris from Birmingham.
SCHOOLS/COLLEGES: Haberdashers Aske; University College London.
ACADEMIC QUALIFICATIONS: BA (Honours) French and German.
HOBBIES AND INTERESTS: Travelling and sculpture.
PERSONAL PROFILE: Head of Production, ITN Factual.

ANTONY LOUCA
Accountant

DATE OF BIRTH: 24.02.46
PLACE OF BIRTH: Kaimakli, Nicosia, Cyprus.
MARITAL STATUS: Married to Ann, a Housewife, from Maidstone, Kent.
CHILDREN: Athos, accountant; Andrea, BA Honours; Christian, university student.
SCHOOLS/COLLEGES: Pancyprian Gymnasium, Nicosia; City of London University.
PROFESSIONAL QUALIFICATIONS: Chartered Certified Accountant.
MEMBERSHIPS: Fellow of the Association of Chartered Certified Accountants.
HOBBIES AND INTERESTS: Skiing, football and snooker.
PERSONAL PROFILE: Senior Partner of Louca & Co. Member of governing body of Mid-Kent College (15 000 students).

LOUCA ANDREAS LOUCA
University Lecturer

DATE OF BIRTH: 30.06.62
PLACE OF BIRTH: London. Father from Chirokitia; Mother from Ayios Sergios, Famagusta.
MARITAL STATUS: Married to Niki Louca, a secretary (father from Ayios Nikolaos; Mother from Styllous).
CHILDREN: Elaine and Andrea.
SCHOOLS/COLLEGES: Thames Polytechnic; University of Surrey; Imperial College London.
ACADEMIC QUALIFICATIONS: BSc (Honours), MSc, DIC, PhD.
MEMBERSHIPS: Graduate Member – Institute of Civil Engineers, Institution of Structural Engineers.
HOBBIES AND INTERESTS: Scuba diving and keeping fit.
PERSONAL PROFILE: Lecturer at Imperial College London in the Department of Civil & Environmental Engineering.

JASON LOUKIANOS
Businessman (Deceased)

DATE OF BIRTH: 22.11.17
PLACE OF BIRTH: Ayia Triada, Yialousa.
MARITAL STATUS: Married to Adoulla, from Ayios Theodoros, Karpassia.
CHILDREN: Andy, Computer Analyst; Barbara, Teacher.
SCHOOLS/COLLEGES: Rizokarpasso Gymnasium; Regent St Polytechnic.
HOBBIES AND INTERESTS: Playing tennis.
PERSONAL PROFILE: Came to England in 1932. Was in the Import/Export Business, then a dress manufacturer. Greek Cypriot Brotherhood committee member and Chairman for 25 years. Chairman of All Saints Church in Camden Town. Worked for Greek consulate in Cardiff. Helped found first Cypriot employment agency in the UK. Was an active member of the Liberal Party.

STAVROS LOUCA
Actor

DATE OF BIRTH: 12.07.80
PLACE OF BIRTH: London. Parents from Pyla and Lapathos.
MARITAL STATUS: Single
SCHOOLS/COLLEGES: Langham; Mountview Theatre School; Chickenshed Theatre; Theatro Technis.
ACADEMIC QUALIFICATIONS: BTech in Performing Arts.
MEMBERSHIPS: Equity.
HOBBIES AND INTERESTS: Bingo.
PERSONAL PROFILE: Actor, singer and dancer. Has appeared in *Casualty*, *Family Affairs*, *The Human Body*. Film work includes *Wicked and Dangerous Neighbours*, *Phases of Life*. Stage work: *A Taste of Honey*, *Cinderella in Boots*. Also appeared in an Alliance & Leicester commercial.

MARIA LUCA
Psychotherapist

DATE OF BIRTH: 27.03.56
PLACE OF BIRTH: Lympia, Nicosia, Cyprus. Migrated to England in 1972.
MARITAL STATUS: Divorced
CHILDREN: Andros Andreou, married and currently studying for a Psychology degree with the OU; Kyriacos Andreou, a mechanic, now working as a car dealer.
SCHOOLS/COLLEGES: Primary school in Lympia until the age of twelve, then spent one year at the KASA Secondary School in Larnaca. Attended the Anglo-French School Pallari in Nicosia.
ACADEMIC QUALIFICATIONS: Currently completing a PhD in Psychotherapeutic Studies (by research) at Kent University in Canterbury; MA in Psychotherapy & Counselling, City University; BA (Honours) Social Science, Middlesex University.
PROFESSIONAL QUALIFICATIONS: United Kingdom Council of Psychotherapy (UKCP) – Accredited Psychotherapist; British Association of Counselling & Psychotherapy – Accredited Psychotherapist.
MEMBERSHIPS: School of Psychotherapy & Counselling at Regent's College; The Society for Psychotherapy Research (SPR).
HOBBIES AND INTERESTS: Dance, especially Greek traditional and ballroom dancing; theatre and classical music; traditional Greek-Cypriot and Middle Eastern cooking; philosophy and psychoanalysis.
PERSONAL PROFILE: Director and Lecturer of the MA in Psychotherapy at Regent's College. Clinical Psychotherapist at St Ann's Hospital in Haringey, and Clinical Supervisor & Consultant at Newham General Hospital. External examiner for Surrey University's undergraduate courses in Counselling. Has published various articles in scientific journals of psychoanalysis and psychotherapy.

CHRISTOS LYMBOURIDES
Former President of Morphou Association

DATE OF BIRTH: 29.09.36
PLACE OF BIRTH: Morphou, Cyprus.
MARITAL STATUS: Married to Tina, fashion designer, from Asha, Cyprus.
CHILDREN: Natalie, BSc in Computing, Westminster University; Angie, BA in Languages, University of Manchester.
SCHOOLS/COLLEGES: Greek Gymnasium, Morphou; Teacher Training College; Brunel College; University of London.
ACADEMIC QUALIFICATIONS: Teaching diploma; diploma in mathematics.
HOBBIES AND INTERESTS: Fashion.
PERSONAL PROFILE: Has been a teacher and clothing manufacturer. Former Chairman of Omonia Football Club. Ex-President of Morphou Association. Member of Union of Apodimon Morphou. Member of Committee for Undeclared Prisoners of War.

ANDREAS SYMEON LYSANDROU
Record Co-director

DATE OF BIRTH: 25.07.70
PLACE OF BIRTH: England. Father from Ayios Andronikos; Mother from Piyi.
MARITAL STATUS: Single
SCHOOLS/COLLEGES: Montem Primary School; George Orwell Secondary School.
MEMBERSHIPS: MCPS (Mechanical Copyright Protection Society); PRS (Performing Right Society).
HONOURS/AWARDS: Various gold discs, including one featuring Victoria Beckham and Dane Bowers (*Out of Your Mind*), which reached number two in the charts.
HOBBIES AND INTERESTS: Cars.
PERSONAL PROFILE: Company Director of his own record and publishing company, Ice Cream Records. Also Head of A&R, and a freelance record producer and songwriter. Occasionally presents shows on various radio stations. To date, has been involved with six records that have reached the national charts.

Address: PO Box 3557, London N7 7QW
email: andy@icecreamrecords.fsnet.co.uk

ANTONIS MAKRIDES
Dental Surgeon

DATE OF BIRTH: 10.02.56
PLACE OF BIRTH: Nicosia.
MARITAL STATUS: Married to Katrine, a Fashion Designer, London.
CHILDREN: Stefan and Elena, both at school.
SCHOOLS/COLLEGE: Pancyprian Gymnasium, Nicosia.
ACADEMIC QUALIFICATIONS: Aristotelio University, Salonica, Greece.
PERSONAL PROFILE: Dental Surgeon with own practice in Palmers Green.

DR ANDREAS MAKRIS
Consultant & Senior Lecturer in Oncology

DATE OF BIRTH: 07.01.61
PLACE OF BIRTH: Nicosia.
MARITAL STATUS: Married to Andrea, a GP, from Wales.
CHILDREN: Thomas and Catherine.
SCHOOLS/COLLEGE: Yerolakkos Elementary School; English School, Nicosia; Raynes Park High School; Oxford & Sheffield Universities.
ACADEMIC QUALIFICATIONS: MA, MB, CHB, MRCP, FRCR, MD.
HOBBIES AND INTERESTS: AFC Wimbledon.
PERSONAL PROFILE: Currently at Mount Vernon Hospital as Consultant & Senior Lecturer in Oncology, specialising in Treatment of Breast and Bowel Cancer.

Address: Senior Lecturer and Consultant, Academic Oncology Unit, Mount Vernon Hospital, Northwood, Middlesex HA6 2RN (UK).

GEORGE MAKRIS
Accountant

DATE OF BIRTH: 06.08.62
PLACE OF BIRTH: Yerolakkos, Nicosia.
MARITAL STATUS: Single
SCHOOLS/COLLEGE: Yerolakkos Elementary School, came to England 1974. Went to Raynes Park High School then Manchester University.
ACADEMIC QUALIFICATIONS: BA Economics.
HOBBIES AND INTERESTS: Wimbledon Football Club.
PERSONAL PROFILE: Worked for KMPG for ten years, where qualified as an Accountant. Worked for four years at Bank of Cyprus as Senior Manager. in 1998 joined Kounnis Freeman & Co as a Partner. Now Partner in the Accountancy firm Freemans and Partners.

DR MICHAEL MAKRIS
Consultant & Senior Lecturer in Haemotology

DATE OF BIRTH: 15.07.59
PLACE OF BIRTH: Yerolakkos.
MARITAL STATUS: Married to Martina from Ireland.
SCHOOLS/COLLEGE: English School Nicosia. Raynes Park High School. Oriel College Oxford, University of London, London Hospital Medical College.
ACADEMIC QUALIFICATIONS: BA Physiological Sciences.
MEMBERSHIPS: MBBS.
HOBBIES AND INTERESTS: Photography, walking computers and football (Sheffield Wednesday).
PERSONAL PROFILE: Worked one London Hospital as Junior Doctor. Two years at Morriston Hospital, Swansea. 1987 till now at Royal Hallamshire Hospital Sheffield as Senior Lecturer in Haemotology & Consultant Haemotologist.

MICHALIS MALLOURIS
Chairman of Hellenic Brotherhood, Manchester

DATE OF BIRTH: 25.11.62
PLACE OF BIRTH: Nicosia
MARITAL STATUS: Married to Anna, Assistant Manager at Nat West Bank Central Office, who is from London (Parents from Agia Varvara, Nicosia).
CHILDREN: Andrea, Elena and Chrystalla.
SCHOOLS/COLLEGE: Woodberry Down Secondary School, London. Kingsway Princeton College, London, Nottingham Trent University, Nottingham, University of Surrey, Guildford.
ACADEMIC QUALIFICATIONS: BSc (Honours) Applied Chemistry, PhD Bioinorganic Chemistry.
PROFESSIONAL QUALIFICATIONS: GRSC, C. Chem.
MEMBERSHIPS: Hellenic Brotherhood, Manchester, Greek Church, Manchester, Hellenes Scientists of Manchester Soc. PITA.
HONOURS/AWARDS: European Sales Person of the Year, 1996 & 97, World Wide Sales Achievements, 8th & 12th 1996 & 97 respectively.
HOBBIES AND INTERESTS: Most sports, cooking, travelling, reading, painting and share dealing.
PERSONAL PROFILE: Business Manager at Buckman Lab Ltd, UK involved with Greek Church in Manchester, Churchwarden, Hellenic Brotherhood, Manchester Secretary. Ex-Committee member of the Leukaemia Society UK in London

Email address: Michael@mallouris.com

STELIOS MAMAS
Deputy Mayor, Royal Borough of Kingston

DATE OF BIRTH: 05.04.34
PLACE OF BIRTH: Astromeritis.
MARITAL STATUS: Single
SCHOOLS/COLLEGE: Kingston College, Kingston Poly, Ruskin College Oxford.
ACADEMIC QUALIFICATIONS: Social Science Diploma.
PROFESSIONAL QUALIFICA-TIONS: Chartered Secretary & Diploma in Municipal Admin.
HOBBIES AND INTERESTS: Politics and arts.
PERSONAL PROFILE: In local Government for 35 years & Local Councillor for 33 years. Presently Deputy Mayor, Royal Borough of Kingston. 2002-2003.

Email address:
stelios.mamas@councillors.kingston.gov.uk

ELENI MAOUDIS
Secretary of Church Committee in Coventry

DATE OF BIRTH: 27.09.48
PLACE OF BIRTH: Kato-Drys.
MARITAL STATUS: Married to George Maoudis, (parents from Kato-Drys).
CHILDREN: Panteli, Chiropodist; Achille, Chiropodist; Margarita, Logistics, 2 Level; Anastasi, Caterer.
SCHOOLS/COLLEGE: Tile-Hill College, Coventry.
QUALIFICATIONS: Florist (NVQ + City & Guilds).
MEMBERSHIPS: SACRG (Standing Advisory Council for Religious Education) Coventry.
HOBBIES AND INTERESTS: Chanter in Coventry Orthodox Church (Psalti).
PERSONAL PROFILE: Secretary of Coventry Greek Orthodox Church Committee. President of Ladies Committee.

PAUL MAOUDIS
Chiropodist

DATE OF BIRTH: 25.05.69
PLACE OF BIRTH: Coventry. (Parents from Kato Drys, Larnaca).
MARITAL STATUS: Married to Helen, a Shop Assistant, from Coventry.
CHILDREN: Naomi, at school and Eleni.
SCHOOLS/COLLEGE: King Henry VIII Junior & Senior School in Coventry. Birmingham School of Chiropody.
ACADEMIC QUALIFICATIONS: 10 O Levels, 3 A Levels.
PROFESSIONAL QUALIFICATIONS: State registered Chiropodist, Diploma in Podiatric Medicine.
MEMBERSHIPS: Society of Chiropodists, Council for Professions Supplementary to Medicine.
HOBBIES AND INTERESTS: DIY and cars.
PERSONAL PROFILE: State Registered Chiropodist 2nd Dan Black Belt in Shotokan Karate. Used to be President of Greek Youth Club (Coventry).

ANDREAS MARCOU
Actor

DATE OF BIRTH: 24.03.33
PLACE OF BIRTH: Xero.
MARITAL STATUS: Married twice. Now married to Helen from Sotera.
CHILDREN: Six children, three from each marriage. Four married, seven grandchildren. Youngest at University, oldest a Detective with the MET.
SCHOOLS/COLLEGE: Famagusta Gymnasium, Guildhall School of Music and Dramatic Art. Webber Douglas School of Singing & Drama.
MEMBERSHIPS: Equity.
HONOURS/AWARDS: 1st prize for Drama at Theatre for Humanity.
HOBBIES AND INTERESTS: Acting profession.
PERSONAL PROFILE: One of the founders of Theatro Technis. Active member in the Theatrical and Cultural life of the Community since 1951. Been on TV, *Dangerman, Casualty, The Bill, Coronation St, London's Burning*. Films include *Cool of the Day* with Jane Fonda, Peter Finch and Angela Lansbury.

MARCOS A MARCOU
Former Chairman Eptakomi Association

DATE OF BIRTH: 22.02.55
PLACE OF BIRTH: Eptakomi, Cyprus.
MARITAL STATUS: Single
CHILDREN: Andreas and Despina.
SCHOOLS/COLLEGE: Eptakomi, Pancyprian Gymnasium, Nicosia, Central Hotel School, Nicosia.
HOBBIES AND INTERESTS: Travel, nature, reading and sports.
PERSONAL PROFILE: Former chairman of Eptakomi Association. Owner of Marcos Trimmings.

HARRY MARCOU, JP
Active Community Member in Birmingham

DATE OF BIRTH: 07.12.55
PLACE OF BIRTH: Galini, Nicosia.
MARITAL STATUS: Married to Krinoula, a Hairdresser - Proprietor, also from Galini.
CHILDREN: Nicholas and Markos
SCHOOLS/COLLEGE: Smethwick Infants, W. Mids; Langley Junior, Warley; Galini Elementary, Galini, Waseley Hills, Worcs; Pitmaston Secondary, Birmingham; Hall Green Tech College, City & Guilds, (metal body repairs).
MEMBERSHIPS: Community Organisations & Assocs., Local Sporting Clubs ie., Golf.
HONOURS/AWARDS: 1998 - Appointed to be a "Justice of the Peace" for the Commission Area of Hereford & Worcester.
HOBBIES AND INTERESTS: Cyprus and its national political problem, religion, golf, shooting (Game) and gardening.
PERSONAL PROFILE: S/E Gaming Machine Operator & Joint Salon Proprietor, Founder Member of "Action for Cyprus" (Midlands), Member of Community Organisations ie., Church Committee. Member of St Andreas, Birmingham.

MARKOS CHRISTOFIS MARCOU
General Dental Practitioner

DATE OF BIRTH: 26.12.72
PLACE OF BIRTH: UK. Father Ayios Elias; Mother Koma Tou Yialou.
MARITAL STATUS: Divorced.
SCHOOLS/COLLEGE: Enfield Grammar School, United, Medical & Dental Schools (Guy's Dental School).
ACADEMIC QUALIFICATIONS: Bachelor of Dental Surgery (BDS).
3 A Levels (Maths, A; Chemistry, B; Physics, B)
MEMBERSHIPS: British Dental Assoc. - General Dental Council.
HOBBIES AND INTERESTS: Eating out, playing football, film/cinema, dancing, news and current affairs and travelling the world.
PERSONAL PROFILE: General Dental Practitioner for five years, in North London, treating a large part of Greek Community.

YIOLA MARCOU
Oncologist at St. Barts Hospital

DATE OF BIRTH: 08.01.70
PLACE OF BIRTH: Paralimni.
MARITAL STATUS: Single
SCHOOLS/COLLEGE: Paralimni Gymnasium, Athens Medical School.
HOBBIES AND INTERESTS: Reading, swimming and cycling.
PERSONAL PROFILE: 1995 started work at Medway Hospital, Gillingham as a medic. Six months at North Middlesex Hospital. Since 1997 Oncologist at St. Barts Hospital.

ARIS GEORGIOS MARCOULLIDES
Dental Surgeon

DATE OF BIRTH: 27.02.48
PLACE OF BIRTH: Larnaca.
MARITAL STATUS: Married to Christine from London (parents from Famagusta).
CHILDREN: Nadia, a Solicitor.
SCHOOLS/COLLEGE: William Ellis School, Royal Dental Hospital, University of London.
ACADEMIC QUALIFICATIONS: BDS (Lond); LDSRCS (Eng).
HOBBIES AND INTERESTS: Travelling to the more remote and interesting parts of the world. Food and wine.
PERSONAL PROFILE: Qualified as a Dentist in 1971. Has been in private practice since 1984. In 1988, opened the Cannon Hill Clinic, a private, multi-disciplinary healthcare centre in North London.

Email address: aris3@btopenworld.com

ANDREAS MARKIDES
Musician

DATE OF BIRTH: 02.06.23
PLACE OF BIRTH: Limassol.
MARITAL STATUS: Married to Iro, a Housewife, from Xeros Cyprus.
CHILDREN: Peter, Hairdresser, Musician; Helen, Housewife.
SCHOOLS/COLLEGE: Limassol Gymnasium.
QUALIFICATIONS: A. Mus. LCM London College of Music.
MEMBERSHIPS: Musicians Union, Performing Right Society.
HONOURS/AWARDS: Honorary member of Musicians Union, awarded for continous membership of the Union since 1947.
HOBBIES AND INTERESTS: Reading and sports.
PERSONAL PROFILE: Musician, Bandleader, Composer, Arranger & Music Teacher.

ANDREAS MARKIDES
Chartered Civil Engineer

DATE OF BIRTH: 08.03.59
PLACE OF BIRTH: Kyra Morphou, Nicosia.
MARITAL STATUS: Married to Kay Swift, a Teacher, from Stoke-on-Trent.
CHILDREN: Eleni, Nike, Stephanie and Alexander, all at school.
SCHOOLS/COLLEGE: The English School Nicosia - O Levels. Felsted School, Essex - A Levels.
ACADEMIC QUALIFICATIONS: BSc (Honours), MSC.
PROFESSIONAL QUALIFICATIONS: CEng, MICE, FIHT.
MEMBERSHIPS: Member of the Institute of Civil Engineers, Fellow of the Institute of Highways & Transportation.
HOBBIES AND INTERESTS: Football, tennis and literature.
PERSONAL PROFILE: Chartered Civil Engineer with a specialisation in Transport. Now a Board Director of Colin Buchanan & Partners which is the foremost independent transport & planning Consultancy in the country. Has offices in London, Bristol, Manchester Dublin and Edinburgh and employs 200 staff. Currently Honorary Secretary of the London Branch of the Institute of Highways and Transportation, and has presented papers at several conferences around the country.

Email: andreas.markides@cbuchanan.co.uk

CONSTANTINOS MARKIDES
Professor at London Business School

DATE OF BIRTH: 24.11.60
PLACE OF BIRTH: Nicosia.
MARITAL STATUS: Single
SCHOOLS/COLLEGE: Boston University: Harvard University.
ACADEMIC QUALIFICATIONS: BA (1983), MA (1984); MBA (1985), DBA (1990); Doctorate in Business Studies.
MEMBERSHIPS: Member of the Academic Board of the Cyprus International Institute of Management.
HOBBIES AND INTERESTS: Football, tennis and theatre.
PERSONAL PROFILE: Author of three books. Fellow of the World Economic Forum of Davos, Non-Executive Director of Amathus (UK) Ltd. Associate Editor of the European Management Journal. Professor at London Business School.

Address: London Business School, Regents Park, London NW1 4SA

DEMETRIS MARKOU MBE
Accountant

DATE OF BIRTH: 07.02.44
PLACE OF BIRTH: Nicosia.
MARITAL STATUS: Separated
CHILDREN: Marcus, Journalist; Andrea, Computer Programmer; Constantinos, Tourism & Leisure Ind, Salford University.
SCHOOLS/COLLEGE: Economics Gymnasium, Nicosia. 1962 Handsworth Technical College.
ACADEMIC QUALIFICATIONS: O & A Levels.
PROFESSIONAL QUALIFICATIONS: FCA Chartered Accountant.
HONOURS/AWARDS: MBE
HOBBIES AND INTERESTS: Skiing and politics.
PERSONAL PROFILE: 1970 opened own Practice in Birmingham called Marcus & Co. Helped the Greek Church in Birmingham & the ESTIA. Officer of the Conservative Party occuping many posts over 25 yrs. 1992 John Major recommended him for MBE which was awarded to him in 1992 for Political & Charitable work.

MARCUS MARKOU
Journalist

DATE OF BIRTH: 21.01.71
PLACE OF BIRTH: Sutton Coldfield, Birmingham.
Father, Demetrious, from Nicosia; Mother Christalla, born in Birmingham.
MARITAL STATUS: Married to Victoria.
SCHOOLS/COLLEGE: Eversfield School, Solihull, Bloxham School, Banbury, Birmingham University, University College London, London Academy of Music & Dramatic Art.
ACADEMIC QUALIFICATIONS: 7 O Levels, 4 A Levels, BA Honours in Modern History and Political Science (2:1), MA Legal & Political Theory.
PROFESSIONAL QUALIFICATIONS: Diploma in Classical Acting.
PERSONAL PROFILE: Journalist - launched, edited and wrote for magazine industry. Currently writing regular column for *Management Today*. Currently Managing Director for www.BusinessesForSale.com (global website for buying & selling small & medium sized businesses).

ADAMOS MARINOU
Former-Chairman of Greek Orthodox Community in Margate

DATE OF BIRTH: 30.01.41
PLACE OF BIRTH: Avgorou.
MARITAL STATUS: Married to Marina.
CHILDREN: Marinos, Fish & Chip Shop owner; Florentia, School Teacher.
HONOURS/AWARDS: Honoured by Greek Orthodox Church in UK.
PERSONAL PROFILE: Former Chairman of the Greek Orthodox Community in Margate.

THEO MASSOS
Actor

DATE OF BIRTH: 24.07.59
PLACE OF BIRTH: Kalo Chorio, Limassol.
MARITAL STATUS: Married to Jacky, a Housewife, from Weybridge, Surrey.
CHILDREN: Angelo, Jason and Costa.
SCHOOLS/COLLEGE: Arnos Grove, N. London, Drama Studio, London.
QUALIFICATIONS: Drama Diploma.
MEMBERSHIPS: British Actors Equity.
HOBBIES AND INTERESTS: Arsenal FC.
PERSONAL PROFILE: Actor. Has performed in London's 'West End'. Played Victoria Palace, Palladium and Strand Theatres. UK and European Tours, TV/ Film, home and abroad.

MICHAEL MATSOUKAS
Parikiaki Newspaper

DATE OF BIRTH: 04.04.40
PLACE OF BIRTH: Palechori.
MARITAL STATUS: Married to Katerina, a Housewife.
CHILDREN: Marina and Georgoulla.
SCHOOLS/COLLEGE: London School of Printing & Commercial School Samuel - Cyprus.
PERSONAL PROFILE: Worked for Vema Newspaper now works for Parikiaki Newspaper.

CHRISTIANA INGRID MAVROMATIS
Musician

DATE OF BIRTH: 08.11.78
PLACE OF BIRTH: Aberystwyth, Wales. Father from Larnaca.
MARITAL STATUS: Single
SCHOOLS/COLLEGE: Penglais School, Aberystwyth (1990-95) The Purcell School, London (1995-98) both Secondary Schools. Guildhall School of Music and Drama, 1998-2002 (London conservatoire).
ACADEMIC QUALIFICATIONS: B.Mus, Performance Diploma (Violin).
HONOURS/AWARDS: Government Scholarship to a specialist Music School (The Purcell School, London) Member of the Cardiff Bay Chamber Orchestra.
HOBBIES AND INTERESTS: Playing violin in orchestras or chamber groups for charity and professionally.
PERSONAL PROFILE: Former member of National UK Children's Orchestra & of National Youth Orchestra of Wales. Leader of Dyfed Youth Orchestra 1993-2000. Led the Chamber Orchestra for the 1998 Investiture Ceremony, Buckingham Palace. Soloist 1st prize, National Eisteddfod.

NICHOLAS CHRISTOPHER MAVROMATIS
Statistics Tutor, University of Wales

DATE OF BIRTH: 26.12.74
PLACE OF BIRTH: Aberystwyth, Wales. Father from Larnaca.
MARITAL STATUS: Single
SCHOOLS/COLLEGE: Penglais School, Aberstwyth 1986-93, University of Oxford, (St. Peter's College) 1993-96, University of Kent 1996-97.
ACADEMIC QUALIFICATIONS: MA. (Oxon), MSc (Kent)
MEMBERSHIPS: London Mathematical Society, Operational Research Society, UK.
HOBBIES AND INTERESTS: Violin, football, karate and astronomy.
PERSONAL PROFILE: Statistics Tutor, University of Wales, Aberystwyth 1997. Higher Scientific Officer, Government Operational Research Group. Committee member: Young Operational Researchers Society, UK.

VASSILI C. MAVROMATIS
Reader in Mathematics, University of Wales, Aberystwyth

DATE OF BIRTH: 24.09.44
PLACE OF BIRTH: Larnaca.
MARITAL STATUS: Married to Anastasia, Hotel Management (LHCIMA), from Plymouth UK. (father born Famagusta).
CHILDREN: Nicholas, Government Operational Research Service MA (Oxford) Mathematics, MSc (Kent) in Statistics. Christine, B.Mus (with Violin Performance) - final year student at Guildhall School of Music, London.
SCHOOLS/COLLEGE: St. Marylebone School, 1955-60, Owen's School 1960-63 (London). Selwyn Collage, Cambridge University 1963-6 Westfield College, London University 1966-9.
ACADEMIC QUALIFICATIONS: MA (Cambridge) MSc, PhD. (London).
MEMBERSHIPS: FIMA (Fellow of Institute of Maths, & its Applications).
FICA (Fellow of Institute of Combinatories & its Application).
PERSONAL PROFILE: Reader in Mathematics, & Director of Postgraduate Studies, Maths, Dept. University of Wales, Aberystwyth.

DR VASSILLIS MAVROU
Chairman of EKA

PLACE OF BIRTH: Famagusta.
MARITAL STATUS: Single
SCHOOLS/COLLEGE: CTL Academy, Famagusta, Greenwich University, Guildhall University, City University.
ACADEMIC QUALIFICATIONS: BA Political Economics MA Politics, Doctorate in Ethnicity.
HOBBIES AND INTERESTS: Politics, community work, reading, karate, dancing and travel.
PERSONAL PROFILE: Former Lecturer at City of London College for Business Studies, Economics Lecturer at Greenwich University & Lecturer in Sociology at North London University. Now the owner of a lettings Agency called Varosi Lettings. He is also the Chairman of Union of Cypriots in Britain (EKA).

LOUKIS MELEAGROS
Consultant Surgeon

DATE OF BIRTH: 10.06.53
PLACE OF BIRTH: Nicosia
MARITAL STATUS: Married to Lynn, a Hospital Manager, from Leeds, UK.
CHILDREN: Evie, Woodhouse College; Yiannis, Haberdashers' Aske's School; Kerynia, Palmers Green High School.
SCHOOLS/COLLEGE: Kykkos Pancyprian Gymnasium - Nicosia, Haberdashers' Aske's School - UK, University College - London, St. George's Hospital Medical School - London.
ACADEMIC QUALIFICATIONS: BSC, MBBS, FRCS (England), MD - University of London.
MEMBERSHIPS: Assoc. of Surgeons of GB and Ireland, British Soc. of Gastroenterology, British Assoc. of Surgical Oncology, President Hellenic Medical Soc. 2001-2.
HONOURS/AWARDS: British Heart Foundation (1986-88) Research Fellow.
HOBBIES AND INTERESTS: Swimming, keep fit/walking, Greek music/Bouzouki music, Blues music/Jazz music, fooball/athletics and theatre.
PERSONAL PROFILE: Consultant Surgeon - North Middlesex University Hospital, Formerly: Senior Lecturer in surgery - Medical College of St. Bartholomew's and Royal London Hospitals (1994-2000), Lecturer in surgery - University College & Middx Hospitals Medical School (1990-94), Specialist Surgeon in Abdominal/Intestinal Diseases. Laparoscopy & Endoscopy & Hernia Surgery, Medico-legal Expert.

STAVROS MELIDES
Secretary, Greek Orthodox Community, Nottingham

DATE OF BIRTH: 03.09.60
PLACE OF BIRTH: Limassol.
MARITAL STATUS: Married to Christala, from Sleaford, England. (family from Mazotos, Larnaca, Cyprus).
CHILDREN: Three children.
SCHOOLS/COLLEGE: Larnaca High School, Cyprus, Dingwall Academy, Scotland, Nottingham Trent University.
ACADEMIC QUALIFICATIONS: MBA.
MEMBERSHIPS: Fellow Assoc. of Professional Recruitment Consultants, Fellow Faculty of Management Science, FSB Chamber of Commerce (Many More).
HOBBIES AND INTERESTS: Hiking, camping, skiing, diving, abseiling and charity work.
PERSONAL PROFILE: Human Resources Consultant, Secretary Greek Orthodox Community Nottingham.

ANDREAS MENELAOU
Chairman of Anglisides Association, UK

DATE OF BIRTH: 10.01.32
PLACE OF BIRTH: Perivolia, Larnaca.
MARITAL STATUS: Widower, was married to Christalla Charalambous from Anglisides.
CHILDREN: Three children, five grandchildren. Katerina, Medical Receptionist; Mirianthi, Beauty Therapist and Menelaos, Antique Dealer.
SCHOOLS/COLLEGE: Perivolia Elementary School.
MEMBERSHIPS: MBIM (Member of British Institute of Management); ACI (Associate of the Institute of Commerce); Cyprus Philatelic Society.
HOBBIES AND INTERESTS: Reading, antiques, stamp collecting, antique books and travel.
PERSONAL PROFILE: Chairman of Anglisides Association UK. Former Secretary of Haringey Cypriot Association.

GEORGE MENICOU
Telecommunications

DATE OF BIRTH: 28.02.32
PLACE OF BIRTH: Limnia Famagusta.
MARITAL STATUS: Married to Angela Georgiou, a Dress designer and later, Housewife, from Phlamoudi Famagusta.
CHILDREN: Nicolas, Maria and Adonis.
SCHOOLS/COLLEGE: Greek Gymnasium of Famagusta (1950), City University of London.
QUALIFICATIONS: Diploma in Electrical (Dip.EE) Charter Engineer (C.Eng) Telecommunications Consultant.
MEMBERSHIPS: Fellow of The Institute of Electrical Engineers (FIEE).
HOBBIES AND INTERESTS: Gardening, computing and television.
PERSONAL PROFILE: Senior Telecommunication Consultant with ITT. Participated in the Development of the 1st Digital Telephone Exchange in the world. His work has required extensive travelling, and he has visited about 42 countries. Retired from the company in 1991, though continued to work as a freelance consultant for a few years. Now fully retired. Has a number of patents for basic inventions in telecommunications.

MICHALIS MENICOU
Engineer

DATE OF BIRTH: 05.05.72
PLACE OF BIRTH: Nicosia.
MARITAL STATUS: Married to Christiana.
SCHOOLS/COLLEGE: Higher Technical Institute, Cyprus; University of Sheffield; Sheffield Hallam University.
ACADEMIC QUALIFICATIONS: HND; B.Eng; MSc; MBA; PhD
MEMBERSHIPS: Institute of Industrial Engineers IIE, Institute for Operations research & the management sciences INFORMS.
HOBBIES AND INTERESTS: Gardening, travelling and history of modern Greece.
PERSONAL PROFILE: Has undertaken work as an External Consultant to various organisations.

CHRISTIANA KOUFETTA-MENICOU
Researcher at University of Nottingham

DATE OF BIRTH: 08.08.74
PLACE OF BIRTH: Famagusta
MARITAL STATUS: Married to Michalis Menicou.
SCHOOLS/COLLEGE: University of Cyprus (undergraduate), University of Sheffield (postgraduate).
ACADEMIC QUALIFICATIONS: B.Ed. in Primary Education, Ph.D. in Science Education Piano Diploma.
MEMBERSHIPS: European Assoc. for research in Learning and Instruction.
HOBBIES AND INTERESTS: Music, swimming and Photography.
PERSONAL PROFILE: Occupation: Research Associate, Centre for Research in Development, Instruction and Training, (Credit Centre), Department of Psychology, University of Nottingham.

MERKIS NEOFITOU MERKI
Politics & Education

DATE OF BIRTH: 28.12.35
PLACE OF BIRTH: Pissouri, Limassol.
MARITAL STATUS: Married to Doula from Pissouri Village.
CHILDREN: Christine, Housewife; Vrionakis, Network Consultant.
MEMBERSHIPS: Guild of Master Craftsmen.
HOBBIES AND INTERESTS: Shooting, fishing, gardening, reading and current affairs.
PERSONAL PROFILE: Building Contractor involved in Cypriot Politics and Greek Schools in the UK. Now involved in land and property management in Cyprus.

Website: www.cypruspropertyagents.com
Email: merkis@merki.fsnet.co.uk

VRIONAKIS MERKIS
Physics/IT Teacher

DATE OF BIRTH: 31.07.70
PLACE OF BIRTH: London. Parents from Pissouri Village, Limassol.
MARITAL STATUS: Married to Maria Morfoulis, (Merkis) a Nursery Nurse.
CHILDREN: Zoe.
SCHOOLS/COLLEGE: Ashmole School Barnet, University of Warwick, London Guildhall University.
ACADEMIC QUALIFICATIONS: BSc Physics (Honours).
PROFESSIONAL QUALIFICATIONS: PGCE Secondary Teaching, MCSE (computing) microsoft, CCDP & CCNP (Cisco Certified Networking & Design).
MEMBERSHIPS: Youth Cypriot Associations.
HONOURS/AWARDS: School Awards, Martial Arts Championships winner.
HOBBIES AND INTERESTS: Martial Arts /Instructor, Greek Dance Instructor.
PERSONAL PROFILE: Founded Southgate Greek Cypriot Youth Club, voluntary help & effort in many Greek Cypriot Youth Societies - Community Centre, EKON etc. Is Head of Department in a secondary School (Science), and also works as an IT Consultant to companies.

Email: vmerkis@hotmail.com

KYL MESSIOS
Actor

DATE OF BIRTH: 20.01.77
PLACE OF BIRTH: London, Father from Kalopsida.
SCHOOLS/COLLEGE: Birmingham University, Southgate School.
ACADEMIC QUALIFICATIONS: BA Drama Theatre Arts (2:1 Honours) 3 A Levels, 9 GCSEs.
MEMBERSHIPS: National Youth Music Theatre.
HOBBIES AND INTERESTS: Theatre, Film, Football Charity Organisations.
PERSONAL PROFILE: Studying at LAMDA Film & Theatre work inc NYMT New York & Far East Tours. He has also appeared on TV in *55 Degrees North*.

CHARILAOS K METTIS
Teacher, Journalist

DATE OF BIRTH: 23.01.34
PLACE OF BIRTH: Philia (Morphou).
MARITAL STATUS: Married to Stella Christofi, a Dress Designer, from Dromalaxia Cyprus.
CHILDREN: Anna, Teacher; Kyriacos, Teacher.
SCHOOLS/COLLEGE: Pancyprian Gymnasium (Nicosia), University of Athens, London University.
ACADEMIC QUALIFICATIONS: Degree in Literature and History.
HONOURS/AWARDS: Ecumenical Patriarchate "Teacher Officio".
HOBBIES AND INTERESTS: Reading and writing.
PERSONAL PROFILE: Head of Greek Section at the Greek Archdiocese in GB, Author of articles and books on history & education of Greeks in GB.

ANASTASIS MICHAEL
Chairman of Ayia Varvara Association

DATE OF BIRTH: 23.11.38
PLACE OF BIRTH: Ayia Varvara, Nicosia.
MARITAL STATUS: Married to Angela, from Flamoudi.
CHILDREN: Xenia, Housewife; Helen, Insurance Manager; Georgia, Pharmacist.
HOBBIES & INTERESTS: Sport.
PERSONAL PROFILE: Chairman of Ayia Varvara Association. Self-employed Fish & Chip shop owner.

CHRISTINE MICHAEL - (Née) CHRISOULLA GEORGIOU-LEVENTIS
Estate agent

PLACE OF BIRTH: Rizokarpasso, Cyprus.
MARITAL STATUS: Married to Lakis, from Skarinou, Cyprus.
CHILDREN: Sandra, BA Business Studies, Nicholas, BSc Management Science, MSc Risk Management, CIMA student.
ACADEMIC QUALIFICATIONS: 6 GCE O Levels, Diploma in Commerce, Business Studies and Economics.
MEMBERSHIPS: Fellow member of the National Association of Estate Agents.
HOBBIES AND INTERESTS: Cooking, entertaining socialising, reading, travelling, interior design and naturally, helping people.
PERSONAL PROFILE: Owns and runs Michael Wright Estate Agents, based in Cockfosters for 30 years and serving the North London community.

CHRYSO MICHAEL
President of Greek School in Mansfield

DATE OF BIRTH: 12.11.54
PLACE OF BIRTH: Troulli Larnaca.
MARITAL STATUS: Married to Demetrious, from Troulli.
CHILDREN: Chrystalla, Katerina, Costas and Georgio.
SCHOOLS/COLLEGE: Clarendon College.
ACADEMIC QUALIFICATIONS: O Levels - Shorthand Typing.
PERSONAL PROFILE: Self Employed. President of Greek School Mansfield.

DOULLA MICHAEL
Chairwoman of Bowes Greek School

DATE OF BIRTH: 15.04.57
PLACE OF BIRTH: London. Father, Antonis Yiakoumi, from Leonarisso; Mother, Maria Tsioupra, from Komi Kebir.
MARITAL STATUS: Married to Andy Michael from Famagusta.
CHILDREN: Vasillia, graduated from Sussex University; Anthony and Christopher at School.
SCHOOLS/COLLEGE: Tollington Park School, Tottenham Technical College.
HOBBIES AND INTERESTS: Silversmithing and travelling.
PERSONAL PROFILE: Chairwoman of Bowes Primary School PTA, Chairwoman of Bowes Greek School, Member of Secretariat of OESEKA.

EFSTATHIOS MICHAEL
Solicitor

DATE OF BIRTH: 09.07.71
PLACE OF BIRTH: London. Father from Xylotymbou; Mother from Prastion, Morphou.
MARITAL STATUS: Single.
SCHOOLS/COLLEGE: Bancroft's School, Woodford Green, 1982-89. Worcester College, Oxford University 1989-92.
ACADEMIC QUALIFICATIONS: MA (Law) (Oxon).
PROFESSIONAL QUALIFICATIONS: Law Society Finals.
HOBBIES AND INTERESTS: Sport (especially football), travel and music.
PERSONAL PROFILE: Partner in Law Firm, Slaughter and May. Specialises in Commercial Litigation, Arbitration and Dispute Resolution, including acting for Carlton and Granada in their widely reported successful action against the Football League.

GEORGE STEPHANOS MICHAEL
Accountant/President of Greek Community in Weston Super Mare

DATE OF BIRTH: 21.11.52
PLACE OF BIRTH: Ardana Famagusta.
MARITAL STATUS: Married to Christina, a Health Shop Manageress, from Xylophagou.
CHILDREN: Stephanos, Laura, Yiangos and Savvas.
SCHOOLS/COLLEGE: Agricultural Gymnasium - Morphou, Weston Super Mare Technical College, Aston University, Birmingham.
ACADEMIC QUALIFICATIONS: 12 O Levels, 4 A Levels, BSc (Hons) Maths and Computer Science.
PROFESSIONAL QUALIFICATIONS: FMAAT, Affiliated Member ICAEW & ACCA.
MEMBERSHIPS: AAT, BCS.
HONOURS/AWARDS: Best Science Student in 1974 Weston Super-Mare Technical College.
HOBBIES AND INTERESTS: Christian religion, hiking, walking, football and athletics.
PERSONAL PROFILE: Own Accountancy Practice, President of Greek Community in Bristol for Weston Super Mare. Treasurer of Citizens' Advice Bureau for South West Region.

HELEN 'ELLENE' MICHAEL
Actress/Singer

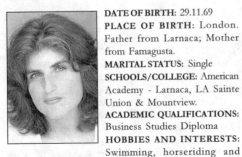

DATE OF BIRTH: 29.11.69
PLACE OF BIRTH: London. Father from Larnaca; Mother from Famagusta.
MARITAL STATUS: Single
SCHOOLS/COLLEGE: American Academy - Larnaca, LA Sainte Union & Mountview.
ACADEMIC QUALIFICATIONS: Business Studies Diploma
HOBBIES AND INTERESTS: Swimming, horseriding and backgammon.
PERSONAL PROFILE: Banker/Entertainer Actor/Singer/Dancer. Has appeared on TV in Cyprus, and in plays in the UK.

MICHAEL MICHAEL
Accountant

DATE OF BIRTH: 12.04.72
PLACE OF BIRTH: Birmingham. Father from Vasili, Leonarisso; Mother from Limassol.
MARITAL STATUS: Single
SCHOOLS/COLLEGE: King Edward School Birmingham, Oxford University.
ACADEMIC QUALIFICATIONS: BA (Honours) in Geography.
PROFESSIONAL QUALIFICATIONS: Chartered Accountant.
MEMBERSHIPS: Securities Institute.
HOBBIES AND INTERESTS: Business, golf, keep-fit, football, (Arsenal fan), socialising and travel.
PERSONAL PROFILE: Corporate Finance Partner with Friend LLP, a niche firm of professional advisors. Also Board Member of Mercia Institute of Enterprise, Connect Midlands Investment Committee and Birmingham Future.

MICHAEL COSTAS-MICHAEL
Councillor, Cardiff County Council

DATE OF BIRTH: 29.09.52
PLACE OF BIRTH: Lympia Nicosia.
MARITAL STATUS: Married to Joyce, a Hairdresser, from Cardiff, Wales.
CHILDREN: Jordan John; James Jack and Zoe Marina.
SCHOOLS/COLLEGE: Kitchener Rd Primary School, Severn Rd, Canton Cardiff, & Market Rd Comprehensive School.
MEMBERSHIPS: Labour Party since 1983, Greek Cypriot Assoc. Fairwater Social Club, Fabians, Assoc. of Labour Councillors.
HOBBIES AND INTERESTS: Sports, politics and environment.
PERSONAL PROFILE: Hairdresser. Elected as Councillor for Cardiff County Council in April 97, Deputy Chair Economic Development 98, Elected 99 Executive Member Environment with responsibility for Highways, Parks Cemeterys, waste Control, Street Cleaning, Recycling. Worked with Fairwater Sports Trust on Sportlot Bid. Worked with Greek Cypriot Association to access Lottery funding for a new community hall in Cardiff.

NEOPHYTOS MICHAEL
Poet

DATE OF BIRTH: 20.01.46
PLACE OF BIRTH: Petra
MARITAL STATUS: Married to Eleni from Sykhari.
SCHOOLS/COLLEGE: Solea Gymnasium, Xeros Technical School.
HOBBIES AND INTERESTS: Writing and music.
PERSONAL PROFILE: Was a qualified Electrician but had problems with vision so became a receptionist in Nicosia General Hospital. Came to England in 1974, did Rehabilitation training for the Blind for three months with RNIB training in Engineering. Worked as a Tool Operator for five year, then Royal London Society for the Blind in Engineering until 1998. Registered partially blind in 1979 and totally blind in 1997. Has written poems entitled *Darling I Love You, My Sweet Lady I Adore You, Baby You're a Dream, Everything For You My Love.* Received letters of thanks from the Queens of the UK, Sweden, Holland, Denmark & Belgium for poems sent to them on different occasions.

NEOPHYTOS MICHAEL, A QUALIFIED ELECTRICIAN, WAS REGISTERED PARTIALLY BLIND IN 1979 AND TOTALLY BLIND IN 1997 AND HAS SINCE BECOME A POET

OLGA MICHAEL
Actress

DATE OF BIRTH: 22.02.75
PLACE OF BIRTH: London. Father from Nicosia; Mother from Paphos.
SCHOOLS/COLLEGE: University of York, Mountview Theatre School.
ACADEMIC QUALIFICATIONS: BA in English Literature (2:1)
PERSONAL PROFILE: Actress & Performance Poet. Recently worked with the Riding Lights Theatre Company touring Britain. Also with LGR & Theatro Technis. As a Poet she has worked for the London Board, & performed at the Poetry Cafe. Is currently working on a cabaret piece about a 'spoof' Greek Pop Group called Zamba!, in which she plays a highly strung Greek singer.

STAVROS MICHAEL
Chairman of Middlesborough Greek Orthodox Community

DATE OF BIRTH: 19.12.33
PLACE OF BIRTH: Perachorio.
MARITAL STATUS: Married to Charoulla from Lithrodondas.
CHILDREN: Chris, Long distance Driver; Panayiota, Runs Takeaway; Pantelou, Holistic Therapist.
SCHOOLS/COLLEGE: Village School.
HOBBIES AND INTERESTS: Music and reading religious literature.
PERSONAL PROFILE: For the past eleven years elected as Chairman of the Middlesborough Greek Orthodox Community.

ANDREW MICHAELIDES
DJ & Radio Presenter

DATE OF BIRTH: 25.05.79
PLACE OF BIRTH: London. Parents from Famagusta, Son of George, Journalist for *Parikiaki* Newspaper and Photini Michaelides.
MARITAL STATUS: Married.
SCHOOLS/COLLEGE: Kingsbury High School, Harrow Weald College, West Herts, Watford.
ACADEMIC QUALIFICATIONS: HND & BA in Media Production Management.
HOBBIES AND INTERESTS: Music and dining out.
PERSONAL PROFILE: A top DJ on LGR. Has worked at Hombres Night Club and at Eros Enfield. Former Radio Presenter at Radio Amore & Asteras in Cyprus, and was a TV Presenter for New Extra TV in Limassol.

CHRISTOPHER MICHAELIDES
Councillor, Bridgend County Borough Council

PLACE OF BIRTH: Barry, South Wales. Father, Michael, from Pedoulas, Cyprus; Mother Gladys, Maud, May Michaelides.
MARITAL STATUS: Married.
CHILDREN: Three daughters.
SCHOOLS/COLLEGE: Gladstone Rd Secondary Modern, Barry, S. Wales, Llandaff Polytechnic.
QUALIFICATIONS: Passed all Department of Transport examinations to become an approved driving instructor.
PERSONAL PROFILE: Formed The Bettws Amenities Society (1990-01), which raised over 1 & 1/2 £million for community projects in village of Bettws, Bridgend, which is an area of social Deprivation. Its population approx 3,000. Founder & President of The Bridgend & Valleys Railway Co. (1985-01) This is a Co which is not for profit, opened officially for business in 2002. Member of the Garw Community Council (1983-01). Cabinet Member responsible for Educ, Leisure, and Community Services, Bridgend County Borough Council, Chairman of Glamorgan Archives, Committee Member of the Board of the Arts Council for Wales.

GEORGE MICHAELIDES
Journalist

DATE OF BIRTH: 01.02.51
PLACE OF BIRTH: Famagusta.
MARITAL STATUS: Married to Photini.
CHILDREN: Vasos, works in Job Centre; Andreas, Radio Presenter.
SCHOOLS/COLLEGE: Famagusta Gymnasium.
MEMBERSHIPS: AKEL Party.
HOBBIES AND INTERESTS: All sports, especially football.
PERSONAL PROFILE: Worked as a Jounalist with *Verna* Newspaper from 1974 - 85, now with *Parikiaki* Newspaper. Also a presenter for LGR & Hellenic TV.

GEORGE PANOS MICHAELIDES
Accountant & Former Chairman of
Independent Greek Schools of UK

DATE OF BIRTH: 09.08.52
PLACE OF BIRTH: Nicosia. Father, Panos, from Nicosia; Mother, Thelma Kofterou, from Ayios Theodoros, Larnaca.
MARITAL STATUS: Married to Stavroulla.
CHILDREN: Two.
SCHOOLS/COLLEGE: Eleneion English School Nicosia, North London University.
ACADEMIC QUALIFICATIONS: BA Accountancy.
PROFESSIONAL QUALIFICATIONS: Chartered Certified Accountant.
HOBBIES AND INTERESTS: Football (Tottenham & Barnet fan) and politics.
PERSONAL PROFILE: Was treasurer of Cypriot Football League from 1977-85. Former Chairman of Potters Bar Greek School, Chairman of Independant Greek Schools of UK. Was first Chairman of Assoc. of Cypriot Qualified Accountants for two years. President of the Association of Chartered Certified Accountants, North London District Society. Partner in ALG Chartered Certified Accountants in North London.

Address: Brook Point, 1412-1420 High Rd, London N20 9BH.
Email address: gpm@alguk.co.uk

OMIROS MICHAELIDES
Chairman of Yerakies Association

DATE OF BIRTH: 19.05.35
PLACE OF BIRTH: Yerakies.
MARITAL STATUS: Married
CHILDREN: One son, three daughters, eight grandchildren, two great grandchildren.
SCHOOLS/COLLEGE: Yerakies Elementary; Pedhoula Gymnasium.
HOBBIES AND INTERESTS: Work and travel.
PERSONAL PROFILE: Came to England in 1953, did National Service in British Army for two years, had Hairdresser, Coffee Bar, Restaurant & Nightclub, Casino in Surrey. 1967 opened Casino in Newcastle was Director in Pleasurama Casinos Division. Now owns the Banqueting Halls Assembly Rooms in Newcastle. Chairman of Yerakies Assoc. UK & Chairman of the Greek Orthodox Church in Newcastle.

Prof. PANTELEIMON MICHAELOUDIS
Musician

DATE OF BIRTH: 07.03.66
PLACE OF BIRTH: Famagusta. Father, Michalakis, former Principal Conductor of the Famagusta Municipal Band.
MARITAL STATUS: Single
SCHOOLS/COLLEGE: 1974, came to London Royal College of Music.
ACADEMIC QUALIFICATIONS: DIP RCM, ARCM.
HOBBIES AND INTERESTS: Sports and reading.
PERSONAL PROFILE: Taught six years at the Royal College of Music, now busy recording and performing in Concerts and Touring. He has given concerts in many international Guitar Festivals and appeared on Radio and TV.

www.panteleimon.com
email: panteleimon-michaeloudis@hotmail.com

CHRISTOS KALLONAS MICHAELS
Head of Legal & Business Affairs at
Icon Entertainment

DATE OF BIRTH: 30.05.70
PLACE OF BIRTH: London. Father, George, from Larnaca; Mother, Antigoni Kallonas, from Latsia.
MARITAL STATUS: Single
SCHOOLS/COLLEGE: Lochinver House School, (Junior School), St. Albans, (Senior School), Leeds University (Degree), Kings College, London (Post Grad Diploma).
ACADEMIC QUALIFICATIONS: LLB.
PROFESSIONAL QUALIFICATIONS: LSF.
MEMBERSHIPS: Law Society, New Producers Alliance.
HOBBIES AND INTERESTS: Film making, acting and Greek dancing.
PERSONAL PROFILE: Head of Legal & Business Affairs at Icon Entertainment & Icon Film Distribution, Director of Sound Films. Interviewed Margaret Thatcher on "CBTV" on ITV at the age of thirteen as Cyprus Representative.

REV. ANDREAS MICHAILIDIS
Priest

DATE OF BIRTH: 07.12.37
PLACE OF BIRTH: Lefka.
MARITAL STATUS: Married to Alkmini, from Greece.
CHILDREN: Anastasios, killed in accident in Greece; Eleni, Student at University in Germany; Menelaos, now Father Niphon, a Monk at the Monastery Mahera, Cyprus; Michael, in Cosmetics business in Greece; Eftychia, at Nottingham University.
SCHOOLS/COLLEGE: Pancyprian Gymnasium Nicosia, Columbia University USA, University of Athens, University of Thessaloniki.
HOBBIES AND INTERESTS: Writing books & poems. One has been published (*The Lexicon of Byzantine Music*).
PERSONAL PROFILE: Greek Orthodox Priest of the Church Virgin Mary in Nottingham. Former teacher and translator in Cyprus and Thessaloniki, Greece, Teaches translation for MA in Linguistics as a visiting Lecturer at the University of Sheffield. Also responsible for the Greek schools of Nottingham and Derby.

LEFKOS MIDDLETON MD
Vice President & Worldwide Head of the Medical Genetics Division of GlaxoSmith Kline R&D

DATE OF BIRTH: 21.12. 50
PLACE OF BIRTH: Nicosia
MARITAL STATUS: Married to Georgia Demetriades from Nicosia.
CHILDREN: Theodore, Law Student; George, Military Service, Cyprus; Constantinos, at school.
SCHOOLS/COLLEGE: Pancyprian Gymnasium, Louis Pasteur University in Strasbourg, France.
HONOURS/AWARDS: Awarded the European Federation of Neurological Societies Investigator Award in 1994 & the Italian Caetano Conte Academy Prize in 1996.
HOBBIES AND INTERESTS: Music, theatre and travel.
PERSONAL PROFILE: Joined GlaxoSmith Kline R&D in 1999, based in London. In 1990, founded the Cyprus Institute of Neurology and Genetics, and introduced the State of the Art medical services to both communities of Cyprus and the region, including prevention of genetic diseases. He identified two new diseases and mapped genes of four diseases in the Mediterranean region. Served as Nicosia Municipal Councillor from 1985-1990 and initiated the creation of the Nicosia Centre of Contemporary Arts in the Old City (Palia Electriki).

HELEN CHRISTA MIKELLIDES
Chiropodist

DATE OF BIRTH: 23.12.70
PLACE OF BIRTH: UK. Father from Nicosia; Mother from Famagusta.
MARITAL STATUS: Single
SCHOOLS/COLLEGE: Bishop Douglas Secondary, Southgate College, University of Westminster, Leaf Hospital, School of Podiatric Medicine, University of Brighton.
ACADEMIC QUALIFICATIONS: BSc (Honours) Podiatry.
PROFESSIONAL QUALIFICATIONS: State Registered Chiropodist/Podiatrist.
MEMBERSHIPS: Council Professions Supplementary to Medicine CPSM, Society of Chiropodists and Podiatrists.
HOBBIES AND INTERESTS: Singing, playing accordion, summer concerts on the lawn! Learning violin and in Gospel choir.
PERSONAL PROFILE: Sang as a backing singer in the Group *Neos Kosmos* for the Eurovision Song Contest in Cyprus. Part of a Greek Dancing Group that performed on the Generation Game in February 2002.

ANDREAS MIKKIDES (Deceased)
Former Mayor of Haringey

DATE OF BIRTH: 15.02.32
PLACE OF BIRTH: Kythrea Nicosia.
MARITAL STATUS: Married to Eleni from Pano Lakatamia, Nicosia.
CHILDREN: Loakim, Christa and Eraclis.
SCHOOLS/COLLEGE: Pancyprian Gymnasium.
HOBBIES AND INTERESTS: Poetry, published an anthology *Photini Orizontes* & two books entitled *Three Stories Look like Fairy Tails* and *Pages of my Life*.
PERSONAL PROFILE: For years was an active member in the Labour Movement, and took part in many demonstrations, including 'Ban the Bomb', against the war in Vietnam, and against the Apartheid Regime of South Africa. Elected as Councillor at Haringey Borough in 1982, Deputy Mayor 1985 & 1986, then mayor. Was the first Cypriot Mayor in Britain & the whole of Europe and has set a record for two periods in a row.

GEORGE MILIOS
Former Secretary of DACA Association

DATE OF BIRTH: 29.09.34
PLACE OF BIRTH: Cairo, Egypt. Father, Costas, from Leonariso; Mother, Eftichia, from Peristerona, Paphos.
MARITAL STATUS: Married to Kety, a Housewife, from Kilani.
CHILDREN: Constantina, Marketing Manager; Nicholas, Estate Agent.
SCHOOLS/COLLEGE: Greek Ambetios Elementary, St. Georges College in Egypt.
PROFESSIONAL QUALIFICATIONS: Instructor-Assessor NVQ.
HOBBIES AND INTERESTS:
Gardening and sports.
PERSONAL PROFILE: Consultant, NVQ Trainer Assessor, Managing Projects on behalf of Organisations. Former Secretary of DACA Association, and is currently on the committee of the Greek Parents Association.

NICK MILO (MAILOS)
Football Coach

DATE OF BIRTH: 13.11.45
PLACE OF BIRTH:
Marathavounos, Cyprus.
MARITAL STATUS: Married to Sally, a Fashion Model, from Norwich.
CHILDREN: Nathan and Georgia, both at school.
SCHOOLS/COLLEGE: Sir William Collins, Roehampton College.
ACADEMIC QUALIFICATIONS: Certificate of Education.
PROFESSIONAL QUALIFICATIONS: UEFA 'A' Pro Coaching Award, FA 'A' Coaching Licence, FA Tutor/ Assessor Licence, FA Academy Directors Licence.
MEMBERSHIPS: Tutor Assessor Staff Coach - FA Coaches Association, London Coaches Association, Surrey Coaches Association.
HONOURS/AWARDS: Islington & St. Pancras Schoolboy Representative, London Schoolboy Representative.
HOBBIES AND INTERESTS: Music, art, and history.
PERSONAL PROFILE: Came to England aged two (1947). First Anglo-Cypriot to play in Cyprus 1970-71 on contract to Olympiacos & later Salamina FC. Member of Cyprus National Squad. Played with QPR & Millwall Football League, Enfield, Barking, Ilford, Beckenham, Non League. Coach at Kingstonians and Manager at Fisher Athletic. At present, Academy Director at Millwall FC.

ANNA MINA
Teacher

PLACE OF BIRTH: London. Parents from Nicosia.
MARITAL STATUS: Married to Costakis, Greek Cypriot born in London.
CHILDREN: Three sons.
SCHOOLS/COLLEGE: Maria Grey.
PROFESSIONAL QUALIFICATIONS: Cert Ed. Dip Ed.
HOBBIES AND INTERESTS:
Reading, writing poetry and gardening.
HONOURS/AWARDS: Brent Citizenship Award 2002.
PERSONAL PROFILE: Secondary School Teacher of English & Special Needs. English Co-ordinator, Learning Mentor Volunteer on the Committee of the "Association of Cypriots Brent & Harrow" - Secretary and Vice-President for the Greek School in Brent.

email: annie_mina2@yahoo.co.uk

DR MINAS GEORGE MINA
Honorary Secretary of National Federation of Cypriots/Teacher/Lecturer

DATE OF BIRTH: 21.09.53
PLACE OF BIRTH: Makrasyka, Famagusta.
MARITAL STATUS: Married to Katey Michael, a Lawyer, from London (parents from Cyprus).
SCHOOLS/COLLEGE: American Academy, Larnaca, Kingsway-Princeton College, London. Kings College, London.
ACADEMIC QUALIFICATIONS: BSc Ph.D.
MEMBERSHIPS: Institute of Clinical Research.
HOBBIES AND INTERESTS: Politics, world & social affairs and swimming.
PERSONAL PROFILE: Teacher/Lecturer. Scientific Research for many years at Univ, currently also training in Medical Diagnostics, General Secretary of Organisation of Relatives of missing Cypriots (UK). Honorary Secretary of National Federation of Cypriots and member of other community Organisations.

PANTELLIS MINA
Secretary of Achna Association

DATE OF BIRTH: 27.07.45
PLACE OF BIRTH: Achna.
MARITAL STATUS: Married to Pantellitsa from Achna.
CHILDREN: Katerina, BSc Bio- Technology; Joanna, at Hertfordshire University; Eleni, at Middlesex University.
SCHOOLS/COLLEGE: Commercial School Famagusta, Pantion University, Athens. City of London Polytechnic, Guildhall University.
ACADEMIC QUALIFICATIONS: MA Politics & Government.
HOBBIES AND INTERESTS: Reading.
PERSONAL PROFILE: Worked as Journalist in Greece & with the Parikiaki in London. Translator & Interpreter. Secretary of Achna Association UK.

MICHAEL MINAS
Artist/Production Designer

DATE OF BIRTH: 14.08.42
PLACE OF BIRTH: Morphou.
MARITAL STATUS: Married to Jacqueline Goldsmith, Designer-Lecturer from London.
CHILDREN: Miraphora, a Graphic Artist (for films including Harry Potter, Captain Corelli's Mandolin etc).
SCHOOLS/COLLEGE: Greek Gymnasium Morphou, Hornsey College of Art & Crafts.
ACADEMIC QUALIFICATIONS: National Diploma in Design (NDD), Studied Painting.
HOBBIES AND INTERESTS: Writing.
PERSONAL PROFILE: 1967-78 Scenic Designer Thames Television. 1977-96 Five solo exhibitions of his paintings as well as selected group exhibitions Television Work: Design & Art Direction: *Orchestra* C4 with Sir George Solti & Dudley Moore *Operalia-* with Placido Domingo for Televisa, Mexico Art Director for *Joseph & the Amazing Technicolor Dreamcoat* for the Really Useful Group. *The Three Tenors*, Christmas in Vienna 2000 for Sony. Michael Bolton - the Arias-Bellini Theatre, Catania Sicily. Also visiting lecturer, Royal College of Art and Chelsea College of Art.

email: minas@clara.co.uk

GEORGE CHRISTOU MINDIKKIS
Musician

DATE OF BIRTH: 27.06.32
PLACE OF BIRTH: Akanthou, Famagusta.
MARITAL STATUS: Married to Elli Costa, a Dressmaker, from Rizokarpaso.
CHILDREN: Maroulla, Legal Secretary; Christakis, Dentist.
SCHOOLS/COLLEGE: Trinity College of Music London.
ACADEMIC QUALIFICATIONS: ALCM, LTCL (violin Teacher) LTCL (school music).
MEMBERSHIPS: Angloakanthou Aid Society, and Lobby for Cyprus.
HOBBIES AND INTERESTS: Music and compositions.
PERSONAL PROFILE: Has given many concerts and lectures, and worked on several programmes at LGR on History of Ancient Greek Music. Harmonised and arranged the "Cyprus Dances" for Piano and Violin and Piano. Composed music for Channel 4 LTV.

CHRISOULLA MINTIS
Work with Cypriot Elderly

DATE OF BIRTH: 04.10.43
PLACE OF BIRTH: Skarinou.
MARITAL STATUS: Married to Costa Mintis for 40 years, a builder, from Tricomo, Cyprus.
CHILDREN: Mary, Interior Designer; Tony has special needs & lives in supported Housing in Peterborough.
HOBBIES AND INTERESTS: Gardening, walking, reading and socialising.
PERSONAL PROFILE: Has worked with various Cypriot Community Groups since 1977 & started the Mothers of Disabled Children's Group in 1987 which ran for two years & was given funding by the Borough of Haringey. In 1996 was involved in starting the group for people with special needs which is still in existence. Has worked with elderly Cypriots dating back to 1977 as a volunteer, moved to working with the Greek Cypriot Women's Health Group and more recently with Cypriot Elderly & Disabled Group as an out-reach worker.

GEORGE MICHAEL MISHELLIS
Former Chairman of Manor Hill Greek School

DATE OF BIRTH: 20.03.40
PLACE OF BIRTH: Larnaca.
MARITAL STATUS: Married to Antigoni, a Housewife and Partner in Business, from Latsia, Nicosia.
CHILDREN: Andonea Buxton, TV Presenter; Christos, Solicitor; Mishellis, Granada Media Executive.
SCHOOLS/COLLEGE: American Academy Larnaca.
PROFESSIONAL QUALIFICATIONS: Designer - Pattern Cutter.
MEMBERSHIPS: Greek Brotherhood.
HOBBIES AND INTERESTS: Fishing and Arsenal Fooball Club.
PERSONAL PROFILE: Previous business: Manufacturer of Ladies Clothing - Ladies Hairdressing - Hotelier & now Landlord/Property Owner. Helped to create the Independent Greek Schools in London. Chairman to Manor Hill School for six years, two years Vice Chairman, two years Treasurer.

DR CONSTANTINOS MISSOURIS
Consultant Cardiologist

DATE OF BIRTH: 23.12.59
PLACE OF BIRTH: Zodhia, Nicosia.
MARITAL STATUS: Single
SCHOOLS/COLLEGE: The English School Nicosia, St George's Hospital Medical School, London.
ACADEMIC QUALIFICATIONS: BSc, MBBs, MD, MRCP
MEMBERSHIPS: Numerous National & International Societies.
HOBBIES AND INTERESTS: Poetry and classical reading.
PERSONAL PROFILE: Consultant Cardiologist, Heatherwood & Wexham Park Hospital & Royal Brompton Hospital, London.

HAMBIS MICHAEL (MITCHELL)
Former Editor of Vema Newspaper

DATE OF BIRTH: 03.03.20
PLACE OF BIRTH: Hirokitia.
MARITAL STATUS: Married to Maroulla from Ora.
CHILDREN: Michael, Andy and Irene.
SCHOOLS/COLLEGE: Hirokitia Elementary School.
MEMBERSHIPS: AKEL, General & Municipal Workers Union, Communist Party GB, Fleet Leaseholders & Tenants Assoc., Camden Pensioners Action Group.
HONOURS/AWARDS: From National Federation of Cypriots in GB for several years of National & Community work. Medal from AKEL for 50 years membership.
HOBBIES AND INTERESTS: Gardening, walking, reading and TV.
PERSONAL PROFILE: Former Editor of *Vema* Newspaper, Member of the Secretariat of the London District Committee of the Communist Party of GB and Secretary of the Committee. Chairman of the Fleet Leaseholders and Tenants' Association in Camden. Chairman of Hirokitia Association UK.

COSTAS MORFAKIS
Managing Partner of Bond Partners LLP

DATE OF BIRTH: 08.05.63
PLACE OF BIRTH: Finchley. Father from Agios Georgious Kyrenia; Mother, Amygdalia, Greece.
MARITAL STATUS: Widower
CHILDREN: Adam and Zoe.
SCHOOLS/COLLEGE: The Grammar School, Nicosia, Arnos School, Southgate.
PROFESSIONAL QUALIFICATIONS: FCA, FCCA, FCMA, MARBP.
MEMBERSHIPS: Chairman of Institute of Chartered Accountants, small practitioners group of central London.
HOBBIES AND INTERESTS: Classic cars and martial arts.
PERSONAL PROFILE: Managing partner of Bond Partners LLP. Chartered Certified Accountants & Insolvency Practitioners.
Auditor of Greek & Greek Cypriot Community of Enfield Charity
Main sponsor of Pantel FC.

THANOS MORPHITIS
Deputy Director of Education, Islington

DATE OF BIRTH: 05.03.54
PLACE OF BIRTH: London. Father from Morphou; Mother from Athens.
MARITAL STATUS: Married
CHILDREN: Five.
SCHOOLS/COLLEGE: William Ellis School, University of Hull.
ACADEMIC QUALIFICATIONS: BA (Honours).
PROFESSIONAL QUALIFICATIONS: Qualified Youth Worker.
PERSONAL PROFILE: Deputy Director of Education, Islington.

GEORGE MOUKTARIS
Accountant/Secretary of Lobby for Cyprus

DATE OF BIRTH: 25.05.51
PLACE OF BIRTH: Famagusta.
MARITAL STATUS: Married to Christalleni from Dherynia.
CHILDREN: Anastasis, Christina and Stavri.
SCHOOLS/COLLEGE: 1st & 2nd Gymnasium Famagusta; West Norwood Tech College.
PROFESSIONAL QUALIFICATIONS: Chartered Accountant.
HOBBIES AND INTERESTS: Sailing, diving, shooting and parachuting.
PERSONAL PROFILE: Has own Accountancy Practice in Edgware called Mouktaris & Co. Former secretary of Cypriot Qualified Accountants Assoc. in UK, and Chairman of Famagusta Assoc. Chairman of Harrow Independent Greek School, Secretary of Lobby for Cyprus.

Address: Mouktaris & Co Chartered Accountants, 156A Burnt Oak Broadway, Edgware, Middlesex HA8 0AX.
Tel: 020 8952 7717
email: George@Mouktaris.co.uk

ANTHOULLA MOUSIKOU
President of the Greek Orthodox Women's Society in Stoke-on-Trent

DATE OF BIRTH: 23.11.60
PLACE OF BIRTH: Famagusta.
MARITAL STATUS: Married to Panayiotis, owns Fast Food Retail Business, from Oroklini, Larnaca.
CHILDREN: Spyroulla, at Sheffield University; Evangelos, at school; Constantinos, at school; Georgios.
SCHOOLS/COLLEGE: Ardana 1st School, Tricomo High School, Naseby Secondary School, Birmingham.
HOBBIES AND INTERESTS: Reading, photography, listening to music, cooking and travelling.
PERSONAL PROFILE: Housewife, President of the Greek Orthodox Ladies Auxillary Society of Stoke-on-Trent in 1997-98, also currently President of the Greek School of Ayia Marina and Panayia Chryseleousa of Stoke-on-Trent.

GEORGE K. MOUSKAS
Businessman

DATE OF BIRTH: 14.07.53
PLACE OF BIRTH: London. Parents from Famagusta and Nicosia.
MARITAL STATUS: Married to Mary Vavlitis in 1975. (parents from villages Vavla & Kato Drys).
CHILDREN: Elli, graduated from London University in 2001; Kyriacos, reading French at London University; Zela, at school.
SCHOOLS/COLLEGE: Finchley Catholic Grammar School then read Law at Ealing College London.
ACADEMIC QUALIFICATIONS: BA (Honours) Law.
MEMBERSHIPS: Baltic Exchange, Lloyds of London.
HOBBIES AND INTERESTS: Watching football, playing tennis and snow skiing.
PERSONAL PROFILE: Managing Director of Shipping Company Zela Shipping Co, Ltd, established 1963. Currently on the Council of the Trust of Archbishop of Thyateira & GB, which overlooks all Ecclesiastical matters in UK.

KYRIACOS MOUSKAS
Shipowner (Deceased)

DATE OF BIRTH: 25.11.1917
PLACE OF BIRTH: Kato Varosi.
MARITAL STATUS: Was married to Zela Loukiades, from Nicosia, Cyprus.
CHILDREN: Zenon, Gloria and George.
SCHOOLS/COLLEGE: Gymnasium High School, Famagusta, Cyprus.
MEMBERSHIPS: Baltic Exchange since 1955.
HONOURS/AWARDS: Made 'Archonta' by Patriarch of Constantinople in 1968.
HOBBIES AND INTERESTS: His work and family.
PERSONAL PROFILE: Shipowner since 1957, becoming the first Greek Cypriot shipowner. Helped to build Greek school at St Andrews Church, Kentish Town, and helped financially many other Greek schools in the UK. Also built a new hospital wing in Voula-Athens, which comprised eleven operating theatres. This was opened in February 2001 by the Greek Minister of Health. Kyriacos Mouskas was one of the founders of the Church of St John the Baptist in Wightman Road.

ZENON MOUSKAS
Businessman

DATE OF BIRTH: 02.08.41
PLACE OF BIRTH: London. Father from Famagusta; Mother from Nicosia.
MARITAL STATUS: Married to Helen Pittas, born in London (father from Dali, Mother from Larnaca)
CHILDREN: Zela, Housewife; Kyriacos, Shipping Company Director.
SCHOOLS/COLLEGE: Crest Nursery School, Wessex Gardens Primary School, Clarks College Grammar School.
ACADEMIC QUALIFICATIONS: FICS AIARS.
MEMBERSHIPS: Baltic Exchange, Lloyds of London.
HOBBIES AND INTERESTS: Sports, Church, Charities
PERSONAL PROFILE: Co-founder of Zela Shipping Co Ltd. Member of the Council of the "Greek Shipping Co-operation Committee". Trustee & Council Member of the Church of "The Holy Cross & St. Michael" - Golders Green.

JOHN MOUSKIS
Secretary of The Greek Parents Association

DATE OF BIRTH: 08.06.48
PLACE OF BIRTH: Kaimakli.
MARITAL STATUS: Married to Loulla from London (parents from Dromolaxia).
CHILDREN: Andrew, at Bournemouth University; Harry, has a Virtual Reality Company; Jason, at Queen Elizabeth Boys' School.
SCHOOLS/COLLEGE: Pancyprian Gymnasium in Nicosia.
PROFESSIONAL QUALIFICATIONS: Accountant.
HOBBIES AND INTERESTS: Greek Music, socialising, walking and theatre.
PERSONAL PROFILE: Partner in the Accountancy Practise G. George Associates in Wood Green. Chairman of Queenswell Greek School, Secretary of Greek Parents Association, Functions Organizer for OESEKA.

HARRY MOUSKIS
Virtual Reality

DATE OF BIRTH: 13.08.77
PLACE OF BIRTH: London. Parents from Kaimakli and London.
MARITAL STATUS: Single
SCHOOLS/COLLEGE: Queen Elizabeth Boys' School, Bournemouth University.
ACADEMIC QUALIFICATIONS: BSc in Production Design & Manufacture, MA in Digital Entertainment Systems.
HOBBIES AND INTERESTS: Computers, films and music.
PERSONAL PROFILE: Now owner of a Virtual Reality Company in North London called V-real.

ANASTASIOS MOUSTAKA
President of Greek Church St Nicholas in Liverpool

DATE OF BIRTH: 01.08.38
PLACE OF BIRTH: Paralimni.
MARITAL STATUS: Married to Irene, from Cyprus.
CHILDREN: Michael, Shop Manager; Helen, Travel Consultant.

SCHOOLS/COLLEGE: Paralimni School, Famagusta High, Cyprus.
PROFESSIONAL QUALIFICATIONS: Hairdresser.
MEMBERSHIPS: Golf Club.
HOBBIES AND INTERESTS: Golf and music.
PERSONAL PROFILE: Owns Hairdressing Business; President of Greek Orthodox Church of St Nicholas in Liverpool.

KYRIAKOS MOUSTOUKAS
Chairman of Liverpool Greek Society

DATE OF BIRTH: 27.07.62
PLACE OF BIRTH: Liverpool. Parents from Lefkara.
MARITAL STATUS: Married to Panayiota.
CHILDREN: Georgia, studying Human Biology at Loughborough University; Christophora; Nikolaos; Dimitris.
SCHOOLS/COLLEGE: Quarry Bank Comp School, Liverpool, Lancaster University.
ACADEMIC QUALIFICATIONS: BSc (Honours) 2.1, Physics with Electronics.
PROFESSIONAL QUALIFICATIONS: Financial Planning Certificate Parts 1,2,3.
MEMBERSHIPS: MLIA (Dip) (Member of Life Insurance Ass.)
HOBBIES AND INTERESTS: Greek music, Greek dancing, ballroom dancing and Bouzouki.
PERSONAL PROFILE: Financial Adviser with Zurich Advice Network; Founder Member & Chairman of Liverpool Greek Society; Greek Church of St. Nicholas (formerly Committee Member).

GEORGE MYRISTIS
Businessman and Footballer

DATE OF BIRTH: 23.04.37
PLACE OF BIRTH: Livadhia, Larnaca.
MARITAL STATUS: Married to Annika Christodoulou, Larnaca.
CHILDREN: Panicos, has own business; Margarita.
SCHOOLS/COLLEGE: Graduated Commercial Lyceum Larnaca.
ACADEMIC QUALIFICATIONS: 5 O Levels
PERSONAL PROFILE: Consultant in Men's Outdoor clothing - 39 years experience & still going. Also in the Bedlinen Business for 30 yrs as a Manufacturer. Played football in Cyprus, for Pezoporikos & the National Team of Cyprus (1955-58).

JOHN MYLONAS
Managing Director of General Motors Russia

DATE OF BIRTH: 22.12.45
PLACE OF BIRTH: Kato Platres.
MARITAL STATUS: Married to Magdalena from Tyrol, Austria.
CHILDREN: James, working in Bedfordshire Fire Brigade; Tara, in the Tourist Industry.
SCHOOLS/COLLEGE: Mitsis Commercial College, Tottenham Tech, Kingston University.
QUALIFICATIONS: HND in Mechanical Engineering, BSc in Production Engineering, MSc in Air Transport Engineering IE (Industrial Engineering) Practitioner.
HONOURS/AWARDS: GM President Honours Award.
HOBBIES AND INTERESTS: Flying, theatre, football and backgammon.
PERSONAL PROFILE: On completion of Masters Degree worked with BEA for a short period. Joined Vauxhall Motors Luton Plant as Production Operator on assembly line (nobody knew of his qualifications), then progressed through a number of senior appointments. In 1989 took an international assignment for General Motors as the Implementation Director setting up two factories in Hungary for Astra Cars and to manufacture opel engines. Then Operations Director for GM Poland. In 1998 John moved to Moscow, where he is now the Managing Director of GM Russia for the joint venture between General Motors and the Russian Autovaz that produces the Lada vehicles.

email: John.Mylonas@gmrussia.ru

MICHAEL JOHN MYLONAS
Barrister

DATE OF BIRTH: 11.06.66
PLACE OF BIRTH: England. Mother from Amiandos; maternal Grandfather from Pano Amiandos; maternal Grandmother from Hydra.
MARITAL STATUS: Single
SCHOOLS/COLLEGE: Eton College, University of Buckingham, Bar School (London).
ACADEMIC QUALIFICATIONS: LLB (Honours), BAR.
MEMBERSHIPS: International BAR Association, Professional Negligence Bar Association., Personal Injury Bar Association., Hurlingham Polo Association
HONOURS/AWARDS: Scholarship, Grays Inn; Scholarship - Inns of School of Law.
HOBBIES AND INTERESTS: Polo, sailing, skiing and motor racing.
PERSONAL PROFILE: Barrister specialising in medical negligence and major disaster litigation. (Ladbroke Grove Inquiry - Lead Counsel).

JASON NEARCHOU
President of Greek Community in Coventry

DATE OF BIRTH: 16.12.58
PLACE OF BIRTH: Limassol.
MARITAL STATUS: Married to Olga, born in Coventry (parents, Cypriot).
CHILDREN: Christian; Petros; Stefanos; Panayiota.
SCHOOLS/COLLEGE: Limassol Gymnasium.
PROFESSIONAL QUALIFICATIONS: Registrar.
HOBBIES AND INTERESTS: Horse riding, swimming and reading.
PERSONAL PROFILE: President of Greek Community of Coventry and of Midlands Festival Communties.

CHRISTOS DEMOS NEOCLEOUS
Solicitor

DATE OF BIRTH: 26.01.58
PLACE OF BIRTH: London. Parents Demos from Dora Limassol and Maroulla from Mandres Famagusta.
MARITAL STATUS: Married to Anna, (father is from Ayios Sergios Famagusta, mother from Agapnou).
CHILDREN: Two sons.
SCHOOLS/COLLEGE: Sir William Collins School, City & East London College, Chelmsford University, College of Law, Lancaster Gate.
ACADEMIC QUALIFICATIONS: A levels, LLB Degree, passed solicitors' finals at first sitting.
HOBBIES AND INTERESTS: Go karting, clay shooting, race cars, skiing and D.I.Y. Was member of Dora Association UK.
PERSONAL PROFILE: Joined Solicitors Kenneth Shaw & Co in 1981 as a trainee; now Equity Owner in the same practice but now called Christos Wybrew.

LOUCAS NEOCLEOUS
Businessman (Deceased)

DATE OF BIRTH: 07.06.24
PLACE OF BIRTH: Galataria.
MARITAL STATUS: Was married to Ada, from Italy.
CHILDREN: Three daughters, all university graduates.
SCHOOLS/COLLEGE: Limassol Elementary School.
MEMBERSHIPS: AKEL.
HOBBIES AND INTERESTS: Sport and politics.
PERSONAL PROFILE: In 1951 came to England, worked in ABC Bakers as a Pastry cook then a Dress Presser. Started his own Dress Manufacting business in 1960 called Loucas Fashions in Lyme Street, Camden Town. Owned property company called Lathurst Property Investment Ltd. Was a member of the committee of DACA the Dressmakers Association. Was a member of Hendon Greek School Committee also helped Camden Town Greek School.

MARIANNA NEOFITOU
Actress

DATE OF BIRTH: 23.06.89
PLACE OF BIRTH: UK. Father from Kalavasos, Mother from Peristeronopiyi.
MARITAL STATUS: Single
SCHOOLS/COLLEGE: Sylvia Young Theatre School.
HOBBIES AND INTERESTS: Singing, dancing, reading and writing songs.
PERSONAL PROFILE: Has appeared on TV in *Watchdog* and *Eastenders* and various commercials in the UK and abroad. Appeared in the film *Harry Potter* No. 2. and had a role in the West end show *Chitty Chitty Bang Bang* at the London Palladium.

ENTRANTS IN GREEK CYPRIOTS IN THE UK HAVE BEEN NOMINATED FOR THEIR ACHIEVEMENTS AND CONTRIBUTIONS. YOU CAN NOMINATE SOMEONE OR YOURSELF WHO DESERVES TO BE IN THE BOOK. ENTRIES ARE FREE. SEND IN YOUR NOMINATIONS, INCLUDING NAME, CONTACT ADDRESS, TELEPHONE NUMBER AND EMAIL TO GREEK CYPRIOTS IN THE UK 111 ST THOMAS'S ROAD LONDON N4 2QJ TELEPHONE 020 7503 3498 EMAIL cypriotwhoswho@aol.com

YIANNIS NEOKLEOUS
Former Chairman of North London Greek Association

DATE OF BIRTH: 23.11.27
PLACE OF BIRTH: Galataria Paphos.
MARITAL STATUS: Married to Androulla from Koutsoventi, Kyrenia.
CHILDREN: Loukia, Housewife; Koullis, Businessman.
SCHOOLS/COLLEGE: Galataria Elementary School.
HOBBIES AND INTERESTS: Backgammon, football and travelling.
PERSONAL PROFILE: Had a Dressmaking Factory called John Fashions, employing more than 70 Cypriots. Was Vice Chairman of North London Greek Association, where he was honoured for his contribution to the schools of that area. Was a member of Omonia FC UK Committee.

CHRIS NEOPHYTOU
Former Chairman of the 12 Apostles Church in Brookmans Park

DATE OF BIRTH: 29.05.50
PLACE OF BIRTH: Famagusta.
MARITAL STATUS: Married
CHILDREN: N. Neophytou, G. Neophytou.
SCHOOLS/COLLEGE: East London University.
ACADEMIC QUALIFICATIONS: BSc Applied Economics.
HOBBIES AND INTERESTS: Swimming, sailing, diving, cinema, fishing and shooting.
PERSONAL PROFILE: Chairman of Caretower Ltd. One of the Founders and first president of the Church of The Twelve Apostles.

TONY NEOPHYTOU
London Greek Radio Broadcaster

DATE OF BIRTH: 26.08.73
PLACE OF BIRTH: London. Parents from Limassol.
MARITAL STATUS: Single
SCHOOLS/COLLEGE: George Orwell Secondary, Islington 6th form Centre, University of North London.
ACADEMIC QUALIFICATIONS: BSc Honours Politics.
PERSONAL PROFILE: Tony is a Broadcaster on London Greek Radio.

SPYROS J NEOPHYTOU
Director and General Manager, Bank of Cyprus, London

DATE OF BIRTH: 19.04.44
PLACE OF BIRTH: Paphos, Cyprus.
MARITAL STATUS: Married to Angela Neophytou.
CHILDREN: Barbara and Marianna.
SCHOOLS/COLLEGE: Graduate of Paphos Greek Gymnasium.
PROFESSIONAL QUALIFICATIONS: 1972 - Associate Member of the Institute of Chartered Accountants in England and Wales. 1979 - Fellow of the Institute of Chartered Accountants in England and Wales.
MEMBERSHIPS: Council Member of the Cyprus-British Chamber of Commerce and Industry.
HONOURS/AWARDS: Gold Cross of the Archdiocese of Thyateira.
HOBBIES AND INTERESTS: Golf.
PERSONAL PROFILE: Director and General Manager - Bank of Cyprus (London) Ltd. Director - Bank of Cyprus (Channel Islands) Ltd.

SPYROS NEOPHYTOU
Sales Manager of Cyprus Airways, UK

DATE OF BIRTH: 26.06.51
PLACE OF BIRTH: Agios Theodoros, Famagusta.
MARITAL STATUS: Married to Christine from London (parents from Komi Kebir).
SCHOOL/COLLEGE: Famagusta Gymnasium. Then studied Aeronautical Engineering at Delta College, Athens and Hatfield Polytechnic.
CHILDREN: Johnathan, Stockbroker; Melanie, studying Education at Roehampton University.
HOBBIES AND INTERESTS: Keep fit, squash and tennis.
PERSONAL PROFILE: Former Chairman of Manor Hill Greek School and was on the committee of Independent Greek Schools. Sales Manager of Cyprus Airways, UK.

CONSTANTINOS NICOLA
Consultant Civil Engineer

DATE OF BIRTH: 20.08.46
PLACE OF BIRTH: Nicosia, Cyprus.
MARITAL STATUS: Married to Nitsa Pavlou Mitella, an Arla Lettings Consultant, from Nicosia, Cyprus.
CHILDREN: Steven Anthony and Louissa Jane.
SCHOOL/COLLEGE: Upton House Secondary Modern School, London, Kingston University, Surrey.
ACADEMIC QUALIFICATIONS: BSc Civil Engineering (1971), IOD Diploma in Company Direction (1989).
MEMBERSHIPS: Member of the Institute of Civil Engineering, Member of the Institute of Highway and Transportation Engineers.
PROFESSIONAL QUALIFICATIONS: Registered Engineer, Republic of Kenya.
HOBBIES & INTERESTS: Photography, golf and football.
PERSONAL PROFILE: Since attaining Chartered status in 1974, has enjoyed a diverse professional career covering the principal disciplines of Civil Engineering, from an Engineering Design Assistant through to the various stages of Project Management, to General Manager and latterly Managing Director of an International Construction Group of Companies.

Early employment included working as a civil servant for the Department of the Environment involved in the design and construction of Kent's M25 motorway section. Later he worked on infrastructure design for major international building projects with a firm of consultants. He was subsequently appointed to work in Kenya and spent four years in East Africa designing and supervising water supply, airports and infrastructure related projects.

Returned to England in late 1980 and has since worked for a major international construction group where he has coordinated the management of a variety of energy related worldwide contracts.

ALEXIS NICOLAS
Footballer

DATE OF BIRTH: 13.02.83
PLACE OF BIRTH: London. Parents from London, grandparents from Famagusta.
MARITAL STATUS: Single
SCHOOLS/COLLEGE: East Barnet School.
HOBBIES AND INTERESTS: Cars and golf.
PERSONAL PROFILE: Footballer. Captain for Barnet District and Middlesex, was with Arsenal from ten to sixteen years old. Joined and played for Aston Villa reserves & youth. Now with Chelsea - played and captained reserves. Full squad member. Has appeared for first team Cyprus Under-21 International.

ANDRIANA NICHOLAS
Teacher

DATE OF BIRTH: 26.01.59
PLACE OF BIRTH: Famagusta.
MARITAL STATUS: Married to Nicholas, a Chartered Accountant, from London.
CHILDREN: Jon and Andreas, both at school.
SCHOOLS/COLLEGE: Hammersmith County School, W12, Middlesex University.
ACADEMIC QUALIFICATIONS: 2 A Levels, 8 O Levels.
PROFESSIONAL QUALIFICATIONS: Bachelor of Education (Honours)
HOBBIES AND INTERESTS: Reading, theatre and being a mother!
PERSONAL PROFILE: Head of Year and Teacher of English at Broomfield School, Enfield.

ANDY NICHOLAS
Head Teacher

DATE OF BIRTH: 25.06.52
PLACE OF BIRTH: Larnaca
MARITAL STATUS: Married to Helen from Audellero, Larnaca.
CHILDREN: Two sons and one daughter.
SCHOOLS/COLLEGE: Gayhurst Primary School, Hackney, St Davids School, Hornsey, All Saints Teachers Training College.
HOBBIES AND INTERESTS: Vintage cars and family.
PERSONAL PROFILE: First post Teacher at Chesterfield Junior School in Enfield. Then went to Coleridge School as a Senior Teacher, followed by Lea Valley School in 1985 as Deputy Headteacher, then Headteacher with 500 Pupils. Ofsted Inspector for Primary Schools. Magistrate with Haringey.

HELEN MARINA NICHOLAS
Bridal Dress Designer

DATE OF BIRTH: 22.11.42
PLACE OF BIRTH: Swindon, Wiltshire. Father from Komi Kebir.
MARITAL STATUS: Married to Fanos from Komi Kebir.
CHILDREN: Nick, IT Developer; Christie, Actress.
SCHOOLS/COLLEGE: Hornsey College of Arts and Crafts.
HOBBIES AND INTERESTS: Travel, reading, music and art.
PERSONAL PROFILE: Bridal Design. Started Helen Marina, now with over 200 outlets in England, Wales and all over Europe and USA. Designs featured in *Hello* Magazine, *Brides*, *You and Your Wedding Day*, *Bliss*, *Cosmopolitan Bride* and others.

JACK NICHOLAS
Hotelier, Charity Work

DATE OF BIRTH: 01.02.55
PLACE OF BIRTH: London. Parents from Komi Kebir.
MARITAL STATUS: Married to Helen Lambrias, a Sales Assistant in John Lewis, Brent Cross, born in London (family from Neo Chorio Kithreas).
CHILDREN: Joanna, studying Law at Middlesex University; Christina, doing GCSEs.
SCHOOLS/COLLEGE: Middlesex Polytechnic.
ACADEMIC QUALIFICATIONS: Higher National Diploma in Hotel & Catering; Management.
PROFESSIONAL QUALIFICATIONS: Fellow of the Hotel & Catering Institute Management Association.
HONOURS/AWARDS: Head Boy at Prep School and Public School; Hotel of the Year Award, 1987.
HOBBIES AND INTERESTS: Playing golf, watching Arsenal, cricket and rugby.
PERSONAL PROFILE: Has been in the hotel industry several years, holding various positions including General Manager of the *Holiday Inns* at Newcastle and Cardiff, and of the London Marriott, Swiss Cottage. Joined Premier in October 1999 as Director of Operations for London and in March 2000 was promoted to Operations Manager UK. Now responsible for the day-to-day operation of 22 hotels - 15 Express by Holiday Inn Hotel, 4 Howard Johnson Hotels and 3 Days Inn Hotels. Whilst in Cardiff was on the Committee of the RNIB South Wales Looking Glass Appeal and helped raise £100,000 in twelve months for the centre in Cardiff. Was invited to St James's Palace with Committees all over the UK to meet the Queen. Was also one of the founding members of The Komi Kebir Football Club in London in the late 1970s.

KYPROS NICHOLAS
Solicitor

DATE OF BIRTH: 12.11.37
PLACE OF BIRTH: Khirokitia.
MARITAL STATUS: Married to Maria.
CHILDREN: Yiota, Stella and Nicholas.
SCHOOLS/COLLEGE: English School, Nicosia. Inns of Courts School of Law, College of Law, Guildford.
PROFESSIONAL QUALIFICATIONS: Solicitor, formerly Barrister at Law.
HONOURS/AWARDS: Freeman of the City of London 1983. Honourary Chief Enyoma in Nigeria, 1985. Director of the Iwuanyanwu F.C in Nigerian football league. Former Governor of the University of East London.
HOBBIES AND INTERESTS: Tennis, swimming and Arsenal.
PERSONAL PROFILE: Civil Servant - Water Development Department Lawyer at Stikeman Somper & Co 1964-1969. Senior and establishing Partner of the practice Nicholas & Co., established in 1969 (18-22 Wigmore Street, London W1U 2RG) Presidentt of the Greek Orthodox Church in Edmonton, London and Vice Chairman of the Greek Orthodox Communities of Great Britain. Trustee of the Archdiocese of Thyateira & G.B & other Religious and educational charities. Solicitor to the Archdiocese of Thyateira & G.B and formerly to the Cyprus Relief Fund. Trustee of the Cardiovascular Disease & Research Trust (CDER).

NICHOLAS CHRISTOPHER KYPROS NICHOLAS
Solicitor

DATE OF BIRTH: 30.06.71
PLACE OF BIRTH: UK. Parents from Chirokitia, Cyprus.
MARITAL STATUS: Married to Katrina, half-English, half-Armenian.
CHILDREN: Adam.
SCHOOLS/COLLEGE: Bethany Davis College of East Anglia, University of North London, Southbank University.
ACADEMIC QUALIFICATIONS: BA Honours.
PROFESSIONAL QUALIFICATIONS: Solicitor.
HOBBIES AND INTERESTS: Football (Arsenal fan), rugby and general Sport.
PERSONAL PROFILE: Solicitor, Partner in Nicholas & Co.
18-22 Wigmore Street, London W1U 2RG.

STEVEN NICHOLAS
Solicitor

DATE OF BIRTH: 08.10.58
PLACE OF BIRTH: London. Parents from Agios Amvrosios.
MARITAL STATUS: Married to Eleni from Yerolakos.
CHILDREN: Three sons.
SCHOOLS/COLLEGE: William Collins School, Kingsway College, Middlesex Poly, College of Law Guildford.
ACADEMIC QUALIFICATIONS: BA Honours in Law.
MEMBERSHIPS: Cypriot Golf Society.
HOBBIES AND INTERESTS: Spurs, golf, squash and Bouzouki.
PERSONAL PROFILE: Solicitor. Partner in Georgiou Nicholas Solicitors

YIACOUMIS NICHOLAS
Businessman

DATE OF BIRTH: 1925
PLACE OF BIRTH: Komi Kebir.
MARITAL STATUS: Married to Pepa from Yialloussa.
CHILDREN: Nick, Chris, Nina, Julie, Eleni; twelve grandchildren.
SCHOOLS/COLLEGE: Komi Kebir Elementary School.
HOBBIES AND INTERESTS: Gardening, reading, politics
PERSONAL PROFILE: Served in the Cyprus Regiment of the British Army. Formed the Company Nicholas Bros. in 1948, making bridal wear, known all over the world. Known for his philanthropic work within the community.

PROFESSOR ANDREAS NICOLAIDES, FORMER PROFESSOR OF VASCULAR SURGERY AT THE IMPERIAL COLLEGE SCHOOL OF MEDICINE

THEODORA NICKSON
Vice Principal at John Kelly Girls' Technology College

DATE OF BIRTH: 31.08.56
PLACE OF BIRTH: Kingsbury, London. Father from Skylloura; Mother from Skarinou.
MARITAL STATUS: Divorced
CHILDREN: Peter, University of Warwick - MSc Physics; Maria, Stanmore College, BTec National Diploma in Media; Elena, Henrietta Barnett School.
SCHOOLS/COLLEGE: University of Nottingham 1974-78, Downer Grammer School, Edgware 1967-74.
ACADEMIC QUALIFICATIONS: MA, BEd Honours, Cert ED.
HOBBIES AND INTERESTS: Reading, theatre and her children.
PERSONAL PROFILE: Currently Vice Principal at John Kelly Girls' Technology College.

Email: Theonickson@hotmail.com

PROFESSOR ANDREAS NICOLAIDES
Professor of Vascular Surgery

DATE OF BIRTH: 17.10.38
PLACE OF BIRTH: Nicosia.
MARITAL STATUS: Married to Lala Hadji Kyriakou, from Nicosia.
CHILDREN: Nicolas, Banker; Savvas, Information Technology.
SCHOOLS/COLLEGE: Pancyprian Gymnasium, Nicosia, Guys Hospital Medical School, London.
ACADEMIC QUALIFICATIONS: M.B, B.S. (London).
PROFESSIONAL QUALIFICATIONS: L.R.C.P.M.R.C.S. (England), F.R.C.S. (England), MS (London).
HONOURS/AWARDS: Awarded the Jacksonian prize by the Royal College of Surgeons England in 1972 for his work on the prevention of venous thromboembolism.
MEMBERSHIPS: Fellow of the Royal College of Surgeons (England and Edinburgh).
HOBBIES AND INTERESTS: Wildlife photography.
PERSONAL PROFILE: Former Professor of Vascular Surgery at the Imperial College School of Medicine (St Mary's Hospital) and Director of the Irvine Laboratory for Cardiovascular Investigation and Research from 1983-2000. His research group was involved in several areas which included non-invasive vascular screening and diagnostic investigation, early detection and prevention of venous disease. He is Editor-in-Chief

of International Angiology and is on the Editorial Board of many vascular journals. He is Emeritus Professor at Imperial College and an examiner for MS and PhD degrees for London University. Now the Medical Director of the Cyprus Institute of Neurology and Genetics. He is co-author of over 400 original papers and editor of fourteen books.

Address: 9 North Grove, Highgate, London N6 4SH.

PROFESSOR KYPROS NICOLAIDES
Obstetrician & Gynaecologist

DATE OF BIRTH: 09.04.53
PLACE OF BIRTH: Limassol.
MARITAL STATUS: Single
CHILDREN: Erodotos and Despina.
SCHOOLS/COLLEGE: Paphos Primary, English School, Nicosia, Kings College, London.
ACADEMIC QUALIFICATIONS: BSc in Bio-Chemistry, MBBS in Medicine.
PROFESSIONAL QUALIFICATIONS: Now a Professor in Foetal Medicine.
HONOURS/AWARDS: Ian Donald Gold Award of the International Society of Ultrasound in Obstetrics and Gynaecology, Eric Salling award of the World Association of Perinatal Medicine.
HOBBIES AND INTERESTS: Reading, classical and Greek music.
PERSONAL PROFILE: Works at Kings College Hospital. Formed the charity of Foetal Medicine Foundation. Promoting research and training internationally. He has been in over 700 scientific and National publications. Regularly gives TV interviews. The head of the biggest foetal medicine research centre in the world. President of the Cypriot Students Association in the 1970s, member of the National Federation of Cypriots in the 1970s.

PROFESSOR KYPROS NICOLAIDES HEADS THE BIGGEST FOETAL MEDICINE RESEARCH CENTRE IN THE WORLD

ANDREAS NICOLAOU
Solicitor, Vice President of the Democratic Party of Cyprus in the UK

DATE OF BIRTH: 25.09.32
PLACE OF BIRTH: Achna Village, Famagusta.
MARITAL STATUS: Married to Vera Georgiou Sideras from Laxis, Famagusta.
CHILDREN: Constantina; Helena and Susanna.
SCHOOLS/COLLEGE: Achna Elementary School, Greek Gymnasium of Famagusta, Council of Legal Education and College of Law.
PROFESSIONAL QUALIFICATIONS: Barrister at Law, Solicitor.
MEMBERSHIPS: The Law Society and various Organisations of the London Greek Community.
HONOURS/AWARDS: Honoured by the Co Patriarch of Constantinople for services to the Greek Orthodox Church.
HOBBIES AND INTERESTS: Football and athletics, classical and Greek music.
PERSONAL PROFILE: Solicitor (own office, A Nicolaou & Co). Helped All Saints Greek Orthodox Church as its Chairman, organised functions for the UK Thalassaemia Society, helped in the establishment of L.G.R. Member and Vice President of the Democratic Party of Cypriots in England. Legal advisor to the Greek Orthodox Church in GB.

REV ECONOMOS GEORGIOS NICOLAOU
Priest

DATE OF BIRTH: 28.09.41
PLACE OF BIRTH: Eftakomi.
MARITAL STATUS: Married to Christalleni from Eftakomi.
CHILDREN: Nicos, Sotiroulla, Andreas and Angela.
SCHOOLS/COLLEGE: Lanition Gymnasium, Limassol, Theological School, Nicosia.
MEMBERSHIPS: Eftakomi Association. Honorary member of Hellenic Society Bristol.
HONOURS/AWARDS: Silver Cross of the Archdiocese of Thyateira of Great Britain.
HOBBIES AND INTERESTS: Stamp collection (Cyprus), Coin collection (Cyprus) and gardening.
PERSONAL PROFILE: Parish Priest Bristol. Was 1st Chairman of Eftakomi Association.

LAMBROS NICOLAOU
Former General Secretary of Cyprus Youth Club (Deceased)

DATE OF BIRTH: 08.04.34
PLACE OF BIRTH: Vokolida, Cyprus.
MARITAL STATUS: Married to Stella.
CHILDREN: One son, one daughter.
MEMBERSHIPS: AKEL, Cyprus Youth Club.
HONOURS/AWARDS: from KLN for ten years' service, and from AKEL for his services to the party.
HOBBIES AND INTERESTS: Writing, poems and gardening.
PERSONAL PROFILE: General Secretary of Cyprus Youth Club for several years, active in Leyton Cypriot Community activities. Former Chairman of Vokolida Association, UK Former member of Central Committee AKEL in UK.

LORA NICOLAOU
Architect/Urban Designer

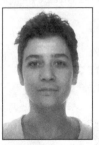

DATE OF BIRTH: 05.03.57
PLACE OF BIRTH: Nicosia.
MARITAL STATUS: Divorced
SCHOOLS/COLLEGE: Palourgiotissa & Acropolis Gymnasium, Nicosia; National Technical University of Athens; Bartlett School of Architecture - University College, London; Oxford Brookes University.
ACADEMIC QUALIFICATIONS: Diploma in Architecture, MSc in Advanced Architectural Studies, MA in Urban Design.
PROFESSIONAL QUALIFICAITONS: Registered Architect-ARB (Architects Registration Board) UK, Institute of Architects & Engineerings-Cyprus, Technical Institute of Architects-Greece.
MEMBERSHIPS: Member of Urban Design Group UK.
HOBBIES AND INTERESTS: Swimming and walking.
PERSONAL PROFILE: Director of Development Planning at DEGW plc, London. Senior Lectureship at Oxford Brookes University.

MARIA K NICOLAOU
Chair of The Leukaemia Society

DATE OF BIRTH: 09.09.61
PLACE OF BIRTH: London. father from Pano Arodhes, Paphos; Mother from Athienou.
MARITAL STATUS: Married to Savvas Nicolaou, Structural Engineer, Assistant Director, born in London (father from St Louca, Famagusta; Mother from Rizakarpasso).
CHILDREN: Twins: John Christopher and Georgia Penny.
SCHOOLS/COLLEGE: Trinity House School for girls, Kingsway Princeton College.
ACADEMIC QUALIFICATIONS: O Levels.
PROFESSIONAL QUALIFICATIONS: YCSW & National Certificate in Supported Housing.
MEMBERSHIPS: Chartered Institute of Housing.
HOBBIES AND INTERESTS: Travel, reading and charity work.
PERSONAL PROFILE: Scheme Manager for Sheltered Housing for Cypriots. Chair of The Leukaemia Society.

NEOPHYTOS NICOLAOU
Organising Secretary AKEL Section in Great Britain

DATE OF BIRTH: 11.12.46
PLACE OF BIRTH: Erimi
MARITAL STATUS: Married to Evoulla, from Limassol.
CHILDREN: One son and two daughters.
SCHOOLS/COLLEGE: Lanition Gymnasium, Limassol. Pitmans London.
MEMBERSHIPS: AKEL, National Fereation of Cypriots, EKA.
HOBBIES AND INTERESTS: Gardening.
PERSONAL PROFILE: Former General Manager of *Parikiaki* Newspaper. Vice Chair of Association of Cypriots in Enfield. Organising Secretary AKEL Section in Great Britain.

NICK NICOLAOU
Consultant Obstetrician and Gynaecologist

DATE OF BIRTH: 23.06.53
PLACE OF BIRTH: London. Parents from Vokolida and Lefkara.
MARITAL STATUS: Married to Eve.
CHILDREN: Erini, Soteri and Katerina.
SCHOOLS/COLLEGE: Guys Hospital Medical School
ACADEMIC QUALIFICATIONS: BSc (Honours) Biochemistry; MD; BS; FRCOG; LAW HBSc (Honours).
HOBBIES AND INTERESTS: Computers, skiing, rugby and football (Chelsea supporter).
PERSONAL PROFILE: Consultant Gynaecologist at Hillingdon Hospital. Senior Gynaecologist at University of London. Examiner of University of London. Former President of Hellenic Medical Society. Junior Vice President of Royal Society of Medicine. UCAS screener for Imperial Medical School.

Email address: Nick.Nicholas@thh.nhs.uk

NICK NICOLAOU
Driving Standards Agency Examiner

DATE OF BIRTH: 20.05.57
PLACE OF BIRTH: London, Parents from Larnaca
MARITAL STATUS: Married to Florentina, born in Manchester, (parents from Avgorou).
CHILDREN: Three children.
SCHOOLS/COLLEGE: St Davids, Southgate Technical.
HOBBIES & INTRESTS: Computers Motor Sport.
PERSONAL PROFILE: Driving Instructor 1990 Driving Standards Agency Examiner.

NICKY NICOLAOU
Footballer

DATE OF BIRTH: 12.10.83
PLACE OF BIRTH: London. Father from Pano Zodia, Morphou; Mother from Ireland.
MARITAL STATUS: Single
SCHOOLS/COLLEGE: Highams Park, E17.
HOBBIES AND INTERESTS: Pool and Snooker.
PERSONAL PROFILE: Played Professionally for Arsenal under 19's and reserves. Originally began as a left winger, now a left back. He played for Southend F.C on loan season 2003-4, then back to Arsenal. Now permanently at Southend, helped them get promoted between 2004/2005.

SAVVAS NICOLAOU
Structural Engineer

DATE OF BIRTH: 06.03.58
PLACE OF BIRTH: London, grandparents from Famagusta.
MARITAL STATUS: Married to Maria K Nicolaou from London, Chair of Leukaemia Society.
CHILDREN: Twins: John and Georgia.
SCHOOLS/COLLEGE: Friern Barnet Grammar School, Imperial College, London.
ACADEMIC QUALIFICATIONS: BSC, MSc, DIC.
PROFESSIONAL QUALIFICATIONS: MICE.
MEMBERSHIPS: Institute of Civil Engineers.
HOBBIES AND INTERESTS: Golf and football.
PERSONAL PROFILE: Associate Director of leading UK Consultants Structural Engineers.

STELLA NICOLAOU
Active Member within the Cypriot Youth Club Movement

DATE OF BIRTH: 08.01.40
PLACE OF BIRTH: Cyprus
MARITAL STATUS: Married to Lambros.
CHILDREN: One son, one daughter.
MEMBERSHIPS: AKEL.
HOBBIES AND INTERESTS: Dancing, music and sports.
PERSONAL PROFILE: Member of Cypriot Women's Association, active within Cypriot Youth Club Movement. Won prizes for Table Tennis. Chairperson of Cypriot Youth Club of Waltham Forest.

NICKY NICOLAOU, PROFESSIONAL FOOTBALLER, HELPED SOUTHEND GET PROMOTED 2004/2005

VASILIS OLYMBIOU
Chairman of Greek School in Maidstone District

DATE OF BIRTH: 16.01.48
PLACE OF BIRTH: Kyrenia
MARITAL STATUS: Married to Thelma, a Secretary, from Famagusta.
CHILDREN: Niki, at university; Andreas, at school.
SCHOOLS/COLLEGE: Pancyprian Gymnasium, Nicosia, Aristotelion university, Salonica.
HOBBIES AND INTERESTS: Travel, reading, sport and politics.
PERSONAL PROFILE: Has worked in a shipping company for 23 years. Has held the position of Chairman, Vice Chairman and Treasurer in the Greek community of Maidstone & District, and has been Chairman of the Greek school since 1992.

MARIOS OLYMPIOS
Accountant & Lecturer

DATE OF BIRTH: 16.07.44
PLACE OF BIRTH: Lymbia Nicosia.
MARITAL STATUS: Married to Chrystalla Alexandrakis, a Secretary, from Alamino Larnaca.
SCHOOLS/COLLEGE: Primary School Lymbia, High Commercial Lykion Nicosia, High Commercial School Nicosia.
ACADEMIC QUALIFICATIONS: Msc with distinction, Finance Accountancy and Management, East London University.
PROFESSIONAL QUALIFICATIONS: Accountant, Mortgage Advisor, Financial Advisor.
MEMBERSHIPS: FCEA - IFA - FFA - MSC.
HONOURS/ADWARDS: Received an award for being an active member of EOKA 1955/59. Award from the Athletic Association Apollon, Award from Lymbia for financial support to the Association.
HOBBIES AND INTERESTS: Athletics, football, travelling, music, reading. Was an athelete at High Commercial Lykion School and a footballer for Apollo Lymbia.
PERSONAL PROFILE: From 1969 to 1978 worked for the RAF British Bases in Cyprus as Storekeeper, and Head Librarian.
Own practice since 1983 as Accountant, Mortgage Advisor and Financial Advisor. From 1984 to 1995 owned fast food businesses in four different locations. Chairman of Education for the Institute of Cost and Executive Accountants and then Chairman of the

Institute for two years. Visiting Lecturer at Guildford College teaching international business and finance Helped organisations such as for the blind, Leukaemia Research Centre and Lymbia Association in UK.

STELIOS ONOUFRIOU
Accountant

DATE OF BIRTH: 01.02.48
PLACE OF BIRTH: London. Father from Famagusta; Mother from Kaimakli.
MARITAL STATUS: Married to Eleni from Exo Metochi.
CHILDREN: Victoria, a Solicitor; Alexander, works for a pharmaceutical company.
SCHOOLS/COLLEGE: Taunton Grammer School.
HOBBIES AND INTERESTS: Music, plays in rock 'n' roll band. Football (Southampton supporter).
PERSONAL PROFILE: Has had an accountancy firm in Southampton for over 20 years.

MELIS ANTONIS OURRIS
Businessman and former president of the Ayios Serglos Famagusta Association

PLACE OF BIRTH: Ayios Sergios, Famagusta.
MARITAL STATUS: Married to Tasoula, from Peristeronopiyi, Famagusta.
CHILDREN: Antonis Melis, Owner and Manager of Anthony Webb Estate Agents; Tom Melis, Manager of Elena Hotel and Owner-Manager of Essex Lettings; Elena Ourris, studying Maths and French at Leeds University.
SCHOOLS/COLLEGE: Educated in Cyprus.
HOBBIES AND INTERESTS: Community work as hobbies.
PERSONAL PROFILE: Treasurer and former president of the Ayios Sergios Famagusta Association. Owner and Managing Director of Ourris Residential Homes, Anastasia Lodge residential home for the elderly. Ourris properties Ltd and Elena Hotel.

ANDRONICOS PALLIKAROS
Involvement with The Greek
Community in Bedford

DATE OF BIRTH: 09.10.36
PLACE OF BIRTH: Gypsos.
MARITAL STATUS: Married to
Margarita from Lefkara.
CHILDREN: One son, two
daughters.
SCHOOLS/COLLEGE:
Lefkoniko High School,
Tricomo High School, Acton
College.
HOBBIES AND INTERESTS:
Community affairs.
PERSONAL PROFILE: 21.11.56 arrested for being a
Member of EOKA - in detention till 1959. Came to
England 12.08.59, became a Teacher at the All Saints
Greek Church at Camden Town. Secretary of the
Committee of the All Saints Church in Camden Town.
Was Also Secretary of the Committee of St Nicholas
Church in Shepherds Bush. One of the Founders of
the St Charalambous Church in Luton and St Mamas in
Bedford.

LOUKIA (LUCY) PALOURTI
Regional Corporate Fundraising Manager

DATE OF BIRTH: 17.04.70
PLACE OF BIRTH: UK. Parents from Avgorou
MARITAL STATUS: Single
SCHOOLS/COLLEGE: Q.E Girls School, Barnet,
Woodhouse Sixth Form College, Finchley, Jesus
College, Cambridge.
ACADEMIC QUALIFICATIONS: BA(Honours) in History
(Class 2:1).
HOBBIES AND INTERESTS: Travel, European, Latin
American literature and trying to keep fit.
PERSONAL PROFILE: Currently Regional Corporate
Fundraising Manager for The Cancer Research
Campaign, securing Partnerships with business's for
the benefit of both parties. In the past
worked for a number of other charities, including
nearly six years with Oxfam.

NICK PANAY
Consultant Gynaecologist

DATE OF BIRTH: 26.03.63
PLACE OF BIRTH: London.
Father from Ayios Amvrosios;
Mother from Limassol.
MARITAL STATUS: Married to
Justine, a General Practitioner,
from England.
CHILDREN: Isabelle and
Thomas.
SCHOOLS/COLLEGE:
Creighton School, Muswell Hill,
University College, London.
ACADEMIC QUALIFICATIONS: BSc, MBBS.
PROFESSIONAL QUALIFCATIONS: MRCOG, MFFP
MEMBERSHIPS: Royal College of Obsygynae, Royal
Society of Medicine (Council), British Menopause
Society.
HOBBIES AND INTERESTS: Tennis, golf, sailing and
skiing.
PERSONAL PROFILE: Consultant Gynaecologist, Queen
Charlotte's & Chelsea Hospital, London.

LILY VARKARIS PANAGI
Media Agent

PLACE OF BIRTH: Varosi, Cy-
prus.
MARITAL STATUS: Divorced
CHILDREN: Zacharias, a Com-
pany Director (Telecoms).
SCHOOLS/COLLEGE:
Highbury Hill High School for
Girls; St Martins School of Art.
ACADEMIC QUALIFICATIONS:
Diploma in Art & Design
(DIPAD).
**PROFESSIONAL QUALIFICA-
TIONS:** Teaching Diploma.
MEMBERSHIPS: On the Board of Agents Association
of Great Britain.
HOBBIES AND INTERESTS: Tennis, dancing, gardening,
history and reading.
PERSONAL PROFILE: TV presenters' agent. Volunteer
for the British Red Cross (20 years).

ANDREW COSTI PANAYI
Accountant

DATE OF BIRTH: 30.04.42
PLACE OF BIRTH: Syghari Kyrenia District.
MARITAL STATUS: Married to Sandra from Portugal.
CHILDREN: Alexandra; and Abraham; Constantine; Chris from a previous marriage.
SCHOOLS/COLLEGE: Pancyprian Gymnasium, Nicosia, City of London Polytechnic.
PROFESSIONAL QUALIFICATIONS: Chartered Accountant.
HOBBIES AND INTERESTS: Travel, swimming, weight lifting and running.
PERSONAL PROFILE: Has own Accountancy Practice, Andrew & Co in Caledonian Road, London.

CHRISTOPHER PANAYI
Actor

DATE OF BIRTH: 10.10.70
PLACE OF BIRTH: London. Parents from Famagusta.
MARITAL STATUS: Single
SCHOOLS/COLLEGE: Holloway School, Arts Educational Drama School, Anna Schers Drama School, North London College Performing Arts Council.
PROFESSIONAL QUALIFICA-TIONS: Drama Diploma, Salsa Teacher/Drama.
MEMBERSHIPS: Equity.
HONOURS/AWARDS: Trophy for Best Stage Fight at Drama School, Shot Putt Winner at school.
HOBBIES AND INTERESTS: Acting.
PERSONAL PROFILE: Actor. Appeared in *Othello* at the Royal Opera House in Covent Garden. Appeared in the film *The Krays*, and the TV Commercial for Malborough Cigarettes.

PROFESSOR GABRIEL PANAYI
Professor of Rheumatology

PLACE OF BIRTH: Kato Drys, Larnaca.
MARITAL STATUS: Married to Alexandra (née Jourrou) (parents from Yialousa).
CHILDREN: Stavros graduated from Cambridge University and is now a Solicitor. Alexander is reading Economics at Cambridge University.
SCHOOLS/COLLEGE: Royal Grammar School, Lancaster, University of Cambridge.
HONOURS/AWARDS: Awarded many honours, including Heberden Orator of the British Society of Rheumatology.
HOBBIES AND INTERESTS: Reading especially Greek poetry, painting and gardening.
PERSONAL PROFILE: Professor of Rheumatology at Guys Kings and St Thomas School of Medicine, Guys Hospital, London SE1. Presently President British Society of Rheumatology. Has written or edited several books on Rheumatology as well as contributing chapters in books and review articles.

JAMES PANAYI
Footballer

DATE OF BIRTH: 24.01.80
PLACE OF BIRTH: Hammersmith, London. Father from Achna.
MARITAL STATUS: Single
SCHOOLS/COLLEGE: St Ignatius Tottenham, Bishops Douglas School.
HOBBIES AND INTERESTS: Football and golf
PERSONAL PROFILE: Signed 01.07.88, played for the 1st team at Watford FC. under Graham Taylor and 1st Greek Cypriot to play in the Premiership.

JAMES PANAYI, PROFESSIONAL FOOTBALLER, WITH WATFORD FC, FIRST GREEK CYPRIOT TO PLAY IN THE PREMIERSHIP

JOHN PANAYI
Chairman of the Leonarisso Association

DATE OF BIRTH: 08.05.38
PLACE OF BIRTH: Leonarisso.
MARITAL STATUS: Married to Nicoulla from Agastina.
CHILDREN: One son, three grandchildren.
SCHOOLS/COLLEGE: Yialousa Gymnasium, Victoria College in Old Street, Regent Polytechnic.
HOBBIES AND INTERESTS: Bowls, clay pigeon shooting and gardening.
PERSONAL PROFILE: Chairman of Leonarisso Association. Past Chairman of District Association of Prudential Assurance Co in Uxbridge. Secretary of the Cypriot Paraplegic Association of the UK.

STAVROS PANAYI
Solicitor

DATE OF BIRTH: 05.07.77
PLACE OF BIRTH: London. Father born in Kato Drys, Mother's parents from Yialoussa.
MARITAL STATUS: Married to Radmila, Russian Catwalk Model.
SCHOOLS/COLLEGE: University College School, Hampstead 1990-1995, Cambridge University 1995-98, Law School 1998-1999.
ACADEMIC QUALIFICATIONS: Law BA Honours, MA.
PROFESSIONAL QUALIFICATIONS: Solicitor of England & Wales.
MEMBERSHIPS: Law Society.
HOBBIES AND INTERESTS: Reading philosophy and history, Bolshoi theatre, good food, wine and cigars.
PERSONAL PROFILE: Lawyer with City Law firm Denton Wilde Sapte, 19 International Offices & around 700 Lawyers worldwide. Specialises in Capital Markets. Worked in the Moscow office from March-September 2001.

VASILLIS PANAYI
Actor/Radio Presenter

DATE OF BIRTH: 17.04.52
PLACE OF BIRTH: Sychari, near Kyrenia.
MARITAL STATUS: Single
SCHOOLS/COLLEGE: Stanisiavsky Drama School, Cyprus, Birmingham School of Speech, Training and Dramatic Art.
HOBBIES AND INTERESTS: Cinema, snooker and shopping.
PERSONAL PROFILE: Actor and Radio Presenter for LGR. Appeared in Theatre Habeus Corpus, Once a Catholic. On TV *Boon*, *Birds of a Feather*, *Soldier, Soldier*, *The Bill*. Film: *Sleeping with the Fishes* with Ewan McGregor. Did voice-over for *Captain Corelli's Mandolin*.

TASOS PANAYIDES
Former High Commissioner of Cyprus in London

DATE OF BIRTH: 09.04.34
PLACE OF BIRTH: Paphos
MARITAL STATUS: Married to Pandora Constantinides.
CHILDREN: Two sons, one daughter.
SCHOOLS/COLLEGE: Paphos Gymnasium, University of London, University of Indiana.
ACADEMIC QUALIFICATIONS: Diploma in Education, MA Political Science.
HOBBIES AND INTERESTS: Swimming, reading and books.
PERSONAL PROFILE: Teacher 1954-1959. 1st Secretary to President Makarios 60-63. Director Presidents Office 1963-1969. Ambassador of Cyprus to Federal Republic Germany, Switzerland & Austria 1969-1978. High Commissioner in UK and Ambassador to Sweden, Denmark, Norway and Iceland 1979-1990. Permanent Secretary, Ministry of Foreign Affairs Cyprus 1990-1994. Ambassador to Sweden, Finland, Norway, Denmark, Latvia, Lithuania & Estonia 1994-1996. Chairman Avra Ship Management SA June 1997.

ANDREAS PANAYIOTOU
Property Developer and Essex Amateur Boxing Champion

DATE OF BIRTH: 09.01.66
PLACE OF BIRTH: Mile End, London. Father from Klonari, Limassol; Mother from Kalochorio, Larnaca.
MARITAL STATUS: Married
CHILDREN: Two sons, three daughters.
SCHOOLS/COLLEGE: Wellington Way, Bow; King Harold, Waltham Abbey.
HONOURS/AWARDS: Essex Amateur Boxing Champion (Middleweight).
HOBBIES AND INTERESTS: Boxing and training.
PERSONAL PROFILE: As a youngster, was a keen amateur boxer. Now a propery developer and investor. In the *Estates Gazette*, rated 31st in the top 200 property owners in the UK. Owns Ability Developments, Ability Investments and Ability Air. Owns and charters private jets and Ability Shipping, which charters ships.

GEORGE KYRIACOS PANAYIOTOU
Known as **GEORGE MICHAEL**
Singer

DATE OF BIRTH: 25.06.63
PLACE OF BIRTH: London. Father from Patriki, Cyprus.
MARITAL STATUS: Single
SCHOOLS/COLLEGE: Kingsbury High School.
HONOURS/AWARDS: The *Faith* album received a Grammy for Best Album in 1988. Two Ivor Novello Awards for songwriter of the year and international hit of the year for *Faith*. In 1996 voted Best British Male at the MTV Europe awards and the BRITS, and at the Ivor Novello Awards he was awarded the title of Songwriter of the Year for the third time.
PERSONAL PROFILE: Singer/songwriter. Formed the group *Wham* with Andrew Ridgeley and they had a string of top 10 hits together. First solo single came in 1984 called *Careless Whisper*. George & Andrew later disbanded the group Wham - this announcement was followed by a unique final concert at Wembley, an emotional farewell in front of 72, 000 people.

JAKE PANAYIOTOU
Night Club Owner

DATE OF BIRTH: 06.11.53
PLACE OF BIRTH: Famagusta. Father Chrysanthos from Paphos; Mother Eleni (Konis) from Engomi.
MARITAL STATUS: Married Irene Smith, in 1972, Director, Wellington Club, born in Plaistow, London.
CHILDREN: Kelly, News International, Wapping; Christian, Wellington Club-Director; Jake Jnr.
SCHOOLS/COLLEGE: Ackland Burghley-Tufnell Park.
HOBBIES AND INTERESTS: Football, family has twelve season tickets at Chelsea.
PERSONAL PROFILE: Jake's dreams of becoming a professional football player with Arsenal were shattered after two serious injuries, sustained whilst playing for their youth team. He then went on to find success with his own company, Browns Chauffeur Hire, along with his three brothers, John, Peter and Angelo. In 1985 he opened Browns Night Club in Covent Garden, which was to become a haven for the stars, including Jack Nicholson, Madonna, Freddie Mercury and Prince. In October 2002, he opened the doors to the exclusive Wellington Club in Knightsbridge, which boasts Mick Jagger, Bono, Mick Hucknall and Kate Moss as founder members.

KELLY PANAYIOTOU
Promotions Manager for The News of the World

DATE OF BIRTH: 26.10.75
PLACE OF BIRTH: London, Father born in Famagusta.
MARITAL STATUS: Single.
SCHOOLS/COLLEGE: King Alfred School, NW11 until age 16 then Camden School For Girls, NW1 for A Levels.
ACADEMIC QUALIFICATIONS: 8 GSCEs and 3 A Levels.
HOBBIES AND INTERESTS: Travel, reading and cookery and hopes one day to write her father's biography.
PERSONAL PROFILE: Joined News International Newspapers at the age of 19 as a junior in the Sales & Marketing department. Cut to seven years later and various positions working on all four of the company's titles (*The Times*, *Sunday Times*, *The Sun*) and is now the Promotions Manager for News of the World - the biggest selling English-language newspaper in the World. Job involves creating and implementing promotions that appear in the paper each Sunday as well as helping to develop long-term marketing strategies.

KYRIACOS PANAYIOTOU AKA JACK PANOS
Horse Breeder

DATE OF BIRTH: 23.04.36
PLACE OF BIRTH: Patriki, Famagusta, Cyprus.
MARITAL STATUS: Married to Lesley Panayiotou. (deceased 26.02.97)
CHILDREN: George Kyriacos, Aka George Michael, Singer/Songwriter, Panayiota, Melanie.
SCHOOLS/COLLEGE: Patriki Elementary School, English High School Tricomo, Cyprus.
ACADEMIC QUALIFICATIONS: English Lower & Higher.
PROFESSIONAL QUALIFICATIONS: Restaurateur & now an Equine Breeder.
HOBBIES AND INTERESTS: Shooting and horse racing.
PERSONAL PROFILE: Horse breeding (thoroughbreds) Kyriacos supports numerous charities.

MIROFORA PANAYIOTOU
Scriptwriter

DATE OF BIRTH: 29.05.77
PLACE OF BIRTH: Northolt, Middlesex. Parents from Ardana, Famagusta.
MARITAL STATUS: Single
SCHOOLS/COLLEGE: Sutton Coldfield Girls School, Warwick University.
ACADEMIC QUALIFICATIONS: BA in Film & Literature.
HOBBIES AND INTERESTS: Photography writing and jogging.
PERSONAL PROFILE: Scriptwriter - made a short film *Vince and Johnny*. Also works in Traffic Link, provides travel news to BBC News.

STRATOS N PANAYIOTOU
Accountant

DATE OF BIRTH: 09.02.76
PLACE OF BIRTH: Limassol.
MARITAL STATUS: Single
SCHOOLS/COLLEGE: Apostles Peter and Paul Lyceum, University of North London, Emile Woolf College and Oxford Brookes University.
ACADEMIC QUALIFICATIONS: BA (Honours) Accounting & Finance.
PROFESSIONAL QUALIFICATIONS: ACCA.
HOBBIES AND INTERESTS: Football, Travelling and Music.
PERSONAL PROFILE: Manager at Gerald Kreditor & Co, Chartered Accountants. Chairman of New Horizons UK.

CHRISTOPHER JAMES PANTELI
Journalist

DATE OF BIRTH: 02.04.78
PLACE OF BIRTH: London. Parents from Larnaca.
MARITAL STATUS: Single
SCHOOLS/COLLEGE: Canon Palmer High School, Ilford, Essex.
ACADEMIC QUALIFICATIONS: A Level Media Studies, English Lanaguage, Photogaphy.
PROFESSIONAL QUALIFICATIONS: Currently studying for a Journalism Diploma.
HOBBIES AND INTERESTS: Enjoys all genres of music and film and is currently writing his first novel.
PERSONAL PROFILE: Journalist, *Ilford Recorder*. Sponsored by Archant on Journalism Diploma Course.

Email: Chris.Panteli@ilfordrecorder.com

DR STAVROS PANTELI
Writer/Lecturer

DATE OF BIRTH: 01.04.47
PLACE OF BIRTH: Phlasou (Solea).
MARITAL STATUS: Married to Floria, Counsellor, Personal Development, born in London, (parents from Famagusta District).
SCHOOLS/COLLEGE: Kingsway, Kilburn, Lincoln's Inn, ASU London University.
ACADEMIC QUALIFICATIONS: BSc (Econ), ACI, PhD.
MEMBERSHIPS: Economic Research Council, Friends of the Public Record Office).
HOBBIES AND INTERESTS: Sports, reading and community care.
PERSONAL PROFILE: Lecturer and Writer. Historian. A Mediterranean Specialist. Author of twelve books, general history and biographies. Private Tutor to several prominent individuals, including royalty. Active member of various Cypriot organisations, National Federation, Solea, Morphou. Founder and co-ordinator of the First Cypriot All England Musical Festival (1984-86), in aid of children with special needs and Kings College Hospital. Regular contributor to London Greek Radio with two weekly programme slots: 'Your own view' and 'Book review'.

MICHAEL LEONIDA PANTELIDES
Urological Surgeon in Bolton

DATE OF BIRTH: 12.12.53
PLACE OF BIRTH: Athienou.
MARITAL STATUS: Married to Kathy, a Physiotherapist, from Manchester.
CHILDREN: Nicholas, Helen, Andrew, Christopher, all at various stages at Bolton School.
SCHOOLS/COLLEGE: 1959-1965 Elementary School at Athienou, 1965-1972, The English School, Nicosia, 1972-1974, Army Service, Military Band, 1974-1979, Manchester University Medical School.
ACADEMIC QUALIFICATIONS: MD- Doctor of Medicine, awarded by Manchester University 1979.
PROFESSIONAL QUALIFICATIONS: Bachelor of Medicine and Bachelor of Surgery 1979 Manchester. FRCS-Fellow of the Royal College of Surgeons of England 1983.
MEMBERSHIPS: British Medical Association, Royal College of Surgeons, British Association of Urological Surgeons, Association of Hellenic Scientists and Professionals of Manchester.
HONOURS/AWARDS: Honours in Pharmacology and Pathology at Medical School.
HOBBIES AND INTERESTS: Mainly music. Enjoys classical music. Still plays the violin but rarely. Enjoys old "popular" Greek music and Cyprus folk music. Fervent Bolton Wanderers Supporter.
PERSONAL PROFILE: After graduation trained in surgery and worked at hospitals within and around Manchester. Specialized in Urological Surgery. Research for the MD thesis related to the use of lasers for the treatment of early prostate cancer. Has published around 20 papers in peer reviewed journals. Appointed Consultant Urologist at Bolton in 1992.

Address: 665 Chorley New Rd, Lostock, Bolton BL6 4AG

ANDROS PANTELLI
Chartered Quantity Surveyor

DATE OF BIRTH: 10.08.54
PLACE OF BIRTH: London. Parents from Larnaca.
MARITAL STATUS: Married to Margarita, a Housewife, from London (parents from Cyprus).
SCHOOLS/COLLEGE: Willesden College, Westminster University.
PROFESSIONAL QUALIFICATIONS: Fellow of The Royal Institute of Chartered Surveyors (FRICS), Member of The Chartered Institute of Arbitrators (MCIAIB).
HOBBIES AND INTERESTS: Reading and skiing.
PERSONAL PROFILE: Chartered Quantity Surveyor, own practice under the name "Pantelli Associates".

CHRISTOS STAVROU PANTZARIS
Bank of Cyprus (London) Chairman

DATE OF BIRTH: 23.02.34
PLACE OF BIRTH: Nicosia
MARITAL STATUS: Married to Annita, (née Colocassides) of Nicosia.
CHILDREN: Avgusta - BA European Studies, Eleni - PhD, Professor Management Sciences, Stavros - Chartered Accountant,
SCHOOLS/COLLEGE: Graduate Pancyprian Gymnasium,
ACADEMIC QUALIFICATIONS: BSc. Civil Eng. (Honours), Manchester University,
HOBBIES AND INTERESTS: Walking, game shooting, classical music and reading.
PERSONAL PROFILE: Bank of Cyprus Group Vice Chairman since 1988, and Chief Executive, since 1995. Bank of Cyprus (London) Chairman (since 01.01.2001). Chairman of KERMIA LTD since 1983, Member of the parent Board of the Bank of Cyprus Group and other Group Subsidiaries since 1974. Chairman Electricity Authority of Cyprus 1974-1979 & 1988-1993. Chairman Cyprus Employers and Industrialists Federation 1970-1972. Played active role in several committees and Boards of the Ministry of Labour & Social Insurance concerned with Industrial Training and Industrial Relations.

ANDREAS PAPACHRISTOFOROU
(Stage name Andy Christo)
Actor

DATE OF BIRTH: 09.05.68
PLACE OF BIRTH: Birmingham. Father from Limassol.
MARITAL STATUS: Single
SCHOOLS/COLLEGE: Lordsworth Boys, Birmingham, Drama School.
HOBBIES AND INTERESTS: Writer, director, keep fit and fencing.
PERSONAL PROFILE: Appeared in *Hollyoaks*, on TV, the film *The Killer*. Appeared in the play Suicide at Theatro Technis.

STAKHAKIS PAPACHRISTOFOROU
President of the Greek Church of Virgin Mary and St Andrews in Birmingham

DATE OF BIRTH: 26.10.41
PLACE OF BIRTH: Limassol.
MARITAL STATUS: Married to June from Birmingham.
CHILDREN: Andreas, Actor; Costas, Electronic Engineer.
SCHOOLS/COLLEGE: Lee Road School in Birmingham.
HOBBIES AND INTERESTS: Football, (Aston Villa fan).
PERSONAL PROFILE: Has eight shops, catering and amusements. President of the Greek Church of Virgin Mary and St Andrews in Birmingham.

ANDREAS S PAPACHRISTOU
President of the Anglo Akanthou Aid Society

DATE OF BIRTH: 15.10.51
PLACE OF BIRTH: Akanthou
MARITAL STATUS: Married
CHILDREN: One son, one daughter.
SCHOOLS/COLLEGE: Akanthou Primary School, Secondary School at Lefkoniko, Higher School of Economics and Commercial Studies (Athens).
ACADEMIC QUALIFICATIONS: Degree in Accountancy and Economics.
MEMBERSHIPS: Member of Neoda (The National Edible Oil Distributors Assocation).
HOBBIES AND INTERESTS: Sailing and antique cars.
PERSONAL PROFILE: Managing Director of catering supply company. President of the Anglo Akanthou Aid Society.

ANDREAS PAPADAKIS
Academic, Architectural Subjects Publisher

DATE OF BIRTH: 17.06.38
PLACE OF BIRTH: Nicosia
MARITAL STATUS: Married to Shelia De Vallee.
CHILDREN: Alexandra at Architectural Association.
SCHOOLS/COLLEGE: Pancyprian Gymnasium, Nicosia, Faraday House, London, Imperial College, London.
ACADEMIC QUALIFICATIONS: DFH, DIC, PhD.
MEMBERSHIPS: Chairman of Chapel at the Archdiocese of Thyatera G.B.
HONOURS/AWARDS: Archon of the Ecumenical Patriarchade.
PERSONAL PROFILE: Academic, Architectural subjects Publisher, Community work.

SYMEON PAPADAMOU
Hotelier and Community Worker in Margate

DATE OF BIRTH: 06.02.37
PLACE OF BIRTH: Avgorou, Famagusta.
MARITAL STATUS: Married to Eleni, born in England, (parents from Aradhippou).
CHILDREN: Theodora, Housewife; Pavlos, Computer Engineer; Kyriacos, Aeronauticed Engineer; Adamos, Hotel & Catering; Andreas, Studying Medicine at University.
SCHOOLS/COLLEGE: Balham and Tooting College of Commerce.
ACADEMIC QUALIFICATIONS: Business adminstration.
PROFESSIONAL QUALIFICATION: Hotel and Catering.
HONOURS/AWARDS: Honorary President of the "Lest we forget" Charity.
HOBBIES AND INTERESTS: Filming, Gardening and Politics.
PERSONAL PROFILE: Hotelier, and does a lot of work within the Cypriot community in Margate.

ANDREA CHRISTOFI PAPADIMITRI
Charity Worker

DATE OF BIRTH: 29.11.38
PLACE OF BIRTH: Leonarisso.
MARITAL STATUS: Married to Anastasia from Peristerona.
CHILDREN: Three sons.
SCHOOLS/COLLEGE: Leonarisso Elementary.
HOBBIES AND INTERESTS: Long distance running, wrestling, boxing and farming.
PERSONAL PROFILE: Fish & Chip shop owner. Charity Worker. Runs London Marathon and other runs to raise money for charity, such as Leukaemia, Thallassaemia Children in Need, Radio Marathon. Runs 70 miles per week. Has used up 36 pairs of running shoes!

ANTONIOS PAPADOPOULLOS
Secretary of Greek Cypriot & Friends
Golf Society

DATE OF BIRTH: 25.10.58
PLACE OF BIRTH: Birmingham.
Parents from Mazotos, Larnaca.
MARITAL STATUS: Divorced
CHILDREN: Marielle, Stephanie,
Christopher and Molly.
SCHOOLS/COLLEGE:
Dartmouth High School,
Sandwell, Aston University.
ACADEMIC QUALIFICATIONS:
BSc (Honours) Civil
Engineering.
MEMBERSHIPS: SPAR.
HONOURS/AWARDS: Reached finals of Independent
Retailer of The Year 2001.
HOBBIES AND INTERESTS: Golf.
PERSONAL PROFILE: Spar Store Owner. Secretary of
Greek Cypriot & Friends Golf Society.

IRENA PAPADOPOULOS
Professor of Transcultural Health &
Nursing

DATE OF BIRTH: 01.10.50
PLACE OF BIRTH: Famagusta.
MARITAL STATUS: Married to
Costas, from Morphou, a
Hairdresser and Property
Developer.
CHILDREN: Panikos, Fitness
Instructor; Chris, Psychology
Graduate/Assistant
Psychologist.
SCHOOLS/COLLEGE: Royal
College of Nursing, London University, Open
University, University of North London.
ACADEMIC QUALIFICATIONS: BA, MA (Ed), PhD.
PROFESSIONAL QUALIFICATIONS: RGN, RM, NDN Cert,
DN, DipNEd.
MEMBERSHIPS: RCN (Royal College of Nursing), Public
Health Alliance, EPISTEME
HOBBIES AND INTERESTS: Reading, writing, socialising
and travel.
PERSONAL PROFILE: Professor of Transcultural Health
& Nursing. Head of Research Centre for Transcultural
Studies in Health, Middlesex University. Co-Founder
and ex-Chief of Directors, Greek and Greek Cypriot
Community of Enfield. Co-Author of one book &
Editor of three others. Author of many research
reports and numerous articles and book chapters.

Correspondence address: Middlesex University.
Archway Campus, 10 Highgate Hill, London N19 5LW.
Email: r.papadopoulos@mdx.ac.uk
Website: http://www.mdx.ac.uk/www/rctsh

LINDA PAPADOPOULOS
Psychologist

DATE OF BIRTH: 03.02.71
PLACE OF BIRTH: Toronto,
Canada. Parents from Limassol.
MARITAL STATUS: Married to
Theo Pitsillides, an Investment
Banker, from Limassol.
SCHOOLS/COLLEGE: York
University, Surrey University,
City University,
ACADEMIC QUALIFICATIONS:
BA (Hons), M.Sc, PhD,
PROFESSIONAL QUALIFICATIONS: CPsychol. (Chartered
Psychologist), AFBPS (Associate Fellow of the British
Psychological Society),
MEMBERSHIPS: British Psychological Society; All
Parliamentary Group on Dermatology; Medical and
Advisory Panel of the Vitilio Society.
HONOURS/AWARDS: Awarded a Readership in
Psychology (one of the youngest in the country);
Nominated for the BPS annual prize in Counselling
Psychology.
HOBBIES AND INTERESTS: Writing, travelling and diving.
PERSONAL PROFILE: Course Director of the MSc in
Counselling Psychology at London Guildhall University
- also holds a research grant. Linda sits on the editorial
board of three academic journals and has authored
three books and numerous research/academic articles.
Has a private practice where she sees patients clinically.
Also contributing editor of *Cosmopolitan* magazine
and appears regularly on TV and radio to comment on
psychosocial matters.

MARIO PAPADOPOULOS
Musical Director Oxford Philomusica

DATE OF BIRTH: 20.12.54
PLACE OF BIRTH: Limassol.
MARITAL STATUS: Married to
Anthie from Nicosia.
CHILDREN: Michael and Stella.
SCHOOLS/COLLEGE: English
School, Nicosia, City Univ.
ACADEMIC QUALIFICATIONS:
Dr of Musical Arts.
PERSONAL PROFILE: Musical
Director of the Oxford
Philomusica appointed
orchestra in residence at the University of Oxford. In
October 2002 the Orchestra was lauched with a concert
at the Barbican. As a recognition of it's work the
orchestra was honoured at a reception at 10 Dowing
Street in April 2002 hosted by Cherie Blair. Appeared
in Paris at Salle Gaveau, Athens, Queen Elizabeth Hall
London. Mario has directed the London Mozart Players,
The Royal Philarmonic Orchestra. He Has conducted
the Magic Flute, Trovatone, The Marriage of Figaro,
with the Greek National Opera.

NICOS PAPADOPOULOS
Journalist, Newscaster London Greek Radio

DATE OF BIRTH: 28.07.52
PLACE OF BIRTH: Nicosia.
MARITAL STATUS: Married to Maria from Karavas, Kyrenia.
CHILDREN: Elena and George.
SCHOOLS/COLLEGE: English College, Cyprus, ABC College, Athens, St Patricks College, London.
PROFESSIONAL QUALIFICATIONS: Journalism, Public Relations, Marketing, Advertising.
MEMBERSHIPS: Cyprus Journalist Union, The Chartered Institute of Journalists, 41 Club and Leukaemia Society.
HOBBIES AND INTERESTS: Travelling, swimming and tennis.
PERSONAL PROFILE: Journalist. Columnist of *Anthropina* at *Eleftheria* Newspaper. News Editor and Newscaster, London Greek Radio.

RENOS KLITOU PAPADOPOULOS
Chartered Clinical Psychologist

DATE OF BIRTH: 17.02.47
PLACE OF BIRTH: Limassol.
MARITAL STATUS: Married to Nina, a University Lecturer, from South Africa.
CHILDREN: Olga and Michelle.
SCHOOLS/COLLEGE: Pancyprian Gymnasium, Nicosia; University of Belgrade; University of Capetown.
ACADEMIC QUALIFCATIONS: PhD in Psychology.
PROFESSIONAL QUALIFICATIONS: Chartered Clinical Psychologist with the British Psychological Society. Analytic Psychologist (Jungian Psychoanalsyt)
MEMBERSHIPS: Member of the International Association for Analytical Psycholology. Registered member of the United Kingdom Council for Psychotherapy
HOBBIES AND INTERESTS: Cycling, reading and watching soccer (Arsenal supporter).
PERSONAL PROFILE: Professor at the Centre for Psychoanalytic Studies of the University of Essex, Consultant Clinical Psychologist at the Tavistock Clinic, Family Therapist and training and supervising Jungian analyst.

ANDREAS PAPAEVRIPIDES
Accountant

DATE OF BIRTH: 24.04.52
PLACE OF BIRTH: Kato Pyrgos Tyllirias.
MARITAL STATUS: Married to Katerina Xenophontos, a Secretary, from Ayios Theodoros, Larnaca.
CHILDREN: Constantinos and Alexandros.
SCHOOLS/COLLEGE: A Gymnasium Morphou (Science Section) 1964-1970, Hackney Technical College 1972-1974, Chelsea College of London University 1974-1977, London School of Accountancy 1978-1980.
ACADEMIC QUALIFICATIONS BSc Economics.
PROFESSIONAL QUALIFICATIONS: F.F.A.
MEMBERSHIPS: Fellow of the Institute of Financial Accountants, Member of the British Institute of Management.
HONOURS/AWARDS: Commendation from National Guard of Cyprus for outstanding service 1972. Honoured by National Union of Cypriots in England.
HOBBIES AND INTERESTS: Politics, history, football and shooting.
PERSONAL PROFILE: Accountant with own practice since 1985. Chairman of Democratic Rally UK since 1994, served in various other positions since 1981, Vice-president of the National Federation of Cypriots in Great Britain since 1995 and Treasurer from 1991-1995. President of the National Union of Cypriot Students in England (E.F.E.K.A.) during 1979/1980 and Non-Executive Director of the Enfield Community Care NHS Trust from 1992-1998. General Seretary of Kato Pyrgos Tyllirias Association since 1977. Vice-Chairman "Conservatives For Cyprus" since 1998. General Secretary of the cypriot football League in England from 1975 to 1981.

ANDREAS PAPAGEORGI
Head of Energy & Economics, National Grid Co

DATE OF BIRTH: 06.02.49
PLACE OF BIRTH: Koma Yialou.
MARITAL STATUS: Married to Maria, a Housewife, from Cyprus Origin-Kakopetria.
CHILDREN: Christina, at University; Demetris, at University; Marianna, at School.
SCHOOLS/COLLEGE: Pancyprian Gymnasium, Kykkou, Woolwich College for Further Education, Catford College, Southampton University, Reading University.
PROFESSIONAL QUALIFICATIONS: BSc Economics (single Honours), MA Business Economics.
MEMBERSHIPS: Institute of Energy, International Institute of Energy Economics.
HOBBIES AND INTERESTS: Reading, swimming and politics.
PERSONAL PROFILE: Head of Energy & Economics, National Grid Company. Chairman of Prospectives Group, Chairman of EuroG Group of Experts, Eurelectric, President of Greek School of Coventry, member of Action for Cyprus Midlands.

DR GEORGE PAPAGEORGIOU
Senior Research Associate for National Institute for Medical Research UK

DATE OF BIRTH: 22.08.57
PLACE OF BIRTH: Anaphotia, Larnaca.
MARITAL STATUS: Married to Alexandra, (née Petrou), a Solicitor, born in London.
CHILDREN: Xanthy; Eleni; Vasiliki; Constantia.
SCHOOLS/COLLEGE: Larnaca Gymnasium, Queen Mary College, University of London, Loughborough University.
ACADEMIC QUALIFICATION: BSc, MSc, PhD.
PROFESSIONAL QUALIFICATIONS: EurChem, CChem MRSC.
MEMBERSHIPS: American Chemical Society, Royal Society of Chemistry.
HOBBIES AND INTERESTS: Gardening, current affairs, and trying to teach his daughters the Greek language.
PERSONAL PROFILE: Senior Research Associate for National Institute for Medical Research UK

Email: gpapage@rimr.mrc.ac.uk

GEORGE MICHAEL PAPAGEORGIS
Barrister

DATE OF BIRTH: 28.09.47
PLACE OF BIRTH: Leonarisso, Famagusta.
MARITAL STATUS: Married to Elizabeth Jane, in 1976, a Housewife, from England.
CHILDREN: Michael David and Sophia Maria, Students.
SCHOOLS/COLLEGE: Greek Gymnasium for Boys, Famagusta, Middle Temple, London.
PROFESSIONAL QUALIFICATIONS: Barrister-at-Law.
HOBBIES AND INTERESTS: Theatre.
PERSONAL PROFILE: Has been practising for over 20 years from 2 Kings Bench Walk, Temple, London. Was The Head of Chambers for over four years. Member of Anglo-Cypriot Lawyers Association.

JOHN KYROS PAPALOIZOU
Deputy Chairman of KOPA

DATE OF BIRTH: 04.06.58
PLACE OF BIRTH: London. Father from Galata. Mother from Nicosia.
MARITAL STATUS: Married, wife from Famagusta.
SCHOOLS/COLLEGE: Stationers Grammar School.
ACADEMIC QUALIFICATIONS: BSc, Building Economics.
PROFESSIONAL QUALIFICATIONS: MRICS.
MEMBERSHIPS: Royal Institute of Chartered Surveyor, Quanity Surveying Division.
HOBBIES AND INTERESTS: Football, tennis and music.
PERSONAL PROFILE: Director of Letting and Property Management Company, Thomas Property Services Ltd. Secretary and Chairman of Greek Football Team Neos Asteras 1970s-1980s. Deputy Chairman and member of KOPA Management Committee.

TASOS PAPALOIZOU
Chartered Accountant

DATE OF BIRTH: 02.05.62
PLACE OF BIRTH: London. Father from Galata; Mother from Nicosia.
MARITAL STATUS: Married to Yasmin, born in London (parents from India).
CHILDREN: Thomas and Alexander.
SCHOOLS/COLLEGE: Friern Barnet Grammar School, Barnet College, University of North London.
ACADEMIC QUALIFICATIONS: BA (Honours)
PROFESSIONAL QUALIFICATIONS: Chartered Accountant.
MEMBERSHIPS: ICAEW.
HOBBIES AND INTERESTS: Football (played for Neos Asteras 1970s-1980s). All forms of sport, travel, cinema and theatre.
PERSONAL PROFILE: Chartered Accountant in own practice, also Director and Shareholder of Property Company.

ANTONIOS PAPAMICHAEL
President of the Greek Orthodox Church in Oxford

DATE OF BIRTH: 10.05.28
PLACE OF BIRTH: Leonarisso.
MARITAL STATUS: Married to Vasoulla, from Famagusta.
CHILDREN: Mario, works for a shipping co in Cyprus; Joanna Kissias, Bank Officer; Athanasia Tracoshas, training to be a Nursery Teacher,
HOBBIES AND INTERESTS: Sings for the local Greek Orthodox Church in Canterbury Road in Oxford.
PERSONAL PROFILE: Was a Tailor/Psaltis in Cyprus. Has been President of Greek Orthodox Church in Oxford for 25 years and head of the choir.

FREDOS PAPANGELOU
Professor of Mathematical Statistics at the University of Manchester

DATE OF BIRTH: 07.10.39
PLACE OF BIRTH: Limassol.
MARITAL STATUS: Married to Elizabeth Lambou from Greece.
CHILDREN: Aris and Markos.
SCHOOLS/COLLEGE: University of Athens.
ACADEMIC QUALIFICAITONS: PhD.
HOBBIES AND INTERESTS: Music and history.
PERSONAL PROFILE: Former Professor of Mathematical Statistics at the University of Manchester. Now Professor Emeritus. Was member of the Interim Governing Board of the University of Cyprus and of the Preparatory Committee of Cyprus University of Applied Sciences and Arts.

THEODOULOS PAPANICOLA
Accountant

DATE OF BIRTH: 12.03.49
PLACE OF BIRTH: Vokholida.
MARITAL STATUS: Married
CHILDREN: Apostola, Nail Technician; Themoulla, Solicitor; Constantina, Student.
SCHOOLS/COLLEGE: Credon School for Boys, Westminster College.
PROFESSIONAL QUALIFICATIONS: FCA, FCCA, FABRP, MCI, ARB.
HOBBIES AND INTERESTS: Travel and cooking.
PERSONAL PROFILE: Chartered Accountant & Insolvency Practitioner.

LILIA HAREKLIA PAPANICOLAOU (née MICHAEL)
Former School Chair, Greek Parents Association

DATE OF BIRTH: 15.10.38
PLACE OF BIRTH: London. Parents from Aradhipou and Larnaca.
MARITAL STATUS: Married to Nicos Andrea Papanicolaou, a Solicitor.
CHILDREN: Andreas, Solictor; Christopher, Solicitor; Thessa, History Teacher.
SCHOOLS/COLLEGE: Waverley Grammar School, Birmingham, University of Birmingham.
ACADEMIC QUALIFICATIONS: B .Social Science (social studies).
PERSONAL PROFILE: Child Care Officer, Office Manager (Nicos & Co Solicitors), School Chairman, Greek Parents Association in late seventies and early eighties.

NICOS ANDREA PAPANICOLAOU
Solicitor

DATE OF BIRTH: 23.06.32
PLACE OF BIRTH: Vokolidha.
MARITAL STATUS: Married to Lilia, (née Michael), an Office Manager, from London.
CHILDREN: Andreas, Solicitor; Christopher, Solicitor; Thessa, History Teacher.
SCHOOLS/COLLEGE: Famagusta Gymnasium, Grays Inn.
ACADEMIC QUALIFICATIONS: Barrister At Law.
PROFESSIONAL QUALIFICATIONS: Solicitor.
PERSONAL PROFILE: Retired Solicitor.

ANTONIOS PAPANTONIOU
Accountant

DATE OF BIRTH: 31.05.48
PLACE OF BIRTH: Pyrga, Famagusta.
MARITAL STATUS: Married to Kika Papantoniou, an Accountant, from Famagusta.
CHILDREN: Stephanos, Marketing Recruitment Consultant; Kyriacos, studying Law & French in Cardiff.
SCHOOLS/COLLEGE: St John's College of further education, Salford Technical College, Aston Polytechnic.
ACADEMIC QUALIFICATIONS: OND and HND Business Studies.
MEMBERSHIPS: Association of Accounting Technicians, Institute of Chartered Secretaries, Administrators.
HONOURS/AWARDS: ACIS-FMATT.
HOBBIES AND INTERESTS: Gardening and reading.
PERSONAL PROFILE: Founder and Owner of Antony & Co Accountants. Has served as Chairman of Action for Cyprus Midlands for about eight years. Currently secretary of the Greek Orthodox Cathedral Of The Dormition of Theotokos & St Andrew in Birmingham.

FRIXOS PAPANTONIOU
Teacher/Artist

DATE OF BIRTH: 01.06.51
PLACE OF BIRTH: Famagusta.
MARITAL STATUS: Single
SCHOOLS/COLLEGE: Middlesex Polytechnic, Kingston University, University of London, Institute of Education.
ACADEMIC QUALIFICATIONS: BA (Honours), A.T.C.
HONOURS/AWARDS: Finalist "Bank of Cyprus Award" 1993.
PERSONAL PROFILE: Teacher in Ceramics in secondary school and community classes in Newham. Held one person and group exhibitions in London.

CHRYSOSTOMOS PAPAPAVLOU
Chairman of Labithos & Karavas Association

DATE OF BIRTH: 27.01.37
PLACE OF BIRTH: Lapithos
MARITAL STATUS: Married to Elsa, a retired Nursery Nurse, born in Denmark.
CHILDREN: Nicholas, working for Haringey council as a Chartered Surveyor; Joanna, Nursery Nurse in school.
SCHOOLS/COLLEGE: Lapithos Gymasium & Primary School, Regent Street Polytechnic.
ACADEMIC QUALIFICATIONS: O.N.C. H.N.C Electrical & Electronic Engineering.
HOBBIES AND INTERESTS: DIY, travelling, languages, French, German and Danish.
PERSONAL PROFILE: Now retired. Former Field Service Engineer with Lansing Forklifts. Member of the Committee Cypriot Community Centre, Wood Green. Chairman of Lapithos & Karavas Association. Former Chairman at Community Centre Edison, ran the Cypriot Youth Club at Edison Centre. Chairman of Greek Parents Association of Rokesley School, Crouch End for many years.

ENTRANTS IN GREEK CYPRIOTS IN THE UK HAVE BEEN NOMINATED FOR THEIR ACHIEVEMENTS AND CONTRIBUTIONS.
YOU CAN NOMINATE SOMEONE OR YOURSELF WHO DESERVES TO BE IN THE BOOK.
ENTRIES ARE FREE.
SEND IN YOUR NOMINATIONS, INCLUDING NAME, CONTACT ADDRESS, TELEPHONE NUMBER AND EMAIL TO
GREEK CYPRIOTS IN THE UK
111 ST THOMAS'S ROAD LONDON N4 2QJ TELEPHONE 020 7503 3498
EMAIL cypriotwhoswho@aol.com

DR ELLI PAPAPHOTI
Founder and Director of the Educational Institute of Great Britain - 1990-1995

PLACE OF BIRTH: Koma Tou Yialou, Famagusta.
MARITAL STATUS: Married to Photis K Papaphotis, served as an Internal Auditor of Laiki Bank, from Akanthou.
CHILDREN: Anastasia, Oxford University Graduate, Internal Auditor of the Bank of Cyprus inEngland; Angelika, Kings College graduate, Accountant.
SCHOOLS/COLLEGE: Famagusta Gymnasium, Nicosia Teachers College, London University.
ACADEMIC QUALIFICATIONS: Associate of the Institute of Education, Academic Diploma in Education, M.A. Education, PhD.
PROFESSIONAL QUALIFICATIONS: Teacher, Head Teacher, Inspector of primary educaion in Cyprus.
MEMBERSHIPS: Member of the Greek Educational Society (based in Athens), Member of K.E.S. (Educational Council of the Archdiocese of Thyateira and Great Britain).
HONOURS/AWARDS: Prizes in all six classes of the Famagusta Gymnasium for being the best student.
HOBBIES AND INTERESTS: Reading, listening to Greek music, theatre, Greek dancing, gardening, socialising and travelling.
PERSONAL PROFILE: Founder and Director of the Educational Institute of Great Britain (1990-1995). An institute educating Greek Teachers, teaching in the Greek Schools in UK. In 1967 was appointed head-teacher of Hatji Georgatsis Kornesios Primary School in Nicosia. Was appointed teacher in the Paedagogical Academy in Nicosia between the years 1985-88. Education Counsellor of the Cyprus High Commission. Education Counsellor of the Archdioceses of Thyateria and Great Britain.

PHOTIS SAVVAS PAPAPHOTIS
President of St Marys Church Camberwell

DATE OF BIRTH: 25.02.25
PLACE OF BIRTH: Akanthou.
MARITAL STATUS: Married to Sousanna, now retired, from Akanthou.
CHILDREN: Maria Allsop, Interior Designer.
SCHOOLS/COLLEGE: Primary School of Akanthou Village.
HOBBIES AND INTERESTS: Reading, walking and socialising.
PERSONAL PROFILE: President of St Marys Greek Orthodox Church, Camberwell, Former President of Anglo-Akanthou Aid Society. Restaurateur.

SAVVAS PAPASAVVAS
Marketing Officer Cyprus Potato Marketing Board

DATE OF BIRTH: 13.12.48
PLACE OF BIRTH: Pano Deftera, Nicosia.
MARITAL STATUS: Married to Androulla, a Bank Manager, from London.
CHILDREN: Irene, University Graduate; Georgia, A Level Student.
SCHOOLS/COLLEGE: West London College, Open University, Middlesex University.
ACADEMIC QUALIFICATIONS: BA, MA.
PROFESSIONAL QUALIFICATIONS: Chartered Institute of Marketing.
MEMBERSHIPS: C.I.M.
HOBBIES AND INTERESTS: Travelling and reading.
PERSONAL PROFILE: Marketing Officer-Cyprus Potato Marketing Board. Treasurer: Deftera Association and Eleni Pericleous Trust Fund.

GLYKERIS PAPASPRYROU
Founder Member of Greek Orthodox Community of Hastings

DATE OF BIRTH: 15.07.23
PLACE OF BIRTH: Ayia Triada, Famagusta.
MARITAL STATUS: Married to Kiki, from Famagusta, now deceased.
CHILDREN: One son, four daughters.
MEMBERSHIPS: AKEL.
HONOURS/AWARDS: Honoured by the Greek Orthodox Church.
HOBBIES AND INTERESTS: Travelling and reading.
PERSONAL PROFILE: Hotel Owner in Hastings. One of the Founder members of Camden Greek School. Founder member of Greek Orthodox Community of Hastings and Chairman for 25 years.

THASIS PAPATHANASIOU
Community Worker

DATE OF BIRTH: 29.05.29
PLACE OF BIRTH: Aradippou
MARITAL STATUS: Married
CHILDREN: Three daughters, four grandsons.
HOBBIES AND INTERESTS: Football, (Fulham Supporter).
PERSONAL PROFILE: Involved with South London Community Greek Schools one of the founders of OESEKA and ESEKA. Was community affairs Secretary and Chairman of OESEKA. One of the Founders of Hammersmith and Fulham Council of Racial Equality for six years Chairman. One of the Founders of the Greek Cypriot Association of Fulham and Hammersmith where he was Secretary and Chairman. One of the Founders and Chairman of the Aradippou Association.

PETER PANAYIOTIS PAPHIDES
Journalist

DATE OF BIRTH: 18.07.69
PLACE OF BIRTH: Birmingham. Father from Kyrenia; Mother from Nea Kifisia in Athens.
MARITAL STATUS: Married to Caitlin Moran, Columnist for *The Times* Newspaper, from London.
CHILDREN: Theodora.
SCHOOLS/COLLEGE: Cottersbrooke Infant and Primary School, Yardley's Secondary School, St David's University College, Lampeter.
ACADEMIC QUALIFICATIONS: 5 O Levels, 4 A Levels, Second Class Honours Degree in Philosophy.
MEMBERSHIPS: AA, The Ramblers Association.
HONOURS/AWARDS: My Salsa Dip has often been declared "The best this side of Holloway Road".
HOBBIES AND INTERESTS: Chips, babies, bidding for rare acid folk vinyl on eBay, driving around the North-West coast of Scotland.
PERSONAL PROFILE: Journalist. Writes in *Time Out*.

KYRIACOS PAPHITIS
Active member of the Cypriot Community in Birmingham

DATE OF BIRTH: 15.01.51
PLACE OF BIRTH: Gerani, Famagusta.
MARITAL STATUS: Married to Anna, a Housewife, from Birmingham.
CHILDREN: Savvas, BA (Honours) Law, Human Resources; Jason, School.
SCHOOLS/COLLEGE: Hall Green College.
HOBBIES AND INTERESTS: Shooting, golf and reading.
PERSONAL PROFILE: M.D of Tasty Bake Ltd. Active Member of Cypriot Community in Birmingham.

THEO PAPHITIS
Business and Football

DATE OF BIRTH: 24.09.59
MARITAL STATUS: Married
SCHOOLS/COLLEGE: Woodberry Down School
HOBBIES AND INTERESTS: Millwall football club, shopping, sport and socialising.
PERSONAL PROFILE: Chairman of four retail chains (La Senza, Contessa, Ryman Stationers and Partners Stationers) comprising over 350 stores. Under his chairmanship his translated ailing businesses to successful ones. As well as retail he has a passion for football was chairman of Millwall FC for eight years during which the club enjoyed its most illustrious period in its history including promotion to the first division and FA Cup Final appearance and European competition.
Recently salvaged the company Red Letter Days out of administration and appeared on the BBC program Dragons' Den as a dragon.

JANET PARASKEVA, CHIEF EXECUTIVE OF THE LAW SOCIETY FOR ENGLAND AND WALES

ZOE PAPHITIS
Actress/Model

DATE OF BIRTH: 30.09.81
PLACE OF BIRTH: Lambeth, London; father from Limassol.
MARITAL STATUS: Single
SCHOOLS/COLLEGE: Claremont Fan Court School, Esher.
ACADEMIC QUALIFICATIONS: GCSEs (Maths, English, Drama, Music) A Level Drama
HONOURS/AWARDS: Grade 5 singing, Grade 3 piano.
HOBBIES AND INTERESTS: Singing, playing saxophone, theatre and football.
PERSONAL PROFILE: Actress/Model. Model: Lingerie for *La Senza* and *Contessa*. Actress: Appeared in *Dream Team* (Sky One); *The Goal* (BBC Worldwide).

STATHIS PAPOUTES
Chief Executive

DATE OF BIRTH: 23.12.50
PLACE OF BIRTH: Strovolos.
MARITAL STATUS: Divorced
CHILDREN: Two sons.
ACADEMIC QUALIFICATIONS: BA Honours degree in Economics, MBA.
HOBBIES AND INTERESTS: Gardening & Architecture
PERSONAL PROFILE: Bank of Cyprus, London 1974-1975. Hungarian International Bank, London 1975-1984, London Forfaiting Company PLC, London, Managing Director 1984-93, Chief Executive 1993 to date.

JANET PARASKEVA
Chief Executive of the Law Society

DATE OF BIRTH: 28.05.46
PLACE OF BIRTH: Newport, Gwent.Parents from Neta, Famagusta.
MARITAL STATUS: Divorced
CHILDREN: Amanda Hunt and Suzanna Paraskeva.
SCHOOLS/COLLEGE: Newport & Hastings High School, Worcester College of Education, Open University.
ACADEMIC QUALIFICATIONS: Cert Ed, BA.
HONOURS/AWARDS: Robert Schuman Silver Medal.
HOBBIES AND INTERESTS: Golf, riding and gardening.
PERSONAL PROFILE: First Chief Executive of the Law Society for England Wales. Director England, National Lottery Charities Board, 1995-2000. Chief Executive, National Youth Agency, 1991-1995. Director, National Youth Bureau, 1988-1991. HM Inspector of Schools, Department of Education and Sciences 1983-1988. Served as a member of the Youth Justice Board at the Home Office. Also as a magistrate for eight years.

Address: 113 Chancery Lane, London WC2A 1PL

PARASKEVAS (Barry) PARASKEVA
Surgeon at Imperial College School of Medicine

DATE OF BIRTH: 29.12.69
PLACE OF BIRTH: London. Father from Makrasyka; Mother from Eptakomi.
MARITAL STATUS: Married to Rebcecca, a Doctor, from London.
CHILDREN: Sophia.
SCHOOLS/COLLEGE: Henry Compton School, Fulham, St Mary's Hospital Medical School, London.
ACADEMIC QUALIFICATIONS: Bachelor of Science BSc (Honours)-Physiology-1st Class, PhD-Molecular Biology of Tumour Metastasis.
PROFESSIONAL QUALIFICATIONS: Bachelor of Medicine & Bachelor of Surgery-MBBS (Honours), Fellow of the Royal College of Surgeons of England-FRCS (Eng).
HONOURS/AWARDS: Queen's Award for Higher Education 2000, Imperial College Award for Teaching excellence in Surgery.
HOBBIES AND INTERESTS: Byzantine art.
PERSONAL PROFILE: Surgeon-St Mary's Hospital London and Lecturer in surgery at Imperial College School of Medicine.

RICHARD PARPERIS
Headteacher

DATE OF BIRTH: 09.08.53
PLACE OF BIRTH: London. Father from Achna.
MARITAL STATUS: Married to Linda from London.
CHILDREN: Victoria Demetra, studying Law.
SCHOOLS/COLLEGE: Ackland Burghley, London, Balls Park College, Hertford, The University of Hertfordshire, Leicester University.
QUALIFICATIONS: BEd, MBA, NPQH.
MEMBERSHIPS: Area Rep for the Hertfordshire Association of Secondary Headteachers (HASSH), member of SHA (Secondary Head's Association).
HOBBIES AND INTERESTS: Travel, reading and education.
PERSONAL PROFILE: Currently a Secondary School Headteacher (11-18 Comprehensive) in Hertfordshire. Started teaching in 1974 and between 1981 and 1991 taught in Haringey, North London. Values Bi-lingual upbringing (thanks to the efforts of his parents). In conjunction with the local Education Authority and the Cyprus High Commission, strove to introduce Modern Greek onto the Curriculum at the school.

DOROS PARTASIDES
Photographer/Film Making/Documentaries

PLACE OF BIRTH: Ayii Omoloyites, Nicosia.
MARITAL STATUS: Married to Vera, from Larnaca.
CHILDREN: Constantine, a Solictor; Marianna, a Journalist.
SCHOOLS/COLLEGE: Technical School, Nicosia.
ACADEMIC QUALIFICATIONS: Diploma, Royal College of Art.
PROFESSIONAL QUALIFICATIONS: AFIAP.
HONOURS/AWARDS: Gold and silver medal of AFIAP.
HOBBIES AND INTERESTS: Football, golf, walks, cinema and art.
PERSONAL PROFILE: Film making/Documentaries, Photographer and Historian, published three books, served on the Committee of The Greek Cypriot Brotherhood.

PAS PASCHALI
Development Editor for the Guardian and Observer

DATE OF BIRTH: 26.05.56
PLACE OF BIRTH: Hammersmith, London. Father born in Achna; Mother born in Komi Kebir.
MARITAL STATUS: Single
SCHOOLS/COLLEGE: Latymer Upper School, Hammersmith/ The City University.
ACADEMIC QUALIFICATIONS: BSc Actuarial Science.
PROFESSIONAL QUALIFICATIONS: AIA (Associate of the Institute of Actuaries).
HOBBIES AND INTERESTS: Painting (oil on Canvas), the arts, cinema, photography and architecture, walking (including several national trails, such as the 193-mile Coast to Coast), Italy (having travelled it extensively, exploring its cities and culture).
PERSONAL PROFILE: Development Editor for the *Guardian* and *Observer* - commissions and edits special supplements for both newspapers. Has been in publishing since 1982, during which time has co-founded an arts magazine, edited two lifestyle magazines, been arts editor for a regional newspaper and a section editor for the *Evening Standard*. In 1979, after deciding not to pursue an actuarial career, he took up freelance design and photography and then journalism.

Email: pas.paschali@guardian.co.uk

CHRISTAKIS PASCHALIDES
Solicitor

DATE OF BIRTH: 20.09.39
PLACE OF BIRTH: Yiallousa.
MARITAL STATUS: Married to Maria from London (parents from Khirokitia and Dohni).
CHILDREN: Two sons, one daughter.
SCHOOLS/COLLEGE: English School, Nicosia, called to the English Bar Nov 1964.
HOBBIES AND INTERESTS: Travelling.
PERSONAL PROFILE: 1964, Legal Advisor to Inland Revenue in Cyprus, 1971, worked as Barrister, 1975, Bank of Cyprus Legal Advisor then Assistant General Manager and Acting General Manager in 1986. Now has own Solicitors office in Grays Inn Road, London and associate offices in Nicosia.

ELLI PASHOURTIDES
Teacher

DATE OF BIRTH: 26.07.57
PLACE OF BIRTH: London. Father, Soteri, from Vokolidha; Mother, Loukia from Lefkara.
MARITAL STATUS: Married to Orthodoxos from Pervolia who works with Cyprus Airways.
CHILDREN: Two sons, one daughter.
SCHOOLS/COLLEGE: Michenden, Froebel Institute of Education, part of university of London.
ACADEMIC QUALIFICATIONS: Certificate in Education
HOBBIES AND INTERESTS: Looking after children, keep fit, dancing and reading.
PERSONAL PROFILE: Teacher - taught at Randel Cremer School in Shoreditch, London Fields Infant School in Hackney. Taught in Cyprus in Dhekelia British Bases. Then in 1986 taught at Winchmore Hill Infants School. Since 1992 has worked with Under-Fives Home School Liason Service working with pre-school children, and home visiting children in the year before school. Former member of Potters Bar Greek School Committee.

PANAYIOTIS PASTOU
Sports and Architecture

DATE OF BIRTH: 24.11.78
PLACE OF BIRTH: London. Father from Athienou; Mother from Trikomo.
MARITAL STATUS: Married to Andrea, a university graduate in Biology, now in Insurance, from London (parents are from Ayios Amvrosios, Cyprus).
SCHOOLS/COLLEGE: Bishops Stopfords Secondary School, Enfield; Greenwich University
ACADEMIC QUALIFICATIONS: BA Honours Degree in Architecture, 8 GCSEs, 3 A Levels.
MEMBERSHIPS: Ayios Amvrosios Committee Member, Athienou Committee Member
HONOURS/AWARDS: BA Honours in Architecture & Community Sports Leaders Award, First Aid Certificate.
HOBBIES AND INTERESTS: Football, athletics, gym and cars.
PERSONAL PROFILE: Director of Eurostars Lettings and PP Property Maintenance. Past Achievments- School Captain. Captain of Enfield Youth Football Club. School Record Holder in Long Jump. Borough Champion in 100 metres & Long Jump. Top Scorer Award School & Youth Team four times.

THEODOROS PASTOU
Director of Kounnis and Partners PLC

DATE OF BIRTH: 18.02.51
PLACE OF BIRTH: Athienou.
MARITAL STATUS: Married to Georgia Mela from Tricomo, daughter of Mouchtari.
CHILDREN: Panayiotis, Architect; Michael, Owner of Italian Restuarant in Upminster; Katerina.
SCHOOLS/COLLEGE: American Academy, Larnaca.
PROFESSIONAL QUALIFICATIONS: Certified Accountant.
HOBBIES & INTERESTS: Football, Omonia Othello Athienou, West Ham, atheletics, music and dancing.
PERSONAL PROFILE: Director of Kounnis and Partners Accountants Plc, 1990-2000. Vice Chair Omonia FC London, 2004. Chairman of Athienou Association; Treasurer of Bowes Greek School.

DESPINA PATIA
Dance Teacher

DATE OF BIRTH: 12.49
PLACE OF BIRTH: Achna, Cyprus.
MARITAL STATUS: Married to Andreas, from Kontea, Cyprus.
CHILDREN: Christina, Lerfteri; Two grandchildren, Nicholas and Stephan.
MEMBERSHIPS: LELA Theatrical (Laiki Enosis Logotchnon Anglia).
HOBBIES AND INTERESTS: Dancing, sports, travelling and acting/drama.
PERSONAL PROFILE: Dancing Teacher at the following schools: Timiou Stavrou in Mill Hill, Canon Independent Green School & Youth Centre, Walker School in Southgate, St Barnabas (Ayios Varnavas) Youth Club, Taking part in the Philhellenes Dance Group & Taking 'O Vassos kei Irinou' to Cyprus.

ELEFTHERIA XENOPHON PATSALOS
Partner & International Tax Advisor, Deloitte & Touche

DATE OF BIRTH: 22.05.54
PLACE OF BIRTH: Aradippou.
MARITAL STATUS: Married to Professor Phillip Patsalos from Pano Lefkara.
CHILDREN: Nicolas and Maria.
SCHOOLS/COLLEGE: American Academy, Larnaca, London School of Economics, City University.
ACADEMIC QUALIFICATIONS: BA Economics.
PROFESSIONAL QUALIFICATIONS: MBA Financial Accounting and Marketing.
HOBBIES AND INTERESTS: Jogging, dance, music and reading.
PERSONAL PROFILE: Partner in Tax Dept Deloitte & Touche, Member of Cypriot Qualified Accountants Association.

PROFESSOR PHILIP N PATSALOS
Director of Pharmacology and Therapeutics at the National Hospital for Neurology and Neurosurgery

DATE OF BIRTH: 01.04.52
PLACE OF BIRTH: Pano Lefkara.
MARITAL STATUS: Married to Eleftheria, an International Tax Advisor, from Aradippou.
CHILDREN: Nicolas and Maria.
SCHOOLS/COLLEGE: Holloway School, Reading University, University of London.
ACADEMIC QUALIFICATIONS: Msc in Neurochemistry, FRCPath, PhD.
PROFESSIONAL QUALIFICATIONS: Doctorate from University of London.
HOBBIES & INTERESTS: Travel, writing and football, (Arsenal Fan).
PERSONAL PROFILE: Professor of Clinical Pharmacology at the Institute of Neurology, University College London.

APOSTOLOS (LAKIS) PATTALIS
Partner, Trehantiri Greek Bookshop

DATE OF BIRTH: 11.09.63
PLACE OF BIRTH: UK. Father (Deceased) from Sisklipos, Kyrenia; Mother from Omorfita Nicosia.
MARITAL STATUS: Married to Maria (parents from Nicosia and Sisklipos).
CHILDREN: Coralena and Andrea.
SCHOOLS/COLLEGE: Stationers Secondary School, Hornsey, Tottenham College, Building Dept, London School of Building.
ACADEMIC QUALIFICATIONS: 4 O Levels, City & Guilds and Advanced City & Guilds in Carpentry and Joinery, A.B.R.AC.
PROFESSIONAL QUALIFICATIONS: I.O.C.B Institute of Chartered Building.
HOBBIES AND INTERESTS: Family, sports and DIY.
PERSONAL PROFILE: Former site Carpenter & Manager Bovis Construction. Now runs Trehantiri with brother Aki.

LEDA PATTICHI
President of Democratic Rally UK Ladies Branch

DATE OF BIRTH: 02.05.43
PLACE OF BIRTH: Lefkoniko. Parents from Famagusta.
MARITAL STATUS: Married to Melis, a baker, from Lefkoniko.
CHILDREN: Kyriakos, Professional Electronics Engineer; Louis, Certified Accountant; Miranda, Solicitor; Odysseas, Accounts Clerk.
SCHOOLS/COLLEGE: Lefkoniko High School, College for Social Workers, Athens.
ACADEMIC QUALIFICATIONS: High School Diploma.
MEMBERSHIPS: President of Democratic Rally (UK) Ladies Branch.
HOBBIES AND INTERESTS: International cooking and cake making.
PERSONAL PROFILE: Receptionist/Carer for elderly mothers. Secretary of The St Andrews Greek Ladies Charity Organisation, The Hellenic Central Fund Raising Committee, Events Organiser of The Lefkonico Association, National Federation of Cypriots in Britain and Trustee of The St Andrews Greek Cathedral.

ANDY PAUL
Singer

DATE OF BIRTH: 18.09.57
PLACE OF BIRTH: Limassol.
MARITAL STATUS: Married to Argentina Pavlou, a Nurse, from Moldova.
CHILDREN: Suzan Valentina, Lisa, Joanne Alexandra, Nicola and Nicolas.
MEMBERSHIPS: Equity.
HOBBIES AND INTERESTS: Computer and his children.
PERSONAL PROFILE: Sang the 1984 Eurovision Song Contest entry for Cyprus.

COSTAS PAUL
Involved with The UK Thalassaemia Society and The Organisation Of Relatives of Missing Cypriots

DATE OF BIRTH: 22.01.39
PLACE OF BIRTH: Famagusta.
MARITAL STATUS: Married to Rita, a Dress Designer, from Larnaca.
CHILDREN: Marianne, Beauty Therapist; Christopher, Actor.
SCHOOLS/COLLEGE: Ayios Memnon Famagusta Elementary, three years at The Famagusta Greek Gymnasium, four years at the Nicosia Technical Institute, three years in London at University Tutorial College and West Ham College of Technology.
ACADEMIC QUALIFICATIONS:8 GCE O Levels. 1 GCE A Level.
PROFESSIONAL QUALIFICATIONS: City and Guilds, Telecoms Certificate.
HONOURS/AWARDS: 1989, Whitbread Community Care Award. 1995, Guardian Jerwood Award Certificate. 1995, Certificate of Merit for services rendered in the prevention of Thalassaemia, Pakistan.
HOBBIES AND INTERESTS: Travelling and gardening.
PERSONAL PROFILE: Ex-British Telecom Manager. Has helped at the UK Thalassaemia Society since 1978. For four years Secretary of The Greek Schools in Enfield. Former Chair of The Church of St Demetrios. Former Chair and organising Secretary of The All Saint's Church Youth Club in the late 50s to early 60s. Also helps with The Organisation of Relatives of Missing Cypriots.

Email: Costas.Paul@virgin.net

PAVLOS PAVLIDES
Assistant Vice President, JP Morgan Chase & Co

DATE OF BIRTH: 12.09.72
PLACE OF BIRTH: Nicosia.
MARITAL STATUS: Single
SCHOOLS/COLLEGE: Falcon School, Nicosia, The Latymer School, City University, London.
ACADEMIC QUALIFICATIONS: B.Sc (Honours) in Economics and Accountancy, M.Sc in Internal Auditing and Management.
PROFESSIONAL QUALIFICATIONS: Member of the Institute of Internal Auditors.
MEMBERSHIPS: Member of the Secretariat of the National Federation of Cypriots in Great Britain. Federation of Overseas Cypriots and the Greek Cypriot Brotherhood.

PERSONAL PROFILE: Secretary, Banking and Financial Services Group, Institute of Internal Auditors UK. Assistant Vice President, JP Morgan Chase & Co. previous positions: First elected President of The National Union of Cypriot Students in the UK (EFEK, UK, which is the umbrella organisation for all Cypriot students societies and asociations, also served as Secretary of SYKFA (EFEK's predecessor organisation). Served as Treasurer, Secretary, and President of Anagennisi Student Union UK, President, British Universities North American Club and Treasurer, Conservative Club, City University. Founding member of Kypros Net Ltd, an internet organisation servicing the overseas Cypriot Communities.

SAVVAS PAVLIDES
Cyprus High Commission Counsellor (Educational Affairs), Primary Education Inspector, Head of Cyprus Educational Mission in the UK

DATE OF BIRTH: 23.06.46
PLACE OF BIRTH: Kyrenia.
MARITAL STATUS: Married to Eleni, a Teacher, from Larnacas Tis Lapithou, Kyrenia.
CHILDREN: Pavlos, Internal Auditor; Mary, Chartered Accountant; Rena, UCL Law Student (LLM); Gloria , European Social & Political Studies at UCL (3rd year).
SCHOOLS/COLLEGE: Larnacas Tis Lapithou Primary School, Pancyprian Gymnasium, Nicosia, Pedagogical Academy, Athens University, The University of Reading UK.
ACADEMIC QUALIFICATIONS: MA in Organisation, Planning & Management in Education (University of Reading); BA in Education (Athens University).
PROFESSIONAL QUALIFICATIONS: Teacher Training Diploma (Pedagogical Academy of Cyprus); Diploma in Byzantine Music (Athens National Odeon).
MEMBERSHIPS: Pancyprian Greek Teachers Organisation (POED); Pancyprian School Inspectors Organization (OEDE); British Educational Leadership Management & Administration Society (BELMAS); The Design & Technology Association (DATA); Byzantine Music Teachers Association; Commandos Ex-servicemen Association (ESEKA); National Association of Head Teachers (NAHT).
HOBBIES AND INTERESTS: Singing, swimming, travelling, poetry, reading and writing.
PERSONAL PROFILE: Chairman of Students Community; Football Player/Referee; Youth Leader/Welfare Officer; Boy Scouts Leader; Member of Pancyprian Refugee Organisation Committee; Church Singer; Head Teacher of Greek Community Schools in Kuwait, UAE and UK; Manager of the Hellenic Centre in London; Commandos Ex-servicemen Officer and first Chairman of the Association; Head of Cyprus Educational Mission.

CHRIS PAVLO
Actor/Writer

DATE OF BIRTH: 06.06.67
PLACE OF BIRTH: London. Father from Famagusta; Mother from Larnaca.
MARITAL STATUS: Single
SCHOOLS/COLLEGE: Ambrose Fleming Secondary School, Webber Douglas Academy.
HOBBIES AND INTERESTS: Football and sports.
PERSONAL PROFILE: Actor/Writer. Performed on TV in *The Bill* and *EastEnders*, *Wendys House*. Appeared in the films *Jeremiah* and *Strong Language*. Appeared in Shakespeare Tours. Regular at the Edinburgh Festival. Wrote and performed in the BBC2 award-winning comedy, *The Harringham Harker*.

ANTONIS PAVLOU
Chairman of Greek Cypriot Orthodox Community in Leeds

DATE OF BIRTH: 02.02.44
PLACE OF BIRTH: Larnaca
MARITAL STATUS: Married to Dimitra.
CHILDREN: Two sons, one daughter.
SCHOOLS/COLLEGE: Elementary School, Ayii Vavatsinia.
HOBBIES AND INTERESTS: Swimming and travel.
PERSONAL PROFILE: Businessman, Chairman of Ayii Vavatsinia Assoc UK. Chairman of Greek Cypriot Orthodox Community in Leeds.

CRITON PAVLOU
Independant Consultant in Obstetrics and Gynaecology

DATE OF BIRTH: 23.01.41
PLACE OF BIRTH: St Neots Hunts. Father from Dhora; Mother from Rizokarpasso.
MARITAL STATUS: Married to Joy from the UK.
CHILDREN: James, Film Industry; Lucy, training in Child Psychotherapy.
SCHOOLS/COLLEGE: St Clement Danes Grammar School, Middlesex Hampstead Medical School.
ACADEMICS QUALIFICATIONS: MB, BS, London.
PROFESSIONAL QUALIFICATIONS: FRCS Ed, FRCOG.
MEMBERSHIPS: British Fertility Society, Hellenic Society, British Society of Cervical Pathology & Colposcopy, British Society of Gynaecological Endoscopy.
HOBBIES AND INTERESTS: Golf, travel, gardening and DIY.
PERSONAL PROFILE: Independent General Consultant Obstetrics and Gynaecology.

MARIA PAVLOU (née CHRISTOU)
Solicitor

DATE OF BIRTH: 10.10.57
PLACE OF BIRTH: London. Parents from Pano Lefkara and Alethrico, Larnaca.
MARITAL STATUS: Married to Costas Christou, also a Solicitor, from Tricomo
CHILDREN: Christopher and Zoe, both at school.
SCHOOLS/COLLEGE: Highbury Hill High School, Kings College London, College of Law Lancaster Gate.
ACADEMIC QUALIFICATIONS: LLB (Honours).
PROFESSIONAL QUALIFICATIONS: Solicitor.
HOBBIES AND INTERESTS: Theatre, opera, tennis, reading, walking and cooking
PERSONAL PROFILE: Would have liked to have been an Opera Singer but fell into the trap of the legal profession.

PAUL PAVLOU
Solictor

DATE OF BIRTH: 13.10.55
PLACE OF BIRTH: London. Father from Rizoakarpasso; Mother from Agastina.
MARITAL STATUS: Married to Vasoulla, an Administrator, from Davlos, Cyprus.
CHILDREN: Constantine, George, and Andreas, all at school.
SCHOOLS/COLLEGE: Tulsehill School, Kings College, London.
ACADEMIC QUALIFICATIONS: Filex LLB.
MEMBERSHIPS: Institute Of Legal Executives.
HOBBIES AND INTERESTS: Football, runs under 10s team.
PERSONAL PROFILE: Solicitor, Committee member of Greek School of St Constantine & St Helen Church Crystal Palace.

STEL PAVLOU
Author/Scriptwriter

DATE OF BIRTH: 1970
PLACE OF BIRTH: UK. Father from Cyprus, Mother, English.
SCHOOLS/COLLEGE: Liverpool University.
PERSONAL PROFILE: Had job in Threshers Off Licence where he wrote the book *Decipher,* a top ten best-selling novel and also the film *51st State,* which starred Samuel L Jackson and Robert Carlyle.

DR ANDREAS PELENDRIDES
General Practitioner

DATE OF BIRTH: 28.10.30
PLACE OF BIRTH: Pelendri.
MARITAL STATUS: Married to Radka Christova from Sofia, Bulgaria.
CHILDREN: Dr Helen Pelendrides, General Practitioner.
SCHOOLS/COLLEGE: Medical School, Sofia, Bulgaria, The Society of Apothecaries of London.
ACADEMIC QUALIFICATIONS: MD, LMSSA.
PROFESSIONAL QUALIFICATIONS: MA (Byzantine Studies), University of London-Royal Holloway College.
HONOURS/AWARDS: MA.
PERSONAL PROFILE: Publication of Two Byzantine Books. General Practitioner.

DR HELEN PELENDRIDES
General Practitioner

DATE OF BIRTH: 16.05.61
PLACE OF BIRTH: Sofia, Bulgaria. Father from Cyprus; Mother from Bulgaria.
MARITAL STATUS: Married to Nicholas Durden, a Medical Doctor, from Finchley London.
CHILDREN: Andrew and Marie, both at school.
SCHOOLS/COLLEGE: South Hampstead High School for Girls London, University of London, Guys Hospital.
ACADEMIC QUALIFICATIONS: MB, BS, DRCOG.
PROFESSIONAL QUALIFICATIONS: University of London, Guys Hospital.
HOBBIES AND INTERESTS: Skiing, keep fit and modern literature.
PERSONAL PROFILE: General Practitioner on three sites in North London (East Finchley, Finchley Central & Wood Green).

PETER PENTAYIOTIS
Freelance Photographer

DATE OF BIRTH: 07.12.48
PLACE OF BIRTH: Pentayia
MARITAL STATUS: Single
SCHOOL/COLLEGE: Pentayia Elementary, Xeros Technical School.
MEMBERSHIPS: Member of the Committee of Pentayia Association, UK
HOBBIES AND INTERESTS: Shooting and golf.
PERSONAL PROFILE: Freelance Photographer, works mainly with *Parikiaki* and *Eleftheria* Newspapers.

**STEL PAVLOU
SCRIPT WRITER OF THE
FILM 51ST STATE
WHICH STARRED
SAMUEL L JACKSON AND
ROBERT CARLYLE**

ANTONIOS LOUI PERDIKIS
Physiotherapist

DATE OF BIRTH: 11.09.51
PLACE OF BIRTH: Limassol.
MARITAL STATUS: Married to Ann Haynes, a PR Consultant, from New Zealand.
SCHOOLS/COLLEGE: East Hearts College, Grays Inn College, School of Physiotherapist at Royal London Hospital, Post Graduate School St Thomas Hospital.
ACADEMIC QUALIFICATIONS: GCE O & A Levels, Chartered Physiotherapist, Diploma in Cyriax Orthopaedic Medicine, State Registered Osteopath.
MEMBERSHIPS: Chartered Society of Physiotherapy Reg no: 41227, Cyriax Organisation Orthopaedic Medicine, General osteopathic Council Reg no: 3659, Australia Physiotherapy Board, Australian Physiotherapy Association.
HOBBIES AND INTERESTS: Golf and keeping fit.
PERSONAL PROFILE: Own private practice of Physical Medicine since 1985. Specializing in Orthopaedic spinal conditions; sports and theatrical dance injuries; Lecturer to various societies; dance schools; Football Societies and universities on sports medicine, diagnosis, prevention and treament. Used to play football for New Salamis Apol and the league team in the Cypriot football league UK.

MINOS PERDIOS
National Team Coach

DATE OF BIRTH: 18.06.67
PLACE OF BIRTH: London. Parents from Larnaca and Akhna.
MARITAL STATUS: Married to Lucia Alexander, a Personnel Manager from Leeds.
CHILDREN: Olivia.
SCHOOLS/COLLEGE: American Academy, Larnaca, Davis College, City University, University of Sheffield.
QUALIFCATIONS: BSc. Actuarial Science and Social Statistics, MSc. Sports Coaching and Exercise Science UEFA B' Licence, SAQ Level 1.
MEMBERSHIPS: FA Coaches Association.
HOBBIES AND INTERESTS: Football, tennis and reading sports autobiographies.
PERSONAL PROFILE: National Team Coach of the St Kitts & Nevis Football Association during the FIFA World Cup 2002 qualifying campaign, Youth Coach at Leeds United Football Club, General Manager at Haringey Borough Football Club, and omonia FC London, Football in the Community Coach at Luton Town football Club.

BOBBY PERICLEOUS
Leukaemia Charity Fund Raiser

DATE OF BIRTH: 31.12.56
PLACE OF BIRTH: London. Father Pantelli Savva from Alethrico; Mother Loiza from Famagusta.
MARITAL STATUS: Married
CHILDREN: Mario and Pantelli.
SCHOOLS/COLLEGE: Alexandra Park School.
HOBBIES AND INTERESTS: Walking, socialising, cooking and fundraising.
PERSONAL PROFILE: Chairwoman of Eleni Pericleous Trust Fund which raises money for Leukaemia to be distributed between Royal Free Hospital and Great Ormond Street Hospital. Was Social Secretary of Potters Bar Greek School.

CHRISTINE PERICLEOUS
Psychotherapist

DATE OF BIRTH: 19.08.55
PLACE OF BIRTH: Ayia Varvara, Nicosia.
MARITAL STATUS: Divorced
CHILDREN: Mary-Louise Pericleous, University Graduate.
SCHOOLS/COLLEGE: Winchmore Secondary, Southgate College.
PROFESSIONAL QUALIFICATIONS: Psychoanalytic Psychotherapist & UKCP.
MEMBERSHIPS: Arbours Association of Psychotherapists.
HOBBIES AND INTERESTS: The arts, theatre, art galleries and hiking.
PERSONAL PROFILE: Was Secretary of the Thalassaemia Society UK. Then worked for Arbours Crisis Centre a residential setting for people with emotional distress. During this time began Psychotherapy training. Currently works as a Psychotherapist in the Cygnet Clinic a private Psychiatric Hospital. Also has a Private Practice offering indivdual Psychoanalytic Psychotherapy.

Email address: christinepericleous@hotmail.com

DR STEPHANOS PERICLEOUS
Surgeon

DATE OF BIRTH: 08.05.74
PLACE OF BIRTH: Nicosia.
MARITAL STATUS: Single
SCHOOLS/COLLEGE: The English School, University College, London Medical School.
ACADEMIC QUALIFICATIONS: MB, BS.
PERSONAL PROFILE: Surgeon.

LEONIDAS PERIKLEOUS
Chairman of the Greek Cypriot Orthodox Community in Leicester

DATE OF BIRTH: 12.03.43
PLACE OF BIRTH: Dora, Limassol.
MARITAL STATUS: Married to Androulla from Limassol.
CHILDREN: One son, one daughter.
SCHOOLS/COLLEGE: Elementary School.
HOBBIES AND INTERESTS: Working and travel.
PERSONAL PROFILE: Chairman of the Greek Cypriot Orthodox Community in Leicester.

MARK PERIKLIS
Solicitor

DATE OF BIRTH: 22.10.64
PLACE OF BIRTH: London. Father from Nicosia; Mother from London.
MARITAL STATUS: Single
SCHOOLS/COLLEGE: University of Hertfordshire, Woodhouse Finchley.
ACADEMIC QUALIFICATIONS: BA (Honours) Law.
PROFESSIONAL QUALIFICATIONS: Life Coaching Academy.
MEMBERSHIPS: Law Society (IFA).
HONOURS/AWARDS: Life Coach.
HOBBIES AND INTERESTS: Squash, photography, writing and travel.
PERSONAL PROFILE: Has own law firm, Mark & Co.

Email: mark@markandcolawyers.co.uk

ALEXANDROS PETRIDES
Music Journalist & Disc Jockey

DATE OF BIRTH: 11.08.64
PLACE OF BIRTH: London. Father from Amiandos; Mother from England.
MARITAL STATUS: Single
SCHOOLS/COLLEGE: Newport Rd, Leyton, Monkswalk School, Boreham Wood College.
HOBBIES AND INTERESTS: Football and skateboarding.
PERSONAL PROFILE: DJ, in clubs all over the world and radio known as Alex P. *Kiss FM* and own show on MTV called *Medonism*. Writes articles in major papers: *Guardian*, *Sun*. Four compilation albums that sold over 150,000 copies each, new album called *Speculaties*. Has done work for Jay Kay, Jamiroquai. Own Velvet Underground Night Club in Charing Cross.

ANDREAS PETRIDES
Stunt Co-ordinator/Stunt Performer

DATE OF BIRTH: 11.11.67
PLACE OF BIRTH: Father from Amiandos; Mother from England.
MARITAL STATUS: Single
SCHOOLS/COLLEGE: Monks Walk, Welwyn Garden City.
HOBBIES AND INTERESTS: Adventure sports and walking.
PERSONAL PROFILE Stunt Co-ordinator and Stunt Performer. Has done work in films such as the last four James Bond films, *Gladiator*, *Braveheart*, *Star Wars*, *The Borrowers*. TV work includes *Casualty*, *Merlin*, *The Professionals*.

CHRYSANTHOS PETRIDES
Partner of Freemans partnership LLP

DATE OF BIRTH: 22.3.55
PLACE OF BIRTH: Nicosia.
MARITAL STATUS: Married to Ann, from Wales.
CHILDREN: Jonathan, Gemma and Alexander.
SCHOOLS/COLLEGE: English School, Nicosia, Warwick University.
ACADEMIC QUALIFICATIONS: BSC.
PROFESSIONAL QUALIFICATIONS: FCA, FCCA.
HOBBIES AND INTERESTS: Squash, golf and skiing.
PERSONAL PROFILE: Accountant Partner of Freemans Partnership LLP.

CHRISTOS PETRIDES
Chairman Omonia, London (Deceased)

DATE OF BIRTH: 09.02.53
PLACE OF BIRTH: Nicosia
MARITAL STATUS: Married to Pantelitsa, a Social worker from Famagusta.
CHILDREN: Costas, Bank Manager; Eugenia, Solicitor.
SCHOOLS/COLLEGE: The English School, Nicosia, Cyprus, City of London.
PROFESSIONAL QUALIFICATIONS: Accountant, AFA.
HOBBIES AND INTERESTS: Football, music and underwater fishing.
PERSONAL PROFILE:
Chairman Omonia London FC.

PETROS PETRIDES
Major Shareholder and First Chairman
of London Greek Radio

DATE OF BIRTH: 06.02.43
PLACE OF BIRTH: Lincoln, UK.
Greek Cypriot Parents.
MARITAL STATUS: Married to
Androula, Company Director,
Chairwoman of the Ladies
Committee, Cypriot Estia of
London, from Famagusta.
CHILDREN: Anthony, Boston
University, business
administration, Company
Director; Eugenios, Fellow of
the Gemmological Associations of the UK and USA.
Company Chairman.
SCHOOLS/COLLEGE: Greek Gymnasium of Famagusta,
London University, Toronto University.
PROFESSIONAL QUALIFICATIONS: B.Sc (Eng), P.Eng,
AMIEE.
MEMBERSHIPS: Institute of Electrical Engineers
HONOURS/AWARDS: Honorary Citizen of the City of
Minneapolis, USA, Who's Who in the World (1984-
1985).
HOBBIES AND INTERESTS: Fishing, hunting and
travelling.
PERSONAL PROFILE: Founder and Chairman of the
Plus Group of Companies with trading and investment
activities in several countries. Holds Directorship in
several companies. Major shareholder and first chairman
of London Greek Radio, Vice Chairman of Cypriot
Estia of London.

ARCHIMANDRITE THEOPHANIS PETROU
High Priest

DATE OF BIRTH: 06.01.42
PLACE OF BIRTH: Kythraia
MARITAL STATUS: Widower,
wife Helen Petrou, died 06.12.98.
CHILDREN: Pierre, Police Press
Executive Officer; Marino,
Manager.
SCHOOLS/COLLEGE: High
Commercial Lyceum, Nicosia.
**PROFESSIONAL QUALIFICA-
TIONS:** High Priest.
HOBBIES AND INTERESTS: Religion and gardening.
PERSONAL PROFILE: High Priest. Available to Greek
Communities throughout the UK.

Tel: 020 7723 4787

MARIO PETROU
Consultant Cardiac Surgeon

DATE OF BIRTH: 20.07.64
PLACE OF BIRTH: London.
Father from Kythrea; Mother
from Kyrenia.
MARITAL STATUS: Married to
Elizabeth from London.
SCHOOLS/COLLEGE: Hackney
Downs Comprehensive School,
Kingsway Princeton College,
University College and
Middlesex School of Medicine.
ACADEMIC QUALIFICATIONS: PhD Cardiac Surgery; Bsc
in Neuroscience.
PROFESSIONAL QUALIFICATIONS: MBBS, frcs (CTH)
HONOURS/AWARDS: William Henry Rean Prize for the
most promising Young Doctor. Mc Cormack Medal
2001.
HOBBIES AND INTERESTS: Classical Music, Snooker
PERSONAL PROFILE: Consultant Cardiac Surgeon, Royal
Brompton Hospital, London.

PETROS PETROU
Businessman

DATE OF BIRTH: 1957
PLACE OF BIRTH: Ayia Phyla,
Limassol.
MARITAL STATUS: Married to
Nina.
CHILDREN: Carmelina.
SCHOOL/COLLEGE: North
London Polytechnic.
HOBBIES AND INTERESTS:
Football and travel.
PERSONAL PROFILE: In 1976 he
joined the National Guard to complete his Military
Service rising to the rank of Lieutenant. Following this
period he emigrated to the UK to further his education
and studied commerce imports and exports which he
chose as his business career. After graduation he
pursued various business ventures one of which was
the Merchant Navy where he gained a valuable insight
into the commercial business practices of other
countries and in particular the catering industry.
In 1989 he teamed with Antonis Antoniades to set up
C&A which was the original Capital Accommodations.

EFTHYMIOS PHEDON
Chairman of the Trustees of the Greek Orthodox Church in Coventry

DATE OF BIRTH: 05.09.38
PLACE OF BIRTH: Ora, Larnaca.
MARITAL STATUS: Married to Maroulla, from Anaphotia.
CHILDREN: Phillip, Marina, Nick, Soulla and Paul.
SCHOOLS/COLLEGE: Ora Elementary School, American Academy, Larnaca.
PROFESSIONAL QUALIFICATIONS: Caterer.
HONOURS/AWARDS: Honoured by the Greek Orthodox Church for services to church community
HOBBIES AND INTERESTS: Travelling, gardening, reading, community work and socialising.
PERSONAL PROFILE: Chairman of the Trustees of the Greek Orthodox Church of Coventry. Retired from successful Catering Business.

DR CONSTANTINOS N PHELLAS
Senior Lecturer in Sociology

DATE OF BIRTH: 24.06.61
PLACE OF BIRTH: Nicosia.
MARITAL STATUS: Single
SCHOOLS/COLLEGE: University of Essex, University of Warwick, City University.
ACADEMIC QUALIFICATIONS: BSc, MSc, MSc, PhD.
PROFESSIONAL QUALIFICATIONS: Taxation Accountant.
MEMBERSHIPS: Institute of Taxation.
HONOURS/AWARDS: Funding from the Government on HIV/AIDS research.
HOBBIES AND INTERESTS: Sports, music and theatre.
PERSONAL PROFILE: Senior Lecturer in Sociology. Published a book on Greek Cultural and Sexual Identities. Area of research: Sexuality, Ethnicity, Culture, Public Health and Health Promotion. He has published extensively on the above-mentioned areas.

Email: cphellas@aol.com

DIMITRI PHILIPOU
Actor

DATE OF BIRTH: 28.12.93
PLACE OF BIRTH: London. Parents from Paphos.
SCHOOLS/COLLEGE: Brettenham School.
HOBBIES AND INTERESTS: Swimming, won medals with Middlesex County.
PERSONAL PROFILE: Actor. Appeared in films *Bad Blood*, *Discovery of Heaven* with Stephen Fry. *Indahouse* with Ali G. Also commercials on TV, appears on Nickelodeon and Fox Kids.

DR GEORGE PHILIPPOU
Cardiac Surgeon

DATE OF BIRTH: 08.10.39
PLACE OF BIRTH: Nicosia.
MARITAL STATUS: Married to Dr Anna Philippou, a Medical Doctor, Consulting Homoeopath, from Sofia.
CHILDREN: Elena Philipou, Administration Manager; Maria Philippou, Beautician.
SCHOOLS/COLLEGE: Pancyprian Gymnasium, Nicosia, Medical University, Sofia.
ACADEMIC QUALIFICATIONS: MD, MB, BS.
PROFESSIONAL QUALIFICATIONS: Cardiac Surgeon.
MEMBERSHIPS: BMA, MDU.
HOBBIES AND INTERESTS: Squash, tennis and reading.
PERSONAL PROFILE: Cardiac Surgeon.

PANICO PHILIPOU
Managing Director of Diesel Menswear and Womenswear

PLACE OF BIRTH: London. Father, Petros, from Yialousa; Mother, May, from Ireland.
MARITAL STATUS: Married to Jessica.
CHILDREN: Petros, Leonidas and Electra.
SCHOOLS/COLLEGE: Sir William Collins School, London University.
ACADEMIC QUALIFICATIONS: BA Econ & Politics.
PROFESSIONAL QUALIFICATIONS: Chartered Certified Accountant.
HOBBIES AND INTERESTS: Football (Arsenal Fan), music and stamp collecting.
PERSONAL PROFILE: Managing Director of Diesel UK, one of the world's leading fashion and design streetwear Co.s. Also involved in labels such as 5S DSL, DSquared, New York Industries, Martin Margiela.

Email: pan_philipou@diesel.com

CHRYS PHILALITHES
Co Founder of Espotting Media

DATE OF BIRTH: 08.12.71
PLACE OF BIRTH: London.
Father from Limassol
Mother from Peyia, Paphos.
MARITAL STATUS: Single
SCHOOL/COLLEGES:
Henrietta Barnett Grammar
School, Woodhouse Sixth Form
College, University of Leeds,
University of Toronto, Canada
Imperial College, University of
London.
ACADEMIC QUALIFICATIONS: BA Honours Economics.
and Politics with North American Studies, Masters in
Business Administration.
HONOURS/AWARDS: Dean's Honours List – University
of Toronto
Awarded the Fulbright Scholarship
Campaign Magazine – Faces To Watch, 2003
The Guardian – 50 Women to Watch, 2003
Wall Street Journal Europe – asked to speak at their
Women in Business Summit, 2003
HOBBIES & INTERESTS: Music, Film, Dance and Scuba
Diving.
PERSONAL PROFILE: Chrys is a founding member of
Espotting Media, and has built one of the most respected
and widely recognised brands in the online B2B
industry. As Marketing Director of Espotting, Chrys is
responsible for group-wide marketing strategy and
execution. Espotting's growth has been explosive – in
three years Chrys has helped grow the advertiser base
from nothing to over 20,000, including names such as
British Airways, eBay and Lastminute.com.
Under Chrys' marketing stewardship, Espotting was
voted the 'Best European Paid Placement Service' by
readers of search industry bible Search Engine Watch,
and was placed at number 27 in the *Financial Times'*
Creative Business 50 for 2002.
Prior to Espotting, Chrys was New Business Manager at
WCRS, one of the UK's Top 20 Advertising Agencies.

CHRISTOPHER PHILLIPIDES
Honorary Consulate of Greece for
Birmingham

DATE OF BIRTH: 1939
PLACE OF BIRTH: Alexandria, Eygpt. Father from
Eftagonia Limassol; Mother from Lymnos.
MARITAL STATUS: Married to Elizabeth.
CHILDREN: Nicholas.
SCHOOLS/COLLEGE: Commercial School Salvagios,
Egypt; Birmingham College.
HOBBIES AND INTERESTS: Travel.
PERSONAL PROFILE: Hotel Proprieter.
Honorary Consulate of Greece for Birmingham since
1975. Involved with the Greek Church in Birmingham

PAUL PHILIPPOU
Teacher/Lecturer

DATE OF BIRTH: 31.10.63
PLACE OF BIRTH: London.
Father from Ayios Serghios,
Famagusta. Mother from the UK.
MARITAL STATUS: Married to
Mary Alexander, a National
Negotiator for UNIFI (Finance
Trade Union), from Perth,
Scotland.
CHILDREN: Cora, Leah and Rosa,
all at school.
SCHOOLS/COLLEGE: University of London, University
of Liverpool.
ACADEMIC QUALIFICATIONS: Msc, DIC in Fluid and
Structural Mechanics; Bsc (Eng); ACGI in Aeronautical
Engineering.
PROFESSIONAL QUALIFICATIONS: PGCE.
HOBBIES AND INTERESTS: Include astronomy,
gardening, poetry, philosophy and left wing and local
history.
PERSONAL PROFILE: Presently writing on local history
and political philosophy. Teaching at Perth High School
and the University of Dundee. Fifteen years teaching
in London and Scotland. Also Associate Lecturer at the
Open University whilst in London. Previously Social
Security Spokesperson for the Scottish Socialist Party.
Labour Party candidate in Fulham for 1994 local
goverment elections. Previously NUT representative,
regional delegate, health and saftey representative. Many
years experience of being a school governor. Previously
weekly columnist for Parikiaki writing on Turkish and
Cypriot political events.

Email: paulphilipou@blueyonder.co.uk

PAUL PHILLIPOU
Secretary of Aris FC

DATE OF BIRTH: 24.07.60
PLACE OF BIRTH: Nicosia.
MARITAL STATUS: Married to Androulla, a Housewife.
CHILDREN: Alex and Eleftheria.
SCHOOLS/COLLEGE: Drayton School, Tottenham.
HOBBIES AND INTERESTS: Football.
PERSONAL PROFILE: Dress Maker, Secretary of Aris FC.

TONY PHILLIPOU
Football Manager in the Cypriot League UK

DATE OF BIRTH: 28.05.67
PLACE OF BIRTH: London. Father from Ayios Dometios; Mother from Nicosia.
MARITAL STATUS: Married to Olga
CHILDREN: Chris, Mario, Andrew and Harry.
SCHOOLS/COLLEGE: Alexandra Park.
HOBBIES AND INTERESTS: Football.
PERSONAL PROFILE: Has been involved with the Cypriot Football League in UK for 17 years. Played for Maronites PAOK New Salamis & Omonia. Also played for the League Representative team. Manager of Omonia - in one year achieved the league title, Cup and LFA Challenge Cup.

ENTRANTS IN GREEK CYPRIOTS IN THE UK HAVE BEEN NOMINATED FOR THEIR ACHIEVEMENTS AND CONTRIBUTIONS. YOU CAN NOMINATE SOMEONE OR YOURSELF WHO DESERVES TO BE IN THE BOOK. ENTRIES ARE FREE. SEND IN YOUR NOMINATIONS, INCLUDING NAME, CONTACT ADDRESS, TELEPHONE NUMBER AND EMAIL TO GREEK CYPRIOTS IN THE UK 111 ST THOMAS'S ROAD LONDON N4 2QJ TELEPHONE 020 7503 3498 EMAIL cypriotwhoswho@aol.com

ANDROS PANAYIOTIS PHOULI
Chairman of Rush Group of Salons

DATE OF BIRTH: 22.03.67
PLACE OF BIRTH: London. Father from Achna, Mother from Odhou.
MARITAL STATUS: Married to Angelina, a Housewife from Kontea, Cyprus.
CHILDREN: Panayiotis, at school.
SCHOOL/COLLEGE: Purley High School, Robert Fielding Hairdressing School.
ACADEMIC QUALIFICATIONS: 2 O Levels.
PROFESSIONAL QUALIFICATIONS: Hairdressing Honours with Distinction.
HONOURS/AWARDS: Andros is the Chairman of Rush Group of Salons whose team have won the following awards:
Guild Photo Stylist, 2001. British Southern Hairdresser of the Year, 2001. Master Hairdresser of the Year, 2001. British F.A.M.E Team Member, 2001 & 2002. Southern Hairdresser of the Year, 2002 & 2004. Guild Art Team of the Year 2002 & 2003. Fellowship for British Hairdressing Team of the Year 2003. British Newcomer of the Year, 2003. British Artistic Team of the Year, 2004.
The above are the biggest prizes you can win in the Hairdressing Industry.
HOBBIES AND INTERESTS: Football, shooting and family.
PERSONAL PROFILE: Chairman of Rush Group of Salons.

XENOPHON PHOTIOU
Senior Bank Officer at the National Bank of Greece

DATE OF BIRTH: 21.09.54
PLACE OF BIRTH: Lagoudera, Nicosia.
MARITAL STATUS: Married.
CHILDREN: One.
SCHOOLS/COLLEGE: Greek Gymnasium of Agros, Morphou, University of Athens.
ACADEMIC QUALIFICATIONS: Bsc Economics
HOBBIES AND INTERESTS: Greek history and music.
PERSONAL PROFILE: Senior Bank Officer at the National Bank of Greece.

KATE PHYLAKTIS
Professor of International Finance, City University Business School, London

DATE OF BIRTH: 20.08.51
PLACE OF BIRTH: Nicosia.
MARITAL STATUS: Married to Akis Phylaktis, an architect.
CHILDREN: Alexandra and George.
SCHOOLS/COLLEGE: Phaneromeni School, Pancyprian Gymnasium Phaneromeni, Brunel University, London School of Economics, City University.
ACADEMIC QUALIFICATIONS: BSc (Econ), MSc (Econ), PhD Banking and Finance.
MEMBERSHIPS: American Finance Association.
HOBBIES AND INTERESTS: Music, swimming, travelling and wine tasting.
PERSONAL PROFILE: Professor of International Finance, City University Business School, London. Previously worked at the International monetary research project at LSE. At the economics office of the now Royal Bank of Scotland. She has held visiting appointments at the research deptartment of the International Monetary Fund. Has published extensively in financial and economic journals. Has written three books: *Financial Data of Banks & Other Institutions, International Finance and the Less Developing Countries* and *The Banking System of Cyprus, Past Present & Future.*

NICKY PLASTIRAS
Team Leader in Community Mental Health

DATE OF BIRTH: 25.11.59
PLACE OF BIRTH: London. Father from Lefkara, Mother from Kalochorio.
MARITAL STATUS: Married to David Phillips, Social Worker from Oxford.
CHILDREN: Audrey and Grace Eleni.
SCHOOLS/COLLEGE: Eleanor Palmer, Tufnell Park, Parliament Hill Girls School, Michenden 6th Form for A Levels, Thames Polytechnic, Surrey University.
ACADEMIC QUALIFICATIONS: Social Sciences, BA Honours.
PROFESSIONAL QUALIFICATIONS: CQSW. MA in Social Work.
HOBBIES AND INTERESTS: Reading, walking and theatre.
PERSONAL PROFILE: Worked for Haringey Council, as a Senior Practitioner in Mental Health Team. Now Team leader in Community Mental Health Team.

PAUL PIERIDES
Solicitor

DATE OF BIRTH: 22.06.48
PLACE OF BIRTH: London. Father from Astromeritis; Mother from Kefalonia, Greece.
MARITAL STATUS: Married to Miroulla from Limassol.
CHILDREN: Maria.
SCHOOLS/COLLEGE: Kingston Grammar School, University College, Oxford.
ACADEMIC QUALIFICATIONS: BA Honours Law, MA Honours Law.
HOBBIES AND INTERESTS: Architecture.
PERSONAL PROFILE: Solicitor specialising in Property Law and Conveyancing. Partner in Gordon Dadds Solicitors.

Address: 80 Brook St, Mayfair, London W1K 5DD

DR KYPROS PILAKOUTAS
University Lecturer

DATE OF BIRTH: 17.02.61
PLACE OF BIRTH: Trachonas, Nicosia.
MARITAL STATUS: Married to Teresa Leonor, a Civil Engineer, Teacher and Translator, from Lisbon Portugal.
CHILDREN: Georgios and Leonora (both at school); Mariana.
SCHOOLS/COLLEGE: The English School Nicosia, Compulsory Service, Cyprus National Guard, Imperial College of Science and Technology (University of London).
ACADEMIC QUALIFICATIONS: BSc (Eng) (1st Class Honours), ACGI, PhD, DIC-Thesis "Earthquake Resistant Design of Reinforced Concrete Walls", 1990.
MEMBERSHIPS: Registered Engineer in Cyprus. MICE Cyprus, Member of the Society for Earthquake and Civil Engineering. 1994: Member of American Concrete Institute, 1995.
HONOURS/AWARDS: Governors Prize for Excellence in written examinations, 1984, Diploma of Iasi Technical University, Romania, Medal of Iasi Technical University, Romania.
HOBBIES AND INTERESTS: Travelling, Greek music and dance, mental games, gardening and football.
PERSONAL PROFILE: University Lecturer at Sheffield University. Visiting Professor - Iasi TU Romania, 2001: Visiting Professor - Artois University, France.

CHRIS PISHIRI
Chartered Surveyor

DATE OF BIRTH: 08.09.69
PLACE OF BIRTH: London. Son of Andrico from Komi Kebir, former owner of Cronos Electronics; Mother Koulla from Komi Kebir.
MARITAL STATUS: Married to Gina from London (parents are from Frenaros and Aglantsia).
CHILDREN: Twins, Andreas & Klair; newborn Kerri.
SCHOOLS/COLLEGE: Ashmole School, Westminster University.
ACADEMIC QUALIFICATIONS: Bsc in Estate Management.
PROFESSIONAL QUALIFICATIONS: Chartered Surveyor.
MEMBERSHIPS: Member of the Royal Institute of Chartered Surveyors.
HOBBIES AND INTERESTS: Football, Arsenal Fan
PERSONAL PROFILE: Partner with brother Jon in Chartered Surveyors Jon Christopher in Finchley who carry out property valuations and surveys for banks and lending institutions.

JON PISHIRI
Chartered Surveyor

DATE OF BIRTH: 22.09.68
PLACE OF BIRTH: London. Father Andrico, previous owner of Cronos Electronics from Komi Kebir; Mother, Koulla, from Komi Kebir.
MARITAL STATUS: Married to Anna Stratis (parents from Akanthou and Troullous).
CHILDREN: Andrianna
SCHOOLS/COLLEGE: Ashmole School, University of Westminster.
ACADEMIC QUALIFICATIONS: BSc in Estate Management.
PROFESSIONAL QUALIFICATIONS: Chartered Surveyor.
MEMBERSHIPS: Associate and member of the Royal Institute of Chartered Surveyors.
HOBBIES AND INTERESTS: Sports, reading, football, (Arsenal Fan).
PERSONAL PROFILE: Partner with brother Chris in Jon Christopher Chartered Surveyors.

CHRISTINA PISHIRIS
Journalist/Scriptwriter

DATE OF BIRTH: 04.02.74
PLACE OF BIRTH: London. Parents from Komi Kebir.
MARITAL STATUS: Single
SCHOOLS/COLLEGE: West Twyford Primary, Ellen Wilkinson, Sussex University.
ACADEMIC QUALIFICATIONS: BA English.
HOBBIES AND INTERESTS: Reading, cinema and internet.
PERSONAL PROFILE: Freelance Journalist, Televisual Trade Magazine & C21. Scriptwriter, written short films.

Email: c_pishiris@hotmail.com

CHRISTOPHER ANTONIOU PISSARIDES
Professor of Economics LSE

DATE OF BIRTH: 20.02.48
PLACE OF BIRTH: Nicosia
MARITAL STATUS: Married to Francesca Cassano, an Economist, from Italy.
CHILDREN: Antony Giulio Christoforou and Miranda Olympia Beatrice.
SCHOOLS/COLLEGE: Eleneion (elementary), Pancyprian Gymnasium (Secondary School), both in Nicosia, Essex University, London School of Economics.
ACADEMIC QUALIFICATIONS: BA,MA (both at Essex), PhD (LSE) all in Economics.
MEMBERSHIPS: Royal Economic Society, Econ-ometric Society, European Economic Association.
HONOURS/AWARDS: Fellow of the British Academy, elected 2002. Fellow of the Econometric Society, elected 1997. Member of Council, Royal Economic Society, elected 1996. Board member, Society for Economic Analysis, elected 1983-1992.
HOBBIES AND INTERESTS: Economics, gardening in Cyprus (thank goodness for computerised watering systems) and cooking.
PERSONAL PROFILE: Currently a Professor of Economics and the Director of the Research Programme on Technology and Growth at the Centre for Economic Performance. Previous three year term as Head of the Economics Department. He has written extensively on unemployment and labour market policy issues. Has written two books (*Equilibrium Unemployment Theory*, now in its second edition, published in 2000 by MIT Press) and several articles and he has been a consultant at the World Bank, the European Commission and the OECD. He is a research fellow of CEPR and IZA and a member of the Monetary Policy Committee of the Central Bank of Cyprus.

LAKIS PITHARAS
Active Member of Cypriot Community in London (Deceased)

DATE OF BIRTH: 03.10.28
PLACE OF BIRTH: Frenaros, Famagusta.
MARITAL STATUS: Married to Marika, from Athens.
CHILDREN: Photis, Dr of Economics at North London University; Lysandros, Dr of Physics; Despina and Tonia, have a Hairdressing Salon.
SCHOOLS/COLLEGE: Famagusta Gymnasium.
PROFESSIONAL QUALIFICATIONS: Apprentice Electrician.
HOBBIES AND INTERESTS: Politics, reading and theatre.
PERSONAL PROFILE: Owner of Dressmaking business, has been active member of the Cypriot Community in London. In the 50s, organised theatres and festivals in the UK and abroad. One of the founders of the National Federation of Cypriots in the UK, and of the Parikiaki newspaper. Former member of the executive committee of Akel UK. Also one of the founder members and chairman of DACA, the Dressmakers Association.

KYRIACOS PITSIELIS
Businessman

DATE OF BIRTH: 31.08.50
PLACE OF BIRTH: Palechori.
MARITAL STATUS: Married to Christina from Rizokarpaso.
CHILDREN: John, Businessman; Marina, housewife, Panicos, Student.
SCHOOLS/COLLEGE: Middlesex University.
ACADEMIC QUALIFICATIONS: BSc Honours Degree.
PROFESSIONAL QUALIFICATIONS: Engineer in Computers.
HOBBIES AND INTERESTS: Politics and golf.
PERSONAL PROFILE: He was a policeman in Cyprus. Came to the UK in 1971 to study. Worked for five years in the computer industry and then began his catering business. Now Co-owner of The Penridge Banqueting Suite.
Committee Member and Co-founder of St Demetrius Church in Edmonton.
Member of the Palechori village Association UK.

JOHN PITTALIS
Accountant

DATE OF BIRTH: 29.03.60
PLACE OF BIRTH: London. Father from Ayios Ioannis, Agros; mother from Agros.
MARITAL STATUS: Married to Sally.
CHILDREN: Kyriacos, Alexi and Xenia.
SCHOOLS/COLLEGE: Lyndhurst House Prep, Clifton College, London School of Economics.
ACADEMIC QUALIFICATIONS: B.Sc (Econ).
PROFESSIONAL QUALIFICATIONS: Chartered Accountant, FCA.
HOBBIES AND INTERESTS: Football, tennis and most sports.
PERSONAL PROFILE: Partner in family accountancy practice. Played for PAOK in Cypriot League UK.

MARIOS PITTALIS
Solicitor

DATE OF BIRTH: 02.01.62
PLACE OF BIRTH: London. Father from Ayios Ioannis, Agros; Mother from Agros.
MARITAL STATUS: Married to Prudence Anne Pittalis, a Registered Nurse, from Wellington, New Zealand.
CHILDREN: Eleni Louise; Zoe Alice; Luca Kyriacos.
SCHOOLS/COLLEGE: Lyndhurst House Prep School, Hampstead, Clifton College Bristol, Kings College, London University, Lancaster Gate, College of Law.
ACADEMIC QUALIFICATIONS: BA Honours, AKC.
PROFESSIONAL QUALIFICATIONS: Solicitor
HOBBIES AND INTERESTS: Sports, football, boxing/kick boxing, skiing, usual arts.
PERSONAL PROFILE: Solicitor (Partner in practice). Played football for PAOK in the Cypriot League UK.

ROGER PITTALIS
Solicitor

DATE OF BIRTH: 18.05.66
PLACE OF BIRTH: London, father from Ayios Ioannis, Agros; Mother from Agros.
MARITAL STATUS: Married to Mary Theresa Pittalis, a qualified Solicitor (father from Armagh, Northern Ireland; Mother from Ayios Ioannis, Agros).
CHILDREN: Miriam Alexandra; Katherine Katerina Barbara.
SCHOOLS/COLLEGE: Lyndhurst House Prep School, Hampstead, Clifton College, Bristol, London University, Chancery Lane College of Law.
ACADEMIC QUALIFICATIONS: BA Honours.
PROFESSIONAL QUALIFICATIONS: Solicitor.
HOBBIES AND INTERESTS: Sports (watching mostly), novels, theatre and cinema.
PERSONAL PROFILE: Solicitor (Partner in practice).

REV. ANDREAS PITTAS
Priest

DATE OF BIRTH: 09.08.37
PLACE OF BIRTH: St Nicholaos.
MARITAL STATUS: Married.
CHILDREN: Maria and Lukia.
SCHOOLS/COLLEGE: Studied as a Priest in Cyprus at School of St Barnabas.
PERSONAL PROFILE: Trustee of St Sozon Philanthropic Society in England. Served as Priest at St Nectarius Greek Orthodox Church in London SW11. Now living in Kiti village, Cyprus.

TONY PITTAS
Solicitor

DATE OF BIRTH: 08.07.59
PLACE OF BIRTH: London. Father from Achna; Mother from Davlos.
MARITAL STATUS: Married to Christina from London (mother, English, father from Davlos).
CHILDREN: Eleni and Maria.
SCHOOLS/COLLEGE: Loxford Secondary in Ilford; Redbridge Technical College; South Bank University.
ACADEMIC QUALIFICATIONS: BA Honours in Law.
HOBBIES AND INTERESTS: Golf (member of Cypriot Golf Society), football.
PERSONAL PROFILE: Solicitor. Senior Partner in Jennings Son & Ash in Holborn.

Address: 1 Waterhouse Square, 138 Holborn, London EC1
Email: TPittas@jenson-ash.co.uk

MAGDA PITZORI
Chairwoman, Midlands Cypriot Festival

DATE OF BIRTH: 13.11.50
PLACE OF BIRTH: Troulli, Larnaca.
MARITAL STATUS: Married to Yiannis from Rizokarpasso.
CHILDREN: Three
SCHOOLS/COLLEGE: Lykeion Larnaca.
HOBBIES AND INTERESTS: Community work.
PERSONAL PROFILE: Chairwoman of the Greek School in Leicester, Chairwoman of the Midlands Cypriot Festival.

MARY PLANT
Artist

DATE OF BIRTH: 28.12.43
PLACE OF BIRTH: Famagusta.
MARITAL STATUS: Married to Guy Hetherington, an Artist, from London.
SCHOOLS/COLLEGE: Chelsea School of Art, London.
ACADEMIC QUALIFICATIONS: BA Painting, MA Painting.
MEMBERSHIPS: IAA (International Association of Art Unesco Paris), EKATE (Cyprus Chamber of Fine Arts), AXIS (Visual Arts Information Service, National Register, Leeds.
HONOURS/AWARDS: Morland Lewis Scholarship, GLA Grant, Bank of Cyprus Award prize-winner.
HOBBIES AND INTERESTS: The study of Literature & Archaeology.
PERSONAL PROFILE: Works as a full-time Artist and has exhibited widely. Two main bodies of work, *Salamis* and *Aphrodite*. Works in many private and Public Collections, including The Leventis Foundation, London, The Bank of Cyprus, London, The Cyprus Popular Bank, London, Cultural Service, Ministry of Education Cyprus.

Web: http://www..axisartists.org.UK

ANDI PLASTIRAS
Health Promotion Specialist Drugs Worker

DATE OF BIRTH: 23.10.62
PLACE OF BIRTH: London. Father from Lefkara; Mother from Larnaca.
MARITAL STATUS: Separated
CHILDREN: Francesca Harrison.
SCHOOLS/COLLEGE: YMCA College, School, Minchenden.
ACADEMIC QUALIFICATIONS: Youth & Community Diploma.
HOBBIES AND INTERESTS: Skiing, reading and exercising
PERSONAL PROFILE: Camden & Islington Health Promotion Service. Health Promotion Specialist Drugs Worker.

ANDY POLYCARPOU
Footballer

DATE OF BIRTH: 15.08.58
PLACE OF BIRTH: London.
Father, Fanos, from Styllous;
Mother, Smyrni, from Komi
Kebir.
MARITAL STATUS: Partner,
Sharon, from Windsor.
CHILDREN: Serena and Sophia.
SCHOOLS/COLLEGE: Wood
Green School.
HOBBIES AND INTERESTS:
Football and antiques.
PERSONAL PROFILE: Professional Footballer, played
for Southend, Cambridge Utd, Cardiff City then
Norwich. Scored the goal when Southend beat Watford
1-0 to play Liverpool in the next round of the FA Cup
in 1978. Now owner of an interior furniture shop in
Windsor.

EVE POLYCARPOU
Actress

DATE OF BIRTH: 28.08.55
PLACE OF BIRTH: Brighton.
Father from Korfi, Limassol;
Mother from Kakopetria.
MARITAL STATUS: Single
SCHOOLS/COLLEGE: St
Angelas   Convent   School,
Southgate College, New College
School of Speech & Drama.
HOBBIES AND INTERESTS:
Tennis, swimming, and walking.
PERSONAL PROFILE: Actress appears in *Donna & Kebab*
with Martha Lewis. Appeared on TV & stage, one
woman show, *Eve in the Beginning*. Did *Big Fat Xmas*
at the Bloomsbury Theatre. Appeared on TV in *Inspector
Morse*, *The Bill* and *Forth Farm*. Music Teacher in Primary
School. Lectures at Southwark College and directed
and devised for them a play at the Soho Theatre.

MICHAEL POLYCARPOU
President of Greek Cypriot Association
of South Wales

DATE OF BIRTH: 25.08.40
PLACE OF BIRTH: Famagusta.
MARITAL STATUS: Married to
Eleni, a retired Senior Midwife,
from   Cheltenham,
Gloucestershire.
CHILDREN: Michael Leventis,
studying   Mathematics   &
Computing; Michael Axios
Paraskevas, studying Business &
IT.
SCHOOLS/COLLEGE: English High School in
Famagusta, Manchester Technical College, Pontypridd
University, Barry College of Further Education.
ACADEMIC QUALIFICATIONS: Electrical Engineer, Court
Translator.
PROFESSIONAL QUALIFICATIONS: Counsellor, Advocate
For Greek Ethnic Minority.
MEMBERSHIPS: Director of Multicultural Cross Roads
in Cardiff, Member of Race Equality Council.
HOBBIES AND INTERESTS: Charities & community,
works on behalf of the underprivileged, gardening &
horticulture and computing.
PERSONAL PROFILE: Greek Ethnic Minority Health
Advocate for Cardiff Social Services. President of The
Greek Cypriots Association of South Wales, Director
of Multicultural Cross Roads in Cardiff.

PEPI POLYCARPOU
Solicitor

PLACE OF BIRTH: Rizokarpasso.
MARITAL STATUS: Single
QUALIFICATIONS: LLB
(Honours); Masters in Business
Law; Solicitor; Advocate in
Cyprus.
PERSONAL PROFILE: Active for
the interests of the Greek
community in London and of
the Cyprus political problem.
Chaired the Association of
Rizokarppasso for many years. Works as a Solicitor at
her established Law Office at 2 Station Parade, Southgate,
London N14 5BJ

Tel: 020 8886 0500
Fax: 020 8886 2899
Email: pepico@btconnect.com

PETER POLYCARPOU
Actor

DATE OF BIRTH: 31.03.57
PLACE OF BIRTH: Brighton. Father from Limassol, (Korfi); Mother from Kakopetria.
MARITAL STATUS: Single
SCHOOLS/COLLEGE: Tottenhall Primary, Southgate Comprehensive, Holmwood School for Boys, Sutton Valance School for Boys, Brighton Polytechnic, Middlesex University.
HONOURS/AWARDS: LRAM in Mime (Licensorship of The Royal Academy of Music); City and Guilds in Web Design.
HOBBIES AND INTERESTS: Makes models and puts ships in bottles; keen cricketer; playing the piano; running marathons for charity; maintaining his own website at www.polycarpou.com.
PERSONAL PROFILE: Actor. Original cast member of Les Miserables at the Barbican & Palace Theatres, taking over the role of Thenadier. Phantom in Andrew Lloyd Webber's *Phantom of the Opera* at Her Majesteys Theatre. Childcatcher in *Chitty Chitty Bang Bang*. RSC and RNT productions include *Titus Andronicus*, *The Jew of Malta*, *A Question of Geography*, *Oklahoma!* and *Metropolis Kabaret*. He created the role of John in the Blockbuster *Miss Saigon* at the Theatre Royal, and played Chris. Theodopoulopoudos in the BBC TV sitcom, *Birds of a Feather*. Appeared as Domingo Mercante in *EVITA*, with Madonna and Jonathan Pryce. Starred as Louis B Mayer in *DE-LOVELY* with Kevin Kline, recently completed for Winkler films. Played Noah for BBC TV/Discovery. Guest appearances in *Holby City*, *American Voices*, and starred opposite Michelle Collins as Yiannis in *Sunburn* for BBC TV. Guest star for ITV's *The Bill*. Also many other stage and television appearances too numerous to mention. Has given one-day workshops in several schools on the *Les Miserables* Schools edition. Active within the Prison Service for three years, teaching and directing drama. Keen supporter and fundraiser for the Anthony Nolan Trust, for which he has run several London Marathons. Patron of the UK Thalassaemia Society. Peter is making his own short film this year called *Mad George*, written by himself and starring Peter and another Cypriot actor, George Jackos.

SAVVAS PONTIKIS
Accountant

DATE OF BIRTH: 05.10.48
PLACE OF BIRTH: Famagusta.
MARITAL STATUS: Married to Soulla, (father from Yialousa; Mother from Famagusta)
CHILDREN: George and Marie Louise.
SCHOOLS/COLLEGE: Greek Gymnasium for Boys, Famagusta, Kingsway College, City Polytechnic.
PROFESSIONAL QUALIFICATIONS: Accountant.
HOBBIES AND INTERESTS: Gym and football.
PERSONAL PROFILE: Has own practise Finlay Pontikis & Associates. Was Vice Chairman and Treasurer of Anorthosis FC UK. Committee Member of The Greek Orthodox Church in Gospel OAK.

DORA POOLE
Executive Member of Greek Parents Association

DATE OF BIRTH: 20.01.53
PLACE OF BIRTH: Lymbia.
MARITAL STATUS: Married to Martin, a Plumber and Heating Engineer, from London.
CHILDREN: Stephanie, Head of Research and Marketing Group based in Hermitage Road Harringay; Laura, at school.
SCHOOLS/COLLEGE: Tottenham Technical College.
ACADEMIC QUALIFICATIONS: City & Guilds Certificate in Hairdresing.
MEMBERSHIPS: Member of O.E.S.E.K.A, Executive member of Greek Parents Association, G.P.A. position held Events Secretary
HOBBIES AND INTERESTS: Helping to maintain our Cypriot Greek Education and Culture for the sake of our children and the generations to follow.
PERSONAL PROFILE: Member of St Mary's GPA Greek School of Cheshunt, held the post of Chairperson for five years on the Parents Committee.

BAMBOS POULLOS
President of Kalopanayiotis Association

DATE OF BIRTH: 26.06.42
PLACE OF BIRTH: Kalopanayiotis.
MARITAL STATUS: Divorced
CHILDREN: Nicholas.
SCHOOLS/COLLEGE: Lykeion Pedhoula, London College of Hairdressing, Wella, Clynol, Loreal, International Inter-Coiffure.
MEMBERSHIPS: Member of Hairdressing Federation.
HOBBIES AND INTERESTS: Gardening, reading and music.
PERSONAL PROFILE: President of Kalopanayiotis Association. Involved in Greek Schools. Arranges beauty demonstrations for raising money within the Greek Community and associations. Has Hairdressing and Beauty Business in Muswell Hill, helping ladies to stay young and beautiful.

Address: 428 Muswell Hill Broadway, London N10 1BS.
Tel: 020 8883 5723

MARIOS ALEXIS POUMPOURIS
Building Surveyor

DATE OF BIRTH: 06.12.72
PLACE OF BIRTH: London, mother from Korfi, Limassol, father from Palekhori, Nicosia
MARITAL STATUS: Single
SCHOOLS/COLLEGE: Winchmore hill, College of North East London
ACADEMIC QUALIFICATIONS: BSc Hons Building Surveying
PROFESSIONAL QUALIFICATIONS: MRICS (Associate Member of The Royal Institute of Chartered Surveyors)
HOBBIES AND INTERESTS: Travelling, dining out, movies, music and socialising.
PERSONAL PROFILE: Project Manager, Construction Consultant & Building Surveyor.

MICHAEL GEORGIOU POUMPOURIS
Vice Chairman of Greek Parents Association

DATE OF BIRTH: 01.11.41
PLACE OF BIRTH: Palekhori, Nicosia.
MARITAL STATUS: Married to Helen Polycarpou, a Travel Agent, from Korfi, Limassol.
CHILDREN: Marios, Chartered Building Surveyor; Alice, Buyer for a National Company.
SCHOOLS/COLLEGE: Elementary School, Palekhori; Nicosia Technical Institute, Nicosia.
ACADEMIC QUALIFICATIONS: GCE O Level English & Maths, GCE A Level Modern Greek.
MEMBERSHIPS: Has been a member of the Greek Parents Association (GPA) since 1978. For a number of years has been an active committee member of Enfield Cypriot Association, previously as Secretary and now as Treasurer.
PERSONAL PROFILE: Travel Agent. Former Chairman of Hazelwood Greek School Parents Association. Vice Chairman of Greek Parents Association.

ANTONITSA POURGOURIDES
Dental Surgeon

DATE OF BIRTH: 27.07.60
PLACE OF BIRTH: Komi Kebir.
MARITAL STATUS: Single
SCHOOLS/COLLEGE: Woodhouse Grammar School, N. Finchley; University College London Dental School.
ACADEMIC QUALIFICATIONS: 11 O Levels, 4 A Levels.
PROFESSIONAL QUALIFICATIONS: LDS.RCS (Eng), BDS (London).
MEMBERSHIPS: B.D.A (British Dental Association), W.I.D (Women in Dentistry).
HOBBIES AND INTERESTS: Travel, cookery, reading and languages.
PERSONAL PROFILE: Dental Surgeon working in General Practice.

EMILIA POURGOURIDES
General Practitioner

DATE OF BIRTH: 14.05.38
PLACE OF BIRTH: Avgorou.
MARITAL STATUS: Married to Kyriacos, a Doctor, from Eptakomi.
CHILDREN: Christina, Consultant Psychiatrist; Effie, Haematologist; Panos, Solicitor.
SCHOOLS/COLLEGE: Famagusta Greek Gymnasium, Medical School, Athens University.
HOBBIES AND INTERESTS: Archaeology and plants.
PERSONAL PROFILE: Practicing GP. Helped in Old Age Homes while in Cyprus.

KYRIACOS POURGOURIDES
General Practitioner

DATE OF BIRTH: 13.03.40
PLACE OF BIRTH: Eptakomi.
MARITAL STATUS: Married to Emilia, a Doctor, from Famagusta.
CHILDREN: Christina, Consultant Psychiatrist; Effie, Haematologist; Panos, Solicitor.
SCHOOLS/COLLEGE: Famagusta Greek Gymnasium, Birmingham University, Medical School.
ACADEMIC QUALIFCATIONS: MB chB, LRCP, MRCS.
HOBBIES AND INTERESTS: Current affairs and politics.
PERSONAL PROFILE: Practicing G.P.

CHRISTOS POUTZIOURIS
Lawyer/Managing Director of Finance Co

DATE OF BIRTH: 21.12.59
PLACE OF BIRTH: Aradippou.
MARITAL STATUS: Married to Soulla.
CHILDREN: Androulla, Zacharias and Porfiris, all at school.
SCHOOLS/COLLEGE: Primary School, Aradippou, Larnaca Gymnasium Agios Georgios.
ACADEMIC QUALIFICATIONS: Athens University - Law School.
PROFESSIONAL QUALIFICATIONS: Lawyer-Advocate.
MEMBERSHIPS: Cyprus Law Bar.
HOBBIES AND INTERESTS: Information and technology, computers, stockmarket investments, technical analysis, sports and shooting.
PERSONAL PROFILE: Lawyer and Managing Director of a finance company.

DR PANICOS POUTZIOURIS
Lecturer/Advisor

DATE OF BIRTH: 4.12.63
PLACE OF BIRTH: Aradippou.
MARITAL STATUS: Married
SCHOOLS/COLLEGE: American Academy, Larnaca, University of Nottingham.
ACADEMIC QUALIFICATIONS: BA Honours Economics, MBA, PhD in Economics, Management-Finance.
HONOURS/AWARDS: Richardson Prize 1999; DTI Small Business Service Award for Best Paper; Best Paper in Small Business & Enterprise Journal 1999.
MEMBERSHIPS: Board member of Institute for Small Business Affairs (UK).
HOBBIES AND INTERESTS: Poetry, Musical & Cultural Festivals.
PERSONAL PROFILE: Director of Postgraduate Programmes at the Manchester Science Enterprise Centre. Lectures, publishes and advises on entreprenership, small business management and family firms.

PANAYIOTIS ANDREAS POYIADZIS
Accountant

DATE OF BIRTH: 25.01.51
PLACE OF BIRTH: Famagusta.
MARITAL STATUS: Married to Stella (née Hanna) from Kato Varosi.
CHILDREN: Demetra, studying Accountancy and Media; twin sons Alexi and Antoni, both at University.
SCHOOLS/COLLEGE: Upton House Secondary School in Hackney, Southgate Technical College for A' Levels and Hendon College of Technology for HND Business Studies.
ACADEMIC QUALIFICATIONS: HND in Business Studies.
PROFESSIONAL QUALIFICATIONS: Fellow Member of Association of Accountants Technicians.
MEMBERSHIPS: A member of Enfield Golf Club and Cypriot Golf Society.
HOBBIES AND INTERESTS: Golf, reading and listening to music and travelling.
PERSONAL PROFILE: An Accountant with own practice PAP & CO in North London. Was Vice Chairman of Hazelwood Greek School and Co-opted Governor of Hazelwood English School. Currently Secretary of the Cypriot Golf Society.

ARISTIDES GEORGE PRATSIDES
Osteopath

DATE OF BIRTH: 25.09.57
PLACE OF BIRTH: London. Parents from Morphou.
MARITAL STATUS: Married to Chryso Christou, runs own Upholstery and Soft Furnishings Business, from London (Cypriot parents).
CHILDREN: Adonis Constantine Pratsides and Joanna Elena Pratsides, both at school.
SCHOOLS/COLLEGE: Wembley High School, Harrow Technical College, University of Hearts, British School of Osteopathy, London.
ACADEMIC QUALIFICATIONS: BSc (Honours) in Applied Biology (2.2).
PROFESSIONAL QUALIFICATIONS: Diploma in Osteopathy (DO).
MEMBERSHIPS: General Osteopathic Council.
HOBBIES AND INTERESTS: Music, cinema, football, watching his children's development.
PERSONAL PROFILE: Registered Osteopath. Has own practice, involved in NHS work and with local general practice.

www.stevenpratsides.co.uk

PAULA KATE PROCOPI
Fashion Consultant

DATE OF BIRTH: 01.04.63
PLACE OF BIRTH: Bicester, Oxfordshire. Parents from Petra, Soleas.
MARITAL STATUS: Married to George Procopi, a Hairstylist and Business Owner, from Stavro, Famagusta.
CHILDREN: Nicole and Christaleni.
SCHOOLS/COLLEGE: John Bunyan Upper School, Bedford, UK, Gregory Grammar School, Nicosia, Barnfieds College, Luton, Beds, North London Consortium- Teacher Training.
ACADEMIC QUALIFICATIONS: 6 O Levels, 2 A Levels, BA Degree in Design, P.Gce Teaching Qualification.
PROFESSIONAL QUALIFICATIONS: Q.T.S, CCNA= Networking Qualification (CISCO).
HOBBIES AND INTERESTS: Music, reading, ballet & opera, riding my bike and Swimming.
PERSONAL PROFILE: Worked for 16 years for many manufacturing companies, as Chief Designer, incl. ITOCHU, a large Japanese Company where acted as Jeff Banks' Fashion Consultant. Worked in Italy & France. Involved with fundraising events to do with Cancer Research, especially within the school where she now teaches.

ANDREW PRODROMOU
Developer of Plasma Televisions

DATE OF BIRTH: 05.06.48
PLACE OF BIRTH: London. Parents from Achna Village.
MARITAL STATUS: Married to Louisa, theatre producer, from Limassol.
CHILDREN: Nadia, completed university; Melina, at UCL studying Geography.
SCHOOLS/COLLEGE: St Clement Danes Grammar School, London.
ACADEMIC QUALIFICATIONS: Chartered Accountant.
PROFESSIONAL QUALIFICATIONS: Fellow of the Institute of Chartered Accountants.
HONOURS/AWARDS: Awarded in 1998 at the North American Broadcast Show, award jointly with Fujitsu for enhancement of television.
HOBBIES AND INTERESTS: Golf, theatre, football, (watching Arsenal).
PERSONAL PROFILE: Founder of Direct Digital Plasma, involved in manufacturing own brand *Delphi*. Plasma TV has won numerous awards. In 1978 granted a patent for multiscreen display technologies.

DR CHRYSOSTOMOS PRODROMOU
Researcher

DATE OF BIRTH: 20.05.62
PLACE OF BIRTH: London. Father from Singrassi; Mother from Limnia.
MARITAL STATUS: Married
CHILDREN: Nicholas.
SCHOOLS/COLLEGE: Stationers Company, Chelsea College, Queen Mary College.
ACADEMIC QUALIFICATIONS: BSc, PhD.
MEMBERSHIPS: British Sub- Aqua Club.
HONOURS/AWARDS: Dive Leader.
HOBBIES AND INTERESTS: Surfing, sub-aqua diving and weight training.
PERSONAL PROFILE: Research Associate at the Institute of Cancer Research. Internationally recognised for research into HSP90 (Heat Shock Protein 90).

HAMBIS PRODROMOU
Media and Sports

DATE OF BIRTH: 29.05.41
PLACE OF BIRTH: Acheritou.
MARITAL STATUS: Married to Margaret, from Larnaca.
CHILDREN: Two sons, two daughters.
SCHOOLS/COLLEGE: Emporiko Lykeon, Famagusta; Teachers College in Athens.
MEMBERSHIPS: AKEL.
PERSONAL PROFILE: Worked with Greek Schools as Teacher, Secretary of Greek Parents Association. Was a Journalist with *Vema* Newspaper later Editor of *Parikiaki* Newspaper. In 1975 was the founder of The Cypriot Football League in the UK where he was Chairman for 20 years. He was formally elected as Honorary President of the Cypriot Football league.

PETER PRODROMOU
Head of Aerodynamics, Mclarens Formula One Racing Cars

DATE OF BIRTH: 14.01.69
PLACE OF BIRTH: London. Father from Kontea; Mother from Trikomo.
MARITAL STATUS: Married to Salima, a GP.
CHILDREN: One son, one daughter.
SCHOOLS/COLLEGE: Ashmole School, Imperial College, London University
ACADEMIC QUALIFICATIONS: BENG in Aeronautical Engineering; MSc in Computational Fluid, Dynamics & Structural Mechanics.
HOBBIES AND INTERESTS: Football and motor racing.
PERSONAL PROFILE: Head of Aerodynamics at Mclarens Formula One Racing Cars.

PRODROMOS PRODROMOU
Deputy Headteacher

DATE OF BIRTH: 16.05.54
PLACE OF BIRTH: London. Father from Kontea; Mother from Trikomo.
MARITAL STATUS: Married to Agnes, Alitalia Airline Personnel, from Ireland,
CHILDREN: Natasha, reading Sociology at Surrey University; Alexander, at Southampton University.
SCHOOLS/COLLEGE: Ashmole School, Southgate N.14, Middlesex University.

ACADEMIC QUALIFICATIONS: 4 A Levels (Maths, Physics, Zoology, Art).
PROFESSIONAL QUALIFICATIONS: BEd (Honours) Maths/Education.
MEMBERSHIPS: Association of Maths Teachers.
HOBBIES AND INTERESTS: Sport, keeping fit and travel.
PERSONAL PROFILE: Present Post Director of Post 16 Education, Deputy Headteacher at King Solomon High School, Ilford.

XENOPHON SOCRATES PROTOPAPAS
Solicitor, President of the Greek Orthodox Community of Barnet - Holy Cross and St Michaels

DATE OF BIRTH: 14.02.47
PLACE OF BIRTH: Nicosia.
MARITAL STATUS: Married to Zoe (née Economides), a Solicitor, from Larnaca, Cyprus.
CHILDREN: Socrates, Chrysanthos (Chryssis).
SCHOOLS/COLLEGE: Kilburn Polytechnic, Ealing School of Law (Now Thames Valley University), The College of Law, London.
ACADEMIC QUALIFICATIONS: BA in Law.
PROFESSIONAL QUALIFICATIONS: Solicitor of the Supreme Court.
HOBBIES AND INTERESTS: Greek/Cypriot community affairs, the Cyprus question, theatre, politics and world affairs.
PERSONAL PROFILE: Senior partner in Protopapas Solicitors. President of the Greek Orthodox Community of Barnet (Holy Cross & St Michaels), Chairman of the Police Liaison Committee for Barnet (South Sector), General Counsellor to the Association of Greek Orthodox Communities of Great Britain. Member of the Hellenic Community Trust.
Positions previously held: Vice Chairman Democratic Rally UK, Branch President Finchley Conservative Party. Member of the Secretariat of the Federation of Greek Cypriot Organisations, Member of the Hellenic Centre Executive Committee.

Address: Protopapas Solicitors, Queens House, 180 Tottenham Court Rd, London W1T 7PD
Tel 0044 (0) 207 636 2100
Email: xenophon@protopapas.co.uk

ZOE PROTOPAPAS
Solicitor, Chair of Independent Greek Schools of England

DATE OF BIRTH: 14.02.59
PLACE OF BIRTH: Nicosia
MARITAL STATUS: Married to Xenophon, a Solicitor from Ayios Andronicos, Karpasias, Cyprus.
CHILDREN: Socrates, Chrysanthos (Chryssis).
SCHOOLS/COLLEGE: Various schools in Cyprus and London; South Bank University, London; Inns of Court School of Law, London.
ACADEMIC QUALIFCATIONS: BA (Honours) Law.
PROFESSIONAL QUALIFICATIONS: Solicitor of the Supreme Court, Barrister-At-Law, Advocate Member of the Cyprus Bar.
MEMBERSHIPS: The Law Society, The Conservative Party, Democratic Rally UK, Greek Orthodox Community of Barnet (Holy Cross & St Michaels), The Hellenic Centre.
HOBBIES AND INTERESTS: Greek education and other matters concerning the Greek Community in the UK. Theatre, politics and world affairs.
PERSONAL PROFILE: A partner in Protopapas Solicitors, specialising in Commercial Property. Chair of the Independent Greek Schools of England, Treasurer of EFEPE, Vice Chair of Woodhouse Greek School, Trustee of the Hellenic Educational Establishment, Trustee of St Cyprian's Greek Orthodox Denominational School, Member of the Hellenic Community Trust.

Address: Protopapas Solicitors, Queens House, 180 Tottenham Court Rd, London W1T 7PD Tel 0044 (0) 207 636 2100
Email: zoe@protopapas.co.uk

GEORGE PSARIAS
Restaurateur

DATE OF BIRTH: 10.07.48
PLACE OF BIRTH: Philousa, Chrysochous, Paphos.
MARITAL STATUS: Married to Vasoulla (née Solomonides) from Avgorou Famagusta.
CHILDREN: Vicki, Independent Film and Television Producer and Director; Solos Psarias, 3rd year Business Studies student at the University of Manchester.
SCHOOLS/COLLEGE: Greek Lyceum, Larnaca 1960-1961, American Academy, Larnaca 1961-1964, Holloway School, London 1964-68.

ACADEMIC QUALIFICATIONS: 7 O Levels, 3 A Levels, B.Sc Materials Science and Technology, University of Bradford 1974, Graduate Diploma (Grad Dip) Management and Administration University of Bradford 1975, MBA (Master of Business Administration) University of Leeds 1997.
MEMBERSHIPS: Member of the Chartered Institute of Marketing, Member of The Institute of Management.
HONOURS/AWARDS: Guiness Book Of Records Longest Kebab 1990 (325 metres), Guiness Book of Records, Biggest Milkshake 17,425 Litres 1999.
HOBBIES AND INTERESTS: Walking, swimming, wining and dining, football matches, a keen Arsenal Supporter.
PERSONAL PROFILE: Restaurateur, owns the Olive Tree Greek Restauant in Leeds, West Yorkshire with wife Vasoulla. Have been listed in: *The Good Food Guide*, *The Hardens UK Restaurants Guide*, *Les Routiers*, The *International Vegetarian Guide*, *Yorkshire Post Restaurant of The Year*. Radio appearances: BBC Radio Leeds, Pulse Radio (Bradford), Radio Aire (Leeds), BBC Radio 4, LGR "Recipe of The Day, Mon-Fri every week. TV appearances: Yorkshire Television, BBC 2 *Food & Drink*, BBC 2 *Money Programme*, Sky *UK Food*.

VICKI PSARIAS
Independent Film and Television Producer and Director

DATE OF BIRTH: 16.11.80
PLACE OF BIRTH: Leeds, England. Father from Philousa Chrysochous Paphos; Mother from Avgorou Famagusta.
MARITAL STATUS: Single
SCHOOLS/COLLEGE: Leeds Girls High, Notre Dame Sixth Form College Leeds, Goldsmiths (University of London).
ACADEMIC QUALIFICATIONS: BA in Media & Communications; MA in Screen Drama.
HONOURS/AWARDS: Won first prize for *Chocolat* for short film in Notting Hill (London) Film Festival
PERSONAL PROFILE: Independent writer and director Recently directed *Rifts*, a film about two warring kebab shop owners, one Greek Cypriot and one Turkish Cypriot, who, 29 years after the political events of 1974, are still at war. However, it is a positive film, encouraging resolution.

ORESTIS ROSSIDES
Director of the Cyprus Tourism Organisation, London

DATE OF BIRTH: 09.05.53
PLACE OF BIRTH: Budapest Hungary. Father, Iacovos, from Famagusta, Mother, Milka, from Vissinia, Greece.
MARITAL STATUS: Single
SCHOOLS/COLLEGE: Secondary: Pancyprian Gymnasium, Nicosia (1965-1971), University: (1973-1978) BA Economics, Washington State University, USA, MA Economics, Washington State University, USA.
MEMBERSHIPS: Association of National Tourist Office Representatives (ANTOR), (Committee member 1991-date, Chairman 1994-95). ABTA-ANTOR committee, 1991-date.
HONOURS: Sport and music awards, Pancyprian Gymnasium (sang and played the trumpet in school choir); First President of Association Of Cyprus Track & Field champions 1987-88; Captain, Washington State University track and field team 1974-76.
HOBBIES AND INTERESTS: Held the national Cyprus record for discus throw, 1976-2000. Still holds the national Cyprus record for the hammer throw (since 1981). Helped numerous Cypriot athletes study with scholarships in American Universities. Has contributed to travel related articles to Cypriot newspapers 1983-1988.
PERSONAL PROFILE: Occupation: Director, office of the Cyprus Tourism Organisation in London from 1989 to date.
Career progression: Lecturer in Economics, Washington State University, 1977-1979. Economics officer, Ministry Of Finance, Cyprus 1980. Tourist Officer, Cyprus Tourism Organisation, 1981-1988.

ORESTIS ROSSIDES HELD THE NATIONAL CYPRUS RECORD FOR DISCUS THROWING 1976-2000

DR MARIA ROUSSOU
Education

DATE OF BIRTH: 15.10.48
PLACE OF BIRTH: Nicosia
MARITAL STATUS: Divorced
CHILDREN: Constantinos, Computer Programmer.
SCHOOLS/COLLEGE: Pancyprian Gymnasium Nicosia, Teacher training college, Birkbeck college University of London.
ACADEMIC QUALIFICATIONS: BEd, BA Classics.
PROFESSIONAL QUALIFICATIONS: Sociology & Psychology of education, PHD Social Anthropology.
MEMBERSHIPS: The Greek Diaspora Studies Trust, British Associations of Applied Linguistics, The Authors Society, Hellenic Centre.
HONOURS/AWARDS: Award from the National Council for Mother Tongue Teaching for work as Vice Chair of the Organisation. Honoured as Honorary member of the Cypriot Brotherhood of South Africa in 1991.
PERSONAL PROFILE: Consultant to the Cyprus Ministry of Justice & Social order for the compilation of data and writing up of the second Cyprus National report to the UN. Written several publications. Weekly contributions to the Fileleftheros newspaper in Cyprus. 1974-1979 worked with the Ministry of Education in Cyprus, Educator & Counsellor for refugee children & displaced Cypriots. Senior Lecturer in Education at the University of Aegean.

DEMETREOS SOCRATES ROUSSOUNIS (Stage name JIMMY)
Actor

DATE OF BIRTH: 08.04.68
PLACE OF BIRTH: Hastings. Parents from Pano, Arodhes.
MARITAL STATUS: Single.
SCHOOLS/COLLEGE: Middlesex University, Lee Strasberg Institute New York.
ACADEMIC QUALIFICATIONS: BA Econ & Geography.
HOBBIES AND INTERESTS: Soccer, pubs and reading.
PERSONAL PROFILE: Actor. Performances include films *The World is not Enough, Snatch, Tomb Raider, Hot Gold, Road to Ithaca* (in Cyprus). TV work: *The Bill, Lee Evans So What Now.* Stage work: *A View From the Bridge.*

DR SOCRATES HERCULES ROUSSOUNIS
Consultant Paediatrician

DATE OF BIRTH: 30.08.37
PLACE OF BIRTH: London. Father from Arodhes and Mother from Arsos, Limassol.
MARITAL STATUS: Married to Lucy Roussounis, a Teacher from Cyprus.
CHILDREN: Alexander, Electrician; Eracles, IT; Stephan, postgraduate.
SCHOOLS/COLLEGE: Howardian High School, Cardiff, King's College, St George's Hospital Medical School London
ACADEMIC QUALIFICATIONS:
M.B, B.S. (London) MRCP (London) DCH (London)
MEMBERSHIPS: British Paediatric Neurology Association.
HONOURS/ADWARDS: FRCP (Fellow of the Royal College of Physicians), FRCPCH (Fellow of the Royal College of Paediatrics and Chief Health).
HOBBIES AND INTERESTS: Golf and photography.
PERSONAL PROFILE: Consultant in Paediatric Neurology at St James's University Hospital, Leeds. Many publications on Child Development, Epilepsy and Cerebral Palsy. Last five years helped pioneer development of clinical use of Botulinum Toxin a new treatment for spasticity for children with Cerebral Palsy and other movement disorders. Director of Yorkshire Regional Child Development Centre, Leeds. Also visiting consultant Red Cross Home For Sick children Limassol Cyprus.
Also first consultant Paediatrician of Cypriot origin to be appointed in England For the NHS.

PAUL ANGELO SAMPSON
TV Presenter

DATE OF BIRTH: 25.08.78
PLACE OF BIRTH: London. Parents from Larnaca.
MARITAL STATUS: Single
SCHOOLS/COLLEGE: University College School, Hampstead, Sussex University.
ACADEMIC QUALIFICATIONS: 3 A Levels, BA Honours in Politics.
HOBBIES AND INTERESTS: Music and football.
PERSONAL PROFILE: T.V. Presenter (ITV, *Dial A Date*) Series Producer (*Dial A Date*). Producer (D-A-D and ITV, *The Dance Years*). Development Executive, Hewland International.

SAMPSON SAMPSON
Judo Champion Coach

DATE OF BIRTH: 17.02.60
PLACE OF BIRTH: Ormidhia.
MARITAL STATUS: Married to Karen, a Housewife, from UK.
CHILDREN: Maria, Andrianna and Sampson.
SCHOOLS/COLLEGE: Pakeman Primary, Tollington Park, City and East London College.
ACADEMIC QUALIFICATIONS: 3 O Levels, 5 GCSEs, 1 A Level.
PROFESSIONAL QUALIFICATIONS: Teachers Diploma in Judo and teachers certificate. Certificate in Hairdressing.
HOBBIES AND INTERESTS: Judo, kendo, karate, goshin jutsu, martial arts, gymnastics, athletics and fitness training
PERSONAL PROFILE: 1st and 2nd Dan Black belt in Judo in Europe. Youngest 3rd Dan Black belt in Judo in the world at the age of 16 and in the shortest time ever recorded. 2nd person ever to reach 5th Dan contests grade in British Judo Council's history. Youngest 5th Dan in Europe and in history of British Judo Council. Youngest ever qualified teacher with diploma for Judo. National & British Kata Champion 15 years running, and still holds the title. Junior national champion, senior national champion 15 times, area champion 28 years. Also promotes, encourages and trains the Cypriot Olympic team in preparation for major international tournaments which involves world and Olympic categories. Has helped under-privileged children and disabled children using Judo to help further their ability, mentally and physically. Has 324 medals 300 of them are gold. Sportsman of Year for two years 1974/75
Email: judosampson@hotmail.com

PROFESSOR PHILLIP SAMOUEL
Professor of Business Economics

DATE OF BIRTH: 15.12.47
PLACE OF BIRTH: Larnaca.
MARITAL STATUS: Married to Maria, a Teacher, from Limassol.
CHILDREN: Paul, in Marketing; James and Irene, both at school.
SCHOOLS/COLLEGE: Enfield College of Technology London School of Economics, Imperial College, Henley Management College.
QUALIFICATIONS: BA (Soc Sc), MSc (Econ), MSc (Man Sc), DBA.
MEMBERSHIPS: FRSA, FIMgt.
HOBBIES AND INTERESTS: Farming.
PERSONAL PROFILE: Professor of Business Economics, Owner of Ladyland Farm, the Living Classroom.

PETER SANDAMAS
Former Chairman & Secretary of the Cypriot Golf Society

DATE OF BIRTH: 02.04.47
PLACE OF BIRTH: Kontea, Famagusta.
MARITAL STATUS: Married to Connie, a Housewife, from London.
CHILDREN: Tony and Brian, both Heating Engineers.
SCHOOLS/COLLEGE: Kontea Primary School, Lykeion of Famagusta.
MEMBERSHIPS: Cypriot Golf Society, Kontea Association, Muswell Hill Golf Club, CORGI, HVCA.
HOBBIES AND INTERESTS: Golf, travel and grandchildren.
PERSONAL PROFILE: One of the founders of the Kontea UK Association. One of the Founders, and former Chairman and Secretary of the Cypriot Golf Society. Won the Bank of Cyprus Captains Cup in 1999. Partner with sons in Plumbing Supplies and Gas Installations Company.

DR GEORGE SANTIS
Consultant Physician to Guy's & St. Thomas NHS Trust

DATE OF BIRTH: 02.12.58
PLACE OF BIRTH: UK. Parents from Cyprus.
MARITAL STATUS: Married to Loelia (née Plunket)
CHILDREN: Lara
SCHOOLS/COLLEGE: University of Leicester.
QUALIFICATIONS: MB ChB MRCP, MD, FRCP
Distinctions in Medicine and Paediatrics.
PERSONAL PROFILE: Consultant physician to Guy's & St Thomas' NHS Trust. Reader in respiratory medicine GKT School of Medicine. Chairman Southeast Lung Cancer Task Force.

ANNA SAVVA
Actress

PLACE OF BIRTH: UK. Father from Kiti, Mother from Pera Orinis.
HOBBIES AND INTERESTS: Salsa dancing.
QUALIFICATIONS: LAMADA, London Academy of Dramatic Art.
MEMBERSHIPS: Equity.
HONOURS/AWARDS: Best Actress, *Time Out* nomination for her performance as Frida in *Frida & Diego*.
PERSONAL PROFILE: Actress: Appeared on T.V.; *The Chief, London's Burning, Minder* Theatre; *Frida Diego, Carmen, Midsummer Night Dream*. Worked on Radio 4.

ELEFTHERIOS SAVVA
Councillor

DATE OF BIRTH: 19.09.46
PLACE OF BIRTH: Ayia Anna, Larnaca.
MARITAL STATUS: Married to Androulla, a Professional Carer, from Inia Paphos.
CHILDREN: Chrissy, workforce development co-ordinator.
SCHOOLS/COLLEGE: School of Life.
HOBBIES AND INTERESTS: Rotarian, raises money for charity.
PERSONAL PROFILE: Councillor for Enfield. A professional foster carer for children of home abuse with behavioural and other complex problems. Trustee of Saint Demetrius Church in Edmonton. Assistant Co-ordinator of the Association of the Greek Orthodox Communities of Great Britain. School Governor of Edmonton County School and Bush Hill Park Primary Schools.

GEORGE SAVVA MBE
Former Mayor of Enfield

DATE OF BIRTH: 26.09.49
PLACE OF BIRTH: Lefkara.
MARITAL STATUS: Married to Eleni, from Kalopsida.
CHILDREN: Tasos, Fitness Instructor; Costakis, at Luton University; Marios, at Thames Valley University; Andreas, at school.
SCHOOLS/COLLEGE: Holloway School, London College of Fashion.
MEMBERSHIPS: Labour Party.
HONOURS/AWARDS: MBE for services to the community and London Borough of Enfield.
HOBBIES AND INTERESTS: Gardening, badminton and football.
PERSONAL PROFILE: Councillor in the London Borough of Enfield. Served as a Deputy Mayor in 1994/1995 and a Mayor in 1995/1996. One of the founders of the Lefkara Association. Has helped towards the establishment of the community centre in Edmonton.

GREGORY SAVVA
Footballer

DATE OF BIRTH: 14.08.55
PLACE OF BIRTH: Pera Orinis.
MARITAL STATUS: Married to Marina from Ireland.
CHILDREN: Harry, Louis, Lydia and Marcus.
SCHOOLS/COLLEGE: Croydon Secondary Technical School.
ACADEMIC QUALIFICATIONS: City & Guilds Hotel & Catering. FPC1, FPC2, FPC3.
HONOURS/AWARDS: Cyprus footballer of the year 1975. Athlete of the year 1975. Captain of National team. 20 caps for Cyprus National Team.
HOBBIES AND INTERESTS: Golf, all sports.
PERSONAL PROFILE: Financial advisor. Qualified Chef. Played football for Omonia Nicosia, Olympiakos in Greece, and Cyprus national team.

MARIA SAVVA
Teacher

DATE OF BIRTH: 27.01.56
PLACE OF BIRTH: Bristol. Father from Leukoniko.
MARITAL STATUS: Married to Constantinos, from Torquay.
CHILDREN: One son, one daughter
SCHOOLS/COLLEGE: St. Ursulas, St. Mathias Teachers Training College.
HOBBIES AND INTERESTS: Reading and family.
PERSONAL PROFILE: Teacher. Taught at the Grammar School in Nicosia and Elmlea School in Bristol. Helped found the Greek Community School in Bristol. Runs Greek dance group and set up Bristol Community Youth Club.

MARIOS SAVVA
President of Greek Cypriot Shooting Association/Property Developer

DATE OF BIRTH: 31.07.60
PLACE OF BIRTH: UK.
MARITAL STATUS: Single
SCHOOLS/COLLEGE: Crockham Court.
MEMBERSHIP: Greek Cypriot Shooting Association.
HOBBIES AND INTERESTS: Clay pigeon shooting and golf.
PERSONAL PROFILE: Chairman Greek Cypriot Shooting Association (65 members). Helps Leukaemia charities. Property Developer.

MARY SAVVA
Actress

DATE OF BIRTH: 04.11.72
PLACE OF BIRTH: Croydon Father from Pera Orinis.
MARITAL STATUS: Single
SCHOOLS/COLLEGE: Riddlesdown High School, Croydon, Italia Conti Theatre School.
QUALIFICATIONS: 6 GCSES 3 year Performing Diploma A.I.S.T.D qualified teacher of dance, modern, jazz and tap.
MEMBERSHIP: Equity.
PERSONAL PROFILE: Appeared on Stage in *The Golden Land*; *Goodbye Girl*; *Rocky Horror Show*. TV work includes *The Bill*. Films: *Treasure Island, Road to Ithaca*.

MIKE SAVVA
Gynaecologist and Obstetrician

DATE OF BIRTH: 1957
PLACE OF BIRTH: Aradippou.
MARITAL STATUS: Married to Jane.
CHILDREN: Two sons.
SCHOOLS/COLLEGE: Holloway School. London Hospital Medical College.
ACADEMIC QUALIFICATIONS: MBBS, FRCOG.
HOBBIES AND INTERESTS: Greek & Cypriot History and football, Arsenal.
PERSONAL PROFILE: Gynaecologist, Consultant at Kings College Hospital. Former President of Hellenic Medical Society. Vice President of the Royal Society of Medicine-Section of Obstetrics and Gynaecology.

NICK SAVVA
Greyhound Trainer

DATE OF BIRTH: 27.04.34
PLACE OF BIRTH: Rizokarpasso.
MARITAL STATUS: Married to Natalie, from London.
CHILDREN: Liza and Nicola.
PERSONAL PROFILE: Dog racing and breeding full time since 1967. Owner of dog 'Toms the Best', who won the English Derby in 1997 and Irish Derby in 1998. 'West Mead Chic' won the Oaks in 1990. Most of the classics won by his own home bred dogs.

SAVVAKIS ANDREAS SAVVA
President of Southend Greek School

DATE OF BIRTH: 23.09.64
PLACE OF BIRTH: Kornos.
MARITAL STATUS: Married to Anna, a Hairdresser, born in London (Cypriot parents).
CHILDREN: Mario and Georgia
HOBBIES AND INTERESTS: Football.
PERSONAL PROFILE: Barber. President of Greek School Southend on Sea.

SAVVAS SAVVA
Businessman

DATE OF BIRTH: 06.11.57
PLACE OF BIRTH: London. Father from Alethrico; Mother from Kato Varosi.
MARITAL STATUS: Married to Maria, from London.
CHILDREN: Ellis and Helena.
SCHOOLS/COLLEGE: Highgate Public, Tottenham Technical
HONOURS/AWARDS: Freedom of the City of London.
HOBBIES AND INTERESTS: Football, golf, reading
PERSONAL PROFILE: Director of Property Company. Philanthropist, Greek School, Churches, Leukaemia. Played for Anorthosis and Cypriot League Team in London.

ANDREAS SAVVAS
Chairman of the Greek Cypriot Community in Enfield

DATE OF BIRTH: 22.02.62
PLACE OF BIRTH: Droushia.
MARITAL STATUS: Married to Chrisy Petrou, a Student Liaison Officer, from Akanthou.
CHILDREN: Chloé, Alexandros and Harry.
SCHOOLS/COLLEGE: Winchmore School, Garnet College, Imperial College, Greenwich University, Hertfordshire University.
ACADEMIC QUALIFICATIONS: M..Eng, PGCE, PDLB.
PROFESSIONAL QUALIFICATIONS: Chartered Institute of Transport, Certificate Professional Competence.
MEMBERSHIPS: RSGB.
HONOURS/AWARDS: LCG.
HOBBIES AND INTERESTS: Assisting voluntary organisation in their day to day activities.
PERSONAL PROFILE: Training Consultant. Chairman of the Greek & Cypriot Community, Enfield.

DEMITRIS SAVVIDES
Accountant

DATE OF BIRTH: 27.04.44
PLACE OF BIRTH: Kato Platres.
MARITAL STATUS: Married to Vivian, Greek American.
CHILDREN: Constantinos, at College; Christopher, at University.
SCHOOLS/COLLEGE: Mitsis School, Cyprus College of Commerce, Birmingham.
HOBBIES AND INTERESTS: Travelling, Birmingham City Football Club.
PERSONAL PROFILE: Accountant. In 1980 formed his own practice Savvides & Co. Involved with the Greek Orthodox Church in Birmingham and the Cypriot Estia.

ELENI SAVVIDES
Teacher

DATE OF BIRTH: 20.03.70
PLACE OF BIRTH: London. Father from Komi Kebir; Mother from Ayia Triada.
MARITAL STATUS: Single (living with partner Paul).
CHILDREN: Theo
SCHOOLS/COLLEGE: Caterham School, Ilford, Essex Huddersfield University, Sussex University, Open University.
QUALIFICATIONS: BA (Honours) Humanities; PGCE, BSc Psychology.
HOBBIES AND INTERESTS: Netball, swimming, reading and travelling.
PERSONAL PROFILE: Teacher for nine years. First taught history in secondary school, now teaches at a primary school in Colchester

GEORGE SAVVIDES
Actor

DATE OF BIRTH: 24.08.54
PLACE OF BIRTH: Famagusta.
MARITAL STATUS: Single
SCHOOLS/COLLEGE: Greek Gymnasium, Famagusta, Middlesex Polytechnic, Welsh College of Music and Drama.
QUALIFICATIONS: BA Advanced certificate in Drama Stage Management and Design.
HOBBIES AND INTERESTS: From 91-93 a judge for the London Fringe Theatre Awards-Awarded best judge for both years.
PERSONAL PROFILE: Currently drama assessor for London Arts. Judge for the International Playwriting Festival. Film critic for the Leeds Guide. Film and drama journalist for Parikiaki. Parts in the TV Series; *The Bill, Soldier Soldier, September Song, Harem* and *Touching Evil*. Films include *The Fool, Memories of Midnight, Britannia Hospital* and *Red Thursday*.

Email address: gssavvides@hotmail.com

SAVVAS TOUMAZIS SAVVIDES
Football

DATE OF BIRTH: 13.02.30
PLACE OF BIRTH: Komi Kebir.
MARITAL STATUS: Married to Niki, from Ayia Triada.
CHILDREN: Tom, TV Presenter; Yianno, Komi Kebir Football Club Player/Captain; Katerina, Teacher; Eleni, Teacher.
SCHOOLS/COLLEGE: Famagusta Gymnasium, Teachers Training College Morphou, University of Athens.
HOBBIES AND INTERESTS: Football and politics.
PERSONAL PROFILE: Teacher in elementary schools in Cyprus. Formed Othello Football Club in Famagusta which became a member of the Cypriot league. In 1964 came to England where he was involved in clothing, until retirement. Involved with Komi Kebir football club Manager for several years. Active member of Komi Kebir Association

KATERINA SAVVIDES
Teacher

DATE OF BIRTH: 24.03.68
PLACE OF BIRTH: London. Parents from Komi Kebir and Agia Triada.
MARITAL STATUS: Married to Richard, from Manchester.
CHILDREN: Nikita.
SCHOOLS/COLLEGE: Caterham High School, Bangor University.
ACADEMIC QUALIFICATIONS: BA Hons, postgraduate teaching qualification.
HOBBIES AND INTERESTS: Gymnastics, trampolining, dancing, gym and travelling.
PERSONAL PROFILE: Teacher. Taught one year in Germany. Then a Tour Guide for a Swiss Company, 1996. Began teaching in a Sussex secondary school, teaching German. Also head of year.

Address: Flat 5, 26 Granville Rd, Hove, East Sussex, BN3 1TG

TOM SAVVIDES
TV Presenter

DATE OF BIRTH: 06.03.69
PLACE OF BIRTH: London. Father from Komi Kebir Mother from Ayia Triada.
MARITAL STATUS: Single
SCHOOLS/COLLEGE: Caterham High School, Ilford; Portsmouth Polytechnic.
QUALIFICATIONS: BA Honours in French and German. Postgraduate diploma in Broadcast Journalism.
HOBBIES AND INTERESTS: Tennis and DIY.
PERSONAL PROFILE: Taught English at University in Paris for three years. Then worked in local radio stations as a presenter and reporter, Thames FM, County Sound Radio. Also reported for News Direct 97.3 FM. Currently at Meridian TV as a TV Reporter.

DORA SCHOLARIOS
University Lecturer, Organisational Analysis

DATE OF BIRTH: 23.10.64
PLACE OF BIRTH: Glasgow. Parents from Larnaca.
MARITAL STATUS: Married to James Malley, From Pittsburgh, USA.
SCHOOLS/COLLEGE: Hutchesons Grammar School, Glasgow, University of Glasgow, George Washington University, USA.
QUALIFICATIONS: PhD., Industrial/Organisational Psychology. M.Phil., Industrial/Organisational Psychology. M.A., Psychology.
HOBBIES AND INTERESTS: Fitness training and Greek dancing.
PERSONAL PROFILE: Senior University Lecturer in Organisational Analysis at University of Strathclyde, Glasgow. Has written in several publications. Involved with the youth community of St. Lukes Greek Church in Glasgow.

FIVOS SCHOLARIOS
Former President of the Cypriot Community, Glasgow

DATE OF BIRTH: 04.01.32
PLACE OF BIRTH: Xylotymbou.
MARITAL STATUS: Married to Georgia Petropoulou, a Housewife, from Pano Lefkara.
CHILDREN: Soteris, Nicos and Theodora.
SCHOOLS/COLLEGE: Pancyprian Commercial Lyceum, Larnaca.
HOBBIES AND INTERESTS: Sports and politics.
HONOURS/AWARDS: At the recommendation of Archbishop of Thyateira Gregorios, was awarded by the Ecumenical Patriarch of Constantinople the title of 'Ekdikos' in recognition of services to the community.
PERSONAL PROFILE: Former District General Secretary (Larnaca District) of the Nationalist Organisation PEON (created by Archbishop Makarios in 1952).
As a player of PEZOPORIKOS in the 1950's and as Captain (56-59), won five medals (two gold and three silver) in the first division of the Cyprus Football league. Member, Secretary, Vice President and President of the Greek community's governing Council in Glasgow (presently serving as a member of the Council).

NICOS SCHOLARIOS
Solicitor

DATE OF BIRTH: 21.07.58
PLACE OF BIRTH: Famagusta.
MARITAL STATUS: Married to Christine from Cardross, Scotland.
CHILDREN: Katerina, Andrew & Peter (twins).
SCHOOLS/COLLEGE: Hutcheson's Grammar School, Glasgow University.
QUALIFICATIONS: Graduated with Honours, LLB (Hons), NP, Solicitor.
HOBBIES AND INTERESTS: Soccer, volleyball and athletics.
PERSONAL PROFILE: Acted as chairman of the Scotland Volleyball Association for two years and vice-chairman for four years.

SOTERIS SCHOLARIOS
Regional Director for Stanley Leisure plc

DATE OF BIRTH: 25.03.55
PLACE OF BIRTH: Scotland. Parents from Xylotymbou and Pano Lefkara.
MARITAL STATUS: Married to Linda.
CHILDREN: Fivos and Niki.
SCHOOLS/COLLEGE: Hutchesons Grammar School, Glasgow University.
ACADEMIC QUALIFICATIONS: MA in Logic and Moral Philosophy.
HOBBIES AND INTERESTS: Football and fitness training.
PERSONAL PROFILE: Currently a holder of the Gaming Board for Great Britain's White Certificate of Approval for Directors. Holder of the Chartered Insurance Institute's Financial Planning Certificate, and the Life Insurance Association's MLIA Diploma.
Local Government Independent Community Councillor. Served as Secretary of the Committee of St. Luke's Greek School in Glasgow, past member of the Governing Council of St. Luke's Greek Church in Glasgow.

NINA SEBASTIANE
TV and Radio Presenter

DATE OF BIRTH: 15.11.69
PLACE OF BIRTH: London. Parents, Cypriot.
MARITAL STATUS: Divorced
SCHOOLS/COLLEGE: Toronto & London.
HOBBIES AND INTERESTS: Skiing, snowboarding, golf, motorbikes, walking and reading.
PERSONAL PROFILE: Currently hosting Speedway Grand Prix and also Blue Eskimo Challenge for Channel 4. Other projects include Ski America for the Travel Channel for which Nina produced, directed and hosted. A fluent Greek speaker, she has also read the Greek News in English for LGR.

Web address: ninasebastiane.com

PHIVOS SEBASTIANE
Record Producer

DATE OF BIRTH: 29.11.72
PLACE OF BIRTH: London. Parents, Cypriot.
MARITAL STATUS: Single
SCHOOLS/COLLEGE: Nicosia Grammar School Mount Grace School.
HOBBIES AND INTERESTS: Music and photography.
PERSONAL PROFILE: Live PA Internationally/Producer resident at Fabric. Own record labels. B+ Positive, P.S Communications. Worked with Mica Paris, Malcolm McClaren and Terry Hall

DEMETRIS SERGI (Jimmy)
Treasurer of Greek Orthodox Church of St. Nicholas, Liverpool

DATE OF BIRTH: 07.08.45
PLACE OF BIRTH: Maroni.
MARITAL STATUS: Married to Maro, a Housewife, from Paphos.
CHILDREN: Christella, married; Michael, Accountant; Antonia, Student.
SCHOOLS/COLLEGE: Pershore House Private School, Hollings University College, Manchester.
ACADEMIC QUALIFICATIONS: HND Business Studies and Management.
HOBBIES AND INTERESTS: Travelling.
PERSONAL PROFILE: Company director and owner of property company and catering organisation. Treasurer of Greek Orthodox Church of St. Nicholas, Liverpool. Justice of the Peace.

MARO SERGI
Former Chairwoman of Greek School

DATE OF BIRTH: 12.12.53
PLACE OF BIRTH: Paphos, Cyprus.
MARITAL STATUS: Married to Demetris.
CHILDREN: Christell, married; Michael, accountant; Antonia, Student, four Grandchildren.
SCHOOLS/COLLEGE: Richard Cobden, Star Cross.
HOBBIES AND INTERESTS: Computers.
PERSONAL PROFILE: Former Chairwoman of Greek School, St Nicholas Church, in Liverpool, served for twenty three years.

MICHAEL SERGI
Chartered Accountant

DATE OF BIRTH: 09.11.73
PLACE OF BIRTH: Wirral, Merseyside. Father from Maroni, Mother from Paphos.
MARITAL STATUS: Single
SCHOOLS/COLLEGE: Birkenhead Boys School Sheffield Hallam University.
ACADEMIC QUALIFICATIONS: 9 GCSEs, 4 A Levels, BA Hons
PROFESSIONAL QUALIFICATIONS: ACA.
HOBBIES AND INTERESTS: Tennis and golf.
PERSONAL PROFILE: Chartered Accountant.

EVRIDIKI SERGIDES
Barrister

DATE OF BIRTH: 01.02.77
PLACE OF BIRTH: London.
Father from Limassol;
Mother from Linou/Soleas.
MARITAL STATUS: Single
SCHOOLS/COLLEGE: Highbury
Fields Secondary School,
Woodhouse College
Queen Mary and Westfield
College, University College
London.
QUALIFICATIONS: Law Degree and Masters.
Bar Vocational Qualifications - 'very competent'.
MEMBERSHIPS: The Honourable Society of Inner
Temple.
PERSONAL PROFILE: After completing Bar school
entered into a 12 month Criminal Pupillage at six Gray's
Inn Square. Qualified as a Barrister.

JOHN (YIANNI) SERGIDES
Doctor

DATE OF BIRTH: 24.05.75
PLACE OF BIRTH: London.
Father from Limassol; mother
from Linou/Soleas.
MARITAL STATUS: Single
SCHOOLS/COLLEGE: Highgate
Senior,
Royal Free Hospital.
QUALIFICATIONS: GCSEs, A
Levels, MBBS, BSE.
MEMBERSHIPS: Royal College
of Surgeons.
HOBBIES AND INTERESTS: Football and cars.
PERSONAL PROFILE: Doctor.

MARINA SERGIDES
Barrister

DATE OF BIRTH: 05.07.78
PLACE OF BIRTH: London. Father from Limassol,
Mother from Linou/Soleas.
MARITAL STATUS: Single
SCHOOLS/COLLEGE: Highbury Fields Secondary
School, Woodhouse College, Queen Mary and Westfield
College.
ACADEMIC QUALIFICATIONS: Law Degree LLB.
PROFESSIONAL QUALIFICATIONS: Bar Vocational
Qualifications - 'very competent'.
MEMBERSHIPS: The Honourable Society of Inner
Temple.
HOBBIES AND INTERESTS: Art, galleries and travelling.
PERSONAL PROFILE: Barrister. Work with Amnesty
International. Recently joined Lobby for Cyprus.

NITSA SERGIDES
Head Teacher

DATE OF BIRTH: 03.02.51
PLACE OF BIRTH: Linou, Soleas.
MARITAL STATUS: Married to
George Y. Sergides, a Civil
Engineer, from Limassol.
CHILDREN: Vicky, Barrister;
Yiannis, Doctor; Marina,
Barrister.
SCHOOLS/COLLEGE: Starcross
and St. Gabriels
Degree in education and
psychology of children with special needs.
QUALIFICATIONS: English Diploma
Bilingualism Diploma
PERSONAL PROFILE: Head Teacher of a 'Beacon'
Primary School. Investor in People. Presented to the
Queen for high achievements in education
Chair of St. John & St. Anthony church in Westbourne
Rd for ten years. Greatest achievements are her three
children.

DR ANDREAS N. SERGIS
Lecturer, Tutor, Research Scientist

DATE OF BIRTH: 11.05.60
PLACE OF BIRTH: Nicosia
MARITAL STATUS: Married to
Stella, a Civil Servant from
Limassol.
CHILDREN: Andrea and
Sophia
SCHOOLS/COLLEGE:
Southwark College, University
of Greenwich, London.
QUALIFICATIONS: BSc Honours,
PhD (Doctorate in Chemistry), Chartered Chemist,
CChem, MRSC, Cert-Ed (FE), ATP.
MEMBERSHIPS: Professional member of the Royal
Society of Chemistry and Society of Chemistry and
Industry. Awarded membership of the New York
Academy of Sciences and the Institute of Education
HOBBIES AND INTERESTS: Swimming, karate
(coaches students) and chess.
PERSONAL PROFILE: Lecturer, tutor and Research
Scientist. Developed new anti-cancer drugs and medical
compounds; helped Hammersmith Hospital, University
of Greenwich and University of Westminster. Currently
teaching and writing textbooks for 'A' Level and Degree
level students. He is a Governor of two local
schoolsAlso set up a private tuition centre. The centre
offers courses at key stages 1-4, GCSE A Level, BSc,
MSc and PhD Level.
Address: 97 Dartford Avenue, Edmonton, London N9
8HE
Email: andrewstella@supanet.com

NICHOLAS SHAKALLI
Footballer

DATE OF BIRTH: 28.12.56
PLACE OF BIRTH: Nicosia.
MARITAL STATUS: Married to Terry Jennifer Banks, a Lloyds Bank Customer Service Staff, from Bow, London.
CHILDREN: Charlotte and Christopher.
SCHOOLS/COLLEGE: St. Marys Infants, London; Ashgate Junior School, Derby; Haverstock Senior and Paddington College, London.
HOBBIES AND INTERESTS: All sports and computers.
PERSONAL PROFILE: Represented London District Schools. Played for Derby under 10s. Played semi professional for; Wembley F.C., Maidstone United, Faversham Town, Olympiakos F.C., Cyprus, in the UK played for AEK, Olympiakos, AEL, Cosmos F.C. and Apoel and the League team.
Played F.A. Cup matches against Jimmy Greaves, John Radford. Charity matches with Trevor Brooking, Billy Bonds, Kenny Samson.
Has F.A. Coaching Football Badge. Managed Cosmos F.C. for six years. Ran marathons in aid of Baby Trust care units in Chatham Hospital.

Email address: shakalli@btinternet.com

SOTIRIS SHANGOLIS
Banker/Teacher

DATE OF BIRTH: 24.12.68
PLACE OF BIRTH: London. Parents from Rizokarpaso.
MARITAL STATUS: Single
SCHOOLS/COLLEGE: Imperial College Management School; London Institute of Education; Queen Mary & Westfield College.
ACADEMIC QUALIFICATIONS: MBA - Masters Business Administration. PGCE - Postgraduate Certificate in Education. BSc (Honours) Physics.
HOBBIES AND INTERESTS: Music - plays bouzouki and guitar. Classic car enthusiast.
PERSONAL PROFILE: Worked with Laiki Bank in Client Management from 1990-94. Teacher at Winchmore School in Physics, Science and Maths (1995-98). Now working at the Bank of Cyprus in Corporate banking.

Email address: shangolis@yahoo.co.uk

CONSTANTINOS SHIATIS
Solicitor/Consultant

DATE OF BIRTH: 04.02.65
PLACE OF BIRTH: London. Family from Sha, Dali.
MARITAL STATUS: Single
SCHOOLS/COLLEGE: Dulwich College, Oxford University, College of Law Guildford, Insead Business School, France.
ACADEMIC QUALIFICATIONS: MA Law Oxford University.
PROFESSIONAL QUALIFICATIONS: Solicitor. MBA.
MEMBERSHIPS: Hellenic Centre, Hellenic Society.
HOBBIES AND INTERESTS: Winetasting, classical, opera, jazz music, theatre, art, hiking, squash, tennis and history (ancient & modern).
PERSONAL PROFILE: Consultant Solicitor. Former Director, Telecoms Team, GE Capital. Previously principal banker, EBRD, London. Supports SW Thames Kidney Association Charity.

Email: cshiatis@dircon.co.uk

DIMITRIS MICHAEL SIAKALLIS
Former Chairman of Agios Amvrosios Association

DATE OF BIRTH: 08.10.41
PLACE OF BIRTH: Agios Amvrosios.
MARITAL STATUS: Married to Foteni Papamichael from Agios Amvrosios.
CHILDREN: Two daughters.
SCHOOLS/COLLEGE: Agios Amvrosios Elementary.
MEMBERSHIPS: Hellenic Bankers Association.
HOBBIES AND INTERESTS: Fishing and shooting.
PERSONAL PROFILE: Worked as a banker in Alpha Bank - relationship manager in head office of the City of London. Was Chairman of Agios Amvrosios Association UK for several years.

ANDRONIKOS COSTANTINOS SIDERAS
Businessman

DATE OF BIRTH: 29.03.62
PLACE OF BIRTH: London. Father from Kontea, Famagustas; Mother from Peyia, Paphos.
MARITAL STATUS: Married to Kyriakoulla (Pieri), a Secretary, from London.
CHILDREN: Costantina Maria; Vasili; Costantino, all at school.
SCHOOLS/COLLEGE: St. Barnabas Greek School, Hazelwood Greek School, Alexandra Park Secondary, Tottenham College of Technology, Middlesex University.
ACADEMIC QUALIFICATIONS: 10 O Levels, 3 A Levels.
PROFESSIONAL QUALIFICATIONS: Accountancy, Credit Management, Sales & Marketing.
MEMBERSHIPS: Board of Directors Haringey Business Development Agency. Board of Governors St. Barnabas Greek School.
HONOURS/AWARDS: Pork Product of the Year award 1999.
HOBBIES AND INTERESTS: Football, badminton, shooting, swimming, karate, cooking dancing and travelling.
PERSONAL PROFILE: Joined family business - Dinos & Sons Continental Foods Ltd in 1982 and helped with expansion. Became Managing Director in 1990. Donates regularly to charities, churches and Cypriot community organisations.

DINOS GEORGIOU SIDERAS
Businessman

DATE OF BIRTH: 26.10.32
PLACE OF BIRTH: Kontea, Famagusta.
MARITAL STATUS: Married to Aspasia (née Charalambous), from Peyia, Paphos.
CHILDREN: Andronikos, Charoulla and Marios.
SCHOOLS/COLLEGE: High School Famagusta Commercial School Limassol, Pitmans college, London.
PROFESSIONAL QUALIFICATIONS: Butchery, meat products manufacturing.
MEMBERSHIPS: Haringey Cypriot Association. Cypriot Community Centre.
HONOURS/AWARDS: Highly commended, Pork Product of the Year award 1999.
HOBBIES AND INTERESTS: Swimming, walking, reading, writing

PERSONAL PROFILE: Own business since 1960. Meat manufacturers imports, exports, nationwide distribution of Cypriot halloumi and cheese products. Contributes to cancer research, children with special needs, Akel Party, orphans around the world.

MARIOS SIDERAS
Businessman

DATE OF BIRTH: 15.09.64
PLACE OF BIRTH: London. Father from Kontea, Famagusta; Mother from Peyia.
MARITAL STATUS: Married to Carmella, (Giarnese), a Secretary, from London (Parents, Italian).
SCHOOLS/COLLEGE: Alexandra Park School St. Barnabas & Hazelwood Greek Schools, Southgate College of Technology.
QUALIFICATIONS: 7 O Levels. OND in Electrical, Electronic Engineering. HND Electrical Engineering Qualified First Aider.
HOBBIES AND INTERESTS: Swimming, volleyball, badminton, go karting, shooting, model building and DIY.
PERSONAL PROFILE: Joined family business, Dinos & Sons, in production 1986 and helped with expansion. Became Production Director in 1990. Donates regularly to charities, churches and Cypriot community organisations.

LOUIS GEORGIOU SIDERAS
Residential Care Provider for people with learning disabilities

DATE OF BIRTH: 28.09.38
PLACE OF BIRTH: Kontea, Famagusta.
MARITAL STATUS: Married to Eleni, a Co-Director, from Kalopsida Famagusta.
CHILDREN: George, Physiotherapist & Co-Director; Renos, Chartered Accountant and Co-Director; Demetrios, Lecturer to Carers for people with special needs.
SCHOOLS/COLLEGE: Primary and two years at English High School, Famagusta.
MEMBERSHIPS: AKEL Party, Institute of Advanced Motorists, Road Haulage Association.
HOBBIES AND INTERESTS: Swimming, abseiling, scuba diving, fishing, skiing, walking, cycling, hunting and private air pilot.
PERSONAL PROFILE: Own Transport Haulage business for 16 years. Residential care provider for people with learning disabilities for 16 years. Co. Director. Donations to Cyprus Community Centre, Cancer Research, Water Aid, Help the Aged, Orphans and AKEL.

RENOS SIDERAS
Chief Executive Healthcare Provider

DATE OF BIRTH: 04.11.63
PLACE OF BIRTH: London. Father from Kontea, Famagusta; Mother from Kalopsida.
MARITAL STATUS: Married to Axiothea who has the most important job of all; bringing up the children.
CHILDREN: Louis, Maria, Pavlos.
SCHOOLS/COLLEGE: Alexandra Park School, Tottenham College.
QUALIFICATIONS: Association of chartered certified accountants, Association of accounting technicians. Private pilot license.
MEMBERSHIPS: ACCA, MAAT.
HOBBIES AND INTERESTS: Flying, five-a-side football and shooting.
PERSONAL PROFILE: Qualified Accountant, qualified Pilot. Joined family business fulltime in 1992 as Finance Director. Promoted to Chief Executive in 2001.

EVATHIA EL' SIWIDY
Head Teacher

DATE OF BIRTH: 17.11.55
PLACE OF BIRTH: London. Parents from Sykhari near Nicosia.
MARITAL STATUS: Married to Mr M. El' Siwidy from Egypt.
CHILDREN: Monica.
SCHOOLS/COLLEGE: Sara Siddons Girls School, Loughborough University of Technology.
QUALIFICATIONS: Educated to A Level Standard. Primary Teachers Certificate, passed with credit.
HOBBIES AND INTERESTS: Swimming.
PERSONAL PROFILE: Teaching for 24 years. Head teacher of a primary school for seven years in the Barnet Education Authority.

GEORGE SOCRATES
Former Senior Lecturer in Materials Science & Technology at Brunel University (Deceased)

DATE OF BIRTH: 01.08.37
PLACE OF BIRTH: London. Parents from Komi Kebir and Strovolos.
MARITAL STATUS: Married to Jeanne from London.
CHILDREN: Anne Zoe, Hypnotherapist; Nicholas John, Dentist.
SCHOOLS/COLLEGE: Kings College, University of Westminster, University of Surrey.
ACADEMIC QUALIFICATIONS: BSc MSc Phd.
PROFESSIONAL QUALIFICATIONS: F.INST.P, C.PHYS, FRIC, C.CHEM
MEMBERSHIPS: Royal Chemical Society, Institute of Physics.
HOBBIES AND INTERESTS: Sailing, skiing, diving, windsurfing and badminton.
PERSONAL PROFILE: Was Senior Lecturer in Materials Science & Technology at Brunel University. Author of numerous publications in Scientific Journals and Author of Scientific Books in Thermo Dynamics, Infra Red and Raman Spectroscopy. Formerly acted as Scientific advisor to the Fire Brigades Union.

SOCRATES SOCRATOUS
Football Referee

DATE OF BIRTH: 26.10.38
PLACE OF BIRTH: Cairo, Egypt. Father from Peyia, Paphos, Mother from Greece
MARITAL STATUS: Married to Niki, a Housewife, from Tsada.
CHILDREN: Charalambos, Supervisor/Manager Networking UK; Savas, Manager Offshore Chemical Company, Cyprus.
SCHOOLS/COLLEGE: High School in Cairo, Staffordshire Technical College.
PROFESSIONAL QUALIFICATIONS: Degree in Managerment/Food Retail.
MEMBERSHIPS: Council Member of London Football Association. Member of the FA.
HONOURS/AWARDS 15 & 25 year awards as referee. Awaiting 35 year award. 20 years as London Football Association Councillor.
HOBBIES AND INTERESTS: All sports, football, travel, reading & current affairs.
PERSONAL PROFILE: Founder Member of KOPA/ Football Referee Assessor & Examiner/ Vice President Hendon & District Football League. Vice Chairman of LFA Referees Committee. Member of the Golders Green Greek Church Community.

GEORGE SOFRONIOU
Actor

DATE OF BIRTH: 22.03.37
PLACE OF BIRTH: Famagusta.
MARITAL STATUS: Divorced
CHILDREN: Christopher, a Computer Programmer.
SCHOOLS/COLLEGE: Famagusta Gymnasium, Dudley College, Drama School Bristol, Birmingham Theatre School.
HOBBIES & INTERESTS: Politics and reading.
PERSONAL PROFILE: Came to England in 1962. Hotelier in London. Fish & Chip Shop in Birmingham. As an actor appeared in films and plays. Acted with Roger Moore and Tony Curtis in the *Persuaders* and the *Saint*, and Richard Burton in *Villains & Gangsters*. Writes comedies.

ANDREW (Sofoclis) SOFOCLEOUS (Sofos)
Martial Arts Expert

DATE OF BIRTH: 14.12.60
PLACE OF BIRTH: London, father from Polemi, mother from Akanthou.
MARITAL STATUS: Married to Tatiana (Stephanides) from London, (parents from Peyia).
CHILDREN: Athena and Sophia.
SCHOOLS/COLLEGE: Brecknock Primary, Drayton Park Primary, Highbury Grove Secondary.
ACADEMIC QUALIFICATIONS: 6 O Levels, 3 A Levels.
PROFESSIONAL QUALIFICATIONS: Master of Wing Chun Kung Fu for 24 years.
HONOURS/AWARDS World record holder of Roof Tile Breaking in two mins 1997. World Record Breaker of fastest hands on Wing Chun Wooden Man 1990. 1983 European Open Fight Champion
PERSONAL PROFILE: Master Andrew Sofos, Martial Arts expert. Also helps Thalasaemia Society, Great Ormond Street Hospital (CLAPA), Whizz Kidz, NSPCC, Plan International, World Wildlife Fund. Bodyguard and security expert for Lennox Lewis and Bob Geldof.
Email: everyonekungfufighting.com
Freefone: 0800 328 7086

THEMOULA SOFRONIOU
Actress

DATE OF BIRTH: 10.09.66
PLACE OF BIRTH: London. Parents from Nicosia.
MARITAL STATUS: Single
SCHOOLS/COLLEGE: Langham School, Tottenham. Tottenham College, Waltham Forest College, University of East London, Mountview Theatre School.
ACADEMIC QUALIFICATIONS: Diploma in Art & Design. BA Honours in Sculpture. Diploma in Musical Theatre. Diploma in Drama.
MEMBERSHIPS: CAA (Concert Artists Association).
HOBBIES AND INTERESTS: Theatre, cinema, galleries, museums, antiques, archeology, writing, reading, medicine and psychology.
PERSONAL PROFILE: Has been exhibiting her own sculptures and textile art for 15 years and has designed and produced furniture.
Also an Actress in theatre and T.V. Commercials. Appeared on stage, comedy showcase, *Oh What a Lovely War*. Voluntary work for the R.S.P.C.A. and M.E. Association.

CHARALAMBOS MICHAEL SOPHOCLIDES
President of the Federation of Cypriots in the UK

DATE OF BIRTH: 02.08.37
PLACE OF BIRTH: Nicosia, Cyprus.
MARITAL STATUS: Married to Diana Nash, Teacher.
CHILDREN: Michael, Jenny and Tony.
SCHOOL/COLLEGE: The English School, Nicosia, London University, Liverpool University.
ACADEMIC QUALIFICATIONS: Civil and Structural Engineering.
PROFESSIONAL QUALIFICATIONS: Joined current employers, Joannou & Paraskeviades Group in 1962. Worked in Cyprus, Libya, Saudi Arabia, Oman, The United Arab Emirates, and United States.
HONOURS/AWARDS: Archon of the Greek Orthodox Patriarchate of Constantinople.
HOBBIES AND INTERESTS: Collector of Antiquarian books and maps that include references to Cyprus. Also collects old Leica cameras, old fountain pens. Likes wide range of music.
PERSONAL PROFILE: Founder member of Amersham and Chesham Lions Club. Involvement in Cypriot Community affairs since 1970. Served in a number of positions in the Greek Cypriot Brotherhood - President since 1989 - and the Federation of Cypriots in the UK - President since 1997. Vice President of SAE Council of Overseas Hellenes with particular responsibility on Cypriot Affairs since 1999.

KIKI (KYRIACI) SOTERI
Optometrist

DATE OF BIRTH: 19.02.74
PLACE OF BIRTH: London. Father from Ardhana; Mother from Tricomo.
MARITAL STATUS: Married to Dr Bipen Patel.
SCHOOLS/COLLEGE: Henrietta Barnett, Hampstead, City University London.
ACADEMIC QUALIFICATIONS: BSc Honours Optometry.
PROFESSIONAL QUALIFICATIONS: College of Optometrists Membership examinations.
MEMBERSHIPS: 1999-2001 President of N London Association of Optometrists. Since 1998 member of the Hellenic Medical Society. Since 2000 member of the National Federation of Cypriot Youth (NFCY).
HOBBIES AND INTERESTS: Live music, Greek & English, rock, folk etc.
PERSONAL PROFILE: Ophthalmic Optician. Owner of Optikal Opticians in Finchley Central, London.
Email: eyes@optikal.co.uk

MARIOS SOTERIADES
Computer Technician Parikiaki Newspaper

DATE OF BIRTH: 14.09.44
PLACE OF BIRTH: Nicosia.
MARITAL STATUS: Married to
Elli, a Hairdresser from Nicosia.
CHILDREN: Nicholas, Anna-
Maria and Alexander.
SCHOOLS/COLLEGE:
Samuel's Commercial School,
Nicosia.
MEMBERSHIPS: AKEL.
HOBBIES AND INTERESTS:
Music.
PERSONAL PROFILE: Computer Technician on Parikiaki
Newspaper.

MIA SOTERIOU
Actress/Composer

PLACE OF BIRTH: London.
Parents from Styllous and
Flassou.
SCHOOLS/COLLEGE: Lady
Margaret School, Wadham
College, Oxford University,
Royal College of Music.
ACADEMIC QUALIFICATIONS:
BA (Oxon) in English Language
& Literature.
**PROFESSIONAL QUALIFICA-
TIONS:** Associated Board of
Royal Schools of Music in Piano, Theory of Music,
Guitar & Violin.
MEMBERSHIPS: Equity, Musicians Union, PRS.
HONOURS/AWARDS: Sony Awards for radio work.
HOBBIES AND INTERESTS: History, medieval &
traditional music and football.
PERSONAL PROFILE: Actress, Musician, Composer,
Singer. Child prodigy classical pianist, gave up at 17 to
go to university. TV work includes *Holby City*, *Sunburn*,
Absolutely Fabulous, *Smith & Jones*, *Eastenders*. Films
include *Topsy Turvy*, *Secrets and Lies*. Stage work
includes *Lennon* (West End). Music includes composing
for theatre in the West End, National, RSC, BBC Radio
and TV.

PHAEDIAS SOTERIOU
MBE for services to the Police and
Cypriot Community

DATE OF BIRTH: 27.03.41
PLACE OF BIRTH: Morphou
MARITAL STATUS: Married
CHILDREN: One son, a Professional Model, one
daughter, a Stylist.
SCHOOLS/COLLEGE: American Academy Larnaca,
Lanition Gymnasium.
MEMBERSHIPS: Honorary Member of the UK
Thalassaemia Society.

HONOURS/AWARDS: MBE for services to the Police
and Cypriot Community on the 12th June 1999 in
Birthday Honours List
HOBBIES AND INTERESTS: Charity work and gardening
PERSONAL PROFILE: When he first came to England
he was a mechanic then became a Policeman for 31
years in Leyton, Special Patrol Group and CID. 1st Cypriot
Police Officer.

VASILIS SOTERIOU
Treasurer of Greek Orthodox Community of Bristol

DATE OF BIRTH: 10.11.58
PLACE OF BIRTH: London.
Parents from Ardana & Ayios
Elias.
MARITAL STATUS: Married to
Eva, from Bristol (Parents,
Cypriot).
CHILDREN: Michael, Mirian and
Georgia.
SCHOOLS/COLLEGE: Finchley
Catholic High School, City
University London, Brunel University.
ACADEMIC QUALIFICATIONS: BSc (Hons) Mechanical
Engineering. MSc Building Services Engineering.
PROFESSIONAL QUALIFICATIONS: C.ENG, MCIBSE
HOBBIES AND INTERESTS: Astronomy, archery, classical
guitar and history.
PERSONAL PROFILE: Worked originally as an air-
conditioning engineer. Now runs own restaurant.
Treasurer of Greek Orthodox Community of Bristol.
On Church Committee for 16 years. Instrumental in
obtaining £193,000 Lottery Grant for construction of
community centre.

SOTOS SOTIRIOU
FHM Retailer of the Year runner up in
2000 & 2001

DATE OF BIRTH: 08.12.51
PLACE OF BIRTH: London.
Parents from Prastion near
Famagusta.
MARITAL STATUS: Single
CHILDREN: Jordan, Jack and
Charlotte.
SCHOOLS/COLLEGE: Clarkes
College.
**PROFESSIONAL QUALIFICA-
TIONS:** Degree in Technical
Building.
HONOURS/AWARDS: FHM Retailer of the Year runner
up in both 2000 and 2001.
HOBBIES AND INTERESTS: Scuba diving, water & snow
skiing and martial arts.
PERSONAL PROFILE: Menswear retail shop owner/
buyer. Helps local schools, Scout groups, various
charities.

CHARALAMBOS SOZOU
Professor of Mathematics

DATE OF BIRTH: 24.04.37
PLACE OF BIRTH: Tochni, Larnaca.
MARITAL STATUS: Married to Maria, (née Kanari), a retired College Lecturer in Mathematics, from Pighi, Famagusta.
CHILDREN: Sozos Derek-Secondary School Teacher Demitris Peter-Research fellow at the London School of Economics.
SCHOOLS/COLLEGE: Pancyprian Commercial Lyceum, Larnaca. Teachers Training College, Morphou. Chelsea College of Advanced Technology, Queen Mary College London.
ACADEMIC QUALIFICATIONS: BA Honours Mathematics; PhD.
HOBBIES AND INTERESTS: Education, history, politics and economics.
PERSONAL PROFILE: Worked as a Primary and Secondary (Mathematics) School Teacher in Cyprus and an Assistant Lecturer in Mathematics at the City University (London). In 1965 was appointed Lecturer in Applied Mathematics at the University of Sheffield, where he was promoted to Senior Lecturer, Reader and in 1983 Professor of Applied Mathematics. Retired in 1998 and is now a visiting Professor of Mathematics at Imperial College.

ANDREW (Andreas) SPARSIS
Joint Secretary of the Greek Community of Leicester

DATE OF BIRTH: 04.07.52
PLACE OF BIRTH: Kiti Village, Larnaca.
MARITAL STATUS: Married to Gina, Director Corporate Training, from Kiti.
CHILDREN: Katy, Human Resources Manager; Michelle, works in Travel.
SCHOOLS/COLLEGE: Christopher Wren, Kynaston, Acton Tech College, Northern Poly, City University.
ACADEMIC QUALIFICATIONS: 5 O Levels, 3 A Levels, 13 City & Guilds.
PROFESSIONAL QUALIFICATIONS: BSc Elec Eng.
MEMBERSHIPS: East Midlands Care Homes Assoc. Forum for Private Business.
HOBBIES AND INTERESTS: Water skiing, technology and cinema.

PERSONAL PROFILE: Joint Secretary of the Greek Community of Leicester. Actively involved in the restoration of the community church, and the formation of car parking facilities which produce a monthly income for the community. Currently in Residential Care for the Elderly, MD of ALA Care Ltd Has four purpose-built premises looking after 120 people and employing over 60 staff. Planning further 40-bed unit, a 30-place Day Care Centre, and a staff training facility.

Address: 3 Sparsis Gardens, Narborough, Leicester LE19 2BQ
Email: andrew@ala-care.co.uk

PETER SPYRIDES
Won £500,000 on "Who Wants to be a Millionaire?"

DATE OF BIRTH: 16.11.67
PLACE OF BIRTH: London. Father from Gypsos
MARITAL STATUS: Married to Catherine, a full time mother, from New Zealand.
CHILDREN: Emma
SCHOOLS/COLLEGE: Forest School, Snaresbrook E17.
ACADEMIC QUALIFICATIONS: 4 A Levels, 10 O Levels.
HOBBIES AND INTERESTS: Cooking, reading crime fiction, computer games. Arsenal season ticket holder.
PERSONAL PROFILE: Back office manager for Entergy-Kock Trading Ltd (Energy Trading company). Won £500,000 on "Who Wants to be a Millionaire?"

ANDREAS SPYROU
Former Chairman of New Salamis FC (UK)

PLACE OF BIRTH: Nicosia.
MARITAL STATUS: Married to Dora, from Famagusta.
CHILDREN: Spiros, Nico and Chris.
SCHOOLS/COLLEGE: English High School, Famagusta.
HOBBIES AND INTERESTS: Football (Manchester Utd fan).
PERSONAL PROFILE: In Cyprus played for New Salamis for six years. Owns Andrews Shipping and Andrews Travel. Was Chairman of New Salamis FC UK for several years.

MARIA SPYROU
LGR Radio Presenter

PLACE OF BIRTH: Avgorou.
MARITAL STATUS: Married.
CHILDREN: Two.
PERSONAL PROFILE: Chair of Greek Cypriot Women's Organisation of Haringey. Member of the Radio marathon-special needs children commitee. Chair of Avgorou Association in the UK. Chair of the Cypriot Popular Writers Association (LELA). As an advisor on social matters, works closely with LGR, presenting a monthly live programme and a weekly update on the latest changes in benefits and other issues. This enlightens LGR listeners and the Greek community as a whole as to what their entitlements are, where and how they can claim them.

SOULLA SPYROU
Teacher

DATE OF BIRTH: 30.04.57
PLACE OF BIRTH: London. Parents from Cyprus.
MARITAL STATUS: Married to Andreas, a BT Engineer.
CHILDREN: Alexis, Pascalis, Kristofer and Stefanos. All studying.
SCHOOLS/COLLEGE: Ambler Primary, Highbury Hill High Girls Grammar, Birmingham University, Teacher Training.
QUALIFICATIONS: 9 O & 3 A levels. Teachers Certificate. OU degree in Social Sciences (BA), Diploma in teaching English as second language. Practitioner's certificate in reflexology, Diploma in Herbal Medicine.
HOBBIES AND INTERESTS: Reading, pottery, sports, painting, dance, theatre, classical studies. Enjoys travel and loves children and dolphins!
PERSONAL PROFILE: Taught in East End of London prior to birth of sons. Then tutored and continued studying. Recently worked as supply teacher in Edmonton. Committee member of F.A.C.E. (Familites of Autistic Children Embrace), organising leisure activities and raising money.
Email: soullaspyrou@learndirect.net

HELEN STAFFORD
Theatrical/Film Agent

DATE OF BIRTH: 28.02.57
PLACE OF BIRTH: Nicosia.
MARITAL STATUS: Married to Graham, a Computer Consultant.
SCHOOLS/COLLEGE: New College of Speech & Drama (now Middlesex University).
HOBBIES AND INTERESTS: Music and films.
ACADEMIC QUALIFICATIONS: 3 Diploma in Dramatic Art Golders Green, GCSEs O Level, English, Art, History A Level, Art, Sociology, R.E, English Lit, 2 year Diploma in Dramatic Equity Art- London University.
PERSONAL PROFILE: Theatrical/Film Agent, Actors/actresses in many West End musicals and also films and TV. Casting Director for films shot in Cyprus.

Sir REO STAKIS
Hotelier, Philanthropist (Deceased)

DATE OF BIRTH: 13.03.13
PLACE OF BIRTH: Kato Drys.
MARITAL STATUS: Married to Annitsa Petropoulos from Lefkara.
CHILDREN: Rena; Ridi; Niki; Stassia; Andros; Evros.
SCHOOLS/COLLEGE: American Academy Larnaca.
HONOURS/AWARDS: 1986 Honorary Degree Doctor of Law from Strathclyde University. 1991 Honorary Degree Doctor of Arts from Napier University. Knighted by Queen Elizabeth the 2nd.
HOBBIES AND INTERESTS: Shooting.
PERSONAL PROFILE: Retired Hotelier, former chairman of Stakis Hotels and Casinos.

PHILLIPOS STASSOPOULOS
Past Chairman of Marathovouno Association (Deceased)

DATE OF BIRTH: 20.01.17
PLACE OF BIRTH: Marathovounos.
MARITAL STATUS: Married
CHILDREN: Maria, Michael and Gerald.
SCHOOLS/COLLEGE: Pancyprian Gymnasium Nicosia.
HOBBIES AND INTERESTS: Dancing, Latin American & Greek.
PERSONAL PROFILE: Came to England in 1937 and worked in restaurants until 1939. Then joined the Greek Merchant Navy. After one year went to college and became SOS Messenger. 1945 back to England to work as a waiter. Later opened restaurant in Tottenham Court Road, London in partnership with his life long friend Xenofon. Was Chairman of Marathovouno Association for 14 years.

ZENON STAVRINIDES
Associate Lecturer in Philosophy, University of Bradford

DATE OF BIRTH: 22.05.45
PLACE OF BIRTH: Nicosia
MARITAL STATUS: Single
SCHOOLS/COLLEGE: Primary schools in Kyrenia, Famagusta and Nicosia. The English School Nicosia. King's College London, Trinity Hall Cambridge, University of Leeds.
QUALIFICATIONS: BA (London), M.Phil (Cambridge), PhD (Leeds)
MEMBERSHIPS: The Philosophical Society of England, Aristotelian Society, Association for Cypriot, Greek & Turkish Affairs, AUT.
HOBBIES AND INTERESTS: Reading works of literature and history, listening to music and cinema.
PERSONAL PROFILE: Associate Lecturer in Philosophy, University of Bradford.

Email: Z.Stavrinides@lineone.net
Address: Department of Social Sciences & Humanities, University of Bradford, Bradford BD7 1DP

THEOPISTOS (THEO) STAVRINOU
Community Activist/Clothing Manufacturer

DATE OF BIRTH: 09.09.59
PLACE OF BIRTH: London. Father Stelios from Alethrico. Mother Panayiota, from Psematismenos.
MARITAL STATUS: Married to Stavroulla, a Primary School Teacher.
CHILDREN: Pola and Stelios.
SCHOOLS/COLLEGE: Thornhill Primary and Archway Secondary School.
PROFESSIONAL QUALIFICATIONS: All his life he has been in the clothing industry.
HOBBIES AND INTERESTS: Family, football and general affairs.
PERSONAL PROFILE: As a youngster he was very actively involved in the social and cultural life of the community youth clubs, especially in activities relating to traditional dancing and music. Also quite active in charity work within the community. For a number of years now, he has been working in clothing manufacturing, outsourcing work in other countries.

ROULLA STAVRINOU
Teacher

DATE OF BIRTH: 19.09.63
PLACE OF BIRTH: Moscow.
Father, Kyriacos Tsioupras, from Komi Kebir; Mother, Pola, from Lymbia.
MARITAL STATUS: Married to Thiso, from London.
CHILDREN: Pola and Stelios.
SCHOOLS/COLLEGE: Ashmole School, Middlesex University.
ACADEMIC QUALIFICATIONS: BEd Bachelor in Education.
HOBBIES AND INTERESTS: Salsa, travel and martial arts.
PERSONAL PROFILE: Taught at St Aidans School now at Earlsmead School, Tottenham, where she is the ethnic minority achievement coordinator.

STELIOS HARALAMBOS STEFANOU (OBE)
Chief Executive, Accord PLC

DATE OF BIRTH: 06.11.52
PLACE OF BIRTH: Ismailia, Egypt.
Father from Peyia, Cyprus; Mother from Ktima, Cyprus.
MARITAL STATUS: Divorced.
SCHOOLS/COLLEGE: Imperial College, London, Tiffin Boys School, Kingston, Surrey.
ACADEMIC QUALIFICATIONS: BSC Chemistry, Associate of the Royal College of Science.
PROFESSIONAL QUALIFICATIONS: Fellow of Institute of Directors.
MEMBERSHIPS: Royal Automobile Club.
HONOURS/AWARDS: Officer British Empire (OBE).
HOBBIES AND INTERESTS: Photography, food and tennis.
PERSONAL PROFILE: Chief Executive of Accord Plc (the company formed in 1999 following the de-merger of the John Doyle Group) and Chairman of Accord's subsidiary companies. From 1987 to 1999 he was Chief Executive of John Doyle Group and was substantially responsible for a strategy of growth and development resulting in a substantial increase in turnover during this period. Prior to joining John Doyle Group, he had held senior positions at Esso (UK) and Johnson Matthey. He is a Fellow of the Institute of Directors and is currently Chairman of the CBI Local Government Panel, a member of the CBI Public Services Strategy Board, a member of the DTLR *Best Value* Evaluation Panel and a member of the Bank of England Regional Advisory Panel.

Dr ELAINE HAYCOCK-STUART
Lecturer, Dept of Nursing Studies, University of Edinburgh

DATE OF BIRTH: 4.3.64
PLACE OF BIRTH: El Adem, Libya. Mother from Famagusta.
MARITAL STATUS: Married to Dr. Neil Stuart, a University Lecturer, from Cumbria.
CHILDREN: Alethea (Elithia) Stuart.
SCHOOLS/COLLEGE: Scarborough Sixth Form College, University of Edinburgh.
ACADEMIC QUALIFICATIONS: PhD Social Science.
PROFESSIONAL QUALIFICATIONS: RGN, RM, DipHV.
HONOURS/AWARDS Churchill Fellow (1996).
HOBBIES AND INTERESTS: Gardening, sailing and exercise.
PERSONAL PROFILE: Lecturer, Dept Nursing Studies, University of Edinburgh.

HELENA P STYLIANIDES
Woodcarver, Sculptor, Tutor

DATE OF BIRTH: 17.04.60
PLACE OF BIRTH: Carshalton, Surrey. Father's from Gourri, Mother's family from Morphou.
MARITAL STATUS: Married to Brian Leslie Pattenden from Upminster. Musician/Tutor, Sculptor.
CHILDREN: Lukas Christos, Rhea Simone.
SCHOOLS/COLLEGE: Hinchley Wood Secondary, Epsom School of Art & Design, Brighton Polytechnic, Chelsea School of Art & Design.
ACADEMIC QUALIFICATIONS: BA 1st class Honours in Fine Art, Sculpture and commendation for thesis. MA Degree in Fine Art, Sculpture. City & Guilds 730 Qualification in Further & Adult Education Teaching.
HOBBIES AND INTERESTS: Travel, world music, cinema, reading and gardening.
PERSONAL PROFILE: Since 1983 produced major public sculptures sited in Cumbria, Essex, London & Skyros Island in Greece. Numerous art projects & workshops for community groups. Qualified as adult education tutor in 1991 teaching picture framing, Greek and Creative Woodcarving.

Address: 75 Chaucer Drive, Lincoln, LN2 4LU
01522 568655

EUGENIOS STYLIANIDES
Chairman of Paphos Association

DATE OF BIRTH: 09.03.30
PLACE OF BIRTH: Ktima, Paphos.
MARITAL STATUS: Married to Stella, from Lazania.
CHILDREN: George, an Accountant; Akis, in films; Marios, BBC Producer.
SCHOOLS/COLLEGE: Greek Gymnasium, Paphos, Regent Street Polytechnic
PROFESSIONAL QUALIFICATIONS: Accountant
HOBBIES AND INTERESTS: Football (Arsenal fan) and Cricket (Surrey Fan).
PERSONAL PROFILE: Opened own practice in 1974 called E.G Stylianides & Co. One of the founders of DOEK FC, Chairman of DOEK. One of the Founder members of the Cypriot League. Member of KOPA Secretariat was Treasurer, now Vice Chairman. Chairman of Paphos Association. Chairman of Southwark Cypriot Day Centre funded by Southwark Council. It is for both Greek and Turkish Cypriot Communities. Trustee of St Marys Church in Camberwell and Secretary of the Committee of the Church. Was School Governor at Warwick Park School, Peckham.

ANDROULLA STYLIANOU
Founder Member of the Leukaemia Society UK

DATE OF BIRTH: 25.11.55
PLACE OF BIRTH: London. Parents from Aradippou.
MARITAL STATUS: Married to Erodotos from Kapedes.
CHILDREN: Mario, Theodoros and Theodosia.
SCHOOLS/COLLEGE: Ackland Burghley, College of North East London.
ACADEMIC QUALIFICATIONS: O & A Levels. Diploma in Business and Marketing.
PERSONAL PROFILE: One of the founder members of the Leukaemia Society. Worked very hard to help create awareness within our community and encourage people of Greek and Turkish Cypriot origin to register as potential bone marrow donors.

The Leukaemia Society (UK), PO Box 6831, London N22 8XG
Email: info@leukaemiasociety.org

ANDREAS STYLIANOU
Accountant/Director of Kounnis & Partners PLC

DATE OF BIRTH: 16.09.50
PLACE OF BIRTH: Ayios Sergios Farmagusta.
MARITAL STATUS: Married to Maria, from Akanthou.
CHILDREN: Koulla, studying History at UCL. Christopher, Entrepreneurship, Business, IT & Technology at Surrey University.
SCHOOL/COLLEGE: Second Gymnasium, Farmagusta, East London College.
MEMBERSHIPS: Chartered Accountant ACA, Institute of Chartered Accountants.
HOBBIES & INTERESTS: Golf, football, socialising and travelling.
PERSONAL PROFILE: Director of Kounnis & Partners PLC. Captain of Cypriot Golf Society, 2004/2005.

ANGELOS STYLIANOU
Actor

DATE OF BIRTH: 12.04.62
PLACE OF BIRTH: London. Parents from Pyla, Cyprus.
MARITAL STATUS: Single
SCHOOLS/COLLEGE: Sir William Collins for Boys, Minchenden Comprehensive, Mountview Theatre School.
PROFESSIONAL QUALIFICATIONS: Diploma for Acting and Diploma Acting for the Screen.
HOBBIES AND INTERESTS: Acting, music, painting and reading.
PERSONAL PROFILE: Actor. Appeared in the films *The Courier* and *The Party*. On stage in *Extremities*, *Loot*, *MacBeth*, *Tartuffe*, *School for Wives*.

CHRISTAKIS STYLIANOU
Honorary President Assia Association

DATE OF BIRTH: 05.03.38
PLACE OF BIRTH: Assia.
MARITAL STATUS: Married to Christalla, from Livadia, Larnaca.
CHILDREN: Two daughters.
SCHOOLS/COLLEGE: Assia Elementary School.
MEMBERSHIPS: AKEL.
HOBBIES AND INTERESTS: Politics and reading.
PERSONAL PROFILE: One of the founders of Assia Association and Chairman for several years, now honorary President. Was involved in the Greek Parents Association for years. One of the founders of the Cypriot Estia of North London.

CHRISTODOULOS STYLIANOU
Secretary of AKEL in Britain. Manager of the Cypriot Community Centre

DATE OF BIRTH: 21.01.43
PLACE OF BIRTH: Avgorou.
MARITAL STATUS: Married to Katerina from Paphos.
CHILDREN: Maria a Maths Teacher and Eleni, Lecturer at Nottingham University.
SCHOOLS/COLLEGE: Elementary in Cyprus.
HOBBIES AND INTERESTS: Reading, Writing and Football (Manchester United fan).
PERSONAL PROFILE: Former Chairman of Bowes Greek School. Former Chairman of OESEKA. Secretary of AKEL in UK. Manager of Cypriot Community Centre in Wood Green.

DR ELENI STYLIANOU
Lecturer at the University of Nottingham

DATE OF BIRTH: 04.12.62
PLACE OF BIRTH: London. Father from Avgorou; Mother from Paphos.
MARITAL STATUS: Single
SCHOOLS/COLLEGE: North Harringey Infants & Juniors; Alexandra Park School; Royal Holloway & Bedford College; University of London, University of Wales College of Medicine.
ACADEMIC QUALIFICATIONS: (2.1 Honours) BSc Biochemistry, PhD Biochemistry.
HOBBIES AND INTERESTS: Having fun with family and friends, entertaining, cooking, gardening, interior design, walking, reading, current affairs, cinema, theatre, listening to all kinds of music.
PERSONAL PROFILE: University lecturer at the University of Nottingham. Lead own research team interested in understanding the basis of inflammatory diseases eg Rheumatiod Arthritis and Asthma.

STYLIANOS STYLIANOU
Honorary President of the Coventry Greek Orthodox Church

DATE OF BIRTH: 24.03.24
PLACE OF BIRTH: Kato Drys.
MARITAL STATUS: Widower.
CHILDREN: Andreas
SCHOOLS/COLLEGE: Kato Drys Elementary school, High School Lefkara.
HONOURS/AWARDS Awarded the Gold Cross of our Holy Archdiocese for services to the Holy Church.
HOBBIES AND INTERESTS: Church.
PERSONAL PROFILE: Honorary President of the Coventry Greek Orthodox Church and one of the founders of the Church.

MARIA STYLIANOU-TUTON
Teacher

DATE OF BIRTH: 25.02.65
PLACE OF BIRTH: London. Father from Avgorou; Mother from Paphos.
MARITAL STATUS: Married to Karl Tuton, a Teacher, from Hull.
CHILDREN: Christos and Matheos.
SCHOOLS/COLLEGE: Alexandra Park School, Avery Hill College, Thames Polytechnic.
ACADEMIC QUALIFICATIONS: BEd (Honours) 1st class in Mathematics.
HOBBIES AND INTERESTS: Keeping fit, reading, pilates and running.
PERSONAL PROFILE: Teacher at Copthall School as head of Mathematics. Also on Parents Committee of Ashmole School.

DOROTHY THEOPHILOU SUN
Author and Founder of Living Colour

DATE OF BIRTH: 31.10.59
PLACE OF BIRTH: London. Father from Paphos; Mother from Anoyera.
MARITAL STATUS: Married to Howard Sun, a Colour Consultant from Jamaica.
CHILDREN: Triplets: One son Phoenix, two daughters, Elysia and Thea.
SCHOOLS/COLLEGE: Haverstock, City & East London College, School of Colour Therapy.
HOBBIES AND INTERESTS: Swimming, excercise, yoga, painting and cooking.
PERSONAL PROFILE: Author and founder of Living Colour. Colour therapist, colour analyst. Established first colour therapy clinic recognised by Government agencies.

ANDRE SYMEOU
Psychologist

PLACE OF BIRTH: Northampton, parents from Exometochi Cyprus.
SCHOOLS/COLLEGE: Northampton Schools, graduated in London.
ACADEMIC QUALIFICATIONS: BSc. Dip. P. Psy. C.
PROFESSIONAL QUALIFICATIONS: Degree in Psychology & Physiology. Studied abnormal psychiatry at post graduate and professionally qualified in Psychotherapy (Cognitive-Behavioural).
MEMBERSHIPS: Professional Psychotherapy Centre.
HOBBIES AND INTERESTS: Phobias.
PERSONAL PROFILE: Psychologist. Guest on several national TV Shows/Phone-ins with BBC Radio. Featured in ITV documentary about phobias.

ANDREAS SYRIMIS
Consultant Practitioner

DATE OF BIRTH: 17.08.60
PLACE OF BIRTH: Cyprus.
SCHOOLS/COLLEGE: British School of Osteopathy, University of Westminster.
PROFESSIONAL QUALIFICATIONS: BSc Osteopathy, BSc Medical Herbalism, MSc Complementary Medicine.
MEMBERSHIPS: GOs C, MCPP.
PERSONAL PROFILE: Consultant Practitioner, Medical Lecturer, Health-Care Advisor on LGR.

Email: andreas@syrimis.fsnet.co.uk
www.bloomsburyhealthcentre.co.uk

RONNIE TAKKOU
Manager of Maronites FC & Omonia under 18s

DATE OF BIRTH: 17.02.52
PLACE OF BIRTH: Kormakitis.
MARITAL STATUS: Married to Mista.
CHILDREN: Michael, at University in Kent; Tasso, at Barnet College; Anna, at secondary school.
SCHOOLS/COLLEGE: Sir William Collins Secondary, London School of Fashion.
HOBBIES AND INTERESTS: All types of sport particularly football.
PERSONAL PROFILE: Head of quality control for Le Shark Sportswear for men. Helps Maronites Association. Has been involved with community football since KOPA was established. At present manager of Maronites F.C and Omonia U.18s.

MICHAEL TAKOUSHIS
Former member of the Secretariat of the National Federation of Cypriots

DATE OF BIRTH: 21.02.39
PLACE OF BIRTH: Lefkoniko
MARITAL STATUS: Married to Melanie, from Lefkoniko.
HOBBIES AND INTERESTS: Golf and football (Arsenal supporter).
PERSONAL PROFILE: Retired Dress Manufactuer, was a member of the Secretariat of the National Federation of Cypriots. General co-ordinator of DYSY in UK. Member of Ekeka for Lefkoniko Association, also was member of Anorthosis football club commitee.
Now living in Cyprus, involved in estate agency business.

ANDREAS TAMBOURIDES
Council Mayor Barnet 2005/2006

DATE OF BIRTH: 02.06.46

PLACE OF BIRTH: Engomi, Nicosia.
MARITAL STATUS: Married to Joanna, a Secretary, from Lincoln, England.
CHILDREN: Alexandros, Administrator; Aristos, Self Employed.
SCHOOLS/COLLEGE: Elementary & High, Cyprus.
ACADEMIC QUALIFICATIONS: City & Guilds Electronics.
MEMBERSHIPS: Conservative Party, North London Enterprise Club.
HONOURS/AWARDS: C.Y.B.C. Play award 1st prize, Cyprus.
HOBBIES AND INTERESTS: Writing, producing and directing plays for the Greek community in London and Cyprus. For a year was a special course tutor at the Mountview Theatre School for Greek Newscasters.
PERSONAL PROFILE: Since arriving in England in 1964 has had several jobs, including newsreading, presenting programmes and directing musical and comedy shows at several Greek Radio Stations in London including *Voice of the Immigrants, London 88* and *Spectrum Radio*. For several years was editor of two community newspapers, *Ellinikos Typos* and *Parikiaki Simerini*. Now a self-employed businessman. Vice Chairman (voluntary) of the North London Enterprise Club since 1994, which helps local unemployed or redundant people to start their own business, and trains and assists local self-employed people. Was a founder member of their Credit Union.
In 1997 was elected Conservative Councillor for Brunswick Park Ward in the Borough of Barnet which has one of the highest concentrations of Greek Cypriots in London. Governor of Moss Hall Junior School and Osidge Junior School. Played major part in the formation of the lobby group Barnet Conservatives for Cyprus. Council Mayor Barnet 2005-2006.

Tel: 020 8368 5417
Email: tambourides@hotmail.com

GEORGE TARDIOS
Actor and Writer

DATE OF BIRTH: 03.04.44
PLACE OF BIRTH: London.
Father from Famagusta; Mother from Morphou.
MARITAL STATUS: Married to Christine Lily, a School Teacher, from Guernsey, Channel Islands.
SCHOOLS/COLLEGE: St Mary's Primary School & Junior School, Sir William Collins Secondary School, Rolle College, Exmouth, Devon, Exeter University, Lancaster University.
ACADEMIC QUALIFICATIONS: Cert.Ed, BEd (English and Drama), Cert Adv. Ed (Advanced).
HONOURS/AWARDS: One year Writing Scholarship.
HOBBIES AND INTERESTS: Literature, cinema, theatre and travel.
PERSONAL PROFILE: Helped found the Arvon Foundation's Centre in Devon. Member of the General Council of the Nat. Poetry Centre and Chairman of the Development Committee. Organised the first National Poetry competition for the Poetry Society/BBCTV and helped establish the Arvon Foundation Jobserver Competition. Also judged the BBC2 South Bank Show Poetry Competition. Lectured in English in Further Education and led *Stanley's Footsteps* Expedition in Tanzania; three years retracing, on foot, HM Stanley's journey of 1871 in his search for David Livingstone. Actor: appeared in theatre, including *Hamlet, Rules of the Game*. Films include *African Rainbow, Hard Men*. TV work: *Hollyoaks* and *Stanley's Footstep*s.

Prof. SAVVAS A TASSOU
Head of Department of Mechanical Engineering at Brunel University

DATE OF BIRTH: 30.09.53
PLACE OF BIRTH: Kalopanayiotis, Nicosia.
MARITAL STATUS: Married to Maria Rotis, a Housewife, from Episkopio, Nicosia.
CHILDREN: Michelle, student at Goldsmith's College; Alexis; Andreas.
SCHOOLS/COLLEGE: Technical School, Nicosia, Higher Technical Institute, Nicosia, Polytechnic of Central London.
ACADEMIC QUALIFICATIONS: BSc (1st Class Honours) - Mechanical Engineering; PhD Mechanical Engineering; MBA in Business Adminstration.
PROFESSIONAL QUALIFICATIONS: CEng Chartered Engineer, 1983. MIMechE Corporate member of the institute of Mechanical Engineers, 1983. MCIBSE Corporate member of the Chartered Institute of Building Services Engineers, 1996.
AWARDS: Institute of Energy Bone-Wheeler prize in 1983 for research paper titled: 'Modelling of Variable Speed Air-to-Water Heat pumps'.
HOBBIES AND INTERESTS: DIY, home improvements and travel.
PERSONAL PROFILE: Currently Head of Department of Mechanical Engineering at Brunel University. Has previously held posts of Research Assistant at the Polytechnic of Central London (1978-1981), Lecturer in thermodynamics and energy systems at the University of Westminster (1981-1986), Lecturer in thermofluids at Brunel University (1986-1993), Senior lecturer (1993-1996), Reader (1996-1998) and Professor 1998. Current research concentrates on food refrigeration and energy conservation in the environmental control of retail food stores. Author of over 120 technical papers in Journals.

ROBBIE TELFER
Actor

DATE OF BIRTH: 21.05.69
PLACE OF BIRTH: London. Grandmother from Amaryeti, Paphos.
MARITAL STATUS: Single
SCHOOLS/COLLEGE: Salford University, London Academy of Performing Arts.
ACADEMIC QUALIFICAIONS: BA in Spanish & French,Diploma in Acting.
MEMBERSHIPS: Foreign Versions Voice-over Agency.
HOBBIES AND INTERESTS: Private Teacher of Spanish, French and Greek.
PERSONAL PROFILE: Actor (main profession), Voice over in Greek. Appeared on TV in *Hot Pursuits*, a commercial for *Coco Chanel*. Appeared in films *The Cat, Stage Nightout, Gasping, Entertaining Strangers* and *Wildfire*.

STELIOS TERALLI
President of Greek Orthodox Church of Stoke on Trent

DATE OF BIRTH: 17.09.63
PLACE OF BIRTH: Aradippou
MARITAL STATUS: Married to Helen, from Cyprus.
CHILDREN: Louise and Andrea, both at school.
SCHOOLS/COLLEGE: School (Aradippou), High School and University (Thessalloniki Greece).
ACADEMIC QUALIFICATIONS: A Levels.
HOBBIES AND INTERESTS: Golf, piano and football.
PERSONAL PROFILE: Shop owner, President of Greek Orthodox Church of Stoke on Trent since 1991.

THEKLA TERALLI
Chairwoman of the Sheffield Greek School

DATE OF BIRTH: 28.12.69
PLACE OF BIRTH: Newmarket, Suffolk. Parents from Aradippou.
MARITAL STATUS: Married to Andreas, a Fish & Chip shop owner from Aradippou.
CHILDREN: Eleni, Maria and Michaela, all at school
SCHOOLS/COLLEGE: Aelfgar Secondary School.
HOBBIES AND INTERESTS: Travelling, shopping, dancing, music Greek and English and writing plays.
PERSONAL PROFILE: Chairwoman of the Sheffield Greek School. Member of the Ladies Church Commitee in Mansfield.

Prof. NICOS TEREZOPOULOS
Lecturer at Imperial College, London

DATE OF BIRTH: 25.07.36
PLACE OF BIRTH: Kyrenia.
MARITAL STATUS: Married to Evangelia, a Greek Diplomat.
CHILDREN: Zacharoulla, Maria and Georgia.
SCHOOLS/COLLEGE: Kyrenia Gymnasium, Imperial College, Trent Polytechnic, University of Nottingham.
ACADEMIC QUALIFICATIONS: HND. Mining Engineering C.ENG (Chartered Engineer), MPhil (Master of Philosophy, Mining), PhD Mining.
HOBBIES AND INTERESTS: Travel
PERSONAL PROFILE: Lecturer at Imperial College London.

JOHN THEMIS
Musician

DATE OF BIRTH: 13.10.54
PLACE OF BIRTH: Melbourne, Australia. Father from Astromeritis; Mother from Zodia.
MARITAL STATUS: Married to Catherine Anne, Accounts Personnel at Middlesex University, from Derry N.Ireland.
CHILDREN: Emily Jane, Hairdresser; James Phillip & Katerina Louise, at school.
SCHOOLS/COLLEGE: Grammar School, Nicosia, Institute Of Marketing.
ACADEMIC QULIFICATIONS: BSc in Marketing & Management.
MEMBERSHIPS: MCPS/PRS Associate Member.
HONOURS/AWARDS: Grammy Nomination 1999.
HOBBIES AND INTERESTS: Music.
PERSONAL PROFILE: Wrote No 1 hit *What Took You So Long* for Emma Bunton; Wrote top 10 hit for Kylie Minogue *Please Stay*. Has played on albums for George Michael, Dido, Rod Stewart and Gabrielle. Has appeared on many TV Shows, *Top Of the Pops, Lottery Show, Aspel, The Word, Tonite with Jay Leno* in America.

MICK THEO
Actor and Nightclub Owner

DATE OF BIRTH: 11.10.63
PLACE OF BIRTH: London. Parents from Famagusta.
MARITAL STATUS: Married
SCHOOL/COLLEGE: Whitfields.
MEMBERSHIPS: Equity
HOBBIES AND INTERESTS: Boxing and training, Helicopter Pilot.
PERSONAL PROFILE: Owner of Club Ko, Wood Green. Actor, appeared in *Snatch* and in commercials on TV.

CHLOE K. THEOCHARIS
Ladies Team Football Player

DATE OF BIRTH: 27.02.78
PLACE OF BIRTH: London. Father from Myrtou & Yialousa, Cyprus; Mother from Wales.
MARITAL STATUS: Single
SCHOOLS/COLLEGE: Thamesmead Com College.
ACADEMIC QUALIFICATIONS: 8 GCSEs, 2 A Levels.
MEMBERSHIPS: Tottenham Hotspur Ladies FC.
HONOURS/AWARDS: Football medals, awards & cups
HOBBIES AND INTERESTS: Football, music and computers.
PERSONAL PROFILE: Plays for Tottenham Hotspur Ladies FC.

DR PANTELI THEOCHAROUS
Senior Scientist

DATE OF BIRTH: 16.01.68
PLACE OF BIRTH: London. Father from Kato Pyrgos: Mother from Flassou.
MARITAL STATUS: Married to Demetra.
CHILDREN: One son.
SCHOOLS/COLLEGE: 1997-2001, Royal Free and University College Medical School (Royal Free Campus), University of London, 1992-1994 University of Westminster, London, 1988-1991 King's College, University of London, 1979-1987, School of St. David & St Katherine, London.
ACADEMIC QUALIFICATIONS: Ph.D in Cancer Medicine (Clinical Studies), M.Sc. Applied Haematology, State registration with the CPSM (Council for Professions Supplementary to Medicine), GCE A-Levels: Biology, Chemistry, Physics.
AWARDS/HONOURS: Technologist Travel Award - The International Society for Haematotherapy & Graft Engineering (ISHAGE) 2001 Annual Meeting (Que`bec City, Canada). British Journal of Haematology Research Trust Fund Award.
MEMBERSHIPS: Fellow of the Institute of Biomedical Science.
HOBBIES AND INTERESTS: Greek dancing, theatre and music.
PERSONAL PROFILE: Current Profession: Senior Scientist, Cell Biology Group. Associate Head, ONYVAX Limted, St George's Hospital Medical School, Cranmer Terrace, London SW17 0RE

Email: ptheocharous@onyvax.com

EVANTHIS THEODORIDES
Teacher, Former Chairman of the Leukaemia Society

DATE OF BIRTH: 15.06.40
PLACE OF BIRTH: Kalo Khorio, Limassol.
MARITAL STATUS: Married to Chrysanthi, a Housewife from Akaki, Nicosia.
CHILDREN: Anna Vassiliades, Solicitor; Stalo Stefanou, Head of Languages in Public Education.
SCHOOLS/COLLEGE: Primary Kalo Khorio, Limassol, Higher Commercial Lyceum, Nicosia, University of London.
ACADEMIC QUALIFICATIONS: BA (London).
PROFESSIONAL QUALIFICATIONS: P.G.C.E (London) in Teaching History.
MEMBERSHIPS: The Leukaemia Society (U.K.) and Enfield Art Circle.
HOBBIES AND INTERESTS: Travel, gardening, drawing and painting.
PERSONAL PROFILE: Teacher, Head of History Dept in a comprehensive school for seven years, company director in the clothing trade for 17 years. Chairman of The Leukaemia Society (UK), from 1994 to 2002 on a voluntary basis.

ANTONIS KYRIACOU THEODOROU
Vice-President and Trustee of St John the Baptist Church in Harringey

DATE OF BIRTH: 28.04.43
PLACE OF BIRTH: Leonarisso.
MARITAL STATUS: Married to Lella Marcou, Women's Issues Officer (Union of Cypriots in England), from Paralimni.
CHILDREN: Sandra, Housewife; Maria, Senior Manager in Kelly Services (US owned Recruitment Company); Chris, Tennis Player.
SCHOOLS/COLLEGE: Wordsworth Secondary School and Holloway Polytechnic.
ACADEMIC QUALIFICATIONS: 7 O Levels, 2 A Levels.
PROFESSIONAL QUALIFICATIONS: Manufacturing, Textiles and Tent Design.
HONOURS/AWARDS: Honorary award for contributions made and support for causes for disabled children.
HOBBIES AND INTERESTS: Sports, football (Man Utd in particular) and gardening.
PERSONAL PROFILE: Director of Christon Junior Marquees (Tent/marquee manufacturing/hire company). Vice-President and Trustee of St John the Baptist Church in Harringey. Trustee of Ayios Demetrios in Edmonton.

KRISTINA THEODOROU
Assistant VT Editor

DATE OF BIRTH: 05.05.76
PLACE OF BIRTH: North London. Paternal grandparents from Analyionta, Perachorio. Maternal grandparents from Vavatsinia, Vavla.
MARITAL STATUS: Single
SCHOOLS/COLLEGE: Copthall Secondary School, Southgate College.
ACADEMIC QUALIFICATIONS: BTEC National Media Studies (Distinction).
HOBBIES AND INTERESTS: Socialising with friends. Watching nice old classic films, (occasionally) enjoy sketching, and shopping of course.
PERSONAL PROFILE: Currently working as an assistant V.T. editor. Achievement of starting at the company as only a runner and climbing up the ladder with minimal qualifications from school and college.

OLYMPIA THEODOROU
Businesswoman

DATE OF BIRTH: 15.02.54
PLACE OF BIRTH: Hendon. Parents from Vavatsinia and Vavla.
MARITAL STATUS: Married to Steve, an Architectural Photographer.
CHILDREN: Kristina, Assistant Film Editor; Anastasia at Nottingham University; Stefanos at School.
SCHOOLS/COLLEGE: Whitfield Comprehensive.
HOBBIES AND INTERESTS: Music from classical to blues.
PERSONAL PROFILE: Self-employed and Partner in Greek city. Contributor to *Parikiaki* Newspaper and had own programme on LGR.

DR ANDREW THEODOSSI
Consultant Gastroenterologist

DATE OF BIRTH: 14.09.47
PLACE OF BIRTH: Polis, Paphos.
MARITAL STATUS: Married to Anne, Secretary & Nurse, from East Grinstead.
CHILDREN: Alexander, Anthony and Stephen.
SCHOOLS/COLLEGE: Sloane Grammer School, Chelsea University College, London, St George's Hospital Medical School London.
ACADEMIC QUALIFICATIONS: M.D, F.R.C.P.
MEMBERSHIPS: Royal College Physicians, London, British Society Gastroenterology, Royal Society Medicine.
HOBBIES AND INTERESTS: Soccer and philosophy in medicine.
PERSONAL PROFILE: Consultant Gastroenterologist, Mayday Hospital, Croydon.

CHRIS THEODOSSIADES
Businessman

DATE OF BIRTH: 17.07.47
PLACE OF BIRTH: Limassol.
MARITAL STATUS: Married to Pamela, from London.
CHILDREN: Demetris and Glen in business, Zoe, studying at Fine Arts College Hampstead Psychology.
SCHOOLS/COLLEGE: Daneford Modern, Finsbury Park.
MEMBERSHIPS: Member of the Round Table.. Masonic Lodge.
HONOURS/AWARDS: Top *Renault* Dealer in the UK for three years.
HOBBIES AND INTERESTS: Gardening, travel, car racing and football (Arsenal supporter).
PERSONAL PROFILE: Trained as an automotive technician and opened a chain of petrol stations. In 1985 began to franchise new cars *Renault, Fiat, Alfa Romeo, Lancia, Citroen*. Expanded to own Theoco in North London, (properties and motor) and motor claims company Accident Assist Direct PLC.

GEORGE THEODOULOU
Chairman of Assia Village Association UK

DATE OF BIRTH: 02.04.55
PLACE OF BIRTH: Assia, Cyprus.
MARITAL STATUS: Married to Kyri Sofokli Petri, an ex-Bank Clerk, from Achna and Milia.
CHILDREN: Anthea, graduate of Brunel University, PGCE in History, Institute of Education; Sofokli, Civil Engineering Degree at City University; Chris, at Southgate School.
SCHOOLS/COLLEGE: In Cyprus.
PROFESSIONAL QUALIFICATIONS: Registered with National House Building Council of Standards.
MEMBERSHIPS: Chairman of Assia Village Association UK, member of the Omonia football clubs committee, member of AKEL and member of the National Federation of Cypriots Secretariat.
HOBBIES AND INTERESTS: Politics and football, (Manchester United fan) and Omonia, visits Old Trafford with family whenever possible.
PERSONAL PROFILE: George is a Building Contractor. He extended the Cypriot Community Centre in Wood Green, and built new homes in Islington and flats in Enfield. Renovated the National Heritage Public House *The Salisbury*, where Oliver Twist was filmed. Had the privilege of meeting all the Arsenal players and sitting with the manager at Highbury whilst watching them play Omonia in 1992. Also had the privilege of being invited to Number 10 Downing St to meet the Prime Minister, Tony Blair.

Address: 91 Trent Gardens, Southgate, London, N14 4QB.

MICHAEL THEODOULOU
Journalist

DATE OF BIRTH: 27.06.59
PLACE OF BIRTH: Tipperary, Republic of Ireland. Father from Goudhi, Paphos, mother from Tipperary.
MARITAL STATUS: Married to Rachel Gillett, an editor at a quarterly journal called Global Dialogue which is published in Nicosia, from Brighton.
CHILDREN: Lauren, Nicholas and Grace.
SCHOOLS/COLLEGE: Ravenswood School for Boys, Keston, Kent, 1971 to 1977, Exeter University 1978 to 1981, Warwick University 1983 to 1984.
ACADEMIC QUALLIFICATIONS: 2:1 Honours degree in English Literature from Exeter. Postgraduate Certificate in Education from Warwick.

HOBBIES AND INTERESTS: Reading fiction and history, visiting Victorian gothic revival churches in England, walking in the Akamas, gardening, bridge and watching (not playing) football. Michael is a Manchester United fan, although, like many supporters around the world, he has never visted the city. And, he is also utterly addicted to *Eastenders*.
PERSONAL PROFILE: Working life began as a teacher in England at Sydenham High school for Girls in 1982. In 1984 moved to Cyprus and spent three years teaching at the English School in Nicosia.
In 1987 helped lauch a short-lived but fun magazine called Cyprus Life and began freelance journalism for British newspapers and radio, including *The Times*, *The Observer*, *The Express* and *IRN*. Apart from Cyprus, covers the Middle East, specialising in Iran and Iraq.

CHRIS TIMOTHEOU
Managing Director of Tims Dairy

DATE OF BIRTH: 30.06.57
PLACE OF BIRTH: London.
MARITAL STATUS: Married to Christine.
SCHOOL/COLLEGE: Arnos Grove, London.
CHILDREN: Nicola, at BBp Law College, London. Natalie, second year English student at Kings College, London.
MEMBERSHIPS: JDC and The National Trust.
HOBBIES AND INTERESTS: Playing/watching football and keeping fit.
PERSONAL PROFILE: Managing Director of Tims Dairy Ltd, founded in the late 1940s, producing and supplying the local Cypriot Community with natural yoghurt and desserts. He took over the business with his brother, Peter, in the 1970s and they have continually expanded to its present location in the outskirts of London.

PANTELITSA TIMS
Chairperson of Ladies organisation in Manchester

DATE OF BIRTH: 26.07.34
PLACE OF BIRTH: Varosia, Famagusta.
MARITAL STATUS: Married Bryan A Tims, in Hong Kong, a retired Ship's Captain and Marine Superintendent, from Birmingham, England.
CHILDREN: Two daughters from husband's first marriage. Eldest, Ruth, an Accountant at Salford University, Manchester. Anne, Children's Nursery Nurse at Wigan.
SCHOOLS/COLLEGE: Gymnasium in Varosia. Vassilikes Sholes in Crete. Northern Polytechnic College in London.
PERSONAL PROFILE: Presently Chair Person (last three years, retiring after four) of ladies charity organisation in Manchester "The Evagelistria".
Has had poetry recognised and published in newspapers in Greece, London, Liverpool and Manchester.

MARTINOS TIRIMO
Musician

DATE OF BIRTH: 19.12.42
PLACE OF BIRTH: Larnaca.
MARITAL STATUS: Married to Mione.
CHILDREN: One son, one daughter.
SCHOOLS/COLLEGE: Bedales School with Cyprus Goverment Scholarship.Royal Academy.
HONOURS/AWARDS: Prizewinner International Beethoven Competition Vienna 1965. Winner Geneva International Piano Competition 1972. Silver Disc 1988, Gold disc 1994 for recording of Rachmaninov's 2nd concerto and Paganini Rhapsody.
HOBBIES & INTERESTS: Chess, reading and badminton.
PERSONAL PROFILE: First public recital in Cyprus 1949. Conducted seven performances of La Traviata with singers and musicians from La Scala Milan at Cyprus Opera festival 1955. Concerto performance as well as recitals worldwide. Radio & TV appearances worldwide. In 1998 received LISZT Scholarship. Composed film score Odyssey. Recordings include Brahms Piano Concertos, Chopin Concertos, Shuberts Piano Sonatas. Publications include Schubert Piano Sonatas in three volumes. The Olympic Commitee of Athens 2004 have appointed him Artistic director for several projects for the cultural Olympiad. Which will include his own scenes of the Beethoven 32 Sonatas.

STELIOS TJIRKALLI
Accountant, Chairman of Athienou Association UK

DATE OF BIRTH: 19.06.56
PLACE OF BIRTH: Bulawayo, Zimbabwe. Father, Andreas, from Dhikomo; Mother, Eleni Pastou, from Athienou.
MARITAL STATUS: Married to Tasoulla from Nicosia.
CHILDREN: Andreas, Postgraduate at Oxford; Harry and Marios, at school.
SCHOOLS/COLLEGE: American Academy Larnaca 1969-1977, North London University 1977-1979.
PROFESSIONAL QUALIFICATIONS: Chartered Certified Accountant Certificate.
MEMBERSHIPS: Member of Association of Accounting Technicians, Institute of Taxation Certificate, authorised by the FSA to Audit SFA Members.
HOBBIES AND INTERESTS: Football, travelling and sailing.
PERSONAL PROFILE: Stelios did articles with BSG Valentine, Chartered Accountants and served as Audit Manager for six years. Founding partner of Andrew, Steale an accounting and auditing practise in Mayfair, London, Chairman of Athienou Association in UK, founding member of the Independent Greek School of Finchley, where he has served as Treasuer and Vice Chairman, Vice Chairman of St Katherines Greek Orthodox Community in Barnet.

TASOULLA TJIRKALLI
Chairwoman of the Greek Womens Philanthropic Association Of Finchley and Barnet

DATE OF BIRTH: 02.12.58
PLACE OF BIRTH: Nicosia
MARITAL STATUS: Married to Stelios, from Zimbabwe (parents from Cyprus).
CHILDREN: Andreas, Postgraduate at Oxford; Harry and Marios, at school.
SCHOOLS/COLLEGE: The Lapithos Gymnasium for three years but due to the Turkish invasion graduated from the second Gymnasium Soleas. Studied Economics in Greece and also qualified as a Beautician.
PROFESSIONAL QUALIFICATIONS: Economics and Beautician.
HOBBIES AND INTERESTS: Travelling, reading, swimming and helping other people.
PERSONAL PROFILE: Accounts Supervisor at a manufacturing company in Greece, Accounts manager at Andrew Steale an accounting & auditing practise in the West End. First Chairperson of the Mothers Committees Of The Independent Greek School Of Finchley. Chairperson of The Greek Womens Philanthropic Association of Finchley and Barnet

LOUIS ANDREAS TOFALIDES
Assistant General Manager at the Bank of Cyprus (London) Ltd

DATE OF BIRTH: 30.01.57
PLACE OF BIRTH: Nicosia.
MARITAL STATUS: Married
CHILDREN: One son, one daughter.
SCHOOLS/COLLEGE: The English School, Nicosia, The London School of Economics (University of London).
ACADEMIC QUALIFICATIONS: BSc. (Econ).
PROFESSIONAL QUALIFICATIONS: Fellow of the Chartered Institute of Bankers.
HOBBIES AND INTERESTS: Football, theatre, classical music and sailing.
PERSONAL PROFILE: Assistant General Manager, Business Banking, Bank of Cyprus (London) Ltd.

DR KYPROS TOFALLIS
Author, Lecturer

DATE OF BIRTH: 27.12.43
PLACE OF BIRTH: Styllos, Famagusta.
MARITAL STATUS: Married to Katerina Adamou, a Teacher from Kato Deftera, Nicosia.
CHILDREN: Christopher, Assistant Headmaster; Elli, Publishers Editor; and Aristos, University student.
SCHOOLS/COLLEGE: Commercial Lyceum, Famagusta; Barnsbury School for Boys; North-Western Polytechnic; Institute of Education, University of London. Studied History, Classical Greek, Modern Greek, Sociology, Philosophy and Education.
ACADEMIC QUALIFICATIONS: BA, MA, PhD, Diploma in Education, and Diploma of English Studies from University of Cambridge.
MEMBERSHIPS: Fellow of the Institute of Linguists, Fellow of the Royal Society of Arts
HOBBIES AND INTERESTS: Reading, politics, history, literature, travel and theatre.
PERSONAL PROFILE: Lecturer in Modern Greek Studies at North London College (1969-1994) and at University of North London (1993-97) Greek Chief Examiner of the Institute of Linguists for 20 years. He was Examiner and Moderator for the University of London and the University of Cambridge. Founder and Director of the Greek Institute (1969), which promotes Modern Greek Studies and British-Greek and Cypriot Friendship. He has organised many functions for the Greek Institute and invited many British MPs, including Michael Foot when he was leader of the Labour Party, who addressed these functions. When writing his book A History Of Cyprus, he met the late Archbishop Makarios and many Cypriot political leaders. He is also a freelance Journalist and has pulished many articles in the Greek and British press. He has also published several books including *A History of Cyprus from the Ancient Times to the Present.*

Address: The Greek Institute, 34 Bush Hill Road, London N21 2DS Telephone & Fax: 020 8360 7968
Email: info@greekinstitute.co.uk

ZANNETOS TOFALLIS
Journalist, Lecturer

DATE OF BIRTH: 26.01.38
PLACE OF BIRTH: Styllos
MARITAL STATUS: Married
CHILDREN: One son, Chris.
Two grandchildren.
SCHOOLS/COLLEGE: Styllos
Elementary, English High
School. Famagusta, University
Of London.
ACADEMIC QUALIFICATIONS
BA Greek Studies, PhD Greek
Studies.
HONOURS/AWARDS: FIL Fellow of Institute of Linguists.
HOBBIES & INTERESTS: Reading and travel
PERSONAL PROFILE: Journalist at *Vema, Parikiaki*
newspaper and several Greek Journals. Lecturer in
Greek Studies at several universities, schools. Presently
Greek Translator 1st Managing Director of LGR.
Chairman of Styllos Association UK. Chairman of
Barnet Cypriot Association.

DR CRITON TOMAZOS
Artist, Poet, Writer, Architect

DATE OF BIRTH: 13.04.40
PLACE OF BIRTH: Larnaca.
MARITAL STATUS: Single
SCHOOLS/COLLEGE: Larnaca
Commercial   Lyceum,
Famagusta, Gymnasium, Cairo
Greek Gymnasium, Kingsway
Day College, Polytechnic Regent
St, London Academy of TV &
Film.
PROFESSIONAL QUALIFICA-
TIONS: Doctor of Environmental Architecture,
Doctor of Human Relationships, Doctor of Fine
Arts.
MEMBERSHIPS: Poetry Society UK, Writers Guild.
HONOURS/AWARDS 1st prize Poetry Eden International
Youth Festival 1982-1983.
HOBBIES & INTERESTS: Painting, poetry, television &
radio, travel, writing, theatre and cinema.
PERSONAL PROFILE: Worked in mainstream
Architectural Design with leading firms, on projects
such as Hammersmith Hospital, GLC Architects
(Hayward Gallery, National Theatre). Worked part-time
with Theatro Technis as an actor, designer, writer.
Produced many paintings in oils, acrylics & water
colours. Co-founder of the Environmental Forum.
Written many poems in English & Greek. Contributor
to *Parikiaki* newspaper.

Address: 2 Park Terrace, Bell Lane, Enfield, Middlesex
EN3 5EU

TOM TOUMAZIS
Senior Vice-President/MD of Buena
Vista International TV

DATE OF BIRTH: 06.06.61
PLACE OF BIRTH: London.
Father from Komi Kebir;
Mother from Kalavasso, (former
proprietors of La Primavera
Restaurant in Golders Green)
MARITAL STATUS: Married to
Helen.
CHILDREN: Christopher,
Gabriel and Stephanie.
SCHOOLS/COLLEGE: Friern
Barnet Grammar School, Woodhouse, Barnet,
Southbank University, Harvard Business School.
MEMBERSHIPS: BAFTA, Royal Television Society,
SOLUS Club.
HOBBIES AND INTERESTS: Golf and film.
PERSONAL PROFILE: Was Managing Director of
Eurosport, then UK Managing Director of EMAP
Advertising. Now works for Walt Disney Television
International as Head of Buena Vista International TV.

SOPHIA TOUMAZIS
PR Consultant

DATE OF BIRTH: 27.04.60
PLACE OF BIRTH: London.
MARITAL STATUS: Married to
Andros Epaminondas.
SCHOOL/COLLEGE: The Mount
School, London; Southgate
College, London; Warwick
University, Warwickshire.
CHILDREN: Christoforos and
Electra.
ACADEMIC QUALIFICATIONS: 2:1
Philosophy and Literature,
Warwick University; PGCE English and Drama.
HOBBIES AND INTERESTS: Film, writing, cooking and
walking.
PERSONAL PROFILE: Director of PR Consultancy, *tpr*,
whose clients include Channel 4 and Associated Press.

MARKOS TOUMAZOS
Chairman of Greek Orthodox Church in Cheltenham

DATE OF BIRTH: 20.03.39
PLACE OF BIRTH: Neta, Famagusta.
MARITAL STATUS: Married to Andriana from Yialousa.
CHILDREN: Marios, Clerk; Christopher, Professor; Yasmin, Housewife; Niki, Housewife; Andreas, Hairdresser.
SCHOOLS/COLLEGE: Neta Elementary, Yialousa Greek Gymnasium.
HOBBIES AND INTERESTS: Shooting and snooker.
PERSONAL PROFILE: Over 40 years in Catering holding positions as General Manager in Night Clubs, Casinos, Hotels, Restaurants. Chairman of Greek Orthodox Church in Cheltenham.

PETROS TREZOS
Chairman of St Peters & Paul Church in Bristol

DATE OF BIRTH: 26.01.17
PLACE OF BIRTH: Lefkoniko.
MARITAL STATUS: Married to Kyriaki, from Tripimeni.
CHILDREN: Stella, Loulla and Maria. Seven Grandchildren, seven Great Grandchildren.
HONOURS/AWARDS: Honoured by the Greek Orthodox Church for services to the church & Bristol community.
HOBBIES AND INTERESTS: Golf and gardening.
PERSONAL PROFILE: Restauranteur and Fish &Chip shop owner. One of the founders of St Peter & Paul Church in Bristol, Chairman of the church for eight years.

GEORGE ANTONIOU TRIMIKLINIOTIS
Executive member of Brent Youth and Community Service Council Commitee

DATE OF BIRTH: 27.09.26
PLACE OF BIRTH: Pera-pedi, Limassol.
MARITAL STATUS: Married to Vassiliki (formerly Sabatakou) from Kalamata, Greece.
CHILDREN: Maria, Vicky and Antony, all university educated.
SCHOOLS/COLLEGE: Primary school, Pera-pedi, Secondary School, one year at Mitsi School
Lemythou 1939-1940. Part time structural engineering course at Willesden College Of Technology (now College Of North West London) from 1960-1966.

PROFESSIONAL QUALIFICATIONS: Ordinary National Certificate in Building, Higher National Certificate in Building, Certificate Of Supplementary Study.
MEMBERSHIPS: Executive member of Brent Youth and Community Service Council Committee, Greek Parents Association, Cypriot Community Association of Brent, Member of AKEL.
HONOURS/AWARDS: Nominated by Brent Community Relations Council for a community service award in the early nineties.
HOBBIES AND INTERESTS: Politics, reading and theatre.
PERSONAL PROFILE: A structural engineer with the GLC. Former Chairman of the Cypriot Community Association of Brent. Executive Member of Brent Community Relations Council, involved in the running of the local Greek school in Brent.

IOANNIS TRITEOS
Chairman of Kato Pyrgos

DATE OF BIRTH: 01.3.49
PLACE OF BIRTH: Kato Pyrgos.
MARITAL STATUS: Married to Androulla, a Teacher at an English Primary School, from Korakou.
CHILDREN: Stelios, Eliana and Alexandros.
SCHOOLS/COLLEGE: Kato Pyrgos, Tyllirias Elementary School, Kykkos Gymnasium, Cyprus, Isleworth polytechnic, London, Chelsea College of Aeronautical Engineering.
ACADEMIC QUALIFICATIONS: Certificate of Education for 21 subjects (pass level final marks 18/20), Officer in the National Guard, HND in Mechanical Engineering, Aeronautical Engineering Diploma.
HOBBIES AND INTERESTS: Sports activities, gardening, travelling, entertaining and current affairs.
PERSONAL PROFILE: Chairman of Kato Pyrgos, Tyllirias UK Association. Chair of Governors of St Barnabas Greek Community School, North London (900 pupils approx) Organising the 1996 & 1997 I.T.T conferences for 280 people in the Travel and Business world.
Working with the Leukaemia Society in fund - raising for the Anthony Nolan Trust, helping support victims and their families.
Organising a large concert at Wembley Arena for 12,000 people, raising £200,000 for Cyprus. Helping to get top artists from Greece and France for the Wembley event.
Helping to get sponsors and organise for 40 Albanian children to come to England and the right to be baptised and christened and becoming a God parent to one of the children.
One of the founders and the first chairman of A.G.T.A (U.K) and a member of the Committee.

However, one of his greatest career highlights is the creation of Magnum Travel in 1981. After ten years of being successful ABTA and IATA retail agents, the company also became Tour Operators since 1990.

In the years 1997, 1998 and 1999 the success of the company was recognised and it received prestigious awards from Cyprus Airways.

ANDREAS TRITEOS
Accountant

DATE OF BIRTH: 31.10.52
PLACE OF BIRTH: Nicosia, brought up in Kato Pyrgos Tyllyria.
MARITAL STATUS: Married to Maria, from Nicosia.
CHILDREN: Two.
SCHOOLS/COLLEGE: Pancyprian Gymnasium of Kykko.
PROFESSIONAL QUALIFICATIONS: Accountant.
MEMBERSHIPS: DYSY.
HOBBIES AND INTERESTS: Shooting and basketball.
PERSONAL PROFILE: Accountant, Partner in Alexander Neil & CO, member of EFEKA, founder member of Kato Pyrgos Tyllyria Association UK, Founder member of Akritas football club and was Chairman of Woodhouse Greek school for two years.

DR GERA MARIA TROISI
Senior Lecturer in Environmental Toxicology

DATE OF BIRTH: 26.07.70
PLACE OF BIRTH: London. Mother from Tricomo.
MARITAL STATUS: Single
SCHOOLS/COLLEGE: Chamberlayne Road School 1975-1980, Burlington Danes School 1981-86, The London Oratory School 1986-88.
ACADEMIC QUALIFICATIONS: BSc Honours Aquatic Biology & Ecology, PhD in Environmental Toxicology.
MEMBERSHIPS: British Toxicology Society. Society for Marine Mammology, European Cetacean Society.
HOBBIES AND INTERESTS: Music, travel and conservation.
PERSONAL PROFILE: Senior Lecturer (Environmental Toxicology), Kingston University. Involved with several organisations including the Institute for Environmental Health-Medical Research Council, Greenpeace, WWF, RSPCA, Whale and Dolphin Conservation Society.) Invited speaker at several international conferences and is a consultant environmental toxicologist. Director of Wildlife & Human Toxicology Unit, a UK government and charity funded research group based at Kingston University.

MICHAEL TRYPHONIDES
High Technology International Design Consultant

DATE OF BIRTH: 14.10.50
PLACE OF BIRTH: Sinaoros, Nicosia.
MARITAL STATUS: Married to Effi, from London(father from Leonarisso; mother from Aradippou).
CHILDREN: Andrea, Nicholas, and Helena, all University graduates.
SCHOOLS/COLLEGE: University College London.
ACADEMIC QUALIFICATIONS: BSc in Electronic Engineering, MIEE, CEng.
HOBBIES AND INTERESTS: Football (Tottenham supporter), swimming and socialising.
PERSONAL PROFILE: Managing Director Of design consultancy Quartet Technology LTD - Consultants in high technology electronic design. Governor at Latymer School for ten years, local authority appointed Governor. Was Governor at Hadleywood Primary School, also for 27 years has been teaching Maths, Physics and Electronics.

Email: miket@netcomqt.demon.co.uk

LOUCAS TSANGARIDES
Chairman of Pedhoulas Assoc in UK

DATE OF BIRTH: 11.11.37
PLACE OF BIRTH: Pedhoulas.
MARITAL STATUS: Married to Stavroula Loula (née Achillea), born in Margate, (parents from Yialousa).
CHILDREN: Lara, Computer Analyst; Mariana, Fashion Buyer; Joanna, Teacher; Neophytos, at university.
SCHOOLS/COLLEGE: Institute of Chartered Ship Brokers.
ACADEMIC QUALIFICATIONS: Member of the ICSB.
HOBBIES AND INTERESTS: Football.
PERSONAL PROFILE: Ex Managing Director of Troodos Shipping & Trading Ltd, Chairman of the Association of Pedhoulas in UK. Served as Chairman of St Barnabas Greek Church at Wood Green.

FLORA TSAPPARELLI
Health Visitor

DATE OF BIRTH: 25.12.37
PLACE OF BIRTH: Yialousa.
MARITAL STATUS: Married to Louis, retired electronics engineer, from Yialousa.
CHILDREN: Christos, doing a Masters Degree in Computing; Yiannis, Accounts Manager.
SCHOOLS/COLLEGE: High School Yialousa, Loizides Gymnasium Nicosia, Nurse Training at King Edward Memorial Hospital in Ealing, Midwifery training in Scotland, South Bank University course in Health Visiting.
HOBBIES AND INTERESTS: Keep fit, swimming, reading and crosswords.
PERSONAL PROFILE: Health Visitor in Brighton for 25 years, now retired.

KYRIACOS TSAPARELLI
Magician

DATE OF BIRTH: 11.09.55
PLACE OF BIRTH: London. Mother Marika Strakka from Kato Varosi, Famagusta; Father Loizos Tsaparelli from Yialousa.
MARITAL STATUS: Married to Maria Moyseos (father from Deftera, mother from Lythrodontas).
CHILDREN: Louis and Natalya.
SCHOOLS/COLLEGE: George Elliot School, Finchley; Woolverstone Hall, Near Ipswich; Southwark College; East Anglia University; Thames Polytechnic.
ACADEMIC QULIFICATIONS: 3 A Levels, 10 O Levels, BSc Degree in Maths Statistics and Computing.
MEMBERSHIPS: The Magic Circle, Associate of the Inner Magic Circle with a Silver Star.
HOBBIES AND INTERESTS: Music Grade 6 in Piano & Cello.
PERSONAL PROFILE: A magician. In Cyprus has performed on RIK TV with presenter Irene on "Efharisto Savatobrado!" Clients include *Budweiser*, *Walkers Crisps*, Yamaha, *Sony*, *Virgin Atlantic Airways*, *British Airways*.
Now running successful entertainment and promotion company. Recently agreed a deal to promote the new X-Type Jaguar in Park Lane London in a Razzamatazz/ Hollywood style. Recent jobs include taking a team of entertainers to Monte Carlo to play alongside Stevie Wonder and Kool and the Gang.

GEORGE TSAVELLAS
General Surgeon

DATE OF BIRTH: 06.06.65
PLACE OF BIRTH: London. Father from Miliou, Paphos; Mother from Neo Chorion, Paphos.
SCHOOLS/COLLEGE: Winchmore School, Charing Cross & Westminster Medical School, University of London.
PROFESSIONAL QUALIFIC-ATIONS: Bachelor of Medicine, Bachelor of Surgery (London) 1990, Fellow of the Royal College of Surgeons of England 1996, Fellow of he Royal College of Surgeons of Edinburgh 1996.
MEMBERSHIPS: British Medical Association, Association of Coloproctology of Great Britain & Ireland.
PERSONAL PROFILE: A General Surgeon with a specialist interest in colorectal disease. Undertook basic surgical training at the University College and Middlesex Hospitals, and higher surgical training on the Wessex rotation. Formerly a research fellow in the Department of Academic Surgery at the Chelsea and Westminster Hospital, Imperial College School of Medicine, London. Publications include papers on minimal residual disease in colorectal cancer.

FOTINI TSIOUPRA
Secretary of Komi Kebir Association

DATE OF BIRTH: 04.05.65
PLACE OF BIRTH: London. Father, Takis Tsioupras (deceased, was Chairman of OESEKA), from Komi Kebir; Mother, Maritsa, from Zodia, was chairwoman of Cypriot Womens League.
SCHOOLS/COLLEGE: Exeter University, Middlesex University.
ACADEMIC QUALIFICATIONS: BA History & Politics, Diploma in Social Work.
HOBBIES AND INTERESTS: Photography and equal opportunities
PERSONAL PROFILE: Senior Probation Officer in London Probation Area. Secretary of Komi Kebir Asociation, Member of the Executive Committee of the Cypriot community centre Wood Green, Member of the Cypriot Womens League.

GNOSOULLA TSIOUPRA (LEWIS)
Solicitor

DATE OF BIRTH: 14.12.67
PLACE OF BIRTH: London; father Takis Tsioupras (deceased, was Chairman of OESEKA), from Komi Kebir; Mother, Maritsa, from Zodhia.
MARITAL STATUS: Married to Dewi Lewis, a Lecturer in Chemistry at University College, London.
CHILDREN: Christoforos and Maritsa.
SCHOOLS/COLLEGE: Latymer School, Surrey University, Law College Lancaster Gate.
ACADEMIC QUALIFICATIONS: BSc Russian & Law.
PROFESSIONAL QUALIFICATIONS: Solicitor.
HOBBIES AND INTERESTS: Travel & politics
PERSONAL PROFILE: Joined city firm Baker & Mckenzie, specialising in employment law from 1992 to 1999. Now an in-house employment lawyer for United Business Media PLC, named in Chambers Law Directory in 2002 as one of the country's top ten in-house employment lawyers. Committee member of Morphou District Association. Board member of Novas Overtures, a charity working with the homeless, refugees, asylum seekers, victims of domestic violence and people with drug, alcohol and mental health problems.

LOUIZA TSIOUPRA (LEON)
Drama, Secondary School Teacher

DATE OF BIRTH: 03.08.76
PLACE OF BIRTH: London. Father, Kyriacos, from Komi Kebir; Mother, Pola, from Lympia.
MARITAL STATUS: Married to Yonel Leon from Cuba.
SCHOOLS/COLLEGE: Ashmole School, Middlesex University, London College of Printing, University of Wales.
ACADEMIC QUALIFICATIONS: BA Hons in Theatre Studies specialising in Design. PGCE Certificate in Education.
HOBBIES AND INTERESTS: Travelling, theatre, acting and designing.
PERSONAL PROFILE: Was costume assistant for White Horse Theatre Co in Germany and Costume designing for National Cypriot Theatre in Cyprus. Now a drama teacher at a secondary school in North London.

MARITSA TSIOUPRA (née HASSABIS)
Honorary Chairwoman of Cypriot Womens League

DATE OF BIRTH: 10.11.27
PLACE OF BIRTH: Pano Zodhia.
MARITAL STATUS: Married to Takis Tsioupras (deceased), from Komi Kebir.
CHILDREN: Eddie Michael, Performing Rights Society;Des Michael, Performing Rights Society; Fotini Tsioupra, Senior Probation Officer, Gnosoulla Tsioupra-Lewis, a Solicitor.
MEMBERSHIPS: AKEL committee member, Cypriot Women's League founder member & formerly Chairperson, now Honorary Chairwoman. Greek Parents Association, founder member & formerly committee member. Haringey Council, member of Ethnic Minorities Joint Consultative Committee; Cypriot Community Centre, founder member; Hazelwood Greek School, formerly committee member; Morphou District Association, committee member; National Federation of Cypriots in Great Britain, founder member and committee member; Zodhia Association, vice Chairperson,
HONOURS/AWARDS: Awards from AKEL, Cypriot Women's League, Morphou District Association, National Federation of Cypriots in Great Britain and Haringey Council.
HOBBIES AND INTERESTS: Politics, travel and grandchildren!
PERSONAL PROFILE: Honorary Chairwoman of Cypriot Women's League.

NICHOLAS TSIOUPRAS
Solicitor

DATE OF BIRTH: 19.07.69
PLACE OF BIRTH: UK. Father from Komi Kebir; Mother, UK.
MARITAL STATUS: Single
SCHOOLS/COLLEGE: Ashmole School, Southgate College, Middlesex University, College of Law.
ACADEMIC QUALIFICATIONS: A levels, Law Degree LLB (Honours).
PROFESSIONAL QUALIFICATIONS: Post Graduate Diploma in Law.
MEMBERSHIPS: Law Society.
HOBBIES AND INTERESTS: Scuba Diving, running, technology and multi-media.
PERSONAL PROFILE: Qualified as a Solicitor in 2000, specialising in all aspects of Property Law.

KYRIACOS LOIZOU TSIOUPRAS
Former Newspaper Editor and General Manager of LGR

DATE OF BIRTH: 18.12.32
PLACE OF BIRTH: Komi Kebir Village, Famagusta district, Cyprus.
MARITAL STATUS: Married to Pola Christoforou, from Lymbia village, Nicosia district, Cyprus.
CHILDREN: Stavroulla Theopistos Stavrinou, Primary school Teacher; Louiza Leon, Secondary school Teacher.
SCHOOLS/COLLEGE: Elementary school, Komi Kebir; Famagusta Gymnasium; London School of Economics and Political Science.
ACADEMIC QUALIFICATIONS: BSc Economics (Honours)
MEMBERSHIPS: Served as member of the Executive Council of the National Federation of Cypriots in the UK as well as Secretary for the same organisation. Also former Vice President of the World Co-ordinating Committee Justice for Cyprus.
Member of the Komi Kebir association.
HOBBIES AND INTERESTS: Politics, reading and travelling.
PERSONAL PROFILE: Sub-editor Haravgi daily newspaper, Nicosia, editor to *Vema* weekly newspaper, London; editor, Parikiaki weekly newspaper, London and General Manager London Greek Radio, London.

POLA TSIOUPRA
Chairwoman of Lympia Association UK

DATE OF BIRTH: 09.05.41
PLACE OF BIRTH: Lymbia.
MARITAL STATUS: Married to Kyriacos Tsioupras.
CHILDREN: Stavroulla and Louiza, both teachers.
SCHOOLS/COLLEGE: Pancyprian Academy, Nicosia.
HOBBIES AND INTERESTS: Dancing, Greek Schools and women's rights.
PERSONAL PROFILE: Was a businesswoman with a florist shop for several years. Chairwoman of Lympia Association. In secretariat of National Federation of Cypriots. Was Chairwoman of Ashmole Greek School. Member of Cypriot Womens League OESEKA, and Greek Parents Association.

KYRIAKOS TSIRPIS
Former Chairman of the Cypriot Golf Society

DATE OF BIRTH: 24.05.40
PLACE OF BIRTH: Agios Sergios, Famagusta.
MARITAL STATUS: Married
CHILDREN: Vasillia, Architect/ Engineer; Mario, at university studying Marine Biology; Stephanos, at school.
SCHOOLS/COLLEGE: In Cyprus.
HOBBIES AND INTERESTS: Football (Arsenal supporter).
PERSONAL PROFILE: One of the founders and Chairman of the Cypriot Golf Society UK. One of the Founders and ex committee member of Anorthosis FC UK.

HARIS TSIRTSIPIS
Accountant

DATE OF BIRTH: 24.10.59
PLACE OF BIRTH: Athienou, Cyprus.
MARITAL STATUS: Married to Alexandra, from Plymouth.
CHILDREN: Three
SCHOOLS/COLLEGE: Pancyprian Gymnasium, Nicosia, Southend College of technology, London School of Economics.
ACADEMIC QUALIFICATIONS: BSc Mathematical Economics & Econometrics.
PROFESSIONAL QUALIFICATIONS: FCCA.
MEMBERSHIPS: Plymouth and Twelve Apostles Greek Orthodox Churches, Athienou Association UK.
HOBBIES AND INTERESTS: Football, basketball and volleyball.
PERSONAL PROFILE: Accountant and Partner in Freeman & Partners Accountants.

COSTAS SOLOMOU TSOULOUPAS
Accountant/Secretary Cosmos FC

DATE OF BIRTH: 09.12.48
PLACE OF BIRTH: Lapithos.
MARITAL STATUS: Married to Kyproulla, from Agios Theodoros, Larnaca.
CHILDREN: Two sons, one daughter.
SCHOOLS/COLLEGE: Lapithos Gymnasium, Putney College, Kilburn Polytechnic.
PROFESSIONAL QUALIFICATIONS: Chartered Accountant.
HOBBIES AND INTERESTS: Football (Chelsea supporter).
PERSONAL PROFILE: An Accountant. Opened own practice Tsouloupas & Co in Croydon in 1982. Member of Streatham & Lambeth Greek School committee, Secretary of Cosmos FC.

CHRYSSOULA TUCK
Honorary Secretary of the Welwyn Hatfield Ethnic Minorities Group

DATE OF BIRTH: 22.12.38
PLACE OF BIRTH: Nicosia.
MARITAL STATUS: Married to Sidney Tuck who is an Anglo Saxon, born in Camden Town.
CHILDREN: Elita, gone to Heaven 2001, and three step-sons, an Industrial Chemist in the U.K., a Private Jet Designer in the United States and an Art Dealer in London. Three grandchildren.
SCHOOLS/COLLEGE: Ayii Omologites, Pancyprian Gymnasium 1949-1952.
ACADEMIC QUALIFICATIONS: Diploma in Business Studies H.N.D.
PROFESSIONAL QUALIFICATIONS: 1974-1982 Accounting Technician via the Open University.
HOBBIES AND INTERESTS: To travel all over the world - and good food.
PERSONAL PROFILE: Became involved with various organisations, mainly charity work, long before retirement. Kept busy for several years as a founder member of the Greek Orthodox Community of the twelve Apostles Hertfordshire. At present is the Honorary Secretary of the Welwyn Hatfield Ethnic Minorities Group.

COSTAS TZIAMBAZIS
Former Chairman of Cypriot Estia, Birmingham

DATE OF BIRTH: 12.04.45
PLACE OF BIRTH: Aradippou.
MARITAL STATUS: Married to Androulla Panayiotou from London, (parents from Aradippou and Assia)
CHILDREN: Elia, Doctor; Athos, working at Deloite Touche; Constantine, Student.
SCHOOLS/COLLEGE: Pancyprian Gymnasium, Larnaca Lyceum.
MEMBERSHIPS: Greek Cypriot ESTIA, Birmingham.
HOBBIES AND INTERESTS: Poetry (writing), culture, music and choir singing.
PERSONAL PROFILE: Former Chairman, Greek Cypriot ESTIA twice. Was also Chairman of Culture Society for four years in Birmingham

ELIA TZIAMBAZIS
Surgeon

DATE OF BIRTH: 26.11.76
PLACE OF BIRTH: Stoke on Trent, England. Parents from Aradippou.
MARITAL STATUS: Single
SCHOOLS/COLLEGE: King Edward's School, Birmingham, Birmingham University.
MEMBERSHIPS: British Medical Association, Royal College of Surgeons.
HOBBIES AND INTERESTS: 1st XI Bournville Hockey Club, National 1st Division.
PERSONAL PROFILE: Working at Birmingham Heartlands Hospital on the Surgical Rotation.

PETER SAVVAS VANEZIS, OBE
Professor of Forensic Medicine and Science

DATE OF BIRTH: 11.12.47
PLACE OF BIRTH: Nicosia
MARITAL STATUS: Married to Maria Vanezis, a Research Assistant, from Limassol.
CHILDREN: Andrew, at Edinburgh University; Frosini, at Hutchson's Grammar School, Glasgow.
SCHOOLS/COLLEGE: Wanstead High School, Bristol University.
ACADEMIC & PROFESSIONAL QUALIFICATIONS: MB, CHB, MD, PHD, FRCPATH, FRCP (Glasgow), DMJ.
MEMBERSHIPS: All major Forensic Societies, plus BMA, Rsm.
HONOURS/AWARDS: OBE.
HOBBIES AND INTERESTS: Golf and painting.
PERSONAL PROFILE: Regius Professor of Forensic Medicine & Science & Head of Department, University of Glasgow. Director: Human Identification Centre, Centre for International Forensic Assistance. Honorary Consultant in Forensic Medicine to: The Government of the Republic of Cyprus, The Medico-Legal Institute, Santiago Chile, The British Armed Forces

RONIS VARLAAM
Film Maker and Artist

DATE OF BIRTH: 07.05.46
PLACE OF BIRTH: Nicosia.
MARITAL STATUS: Single
SCHOOLS/COLLEGE: Terra Santa College, Nicosia, London Film School.
HOBBIES AND INTERESTS: Photography, travel and reading.
PERSONAL PROFILE: Film Maker and Artist. Produced and directed a number of documentaries for Channel 4, including *The Enthusiasts* and *Well You Didn't*. Was also co-Director for *Green Line*, a documentary on Cyprus for Channel 4. Has exhibited work at the Alsager Gallery, Manchester Metropolitan University and various other galleries.

Email: ronis@eurofilms.tv

CHRISTAKIS KYRIACOS VARNAVIDES
General Medical Practitioner

DATE OF BIRTH: 09.07.45
PLACE OF BIRTH: Nicosia
MARITAL STATUS: Married to Andrea, a Nurse, from Leeds.
CHILDREN: Kyriacos, Police Officer; Charis, Graduate (BA Honours).
SCHOOLS/COLLEGE: Leeds University.
ACADEMIC QUALIFICATIONS: BSc (Hons) Physiology.
PROFESSIONAL QUALIFICATIONS: M.B.ch.B. Dip Obst. RCOG.FRCGP.
MEMBERSHIPS: Fellow of the Royal College of General Practitioners.
HOBBIES AND INTERESTS: Photography, dermatology, plays Badminton (badly), also when the mood takes, writes poetry (also badly).
PERSONAL PROFILE: General Medical Practitioner. Examiner for Membership of the Royal College of General Practitioners. Chairman of The Greek School, Leeds, Author of numerous Medical Papers

LAMBROS KLEANTHIS VARNAVIDES
Managing Director of Shipping at the Royal Bank of Scotland

DATE OF BIRTH: 01.07.49
PLACE OF BIRTH: London. Father, Professor Panayiotis, from Paphos; Mother, Despina, from Famagusta.
MARITAL STATUS: Married to Katie from London, (parents from Kato Drys)
CHILDREN: Elli.
SCHOOLS/COLLEGE: Latymer Upper School, Hammersmith, University College London, London School of Economics.
ACADEMIC QUALIFICATIONS: BSc & MSc in Economics, M.Phil.
HOBBIES AND INTERESTS: Opera, reading and travel.
PERSONAL PROFILE: Joined Williams & Glyns Bank in 1974 as a Shipping Analyst. Now Managing Director of Shipping at The Royal Bank of Scotland.

DR LYSANDROS VARNAVIDES
Researcher in Molecular Haemotology

DATE OF BIRTH: 14.04.41
PLACE OF BIRTH: Neta.
MARITAL STATUS: Married to Eleni, from Achna.
CHILDREN: Andreas and Alexia.
SCHOOLS/COLLEGE: Chiswick Polytechnic, Chelsea College, University College Hospital (London).
ACADEMIC QUALIFICATIONS: BSc Chemistry and Physiology, MSc in Bio-chemistry, PhD in Bio-chemistry (London).
HOBBIES AND INTERESTS: Reading and Byzantine music.
PERSONAL PROFILE: Principal clinical scientist (prenatal diagnosis, Molecular Haemotology) at Kings College Hospital, London.

PANAYIOTIS L VARNAVIDES
Professor of Pure Mathematics
(Deceased)

DATE OF BIRTH: 10.06.12
PLACE OF BIRTH: Paphos
MARITAL STATUS: Married to Despina Lysandrou, from Famagusta.
CHILDREN: Lambros, born London; Mary, born Khartoum.
SCHOOLS/COLLEGE: Athens University, University College, London.
ACADEMIC QUALIFICATIONS: BSC, PhD.
PERSONAL PROFILE: Number Theory Professor of Pure Mathematics, taught at University College, London, University College Khartoum, American University of Beirut, Chelsea College, London University.

ANDRIANA VASILIADES
Member of Network ME

DATE OF BIRTH: 05.07.46
PLACE OF BIRTH: Vouni, Limassol.
MARITAL STATUS: Widowed for the past seven years.
CHILDREN: Georgia, a Linguist; Christina, an Associate Publisher.
SCHOOLS/COLLEGE: Lanition Gymnasium, Limassol: Pitman College; Westminster College; Enfield College; North East London College; Middlesex University.
ACADEMIC QUALIFICATIONS: Sociology Degree Two
MEMBERSHIPS: Member of Action for ME, Greek & Greek Cypriot Community of Enfield, Network ME
HOBBIES AND INTERESTS: Reading, gardening, baking, tapestry and complementary therapies
PERSONAL PROFILE: At nine months old caught Typhoid, luckily survived the ordeal. At 16 caught Glandular Fever, then suffered extreme mental & physical fatigue. Came to London at 20 for a cure. Thought to have had breathing problems, later diagnosed with ME. While recovering from ME was found to be suffering from skin cancer. After three painful operations was given the all clear. Whilst under these treatments did O & A Levels and a Sociology degree at the age of 50. Now works for Network ME a local support group based in Edmonton, which supports ME sufferers and carers.

DINA (Constantinou) VASS
Musician

DATE OF BIRTH: 13.04.74
PLACE OF BIRTH: London. Father from Paphos; Mother from Limassol.
MARITAL STATUS: Single
SCHOOLS/COLLEGE: Coppetts Wood Primary School, Friern Barnet County School, London N11.
ACADEMIC QUALIFICATIONS: GCSE's English, Maths, Art, Biology, Textiles.
PROFESSIONAL QUALIFICATIONS: Diploma in Business Management and Office.
MEMBERSHIPS: MCPS and Musicians Union.
HONOURS/AWARDS: Ice hockey coaching award, Town FM competition for Talent.
HOBBIES AND INTERESTS: Ice skating, hockey, gym and sketching/art
PERSONAL PROFILE: Musician. Signed up by *Go Beat* Records.

ANDREAS VASILIOU
Managing Director of Amathus (UK) Ltd

DATE OF BIRTH: 25.01.48
PLACE OF BIRTH: Saranti.
MARITAL STATUS: Married to Maria, a Greek Language Teacher, from Lemithou.
CHILDREN: Ifigenia, BA Business Studies, Sales Executive in IPC Magazine; Andriani, BA Hons Fine Art.
SCHOOLS/COLLEGE: Agros Apeitium Gymnasium.
PROFESSIONAL QUALIFICATIONS: Fellow of Institute of Travel and Tourism.
MEMBERSHIPS: I.T.T. (Institute of Travel & Tourism).
HONOURS/AWARDS: Cyprus Tourism Organisation, November 2000.
HOBBIES AND INTERESTS: Golf and travelling.
PERSONAL PROFILE: Managing Director of Amathus (UK) Ltd. Commitment to suceed in Travel & Tourism by managing and leading a company specialising mainly in Cyprus and Greece. Served as AGTA Chairman, 1998-2002.

ANDRIANI VASILIOU
Artist

DATE OF BIRTH: 27.01.82
PLACE OF BIRTH: London. Parents from Saranti and Lemithou
MARITAL STATUS: Single
SCHOOL/COLLEGE: Ashmole School, Central St Martins, Art University.
ACADEMIC QUALIFICATIONS: BA Honours Fine Art.
HOBBIES & INTERESTS: Music and travelling.
PERSONAL PROFILE: Artist exhibited in Nicosia Cyprus, Gallery K, Central St Martins, and Vinopolis, London.
In Nicosia, 2002, she exhibited her works at the Lions home, an organisation that cares and protects underprivileged and bereaved children in Cyprus. All profits from the sale of paintings were donated to this foundation.

VASOS VASSILIOU
Teacher

DATE OF BIRTH: 28.04.72
PLACE OF BIRTH: London. Parents from Pervolia and Ayios Theodoros, Larnaca.
MARITAL STATUS: Single
SCHOOLS/COLLEGE: Hazelwood Broomfield, University of Westminster.
ACADEMIC QUALIFICATIONS: BA Honours Business Studies, PGCE.
HOBBIES AND INTERESTS: Football, Arsenal Supporter.
PERSONAL PROFILE: Teacher at Cranford Community College in Hounslow Teaching Business Studies. Head of Year twelve & thirteen. Used to teach Greek Dancing at the Cypriot Community Centre, Member of Datcha Dance Group. Played football for Komi Kebir in Cypriot Football League

KOSTA VAZANIAS
Businessman

DATE OF BIRTH: 09.11.56
PLACE OF BIRTH: London. Parents from Athienou
MARITAL STATUS: Married to Lisa Loizou, a Fashion Designer, from London, UK.
CHILDREN: Andreas, Harry, Michael, all at school; Christopher, at nursery.
SCHOOLS/COLLEGE: Mora Road Primary School, John Kelly Secondary High School, Kingsway Princeton College.
ACADEMIC QUALIFCATIONS: 6 O Levels, 1 A Level
HOBBIES AND INTERESTS: Football, most sports and tropical fish.
PERSONAL PROFILE: Started MK Fashions with brother Michael. Own West & Webb, supplying Ladieswear to multiples. 1995 opened retail outlets called Vestry Shops in Lakeside, Bluewater, Manchester, Oxford Street, Kings Road, Glasgow, Bristol amongst others.

MICHAEL VAZANIAS
Businessman

DATE OF BIRTH: 15.05.50
PLACE OF BIRTH: Athienou.
MARITAL STATUS: Married to Sandra, from London.
CHILDREN: Harry working at Anderson Consulting, Daniel doing a degree in Software Engineering at Sussex University, Nicholas still at school.
SCHOOLS/COLLEGE: John Kelly, Neasden.
HOBBIES AND INTERESTS: Eating out, theatre and travel.
PERSONAL PROFILE: Started as qualified Master Printer. In 1976 started M& K Fashions with brother Costas. Started manufacturing in 1988 under the label West & Webb supplying Ladieswear to the mutiples. In 1995 opened own retail outlets called Vestry selling ladieswear with shops in Lakeside, Oxford Street, Kings road, Bluewater, Manchester, Glasgow, Bristol. One of the founder members of the Cypriot Chamber of Commerce.

NICHOLAS NICOLAOU-VENEDI
Regional Finance Governor for London Unison

DATE OF BIRTH: 19.06.60
PLACE OF BIRTH: London. Father from Kalopsida: Mother from Kyrenia.
MARITAL STATUS: Divorced, ex-wife from Spain.
CHILDREN: Andalucia, at school in Sevillia in Spain.
SCHOOLS/COLLEGE: Cardinal Manning Catholic School, Kensington.
ACADEMIC QUALIFICATIONS: BA (Honours) Degree Politics & Economics.
PROFESSIONAL QUALIFICATIONS: M.I.L (Institute of Linguists).
HOBBIES AND INTERESTS: Politics, current affairs, travelling, socialising, sport.
PERSONAL PROFILE: Regional Finance Governor for Unison since 1998 - membership in London of 150,000 - nationally 1.4 million. Also Chair of London Unison Diversity Forum.

MARIA VIGAR
Actress

PLACE OF BIRTH: Nicosia.
MARITAL STATUS: Married
CHILDREN: Athos and James.
SCHOOLS/COLLEGE: The English School, Nicosia.
ACADEMIC QUALIFICATIONS: MA Text & Performance -Kings College London.
PROFESSIONAL QUALIFICATIONS: Cert in Education & Professional Training for the Theatre.
MEMBERSHIPS: Fellow RSA; Equity; Amnesty International.
PERSONAL PROFILE: Actress, Teacher, Drama Director (Radio/Theatre). Writer (Radio Drama; Stage Plays). Community Development & Fundraising for local Hospice Care. Founder member of the Beckenham and West Wickham Amnesty International Group and now co-Chair.

ANTONIS G VIOLARIS
Consultant Cardiologist

DATE OF BIRTH: 30.01.61
PLACE OF BIRTH: Father and Mother from Paphos.
MARITAL STATUS: Married
CHILDREN: Three daughters.
SCHOOLS/COLLEGE: Stationers, Sheffield University, ERASMUS University Rotterdam, Netherlands.
ACADEMIC QUALIFICATIONS: MB, ChB, MD, Phd, FRCP
MEMBERSHIPS: Fellow of the Royal College of Physicians of London. Member of the British Cardiac Society.
HOBBIES AND INTERESTS: Work and family.
PERSONAL PROFILE: Consultant Cardiologist at North West London Hospitals. Written several books. Works at St Marys Hospital, Paddington.

GLAFKOS P. VIOLARIS
Teacher

DATE OF BIRTH: 13.09.34
PLACE OF BIRTH: Mesana, Paphos.
MARITAL STATUS: Married to Maroulla A. Taliotou, a teacher, from Houlou, Paphos.
CHILDREN: Dr Antonios Violaris, Cardiologist; Miss Salome Violaris, BA Sociobiology-criminology; Dr Patroklos Violaris, Electronic Engineering Director of I.S.S (International Software Services Manchester); Ekaterine E A Kyriakou, Optometrist; Christodoulos Violaris, Optometrist.
SCHOOLS/COLLEGE: Greek Gymnasium of Limassol 1946-1952, Teacher Training College, Morphou, 1953-1955.
ACADEMIC QUALIFICATIONS: Teacher certificate, BA Honours Classical Greek.
PROFESSIONAL QUALIFICATIONS: Teacher from Primary to Secondary and Further Education.
MEMBERSHIPS: Folklore Society, England; Labour Party.
HONOURS/AWARDS: Notarios, Officio of Ecumenical Patriarchade.
HOBBIES AND INTERESTS: Folklore, history, journalism, reading, and writing books.
PERSONAL PROFILE: Teacher retired. Worked as primary teacher in Cyprus. Member of the First Cyprus Education Mission 1969-1972, teacher at Stationers Company School. Honorary President of Paphos Association in England. Secretary of St John the Baptist Greek Orthodox Church in Haringey.

MICHAEL CHRISTOS VOTSIS
Solicitor

DATE OF BIRTH: 24.03.51
PLACE OF BIRTH: London. Parents from Assia and Lefkara.
MARITAL STATUS: Married to Phaedra from London, (parents from Vavla And Kato Drys)
CHILDREN: Christos and Elina.
SCHOOLS/COLLEGE: Quintin St Johns Wood, Hull University, College of Law Guildford.
ACADEMIC QUALIFICATIONS: LLB (Honours).
HOBBIES AND INTERESTS: Football (Chelsea Supporter).
PERSONAL PROFILE: Solicitor. Formed own practice in 1975 called Michael Votsis & Co. In 1995 merged with Yanakas to form YVA Solicitors.

ANTONAKIS NIKOLAS VOUROU
School Governor, Former Secretary of EKEKA and Komi Kebir Association

DATE OF BIRTH: 05.05.55
PLACE OF BIRTH: London. Father from Rizokarpasso; Mother from Komi Kebir.
MARITAL STATUS: Married to Caroline, a Local Goverment Officer, from London.
CHILDREN: Panayiota and Nicolas.
SCHOOLS/COLLEGE: Wood Green School, Polytechnic of North London.
ACADEMIC QUALIFICATIONS: HND.
HOBBIES AND INTERESTS: Flying and travelling.
PERSONAL PROFILE: An Events Programmer and Co-ordinator. Governor of three schools. Involved with various charitable organisations. Former Secretary of Komi Kebir Association, and EKEKA Association.

Tel: 0044 (0) 7802266841
Email: tony@onestopcoordinations.com

ELIZABETH WHINCOP (née LOUKA)
Headteacher

DATE OF BIRTH: 23.02.56
PLACE OF BIRTH: London. Parents from Chirokitia.
MARITAL STATUS: Married to Simon, a Teacher, from England.
CHILDREN: Luke attends St Andrews Primary School in Southgate.
SCHOOLS/COLLEGE: Holy Trinity Primary School, Camden, Haverstock Secondary School, Camden.
ACADEMIC QUALIFICATIONS: 4 GCE A Levels: English Literature, Sociology, British Politics, Art. 8 GCE O Levels: 2 CSEs
PROFESSIONAL QUALIFICATIONS: Certificate of Education (Distinction), Bach. of Education, Advance Diploma in Education.
MEMBERSHIPS: Professional Association (NAHT).
HOBBIES AND INTERESTS: Art, photography, film, theatre, gardening and reading.
PERSONAL PROFILE: Having qualified as a teacher in 1978, travelled to Athens to work as an English Teacher for one year before beginning teaching career in Enfield in 1980. Worked as a primary school teacher at Bowes and Galliard Schools for seven years. Moved to Haringey to become an English Advisory teacher working in a range of schools across the borough. Was then involved in the Haringey Cypriot Workers Forum and the Minorities Book Project, which worked to produce dual language books for primary school children. Became a Deputy Headteacher in 1988 at Holy Trinity School in Hampstead. First Headteacher post was at Christ Church CE School in Regents Park for ten years before taking up current post as the Head of Walker Primary school in Southgate in London in January 2001.

Email: Lwhincop@hotmail.com

**ELIZABETH WHINCOP
(NEE LOUCA)
HEADTEACHER OF
WALKER PRIMARY SCHOOL
IN SOUTHGATE, LONDON**

RENOS EVRYVIADES WIDESON
Photographer

DATE OF BIRTH: 12.12.20
PLACE OF BIRTH: Larnaca.
MARITAL STATUS: Married to Mary (née Petrides), from Nicosia.
CHILDREN: Angelos, an Architect; Odysseus, a Civil Engineer.
SCHOOLS/COLLEGE: Pancyprian Commercial Lyceum, Larnaca.
HOBBIES AND INTERESTS: Photography, painting, woodwork, sailing, languages, in younger days. football, tennis, swimming and water skiing etc.
PERSONAL PROFILE: Civil Services, Cyprus 1937-1941. C.V.F. & Cyprus Regiment, attached to R.A.S.C 1941-1949. Major I/C Supplies Tourist Development Office, Cyprus 1949-1959. 1960-1977 BBC T.V retired as Head of Film Operations. Publications: Cyprus in Picture 1952, Portrait of Cyprus 1955, Cyprus, Images of a Lifetime 1992. Photographic Exhibitions: Nicosia, Larnaca, London, Copenhagen.

MONICA CONSTANTINOU WILLIAMS
Bookseller specialising on Greece and Cyprus

DATE OF BIRTH: 29.12.40
PLACE OF BIRTH: England, Parents from Limassol and Nicosia.
MARITAL STATUS: Married to Fred Williams, a Publisher.
CHILDREN: Alison Richards, a mother; Andrew Stoddart, works in the book shop.
SCHOOLS/COLLEGE: Paddington and Maida Vale Grammar School, City of London Business School.
PROFESSIONAL QUALIFICATIONS: Business Studies.
HOBBIES AND INTERESTS: Theatre, dance and travel.
PERSONAL PROFILE: Bookseller specialising on Greece and Cyprus, 36 years, every aspect, huge range of books.

**RENOS WIDESON
HEAD OF BBC FILM OPERATIONS
1960-1977**

DR CHRYSOULA KYPRIANOU-WORRALL
Psychologist/Psychoanalyst

DATE OF BIRTH: 01.10.39
PLACE OF BIRTH: Karavas.
MARITAL STATUS: Married to an Englishman, Dr Norman Worrall (divorced in 1980).
CHILDREN: Adrian, a Research Psychologist at the Royal College of Psychiatrists London; Alexis, a Multi-Media Artist.
ACADEMIC QUALIFICATIONS: B.A. (Honours), M.A., PhD.
PROFESSIONAL QUALIFICATIONS: Chartered Psychologist and Psychoanalyst.
MEMBERSHIPS: British Psychologist Society, UKCP-United Kingdom Council of Psychotherapy.
HOBBIES AND INTERESTS: Arts, travel, trekking and walking.
PERSONAL PROFILE: Worked as a Lecturer in Educational Psychology at Hertfordshire University where she developed several postgraduate programmes and degrees for the in-service training of teachers from U.K and abroad, including Greece and Cyprus. Works as a consultant in industry and undertakes training for organisations. Also works privately as a Counselling Psychologist and Psychoanalyst with adults and couples who experience personal and relationship difficulties.

LITSA WORRALL (officially PANTELITSA)
Company Secretary & Projects Manager for the Greek and Greek Cypriot Community of Enfield

DATE OF BIRTH: 10.08.55
PLACE OF BIRTH: Father from Larnaca; Mother from Achna.
MARITAL STATUS: Married to Martin Worrall, from England.
CHILDREN: Stephanie, still at school.
QUALIFICATIONS: City & Guilds NVQ level 1 & IIT NVQD32, D33, D34 Assessor and Verifier.
HOBBIES AND INTERESTS: Drama, local theatre, painting.
PERSONAL PROFILE: Helps Cypriots in Enfield with Rena Papadopoulos and Achilles Georgiou without funding and operating from their homes, offering services to those in need - now in its 9th year in existence. Set up to assist all the voluntary groups in the Borough. In this role Litsa was invited to attend a private luncheon reception with her Royal Majesty Queen Elizabeth II and Prince Phillip on the 6th June 2002

CLEO NICOLAIDOU-WRIGHT
Management Consultant and University Lecturer

DATE OF BIRTH: 28.01.62
PLACE OF BIRTH: Limassol
MARITAL STATUS: Married to Dr Jim Wright, a Director for Environmental Resources Management (ERM), a global environmental consultancy, a British National.
SCHOOLS/COLLEGE: 1st Gymnasium, Limassol, The American College in Athens, Greece, San Francisco State University, USA and Henley Management School, UK.
ACADEMIC QUALIFICATIONS: BA, MA, MBA, also a PRINCE 2 Project Management Practitioner.
MEMBERSHIPS: Membership of the Association of MBAs (AMBA); Referee for SYSTEM (Swedish Technology & Education Journal);
HOBBIES AND INTERESTS: Long distance running, cross-country cycling, travelling and playing bridge.
PERSONAL PROFILE: Worked in universities for twelve years as a Lecturer (Kuwait University), Senior Trainer (Exeter University,) and Operations Manager (University of Surrey). More recently has worked as a management consultant and interim manager mainly within the Public Sector in the UK.

GEORGE WRIGHT
Reporter

DATE OF BIRTH: 15.02.74
PLACE OF BIRTH: London. Grandparent from Famagusta.
MARITAL STATUS: Single
SCHOOLS/COLLEGE: Davenant Foundation School, Essex, Royal Holloway College, (London University).
ACADEMIC QUALIFICATIONS: A Levels, Degree in Classical Studies.
PROFESSIONAL QUALIFICATIONS: Journalism Diploma.
HOBBIES AND INTERESTS: Jazz and world music.
PERSONAL PROFILE: Reporter, London Evening Standard.

ALEXANDROS NICHOLAS XENOFONTOS
Composer, Musician

DATE OF BIRTH: 03.10.74
PLACE OF BIRTH: London. Father from Ayia Varvara (Lefkosia); Mother from Akanthou.
MARITAL STATUS: Single
SCHOOLS/COLLEGE: City Polytechnic, London Guildhall University, Newham Academy of Music.
ACADEMIC QUALIFICATIONS: 12 GCSE, OND Music Technology, 2:1 Honours Degree Music Technology.
MEMBERSHIPS: PRS/MCPS, PPL
HOBBIES AND INTERESTS: Sea fishing, shooting and athletics.
PERSONAL PROFILE: Composer, musician. Set up own record label, *Feelgood Records* 2000, releasing primarily his own Dance Music, debut release *I Can Make You* having commercial radio play on Capital Radio (London), Radio 1, Kiss100, Choice etc. Has also written music for American producer, ten part documentary about the middle east, wrote theme and other music for Hollywood Film *My Big Fat Greek Wedding*

Details: info@feelgoodrecords.co.uk
Tel: 07956 404832

ELEFTHERIA A XENOPHONTOS
Chairwoman of Neo Chorio Committee UK

DATE OF BIRTH: 15.2.56
PLACE OF BIRTH: Neo Chorio, Phaphos.
MARITAL STATUS: Married to Andreas Xenophontos, owns and runs fish restaurant, from Nicosia.
CHILDREN: Xenia, studying for a Masters in History of Art.
SCHOOLS/COLLEGE: Primary & secondary in Cyprus. Paddington College, North London College, Stanmore College, Greek Educational Institute of GB, Open University.
ACADEMIC QUALIFICATIONS: HND Business Studies, NNEB Child Nursery Education, Course in 'Children with Special Needs', Diploma in teaching Greek as a foreign language, BA (Honours).
MEMBERSHIPS: Royal Academy of Art, Tate Gallery, Fitness First Health Club.
HOBBIES AND INTERESTS: Visiting museums and galleries, drama, theatre, music, reading and sports such as badminton and swimming.
PERSONAL PROFILE: In the Neo Chorio committee since 1993, when it was first formed. Elected Chair in 1995. The Association has already funded the opening of a health care clinic for the elderly and are now opening an old peoples' home for the residents of Neo Chorio.

ALEXANDROS NICHOLAS XENOFONTOS WROTE THE THEME MUSIC FOR THE FILM 'MY BIG FAT GREEK WEDDING'

NICOS YENIAS
Chairman of Marathovouno Association

DATE OF BIRTH: 10.03.48
PLACE OF BIRTH: Marathovounos.
MARITAL STATUS: Married to Agapi, from Kaimakli.
CHILDREN: Olga, lives in Russia.
SCHOOLS/COLLEGE: Marathovouno Elementary, Lykeion Famagusta.
MEMBERSHIPS: AKEL.
HOBBIES AND INTERESTS: Sports and politics.
PERSONAL PROFILE: Car Mechanic/Panel Beater. Went to Moscow 1971-1973 studying Social Science. Went back to Cyprus 1973 then to England 1975. Chairman of Marathovouno Association, member of Secretariat AKEL UK. Member of EKO and National Federation of Cypriots.

ANTONAKIS YEROLEMOU
Businessman

DATE OF BIRTH: 13.07.42
PLACE OF BIRTH: Komi Kebir.
MARITAL STATUS: Married to Barbara.
MEMBERSHIPS: Leukaemia Research fund, Macmillan Nurses, Greek Cypriot Brotherhood, Estia of London Komi Kebir Association.
HOBBIES AND INTERESTS: Music, reading and travelling.
PERSONAL PROFILE: Joined family business Katsouris Bros in 1964. Responsible for transforming Katsouris Bros from importer for the Cypriot community into one of the most successful specialist importers of Cypriot and Greek products in the UK. This success was due to the creation of the Cypressa brand. Together with his family in 1976 he opened the first Wine & Mousaka restaurant. Its success was instant and two more were to follow. Following his success with the restaurants together with his family he opened Katsouris Fresh Foods Ltd in 1982 to serve as a central kitchen for the restaurants. Today Katsouris Fresh Foods Ltd employs more than 1600 people and they are one of the most successful independent chilled food manufacturers in the UK. Its client base includes Marks and Spencer, J Sainsbury, Waitrose, Tesco, Somerfields and Morrisons. Katsouris Fresh Foods Ltd also exports its products to French Multiples. In 1988 he formed Filo Pastry Ltd, the biggest and most successful Filo producing company in the UK, supplying Filo pastry to the major supermarkets and manufacturers.
Early in 1993, together with his family he took control of Sahib Foods Ltd with a workforce of 180. Sahib Foods Ltd supplies ethnic chilled foods to the Multiples Antonaki is also a member of the Greek Orthodox Archbishop Trust, the Hellenic Centre, founder member of the Cyprus British Chamber of Commerce. Through his group of companies he supports a number of charities, including The Royal Opera Trust.
Recently in 2002, Katsouris Fresh Foods merged with Bakkavor Group a Public Company in Iceland. Antonaki is also on the board of Lanitis Development Group.

MILTOS YEROLEMOU
Actor

DATE OF BIRTH: 24.01.68
PLACE OF BIRTH: London. Parents from Ayios Theodoros, Larnaca.
MARITAL STATUS: Single
SCHOOLS/COLLEGE: Eastbourne Sixth Form College, De Montfort University, Leicester.
ACADEMIC QUALIFICATIONS: A Levels: Law, English, Politics, Economics, Performing Arts (Drama); BA Honours degree.
MEMBERSHIPS: Equity, Screenwriters Guild.
HONOURS/AWARDS: 1985, Eastbourne Herald Award for Best Actor *Nicely Nicely Johnson, Guys and Dolls.* 1986, Eastbourne Herald Award for Best Actor in Bottom In, *Midsummer Nights Dream* 1996, Manchester Evening Standard Nomination for Supporting Actor in *Animal Crackers.*
PERSONAL PROFILE: Actor/Director. Founder member/performer in Might and Main Theatre Company 1991-1996, Royal Shakespeare Theatre 1998-2000, National Theatre, The Ramayana 2001, Puck in *Midsummer Nights Dream English Opera* 1997-1998, Mikey in BBC TV Comedy Hubbub 1996-2001.

GEORGE YEROSIMOU
Assistant Headteacher

DATE OF BIRTH: 21.08.55
PLACE OF BIRTH: London. Grandparents from Akanthou.
MARITAL STATUS: Married to Loulla, from London (father from Akanthou, mother from Mandres).
CHILDREN: Michael, Recruitment Consultant; Elizabeth, Nursery Nurse; Matthew, at school.
SCHOOLS/COLLEGE: St Clement Danes Grammar School, London W12, Borough Road College, University of London, The Open University, The Institute of Education.

QUALIFICATIONS: BA, MA, NPQH, Cert Ed.

MEMBERSHIPS: Naht-National Association of Head Teachers.

PERSONAL PROFILE: Currently a Deputy Headteacher at a comprehensive school in Epping, but aspiring to Headteacher. Class I Football Referee. Has refereed in KOPA for 20 years and has officiated four finals including two Challenge Cup Finals. Formerly played for DOEK, Atlas & Cosmos. Chairman/School Co-ordinator of Caterham Greek School for ten years. Chairman/Secretary of Redbridge Greek Community Association since 1997.

Email: Deputy@St-Johns-eppingessex.sch.uk

GEORGE YIACOUMIS
Honorary President of Cypriot ESTIA Birmingham

DATE OF BIRTH: 28.07.47
PLACE OF BIRTH: Vatili.
MARITAL STATUS: Married to Maria, from Kato Drys.
CHILDREN: Helen, Katerina and Mariana.
SCHOOLS/COLLEGE: Handsworth College.
HOBBIES AND INTERESTS: Football and tennis.
PERSONAL PROFILE: Owner of a small chain of Fish Restaurants. Honorary President of ESTIA. Past President for many years. Member of Executive Committee of the National Federation of Cypriots. Vice President of the Greek Orthodox Communities in the UK.

HELEN GEORGE YIACOUMIS
Solicitor

DATE OF BIRTH: 06.06.73
PLACE OF BIRTH: Birmingham. Father from Vatili; Mother from Kato Drys.
MARITAL STATUS: Single
SCHOOLS/COLLEGE: Edgbaston High School for Girls, Birmingham, Kings College, London 1991-1995, College of Law, London, 1995-1997.

ACADEMIC QUALIFICATIONS: BA combined Honours Hispanic Studies, Modern Greek & Byzantine Studies (1st Class).

PROFESSIONAL QUALIFICATIONS: C.P.E. Diploma in Law (Commendation), Legal Practice Course, Solicitor, trained and qualified at City Shipping Firm Holman Fenwick Willan.

MEMBERSHIPS: Anglo-Cypriot Lawyers Association.

HOBBIES AND INTERESTS: Fitness, an RSA, qualified instructor.

PERSONAL PROFILE: Now works in commercial litigation and dispute resolution at Birmingham Office of Hammond Suddards Edge (top 10 firm). Was Secretary of West Midlands British Cypriot Youth Committee and a representative of British Cypriot Youth at Biannual International Conference for overseas Cypriots.

PANAYIOTIS YIACOUMI
Chairman of the Greek Parents Association

DATE OF BIRTH: 02.02.52
PLACE OF BIRTH: Gypsou.
MARITAL STATUS: Married to Yianoulla, (parents from Ayios Amvrossio and Prodromi).
CHILDREN: Eva, Kynakos and Lia.
SCHOOLS/COLLEGE: Gypsou Primary, Centre of Higher Studies in Famagusta, Harrow College of Further Eduacation, City University, Open University.

ACADEMIC QUALIFICATIONS: 9 O Levels, 4 A Levels, Honours degree in Economics & Political Science.

HOBBIES AND INTERESTS: Family, reading, politics, history, music, travel and sports.

PERSONAL PROFILE: General Secretary of Gypsos Association. Member and Chairman of Greek Parents Association. Magistrate in the Middlesex commission area, adjudicating at Uxbridge Magistrates Court and Isleworth Crown Court.

ANTONIS YIAKOUMI
Former Chairman of the Greek Parents Association and General Manager of Parikiaki newspaper

DATE OF BIRTH: 7.8.24
PLACE OF BIRTH: Vasilli Leonarisso.
MARITAL STATUS: Married to Maria Tsioupra from Komi Kebir.
CHILDREN: Michael, Editor of Greek Cypriots in the UK; Doulla, Chairwoman of Bowes Greek School; Louis, Editor of a motor car magazine.
SCHOOLS/COLLEGE: Elementary School Vasilli.
MEMBERSHIPS: AKEL.
HONOURS/AWARDS: Honoured for 50 years service to AKEL.
HOBBIES AND INTERESTS: Reading, politics and football.
PERSONAL PROFILE: Shoemaker in Famagusta. Served in British Army 1943-45. Came to UK in 1952. Was a restaurant owner then manager of *Parikiaki* newspaper from 1977 to 1990. Ex-Chairman of the Greek Parents Association and in the Secretariat of AKEL UK for several years.

MICHAEL YIAKOUMI

Co Editor of the book *Greek Cypriots in the UK*

DATE OF BIRTH: 08.08.55
PLACE OF BIRTH: London. Father, Antonis, from Vasilli, Leonarisso; Mother, Maria (née Tsioupra) from Komi Kebir.
MARITAL STATUS: Divorced
CHILDREN: Maria, studying Philosophy at University of Herts and Dimitri, at school.
SCHOOLS/COLLEGE: Ambler Primary, Holloway Secondary and Tottenham College.
QUALIFICATIONS: 9 O Levels and 1 A Level.
MEMBERSHIPS: Komi Kebir Association.
HOBBIES AND INTERESTS: Football and travelling.
PERSONAL PROFILE: Co Editor of the book *Greek Cypriots in the UK*. From college he worked in a L'Loyd's insurance underwriting syndicate, then for the advertising section of the *Parikiaki* newspaper.
He has also owned a Ladieswear business, manufacturing, wholesale and retail. Was a Co founder of PAOK and Komi Kebir football club that play in the Cypriot League in the UK and active member of the Komi Kebir Association.
He was a member of the Parent Teachers Associations at Southgate Greek School and Trent Primary School in Barnet.

SOFRONIOS YIAKOUMI

Active Committee Member of the Hellenic Brotherhood of Manchester

DATE OF BIRTH: 09.06.59
PLACE OF BIRTH: Peristeronopygi, Famagusta.
MARITAL STATUS: Married to Katia (Koumbari) from Limnia, Famagusta.
CHILDREN: Jacovos, George, Panayiotis and Sotiris.
SCHOOLS/COLLEGE: Piyi Primary School, Lefkoniko High School, North Trafford College, Manchester.
ACADEMIC QUALIFCATIONS: GCSE O Levels, Ordinary National Diploma Business Studies.
PERSONAL PROFILE: Caterer (Self Employed). Active Committee Member of The Hellenic Brotherhood of Manchester. Member of The Church Wardens Committee of The Greek Orthodox Church of The Annunciation of The Mother of God, 1998-1999 Secretary to the Church Wardens).

Address: 19 Torkington Rd, Gatley, Cheadle, Cheshire SK8 4PR.

CONSTANTINOS YIANGOU

Consultant in General Surgery and Surgical Oncology

DATE OF BIRTH: 28.08.61
PLACE OF BIRTH: Nicosia.
MARITAL STATUS: Single
SCHOOLS/COLLEGE: Pancyprian Gymnasium, Nicosia, St Mary's Hospital Medical School, University of London.
QUALIFICATIONS: BSC (Honours), MB, BS (Honours) FRCS, FRCS (Gen Surg).
MEMBERSHIPS: Fellow of the Royal College of Surgeons of England, The British Medical Association, The British Association of Surgical Oncology, The Association of Breast Surgery at Baso.
HONOURS/AWARDS: Norman Plummer Memorial Prize Award by Charing Cross Hospital in March 1995. Ronald Payen Prize awarded by the British Association of Surgical Oncology in November 1995.
HOBBIES AND INTERESTS: Music, motor racing and the history of Cyprus in the 20th Century.
PERSONAL PROFILE: Consultant at Queen Alexandra & Bupa Hospitals Portsmouth. Honorary Senior Lecturer Academic Department & Surgery, Ports-mouth Uni. On The General Medical Council's specialist Register since 1999. Sub-specialisation: Breast & Endocrine Surgery. Research Interests: Diagnosis & Treatment of Breast & Thyroid Cancers. Named in the list of leading experts in the field of Breast Cancer, by *The Times* and Dr Foster.

YIANNAKIS YIANNA
President of Greek Orthodox Church of St Panteleimon Harrow

DATE OF BIRTH: 12.11.45
PLACE OF BIRTH: Tricomo, Famagusta.
MARITAL STATUS: Married to Militsa, a Housewife, from Nicosia.
CHILDREN: Marina, Bank worker; Peter, Police officer; Christakis, Bank worker.
SCHOOLS/COLLEGE: Commercial Gymnasium, Tricomo.
PROFESSIONAL QUALIFICATIONS: Dress Manufacturer.
HOBBIES AND INTERESTS: Gardening.
PERSONAL PROFILE: President of Greek Orthodox Church of Saint Panteleimon Wembley, Harrow & District.

CHRISTOPHER YIANNAKAS
Solicitor

DATE OF BIRTH: 30.04.63
PLACE OF BIRTH: London. Parents from Larnaca District.
MARITAL STATUS: Married to Xenia.
SCHOOLS/COLLEGE: Friern Barnet Grammar, Highgate School, Middlesex University.
ACADEMIC QUALIFICATIONS: 12 O Levels, 3 A Levels, LLB Honours Law.
PROFESSIONAL QUALIFICATIONS: Solicitor.
MEMBERSHIPS: Law Society and Solicitors Family Law Association.
HONOURS/AWARDS: Accredited Family Law Specialist with Solicitors Family Law Association, Law Society Family Law Board.
HOBBIES AND INTERESTS: Football, squash, world war II history.
PERSONAL PROFILE: Advises at CABs. Regularly advises on LGR and Spectrum Radio regarding legal problems.

Father ANASTASIOS YIANNI
Priest

DATE OF BIRTH: 14.12.29
PLACE OF BIRTH: Troullous, Larnaca.
MARITAL STATUS: Married to Angela Papathemestocli, from Limassol.
CHILDREN: One daughter.
SCHOOLS/COLLEGE: Troullous Elementary, Cotwins College, London.
HOBBIES AND INTERESTS: Reading.
PERSONAL PROFILE: Father Anastasios is the Priest at the Gospel Oak Greek Orthodox Church.

LEON YIANNI
Actor

DATE OF BIRTH: 15.01.65
PLACE OF BIRTH: London. Father from Arsos; Mother from Limassol.
MARITAL STATUS: Single
SCHOOLS/COLLEGE: Islington Green School, Drama Centre.
ACADEMIC QUALIFICATIONS: Diploma in Acting.
MEMBERSHIPS: Member of Green Peace and Amnesty International.
HOBBIES AND INTERESTS: Reading and gardening.
PERSONAL PROFILE: Actor appeared on TV in *The Bill* and *October*. Stage: *A Song at Twilight, The Kitchen*.

ANDREAS YIANNIS
Treasurer for the Cypriot Association Brent

DATE OF BIRTH: 5.08.59
PLACE OF BIRTH: London. Father from Vathylakas; Mother from Kornos.
MARITAL STATUS: Single
SCHOOLS/COLLEGE: Kingsbury High School, Kilburn Polytechnic, City & East London College.
QUALIFICATIONS: 6 O Levels, 1 A Level Institute of Bankers Conversion Course.
HOBBIES AND INTERESTS: Season ticket holder Watford football club.
PERSONAL PROFILE: Worldwide travel on a regualr basis. Committee member of Cypriot Association of Brent and Harrow. Manager funding for The Australia & New Zealand Banking Group Ltd in London - with them for 24 years. Voluntary Helper and Treasurer for The Cypriot Association of Brent and Harrow to maintain the Saturday Kingsbury Greek School and Thursday Youth Club. Regularly involved in fundraising activies

MARIA YIANNIKARIS (née NICOLAIDES)
Bridal Designer

DATE OF BIRTH: 15.10.57
PLACE OF BIRTH: London. Parents from Yerolakos.
MARITAL STATUS: Married to Simeos Dimitrios Yiannikaris, a London Taxi Driver.
CHILDREN: Andrea Simeos, Natassa Georgina.
SCHOOLS/COLLEGE: Alexandra Park School, London College of Fashion
QUALIFICATIONS: 11 GCSEs, City & Guilds College Diploma.
HONOURS/AWARDS: Three times winner of British Bridal Designer Awards.
HOBBIES AND INTERESTS: Travel, reading, writing, cinema and film.
PERSONAL PROFILE: Professional Designer for 23 years, past thirteen years as Mirror Mirror Award Winning Bridal Designer. Celebrity clientele include Zoe Ball, Amanda Holden, Caroline Quentin. Helps husband who is a committee member of London Taxi Drivers Fund for Under-privileged Children. Designed wedding dress for Kym Marsh from *Hear'Say*, who married Jack Ryder from *Eastenders*.

SIMEOS DIMITRIOS YIANNIKARIS
London Black Cab Driver

DATE OF BIRTH: 19.04.62
PLACE OF BIRTH: London. Parents from Limassol.
MARITAL STATUS: Married to Maria Nicolaides, Bridal Designer Mirror Mirror, from London.
CHILDREN: Andreas Simeos, Natassa Georgina.
SCHOOLS/COLLEGE: Southgate College.
ACADEMIC QUALIFICAIONS: 10 GCSEs.
PROFESSIONAL QUALIFICATIONS: City & Guilds.
MEMBERSHIPS: Committee member of The London Taxi Drivers Fund for Under-privileged Children.
HONOURS/AWARDS: Probably the 1st Greek Cypriot to take part in the Lord Mayors Show, Representing the Charity. Attended the Queen's garden party in 2004 for children's charity work.
HOBBIES AND INTERESTS: Reading, travel, sci-fi film, and the charity work.
PERSONAL PROFILE: London Black Cab Driver.

PAUL YIANNAKAS
Solicitor

DATE OF BIRTH: 12.01.37
PLACE OF BIRTH: Kilani, Limassol.
MARITAL STATUS: Married to Maria from London, parents from Lefkara.
CHILDREN: Chris, Solicitor, Katerina, Housewife.
SCHOOLS/COLLEGE: Limassol Gymnasium, Bradford College, Law Society School.
HOBBIES AND INTERESTS: Football, Byzantine music church chanter.
PERSONAL PROFILE: Solicitor at one of the first practices in the Cypriot community. Former Chairman and Secretary of the Cypriot Football League in London. Served the Football League for 26 years. Acting Chairman and treasurer of School of Byzantine music. Chairman of Kilani Association. Trustee and Committee member of Holy Cross of St Michael in the Goldens Green Church. Chairman of Islington Cypriot Community Centre.

ANDREAS YIASOUMI
President of Hellenic Brotherhood in Manchester

DATE OF BIRTH: 12.06.47
PLACE OF BIRTH: Peristeronopiyi, Famagusta
MARITAL STATUS: Married to Elene Photiou from Peristeronopiyi
CHILDREN: Costas Yiasoumi, actuary; Thomas, Chartered Accountant; Panayiotis, Banker, Kiki, at University of Manchester
SCHOOLS/COLLEGE: Grammar School of Lefkonico, Famagusta
MEMBERSHIPS: Hellenic Brotherhood Manchester
HOBBIES AND INTERESTS: Gardening, Football, Game Shooting
PERSONAL PROFILE: President of Hellenic Brotherhood for 8 years. Also a trustee. Restaurant Owner and Property Developer.

GEORGE YIASOUMI
Actor

DATE OF BIRTH: 19.04.59
PLACE OF BIRTH: London, parents from Achna, Famagusta
MARITAL STATUS: Married
SCHOOLS/COLLEGE: Local Comprehensive, E.15 Acting School
HOBBIES AND INTERESTS: Photography
PERSONAL PROFILE: Actor. Appeared in films such as Swept Away, The Man Who Cried, The Borrowers, Greystoke, TV. Sam Game, Lock Stock, Indiana Jones Chronicles, The Bill and others. Theatre: Vanitas Splendide and others. TV commercials: Daewoo, Pizza Hut, Nike, Twix and others.

OURANIOS ANDREAS YIASOUMIS
Businessman

DATE OF BIRTH: 12.03.61
PLACE OF BIRTH: Nicosia
MARITAL STATUS: Married to Dali from Russia
CHILDREN: Marios and Nicholas
SCHOOLS/COLLEGE: University of Westminster
ACADEMIC QUALIFICATIONS: BSc Computer Science
HOBBIES AND INTERESTS: Football, supports Liverpool but has a box at Tottenham.
PERSONAL PROFILE: Owner of Higrade Computers, manufacturers of PCs in Barking, Essex. Turnover 53 million pounds, employs over 200 people.

GEORGE ZACHARIA
Businessman

DATE OF BIRTH: 10.12.47
PLACE OF BIRTH: Eptakomi.
MARITAL STATUS: Married to Julie, from Vokolida.
CHILDREN: Peter, Chrysanthos, Andreas and Pamela.
SCHOOLS/COLLEGE: William Collins School.
HOBBIES AND INTERESTS: Travelling.
PERSONAL PROFILE: George opened the Venus Restaurant in Bethnal Green in 1976, it became one of the Top Restaurants in the East End, famous clientele include Martine McCutcheon and David Beckham.

GREGORY ZACHARIA
Former Chairman, Cypriot Estia Birmingham

DATE OF BIRTH: 10.10.43
PLACE OF BIRTH: Aradippou.
MARITAL STATUS: Married to Maritsa, from Aradippou.
CHILDREN: Three sons, two daughters.
HOBBIES AND INTERESTS: Traditional music and pillotta
PERSONAL PROFILE: Owns a Fish and Chip Shop business. Chairman of Cypriot Estia for two years and a member. Chairman of St Triada Greek School in Birmingham. Member of the Secretariat of the National Federation of Cypriots in the UK. Representative of the Aradippou Association in the Midlands. DYSY representative of the Midlands and Member of the local Education Authority in Staffordshire.

JULIE ZACHARIA
Author *Traditional Greek Cooking from Cyprus and Beyond*

DATE OF BIRTH: 06.12.47
PLACE OF BIRTH: Vokolida, Famagusta.
MARITAL STATUS: Married to George, from Eptakomi.
CHILDREN: Peter Chrysanthos, Andreas and Pamela.
HOBBIES AND INTERESTS: Cooking and swimming.
PERSONAL PROFILE: Julie is a Housewife but wrote the book *Traditional Greek Cooking from Cyprus and Beyond.*

TASOS ZACHARIADES
Journalist

DATE OF BIRTH: 06.05.45
PLACE OF BIRTH: Morphou
MARITAL STATUS: Married to Sophia, Famagusta.
SCHOOLS/COLLEGE: Cyprus Secondary School, College of Journalism, London.
MEMBERSHIPS: National Union Of Journalists, served as President of Enosis Apodimon Morphou.
HOBBIES AND INTERESTS: Theatre, reading and travel.
PERSONAL PROFILE: Journalist, News Editor London Greek Radio, London Correspondent Cyprus Weekly Newspaper.

CHRISTOS ZAVROS
Journalist & Writer

DATE OF BIRTH: 01.04.25
PLACE OF BIRTH: Tseri, Nicosia.
MARITAL STATUS: Married to Maria, a Housewife, from Cyprus.
CHILDREN: Nicos, a Shoe Machinist; Erini, works for Bank Of Cyprus; Lakis, owner of a Computer Company in Australia; Helen, a Nursery Teacher.
SCHOOLS/COLLEGE: School in Tseri, Nicosia.
PROFESSIONAL QUALIFICATIONS: Journalist.
MEMBERSHIPS: AKEL, EKA, LELA.
HONOURS/AWARDS: From AKEL 50 years membership, from Trade Union of Printers in Cyprus, 40 years membership from National Federation of Cypriots in Britain and from LELA.
HOBBIES AND INTERESTS: Politics.
PERSONAL PROFILE: Journalist with *Parikiaki* newspaper. Has written seven books. Former Secretary of AKEL UK.

AFXENDIS DEMETRI ZEMENIDES
Chartered Engineer

DATE OF BIRTH: 26.02.30
PLACE OF BIRTH: Komi Kebir.
MARITAL STATUS: Married to Josephine, a retired Personnel Manager, born in London.
CHILDREN: Deborah Anna Jane and Christopher Adam, both Practising Solicitors.
SCHOOLS/COLLEGE: Northampton Engineering College (now City University).
ACADEMIC QUALIFICATIONS: B.Sc (Engineering).
PROFESSIONAL QUALIFICATIONS: Chartered Engineer, Fellow of the Institution of Electrical Engineers.
HOBBIES AND INTERESTS: Travel, family and photography.
PERSONAL PROFILE: Graduate Apprenticeship with GEC Ltd, Coventry. Three years importing and exporting electronic components. Sealectro Ltd 1961-1990, started as General Manager and became Director (1963), Managing Director (1980-1990). Started Portsmouth Engineering Training Association (now PETA Ltd) in 1969 and served as Governor for some years for Highbury Technical College (Portsmouth), then Portsmouth Polytechnic till retirement in 1990. Trustee for New Theatre Royal, Portsmouth for last six years.

DEMETRIOS COSTA ZEMENIDES
Accountant

DATE OF BIRTH: 08.06.51
PLACE OF BIRTH: Nicosia, but lived in Komi Kebir. Parents born and lived in Komi Kebir.
MARITAL STATUS: Married to Lenia (the daughter of Michael D Christodoulides from the well known family of educationalists that came out of Oikos, Marathasa). Lenia studied Industrial Chemistry and also holds degrees in History and European Humanities.
CHILDREN: Sophie, who is a Medical Student at University College, London and holds an honours degree in Tumour Biology; Michael, who is a Medical Student at University College London and is currently completing his honours degree in Immunology.
SCHOOLS/COLLEGE: Komi Kebir Elementary School, Famagusta Technical School, London School of Accountancy.
PROFESSIONAL QUALIFIATIONS: Fellow Chartered Certified Accountant, IDC Staff Instructor (Professional Association of Diving Instructors).
HOBBIES AND INTERESTS: Travel, poetry, painting, shooting and scuba diving.

PERSONAL PROFILE: Completed Accountancy Exams in record time of two and half years whilst working at Goodman Lawrence & Co where he became a partner and, ultimately took over as the managing partner. Holds several Directorships in the UK and Cyprus.

PANICOS ZEMENIDES
Accountant/Chairman of Komi Kebir Association

DATE OF BIRTH: 04.04.59
PLACE OF BIRTH: Komi Kebir.
MARITAL STATUS: Married to Helen an Accountant, (father from Kalopsida, mother from Rizokarpasso).
CHILDREN: Andrea and Angela.
SCHOOLS/COLLEGE: St Davids and St Katherine School, Hornsey; University of North London, London School of Accountancy.
PROFESSIONAL QUALIFICATIONS: Chartered Certified Accountant.
HOBBIES AND INTERESTS: Squash and reading
PERSONAL PROFILE: An Accountant - worked in practice for 18 years. Now has own practice OMG Chartered Certified Accountants based in Woodford London E18. Chairman of Komi Kebir Association for last six years. On parents committee of Finchley Greek School for five years, Treasurer for two years, Vice Chairman for two years.

Address: 111A George Lane, London E18 1AN
Tel: 020 8530 6765

**PANAYIOTIS ZENIOU,
BRITISH DECATHLON
CHAMPION, EUROPEAN
BRONZE MEDALLIST &
CAPTAIN OF GREAT BRITAIN
EUROPEAN CUP 1977**

ANTHONY ZENIOS
Director CIL International Ltd

DATE OF BIRTH: 11.10.42
PLACE OF BIRTH: London. Father born in Kontea.
MARITAL STATUS: Married to Ray Rachel Zenios, born Alexandria, Eygpt, Independent Financial Advisor.
CHILDREN: Jonathan David Zenios, MD at Barclay Capital; Natailie Desiree Zenios, Housewife. (Both children are qualified Chartered Accountants).
SCHOOLS/COLLEGE: Ambler Primary 1950-1954, William Ellis 1954-1961, London School of Economics 1961-1964.
ACADEMIC QUALIFICATIONS: BSc (Econs).
MEMBERSHIPS: British Philatelic Federation, Jaguar Drivers Club.
HOBBIES AND INTERESTS: Bridge, philately, wine, football, food, literature and music.
PERSONAL PROFILE: Company Director, City Industrial Ltd, CIL International Ltd, CIL involved in major charitable works via The Morris Charitable Trust.

PANAYIODA N. ZENIOU
Poet

DATE OF BIRTH: 23.01.39
PLACE OF BIRTH: Kato Dicomo Kyrenia.
MARITAL STATUS: Married to Nicholas K. Zeniou, a Supervisor in a building business, from Kato Dicomo.
CHILDREN: Andreas, Kyprianos, Elli N. Zeniou all finished college and university and are in full time employment.
MEMBERSHIPS: An active member of (LELA) Laiki Enosi Logotechnon Anglias. Presenting some of their plays in a poetic way, as well as participating, as part of the cast. A member of Academy Club.
HOBBIES AND INTERESTS: Poetic Culture, Greek Civilisation.
PERSONAL PROFILE: Has produced a first book of poetry called *Xerizomeni Lemonia* which has been approved by the Cyprus Department of Education. While this book mainly deals with the Cyprus Tragedy of 1974, Panayioda is currently working on compiling other material, for a second Anthology.

Address: 80 Sydney Rd, London N8 OEX
Tel: 020 8341 1873

DR GEORGE M. ZINTILIS
Chartered Civil & Mechanical Engineer

DATE OF BIRTH: 28.09.52
PLACE OF BIRTH: Nicosia
MARITAL STATUS: Married to Jennifer, Australian, a Company Director and Administrator.
CHILDREN: Andonella.
SCHOOLS/COLLEGE: Pancyprian Gymnasium Nicosia, University College, London.
ACADEMIC QUALIFICATIONS: BSc (Eng) Honours, PhD.
PROFESSIONAL QUALIFICATIONS: Chartered Civil & Mechanical Engineer.
MEMBERSHIPS: MICE, MIMeehe, FEANI, ETEK (Cyprus), American Academy of Forensic Sciences, Expert Witness Institute, Society of Expert Witnesses.
HOBBIES AND INTERESTS: Reading, history, astronomy, films and driving.
PERSONAL PROFILE: Consulting Engineer, worked in Hong Kong, Australia and UK. Set up his own consulting firm (ZACE) in 1993. Part-time University Lecturer. Delivers short specialist courses for Architects and Engineers. Published articles and technical papers overseas.

PANAYIOTIS ZENIOU
British Decathlon Champion

DATE OF BIRTH: 07.02.53
PLACE OF BIRTH: Ormithia, Larnaca.
MARITAL STATUS: Married
CHILDREN: Mixed race children. His son's (Adam) Godfather is Daley Thomson.
SCHOOLS/COLLEGE: Archway Secondary, Kings Way F.E, North London University.
ACADEMIC QUALIFICATIONS: Certificate in Education.
PROFESSIONAL QUALIFICATIONS: Sports Coaching Qualification in ten sports.
MEMBERSHIPS: Life Member of NL Athletes Club
HONOURS/AWARDS: Islington Sportsman of the Year.
HOBBIES AND INTERESTS: My children.
PERSONAL PROFILE: Lecturer at the College of N.E London.
Great Britain Junior International, 1972, Great Britain Senior International, 1984. Vets International 1993-1996 European Bronze medallist (Decathlon). Captain of Great Britain European Cup 1977. British International in two sports, decathlon and bobsleigh.
Competed for Cyprus 1978 & 1982 Commonwealth Games. Held record for GB appearances in Decathlon (25). British Decathlon Champion 1975,1977, second on three occasions. Competed for Great Britain from 1972-1996 provided the Athletics Tournament for EKON.

ANDREAS MICHAEL ZISSIMOS
Scientist/Lecturer

DATE OF BIRTH: 08.09.72
PLACE OF BIRTH: Famagusta, Kato Varosi.
MARITAL STATUS: Married to Andry Antoniou, an Advertising Executive with One2One, second generation Cypriot from Kormakiti.
SCHOOLS/COLLEGE: Kykkos Lyceum, Cyprus, University of North London.
ACADEMIC QUALIFICATIONS: PhD Chemistry, BSc (Hons) First, Certificate of Secondary.
MEMBERSHIPS: Royal Society of Chemistry.
HOBBIES AND INTERESTS: Keen sportsman, likes writing and continental cinematographer.
PERSONAL PROFILE: Since Feb 2000, a Research Fellow at University College, London; 1996-1999, Visiting Lecturer, University Of North London. Dedicated Scientist currently working in drug discovery and development in collaboration with various pharmaceutical companies. Has published various scientific articles in well respected scientific journals. Active within the community since student years, has been involved in the Cypriot Student Movement and has participated in various youth festivals around the world and represented Cyprus in various meetings (Commonwealth Youth Meeting Manchester 1997, youth and student festival in Cuba 1996). Still active in the Cypriot community (member of forum for Friendship and Episteme) and regularly publishes articles in community press.

CHRIS VAKIS ZISSIMOS
Councillor

DATE OF BIRTH: 1922
PLACE OF BIRTH: Famagusta.
MARITAL STATUS: Married
CHILDREN: One son, a Reseacher at university.
SCHOOLS/COLLEGE: Famagusta Elementary and Gymnasium, University of London, studied Economics.
HOBBIES AND INTERESTS: Reading.
PERSONAL PROFILE: Was a Teacher. Has worked alot with the community. Councillor with Haringey Council for 20 years. Created the Islington Advice Centre for Cypriots.

A. K. ZIVANARIS
Businessman

DATE OF BIRTH: 01.03.42
PLACE OF BIRTH: Lefkara.
MARITAL STATUS: Married.
CHILDREN: Theano, Businesswoman.
SCHOOLS/COLLEGE: University of Hull.
ACADEMIC QUALIFICATIONS: B.Sc (Econ) Honours.
MEMBERSHIPS: Institute of Directors, CBI.
HOBBIES AND INTERESTS: Music, reading and sport.
PERSONAL PROFILE: Chairman and Managing Director of Lincoln Group. Member of Variety Club of Great Britain. Was a Director of Middlesborough FC in the 1980s.

MICHAEL P ZOGRAPHOS
Former Chairman of St Catherines Greek Orthodox Church of Barnet

DATE OF BIRTH: 1936
PLACE OF BIRTH: Assia.
MARITAL STATUS: Married to Chloe, from Moutoullas.
CHILDREN: Christina and Maria.
SCHOOLS/COLLEGE: Samuel Commercial School, Nicosia.
HOBBIES AND INTERESTS: Reading and travelling.
PERSONAL PROFILE: Worked for Zeno Booksellers from 1962 then bought it in 1966 and kept it until 1997, when he retired. During these times his main purpose was to promote books about Greece and Cyprus all over the world. A founder member of Assia Association UK. He was secretary for eight years and Chairman for four. Also served as Chairman of St Catherine Greek Orthodox Church of Barnet.

Address: 50 Westbury Road, London, N12 7DP

ALEX ZORBAS
Actor

DATE OF BIRTH: 16.10.73
PLACE OF BIRTH: London. Father from Limassol; Mother from Lefkada, Greece.
MARITAL STATUS: Single
SCHOOLS/COLLEGE: Mountview Theatre School.
HOBBIES AND INTERESTS: Music, Greek dancing, croupier, painting, football, skiing and tennis.
PERSONAL PROFILE: Actor. Television: *The Escape, Benin Tales*. Stage: *Sexual Perversity In Chicago, Street Scene, When Five Years Pass, Blood Wedding, Greenland, Metamorphosis, The Seagull*. Commercial: *Cellnet* Corporate Film.

Andy Nicola - Photographer 1940-1997

Andy was born in Nicosia, Cyprus 4th July 1940, the eldest son in a family who emigrated to England in July 1955.

His early education was in Nicosia where he attended Primary School and later The English School. By 15 he was proficient in English and the only member of the family who could communicate during the family's long voyage to England. On arrival in England, he attended Haverstock Hill Secondary Modern School in Chalk Farm, London.

Andy first studied to be a Civil Engineer but, in the process, discovered the art of photography. His love and understanding of this hobby inspired him to give up the engineering course. He attended a Photography Diploma course at the London College of Printing and in 1965 attained a Diploma in Photography.

Andy worked on a number of projects during the period following his graduation. In particular, he was immensely proud to have been commissioned, together with a writer, to study the various aspects of the Cypriot life in Cyprus by the Times newspaper group.

Andy's role was to undertake all the photography for this project. He later revisited Cyprus on a number of occasions and successfully compiled a black and white photographic dossier of life in Cyprus. His work was recognised and acclaimed by the community and media and many of his photographs were published and displayed in a number of exhibitions in London. Another of his projects was to compile a photographic portfolio of Cypriots living in London, these images were also exhibited at various festivals and exhibitions. He has participated in a number of projects to promote the arts in the Greek-Cypriot community and was involved in the early period of establishing Theatro Technis in Camden.

Unfortunately his creativity and inspirational energy was marred by his illness when in the 1964 he contracted a virus which later lead to kidney failure. For 33 years he struggled to survive and had undergone treatment, having had 12 years of dialysis and finally a kidney transplant in 1983 with his father as the donor. He was involved with the formation of the Royal Free Hospital Kidney Patients Association and for many years served on the committee and later was chairman.

Andy was passionate about his work and was a true artist caring about the Greek-Cypriot community and its cultural survival.

He passed away on 1st November 1997 at the Royal Free Hospital, Hampstead.

Playing backgammon in the cafe
© Andy Nicola

Seven Sisters Road in the 1970s
© Andy Nicola

Shiamishi and lokmades being served outside the church
© Andy Nicola

Kolifa wheat, pomegranates and almonds in sugar is eaten
in memory of the deceased
© Andy Nicola

Reading the future in a coffee cup
© Andy Nicola

Dancing at the Greek wedding
© Andy Nicola

Dancing at a wedding
© Andy Nicola

Little boy in church on Sunday
© Andy Nicola

Christening in the 1970s
© Andy Nicola

Church service in the 1970s
© Andy Nicola

Special Greek pastries and koubes at
All Saints church in Camden town
© Andy Nicola

Selling the Haravgi newspaper outside the All Saints church
in Camden town
© Andy Nicola

Seven Sisters Road in the 1970s
© Andy Nicola

Cypriot youth in the 1970s
© Andy Nicola

Cypriot youth in 1990s
© Peter Pentayiotis

The vision unfolds

- In line with the latest international trends, we have created our new identity
- We have modernised our fleet
- Our Loyalty Schemes reward you with free travel
- We offer online services
- Comfort and care on every minute of your journey

CYPRUS AIRWAYS
Our destination, is you!

www.cyprusairways.com

Jordan Andrews Ltd
80 Park Road
London
N8 8JQ

Tel: 0044-(0)-20-8341-9222
Fax: 0044-(0)-20-8342-5222
Email: jordan@jordanandrews.com
Web: www.jordanandrews.com

Aroma Patisserie

Παραγγελίες για:
- γάμους
- γενέθλια
- αρραβώνες
- βαφτίσια
- ονομαστικές γιορτές

Βάζουμε τη φωτογραφία που θέλετε πάνω στην τούρτα

424 Green Lanes, Palmers Green, London N13 5PB

TEL: 020 8886 8083

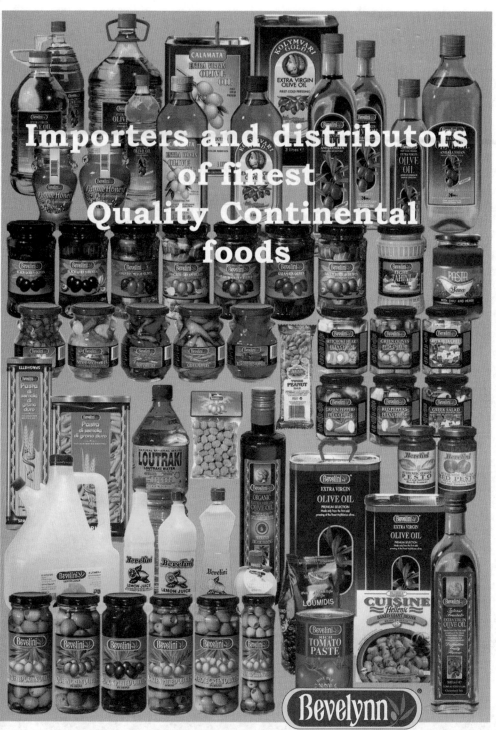

Summer Product Range

Big K Charcoal Merchants Ltd, Unit 20 Millmead Industrial Centre,
Millmead Road,
Tottenham Hale, London N17 9QU

Tel: (01366) 501485 Fax: (01366) 500395 E-Mail: sales@bigk.co.uk www.bigk.co.uk

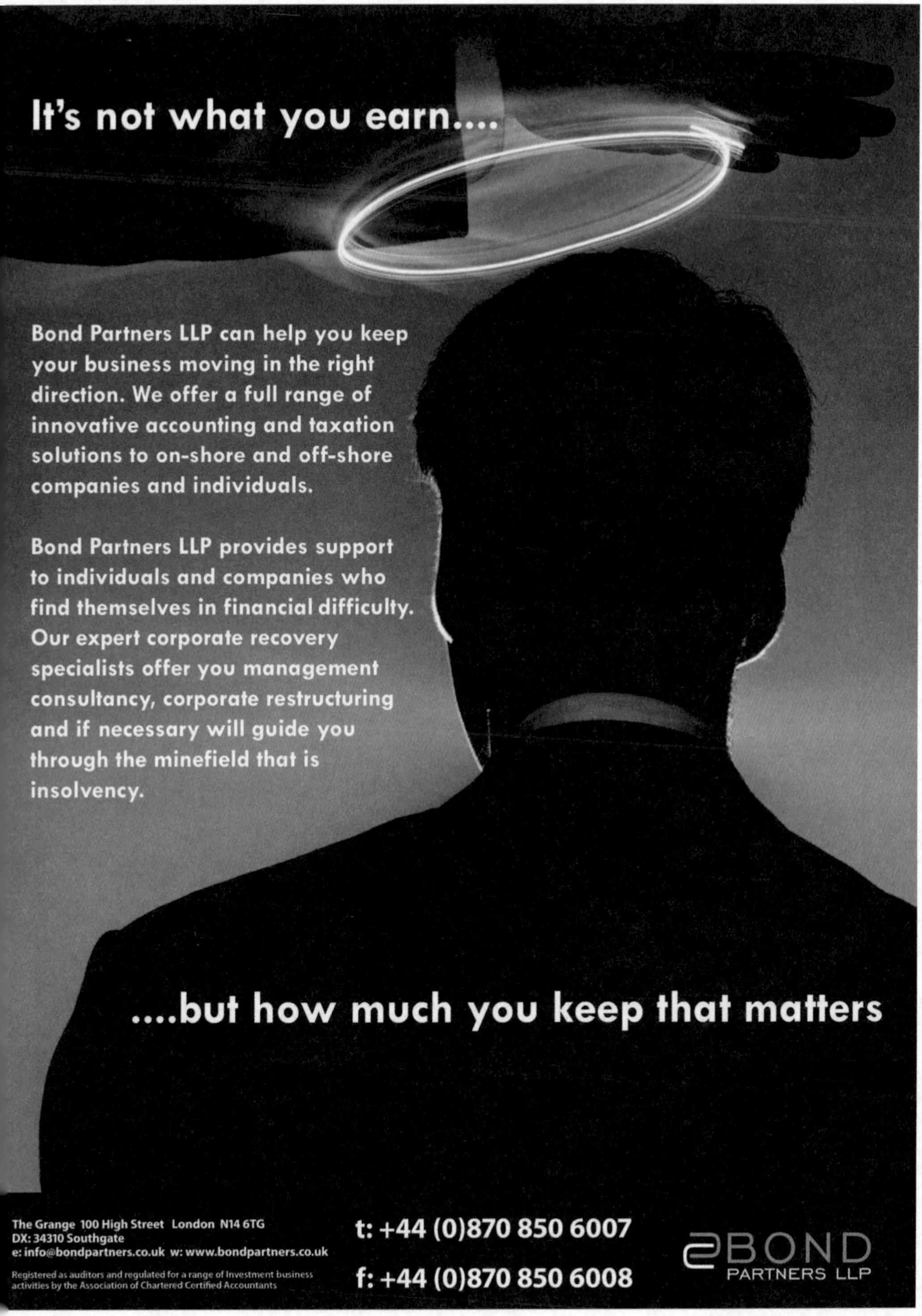

It's not what you earn....

Bond Partners LLP can help you keep your business moving in the right direction. We offer a full range of innovative accounting and taxation solutions to on-shore and off-shore companies and individuals.

Bond Partners LLP provides support to individuals and companies who find themselves in financial difficulty. Our expert corporate recovery specialists offer you management consultancy, corporate restructuring and if necessary will guide you through the minefield that is insolvency.

....but how much you keep that matters

The Grange 100 High Street London N14 6TG
DX: 34310 Southgate
e: info@bondpartners.co.uk w: www.bondpartners.co.uk

Registered as auditors and regulated for a range of Investment business activities by the Association of Chartered Certified Accountants

t: +44 (0)870 850 6007

f: +44 (0)870 850 6008

BOND
PARTNERS LLP

ESTATE AGENTS AND VALUERS

**RESIDENTIAL • COMMERCIAL
LETTING & MANAGEMENT • CONSTRUCTIONS**

<u>HEAD OFFICE:</u>

P.O. BOX 3309
1 TURNPIKE LANE, LONDON N8 0EP

TEL: 020 8342 5555
FAX: 020 8342 5656

**Email: capital@capitalaccommodation.co.uk
www.capitalaccommodation.co.uk**

North London's brand new luxury nightspot

CLUB KO

club KO, 9a the broadway, high road, wood green, N22 6BH
info & membership 020 8888 0202. www.clubko.com

designed @ www.liferide.co.uk

Club Ko, 9a The Broadway, High Road,
Wood Green
N22 6BH

Tel: 020 8888 0202

www.clubko.com

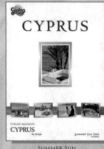
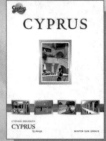

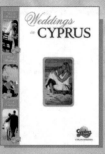

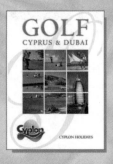

THE DEVELOPING / INVESTMENT COMPANY

YIANIS
GROUP

**Congratulations on producing
the first ever Greek Cypriot
Who's Who**

THE YIANIS GROUP CURRENTLY OWN OVER 3 MILLION SQUARE FEET OF

FREEHOLD PROPERTY AND WE'RE GETTING

BIGGER

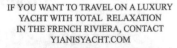

IF YOU WANT TO TRAVEL IN THE
ULTIMATE OF LUXURY AND STYLE ON
A PRIVATE JET, CONTACT US AT
YIANISAIR.COM.

IF YOU WANT TO TRAVEL ON A LUXURY
YACHT WITH TOTAL RELAXATION
IN THE FRENCH RIVIERA, CONTACT
YIANISYACHT.COM

G6a Belgrave Court, 36 Westferry Circus, Canary Riverside,
Canary Wharf, London, E14 8RL

Tel: 020 7519 1000 Fax: 020 7519 6006
Email: sandrapeters@yianis.com
www.yianisgroup.com

GEORGIOU NICHOLAS

SOLICITORS

22 John Street
London WC1N 2BY
Tel: 020 7681 8888
Fax: 020 7831 6345
DX 0047 London

359 Goswell Road
London EC1
Tel: 020 7278 1121

334 Chiswick High Road
London W4 5TA
Tel: 020 8742 5000

E-mail: solicitors@georgiou-nicholas.co.uk
Website: www.georgiou-nicholas.co.uk

Quality Fresh Dairy Products

Tims Dairy Limited

Mopes Farm, Denham Lane, Chalfont St. Peter
Buckinghamshire SL9 0QH

Telephone: +44 (0) 1753 888380
Facsimile: +44 (0) 1753 893538
Email: info@timsdairy.co.uk
website: www.timsdairy.co.uk

A new year, the same personal service

SFSIS is now
Lewis Charles Securities

67 Arlington Road N14 5BB
Louisianaproperties@btconnect.com

Tel 020 8211 3663
Fax 020 8211 3662

VICKEAL LTD. T/A
MARCOS TRIMMINGS
Zips ● Cottons ● Buttons ● Canvas ● Elastics etc.

TAVISTOCK ROAD
LONDON N4 1TD

TEL: 020-8800 9918/9903
FAX: 020-8809 6776

E-mail: eptakomi@aol.com
Website: www.marcostrimmings.com

ZIPS, COTTONS, BUTTONS, CANVAS, ELASTICS ETC.

FOODS LTD

CREATORS OF

Pearl's

DELICIOUS CAKES

UNITS A, B & E.
38 CRAWLEY ROAD,
LONDON N22 6AG

Telephone: 020 8888 8897
Fax: 020 8889 0194
Email: info@pittasfoods.com
www.pittasfoods.com

World of Windows & Doors Limited

9B Garman Road, Tottenham, London N17 0UR

Tel: 020 8885 3009
Fax: 020 8365 0424

Kenville House, Spring Villa Business Park,
Spring Villa Road, Edgware, Middlesex HA8 7EB,
United Kingdom

Tel: +44 (0)20 8099 8099
Fax +44 (0)20 8099 9000

Telex: 886644 (Asb ZELA G)
Website: www.zelashipping.com
Email: mail@zelashipping.com

KATE KUBA

Georgina's 131 Bramley Road N14 4UT

Muswell Hill 71 Muswell Hill N10 3HA

Loughton 209E High Road IG10 1BB

Southgate 49 Chase Side N14 5BU

Brook Street 26 Brook Street W1K 5DQ

Kings Road 22 Duke of York Square SW6 4LY

Richmond 22 Hill Street TW9 1TW

it's all Greek to me!...

Η συχνότητα του Λονδίνου
που μιλάει ελληνικά

Μουσική ,ενημέρωση ,ψυχαγωγία...
βάλτε τον στο πρόγραμμα!

London Greek radio
437 High road London N12 0AP
www.lgr.co.uk
tel 0208349650
fax 02083496970

Mirror Mirror

LONDON

Stockist of the largest collection of Pronovias in the southeast.

Also Mirror Mirror Couture, Cymbeline, Emily Costa,

Linea Raffaelli and Justine Mireil

---

37 Park Road,	56 Penton Street,
London N8 8TE	London N1 9QA
Tel: 020 8348 2113	Tel: 020 7713 9022

By Appointment
www.mirrormirror.uk.com

THE ABILITY GROUP

ANDREAS PANAYIOTOU
GROUP CHAIRMAN

PHILIP SHABATAI
CHIEF EXECUTIVE

DEVELOPMENTS • INVESTMENTS • SHIPPING • AIR

ABILITY HOUSE   7 PORTLAND PLACE   LONDON   W1B 1PP
TEL: 0207 580 1234   FAX: 0207 580 7271   info@theabilitygroup.com   www.theabilitygroup.com

The City College

WHERE STUDENTS COME FIRST

Your Future
Starts Here

Full time courses

- Bachelor of Business Administration (BBA)
- BSc in Computer Science
  (both degrees awarded by Crown University, USA)
- Master of Business Administration (MBA)
  (awarded by Heriot-Watt University)
- Computing & Multimedia
- Hospitality Management
- Travel & Tourism Management
- Secretarial Studies
- English as a Foreign Language

Distance learning courses

- Chartered Institute of Marketing
- Hospitality Management
- Travel & Tourism Management

University House
55 East Road
London N1 6AH
Tel: 020 7253 1133
Fax: 020 7251 6610
e-mail: admissions@citycollege.ac.uk
website: www.citycollege.ac.uk

Recognised as effecient by the
British Accreditation Council (BAC)

Cutwater Construction Limited

12 Corri Avenue
Southgate
London N14 7HL

Telephone: 0208 882 4534
Facsimile: 0208 882 4534
Mobile: 07836 752123

PROPERTY DEVELOPMENT
ARCHITECTURAL PLANNING
DESIGN CONSULTANTS

- *We carry out all Design & Building requirements*
- *Consultation with Client Pre-Design*
- *Consultation on Draft Designs*
- *Submission of plans for approval*
- *Production of detailed quotation*
- *Management and/or completion of development*
- *NHBC guarantee – 10 years (new buildings)*
- *Extensions, Conversions & New Builds*
- *Architectural Landscaping*
- *Complete follow-up service available*

Director: T Efstathiou B.A. Arch   Secretary: G.A. Efstathiou   Registered in England No. 5165369   V.A.T. Registration No. 858 7080 85

MONDIAL
FORWARDING LTD.
Specialist Forwarders to Greece & Cyprus
ESTABLISHED 1974

Head Office:
**46 LOCKFIELD AVENUE
BRIMSDOWN, ENFIELD
MIDDLESEX EN3 7PX
Tel: 020 - 8805 3344 (8 Lines)
Fax: 020 - 8805 2299**

NICHOLAS & CO - Solicitors
Established 1969

* * * * * * * *

18-22 Wigmore Street London W1U 2RG
Tel: 020 7323 4450
Fax: 020 73234401
Email: info@nicholassolicitors.com

SOLICITORS

Kypros Nicholas
Philip Phillippou
Nick Nicholas
Nana Constantinou
Rodney Emmot
Elizabeth Tillyer
Mallika Prinja
Panayiota Ioannou

O A K
INSURANCE
SERVICES

Theobald's Park Road
Crews Hill
Enfield EN2 9BG
Tel: 020 8367 5000
Fax: 020 8367 5600

 **Wedding Co-ordinations**

We have competitive packages available and the expertise to plan your wedding,
engagement or social event down to the last detail.

Our professional team are experts in coordinating your special day.

MANY VENUES AVAILABLE - (Some examples):
London Marriot, Landmark, London Hilton, Inter-Continental, The Brewery, Renaissance, Alexandra Palace, Decorium and many others.

You are only 'One Stop' away from your perfect day.

For more information on our competitive packages and prices please contact
TONY VOUROS

Tel: 020 8445 6720
Mobile: 07802 266 841

Email: info@onestopcoordinations.com
Web: www.Onestopcoordinations.com

P. C. E. FABRICS LTD

ALL FABRICS BOUGHT AND SOLD

Unit 10
407/409 Hornsey Road
London N19 4DX

Tel: 0207-281 2819
Fax: 0207-281 8113
Mobile: 0860 790756

Bank of Cyprus UK

CELEBRATING 50 YEARS IN THE UK

Bank of Cyprus UK is proud to celebrate 50 years of business in the United Kingdom.

The bank opened its first branch in London's Shaftesbury Avenue in 1955. This was a time when Cypriot migration to Britain, and London in particular, started in earnest. The bank developed and grew alongside its entrepreneurial customers and supported their businesses and investments with dedicated personal service. Following the demographic trend of its customer base, the bank expanded to North London and eventually created a branch network spanning North and South London, Birmingham and Manchester.

In 1997, the bank opened a branch of the parent company that operated alongside the UK subsidiary Bank of Cyprus (London) Ltd. Through the capital base of the parent, the branch offered an enhanced lending capacity that served the needs of its larger corporate customers. With the entry of Cyprus into the European Union in 2004, the subsidiary and the branch were merged into the current entity, Bank of Cyprus UK.

Today the bank employs 230 staff and continues to operate in London, Birmingham and Manchester, through a network of business centres, branches, a personal banking centre and a representative office. The bank's strategic focus is business banking and its vision is to continue to meet its customers' needs through dedicated relationship-based service.

The bank's commitment to its customers is reinforced by the development of a new flagship establishment in Southgate which will house the Corporate and Business Banking Centre and a new branch. As part of the celebrations for its 50 years, the bank will be organising various events and will also be supporting a number of community-based projects including sponsorships of local schools.

Commenting on the 50 year anniversary, the bank's General Manager Mr Spyros Neophytou stated: 'The bank has come a long way from relatively humble beginnings in the UK 50 years ago. The bank would like to thank its customers for their contribution to its success over the past 50 years, and looks forward to serving their banking needs with the same commitment and dedication over the next 50 years and beyond.'

YEARS IN THE UK 1955-2005

pōmilo

LADIES CLOTHING

A FRESH APPROACH TO LADIES' FASHION

Come and see our special offers at any of the following stores:

POMILO 64 Church St, Enfield Town	**POMILO** 724 High Rd, North Finchley	**POMILO** 279 High Rd Loughton	**POMILO** 8 Palace Parade High Street Walthamstow

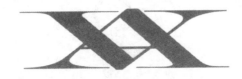

ValentinaGroup

Watkins House
Pegamoid Road
Edmonton N18 2NG
Tel: 0208 887 7100

176 Tollington Park
London N4 3AJ
Tel: 020 7263 8100
Fax: 020 7686 8080

Email: Varosi @varosilettings.co.uk

Registration Number: 4288212

ENTRANTS IN
GREEK CYPRIOTS IN THE UK
HAVE BEEN NOMINATED
FOR THEIR ACHIEVEMENTS AND
CONTRIBUTIONS.

YOU CAN NOMINATE SOMEONE OR
YOURSELF WHO DESERVES
TO BE IN THE BOOK.

ENTRIES ARE FREE.

SEND IN YOUR NOMINATIONS,
INCLUDING NAME,
CONTACT ADDRESS,
TELEPHONE NUMBER
AND EMAIL TO

GREEK CYPRIOTS IN THE UK
111 ST THOMAS'S ROAD
LONDON N4 2QJ
TELEPHONE 020 7503 3498
EMAIL cypriotwhoswho@aol.com

verve clothing co

One of London's leading manufacturers and supplier of ladies garments to the high street retailer.

for further information visit www.verveclothingco.co.uk

VERVE HOUSE, BAIRD ROAD, EN1 1SJ
TEL: 020 8804 9911 FAX: 020 8804 0033

VERVE CLOTHING CO

Your contact in the UK

Your contact in Australia

Your contact in Cyprus

Your contact in Greece

Created by Blackbox www.blackboxpartnership.com

Any question, anywhere, one answer.

At Laiki we give you your own business relationship manager.
One point of contact able to deal with any query, in any country. Someone
who knows you and your business plans in depth. So you don't have to
repeat yourself. Contact: intlbusinessbanking@laiki.com or
by phone +44 20 7307 8419.

 **LAIKI GROUP**

By your side, all your life!

my dental care

www.my-dentalcare.com

New Patients Welcome
Tel: 020 8889 3773

Dentists
Mr Mark Marcou BDS (Lond.)
Mrs Vivian Onu-Nzegbulem BDS
Mr Prem Nair BDS, FDSRCS

Dental therapist/hygienist:
Mrs Mira Shah

141 Myddleton Road, Wood Green, London N22 8NG
Email: smile@my-dentalcare.com
Web: www.my-dentalcare.com

Opening Times:
Monday to Thursday: 9.00am to 6.00pm
Lunch: 1.00pm to 2.00pm
Tuesday late evening appointments available until 8.00pm
Friday: 8.00am to 2.00pm

Private Hygienist / therapist sessions available
Enquire at Reception

NHS Treatment

NHS treatment is FREE if you:-

- are under 18 years of age
- are pregnant
- are a mother and your baby is under 1 year
- are receiving income support
- are receiving pension credit
- are receiving income based job seekers allowance
- are a student who is 18 years and in full time education
- have an exemption certificate i.e. HC2
- receive families tax credit or disability tax credit
- If you are on a low income and none of the above apply please ask the receptionist for a HC2 form for help with NHS charges

Private Dentistry

Some of the private treatments available:-

- Tooth whitening
- Tooth Cleaning – Power Clean treatment
- White fillings / Porcelain fillings
- Tooth coloured crowns / bridges
- Gold crowns and inlays
- Dentures

Under the personal management of
Karageorgis Brothers

13 Percy Street
London W1 9FD

Tel: 020 7636 4804
020 7580 3988
Fax: 020 7323 0679

www.ElyseeRestaurant.com

ALISON HAYES (UK)

361B–363B LIVERPOOL ROAD
LONDON N1 1NL

TELEPHONE: **020 7700 8800**
FAX: 020 7607 1851
Email: ngeorghiades@alisonhayes.co.uk

Broxbourne Dental Care

– Mr S. Efstratiou BDS (RAND) –

Unit 1, The Precinct

High Road

Broxbourne

Herts EN10 7HY

Tel: 01992 478578

Claudia

Claudia House

1324-1326 High Road

Whetstone, London N20 9HJ

Tel: (020) 8445 5484

Fax: (020) 8492 9406

Email: info@claudiainternational.co.uk

GEORGE THEODOULOU

Building Contractor

91 TRENT GARDENS
SOUTHGATE
LONDON N14 4QB

TELEPHONE: 020 8449 9049
MOBILE: 07885 107571
FAX: 020 8440 7696

ESTABLISHED SINCE 1958
RESIDENTIAL & COMMERCIAL AGENTS / SURVEYORS
PROPERTY MANAGEMENT

7 Topsfield Parade

Crouch End Broadway

London N8 8PR

Tel: 020 8348 1111

020 8348 2545

Fax: 020 8348 5902

Email: enquiries@hornseyagencies.com

Web: www.hornseyagencies.com

The Ivory Tower

Furniture & Gifts

464 Muswell Hill Broadway

Muswell Hill

London N10 1BS

Tel: 020 8444 1070

Fax: 020 8444 1071

Acrobell Ltd t/a

Clothing Manufacturers

Unit 6, Sussex Works
Cline Road, London N11 2LX
(entrance Ring Way N11)

Tel: 020 8368 6000
Fax: 020 8368 0703

www.acrobell.co.uk

PARIKIAKI

THE NEWSPAPER OF THE CYPRIOT COMMUNITY IN BRITAIN

OUR NEW ADDRESS
AS FROM
11th SEPTEMBER 2005

140 FALKLAND ROAD

LONDON N8 0NP

TEL: 020 8341 5853

020 8341 0751

FAX: 020 8341 6642

The

Kelmanson
Partnership

CHARTERED CERTIFIED ACCOUNTANTS

REGISTERED AUDITORS
INSOLVENCY PRACTITIONERS

AVCO HOUSE, 6 ALBERT ROAD
BARNET, HERTFORDSHIRE EN4 9SH
TELEPHONE: 020 8441 2000
FACSIMILE: 020 8441 3000

EMAIL: tkp@kelpart.co.uk
WEBSITE: www.kelpart.co.uk

THOMAS PROPERTIES

Tel: 020 7281 2000 Fax: 020 7281 2001

LANDLORDS

- GUARANTEED RENTS
- NO COMMISSION CHARGED ON CERTAIN SCHEMES
- FREE VALUATIONS
- MAINTENANCE SERVICE AVAILABLE
- FRIENDLY PROFESSIONAL SERVICE
- ESTABLISHED BUSINESS WITH 10 YEARS EXPERIENCE

TENANTS

- GOOD QUALITY PROPERTIES AVAILABLE
- LOW DEPOSITS
- FAST REFERENCING PROCEDURES
- HOUSING BENEFIT MAY BE CONSIDERED

167 STROUD GREEN ROAD, LONDON N4 3PZ

'Delivering excellence, efficiency and Best Value'

Accord has a track record as a leading service provider, principally to the public sector. We have particular expertise in multi-disciplined services, which are provided on a client-focused, partnering basis.

Our aim, at Accord, is to be flexible in our business approach, enabling us to integrate the provision of our services within our customers' business, social and community objectives.

For more information on Accord's services
please contact David Brazier on: 01707 367000

ACCORD
www.accordplc.com

THE INSTITUTE OF
CHARTERED
ACCOUNTANTS

IN ENGLAND & WALES

ALEXANDER LAWSON & CO
·

BUSINESS RECOVERY & INSOLVENCY

NINOS KOUMETTOU FCA FCCA FABRP

641 GREEN LANES
LONDON N8 0RE
TELEPHONE: 020 8348 0183
FAX: 020 8340 9115
E-Mail: Alawco@aol.com

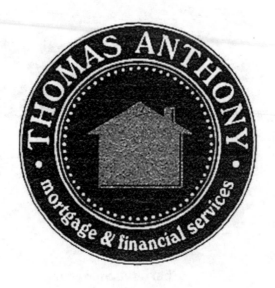

Jon Christopher

Chartered Surveyors

7 Fortis Green
East Finchley
London N2 9JR

Tel: 020 8444 0055
Fax: 020 8444 0222

Email: info@jonchristopher.com
Web: www.jonchristopher.com

RICS

FUNERAL DIRECTORS

&

Monumental Masons

ΤΟ ΠΡΩΤΟ ΚΑΙ ΜΟΝΑΔΙΚΟ ΕΛΛΗΝΟΚΥΠΡΙΑΚΟ ΟΡΘΟΔΟΞΟ
ΓΡΑΦΕΙΟ ΚΗΔΕΙΩΝ ΤΗΣ ΠΑΡΟΙΚΙΑΣ

24ΩΡΗ ΕΞΥΠΗΡΕΤΗΣΗ ΣΕ ΟΛΑ ΤΑ ΜΕΡΗ ΤΟΥ ΛΟΝΔΙΝΟΥ

Specialists in repatriation to Greece, Cyprus, and all over the world

EXHUMATIONS

CREMATIONS

ΤΑΦΟΠΕΤΡΕΣ ΚΑΙ ΣΤΑΥΡΟΙ

131-133 MYDDLETON ROAD
WOOD GREEN
LONDON N22 8NG
TEL: 020 8889 9888 (24 ώρες)
FAX: 020 8888 9205
EMAIL: info@ d-e.co.uk

D.G.S.

Digital Grading Service
Precision Graders and Marker-makers

Unit 1, Tiverton Foundry

Tiverton Road

London N15 6RP

Tel: 020 8800 1343

Fax: 020 8800 3553

J&P
Joannou & Paraskevaides Group

International
Building & Civil Engineering Contractors

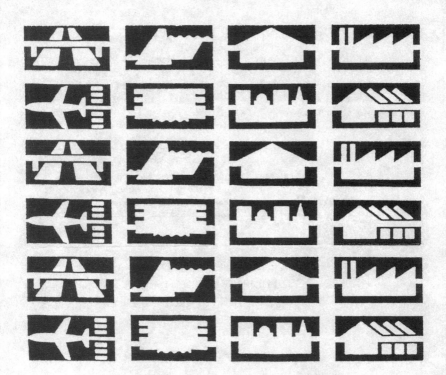

UK Representative Office
16 Hanover Street London W1S 1YL
Tel: +44 (020) 7462 5000 Fax: +44 (020) 7493 0059
Email: London@jandp.org

Kounnis And Partners Plc

Chartered Certified Accountants

Incorporating
Shears Schryer Carlton & Co.
Graff & Graff
Theo & Co
John Lewis & Co

DIRECTORS

D.K. Kounnis FAPA, FAIA
A.C. Stylianou, ACA, FCCA
C.A. Joannou, BSc, FCCA
N.S. Roberts, BSc., FCA
M.J. Carlton, FCCA

CONSULTANTS

A.P. Freeman, FCCA
T. Papapavlou, ACPA, FIAB
J.E. Lewis, FCA, FCCA

*We are a dynamic company of Chartered Certified Accountants
offering clients the highest level of service and support.
We provide a wide range of audit, accountancy and taxation services for
sole traders, partnerships and small and medium sized companies.*

STERLING HOUSE
FULBOURNE ROAD
LONDON E17 4EE

Tel: 020 8498 2777 (15 Lines)
Fax: 020 8498 2775
Email: info@kounnis.com   Website: www.kounnis.com

*Registered in England and Wales No. 4205389
Registered to carry out Audit work by the Association of Chartered Certified Accountants*

Best Wishes
from

THE A.G. LEVENTIS GROUP

OF COMPANIES

CHARTERED ACCOUNTANTS & REGISTERED AUDITORS

RYLAND HOUSE
44/48 Bristol Street, Birmingham B5 7AA
Tel: 0121-622 3633 Fax: 0121-622 5845

****

Cypressa
foods of the sun

CONGRATULATIONS ON PRODUCING

THE GREEK CYPRIOT

WHO'S WHO

Katsouris Brothers Ltd

100 Queensbury Road
Wembley
Middlesex HA0 1WP

Telephone: 020 8991 6080
Fax: 020 8991 6090

www.cypressa.co.uk

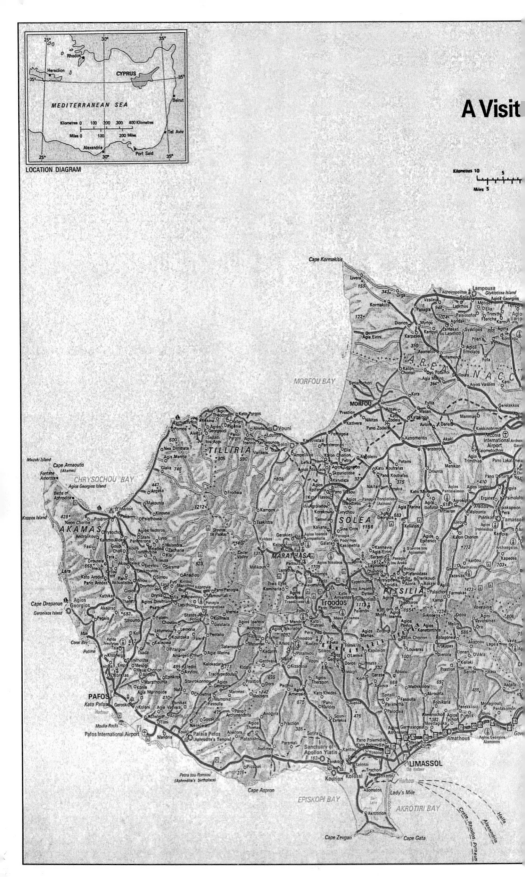

A Visit